SIDNEY HERBERT

TOO SHORT A LIFE

Sidney Herbert, photograph, late 1850s

Sidney Herbert
TOO SHORT A LIFE

R.E. Foster

THE HOBNOB PRESS

First published in the United Kingdom in 2019

by The Hobnob Press,
8 Lock Warehouse, Severn Road, Gloucester GL1 2GA
www.hobnobpress.co.uk

© R.E. Foster, 2019

The Author hereby asserts his moral rights to be identified as the Author of the Work.

All rights reserved. No part of this publication may be reproduced, stored in a retrieval system, or transmitted in any form or by any means, electronic, mechanical, photocopying, recording or otherwise, without the prior permission of the publisher and copyright holder.

British Library Cataloguing in Publication Data
A catalogue record for this book is available from the British Library

ISBN 978-1-906978-69-3 (paperback)
      978-1-906978-70-9 (casebound)

Typeset in Adobe Garamond Pro 11/14 pt.
Typesetting and origination by John Chandler

Front cover illustration:
Sidney Herbert, from the drawing by George Richmond, 1847

Back cover illustration:
Colour woodcut of Wilton House, 1865

Contents

Abbreviations vi
Maps and Illustrations vii
Preface and Acknowledgements ix

Introduction. Sidney Herbert: Saint *and* Sinner 1
1. Gilded Youth 1810-1832 14
2. Setting Course 1832-1837 40
3. Rising Reputation 1837-1841 64
4. Debatable Progress 1841-1845 86
5. Treacherous Times 1845-1846 109
6. Halcyon Days 1846-1850 140
7. Progressive Conservative 1850-1852 179
8. Crimean Prelude 1852-1854 220
9. Crimean Controversies 1854-1855 257
10. Confronting Obloquy 1855-1857 297
11. Allied Reformers 1857-1859 339
12. Cumulative Burdens 1859-1861 381
Afterwards. El Cid? Relocating Herbert 425

Bibliography 469
Index 479

Abbreviations

BL Add. Mss.	British Library Additional Manuscripts
CWFN	*Collected Works of Florence Nightingale*
DWG	*Devizes and Wiltshire Gazette*
EH	Elizabeth Herbert
FN	Florence Nightingale
HRO	Hampshire Record Office
Hansard	*Hansard's Parliamentary Debates: Third Series*
HLPP	Hartley Library, Palmerston Papers
JRG	Sir James Graham
LMA	London Metropolitan Archives
LRO	Liverpool Record Office
NUL	Nottingham University Library
ODNB	*Oxford Dictionary of National Biography*
Pam	Palmerston
PGL	Palace Green Library, Durham
PP	Parliamentary Papers
SH	Sidney Herbert
Stanmore	Lord Stanmore, *Sidney Herbert. Lord Herbert of Lea. A Memoir*
SWJ	*Salisbury and Winchester Journal*
TNA	The National Archives
WEG	William Ewart Gladstone
WSHC	Wiltshire and Swindon History Centre
WSRO	West Sussex Record Office

Maps and Illustrations

Between pages 256-7
Map 1. The Black Sea
Map 2. The Crimean Campaign
1 George Augustus, 11th Earl of Pembroke
2 Catherine Woronzow, Countess of Pembroke
3 Pembroke Lodge
4 Simon Woronzow and his secretary
5 Wilton House
6 Mount Merrion
7 Robert, 12th Earl of Pembroke
8 William Ewart Gladstone
9 The Duke of Newcastle
10 The Duke of Wellington and Sir Robert Peel
11 Sidney Herbert
12 Elizabeth Herbert
13 Herbert's room at Wilton
14 49 Belgrave Square
15 Elizabeth Herbert with Mary and George Herbert
16 Appeal leaflet on behalf of the Female Emigration Fund
17 The Earl of Malmesbury
18 Viscount Palmerston
19 The Earl of Aberdeen
20 Sir James Graham
21 Lord John Russell
22 The Earl of Derby
23 Benjamin Disraeli
24 The Aberdeen Cabinet

25 Florence Nightingale
26 Earl de Grey and Ripon
27 St Mary and St Nicholas' Church, Wilton
28 St John's Church, Sandymount
29 St Mary's, Star of the Sea, Sandymount
30 St John's Church, Bemerton
31 Sidney Herbert
32 Lady Herbert
33 Herbert memorial, Wilton Church
34 Herbert statue, Salisbury
35 Herbert statue, War Office
36 Nightingale visits the Herbert Hospital
37 Casting of an Armstrong gun
38 London volunteer rifle corps
39 Herbert statue, Waterloo Place
40 Herbert statue, Victoria Park
41 Sidney Herbert, drawing by George Richmond, 1847

Credits
Figures 1,2, 12, 13, 15, 16, 35 and the frontispiece photograph of Herbert appear by courtesy of Lord Pembroke. The remainder are from the author's collection. Maps appear by courtesy of Michaela Foster.

Preface and Acknowledgements

I first encountered Sidney Herbert as an 'A' level history student during the late 1970s. He crossed my path again whilst I was reading for undergraduate and postgraduate degrees at the University of Southampton during the 1980s. A more tangential meeting followed during the 1990s when I was a teacher at Embley Park, the erstwhile home of Herbert's friend and associate, Florence Nightingale. At none of these junctures can I claim to have thought about Herbert in his own right. I only started to do that in 2014 when I was invited by the History of Parliament Trust to write the Wiltshire entries for the 1832-68 period: Herbert sat for South Wiltshire between 1832 and 1861. The interest thus sparked was heightened when I joined the guiding team at Wilton House in 2016. What follows, therefore, might be counted as the final destination in a circuitous journey lasting four decades.

Herbert was a national figure but a Wiltshire man, hailed on his death as one of its greatest sons. He was the de facto head of its largest estate, and a leading figure in county affairs for over thirty years. His electoral power base was in Wiltshire. He relished representing the county at Westminster: the decision to resign his parliamentary seat in 1861 was an emotional wrench for him. Following Herbert's life in Wiltshire, therefore, reveals a good deal about his interests, character, and modus operandi. Above all, it tells us that Herbert idealised his family's ancestral seat at Wilton, Wiltshire's ancient county town. Wilton House was the home to which he insisted on returning to die in 1861. It is appropriate that Herbert has found a publisher whose focus is the locality with which he so strongly identified.

Numerous debts have been incurred whilst preparing this book. First and foremost, I should like to thank John Chandler of The

Hobnob Press, who responded with enthusiasm to my proposal for a book about Herbert. The 18th Earl of Pembroke, Herbert's great-great-great-grandson, has been supportive of my researches, in particular by allowing me to use letters and photographs in his possession. Herbert family papers in the public domain can be consulted at the Wiltshire and Swindon History Centre in Chippenham. The staff who look after them have been unfailingly helpful as I worked my way through the relevant boxes, bundles and volumes. No less can be said for those who have eased the labours of my research in the following repositories: the Bodleian Library, Oxford, the British Library, the National Archives, the University of Durham (Palace Green Library), Liverpool Record Office, the University of Nottingham (Manuscripts and Special Collections), the University of Southampton (Hartley Library), St Deniol's Library, Hawarden, the National Maritime Museum (Caird Library), Hampshire Record Office, West Sussex Record Office, and Salisbury City Library. Those with smaller collections of relevance to me who have kindly answered queries include: the London Library, Gloucestershire Archives, Surrey History Centre, the Wellcome Library, the London Metropolitan Archives and Devon Record Office.

Amongst the host of individuals who have been generous with their knowledge are: Professor David Brown, who supplied transcripts from Lord Shaftesbury's diary; the Reverend Geoffrey Cooke, for advice about the Victorian High Church; Mick Crumplin, for information about Bright's Disease; Dr Richard Gaunt, for help with the Newcastle archive; Dr Rory Muir, for pointers in the direction of army reform; Rob Petre, for arranging for me to see Herbert's portrait in the Fellows' Common Room at Oriel College, Oxford; Christopher Rogers, for advice on architectural questions; and Dr Philip Salmon, my editor at the History of Parliament Trust. The latter might have mixed feelings that his invitation to write a 2,000 word article on Herbert has mutated into a 170,000 word book.

His Excellency Renato Carlos Sersale di Cerisano, Argentina's Ambassador to the Court of St James, kindly allowed me to view his official residence, 49 Belgrave Square. Architecturally, it is not much changed since Thomas Cubitt finished building it for Sidney Herbert in 1851. Closer to home, I am grateful to all those who work on the

Wilton Estate for helping me to gain greater access and insight into the Herbert family: Chris Rolfe, Nigel Bailey, Louise Vincent, and of course all my guiding friends and colleagues. Sarah King and Ros Liddington allowed me to see items in their care. For providing cut-price (or better!) accommodation during my visits to archival centres, I am grateful to Andy and Jackie Waring, Susanna Foster, James Harcourt-Flynn, and Jennie Beckwith. For comments on chapter drafts, I am obliged to Carol Kitching, Edd Foster, and especially Susanna Foster. To anybody who feels aggrieved that they have not been acknowledged, I apologise. For remaining errors of fact or interpretation, I assume sole responsibility and apologise to the reader.

Far and away my greatest debts, however, are the ever-multiplying ones owed to my wife, Michaela. Beyond her official duties as wife and mother, she has acted variously as chauffeuse, research assistant, map drawer, proof-reader and critic. In the process she has become far more of an authority than me on many aspects of the Herbert family. She is, in the words Herbert used so often to his wife, 'My Dearest Heart.' It would be totally invidious to dedicate the book to anyone else.

Introduction
Sidney Herbert: Saint *and* Sinner

Sunday 3 May 1953. Alderman F.H. Wort stood musing beside the grave of Florence Nightingale at East Wellow in Hampshire. What would the good lady have thought, he wondered, about Salisbury City Council's proposal to remove Sidney Herbert's statue from its pre-eminent position in the city's Market Square? His view, which Nightingale would have shared, was that they were debasing Herbert's memory. Venting his spleen at the next day's council meeting, Wort declaimed that Herbert and Nightingale had done more for nursing 'than anyone in the history of the world'. The debate is revealing: Herbert was remembered, if at all, as the junior partner in a legendary relationship during the Crimean War. By eighteen votes to seven, councillors ratified the proposal to move his statue to an unremarkable site on the outskirts of the city.[1]

Such a development would have shocked Herbert's contemporaries. Sir James Graham, a close ally and senior statesman, had told W. E. Gladstone when Herbert died that his 'friends need not be under any anxiety with respect to his memory. He so lived that he will not be forgotten by the present generation, and in after times he rests under an edifice, reared by himself and dedicated to his God, which is a worthy and a lasting monument of him'.[2] Graham was referring

1 *SWJ*, 8 May 1953.
2 Parker, *Graham*, II, p. 415, JRG to WEG, 24 Aug. 1861.

to Wilton's parish church, built largely on Herbert's initiative during the 1840s. Dublin boasts Herbert Avenue, Pembroke Street, Sydney Terrace and Lea Road. Further memorials include Herbert Sound in Antarctica, the town of Pembroke in Canada, the small settlement of Herbert, and Mount Herbert, in New Zealand. Gladstone named a son for one of the few men he confessed to have loved: Herbert Gladstone became Home Secretary in 1905. Dr Sidney Herbert Brown, a senior medical officer at University College Hospital, was another probably baptised in his memory; so too, Sidney Herbert Ray, an authority on the languages of Polynesia.[1] Virtually all those who encountered Herbert extolled his virtues. Nightingale remembered him as 'a man of the most varied and brilliant conversational genius I have ever known'. Speaker Denison told Herbert directly that he was 'the pleasantest Gentleman in England'.[2] There was also widespread agreement about what Herbert would have become. Lord Aberdeen, a former Prime Minister well placed to know, 'expressed his strong opinion' to the Queen in September 1860 'that "Sidney was the only man fit to be Prime Minister."'[3] Small wonder then, that Herbert's death in August 1861, a few weeks short of his fifty-first birthday, was 'mourned as premature and counted for a national calamity'.[4]

Today, however, Herbert stands in danger of being written out of history. There is no blue plaque outside his former home in Belgrave Square, the point of departure for the party of nurses who accompanied Nightingale to the Crimea in 1854. A biography of Herbert, due to appear in the 1980s, was never published. Richard Shannon's 550 page life of Gladstone contains no reference to Herbert in its index. Named in his honour, the Royal Herbert Hospital closed in 1977. By 1995 it had become a complex of flats and apartments with amenities that included a swimming pool and outdoor nature reserve. Whilst it may be true, as one perplexed reviewer noted in 1906, that 'it is not quite

---

1 *The Times*, 23 June 1906, 4 Dec. 1907.
2 *CWFN*, VII, p. 733; WSHC 2057/F4/54, Denison to SH, 5 Jan. 1861.
3 WHSC 2057/F6/98, 'Character of Sidney Herbert', p. 9.
4 *Fraser's Magazine*, 'Herbert', p. 198.

easy to understand the impression he made on his contemporaries', the neglect of Herbert has surely been allowed to go too far.¹

Any new assessment of Herbert must address the reasons why he is 'so often depicted as little short of a saint'.² Several have already been mentioned: his association with a secular saint, his premature demise, the sense of a lost leader, his personable nature. One could add the fact that Herbert was worked to death in the service of his country, leaving behind a young family. The chief reason for his character standing so high, however, is that there has been no major study of him for well over a century, let alone a critical biography. Historians have had no option but to rely on obituaries or the essay by Harriet Martineau (a friend of Nightingale's) which appeared in 1869 as one of her *Biographical Sketches*. Both sources were influential in shaping the 1891 entry on Herbert written by J.A. Hamilton for the *Dictionary of National Biography*. The *éminence grise*, though, in creating Herbert's posthumous reputation, was Elizabeth A'Court, better known from 1846 as Mrs Sidney Herbert.

Left distraught by Herbert's death, and dedicated to preserving his memory as she perceived it, Lady Herbert spent a portion of her later years ensuring that his biography was written. Having flirted with the idea of writing it herself, she secured the services of Arthur Hamilton-Gordon. Ennobled in 1893 as Lord Stanmore, the putative biographer was the youngest son of the 4th Earl of Aberdeen, Prime Minister for much of the Crimean War. Stanmore had got to know Herbert a little when serving as his father's private secretary during the 1850s. A distinguished career as a colonial administrator followed, including spells as governor of Trinidad, Mauritius, Fiji and New Zealand. For Lady Herbert, Stanmore's retiring to England in 1890 was serendipitous. With time on his hands, access to both his father's and Gladstone's papers, and with High Church sympathies to boot, few people were better qualified to undertake the heavy responsibility she entrusted to him.³

1   *London Evening Standard*, 12 Dec. 1906.
2   Hoppen, *Mid-Victorian Generation*, p. 139.
3   ODNB.

Few people at the time, and few historians since, have appreciated just how far Lady Herbert participated in producing the 'perceptive official biography' which resulted.[1] She responded to Stanmore's request for information about Herbert's private life, providing details of his philanthropic works and insights into his religious beliefs.[2] In addition Stanmore saw two earlier and overlapping memoranda which she had written for the benefit of children too young to remember their father: one, a description of Herbert's personal attributes; the other, a narrative of the final eighteen months of his life. Stanmore made substantial use of them, incorporating unacknowledged extracts into his narrative. When he writes, for example, of Herbert's qualities, that 'the one which always struck one so forcibly was his wonderful modesty and humility', that he had a 'sweetness of temper', and that 'I never saw it ruffled under the most trying circumstances', we are reading pure Lady Herbert. So too the story of how once, when out hunting in Wiltshire, Herbert was approached by a tenant who complained that his daughter, afflicted by a deformity, was the victim of merciless bullying by neighbours. Herbert dismounted, said 'I'll see to that', and walked arm in arm with her through the village. Needless to say, the young lady was not troubled again.[3]

Lady Herbert's desire to ensure that literally no word should appear in print that might damage her husband's reputation was one reason (though by no means the only one) why Stanmore's labours were so protracted. In November 1899, for example, fearing that it might be misconstrued, she objected to Stanmore's seemingly innocuous use of 'striking'. The author replied that he had employed it in the sense of 'noted', not 'hitting'. And in April 1904, having read a full draft, she returned it with the instruction that more of Herbert's character, as she portrayed it, should be in evidence.[4] Some fifteen years after he had agreed to take on the project, one can understand why Stanmore's letters to her sometimes betray a sense of frustration. Nevertheless, when the volumes finally appeared in 1906 Stanmore dedicated them

1 Conacher, *Aberdeen Coalition*, p. 45, n.
2 BL Add. Mss. 49270, fols. 141-50.
3 WSHC 2057/F6/98, 'Character of Sidney Herbert', pp. 9, 13-15, 17.
4 WSHC 2057/F4/52, Stanmore to EH, 7 Nov. 1899, 24 Apr. 1904.

to Lady Herbert 'with respect and affection'. Only the two of them really knew how far she had been co-author. The decision to subtitle the work a memoir, not a biography, might have roused the discerning reader's suspicions. If so, they were quickly dampened by reference to the index. There is just a single entry under her name: 'A'Court, Elizabeth, her marriage to S. Herbert'.

Ignorance as to who lay behind Stanmore's tome goes some way towards explaining the mixed reviews which it received. The *London Evening Standard*, reasonably presuming Stanmore to be the memoirist, confessed disappointment that he had not drawn on his own recollections as Aberdeen's secretary. Reaching the opposite conclusion from its author, the *Morning Chronicle* thought volume two (covering the years from 1855) 'a pathetic record of unachieved reforms'. Herbert Paul, writer and Liberal MP, was particularly dismissive of 'The Saint of the Peelites', a man who though he 'fancied himself a Liberal, was an aristocratic Conservative'. More common criticisms were that the work was prolix (nearly 950 pages) and, being 'filled with interminable political letters', rather dull.[1] Other reviews, to be fair, identified the letters as one of the strengths of the volumes, affording as they did, insights into the minds of some of the great political actors of the day. As such, *The Globe* thought Stanmore's work of 'permanent value'. Most modern scholars concur.[2]

Something of a perfectionist ('It is out of my power to write hurriedly, I cannot do it'), Stanmore was aware of limitations in his biography. He bemoaned the failure of Herbert's family to supply him with illustrative material. So far as the text was concerned, he confessed to there being 'too much of the minister & member of Parliament, too little of the <u>man</u> himself', that is to say his 'personal and inner life'.[3] George Russell took up the point. Having recently read Disraeli's representation of Herbert, transparently disguised as Sidney Wilton in

1 *The Speaker*, 12 Jan. 1907; *London Evening Standard*, 12 Dec. 1906; *Liverpool Daily Post*, 19 Dec. 1906.
2 BL Add. Mss. 49270, fols. 183-4, Russell to Stanmore, 13 Dec. 1906; *The Globe*, 19 Dec. 1906.
3 WSHC 2057/F4/52, Stanmore to EH, 7 Nov. 1899, 11 Nov. 1901; Stanmore, I, pp. vii-ix.

Endymion, he observed inquisitively 'that it suggests one trait which does not appear in your book i.e. a peculiar susceptibility to looks, charms, and indeed, a "flirtatious" disposition'.[1] The fault, if fault it was, was not Stanmore's. Lady Herbert, for all that she was happy to provide an idealised portrait of her husband, allowed Stanmore very limited sight of the personal correspondence between them. But whilst that was her choice, the decision to gloss over the nature of Herbert's religious beliefs was Stanmore's. It was universally acknowledged that Herbert was a staunch High Churchman. To have followed the line taken by Lady Herbert in her notes that only calculations of political pragmatism prevented Herbert from going over to Rome (she had done so in 1865) would have been, to say the least, tendentious.

Stanmore also rightly conceded that there was 'a certain unevenness in the narrative'. Late-Victorian literary convention resulted in there being only a single reference to Herbert's funeral, and no serious consideration of posthumous reputation. The unevenness also reflects the range of sources available to Stanmore. Herbert did not keep copies of many of his letters.[2] Stanmore was able to compensate for this by seeing most of Herbert's letters amongst Gladstone's, Graham's and Nightingale's papers but he did not have access to others such as Palmerston's and Newcastle's. There were other collections which he was aware of but unable to locate. A Mr Purcell claimed to have 'many' letters from Herbert to Manning. As they have yet to find their way into the public domain, one can only agree with Stanmore that they would certainly be revealing.[3] There is also virtually nothing documenting Herbert's problematic relationship with his half-brother Robert, 12th Earl of Pembroke. By contrast we have plenty of material for Herbert's school years, the avalanche of congratulatory notes triggered by news of his engagement, hundreds of letters concerning arcane militia business, and an excruciatingly intrusive account of his final hours.

1   BL Add. Mss. 49270, fols. 183-4, Russell to Stanmore, 13 Dec. 1906.
2   Stanmore, I, pp. vii-ix; WSHC 2057/F4/52, Stanmore to EH, 7 Aug. 1895.
3   WSHC 2057/F4/52, Stanmore to EH, 22 July 1896.

Considering the volumes as a whole, Stanmore is also open to the charge that he devotes too little space to Herbert's early career. Just 27 pages cover the period from 1810 to 1841. Sixty percent of Herbert's life, in other words, is crammed into the first three percent of the biography. By comparison, Stanmore allocates over 30 pages to the China war of 1859-60, much of it comprising letters and despatches received by Herbert from the commander of the British forces. These do not tell us much about Herbert. They do explain why some reviewers thought the work more an account of Herbert's times than a biography.

Whilst one can excuse there being little on Herbert's childhood, it will not do that Stanmore assigns barely nine pages to his first nine years in the Commons. It is true that Herbert was relatively inactive in the parliamentary arena before 1841. It is also unfortunate that very little of his correspondence for the 1830s survives. But important details relating to the evolution of Herbert's politics might have been gleaned from electoral ephemera and newspapers. Herbert made some important speeches on the hustings in Wiltshire and at other public gatherings in the county. Taking account of them helps us to understand why he was sometimes at the centre of controversy. Was it really the case, as Stanmore avowed, that he found the requisite materials difficult to obtain?[1] And why did he not use the unconscionable delay between the commissioning and publication of his book to utilise the various printed sources to appear during the intervening period? The most plausible explanation is political bias. Stanmore, a Gladstonian Liberal, wished to downplay the Toryism of the younger Herbert. But Herbert's Tory years have to be properly considered if one wants to obtain a truly rounded picture of his political career. Without them, his story risks becoming the improbable tale of an immutable liberal saint; with them we have the far more interesting narrative of how an imperfect human being provides 'an illustration of the progressive liberality of political sentiments, and the gradual abandonment of narrow prejudices for wide, generous, and enlightened principles'.[2]

1 WSHC 2057/F4/52, Stanmore to EH, 17 Mar. 1904.
2 *SWJ*, 3 Aug. 1861.

One need spend only a few minutes immersed amongst Herbert's papers to encounter a very different man to the one presented to us by Stanmore. Doing so brings to mind the cryptic footnote Lady Herbert inserted that 'None of us will ever forget the happy, joyous laugh, the droll way of putting things, the vivid descriptions of things or people, or places he had seen'.[1] This was the Herbert largely excised from Stanmore's volumes. Let there be no doubt, however, that the usually placid and charming gentleman had another side, one that was often endearingly puckish but sometimes merciless. It was this Herbert who wrote in his journal in 1829 that Lady Amherst, of whom he was fond, 'looks far too much like a crocodile to be pleasant'; or the Herbert who, in 1831, judged a Reverend Davis to be 'an ineffable blockhead'.[2] Whilst this was relatively harmless, woe betides the recipient of Herbert's vituperation when he was angry. The truth of Lord Stanley's judgement that he was 'bitter in his invective' was never better illustrated than during a parliamentary debate in 1852. Disraeli, with his well-known Jewish antecedents, was the unfortunate target: 'how', Herbert asked, 'could it be expected that any man would become a convert to a faith, the profession of which must begin with a surgical operation?' Mr Gladstone was so discomfited by his friend's language that he could not sleep that night.[3] He would have been even more discombobulated had he seen the letter Herbert wrote to Palmerston cautioning the then Prime Minister that 'His [Gladstone's] temperament [...] is such, that if not in the government, he will soon be in opposition to it'. Similarly, Herbert wrote anonymous pieces in the *Morning Chronicle* lambasting Lord Malmesbury, a lifelong friend, for his inexperience on being appointed Foreign Secretary.[4] Herbert's attack on Disraeli was cruel; his insinuations about Gladstone and Malmesbury unworthy.

---

1   WSHC 2057/F6/98, 'Character of Sidney Herbert', pp. 20-1.
2   WSHC 2057/F5/13, journal entry, 21 Aug. 1829; WSHC 2057/F5/15, journal entry, Sept. 1831.
3   Vincent, *Stanley Journals*, p. 174, 14 July 1861; Hansard, 26 Nov. 1852, CXXIII, col. 610; Shannon, *Gladstone. Peel's Inheritor*, p. 256.
4   HLPP GC/HE/66, SH to Pam, 6 Apr. 1860; *ODNB*.

For all that, Herbert remains an attractive character. Florence Nightingale admired his 'simplicity and candour' and his 'extreme quickness of perception'.[1] He was a voracious reader, consuming anything from Plato and Aristotle to the latest plays, novels and newspapers. On Christmas Day 1845, at the height of the Corn Law crisis, one of his chief queries to his friend, Lord Lincoln, was whether he had 'seen the new punch [sic] with the two tea boys'.[2] Herbert also travelled extensively both at home and abroad, usually in one of the seven carriages he kept at Wilton or, increasingly, by train. He was a trustee of both the National Gallery and the National Portrait Gallery. No mean artist, Herbert was well qualified to add to Wilton's already impressive collection of paintings; he also bought busts of Dante, Oliver Cromwell and Benjamin Franklin for himself. His passion for churches, meanwhile, was proverbial. Returning from Italy in 1848, he brought with him 'an immense quantity of Alexandrine mosaics, a whole altar of it, many fine twisted columns of it, and some beautiful large columns of richly coloured marble'.[3] Some of it was incorporated into his new parish church in Wilton; other pieces within the grand home he created in Belgrave Square. Blessed with 'a very sweet tenor voice', Herbert spoke well, variously as a student in the Oxford Union, outdoors when addressing gatherings of his Wiltshire constituents, or indoors speechifying before his peers in the more rarefied atmosphere of the House of Commons. Elizabeth recorded that he was in the habit, after a speech there, of coming up to see her in the Strangers' Gallery and saying that 'I feel I did not do it as I wished'.[4] He usually did; his diffidence too was winning. The most salient objects in Herbert's private room at Wilton, however, were not copies of Hansard and fine art (though William Owen's portrait of his father took pride of place), but an assortment of at least 30 pistols and hunting pieces. Herbert's habits as a sportsman, remembered his son, had been the subject of an article. Sadly, he could not remember when and where. Thankfully, Herbert at the peak of his abilities was

1   Cook, I, *Nightingale*, p. 366.
2   NUL Ne C 11927 SH to Lincoln, 25 Dec. 1845.
3   Mozley, *Reminiscences*, II, p. 161.
4   WSHC 2057/F6/98, 'Account of Sidney Herbert', pp. 9-10, 12.

captured in chalk, oils, and marble by George Richmond, Sir Francis Grant and Lawrence Macdonald.[1]

Some critics looked to the above, however, as evidence that Herbert was effete; Nightingale identified his 'excessive eclecticism' as a weakness. Herbert did not help himself by protesting that 'he was naturally idle, loving pleasure, and sport, and travelling, and anything better than work!' On one occasion he was reported to be engrossed in a classical text whilst nonchalantly signing papers that crossed his desk in the War Office.[2] One word which does undeniably attach itself to him is 'weak'. Lytton Strachey, in a metaphor employed to characterise Herbert's relationship with Nightingale, likened him to a stag, 'a comely, gallant creature springing through the forest; but the forest is a dangerous place. One has the image of those wide eyes fascinated suddenly by something feline, something strong; there is a pause; and then the tigress has her claws in the quivering haunches; and then – !' The Duke of Argyll maintained that even Herbert's statue in Pall Mall conveyed 'an attitude that wants power and strength'.[3] Herbert's image, in other words, told against him. He was tall and willowy, remembered at Oxford as having been 'a head and shoulders taller than any of us'. He was only half joking when he said that 'My height has been against me in everything. In hunting, and in politics, and in everything I care for most'. Unlike Palmerston, Herbert bore no resemblance to John Bull, the sort of Englishman who could lead his country in war. Contemporaries were agreed he looked far more like his celebrated ancestor, the poet and priest George Herbert, who had died of consumption, aged 39, in 1633. How they knew this and not, like Goldwin Smith, that 'He had, however, beneath a quiet bearing,

---

1   BL Add. Mss. 49270, fols. 178-9, Pembroke to Stanmore, nd, 1906; WSHC 2057/D5/13, inventory of SH's effects.
2   Cook, I, *Nightingale*, p. 366; WSHC 2057/F6/98, 'Character of Sidney Herbert', p. 16.
3   Strachey, *Eminent Victorians*, p. 148; Argyll, *Autobiography*, I, pp. 380-1.

and a slight appearance of aristocratic listlessness, plenty of courage and not a little force of character', is far from clear.¹

Towards his end, Herbert did suffer a rapid physical decline: photographs taken of him in the 1850s are barely recognisable as the same man who appears in the portraits of the late 1840s. But anybody who thinks that Herbert was a lightweight will be disabused if they bother to read his testimony to the 1860 Select Committee on Military Organisation. The acuity of his mind and the grasp of detail contained therein are remarkable.² The truth is that Herbert, perhaps more than most, was a compendium of paradoxes. These included the dutiful Herbert who twice refused offices he found uncongenial, Herbert the pillar of the Anglican Church who was suspected of at least closet Catholicism, and Herbert the epitome of moral probity who enjoyed a flutter: he wagered £127 (roughly £10,000 today) on various horses in the 1850 Derby.³ There was also Herbert the model husband who was linked with the morally dubious Mrs Caroline Norton, Herbert the champion of the landed interest who became an apostle of free trade, and the half-Russian Herbert who was lauded as a great British patriot. In consequence Herbert was at various times assailed as a traitor to his party, his faith, his class and his country.

But Herbert does matter. He was appointed to office on six different occasions by three different Prime Ministers; he declined offers to enter government from two others. Of ten years spent in office, more than half found him seated at the cabinet table. He made over 650 recorded interventions in parliamentary debate. Moreover, it was the quality of his speeches that was noteworthy. One memorial essay would remember how 'an attentive silence, meet honour for some Nestor of debate, would greet Sidney Herbert rising for a speech'.⁴ Herbert delivered much praised orations during some of the finest

1   Mozley, *Reminiscences*, II, p. 157; *London Daily News*, 21 Dec. 1906; Haultain, *Reminiscences by Goldwin Smith*, p. 202. George Herbert (1593-1633) was descended from a younger brother of the 1st Earl of Pembroke. He became rector of Bemerton on the Wilton estate.
2   PP 1860 (441), VII, pp. 503-73.
3   WSHC 2057/A6/66.
4   *Fraser's Magazine*, 'Herbert', p. 210.

debates ever to have taken place in the House of Commons. He was doing so at a time when, because of the fluidity of parties, a speech was capable of swaying the allegiance of some Members. It was small wonder that he was one of those few singled out as an asset worth recruiting by all five Prime Ministers who held office during the last fifteen years of his life. Behind the scenes too, Herbert was a significant player in the kaleidoscopic game of high politics which followed the split in the Conservative party in 1846. He was never far from the centre of the action in the dramas surrounding the making and unmaking of governments during the 1850s. In 1859 he was foremost in promoting the meeting which has come to be seen as marking the formation of the modern Liberal party.

Yet there was also something of the shooting star about Herbert – a glowing brilliance which disappeared all too quickly. Critics were apt to conclude that his achievements were correspondingly nebulous. At first, it is true, his accomplishments were modest. Even so, he used his tenure of junior office down to 1846 not only to gain experience but to push for reform in the navy and army. During the Crimean War, although occupying an office of less importance than was popularly presumed, he did his best to make the most of an administrative system unequal to its task. His most impressive work, however, was undertaken after the war. This is now remembered as being synonymous with the work of Florence Nightingale. Their initiatives to improve conditions for the home army in peacetime were both ground-breaking and impressive. But at the time of his death Herbert was recognised, more than anybody else of his generation, as having been an army reformer in toto. He had grappled with issues such as the education of officers, the practice of buying and selling commissions, the conundrum of how best to supplement regular forces in wartime, and the overarching concern of ensuring the nation's security against foreign invasion. It was his fate – and prejudicial to his prospects for success – to hold real power for only a brief period whilst pitted against a formidable battery of opponents. As such, he was able only to sow the seeds of reforms that would come to fruition a decade and more after his premature death. It is striking indeed, that of the people whose lives were most intertwined with his own, Gladstone lived until 1898 and Nightingale until 1910. Lady Herbert survived until 1911, thus outliving him almost as long as he had lived. Sidney Herbert's truly was a life too short.

Although Herbert never lived long enough to become a political giant, he moved amongst them. He did not especially like the Earl of Derby or Lord John Russell. His dislike of what he conceived of as Palmerston's immoral gung-ho politics was exceeded only by his atavistic loathing of Disraeli. By contrast, something approaching reverence was afforded to Sir Robert Peel. When Peel died in 1850 Herbert became one of the self-appointed guardians of his political credo. Part of the void created by the death of his political godfather was filled by the Earl of Aberdeen and, increasingly during the later 1850s, by Sir James Graham. Had Herbert lived the allotted three score and ten he would have joined the ranks of those giants. It is just about conceivable that he could have returned to the Conservative fold – in which case Disraeli might never have climbed to the top of the greasy pole. Far more likely he would have provided what many (from the Crown downwards) wanted, a viable alternative to Gladstone as heir to Palmerston and Russell for the leadership of the Liberal party. A Herbert government following Palmerston's death in 1865 would have been more progressive than its predecessor. A moderate Reform Bill would have been enacted; a more robust foreign policy would have been adopted than the pacific one which proved so costly to the party under Gladstone. The reconfigured Liberal consensus with Herbert at its centre would have deprived history of the celebrated duel between Gladstone and Disraeli; the Conservatives would have been denied their end of century hegemony.[1] Had Sidney Herbert lived, the story of mid-Victorian politics would have been very different.

1   Aldous, *The Lion and the Unicorn*, pp. 140-1.

1
Gilded Youth 1810-1832

'*Ung je serviray*' proclaims the Herbert family motto at Wilton House, Wiltshire seat of the earls of Pembroke. The Norman-French wording, rendered in modern English as 'the one I will serve', is ambiguous. Does it denote service to the Crown or God? Cynics suggest that the evidence of nearly five centuries points to the baser motive of the family serving its own interests. Perhaps the motto always was intended as a conflation of all three. Whatever the truth, Sidney Herbert was exposed to its stricture from his earliest days.

Herbert, it was universally agreed, 'possessed the advantages of birth and family'.[1] He boasted a distinguished Welsh lineage dating back to at least the fifteenth century: William Herbert, a Yorkist, was ennobled as the Earl of Pembroke of the eighth creation in 1468. Before Lancastrian forces captured and beheaded him at Northampton a year later, he had fathered an illegitimate son, Richard (d.1510), who became a Gentleman Usher to Henry VII.[2] His son, another William (*c.* 1506-1570), made what turned out to be a prescient match when he married Anne Parr, younger sister of Henry VIII's sixth wife. In 1544 he was granted the 45,000 acre estate of the former Wilton Abbey, which had been dissolved in 1539. A member of Edward VI's Regency Council, he became 1st Earl of Pembroke of the tenth creation in

1   *SWJ*, 24 Aug. 1861.
2   Lever, *Herberts of Wilton*, pp. 2-3.

October 1551.[1] By then a grand Tudor house on the footprint of the medieval abbey was nearing completion. His son, Henry (1540-1601), who succeeded as 2nd Earl, married as his third wife Mary Sidney (1561-1621), 'the greatest patroness of wit and learning of any lady in her time'. Her brother, Sir Philip Sidney, composed part of his *Arcadia* at Wilton. Other luminaries who graced its portals included Ben Jonson, Edmund Spenser, and William Shakespeare.[2]

The Sidney name would be re-employed for Herbert's forename two centuries later. In the interim, Herbert's forebears stamped a generally modest imprint upon history. William, 3rd Earl (1580-1630), was instrumental in founding Pembroke College, Oxford, in 1624. He and his younger brother, Philip (1584-1649), Earl of Montgomery in his own right since 1605, and 4th Earl of Pembroke from 1630, were the 'incomparable brethren', the dedicatees of the First Folio of Shakespeare's plays. Philip also served as Lord Chamberlain to Charles I. In deference to his royal master, who was a frequent summer visitor, he added new state rooms to Wilton. At their heart, the Inigo Jones-inspired 'Double Cube' consummated Wilton's reputation as an idyllic retreat – and continues to awe the visitor.[3] After the family's fortunes were temporarily jeopardised by Philip, the 7th Earl (1652-1683), who lived up to his reputation as 'the most violent homicide of his age', stability was restored by his polymath brother, Thomas. The 8th Earl (1656-1733), amassed an unrivalled collection of classical statuary, paintings and coins; and established Wilton's famous carpet factory. His son Henry, 9th Earl (1689-1750), though according to Sarah Churchill 'sometimes mad, and always very odd', retained sufficient faculties to oversee construction of the famous Palladian Bridge across the River Nadder.[4] Sidney Herbert's love of the arts hailed from a distinguished pedigree.

Henry, 10th Earl (1734-1794), Sidney Herbert's paternal grandfather, was a man with less aesthetic interests. By his own admission

1   *ODNB*; Lever, *Herberts of Wilton*, chs. 1-2. Anne Boleyn had been made Marchioness of Pembroke of the ninth creation in 1532.
2   *ODNB*; Lever, *Herberts of Wilton*, ch. 3.
3   *ODNB*; Lever, *Herberts of Wilton*, ch. 5.
4   *ODNB*; Lever, *Herberts of Wilton*, ch. 8.

'Horse mad', Earl Henry built a riding school at Wilton. To proselytise his passion he wrote *A Method of Breaking Horses, and Teaching Soldiers to Ride* (1761). It went through several editions and became a standard text for British cavalrymen. Presumably it helped to inform some of those who took part in the Charge of the Light Brigade – about which Sidney Herbert would have mixed feelings. His grandfather also put theory into practice; he saw active service in the Seven Years' War, and became a full general in 1782.[1] But military discipline was sadly lacking in his private life. Having married Elizabeth Spencer, daughter of the 3rd Duke of Marlborough, Henry brought scandal on the family when, in 1762, he eloped to France with Miss Catherine (Kitty) Hunter, daughter of a Lord of the Treasury. An illegitimate son followed before the Earl returned to England in 1763 to be reconciled with his wife. He soon strayed again, fathering at least one illegitimate daughter and adding further insult to his injured wife by displaying prints of one of his mistresses, the ballerina Giovanna Zanerini, in his private apartments. Perhaps the most damning comment came from Horace Walpole: he was 'not surprised at any extravagance in his Lordship's morals'. His Lordship was rarely at Wilton after 1784. He spent most of his final decade abroad, dissipating much money in the process. George, his increasingly despairing heir, feared that Wilton's great art treasures would be lost.[2] Sidney Herbert never knew his grandfather but he shared his father's view that Earl Henry was immoral and stood convicted of at least putative cultural vandalism. As he explained to the Irish politician and author, J.W. Croker, in 1838:

> Strange to say, we have not in the library even the first edition of Shakespeare, and as it must originally have been here, it very probably disappeared through the knavery of my worthy grandfather, who had but little respect for entails, and, when in money difficulties,

---

1   *ODNB*; Lever, *Herberts of Wilton*, chs. 9-10.
2   Herbert, *Pembroke Papers*, pp. 352-3, 439-41, 447-50. The long-suffering Countess survived until 1831.

appropriated and sold pictures, and probably other things belonging to the Wilton collection.¹

Herbert's father, George Augustus, 11th Earl (1759-1827), was an 'honourable and retiring man of amiable disposition'. Joining the army as an ensign in the 12th Foot in 1775, his later service abroad saw him take charge of the 2nd and 3rd Dragoon Guards in Flanders. In 1812 he became a full general. By then, however, his political and diplomatic interests had supervened. In politics he was a Pittite Tory. He sat in the Commons from 1780 as MP for Wilton borough, transferring to the Lords in 1794 when he succeeded to the earldom. Appointed Lord Lieutenant of Wiltshire the same year, he was appointed a Knight of the Garter in 1805, and served as Ambassador Extraordinary on what proved to be an abortive mission to secure an alliance against Napoleon in 1807.² Closer to home the 11th Earl engaged the architect James Wyatt to remodel the north and west wings of Wilton House. Reports claimed that he also invested in excess of £200,000 improving the estate, thereby increasing the rent rolls from £35,000 to £100,000 per annum. Even when allowance is made for the favourable economic conditions for landowners created by the long war with France, this seems improbable: in 1870 the estate's 42,244 acres realised £40,500 in rental.³ Herbert, though he objected to the 'thorough ransacking' of the house 'during the immense and unfortunate alterations made by Wyatt', was nevertheless in no doubt that the family was in his father's debt. As his half-sister Diana put it, the Earl had found Wilton 'in a very bad way on his coming to the title [and he] spared no trouble to bring it all to rights as he left it'. Spread over more than thirty parishes, the Pembroke estate was outstripped only by the likes of the Duke of Bedford at Woburn, and the Duke of Devonshire at Chatsworth.⁴

1 Jennings, *Croker Papers*, II, pp. 332-3, SH to Croker, 4 Nov 1838.
2 ODNB.
3 Thompson, *English Landed Society*, ch. 2; Bateman, *Great Landowners*, p. 355.
4 Jennings, *Croker Papers*, II, pp. 332-3, SH to Croker, 4 Nov 1838; HRO 21M57/3A/1, Lady Normanton to Somerton, 17 Oct. 1841.

Encouraged by his father in January 1787 to consider marrying a foreign heiress, the future 11th Earl had retorted that 'My objections to a foreign wife, I hope, will never cease. Let her be perfection, her husband must be immediately connected with a pack of foreigners, her country people, relations, & friends, & that would never do'.[1] Three months later, as if to prove his point, he married a relatively impoverished cousin, Elizabeth Beauclerk. Their happy union produced two sons, who died before the age of six, and a daughter, Lady Diana, who married Welbore Ellis Agar, 2nd Earl of Normanton. A third son, Robert, born 19 September 1791, survived to become Lord Herbert and heir to the earldom. But the Countess died in March 1793, aged 26.

In January 1808, ignoring his self-imposed edict of 1787, the 11th Earl re-married. For some years he had been friendly with Count Simon Woronzow, the Anglophile Russian ambassador to the Court of St James. Palmerston, who encountered him at Wilton on several occasions, judged him 'remarkably pleasant [...] full of anecdote [...] a staunch & enthusiastic Pittite'.[2] Woronzow's son, Michael, 'heir to 24,000 souls', was in the course of distinguishing himself against Napoleon and would rise to become Commander-in-Chief in the Caucasus. The Earl's eye, however, had been drawn to Count Simon's daughter, Catherine, 25 years his junior. Their match inevitably raised eyebrows. Harriet Martineau, though admitting 'The Woronzoffs [sic] were very like English people, certainly', wrote that, 'there is something peculiar in such a connection with Russia'.[3] Those who knew the couple took a different tack. A few days before the event, Palmerston reported that the wedding had:

> given great pleasure to all her [Catherine's] friends. Ld Pembroke is certainly a good deal older than she is, but her habits are more formed than those of most young women of her age, and he bears his

1 Herbert, *Pembroke Papers*, pp. 326-7, Herbert to Pembroke, 10 Jan 1787.
2 Bourne, *Palmerston-Sulivan*, pp. 29-30, 73-5, Pam to the Sulivans, 5 Sept. 1804, 16 Dec. 1806.
3 Martineau, *Biographical Sketches*, p. 316.

years lightly, and as they have been intimate from her childhood the objection is not strong.[1]

Gladstone would later reflect that Catherine 'was really of herself a kind of bond between the two countries'.[2]

Catherine Woronzow soon filled Wilton with furniture by William Kent and Thomas Chippendale; she also oversaw the remodelling of the formal gardens. By 1819 she had produced five daughters who could play in them. All would make propitious marriages: Elizabeth (1809) to Richard, 3rd Earl Clanwilliam; Mary (1813) to George, 2nd Marquis of Ailesbury; Catherine (1814) to Alexander, 6th Earl of Dunmore; Georgiana (1817) to Henry, 4th Marquis of Lansdowne; and Emma (1819) to the 3rd Viscount de Vesci. In danger of being lost amongst the brood was a son, Sidney.

Sidney Herbert was born at Pembroke Lodge on 16 September 1810. It had been intended that he would enter the world at Wilton, not the former mole catcher's cottage turned Georgian home in Richmond Park gifted to his grandmother by George III. Family lore has it that his early arrival necessitated borrowing swaddling clothes from the nearby workhouse. True or not, 'Boysey' was idolised by his parents. Lady Pembroke enthused that he was angelic when, as an infant, she dressed him to portray Cupid.[3] A more objective source reports that he possessed an 'unusual combination of light golden hair with dark eyes shaded by long thick eyelashes'.[4]

Herbert's strikingly handsome appearance was something that contemporaries would remark upon throughout his life. Thomas Sotheron Estcourt, later a parliamentary colleague, recalled the eight-year-old Herbert with 'his graceful form, his expressive eyes and his elegant bearing'.[5] The boy he saw enjoyed a happy childhood. Herbert's future wife recorded that he 'used to say that the only scolding he ever

1   Bourne, *Palmerston-Sulivan*, pp. 97-8, Pam to the Sulivans, 24 Dec. 1807.
2   WSHC 2057/F4/60, WEG to EH, 13 Jan. 1893.
3   Stanmore, I, p. 3.
4   Stanmore, I, pp. 3-4.
5   *SWJ*, 24 Aug. 1861.

recollected having received from his Father was for not having opened a door for a person not quite a lady who was going out of the room'.[1] Forty years later, in a burst of romantic nostalgia, Herbert chided his eleven-year-old daughter for having allowed the family cat to consume Wilton's resident rodents: 'I used to coax the mice into my room with crumbs. They are such dear little bright eyed things'.[2] James Harris, later 3rd Earl of Malmesbury who, as a boy spent the winter months at Wilton, confirms the picture of the Herberts as a happy family unit. He found the girls to be 'charming children', adding that 'Sidney Herbert and I have always been like brothers'.[3] The two of them played together with what Lady Pembroke labelled 'Sidney's Equestrian Plaything', still extant with cut-out figures including a Cossack and Russian general. And they probably watched together as the Grand Duke Nicholas (later Czar Nicholas I) planted a Turkish oak during a stay at Wilton before departing for the obligatory tourist destinations of Salisbury Cathedral and Stonehenge.[4] In Harris's absence, Herbert forged deep and lasting bonds with his sisters. The pet names they coined for each other included Betty, Tooty and Polly Plump. Sidney, presumably because of his youngest sisters' inability to pronounce his name, was most commonly 'Tid' or 'Tiddens'. His earliest surviving letter suggests that he bore them no ill-will for it. Baby Georgiana, he related, had been 'rather grumpy', leaving him to amuse his other three sisters: 'we made a house, the two dolls were very ill, so I was the doctor. I felt the pulse of each doll, one was very quick and the other very slow. I wrote a prescription'.[5]

In 1819 Herbert was sent to Hall Place School in Beaconsfield, Buckinghamshire. An early letter home thanked his sister Elizabeth for the Russian leather purse she had sent him, and informed the family that 'we race a great deal, for it is our chief amusement'.[6] The following year he reported to his mother that 'my cough is a good

1 WHSC 2057/F6/98, 'Character of Sidney Herbert', p. 12.
2 BL Add. Mss. 59671, fols. 50-1, EH to M. Herbert, 31 Jan. 1861.
3 Malmesbury, *Memoirs*, I, pp. 17, 169-70.
4 *SWJ*, 3 Mar. 1817; WSHC F7/1.
5 WSHC 2057/F4/49, SH to Lady Pembroke, 15 Feb. 1819.
6 WSHC 2057/F4/50, SH to E. Herbert, 28 May 1819.

deal better', juxtaposed with the more momentous news of rumours that Napoleon had escaped from St Helena – gossip corrected in the same letter as 'all a ridiculous story'. His epistle also informed Lady Pembroke that he was reading *Caesar* 'and I like it very much'. But there were also suggestions of homesickness: he hoped that both his parents would fulfil a promise to visit him soon.[1] A month later he penned lines celebrating not just the festive season but his joy at being once more at Wilton:

> Now in these merry days we see;
> In Wilton Hall with sprightly glee
> A set of boys who come to sing,
> Till the great dinner-bell does ring.[2]

It is the first recorded expression of his lifelong love for the family seat.

Herbert entered Harrow in April 1824. He found the regime demanding: 'it was really quite terrible turning out of bed with the damp night air' in the 'pitch black' at 6.30 a.m., he recalled in February 1825. Illness severely curtailed his participation in sport that summer. He would have done better than to inform his anxious mother in April 1826 that a boy who had entered the school just a week earlier had drowned 'in our bathing place called Duck puddle'.[3] Other letters home suggest some continuation of the homesickness he had experienced at Hall Place. His earliest extant letter from Harrow, however, had announced, with unconcealed delight, that he had been placed in the first remove (and 'that you may think I am not mistaken – now f-i-r-s-t, first, or in figures 1st)'.[4] Subsequent epistles reveal that Herbert was in danger of becoming sanctimonious. He expressed his abhorrence of foul-mouthed schoolfellows, contrasting them with 'those boys who never swear [...] who are spoken of in the highest terms'; and others who had run up debts. He was surely gratified to

---

1 WSHC 2057/F4/49, SH to Lady Pembroke, 3 Nov. 1820.
2 WSHC 2057/F4/49, nd, Dec. 1820.
3 WSHC 2057/F4/49, SH to Lady Pembroke, 7 Feb. 1825, 20 Apr. 1826.
4 WSHC 2057/F4/49, SH to Lady Pembroke, 1 May 1824.

read his housemaster's (the Reverend Samuel Ellis Batten) report that he had 'never seen a boy of so pure a mind, so perfectly uncorrupted by bad example'.[1] Further evidence of Herbert's desire to keep it that way is contained in a letter of 1826. He asked his mother to send him a copy of the Reverend William Paley's 1785 tome, *The Principles of Moral and Political Philosophy*, in which God was famously portrayed as a watchmaker.[2]

The picture of Herbert as the 'all work and no play' goody-goody schoolboy should not be overdrawn. He enjoyed playing cricket; he confessed to his mother in 1825 that he had been so distracted by it that he had not had sufficient time to write to her. As the next cricket season approached, he greeted the end of examinations with the heartfelt confession that 'I can assure you I am not sorry for it'.[3] And the Herbert who abhorred debt-ridden peers, who boasted that 'I am keeping my accounts quite tidily,' was forced to grovel barely six months later that 'I am rather short of money and would be much obliged to you to send me some'.[4] The truth is that Herbert's school years were unremarkable. Like others who attended English public schools during that era, he had been exposed to 'an essentially Christian brew, composed of earnestness, gentleness, truth-telling, dutifulness, compassion, and turning the other cheek'.[5] Herbert enjoyed his time at Harrow. By the autumn of 1826 he was writing that 'I am a great man here now'. As the end of the academic year approached he wrote home asking for a new blue cloth coat and white silk stockings to wear at his final Speech Day. 'I intend', so his sister was informed, 'to electrify the public most astonishingly. I am to personate Evander

---

1 Stanmore, I, pp. 5-6. Batten (1792-1830), a graduate of Pembroke College, Cambridge, was an assistant master at Harrow from 1815 until his death.
2 WSHC 2057/F4/49, SH to Lady Pembroke, 20 Apr. 1826.
3 WSHC 2057/F4/49, SH to Lady Pembroke, 19 Apr., 18 June 1825, 3 Mar. 1826.
4 WSHC 2057/F4/50, SH to Polly, 15 Sept. 1826; WSHC 2057/F4/49, SH to Lady Pembroke, 22 Mar. 1827.
5 *Fraser's Magazine*, 'Herbert', p. 198; Hilton, *A Mad, Bad and Dangerous People*, p. 466.

an old king according to Virgil'.¹ History does not record whether Herbert fulfilled his boast. But he did remain a prominent subscriber to the annual dinner for Old Harrovian gentlemen for the rest of his life.

The Reverend Mr Batten, Herbert's housemaster, took his young charge with him when he went up to Cambridge to receive his MA in April 1826. They stayed in Queens' College, viewed King's ('very beautiful'), dined at Trinity ('infinitely finer than Christchurch at Oxford'), and then visited the Fitzwilliam Museum, to whose founder Herbert would soon have reason to be profoundly grateful. His letter describing the visit also contains early intimations of political connections: he saw Palmerston, Secretary at War, 'whom I know'; and Henry Goulburn, Chief Secretary for Ireland, 'whom I now know'. W.J. Bankes, on the other hand, MP for the University, he hoped he would not get to know, 'for he is an immense talker and a little wizen sour looking-man'.²

On 26 October 1827 'Tiddens' received a letter from his sister, Mary, detailing the death of their father earlier that day at Pembroke House in Whitehall. The 11th Earl had been unwell for several years but his passing, as Palmerston put it, 'though an event that one has long considered not improbable his improvement latterly had made one cease to entertain any immediate fears of'. Herbert, only recently turned seventeen, returned home to Wilton for the funeral on 8 November.³

Palmerston, 'truly grieved' by the Earl's death, wrote of his hope 'that he has been able to make such arrangements as will render her [Lady Pembroke] independent in all ways of Ld Herbert'. His reference was to the man Herbert and his sisters knew as Uncle Bobby. In reality he was their half-brother, Robert, who now succeeded as

1   WSHC 2057/F4/50, SH to E. Herbert, 20 Dec. 1826, 26 June 1827.
2   WSHC 2057/F4/49, SH to Lady Pembroke, 20 Apr. 1826.
3   WSHC 2057/F4/50, M. Herbert to SH, 26 Oct. 1827; Bourne, *Palmerston-Sulivan*, pp. 202-4, Pam to E. Sulivan, 3 Nov. 1827; *SWJ*, 12 Nov. 1827.

12th Earl.[1] The earnest 11th Earl had viewed his heir with the same low regard previously reserved for his wayward father. General opinion agreed with him. Robert was, as one report put it, 'more fair than wise or good'.[2] His reputation derived from his unfortunate relationship with Octavia Spinelli. Daughter of the Duke of Laurino, a Sicilian nobleman, Robert had met Octavia whilst holidaying in Sicily in 1814. At the time she was married to the elderly Prince Buttera de Rubari. Robert, smitten by Octavia, promised to marry her when Rubari died. The prince duly played his part by departing the world in June; Octavia and Robert married on 17 August. A day later the 11th Earl reached Sicily, too late to prevent what he considered to be an unsuitable union. Robert returned to England in December 1814 where he quickly came to share his father's view. But Octavia followed him to London, styled herself Lady Herbert, and had a British court rule that their marriage was legal. Robert responded by moving abroad, eventually setting up home in Paris. Octavia abandoned the pursuit and returned to Italy, thence receiving what the Earl regarded as £1,200 per annum palimony.[3] How the domestic status quo and the fortunes of the Wilton estate would be affected by Robert's succeeding to the earldom was an open question. But there seems to have been considerable support for the popular view that 'The Earl of Pembroke, who passes his time more at Paris than anywhere else, is notorious for being an obstinate ninny'.[4]

In what he clearly conceived of as an exercise in damage limitation, the 11th Earl left Robert a relatively modest £10,000 in his will.[5] The bulk of his personal estate was bequeathed to Herbert. Much of this had been inherited as recently as 1816 from Richard, 7th Viscount Fitzwilliam, his father's kinsman by marriage, who lacked a

1 Bourne, *Palmerston-Sulivan Letters*, 202-4, Pam to E. Sulivan, 3 Nov. 1827; WSHC 2057/F4/50, E. Herbert to SH, 8 June 1828.
2 WSHC 2057/F1/12, unidentified press cutting, 1830.
3 WSHC 2057/A6/61.
4 Lever, *Herberts of Wilton*, pp. 205-7, 214-15; WSHC 2057/F1/12, unidentified press cutting of 1830.
5 *SWJ*, 10 Dec. 1827.

male heir. Legend has it that Fitzwilliam's munificence stemmed from the occasion:

> when one morning, at breakfast, the expectant heir [Lord Onslow, another relation] after helping himself to cream, brought the rim of his cup in contact with the rim of the cream jug, to prevent a drop from falling. Lord Fitzwilliam contended that this was ill-bred, and showed want of refinement, inasmuch Lord Onslow's lip might have touched the part of the cup which touched the rim of the jug [...] his name was forthwith erased from the will.[1]

More likely, Fitzwilliam's generosity was the consequence of a longstanding friendship with the Herberts which had seen both the 10th and 11th Earl return him as one of the Members for Wilton. What matters, though, is not the origin but the scale of the fortune. Sidney Herbert's 2,301 acres of prime real estate in and around southern Dublin would realise an annual rental of £35,586, over £2 million at current rates. It made him, in economic terms at least, an aristocrat, with the freedom denied many younger sons of being able to pursue any course he chose.[2]

Following his father's funeral, that course was foreign travel. Herbert was in Rome at the end of 1827; he was disappointed by the Eternal City. It provided evidence, he told his mother, of Clarendon's remark, 'that of all classes & professions clergymen made the worst administration of public affairs'.[3] When Herbert came home, he went to Chilmark, nine miles west of Wilton, where he was tutored for several months by its rector, the Reverend Francis Lear, and Lear's brother-in-law, George Majendie.[4] Herbert welcomed the solitude that Chilmark provided ('you cannot think how comfortable it is to be

---

1 'Wills and Will-making', *Quarterly Review*, CVIII (1860), p. 449. Fitzwilliam's art treasures formed the nucleus of the Fitzwilliam Museum, Cambridge. It opened in 1848.
2 Bateman, *Great Landowners*, p. 355; Thompson, *English Landed Society*, pp. 70-1.
3 WSHC 2057/F4/49, SH to Lady Pembroke, 22 Dec. 1827.
4 Lever, *Herberts of Wilton*, p. 209.

in a nice little country church after that great noisy [Harrow] chapel') as somewhere where he could reflect on the loss of his father and the world they had inhabited together:

> I like [...] being so near Wilton, so many things here ever bringing to mind all he said and did – all the places I have ridden with him, and the home where we used to be so happy. In short there is not a spot about Wilton which I do not love as if it were a person.[1]

Herbert's regime at Chilmark was a congenial one. Mornings were spent 'employed in classical studies, in riding, and occasionally shooting; the evenings in English reading and the recreations of music and drawing'.[2] He wrote letters thanking his adoring sisters for books on the French Revolution, and works by Horace. Greater excitement was occasioned by receiving a hat that 'fits me capitally', and in bagging five of the fourteen brace of pheasants shot when out with 'Lear and the Archbishop'. However, Herbert's propensity for priggishness remained. In a letter to his eldest sister, Elizabeth, thanking her for the present of *Thorpe's Catalogue*, he concluded that 'your conduct in so doing was highly sisterly, & as such I commend it much'.[3]

Herbert returned to a more populous environment when he matriculated at Oriel College, Oxford, on 19 May 1828. The university experience for the landed order in the early nineteenth century has fairly been described as having:

> virtually no intellectual content [...] the sons of the nobility got to know their peers, made the friendships and contacts that would form the structure of their later social life and assist them in their political groupings if inclined to that life, and tried out their paces in the ways of the great world away from parental supervision. They proceeded to

---

1 WSHC 2057/F4/49, SH to Lady Pembroke, 18 Nov. 1827.
2 Stanmore, I, pp. 9-10.
3 WSHC 2057/F4/50, SH to E. Herbert, 15 June, 9, 28 Sept., 14 Dec. 1828.

degrees without qualification or examination, purely on the basis of satisfying the terms of residence.[1]

To be fair to Herbert, he was amongst those who evinced signs of wanting to extend their minds. Majendie assured his mother that he had quickly adopted 'the habits of discipline and study required of him' and that he 'has got into a small set of very respectable and reading young men in his own college'. Such wine parties as he attended were 'quite harmless and free from all intemperance'.[2]

Oriel suited Herbert. It is probable that he went there because of its reputation as one of the more God-fearing colleges.[3] His Pembroke ancestors had not been notable for the strength of their religious convictions (the 1st Earl had craved forgiveness on his knees when Mary Tudor restored nuns to Wilton only to turn them out as whores when her half-sister Elizabeth ascended the throne), but there can be no doubting Herbert's religiosity. This was the thirteen-year-old boy who, in an early letter from Harrow, beseeched his mother to despatch post haste 'a little black prayer-book, which I got out to pack [...] but entirely forgot'; and the fifteen-year-old teenager who asked his sister for 'a good long account' of the Consecration of Fugglestone St Peter.[4] Two years later, he was denouncing pluralities to his mother: 'a parish can never be so properly looked after by a curate with 100 as by the incumbent himself with 4 or 500£ per annum'. He was also looking forward to a meeting of the Christian Knowledge Society in Montgomery.[5] Above all, the young Herbert was unequivocal about his allegiance to the Established Church. Although he had just slept, not for the first time, through a 'bad sermon' from an Anglican priest ('Dissent in this has an advantage over us'), he confided in his private journal that:

1   Thompson, *English Landed Society*, pp. 86-7.
2   Stanmore, I, p. 10.
3   Neither Herbert's father nor his grandfather entered university; the 8th and 9th Earls had been at Christ Church.
4   WSHC 2057/F4/49, SH to Lady Pembroke, 1 May 1824; WSHC 2057/F4/50, SH to E. Herbert, 18 Feb. 1826.
5   WSHC 2057/F4/49, SH to Lady Pembroke, 8 July 1828.

I hold conformity to be a moral duty [...] a man had better keep his doubts to himself. A man will not go to heaven or to hell because to his taste Calvin wrote in a pleasanter style than Luther or vice versa.[1]

There exists some confusion as to who most influenced Herbert's religion when an undergraduate. His going up had more or less coincided with the 'casual discussions within the senior common room at Oriel College' which would take shape as the Oxford Movement.[2] Herbert had gone down before John Keble delivered the assize sermon of 14 July 1833 that is generally recognised as marking the start of the Movement, but he was familiar with some of the High Churchmen who would call for the re-integration of some older Catholic elements of the Christian faith into mainstream Anglicanism. Keble had been a Fellow of Oriel until 1823; Edward Bouverie Pusey became one that same year. But it was John Henry Newman, a Fellow from 1822 before succeeding as vicar of St Mary's in 1828, whose name was most linked with Herbert's. Elizabeth Herbert would insist that Newman had been his tutor and that 'my husband had been his old and favourite pupil'. The Reverend Thomas Mozley, a pupil and intimate of Newman's, wrote that any redeeming features Herbert possessed were the product of Newman 'surrounding him and penetrating him, in spite of a wilful and stubborn resistance, and asserting possession of him in due time'. Most of this is simply untrue. Newman was never Herbert's tutor; Mozley also adds, even if he does not explain why, that 'there ensued a great coolness, and more than coolness, between him and Sidney Herbert'.[3]

The greatest Oxford influence on Herbert was, more accurately, Richard Hurrell Froude. Just seven years older than Herbert, it was Froude, a Fellow of Oriel since 1826, who was his tutor. Froude has been described (as the later Herbert might well have been himself) as 'an advanced High Churchman, one of the very few who were not, like the rest of English society, strongly anti-papalist and who believed

---

1   WSHC 2057/F5/15, journal entry, Aug. 1832.
2   Yates, *Oxford Movement*, p. 11.
3   BL Add. Mss. 49270, fol. 148; Herbert, *How I Came Home*, p. 6; Mozley, *Reminiscences*, II, pp. 159,161.

that if the Church of England was to truly recover its Catholic heritage then some sort of rapprochement with Rome was unavoidable'.[1] Before he died from consumption at the age of 32 in 1836, Froude was one of the co-founders of *Tracts for the Times*, the theological publications inimical with the Oxford Movement. The appearance in print of his diary, *Remains* (1838-9), because it appeared to reveal evidence of Catholic leanings, would prove particularly controversial. For those in Protestant England less nuanced in their judgements, Herbert's supposed sympathies for Rome, which this and other Oxford associations implied, would be a major source of the mid-century antipathy which existed towards him.

But it is important to see matters in their proper perspective. The Oxford Movement only really became politically consequential from the late 1830s. Those who first saw Herbert during his university years were struck not by the intensity of his religion but by the charm of his demeanour. Gladstone recalled that 'The beauty and grace of his appearance, exhibiting him as one of Nature's nobles, made an indelible impression on me'. Mozley's view was that Herbert was 'the grandest and most historic figure then at Oxford'. Charles Greville, Clerk to the Privy Council, thought him 'the best sort of youth I have seen for a long while'.[2] Insofar as Herbert was the product of nurture, the credit is due principally to five people, most obviously his parents. Herbert idealised his father. He returned to Chilmark on the first anniversary of the 11th Earl's death to reflect that pain mixed with feelings that 'rouse and excite in me the desire of doing right and making myself as far as I can worthy of him'.[3] Herbert was no less devoted to his mother; commentators concurred that she had 'admirably supplied' the years of parenting that fell to her alone.[4] But three other men stand out. One was the Reverend Mr Batten, Herbert's housemaster at Harrow. Herbert described him as 'a very uncommon person' and

---

1   Yates, *Oxford Movement*, pp. 11, 17-18. Stanmore, I, p. 10, refers only once to Froude, and then only in passing.
2   Mozley, *Reminiscences*, II, p. 157; Magnus, *Gladstone*, pp. 142-3; Reeve, *Greville Memoirs*, pt. 1, I, p. 267, 2 Jan. 1830.
3   WSHC 2057/F4/49, SH to Lady Pembroke, 26 Oct. 1828.
4   *Fraser's Magazine*, 'Herbert', p. 198.

that among his talents, 'none was more remarkable than the power he had of engaging one's affections'. Herbert was chiefly responsible for the monument raised in Batten's memory in the north transept of the chapel at Harrow.[1] The other formative influences were Majendie and Lear, his tutors at Chilmark. An indication of his regard for the former was the fact that he bequeathed £2,000 to him in the first version of his will. Lear, meanwhile, was set to receive £4,000.[2] He already enjoyed the emoluments of Chilmark and Bishopstone, the latter a living in the Herbert family's gift worth £1,000 per annum. Herbert's influence would later secure him the Deanery of Salisbury. When Lear died in March 1850 Herbert wrote that of all those who had taught him, Lear was 'the one I had known the longest and loved the best'. He headed the list of subscribers to a window in Lear's memory in Salisbury Cathedral.[3] It was but one example testifying to the fact that the Herbert who entered adulthood was one who viewed life as possessed of a moral purpose, grounded in his sense of religious duty and with an awareness of his social obligations.

Oxford doubtless reinforced these tendencies in Herbert but it was more important for confirming something else: a passion for politics, fortified by a prowess in debating. The first evidence for the former is a letter from school of 1827 assuring his sister that 'my politics are perfectly unchanged, and I read the papers and every evening make Harangues & c & c to the great annoyance of one or two boys, who hate politics; for Thornton the boy with the red nose and I go on talking about it unceasingly'.[4] Herbert's nascent interest was only first appreciated as a talent, however, when he became 'an interested and active member of the Union Debating Society'. Founded in 1823, the Union provided the forum in which Herbert and his contemporaries 'practised their early oratorical powers'.[5] He

1   WSHC 2057/F4/50, SH to E. Herbert, 30 June 1830; Stanmore, I, pp. 6-7.
2   WSHC 2057/D5/13, will dated 13 Feb. 1832.
3   Lever, *Herberts of Wilton*, p. 214; *Fraser's Magazine*, 'Herbert', p. 198; *The Times*, 27 Mar. 1850.
4   WSHC 2057/F4/50, SH to E. Herbert, 26 June 1827.
5   *Fraser's Magazine*, 'Herbert', p. 198; *The Times*, 5 Oct. 1872.

was elected President for Hilary term in 1830. There is scant record of what took place during his stewardship other than a reference in Gladstone's diary, 12 November 1830, noting that he and Herbert had just picked over the bones of the Union's debate on the motion that Wellington's government was undeserving of the nation's confidence.[1] Over forty years later, however, at the Union's jubilee dinner, Herbert's was one of the few names singled out by Cardinal Manning as those he remembered as having shone during its early years.[2]

It was through the Union that Herbert first met Henry Manning, apparently the only undergraduate who could rival him in popularity, and later one of the greatest lights of the Oxford Movement. His friendship and his conversion to Rome in 1851 would inevitably fuel speculation as to the true nature of Herbert's religious allegiances. Among other leading members of the Union, those whom Herbert would encounter again in politics included Lord Dalhousie, Lord Elgin and Lord Canning.[3] However, two people stand out, both High Churchmen, both presidents of the Union. One was the ill-starred Henry Pelham-Clinton, 12th Earl of Lincoln, later 5th Duke of Newcastle. Lincoln's career would follow Herbert's closely: he served as Secretary for War and the Colonies (1852-4), Secretary for War (1854-5), and Secretary for the Colonies (1859-64). The other was the force of nature that was William Ewart Gladstone. Son of a Liverpool merchant, and a year older than Herbert, he gained a rare Double First in 1831. Herbert recorded in his journal that 'I am very glad of it for he has my respect in every department in talents & character he is sterling'. His first surviving letter to Gladstone is one congratulating him on the achievement.[4]

1   Foot, *Gladstone Diaries*, I, p. 329, 12 Nov. 1830.
2   *The Times*, 23 Oct. 1873.
3   Dalhousie served as President of the Board of Trade and Governor-General of India; Elgin served as Governor of Jamaica, Governor-General of Canada and Viceroy of India; Canning served as Postmaster-General and Governor-General of India.
4   WSHC 2057/F/5/15, Dec. 1831; BL Add. Mss. 44210, fols. 1-2, SH to WEG, 18 June 1831.

Gladstone was politic enough not to respond in kind when Herbert was awarded his degree. It is difficult to imagine him emulating Herbert's decision to adorn a pro-forma signed by his three examiners with less than flattering caricatures. Herbert's verdict on the 'two or three days' he spent in Schools in November 1831 was that 'the examination is really nothing'. Unlike Gladstone, but like most young men from his background, he had not opted to try for a degree with Honours. His papers nevertheless sufficiently impressed the examiners that they 'invited him to try for a Class'. When he declined, 'they gave me a fourth'. The Oxford Fourth had been introduced just months earlier. It was intended for 'candidates for pass degrees who had shown more than ordinary diligence or ability'. It was not intended to be seen (though it quickly was) as derogatory in character. Rather the opposite.[1] Herbert was formally admitted to his degree in Classics as a Grand Compounder on 10 November. He left Oxford 'not without regret [...] I have spent some very pleasant time there & leave one or two valuable friends'.[2]

Herbert interspersed his Oxford years with travel. During the summer of 1829 he went with his mother and sisters to Wales. The journal he kept is replete with his sardonic wit. En route, they stay a night at Moreton-in-Marsh in a house 'occupied by the Landlady, the chambermaid the waiter & the rats; all seemed very active but particularly the last. We were the first persons who had slept there for some time & will probably be the last'.[3] No less memorable is his description of a Sunday evening service where the priest, a deaf landowner and a drunken butler attempted unsuccessfully to coordinate their response to the prayers: 'it really was terrible it was so impossible to resist laughing [...] I would not have to go through it again for any money. We all sat pinching ourselves and our neighbours

---

1   HP 2057/F5/15, 8 Nov. 1831; Brock and Curthoys, *History of the University of Oxford*, VI, p. 345.
2   WSHC 2057/F5/15, 8 Nov. 1831; *London Evening Standard*, 11 Nov. 1831. Grand compounders were those with incomes of more than £300 per annum.
3   WSHC 2057/F5/13, journal entry, 17 Aug. 1829.

in agony'.[1] But Herbert reveals another side to his nature when he waxes lyrical about place, whether it be Powis Castle where there was a 'beautiful view of the mountains & fine old trees standing about', or the road to Beaumaris which 'is as lovely a drive along the sea coast as can be imagined'. Even Liverpool, where the family briefly detoured, 'is really a very interesting place. We may be a nation of shopkeepers but here is a [...] gallantry in our housekeeping which distinguishes [us] from all others'.[2]

Less well documented, Herbert passed some of the long vacation of 1830 on a riding tour of Normandy. He was accompanied by his friend George Moberly, subsequently Bishop of Salisbury.[3] Herbert was particularly impressed by the great churches of Abbeville and Rouen. Rouen, he informed his mother, was a 'magnificent cathedral faintly lit by a few lamps & arches & windows just glimmering thro' the darkness [...] beautiful to a degree I cannot describe'.[4] The tour clearly confirmed his love for the church architecture of Catholic northern Europe. He would be more ambivalent in his feelings as he contemplated his first visit to Ireland.

The story of John Bull's other island would help define Herbert's career in politics as it did many others during the nineteenth century. Although Ireland had its own parliament until 1800, more than three-quarters of the land was in the hands of frequently absent English landlords. And whilst they were overwhelmingly Protestant, 93% of Ireland's peasant population was Roman Catholic. It was a recipe for both social and political unrest. One such manifestation, the rebellion of 1798, had precipitated the 1800 Act of Union which abolished the Irish parliament and transferred its legislative powers to Westminster. This merely recast the problem since Catholics were denied the right to sit there. Daniel O'Connell, a Catholic lawyer, spearheaded a campaign to secure equal political rights. The issue was forced when he was elected at a by-election for County Clare in 1828. Wellington's

1 WSHC 2057/F5/13, journal entry, 29 Aug. 1829.
2 WSHC 2057/F5/13, journal entries, 25 Aug., 17, 23 Sept. 1829.
3 George Moberly (1803-1885), Bishop of Salisbury from 1869 until his death.
4 WSHC 2057/F4/49, SH to Lady Pembroke, 15 Sept. 1830.

Tory government introduced Catholic Emancipation as the alternative to possible revolution.¹ It is unsurprising to find the seventeen-year-old Herbert ending a letter to his mother with the postscript: 'That wretch O'Connell!!'² He had, after all, recently acquired more than a passing interest. His Fitzwilliam inheritance included developments south of Dublin's city centre increasingly popular with its middle class citizens. The remainder of Herbert's Irish property lay in Ringsend, a mile east of the city centre; then, moving south around Dublin Bay, Irishtown and Sandymount to Ballsbridge, Dundrum and the main seat at Mount Merrion Park.³

Herbert had planned to visit Ireland with his family as part of their summer wanderings in 1829; he had even learnt a few Gaelic phrases in anticipation.⁴ In the event he was easily persuaded 'to take up with a Welsh tour instead in which we should see much more beauty'.⁵ Even the insalubrity of the earlier mentioned hostelry at Moreton-in-Marsh, with its quarter inch of dirt, he reckoned likely to be a 'palace [compared] to what we should meet with in Ireland'.⁶ His information, and prejudices, presumably derived from the depressing accounts received from Cornelius Sullivan, his land agent in Ireland. Distress in the Dublin suburbs, he noted in his journal in 1831, 'is very great', adding the sombre afterthought that 'the cholera when it comes will revel in the liberties'.⁷ Herbert had at least responded to Sullivan's bulletins with largesse. In April 1831, for example, he subscribed, via Sullivan, £50 to an Irish distress committee.⁸ Sullivan, as a moving force in the Sandymount, Ringsend and Irishtown Benevolent Institution, subsequently orchestrated a vote of thanks to Herbert as 'a truly kind and benevolent landlord'. This was not, as

1   Foster, *Modern Ireland 1600-1972*, ch's. 12-13.
2   WSHC 2057/F4/49, SH to Lady Pembroke, 8 July 1828.
3   http://humphrysfamilytree.com/Herbert/dublin.estate.html accessed 21 Feb. 2019.
4   WSHC 2057/F5/13, journal entry, 17 Aug. 1829.
5   WSHC 2057/F5/13, journal entry, 25 Aug. 1829.
6   WSHC 2057/F5/13, journal entry, 17 Aug. 1829.
7   WSHC 2057/F5/15, journal entry, Dec. 1831.
8   *Morning Chronicle*, 25 Apr. 1831.

one might suspect, simply stock formulary but a genuine response to Herbert's instruction that Sullivan spend £500 on food, clothing and employment for his tenants. The objective was to provide 'cleanliness and comfort' to the poor of the various districts 'without regard to the religious persuasion of recipients'.[1] Herbert was the recipient of further thanks in March 1832. On this occasion he had gifted the Taney Charitable Association with 50 blankets, 20 rugs, 50 pairs of men's stockings (and, incongruously, only 29 pairs of women's stockings), the whole to be sold to the poor at half price.[2]

A month later Herbert finally arrived to view his Irish inheritance in person. It was a trip during which he intended mixing business with pleasure. He was not especially enamoured by his first sight of Mount Merrion House, five miles south of Dublin. Built for the 5th Viscount Fitzwilliam a century before, it 'consisted of two distinct buildings, joined together by a two-storey structure, built upon arches, spanning an open courtyard'. Its charm was perhaps hidden by the fact that it was surrounded by an eight-foot-high granite wall. But Herbert was unequivocal in his feelings about its setting overlooking Dublin Bay: 'The view is something more lovely than I know anywhere as a sea view. With a different house in a different situation it would be one of the most beautiful things in Ireland'.[3] It stood in stark contrast to the rural poverty surrounding it.

During the ten days he spent in Ireland, Herbert was reported to have donated £500 to various causes, a figure 'represented to have been the theme of general admiration'. This included £50 for the Dublin mansion house relief committee and contributions 'to nearly all the charitable institutions of Dublin'. An address purporting to be from the poorest tenants on his estate declared that 'it is mainly owing to your unbounded liberality [...] in supplying food, fuel and clothing to the Poor' that they had been enabled to escape the worst deprivations of the past year. Herbert returned thanks on 5 May, insisting that his

1 *Dublin Morning Register*, 28 Dec. 1831.
2 *Saunders's News-letter*, 9 Mar. 1832.
3 WSHC 2057/F4/49, SH to Lady Pembroke, 26 Apr. 1832; Curtis, *Mount Merrion*, p. 15. The house was sold to the Catholic Church in 1936; much of it was demolished during the 1970s.

agents and local clergy were no less deserving of credit.[1] The tone of a private letter sent to his mother a few days earlier could hardly have been more different. In it he related dining 'at the Beefsteak Club, which comprises a hundred and fifty of the principal people here – all Tories, or nearly so. They drank my health, and I had to make a speech, in which I lied like a pig'.[2]

Herbert's private journal makes virtually no mention of his visit to Ireland. His thoughts at this time were focused on the struggle about to culminate with the passage of the Great Reform Act. The Act marked the third breach of the 'old' constitution of 1688. The first, in 1828, had seen parliament repeal the Test and Corporation Acts, formally ending the exclusion of Protestant Nonconformists from civil offices. Roman Catholic Emancipation had followed in 1829. The Tory party, badly split over the latter question, was mostly committed to resisting the popular pressure for reform of the electoral system which increased during 1830. Wellington's Tory government fell in November. The Whig-Reformer ministry which succeeded it introduced a Reform Bill in March 1831. This proposed abolishing the worst of the so-called rotten boroughs, and extending the franchise. A general election in May 1831 returned a clear majority in favour of the measure. But it took King William IV's threat to swamp the Tory-dominated Lords with Reformer peers before the Upper House gave way to the will of the people. Their doing so was interpreted by many to mean that the long hegemony of the Protestant landed order had been broken.

Thirty years later, liberals writing Herbert's obituary made at most passing reference to his life during this period of constitutional upheaval. One can understand why. His sister Elizabeth, in a letter sent to him at Oriel in March 1829, addressed him as 'my dearest & I hope Protestant Tory boy'. 'I hope', she added, that 'the pure constitutional air of Oxford has strengthened all your loyal Protestant feelings'.[3] In May 1831 Herbert took part in the famous Oxford Union debate

---

1   *Dublin Morning Register*, 2 May 1832; *Saunders's News-letter*, 7 May 1832; *London Evening Standard*, 21 May 1832; *SWJ*, 28 May 1832.
2   WSHC 2057/F4/49, SH to Lady Pembroke, 26 Apr. 1832.
3   WSHC 2057/F4/50, E. Herbert to SH, 1 Mar. 1829.

calling for the members of Grey's government to be impeached.[1] Of more practical use, he was prominent in helping to raise £800 for the Tory cause in the ongoing general election campaign. His journal then relates how he, Gladstone and Christopher Wordsworth (nephew of the poet and co-founder of the Boat Race) determined to get up a petition against the Reform Bill by convening a meeting of 'the influential Tories' in the various Oxford colleges. The resulting petition, of which Herbert was probably chief author, predicted that the Reform Bill would disturb the vital balance of power between the aristocratic and popular elements of the constitution. It would 'admit an alarming Proportion of Roman Catholic influence into Parliament'; popular clamour for change 'ought never to carry any weight except in cases where its sentence is found on independent grounds to be reasonable'. Herbert claimed that 770 of 1,100 undergraduates had supported the petition.[2] It was presented to parliament by Lord Mahon on 1 July. 'Upon the whole', Herbert reflected, 'I think the Petition did good, and certainly it is a good proof of the opinion of the Gentry, political opinions being for the most part hereditary in young men [...] I certainly do not regret the part I took in this matter'. At least one commentator in the press agreed: the petition 'proves how decidedly the rising talent of the country is opposed to any hasty and ill-considered innovations'.[3]

Herbert was dispirited for most of the summer of 1831. Anti-Reformers had been trounced in the general election; he felt unwell a day after meeting the Duke of Wellington at Lord Farnborough's. Plans for foreign travel were postponed: 'all this summer I spend in illness', he complained to Gladstone in August. Herbert's next letter, in September, was more upbeat. He and a friend had gone to Broadstairs where they found lodgings with a fisherman and were 'improving both our minds & bodies'. Buoyed, he returned to London to celebrate his

1 Shannon, *Gladstone. Peel's Inheritor*, p. 31.
2 WSHC 2057/F5/15, unidentified press cutting; journal entry, June 1831.
3 BL Add. Mss. 44210, fols. 5-6, SH to WEG, 2 July 1831; Hansard, 1 July 1831, IV, cols. 580-2; WSHC 2057/F5/15, unidentified press cutting; journal entry, June 1831.

coming of age on 10 September.¹ A month later, though, his mood had darkened again in response to the news that popular violence had erupted when the House of Lords rejected a revised version of the Reform Bill. Herbert was in no doubt that 'Grey and Place' (the latter the Radical tailor who was the de facto leader of the campaign for Reform in London) were to blame. Political Armageddon was not yet so certain, however, as to deter him from spending £100 on a mare 'to hunt like an angel'.² Herbert still clung to the hope that the Upper House would remain resolute, though his comment in February 1832 that 'I think the Lords will lose much character in the country by giving way so soon' implies the recognition that he now thought some form of compromise on the Reform Bill inevitable. Herbert was, however, disgusted that their Lordships capitulated in face of the King's threat to overwhelm them with Reformers. His journal records simply that 'the House of Lords is destroyed'.³ His wider fears for the consequences that would follow were reinforced en route to Ireland in April 1832. Herbert described travelling through:

> the horrible country from Birmingham to Wolverhampton, which is a continuation of furnaces and steam-engines, which suffocated us with smoke, all Sunday though it was. The people [...] looked more miserable and squalid and villainous than anything I ever saw before, and did not raise my opinion of the £10 householders and intellectual political unionists, whom Brougham so much lauded in his first speech on Reform.⁴

Herbert's dystopian vision of the Black Country, an example of the new Britain being created by the Industrial Revolution, was partly a result of his background as a conspicuously privileged member of the old landed order. In metaphorical terms, Birmingham and

---

1   BL Add. Mss. 44210, fols. 8-12, SH to WEG, 17 Aug., 8 Sept. 1831; WSHC 2057/F5/15, journal entries, July, Sept., 10 Oct. 1831.
2   WSHC 2057/F5/15, journal entries, Dec. 1831.
3   WSHC 2057/F5/15, journal entries, Feb, 15 May 1832.
4   WSHC 2057/F4/49, SH to Lady Pembroke, 26 Apr. 1832. Brougham was Lord Chancellor.

Wolverhampton were light years from the dreaming spires of Oxford, let alone Arcadian Wilton. His Tory politics were understandable; his disdain for urbanisation and the labouring masses undisguised. How would these worlds accommodate each other in the generation ahead? That was one of the great challenges facing Herbert's political generation. With his personal gifts it was no surprise that he was tipped to be amongst its leaders. The young Herbert was not inclined to demur: 'there are very few clever men in the world', he announced in August 1832. There could hardly have been a more exciting moment for the would-be Member of Parliament to join the political fray.

2
Setting Course 1832-1837

Harriet Martineau wrote that 'it was simply a matter of course that Herbert should enter Parliament as soon as he was old enough'.¹ Given his background this was true but it was by no means certain where he would stand in the general election of 1832. His Irish friends had been keen to enlist him as a candidate during his visit in April: 'Two or three people spoke to me about the representation of the county [Dublin], where they say one or perhaps two Tories might be brought in at the next election'.² Rumours persisted until the autumn that he would come forward. In the face of them, a hostile *Dublin Evening Post* mocked that 'There is a certain Mr Herbert, or Sir Sidney Herbert, or Lord Sidney Herbert – we really do not know his designation – but we know he represents great property in the neighbourhood of Dublin'.³ Herbert, unpersuaded that he could win Dublin, was never seriously tempted to throw his hat into the ring. His contribution was limited to the £100 which he subscribed to the Protestant Conservative Society. He was duly thanked for this display of his 'soundest constitutional principles'.⁴

Wilton was the obvious constituency. Long before the Herberts set foot there it had been an important royal centre and Wiltshire's

1   Martineau, *Biographical Sketches*, p. 318.
2   WSHC 2057/F4/49, SH to Lady Pembroke, 26 Apr. 1832.
3   *Morning Chronicle*, 11 Sept. 1832; *Saunders's News-letter*, 17 Oct. 1832.
4   *Dublin Evening Packet*, 19 July 1832; *Dublin Evening Mail*, 10 Oct. 1832.

county town. By 1832 it had long been eclipsed by Salisbury, three miles to the east. Even the town's famous carpet business encouraged by Herbert's Pembroke ancestors, was in decline. The borough's otherwise small agriculturally-based community sat incongruously alongside the grand Palladian house which dominated it.[1] But though Wilton boasted a population of only 1,997 in 1831 (unenfranchised Birmingham, which so repelled Herbert in April 1832, had over 146,000), it had continued to return two MPs. And since the Earls of Pembroke effectively controlled the corporation of roughly twenty members which constituted the electorate, it was a classic example of a proprietary borough. There had been no contested election there since 1710.

Remarkably, Wilton did not fall victim to the disfranchising clauses of the Reform Bill 'as I [Herbert] had feared'.[2] Instead the framers of the Reform Bill contented themselves with remodelling the parliamentary borough. One seat was abolished and the boundaries extended: by incorporating into it part or all of seventeen contiguous parishes, the parliamentary borough of Wilton grew from 0.2 to 49.4 square miles in size. Even so, the new constituency contained only 298 properties estimated to be worth the requisite £10 per annum which qualified their occupants to vote.[3] And since virtually all of them came under the sway of the Pembroke estate there would have been nothing easier than to install Herbert as the incumbent Member for life. As the *Morning Chronicle* put it, the Reform Act found Wilton 'a nomination borough, under the direct influence of the Earl of Pembroke, and, after the passing of that Bill, it remains as much under the influence of that nobleman as ever'.[4] Not wanting to be backward in coming forward, Herbert wrote to his brother in June 1832, effectively asking for the seat. Robert Pembroke was obliging. He replied at once to his half-

1 https://www.historyofparliamentonline.org/volume/1820-1832/constituencies/wilton, accessed 12 Feb. 2019.
2 WSHC 2057/F5/15, journal entry, Dec. 1831.
3 Gash, *Politics in the Age of Peel*, pp. 70, 432-3.
4 *Morning Chronicle*, 7 Jan. 1835.

brother with the news that he had instructed the elderly incumbent to stand aside.[1]

In the event, Herbert was persuaded to stand for the newly created South Wiltshire constituency instead: populous county seats were more prestigious than small borough ones.[2] The possibility had first been touted to Herbert in May. He was flattered to discover, during a visit to Salisbury, that his name commanded 'great support, some unexpected'; even more by being told that he was the Tory candidate most likely to be elected.[3] Against this, however, Herbert had to weigh the fact that though he would be returned for Wilton with minimum fuss, winning in Wiltshire was by no means certain. Robert Pembroke for one was doubtful; he generously offered to keep the Wilton seat open. He knew that John Benett and John Dugdale Astley stood in Herbert's path. Both supporters of the Reform Bill, Benett and Astley had been returned unopposed for the old, undivided Wiltshire constituency since 1820. The widespread presumption was that they would make a seamless transition to represent South Wiltshire.[4] But when Herbert announced his candidacy it was Astley who blinked first; he opted to run for North Wiltshire instead. Herbert's formal election address appeared on 26 June. In language typical for an aspiring county MP he proclaimed that 'I appear before you perfectly independent, unshackled by any pledges, and determined to act entirely as my conscience and my judgement shall dictate'.[5]

In a letter to the press which suggests imperfect historical judgement, Herbert was trumpeted as 'a man amongst the descendants of those illustrious chiefs' who had helped 'lay the foundation of the power and glory of England'. His coming forward 'at so early an age,

1 WSHC 2057/F4/70, Pembroke to SH, 16 June, 11 July 1832.
2 The English political nation was divided into 144 county, 323 borough and 4 university seats. Like most counties Wiltshire was divided in two by the Reform Act, each new constituency returning two members. The principle qualification for the vote was possession of freehold land worth £2 a year.
3 WSHC 2057/F5/15, journal entry, 19 May 1832.
4 *Reading Mercury*, 11 June 1832.
5 *SWJ*, 2 July 1832.

and at a moment of such peculiar difficulty', it added, 'is the surest presage of future eminence and distinction'.[1] The sentiments contrasted sharply with those expressed in another letter of the same day. Did South Wiltshire's freeholders really want to see Herbert 'returned by dumb show', to be represented by 'a stripling [...] a youth just come of age, without experience, stability, or a sufficient knowledge of the affairs of men [?]'[2] The writer had a point: it was unusual for somebody so young to represent a county constituency. A more serious objection, given the popular mood, was that Herbert had opposed the Reform Bill. Oddly, his opponents made relatively little of this. They were presumably unaware of how prominent a part he had played in the campaign against it at Oxford. Even so, Herbert deemed it politic to issue a second address on 7 July. In it he denied any imputation that he was a reactionary, adducing as proof his desire to see economy and the correction of abuses in the State.[3] Unconvinced, the Earl of Radnor, de facto leader of South Wiltshire's Reformers, issued a letter from his seat at Longford Castle (seven miles from Wilton) demanding that Herbert be opposed. Herbert was 'very glad of it', believing that it had 'decidedly given me a helping hand'.[4] Radnor had indeed miscalculated. Convention dictated that peers abstain from such overt intervention in electoral matters; instead Radnor laid himself open to the charge that he was attempting to dictate the constituency's affairs. He and Herbert exchanged sharp letters on the subject.[5]

The substantive point was that, by mid-July, no third candidate would enter the field: Herbert would be returned unopposed alongside the Reformer, John Benett. This was ultimately recognition of reality. Popular sentiment may well have been against Herbert; the political influence that came with the possession of many acres was not. The 40,000 acre Wilton estate was far and away the largest in

1 *SWJ*, 9 July 1832 for Edward Hinxman's letter of 7 July.
2 *SWJ*, 9 July 1832 for John Leach's letter of 7 July.
3 *Hampshire Advertiser*, 23 June 1832; *SWJ*, 25 June, 2, 16 July 1832; *DWG*, 28 June 1832.
4 WSHC 2057/F5/15, journal entry, July 1832.
5 *Hampshire Advertiser*, 7 July 1832; *SWJ*, 9 July 1832; WSHC 2057/F4/70, Radnor to SH, 1 July 1832; SH to Radnor, 9 July 1832.

the constituency. Second largest was Radnor's 17,000 acres, but some of those lay in North Wiltshire. No other family could boast more than 10,000 acres: next in size was the Earl of Normanton's 9,800 acre Somerley Park estate. And Normanton, it will be remembered, was married to Herbert's half-sister, Diana. The combined acreage of Tory landowners in the constituency was roughly twice that of Reformers. Herbert was therefore always fairly confident that he would prevail: 'Country gentlemen', he wrote in his journal, 'have a good deal of esprit de corps [...] they must always stick by a member of their Club'.[1] Reformers, as one of their number subsequently put it, had to cling to the belief that Herbert 'appeared amiable and talented, and [...] would adhere to his pledge to be independent'.[2] Even so Herbert took nothing for granted. He got caught up in the excitement of a 'canvass going on full tilt', albeit mixed with the frustration of being obliged to dissemble: 'when I am asked whether I am a reformer I say the question is passed & therefore I cannot be called upon for an opinion upon it'. He had 'much rather say I am an antireformer & a gentleman & be d__d to you'.[3]

Nomination day, 17 December, was something of a parade. It began with an election breakfast for Herbert and his principal supporters at Wilton House. Then 'we had a capital procession from Wilton [to the hustings at Salisbury] of four or five hundred horsemen, and a very fine day'.[4] Herbert was introduced on the hustings as 'a young man of honour and integrity', and less accurately as the bearer of a name which 'appeared prominently in Magna Charta'.[5] Although 'received with some sneers' when he rose to speak, Herbert was defiant in his insistence that he would oppose measures which he judged as tending to 'destruction'. Repeating the claim made in his electoral

1 WSHC 2057/F5/15, journal entry, Aug. 1832.
2 *SWJ*, 28 Jan. 1833 for Mr Peniston's speech at the Reformer dinner in Salisbury.
3 WSHC 2057/F5/15, journal entry, 19 May 1832.
4 WSHC 2057/F4/49, SH to Lady Pembroke, 17 Dec. 1832; *DWG*, 20 Dec. 1832.
5 It was William Marshal, son of the Earl of Pembroke of the second creation, who was numbered amongst the signatories of Magna Carta.

address that he was 'no reactionary Tory', he nevertheless promised to support proposals for reform that he considered beneficial. Commutation of tithes was cited as an example. Until a sharp shower brought a premature end to the proceedings, Herbert appears to have enjoyed his experience of the rough and tumble of nineteenth-century electioneering.[1]

For all that South Wiltshire's Reformers wanted to believe that Herbert would be an independent at Westminster, the facts suggested otherwise. Robert Pembroke had supported his half-brother's standing with the endorsement that 'you are a staunch and honest Tory, and will I am sure from all I have heard distinguish yourself as a speaker, and thereby I hope keep in subjection [the] radical opinion of our county'. Lord Stanmore was therefore right to say that it was as 'a Tory and a follower of the Duke of Wellington' that Herbert took his seat in the House of Commons.[2] The Tory party, however, was in a state of flux. More than a generation of essentially Tory administrations had come to an end in 1830. Opposing the Reform Bill had resulted in substantial Tory losses at the general elections of 1831 and 1832. As the party looked to regroup, in the Lower House at least, it was less to the Iron Duke than Sir Robert Peel that it looked for leadership.

In terms of personnel, the 1833 parliament differed considerably from its predecessor. Herbert was one of 252 new Members. In addition, he was one of only 42 Members to have been returned as a Tory for an English county seat. More pertinent than either of those statistics, Herbert was one of only 147 Tory MPs who found themselves confronted by 511 Reformers.[3] Admittedly that label encompasses a mix of Whig, moderate liberal, Radical and Irish Members, but if Herbert had entered parliament harbouring ambitions of office, he had clearly tied his fortunes to the wrong party. Charles Greville remarked that 'the Tories are few and scattered'; among the new Members 'not one of them of shining or remarkable talent'.[4] At least Herbert had two

1 *SWJ*, 24 Dec. 1832.
2 WSHC 2057/F4/70, Pembroke to SH, 11 July 1832; Stanmore, I, p. 18.
3 Woolley, 'The Personnel of the Parliament of 1833', pp. 240-62.
4 Reeve, *Greville Memoirs*, pt. 1, II, p. 353; III, p. 27.

kindred spirits for companionship: Lord Lincoln had been returned for South Nottinghamshire; Gladstone for Newark. One reason why all three had the chance to shine was that Tory lights were otherwise so dim.

The extent of Herbert's Toryism during his early days in parliament is difficult to measure. He informed his mother before taking his seat that 'there is no danger of my committing myself about Politics, and I am as cautious as a fidge'.[1] Such evidence as there is points to his having been more of an independent Tory than a partisan one. In February 1833 he opposed a motion tabled by the Radical, Joseph Hume, declaring army and navy sinecures to be unnecessary; likewise Hume's motion of April that flogging in the army by commissioned officers should be abolished. Herbert was also amongst the majority who saw off the Radical George Grote's proposal of 25 April that the secret ballot should be introduced for future elections. As one would expect of a county Member, however, he joined in supporting demands for a select committee on distress, on 23 March, even though it was moved by a Radical.[2] The following month Herbert was one of sixteen county Members who prided themselves on having supported a motion calling for a reduction in the duty on malt (a particular bugbear in agricultural constituencies) to ten shillings a quarter. Taking ministers apparently by surprise ('the fools!!' noted Herbert in his journal), the motion passed by 162 votes to 152.[3] But the latter two votes were flimsy evidence for the claim made by a speaker at a dinner of Salisbury Reformers in 1833 that 'well-founded hopes might be entertained of the Hon. Sidney Herbert becoming a supporter of the rights and liberties of the people'.[4]

Given Herbert's indifferent attendance record later in the decade, it would probably be truer to say that he was a lax attender. Certainly he was far from well. He recorded that he was suffering 'vexations of spirit!!' during the early spring. Newspapers reported that illness prevented him from attending the House during May. In

1   WSHC 2057/F4/49, SH to Lady Pembroke, 20 Dec. 1832.
2   *SWJ*, 25 Mar. 1833.
3   WSHC 2057/F5/15, journal entries, Feb., Apr., 1833.
4   *SWJ*, 10 June 1833.

the summer he was debilitated 'with a large swelling in the side'. His response was of doubtful efficacy: he took mercury 'in great quantities wh. so weakened me I can scarce walk ten yards and look like a ghost'.[1] Laid low, he was prone to introspection. His life thus far, he reflected, had been a mixture of pleasure and pain:

> Had I a little more virtue & a little less conscience I sh be a happier man [...] They say the good are happy. But they are so few we cannot take them into consideration when speaking of mankind. The mass who are bad certainly are not happy in this world nor probably in the next [God] made his creatures so & so balanced their temptations & frailties that the majority must perish & being prescient he must have so intended it.

Life, Herbert concluded, could only be endured because of his belief in the certainty of the world to come.[2]

Herbert's body and mood were sufficiently recovered for him to be able to resume his foreign travels later that summer. After a 'very rough passage' to Le Havre, he found the cathedral at Chartres 'magnificent & such windows'. Orleans too, was 'very beautiful & very perfect'. From France he continued on to Monaco and then Italy. Pisa's cathedral, and the city's celebrated tower, he recorded, 'are well worth seeing and all [...] together for the convenience of travellers'.[3] He returned refreshed for the parliamentary fray.

For the first half of 1834 Herbert remained a largely anonymous Member. He seems to have done little beyond assisting his Wiltshire colleague, John Benett, in steering a minor enclosure Bill through the House.[4] In the voting lobbies he continued to oppose abortive proposals from Radicals who wanted further constitutional reform, for example Tennyson's motion to reduce the maximum life of a parliament from seven years. Mindful of his duty to his constituents,

---

1 WSHC 2057/F5/15, journal entries, Feb., Apr., July 1833; *The Times*, 24 May 1833.
2 WSHC 2057/F5/15, journal entry, July 1833.
3 WSHC 2057/F5/15, journal entries, July-Aug. 1833.
4 *Commons Journal*, 19, 25 Feb., 7, 10 Mar., 17 Apr., 2 May 1834.

he also opposed a motion to introduce a low fixed duty on corn but supported those calling for a repeal of the malt tax and the setting up of a select committee to consider the question of agricultural distress.

Unsurprisingly, it was Church-related questions which galvanised Herbert into making his parliamentary mark. In 1833 Grey's government introduced the Irish Church Temporalities Bill. This proposed abolishing some Anglican bishoprics and diverting the money saved to lay purposes. To High Churchmen such as Herbert, this was anathema: the State should not interfere in the affairs of the Church, the more so if such intrusions threatened to weaken the Establishment. Illness prevented Herbert from joining Lincoln and Gladstone to vote against the proposals but he was anxious that the press report his 'indisposition' as the reason for his not doing so.[1]

But Herbert was well enough to join the next big political battle in defence of Anglicanism. Anxious to appease its Nonconformist allies, the government supported a Bill allowing them to enter Oxbridge. On 20 June Herbert rose from his seat on the backbenches to speak against the Second Reading.[2] By convention, maiden speeches were brief and uncontentious, and as such listened to without interruption. Herbert's first essay in parliamentary oratory was therefore atypical: a substantial exposition on a burning question of the moment. The ancient universities, he began, were not just educational institutions but Anglican ones too. How therefore:

> could a Dissenter become a master in any of the colleges, when, to be one, a complete knowledge of the tenets of the Established Church was necessary? No matter how great a proficient in learning he might be – no matter how brilliant were the talents with which nature endowed him, a religious education was a sine qua non [...] Even the Dissenters themselves, when such was the fact, ought not to wish to enter these colleges, and be under such masters, and be continually

---

1 Evans, *Forging of the Modern State*, pp. 239-41; *The Times*, 24 May 1833.
2 Hansard, 20 June 1834, XXIV, cols. 640-3.

present in a place where a system of religious education was adopted from beginning to end.

Herbert was even more concerned about the possible consequences for Anglican students of admitting Nonconformists to study alongside them:

> Could it be expected, that those pupils would ever look with much reverence on the religion of the Established Church, when they saw it treated with indifference, as it would be if the Dissenters were allowed to become masters? In these times of trouble – in these times of dissension of every species – the admission of Dissenters into the Universities would be nothing less than opening them to conflicting opinions, and making them an arena for religious animosity, instead of allowing them to be the quiet seats of study.

The longer-term consequences of the Bill, he prophesised, would be little short of apocalyptic:

> under its cloak infidels and atheists would creep into the Universities [...] the noblemen and gentry of the country would cease to send their sons to the Universities [...] it would prevent them from forming, at the University, attachments with those who would become afterwards ministers of religion [...] By breaking off the early acquaintance that might be formed between the minister and the gentlemen among whom he might afterwards reside [...] a stop would be put to the mutual assistance they would afford to each other in making the stream of benevolence flow more rapidly and broadly.

There was though, he suggested, a simple solution:

> Let the Dissenters erect their own colleges, and, if they should happen to produce, as the English Universities already had, great and eloquent statesmen, profound philosophers, and men who would be an ornament to society, then would their country be grateful to them for the benefit they had bestowed upon it.

The Tory press lauded Herbert's speech; Gladstone too, judged it 'very successful'.[1] Later liberal apologists found it more problematic. Harriet Martineau explained it away as 'the speech of a very young man, though a strong Conservative'. Stanmore chose to focus on style, not substance: the speech was an example of a time when 'arguments were used with confidence, and indeed assumed as postulates, which would now, if used at all, be advanced with far greater hesitation'.[2] The latter in particular was pulling his punches. Herbert's speech had revealed him to be a contender for the accolade of being (in the famous phrase Macaulay would use of Gladstone) the 'rising hope of those stern and unbending Tories'.

Well before Herbert made his maiden speech, he had been more agreeably labelled as 'one of the wealthiest commoners in the gay world'.[3] Blessed with many personal virtues and heir to an earldom, he was among the most eligible bachelors of his time. His first recorded acknowledgment that he was an object of desire dates from his journey through Wales in 1829: a 'Miss Shipley', he observed, 'is making a dead set at me'. Stories inevitably circulated thereafter that he was about to be ensnared. During the summer of 1832 it was widely reported that he had chosen for his life-partner 'one of the fairest ornaments of our fashionable circles' – but no name was provided.[4] A few weeks later the Wiltshire press thought it had a scoop when it identified Herbert's intended as the daughter of Lord Arundell of Wardour Castle. It was a match that would have raised eyebrows: the Arundells were amongst Wiltshire's most prominent Roman Catholic families. Herbert certainly visited Wardour at least twice that summer; when he ventured into Salisbury in September bells were pealed in anticipation of an announcement. Such anticipation is baffling, however, not least because Lord Arundell was childless.[5] At least the

---

1 *London Evening Standard*, 21 June 1834; Morley, *Gladstone*, I, p. 112. The Bill passed the Commons only to be lost in the Lords.
2 Martineau, *Biographical Sketches*, pp. 318-19; Stanmore, I, pp. 18-19.
3 *London Evening Standard*, 29 May 1833.
4 WSHC 2057/F5/13, journal entry, 27 Sept. 1829; *Saunders's Newsletter*, 10 July 1832.
5 *SWJ*, 22 July, 9 Sept. 1832; Williamson, *Arundells of Wardour*, ch. 10.

London Evening Standard was prepared to produce a name: Herbert, it reported in May 1833, would soon become engaged to Lady Honoria Cadogan, second daughter of the 3rd Earl of Cadogan. The rumours quickly evaporated; Lady Honoria died unmarried in 1904. So far as the identity of Herbert's bride was concerned, the gossip was set to continue for another decade and more.[1]

There was at least substance to reports in the early 1830s that Herbert was to set up home at Wilton House. That fact necessitates that we re-think the image of Robert Pembroke as the pariah of the family. It was true that his marriage was unfortunate, that he had offended his father, that he liked living in Paris, and 'disliked' England.[2] And the young Herbert seems to have been ambivalent about him. He was, after all, only four-years old when Robert contracted his *mésalliance*. From Harrow in 1825 he wrote that he was 'very anxious' to hear that 'poor Robert' was ill in Paris. Three years later, however, it was a holier-than-thou Herbert who expressed 'fears' that Robert had appointed clergymen to two benefices in his gift when he self-evidently knew nothing about them. And when Herbert received news that Robert was coming to England briefly in 1829 he admitted that 'I somehow or other feel very nervous about this visit'.[3] Nearly twenty years older, Robert was like a distant uncle to him.

But was Robert really such a black sheep? He had been present at his father's deathbed in 1827. On entering into the earldom, he invested £20,000 for his half-siblings: they were paid any interest accrued on a half yearly basis.[4] More importantly, Robert was generous to a fault in his conduct towards Herbert when the latter gave notice of his wish to enter parliament for Wilton in 1832. He was no less amenable when his half-brother inconvenienced him by switching his ambitions to South Wiltshire instead. As a matter of courtesy Robert had also insisted on securing his step-mother, the Dowager Lady Pembroke's acquiescence in the plan (Herbert's mother was only

1 *London Evening Standard*, 29 May 1833.
2 BL Add. Mss. 49270, fol. 141.
3 WSHC 2057/F4/49, SH to Lady Pembroke, 7 Feb. 1825, 8 July 1828; WSHC 2057/F5/13, journal entry, 14 Oct. 1829.
4 WSHC 2057/A6/61.

six years older than Robert) before implementing it: 'there has been hostility & civil war enough in the family, this might again fan the flame in some parts'. He proceeded then to tease Herbert for choosing to base himself in Salisbury, not Wilton, for the South Wiltshire campaign. It had, the Earl presumed, been done for political reasons:

> otherwise I should feel much hurt at your not having taken up yr abode at yr natural home, the home of your forefathers, at least when you are not in the Emerald isle [...] If you play such tricks again, when I set up shop at Wilton, I shall be forced to write on the gate (Pembroke & Sidney Herbert are Partners) otherwise people will imagine you have nothing to do with the Firm.

He could, he assured his young half-brother, 'always find you a mutton chop & a bottle of claret, very wholesome food for canvassers'. Robert ended that particular letter by asking Herbert to send his love to his half-sisters and signed off as 'Ever yr most affectte fratello mio, Pembroke'.[1] Neither his words nor his actions as this time merit saddling him with the label of *persona non grata*.

However, Herbert's coming of age and return for South Wiltshire may well have been the triggers for the 12th Earl's deciding that he did not, after all, want to 'set up shop' at Wilton. According to a later account, it had been a grudging Robert who 'came down to Wilton for the ceremony of taking charge of the property' when his father died.[2] Wilton therefore needed a custodian; Herbert, as county Member from December 1832, needed a home. The solution was obvious. As Elizabeth Herbert put it, 'it was decided by the wish of his Brother that he should return to Wilton as the place was suffering in all ways from the absence of the proprietors'.[3] Herbert's mother, who had been living in London since the 11th Earl's death in 1827, came with him. The Wiltshire press in due course confirmed that Robert had 'lent his superb chateau, Wilton House, near Salisbury, to the Hon. Sidney Herbert'. 'The Dowager Countess and the Ladies Herbert,' it

1   WSHC 2057/F4/70, Pembroke to SH, 11 July 1832.
2   BL Add. Mss. 49270, fol. 141.
3   BL Add. Mss. 49270, fol. 141.

added sardonically, 'are to become inmates'. In August 1834, having entrusted his proxy vote in the House of Lords to Wellington, it was reported that Pembroke had decided on a permanent move to Paris.[1] In Robert's absence Herbert now assumed responsibility, therefore, for the day to day running of the vast Wilton estate, as well as the less onerous task of overseeing the affairs of the parliamentary borough. He remained mindful, however, that he was essentially a tenant in his brother's house. Whilst travelling in Europe in 1833, for example, his journal records how he came across a statue similar to 'a statue now in the possession of Lord Pembroke [...] at Wilton'. So far as outside observers were concerned, though, Sidney Herbert was now the one to 'live & rule at Wilton'.[2]

Possibly because he was still coming to grips with his new role at Wilton, Herbert did not go abroad in 1834. He could, however, be seen supporting race meetings at Salisbury and Goodwood.[3] When the parliamentary race was resumed in the autumn, William IV brought down the frontrunner: Lord Melbourne, who had only become Prime Minister in July when Grey retired, was dismissed on 14 November. The King had objected to Melbourne advancing Lord John Russell to be Leader of the House, owing to the latter's desire to revive the question of the Irish Church. In the game of political musical chairs which followed, Wellington was appointed head of a caretaker ministry pending Sir Robert Peel's return from holiday in Italy. Peel accepted the King's invitation to form a ministry on 10 December. Since his government was in a minority in the Commons, Peel also secured the monarch's agreement to call an election in an attempt to strengthen his parliamentary position.

The January 1835 election is chiefly memorable for the letter Peel addressed to his constituents on 18 December 1834. Clearly intended for a national audience, it has become known as the Tamworth Manifesto. By appealing 'to the good sense and calm judgement of the people', Peel attempted to regain the political middle ground for the

1 *Dublin Morning Register*, 30 Aug. 1834; *SWJ*, 30 Oct. 1834.
2 WSHC 2057/F5/15, journal entry, July 1833; HRO 21M57/2A1/5/5-6, SH to Normanton, 9 June 1841.
3 *London Evening Standard*, 29 July 1834; *SWJ*, 1 Sept. 1834.

Tories, not least by rebranding them as Conservatives. He drew a line under the 1832 Reform Act by accepting it as 'a final and irrevocable settlement of a great constitutional question'. For the future, he promised to act in its spirit. This he defined as meaning 'a careful review of institutions, civil and ecclesiastical, undertaken in a friendly temper combining, with the firm maintenance of established rights, the correction of proved abuses and the redress of real grievances'.[1] Herbert's election address of 31 December duly took its cue from Tamworth. He promised to:

> support every Reform, which by removing their defects, may add fresh strength and efficacy to our Institutions, whilst I will as strenuously oppose all such innovations as may tend to weaken or destroy them. I am a sincere friend to economy and retrenchment, and will advocate such measures only as promise security and prosperity to the various Interests of the Empire.[2]

To outward appearances Herbert was enjoying the holiday period. He had forsaken his 'suburban residence in Wilts' to spend Christmas 'in pursuit of the feathered tribe' with the Malmesbury family at Heron Court near Ringwood.[3] In reality his mind was unsettled. On 21 December Peel had offered him junior office as a Lord Commissioner of the Treasury. This was essentially a sinecure post carrying no significant responsibility. His friends Gladstone and Lincoln had received, and accepted, the same invitation. Herbert declined. Early biographies attributed his refusal to moral scruple: that he was not prepared to take payment from the public purse in exchange for a nominal workload.[4] The truth lies elsewhere. Herbert had promised his constituents in 1832 that he would be independent, untrammelled by party. Freeholders expected no less. Joining the government, however junior the position, would render that pledge hollow. It would quite possibly provoke a potentially expensive election

---

1   Gash, *Peel*, pp. 93-9.
2   *SWJ*, 5 Jan. 1835.
3   NUL Ne C 11822/1-3, SH to Lincoln, 2 Jan. 1835.
4   *Fraser's Magazine*, 'Herbert', p. 199.

contest. Even if successful it would leave him with the dilemma of having to decide where his priorities lay if loyalties to government and constituency conflicted. Of course, Herbert did not put it like this to Peel. His letter declining office was self-effacing in tone:

> I [...] think the support I might succeed in giving to your administration as an independent co. member wd be better worth your acceptance than any service I cd now give as an official man [...] I am determined to do whatever may be most useful.[1]

He might have added 'for myself'.

Peel responded by interrupting Herbert's sport on New Year's Day with the offer of a more prestigious post: one of the two Secretaryships at the Board of Control. It was, Peel flattered him, 'one of the most important and interesting (I fear I must add laborious) offices connected with the Government'.[2] Herbert capitulated. News of his appointment excited scorn in some circles. Charles Greville, unaware of Peel's first offer to Herbert, regarded it as a clear case of over-promotion:

> He is about twenty-two or twenty-three years old, unpractised in business, and never spoke but once in the House of Commons, when he made one of those pretty first speeches which prove little or nothing, and that was in opposition to the Dissenters. He may be very fit for this place, but it remains to be proved, and I am surprised he did not make him begin with a Lordship of the Treasury or some such thing, and put Gladstone, who is a very clever man, in that post.[3]

Greville ascribed Herbert's elevation to Peel's penchant for 'the old aristocratic principle of taking high birth and connection as substitutes for other qualifications'. There was some force in his criticism – at least two modern authorities have concurred – but the

---

1   WSHC 2057 F4/53, SH to Peel, 22 Dec. 1834.
2   WSHC 2057/F4/53, Peel to SH, 1 Jan. 1835.
3   Reeve, *Greville Memoirs, Journal*, pt. 1, vol. 3, pp. 193-4, 12 Jan.1835.

fault was not Herbert's.[1] And neither was it entirely fair. Herbert was 'regarded as a graceful and accomplished young Tory, an ornament to a party then in disgrace and under chastisement'. This was clearly the view of Peel himself, a view formed at first hand. Herbert had been amongst the select group invited to an evening party at his London home in April 1834.[2] There was an easy familiarity from a man renowned for his formality in Peel's letter to 'my very dear Sidney', offering him office.[3] For his part, Herbert had entertained high regard for Peel since at least 1829, when he encountered him as Member for Oxford University. Peel's conduct then, trying vainly to persuade his listeners of the necessity to grant Catholic Emancipation, 'has been so much more open & manly than heretofore that he is raised 3 pegs in my estimation'.[4] Personal regard for Peel, what Peel stood for, a sense of duty, the desire to serve with his friends, the offer of a more attractive job, ambition too, all played their part in effecting Herbert's change of heart.

There remained the ticklish problem of how Herbert's taking office would play in Wiltshire. His fears were confirmed when he returned from the hunting field on 5 January to find a letter from Thomas Grove of Ferne House, near Shaftesbury, hitherto one of his most zealous supporters. Grove expressed disappointment that Herbert appeared to be compromising his political independence. Although still prepared to vote for Herbert, Grove did not feel that he could second his nomination at the hustings as he had in 1832. A 'pained' Herbert replied that were the government to adopt principles of which he disapproved, 'I at once resign the situation I have accepted'. With a certain defiance he added that what he was doing 'is a complete sacrifice of time and pursuits: but I wish to make myself useful. It is a fair object of ambition which I shd be ashamed of myself if I had not'.[5]

1 Gash, *Pillars of Government*, p. 158; Kitson Clark, *Peel and the Conservative Party*, p. 204.
2 Martineau, *Biographical Sketches*, p. 318; *Morning Post*, 16 Apr. 1834.
3 WSHC 2057/F4/53, Peel to SH, 1 Jan. 1835.
4 WSHC 2057/F4/50, SH to Lady E. Herbert, 8 Mar. 1829.
5 WSHC 2057/F4/70, Grove to SH, 5 Jan. 1835; SH to Grove, 5 Jan. 1835.

In truth Herbert was more alarmed than defiant. Not least because of his speech against admitting Nonconformists to Oxbridge, he knew that 'The Dissenters [were] very anxious at all risks to get up an opposition to me'. The news that Grove was, in a way, abandoning him, 'may assist them very much'. He wrote immediately to Sir Edmund Antrobus, a family friend, admitting that 'I am very anxious not to appear to be deserted by the gentry at this moment'. He asked Antrobus to second his nomination.[1] In an attempt to mitigate further criticism, Herbert also rushed out a second address in which he rehearsed the arguments used in his letter to Grove: that he entertained a 'sincere desire' to be 'useful to my country', that he 'felt it my duty to comply' with Peel's offering him 'an efficient and active office'. It would not, he promised South Wiltshire's freeholders, in any way compromise his independence in serving them.[2]

Herbert's initiatives did not defuse the issue. But his worst fears were not realised; there was no formal opposition to his re-election. Perhaps partly in relief, Herbert invited Benett's supporters to rendezvous with his at Wilton on nomination day, 14 January. It was therefore a joint procession of an estimated 800 people that proceeded to the hustings in Salisbury. Even so, the proceedings were lively. As one report in the local press put it, 'some disapprobation was manifested by the unwashed artificers below the hustings'; the disturbance resulted in Herbert's proposer having to abandon his speech.[3] Herbert too experienced some interruption when he rose to speak, especially when he said that Peel's Tamworth address 'met his entire approval'. However, most of his remarks were devoted to religious questions. Declaring his love for the Church, 'the almoner of the poor', he nevertheless repeated the pledge that he had made in 1832, that this did not preclude reforming it. Whether any Nonconformists present believed him when he said that this included redressing legitimate Dissenters' grievances is another matter. But the day at least ended on an amicable note. Supporters of both Members attended a dinner in

1   WSHC 2057/F4/70, SH to Antrobus, 5 Jan. 1835.
2   *SWJ*, 12 Jan. 1835.
3   *DWG*, 15 Jan. 1835; *SWJ*, 19 Jan. 1835.

Salisbury's Assembly Rooms, an occasion enlivened by Mr Newman the ventriloquist. In the toasts which followed, J.T. Mayne, a well-known local solicitor and rabid anti-Tory, conceded that Herbert was 'doubtless an excellent and amiable man; and the Tories had played their best card when they brought forward that gentleman'.[1]

So far as the nationwide political picture was concerned, Herbert concluded that 'upon the whole [...] the elections are gone pretty well'.[2] He was in similarly optimistic vein at the beginning of February. Speaking in Salisbury, he declared that he and his Reformer colleague, Benett, were 'two men who belonged to no party [...] the only party from whom danger to the institutions of the country was to be apprehended was a small party; the two leading parties of the state had merged into one – had united for the preservation of all that was valuable to them'.[3] This was at best self-deception. Even with a gain of approximately 100 seats in the election, the Conservatives faced a mammoth uphill task in the Commons: they could muster approximately 273 supporters; their opponents 385. Within two months of Herbert's speech, Whig, Reformer, Radical and Irish Members met at Lichfield House in London. Here they agreed a 'Compact' to oust Peel from office. After several defeats in the Commons, Peel resigned on 8 April.

Herbert's first taste of office was consequently fleeting. As joint Secretary to the Board of Control he became part of the body set up in 1784 to manage the affairs of British India and the East India Company. Hitherto the job of secretary had been vested in a single individual. Herbert, however, was appointed to serve alongside Winthrop Mackworth Praed, another young Member identified by Peel as destined for greater things. In the event, the brilliant Praed, who already enjoyed a reputation as a poet, was to die of tuberculosis, aged 36, in 1839. For the moment he and Herbert were charged with assisting the President of the Board, Lord Ellenborough.

1   *DWG*, 15 Jan. 1835; *SWJ*, 19 Jan. 1835.
2   HRO 21M57/2A1/5/1, SH to Normanton, 12 Jan. 1835.
3   *Gloucestershire Chronicle*, 14 Feb. 1835.

Greville described the office of Secretary as one 'of great labour and involving considerable business in the House of Commons'.[1] Peel defined it in more positive language, stressing to Herbert that it 'would afford great opportunities of acquiring political knowledge, and an insight into the complex machine of government'. Sugaring the pill further, Peel suggested that since Praed was effectively the senior Secretary he 'would no doubt relieve his colleague from the main part of the legal business that might come under review; the other secretary would have the financial department and a share of the political'.[2] But this was incidental. The important point was that Peel, in his typical fashion, was seeking to test a promising young man in the humdrum of routine administration, essential if Herbert were to be considered for further advancement up the ministerial ladder. Also characteristic of the Prime Minister's managerial acumen was his placing Herbert in an unfamiliar environment. It would serve to broaden Herbert's experience and perhaps soften the perception highlighted in his maiden speech that he was simply a High Church Tory.

Peel's intentions were scuppered by the fact that his ministry lasted barely the hundred days by which it is known in history. Evidence for Herbert's activity whilst in office is extremely sparse. The one public reference was the appearance in the press of a long letter he wrote on 16 March relating to the proposed division of the government of the Bengal Presidency.[3] His private papers contain only a list of Indian civil servants with their respective salaries, a query regarding the Indian government's salt monopoly, data concerning the relative pay of officers in the royal and Indian navies, a memorandum on the state of the North-West Province of the Bengal Presidency, and suggestions that a committee might be formed to examine the affairs of the East India Company. Otherwise there is only a memorandum of 13 February, listing possible routes for a steam navigation service to India. The most promising, Herbert thought, was through the

1 Reeve, *Greville Memoirs*, pt. 1, III, pp. 193-4, 12 Jan. 1835.
2 WSHC 2057/ F4/53, Peel to SH, 1 Jan. 1835.
3 *Public Ledger and Daily Advertiser*, 3 Apr. 1835.

Euphrates Valley with the possibility that one day a waterway might be constructed through the Gulf of Suez.[1]

Denied the necessity to contemplate such questions following Melbourne's return to power in April, the salient feature of Herbert's record for the rest of the parliament was his absence from it. He would later complain that he found the pugnacious mood prevalent in the Chamber to be distasteful, but this hardly constituted valid grounds for non-attendance.[2] More excusable were the enforced absences arising from his recurring ill-health. Only weeks after leaving office he was reported to be suffering from a 'severe indisposition'. During 1836 he was laid low for a more extended period. He was present for just four votes that year, three of which took place the same day, 14 April.[3] The next occasion on which he is listed as being present for a division is 1 February 1837. In better health by then, he nevertheless attended only thirteen divisions before parliament was dissolved in June. When present, religious concerns were clearly the subject which interested him most: three of his votes related to the question of church leases; another to the Church Rates Regulation Bill.

On paper at least, Herbert was more active in the committee work of the House. Given his recent ministerial experience there was logic in his being appointed to the 1835 Select Committee to Consider the East India Maritime Officers' Petition, the 1836 Select Committee on the Supply of Salt for British India, and the 1837 Select Committee on Steam Communication with India. More important, certainly so far as his constituents were concerned, was his being a member of the Select Committee on the State of Agriculture, set up in February 1836.[4] Given Herbert's absence from the division lobbies however, it is not certain how often – or even if – he managed to attend the various hearings. He was also virtually anonymous in debate. His only recorded intervention was a brief protest against Melbourne's decision to cancel Peel's appointment of Lord Heytesbury as Governor-General

1 WSHC 2057/F8/1/A-C; Stanmore, I, pp. 20-1.
2 *SWJ*, 7 Aug. 1837.
3 *SWJ*, 11 May 1835; *Saunders's News-letter*, 16 June 1836.
4 PP 1835 (242), XVIII; 1836 (518), XVII; 1837 (539), VI;1836 (79), VIII; *SWJ*, 15 Feb. 1836.

of India. Charging, not unreasonably, that Heytesbury was the victim of blatant partisanship, Herbert's motivation was more probably personal. Heytesbury's family, firm Wiltshire friends, was destined to play a pivotal part in his life: Herbert would marry one of Heytesbury's nieces.[1]

Herbert's life outside parliament during this period was undramatic. Early in 1835 he found time to visit Robert Pembroke in Paris. Back in London, he was to be seen at exclusive social gatherings such as the Earl and Countess of Jersey's dinner for the Duke of Cambridge. In Wiltshire, he was a notable patron of local charities, remained an enthusiast for horseracing, and regularly participated in both fox and stag hunting. In his guises as large landowner and MP he was present at both quarter sessions and the assizes.[2] A particular highlight during the autumn of 1835 was a visit to Drayton Manor, Peel's seat in Staffordshire. Further confirmation, were it needed, of the high regard in which he was held by the Conservative leader, Herbert found himself one of a very select group of guests. The others included two older men who would become important colleagues: Sir James Graham, First Lord of the Admiralty under Grey but now morphing towards Conservatism; and Sir Henry Hardinge, who had lost his left hand in the Waterloo campaign and more recently been Peel's Chief Secretary for Ireland. There was also the ubiquitous, loquacious Irishman, John Wilson Croker. Herbert's journal records how Peel recounted to them the story of how he had been summoned home from Italy in November 1834; Graham joined him in reminiscences of George IV and Queen Caroline. Both were upstaged by Hardinge who regaled them with memories of Wellington's campaigns: the Duke, apparently, ranked Waterloo only the third best of his battles. But even Hardinge was trumped by Croker who dominated the conversation with what Herbert called 'very brilliant [...] graphic [...] descriptions of the House of Commons'. The man possessed of the chutzpah to tell

---

1 Hansard, 29 June 1835, LIX, cols. 51-2.
2 *Morning Post*, 2 Feb. 1835; *SWJ*, 11, 25 May 1835; *Morning Chronicle*, 15 June 1835.

Wellington what had really happened at Waterloo thought nothing of lecturing Herbert about Wilton House and its treasures until 1 a.m.[1]

Less gripping but still worthy, Herbert took the lead in forming a Salisbury Literary and Philosophical Society at the beginning of 1836. A sign of changing times, he also agreed to join the management committee for a projected South Western railway.[2] Illness (the symptoms go unrecorded) returned to stalk him by the summer; he was 'induced by his medical advisers to try the waters of Germany'. Hardly, one suspects, needing much persuasion, Herbert's travel journal for July records passing through Brussels, Louvain and Liege en route to various German states. 'The unfinished cathedral at Cologne is very beautiful', he noted, 'the choir quite wonderful'. From Cologne Herbert continued on to Weisbaden, Frankfurt and Augsburg where there was 'very ugly country'; thence to Munich where, by contrast, he set eyes on 'varied and fine woods'.[3] Herbert may well have entertained further plans for travel abroad during the summer recess of 1837. If so they had to be set aside. By convention, the death of the Sovereign required that there be a general election; the death of William IV on 20 June led to the dissolution of parliament.

In the half-decade since leaving Oxford, Herbert had begun to make a mark. Socially he mixed in the highest circles; out of town he was becoming established at Wilton. Two personal uncertainties threatened to dog him. With three of his five sisters already married (Elizabeth in 1830, Catherine in 1836 and Mary in 1837), Herbert's bachelorhood was cause for anxiety, at least with siblings and relations. As heir to his half-brother, it was increasingly probable that only his producing a son could ensure the continuation of the 300-year Herbert line at Wilton. A related concern was his health. Although only in his mid-twenties, Herbert had already had to endure debilitating bouts of illness in 1825, 1831, 1833, 1835 and 1836. This was surely more than the gout which was said to be hereditary in the family. Most likely his

---

1 *London Evening Standard*, 9 Oct. 1835; WSHC 2057/F5/15, journal entries, 23, 25 Sept. 1835.
2 *SWJ*, 8 Feb., 28 Mar. 1836.
3 *DWG*, 21 July 1836; WSHC 2057/F5/15, journal entries, July 1836.

afflictions were early manifestations of the kidney disease described by Dr Richard Bright in 1827.

Politically meanwhile, Herbert's raw Toryism had shown signs of mellowing. He stood in the 1832 election as an independent Tory; in 1835 he ran as a Peelite Conservative. A brief tenure of minor office had given notice, as he put it, 'that he might not remain a drone in the hive'.[1] Others, most importantly Sir Robert Peel, agreed: if he was not quite the best of his generation, he was certainly among the brightest. Herbert's core political beliefs, however, were far from settled. By 1835 he was talking the Peelite language of moderation, the middle way between Tories and 'Destructives', but it was anodyne stuff. And he had very obviously equivocated about taking office. Peelite Conservatism was as yet a bolt-on to his deep-rooted High Church Toryism. For all that he had set course, therefore, it was in several important respects still far from clear in which direction Herbert would be travelling.

1 *DWG*, 15 Jan. 1835.

3
Rising Reputation 1837-1841

Herbert's address for the 1837 election, issued on 21 July, pledged 'Loyalty to the Queen, reverence to the Church, and attachment to those free institutions, which give stability to the Crown, and happiness to the people'. He added his determination to safeguard the House of Lords and his desire to see the nation pursuing a less interventionist foreign policy. The latter two were issues that would exercise his mind during the next parliament.[1] For the moment he enjoyed his third unopposed return alongside Benett on 2 August. Owing to 'extremely unpropitious weather', the nomination was a tame affair. The election breakfast too, incurred only moderate costs: £20 1s 5½d was sufficient for 60 fowls, 12 ducks, 19 pigeons, 151 pounds of beef, 33 pounds of veal, 300 prawns, 23 lobsters, lemons, and 50 gallons of bread.[2]

Far more interesting was the speech Herbert delivered to 200 guests at the Salisbury Assembly Rooms during the celebration dinner held afterwards. 'The Tories', he claimed, 'had ceased to exist as the country had gone beyond them – and the Whigs because they had gone beyond the country. Both parties had found it necessary to enlarge the bases on which they were originally formed. Thus the old Tory had become a liberal Conservative'. Amongst the latter, of course, he included himself.[3] It was his fullest public statement yet of

1 *SWJ*, 24 July 1837.
2 WSHC 2057/F4/70.
3 *SWJ*, 7 Aug. 1837.

his commitment to the middle way that was the hallmark of Peelite Conservatism.

Herbert's remarks are also revealing of the typical Conservative's take on the unfolding story of national party politics, namely that their opponents were moving dangerously to the left. Roughly forty MPs who could be categorised as Reformers in 1832 (notably Lord Stanley and Sir James Graham) were more properly to be labelled as Conservatives by 1837. This made Melbourne's government more dependent for its survival on the support of Irish and Radical Members. Further reform was the expected price for that support. Daniel O'Connell, leader of the Irish contingent, could reasonably expect moves on Irish corporations, tithes and the poor law. Nonconformists, having secured the right to marry in Dissenting Chapels and the civil registration of births, marriages and deaths, could turn their attention to the running sore of church rates. And Radicals of all shades could look to curbing the veto, and even the very existence, of the Tory-dominated House of Lords. Hence the allusions to protecting the Lords in Herbert's election address. This and 'the Church in danger' cry proved to be the most potent election issues in 1837. They gained greatest traction with the Conservatives. A gain of 40 seats left them in a minority of 345 to 313 in the House.[1]

Herbert doubtless discussed this encouraging picture on his many visits to the Tory Carlton Club. Established in 1832, he had been elected one of its ten-member executive committee in 1834. With the Reformer government now vulnerable, it ought to have been incumbent on him to adopt a high profile in the Commons too. But Herbert was far from being the most reliable piece of cannon fodder.[2] He did not appear in a single division in the new parliament until 16 January 1838, even if the fifty votes cast that year did represent his most active year in the lobbies to date. Thereafter, however, his record nosedived. He was present for fewer than a hundred divisions 1839-41, a figure well below the average for Members as a whole.

---

1 Gash, *Peel*, pp. 193-6.
2 WSHC 2057/F5/15, journal entry, 20 Jan. 1838; *Derry Journal*, 18 Feb. 1840.

Explanation for Herbert's less than impressive devotion to the Conservative cause lies partly in his continuing predilection for foreign travel. His absence from Westminster between July 1839 and January 1840, for example, was the consequence of his visiting his maternal uncle, Count Michael Woronzow, then Governor-General of New Russia. The seemingly exotic nature of this expedition, at least in the eyes of the Wiltshire press, ensured that Herbert's progress received much notice as he set off for the Black Sea port of Odessa. He returned via St Petersburg, Hamburg and Nice where he and his mother were reported as intending to spend the winter.[1] Herbert's early return home from Rome in January 1840 may possibly have been in response to exhortations from the Conservative leadership. If so, they were ineffectual. During 1840 Herbert was present for just 45 of the 256 divisions which took place, poor even by the standards of his fellow Wiltshire MPs. As the parliament neared its end, and several votes became cliff-hangers, he incurred further criticism when he chose to attend his sick sister rather than the division lobbies.[2]

We are on safe ground, therefore, in asserting that Herbert contributed more to the Conservative cause by his speeches than his votes during the 1837 parliament. Lord Stanmore went so far as to claim that he 'rapidly acquired reputation as a speaker'.[3] The first of seven noteworthy speeches was made on 15 February 1838: he led the debate against the latest motion from Radical Members to introduce the secret ballot. His arguments, however, were unoriginal. Voting in secret, he contended, was 'un-English [...] he felt himself strongly averse to the introduction of any new principle alien to our habits'. Further, since the vote was a trust, 'both electors and non-electors had a right to know in what manner their fellow countrymen exercised the franchise'. 'Senatoriensis', who mistakenly believed this to be Herbert's maiden speech, judged that it 'personified bashful nonsense'. Herbert, he prophesied, would become 'the most insufferable of jabberers,

---

1   *SWJ*, 16 Sept., 18 Nov. 1839; *Wiltshire Independent*, 26 Dec. 1839. At the time of writing, New Russia is part of The Ukraine.
2   *SWJ*, 28 Sept. 1840; *Leicester Journal*, 5 Mar. 1841.
3   Stanmore, I, p. 22.

the most constant of praters, the most unendurable of talkers'.[1] The Radical motion was defeated by 395 votes to 198.

Just over a month later Herbert delivered his first lengthy speech on foreign affairs. It concerned the conflict which had erupted in Spain in 1833 known as the First Carlist War. The protagonists were the teenage Queen Isabella, a supposed liberal-constitutionalist, and Don Carlos, an autocratic uncle who was attempting to usurp her. The government backed Isabella, not least by suspending the Foreign Enlistment Act, thereby allowing a British Legion to enter her service. With the war dragging on, Herbert was amongst those who held that the Legion should be withdrawn. He doubted that Isabella, even if victorious, 'would exhibit any extraordinary extent of freedom and civilisation', in particular that she would 'fully and fairly carry into execution [...] the suppression of the slave trade'. His wider anxiety was the one he had voiced at the 1837 election, that 'The people of England [...] always looked with jealousy upon any interference in the purely domestic concerns of a foreign country'.[2] Although Herbert chose to ignore the government's line that British commercial interests were at stake, his was a powerful speech in a debate which saw Melbourne's majority cut to eight. Taken together, these two speeches were the basis for the claim made by *Fraser's Magazine* in July 1838 that he was a man whose star was on the rise.[3]

Herbert's second intervention on a question of foreign affairs was provoked by an issue which would come up several times during his life. It was sparked, in July 1839, by the Chinese government's seizing the opium being imported into Canton by British merchants. The offending poppies, complained the Chinese authorities, were having deleterious effects on its people. Palmerston, the Foreign Secretary, responded by demanding compensation and protection for British merchants. When the Chinese refused, he despatched an expeditionary force to Canton. Replying to a speech defending the

---

1 Hansard, 15 Feb. 1838, XL, cols. 1166-8; *Bell's Weekly Messenger*, 18 Feb. 1838.
2 Ridley, *Palmerston*, ch. 15; Hansard, XLI, 27 Mar. 1838, cols. 1350-3. The war ended when Don Carlos was defeated in 1839.
3 *Fraser's Magazine*, XVIII (1838), p. 122.

government by Sir George Staunton, an acknowledged authority on Chinese affairs, Herbert took the moral high ground:

> He deeply regretted to think that the country had engaged in a war of doubtful justice, that we were expending £6,000,000 to recover £2,000,000; that we were sending good money after bad, and that we were contending with an enemy whose cause of quarrel was better than ours.[1]

But it was Palmerston and realpolitik that prevailed. Canton was bombarded and captured in May 1841. The resulting 1842 Treaty of Nanking was concluded by a Conservative government of which Herbert was a member. Its provisions included special trading status for British merchants at five Chinese ports and a lease on Hong Kong. But Herbert's speech had been 'ably advocated', managing as it did to balance the tightrope of 'defend[ing] his party from the insinuation, that they had been capable of rejoicing at the failure of British troops, even in a cause which was not to be approved'.[2]

Herbert's early parliamentary forays into foreign affairs, especially on China, were at least part personal in motivation. He had little regard for Staunton, a man who was 'always asking questions about tea & indigo'. And he did not disguise his schadenfreude when he heard that Staunton and his fellow Reformer Member for South Hampshire would be ousted at the 1835 election: 'It would be a glorious triumph & a complete extinguisher to our friend Cupid'.[3] 'Cupid', of course, was the womanising Lord Palmerston, and far more than Staunton's, a name that would stick in Herbert's craw. Divining the sources of Herbert's dislike for a man who had been a frequent and welcome visitor to Wilton during his father's lifetime is therefore of some consequence. They are not difficult to identify. Palmerston, born in 1784, was the epitome of Regency decadence. More than immoral, Palmerston bordered on the ungodly: it would later be said that he could not tell the difference between Moses and

---

1   Hansard, 7 Apr. 1840, LIII, cols. 745-8.
2   Ridley, *Palmerston*, ch. 18; *Ipswich Journal*, 31 Mar. 1838.
3   HRO 21M57/2A1/5/1, SH to Normanton, 12 Jan. 1835.

Sydney Smith. His bombastic and unashamedly patriotic style at the Foreign Office, therefore, was only to be expected. Behind his back, Herbert was more consistently contemptuous of Palmerston than of any other leading political figure except Disraeli. He continually and dangerously underrated him. The genial Palmerston, it might be noted, was usually complimentary about Herbert.

But this is to anticipate. Herbert's last significant speech of the 1830s, in April 1839, was provoked not by Palmerston but by the government's resisting demands from the House of Lords to institute an inquiry into the state of Ireland. Herbert's peroration went beyond the Emerald Isle to embrace questions relating to the governance of the United Kingdom as a whole. Melbourne's government, he charged, was one which 'was composed of all classes of Reformers, and which was upheld by those who were striving to overthrow the whole fabric of the Constitution'. Specifically, they wanted 'to annihilate the House of Lords'. He was adamant, however, that they would not succeed:

> The House of Lords had recovered all their former influence in the country—an influence which they owed to their great talents and their great virtues; but, above all, to the enlightened patriotism of the Duke of Wellington. The House of Lords were strong in their right to inquire into the state of the country when its grievances were brought before them.

In 'a short but striking speech', reported the *London Evening Standard*, Herbert had 'produced a great effect on the House'.[1]

Herbert's contribution to the foregoing debate, though delivered as a Conservative Member for an English county, was consciously the speech of an Irish landlord. Resenting the charge from the Opposition benches that he and his ilk were responsible for the outrages in that unhappy island, Herbert called for a proper parliamentary investigation 'to afford them an opportunity of establishing their innocence [...] black is not white'.[2] It was a sensitive subject for Herbert, not least

---

1 Hansard, 16 Apr. 1839, XLVII, cols. 142-4; *London Evening Standard*, 17 Apr. 1839.
2 Hansard, 16 Apr. 1839, XLVII, cols. 142-4.

because there is limited evidence for him visiting Mount Merrion and his Irish property during these years. Following his appearance at a grand ball in Dublin Castle in April 1834, he does not appear to have set foot in Ireland again until April 1840. On that occasion he met with representatives of the Kingston Railway Company regarding claims for compensation from a number of his tenants near Sandymount: their properties had been flooded the previous year, allegedly because of shortcomings on the part of the company.[1] But it was Herbert's absence rather than his presence that attracted the more colourful stories. A critical *Dublin Evening Post* maintained that he preferred to spend the £30,000 to £40,000 accruing annually from his Irish property 'among the London clubs and his English tenantry rather than to gratify the craving maw of the Dublin Orangemen'.[2]

This was neither fair nor true. Even if he was rarely there, Irish affairs were a continuing preoccupation of Herbert's throughout the 1830s. Reports of his ongoing munificence included a £25 donation in 1834 to the Benevolent Society of St Patrick (whose anniversary meeting at the Freemason's Tavern in London he attended), £50 towards the relief of distressed Irish clergy in 1835, £40 to the Society for the Suppression of Street Begging in Dublin in 1839; and cheap land, together with £200 for a new Catholic church, near Dublin's Upper Baggot Street. He also contributed to a fund for the founding of the Catholic Sisters of Mercy Convent, next to Booterstown Church, in 1838.[3] But if this shows a Herbert who continued to be blind to any religious divide when charitable concerns were uppermost, he remained fearful of the potentially pernicious effects of the Irish Catholic priesthood. That fear had helped to inform his speech against the secret ballot in 1838. How, he asked:

1 *Dublin Observer*, 14 Apr. 1834; *Dublin Morning Register*, 22 Aug. 1839;*Kilkenny Journal*, 27 Nov. 1839; *Dublin Weekly Herald*, 17 Aug. 1840; *Dublin Evening Packet*, 1 Sept. 1840.
2 *Dublin Evening Post*, 3 Jan. 1835.
3 *Dublin Weekly Mail*, 19 Mar. 1834; *Dublin Morning Register*, 22 May 1835; *SWJ*, 21 Dec. 1835; *Dublin Morning Register*, 18 Dec. 1839.

would the ballot guard against priestly influence in Ireland? Did they expect that law would overcome superstition or that it would prove a remedy against the confessional as a mode of communicating secrets? [...] Father Maher told the electors, previous to the election, that if they did not vote in a particular way, he would visit them in the mitigated penalty of massacre in this life, and eternal damnation in the world to come.[1]

Herbert's more mundane work at Westminster likewise included a substantial smattering of Irish-related topics. He served on the March 1833 Select Committee on the Newry Borough Election Petition, attending all three days of its less than exciting deliberations, as well as the 1834 Select Committee to Inquire into the Present State of Navigation of the River Shannon.[2] Proposed legislation for Ireland was also something that could induce this less than assiduous Member to attend divisions. In February 1838 he was one of the Conservatives who (unlike Peel and Gladstone) voted for the Poor Relief (Ireland) Bill. The following March he backed the Second Reading of the Municipal Corporations (Ireland) Bill. And in 1840 no fewer than nine of the thirty-nine votes he cast were on a single measure: the Registration of Voters (Ireland) Bill. It was perhaps not entirely surprising that when Peel appointed Herbert as Secretary to the Board of Control, some Irish newspapers reported it as being to the non-existent post of the Irish Board of Control.[3]

The notable Irish dimension to Herbert's political profile 'and his long purse', inevitably led to renewed rumours that he would contest an Irish constituency. He was touted as a possible candidate for Dublin City at the 1835 general election. There was never a realistic possibility, of course, that he would quit South Wiltshire. As a hostile newspaper put it bluntly, 'he does not see why he should throw ten or twelve thousand pounds among the rotten Freemen of Dublin. Mr Herbert, though a huge Tory, and a little man is, however, a sensible

---

1 Hansard, 15 Feb. 1838, XL, cols. 1166-8.
2 PP 1833 (76), X;1834 (532), XVII.
3 *Berkshire Chronicle*, 17 Jan. 1835.

one'.¹ But Herbert did not completely abstain from involving himself in Irish politics. He agreed for his name to be added to the committee for the Orange Registry Association set up in response to the Liberal Association in 1836. He was also reputed to have given £500 to the campaign fund of West and Hamilton, the Conservative candidates for the borough of Dublin in 1837. His opponent at the 1841 South Wiltshire election claimed that he had recently visited Dublin to urge electors to vote against O'Connell and his campaign to repeal the Act of Union.² There was certainly no love lost between the pair. O'Connell singled out Herbert for criticism at a meeting held in Dublin's Corn Exchange in December 1837, alleging that though he received up to £20,000 in rent from his Irish property he paid no poor rates. At the same venue two years later, O'Connell said that Herbert's having had 'sedulously and zealously [...] used all his Irish influence against the welfare and happiness of this country is notorious to you all'.³ Herbert doubtless had such taunts in mind when O'Connell interrupted his encomium on Wellington's leadership of the Lords in 1839 with an ironic 'Hear, hear'. Rounding directly on the Irishman, Herbert riposted that 'He did not expect the assent of the hon. Member for Dublin to the opinion which he had expressed. But the hon. Member was not in the Corn Exchange'.⁴

Ireland was but one ingredient in a cauldron of social and economic woes which many feared would boil over in the years after 1837. The 1834 Poor Law Amendment Act, which heralded a relatively draconian workhouse regime, was popular with the ratepayers who funded it, but not the indigent who experienced it. Protest against the New Poor Law helped fuel the working class movement known as Chartism. There were never many Chartists in rural South Wiltshire but Herbert was present for the division of 12 July 1839 at which

1 *Dublin Morning Register*, 26 Dec. 1834; *Morning Post*, 29 Dec. 1834; *Dublin Evening Post*, 3 Jan. 1835; *SWJ*, 12 Jan. 1835; *Dublin Evening Post*, 3 Jan. 1835.
2 *The Pilot*, 10 Feb. 1836; *Morning Chronicle*, 28 July 1837; *Wiltshire Independent*, 19 Aug. 1841.
3 *Saunders's News-letter*, 22 Dec. 1837; *Northern Whig*, 9 Sept. 1841.
4 Hansard, 16 Apr. 1839, XLVII, cols. 142-4.

Members rejected (by 235 votes to 46) the motion to consider the Charter's famous Six Points.[1] Middle class complainants, meanwhile, were focused increasingly on the Corn Laws. Introduced in 1815 to protect British growers, the Laws imposed a fixed duty designed to maintain grain prices in face of increased foreign competition after Waterloo. Although modified in 1828 in favour of a sliding scale, they remained open to attack as a piece of naked class legislation: landlords and farmers benefitted from inflated prices at the expense of the masses saddled with artificially high bread prices. In face of economic recession, the Anti-Corn Law League was launched in 1839. The cause made more headway in parliament than Chartism; nearly 200 Reformer MPs supported a Repeal motion that year. Herbert, as one would expect of a member of the privileged landed order, did not.

All this and more was the context for Herbert's most wide-ranging speech to date, delivered during a no confidence debate at the end of January 1840.[2] He attacked the government's Irish policies as ones 'which dealt out penalty and punishment to the weak and impunity to the strong'; he warned of the 'anxious agitation' fomented by Chartists and protesters against the New Poor Law; and he charged ministers with ambivalence, 'particularly dangerous', in face of the campaign against the Corn Laws: 'it peculiarly became the Government to exert a moral influence, without which no Government ought to be in existence'. Compounded by 'the alarming yearly deficiency in the revenue of the country', the time was ripe, in his view, for a vigorous Conservative government:

> a strong, compact phalanx, under a leader with whose value they were fully acquainted [...] that public man who, from his tried principles and able conduct in the service of the State, might be safely depended upon to guard the property and the liberty of her Majesty's subjects, and stand as an insuperable barrier between democratic encroachment and her throne.

1   Manhood suffrage, secret ballot, abolition of the property qualification for MPs, payment for MPs, equal-sized constituencies, and annual parliaments.
2   Hansard, 30 Jan. 1840, LI, cols. 881-5.

Melbourne's Reformer ministry would survive the no confidence motion by just 308 votes to 287. But Herbert's speech had 'showed, with considerable effect, that the confidence of very many Ministerial Members was not placed in the government, but on the inefficiency of it'.[1]

By the time that Herbert made his final major speech of the parliament in May 1841, the ministry was entering its death throes. In an attempt to resurrect its fortunes Sir Francis Baring, Chancellor of the Exchequer, presented a free trade budget. By proposing to lower tariffs on imported consumer products, principally sugar, corn and timber, he gambled that he could boost revenues by stimulating consumption. The Opposition, since it raised the emotive question of slavery, adopted the strategy of attacking along the sugar front only. Sugar was imported from Britain's West Indian colonies, harvested since the abolition of slavery in the British Empire in 1833, by freed workers. Sugar prices had consequently risen, but tariffs had protected West Indian sugar against competition from slave-labour based producers. Whilst reducing sugar tariffs might reduce sugar prices, therefore, the government could be accused of putting financial considerations ahead of moral ones.[2]

Herbert's speech in the ensuing debate, at any event, was insistent that slavery was the point at issue:

> if we were to permit the introduction, of slave-grown sugar, we should stultify all the exertions that we had made for the suppression of the slave trade [...] By the introduction of slave-grown sugar into this country, its consumption would be increased; its production would likewise be increased; and by opening new markets for those slave-grown products you would create a necessity for an additional supply of slave-labour. They should recollect the claims to their consideration which the West Indies possessed [...] that it was only fair to allow them a moderate protection, to enable them to compete on fair terms with other countries [...] They had contended for the principle that it

---

1 *Cheltenham Chronicle*, 6 Feb. 1840.
2 Newbould, *Whiggery and Reform*, pp. 298-304; Gash, *Peel*, pp. 254-6.

was possible, that sugar could be successfully cultivated by free labour, and they had in this respect given an example to other nations in the suppression of slavery. But if we now show, that sugar cannot be so cultivated, we shall have only tried the experiment of abolition to demonstrate its failure. With what face shall we go to other countries to ask them to follow our example, and pursue a course which we shall have just shown them to be impossible. Instead of an example, we shall be a warning, and our abolition will only have served to rivet the chains of slavery by showing the impossibility of free labour to compete with it.[1]

It was later claimed that Herbert's speech 'was one of those which largely contributed to the defeat of Lord Melbourne's Government'.[2] This must be considered doubtful. His was just one of over eighty speeches in a debate which lasted eight nights. Though the government did lose that particular division by 317 votes to 281, it limped on for another three weeks before losing a confidence debate in which Herbert did not speak. An equally bold claim was that Herbert's speech 'contained the first glimmerings of an alteration of opinion with regard to the free-trade theory'.[3] It is true that he had referred to the question:

> Nobody could dispute the theory [...] Why, so simple was the theory of the principles of free trade, that a child might understand it, provided, that those principles were to be applied as an inflexible mathematical rule. It might be easy to apply those principles if they were not bound to consider the particular circumstances under which they were to be applied, and if men were to shut their eyes in the application of those principles, without reference to existing circumstances in a great commercial country like this.

But his words must be seen in context. They were part of a preamble to a speech about the moral issues raised by the realities of sugar

[1] Hansard, 12 May 1841, LVIII, cols. 297-300.
[2] *SWJ*, 3 Aug. 1861.
[3] Stanmore, I, p. 25.

production, not the rights and wrongs of free trade. And he was referring in this instance specifically to the revision of the Corn Laws by a Tory government in 1828, not prophesying what its Conservative successor would do in 1846. If Herbert's words do contain a clue to his guiding political principles, it is that he thought it best to act pragmatically. Even so, the speech as a whole was an important one, 'so able as fully to justify the promise he gave on one or two previous occasions'.[1]

For substance as to where Herbert stood on the Corn Laws in 1841, we need look no further than his unopposed return for South Wiltshire at the general election. The Reformers had made the Corn Laws a key election issue by proposing that a fixed duty of eight shillings a quarter should replace the sliding scale. Herbert responded to it in his address of 18 June when he said that 'I have resisted the attempts which are being made to deprive the Agriculturist of that fair protection to which he is entitled, and which is essential to the prosperity of the labouring part of the population'. He enlarged on the theme at the hustings on 7 July. Having seen the supposed advantages of cheap bread whilst on his travels in Germany, he told the assembled freeholders, it was the poor who suffered most from such a policy. He would not touch it 'with a pair of tongs'. Let there be no doubt that 'He had opposed, and would continue to oppose, the alteration sought to be made in the corn-laws'.[2] The county election was otherwise unremarkable. At the post-election dinner in Salisbury's Assembly Rooms he rallied supporters with a speech in which:

> he trusted that an honourable party was about to be elected in the kingdom which would pursue a medium course [...] The party with whom he acted had lain still, merely contenting themselves with defending those parts of the constitution which had been attacked, until, like the Duke at Waterloo, they had availed themselves of the opportunity presented to them, and the cry had been, 'Up, Guards, and at them'.

---

1   Hansard, 12 May 1841, LVIII, col. 298; *Morning Post*, 13 May 1841.
2   *SWJ*, 21 June, 12 July 1841.

The bill for the election breakfast came to £41 15s 2d, the increase on that of four years before occasioned chiefly by the inclusion of sixty bottles of sherry and twelve each of brandy and port.[1]

Herbert's name, the bonhomie of the above celebrations notwithstanding, had been 'received with mingled tokens of applause and disapprobation' at the nomination in Salisbury's Market Square.[2] The mixed response reflected rumours that he had been meddling in the city's politics. Since 1832 Salisbury's two seats had been shared, unopposed, between a Reformer and a Conservative. Emboldened by the electoral currents running in favour of Conservatism, however, Salisbury Reformers believed Herbert to have been behind the candidacy of the Hon. Anthony John Ashley Cooper, son of the Earl of Shaftesbury, in an attempt to seize both seats. It was a belief reinforced by the fact that the Earls of Pembroke and Shaftesbury enjoyed past political ties and that Ashley Cooper had been a welcome guest at Wilton throughout his campaign. Herbert found himself accused of 'highly unconstitutional interference', in particular that he had attempted to coerce or intimidate up to 50 Reformer voters into changing their political colours. In the fracas which followed the nomination, one person died, unrest which would have been avoided had there been no contest. Herbert's role in promoting it drew the charge from the incumbent Reformer Member that he had been 'incautious'.[3] Herbert's efforts were also unavailing; Ashley Cooper lost the election by 59 votes.

Part of the resentment over Herbert's suspected involvement in Salisbury politics was that he 'had Wilton at his disposal'. In the absence of his half-brother, the practical business of disposing of Wilton's borough seat had indeed fallen to him. In July 1837 Herbert was present to witness the return of Colonel Edward Baker, 'an intimate friend' of his late father. Formalities concluded, Herbert oversaw Wilton's idiosyncratic election ritual whereby coins were showered from the town hall on supporters (there were, strangely,

1 *SWJ*, 12 July 1841; WSHC 2057/F4/70.
2 *SWJ*, 12 July 1841.
3 *SWJ*, 21 June, 5 July 1841; *DWG*, 8 July 1841.

no opponents) gathered below.[1] What followed four years later when Baker retired was, by Wilton's standards, tantamount to electoral excitement. It also revealed a more punctilious Herbert than the one allegedly then indulging in skulduggery in Salisbury. The Earl of Normanton, by dint of a former promise made by the 11th Earl of Pembroke, presumed that the Wilton vacancy was earmarked for his son, Viscount Somerton, a grandson of the 11th Earl. A resolute Herbert thus incurred Normanton's ire when informing him that 'An offer to Somerton might be a natural one as a matter of feeling on the score of relationship but cannot be as a matter of right'.[2] Ostensibly with the absent 12th Earl's blessing, Herbert offered the seat instead to James, Viscount Fitzharris, his friend since boyhood. Fitzharris was in turn nonplussed by his patron's insistence that electoral niceties be observed:

> He says that he has consulted precedents, but cannot find that in the memory of man anybody has ever put out an address for that borough, but that I must canvass it exactly as if it were Birmingham, and I had Lord John Russell standing against me [...] I completed a most tiresome and uninteresting canvass, there being no opposition to me, but it is an extensive borough, entirely agricultural, and necessitated long drives from one point to another.[3]

To add injury (of sorts) to what he considered insult, Fitzharris succeeded his father as 3rd Earl of Malmesbury two months later, thus quitting Wilton borough before he could take his seat in the Commons. Somerton was installed in his stead.

Herbert's machinations at the 1841 election remind us that, for all that his national star was rising, Wilton and Wiltshire affairs continued to impose on his time. As county MP he was a prominent member of the provisional committee lobbying for rail connections to be established from London through Wiltshire. He was also expected to appear at formal political occasions such as County

1 *SWJ*, 24 July 1837.
2 HRO 21M57/2A1/5/5-6, SH to Normanton, 9 June 1841.
3 Malmesbury, *Memoirs,* I, pp. 133-4; *SWJ*, 5 July 1841.

Meetings, official gatherings of freeholders convened sporadically by the High Sheriff. In 1840, for example, he seconded the resolution at the County Meeting held in Devizes to congratulate the Queen on having survived Edward Oxford's attempt to shoot her on 10 June. A more partisan event in the town two years previously had seen him tell Conservatives, in an after dinner speech, that Peel's party faced an 'uphill struggle'.[1] Meanwhile, one of the various requests for patronage to which he acceded as representative for South Wiltshire was agreeing to become President of the Salisbury and Wilton District Board of Education in January 1840. Another, with portents for the future, was when he became chairman of the governing committee of the Salisbury General Infirmary in 1842. These were not necessarily bodies of which he was simply a token figurehead. He 'laboured one whole winter' remodelling the Infirmary: not that the modern reader would have much sympathy with his complaint that he had given 'up the best days' hunting or shooting' in order to do so.[2]

Unlike many MPs, Herbert chose to play an active part in local government. There was nothing glamorous about attending the meeting held in Wilton's town hall in November 1838 to determine the assessment for the new parish rate.[3] At least this was only an annual chore. More regular duties undertaken when in Wiltshire were those as one of the county's magistrates. These might be at the weekly petty sessions held in Salisbury to deal with lesser crimes and nuisances, or less frequently, in full meetings of the county's JPs in quarter sessions. He was, for example, active in the deliberations which took place in January 1841 as to the expediency of Wiltshire's appointing a second county coroner.[4] Magistrates moreover, were ex-officio members of their local board of Poor Law guardians. Creations of the 1834 Poor Law Amendment Act, guardians were entrusted with overseeing the implementation of the new workhouse regime. Herbert related to his fellow MPs how, as a member of the Wilton board, 'he for one had

1 *DWG*, 19 Apr. 1838; *SWJ*, 29 June 1840.
2 *SWJ*, 2, 20 Jan. 1840; WSHC 2057/F6/98, 'Character of Sidney Herbert', p. 24.
3 *SWJ*, 5 Nov. 1838.
4 *SWJ*, 3 Dec. 1838; *Wiltshire Independent*, 7 Jan. 1841.

not hesitated to do his duty week after week watching the operation of the act, and thus incurring the odium and unpopularity which such a course of conduct was sure to bring upon all its supporters'.[1] And, as ever, there were the never-ending demands on his (admittedly capacious) wallet. Coal, blankets and potatoes were regularly distributed to the poor of Wilton in his mother's name.[2] Herbert himself donated £20 towards the restoration of Norton Bavant Church in July 1837, and £100 for the relief of the poor following major floods around Shrewton and Maddington at the beginning of 1841. More congenial was the fete with fireworks which he and his mother hosted in Wilton Park in August 1840.[3]

Herbert was also a prominent and enthusiastic member of Wiltshire's yeomanry cavalry. First set up in 1794 as an adjunct to home defence, yeomanry corps nationally had languished after Waterloo only to be rejuvenated following rural disorder in southern England in 1830. Constituent troops comprised a cross-section of farmers and rural tradesmen officered by landed gentlemen, all volunteers. Motivated by a desire to save money, and a suspicion that most rank and file yeomen were Tories, Melbourne's government made drastic reductions in the number of yeomanry troops in 1838.[4] Herbert spoke out strongly against this and subsequently played an active part in ensuring that the Royal Wiltshire Yeomanry survived. He was promoted to lieutenant in the Everley troop in June 1838 and is regularly listed as being present for its statutory periods of permanent duty and exercise.[5] In May 1840 he was advanced to the captaincy of the Warminster troop, promptly inviting his men to join him in a public breakfast at Wilton. The following spring, Herbert's was one of the regiment's ten troops which assembled at Warminster. There he met George, Lord Bruce, his commanding officer and brother-in-law; and Major Walter Long, one of the Conservative Members for North Wiltshire. His fellow captains

1 Hansard, 30 Jan. 1840, LI, cols. 882-3.
2 *SWJ*, 29 Dec. 1834.
3 *SWJ*, 23 July 1838, 17 Aug. 1840, 25 Jan. 1841.
4 Foster, *Politics of County Power*, pp. 85-9.
5 *DWG*, 19 Apr. 1838; *SWJ*, 18 June 1838.

comprised friends, neighbours and relations from across the political divide.¹

Equestrian diversion of a more leisurely type was provided by the hunting field. Herbert was regularly reported to be out with Lord Bruce's staghounds in Savernake Forest near Marlborough.² Field sports more generally were not confined to Wiltshire. They figured prominently when Herbert paid another visit to Sir Robert Peel at Drayton Manor in September 1838. Whilst his host regaled him with stories about Polignac, Herbert bagged 62 brace of pheasants.³ Herbert's greatest sporting passion during these years, though, was the turf. The press records him entering four horses for the Winchester races in July 1838; three months later, during a stay at Heaton Park in Lancashire, he attended Doncaster races. On home turf for the Salisbury races in 1839 (the racecourse was on Pembroke land), 'The Hon Sidney Herbert was indefatigable in his exertions to give *eclat* to the sport'. The latter may partly have been a case of putting on a brave face: a few months earlier Herbert's horse, Clarion, had finished unplaced when strongly tipped to win the Epsom Derby.⁴

Reference to Herbert's being either hunting or shooting litter the late-1830s diary of his favourite sister, Mary. He desisted long enough to give her away at her wedding to Lord George Charles Bruce in May 1837.⁵ Tottenham Park, her new home near Marlborough, was thence his second favourite country retreat after Wilton. Competition for a brief while was provided by Bowood House near Chippenham, seat of the Marquis of Lansdowne. Henry, Lord Shelburne, son of the 3rd Marquis, married Herbert's youngest sister, Georgiana, at Wilton on 18 August 1840. Aged 23, Georgiana fell unwell with 'a painful illness' only months later. Herbert wrote to Lincoln on 25 February about his prayers for a miracle. It did not happen. Georgiana, the grumpy baby about whom he had complained in 1819, died three

1 *SWJ*, 25 May 1840, 17 May 1841.
2 *DWG*, 23 Apr. 1838.
3 *SWJ*, 24 Sept. 1838; WSHC 2057/F5/15, journal entry, Sept. 1838.
4 *SWJ*, 16 July 1838; *Wiltshire Independent*, 11 Oct. 1838, 22 Aug. 1839; *Morning Post*, 6 May 1839.
5 WSHC 2057/F5/12a.

days later. The family united in grief. Robert Pembroke, who had regularly entertained his young half-sisters in Paris, and much to Herbert's satisfaction, came over especially from France for the funeral at Bowood.[1]

Georgiana's death marked the personal low point of this period in Herbert's life. The political highpoint was the Conservatives' return to office. The July 1841 election had given them 367 seats, some 76 more than their 291 Liberal opponents. Melbourne's ministry accepted the inevitable and resigned on 30 August. Rumour spread that Herbert would be appointed Chief Secretary for Ireland. Given that he was a rising political star and owned property in and around Dublin, it is easy to understand why. In the event the office went to Lord Eliot.[2] Herbert, it was announced, would be First Secretary of the Admiralty with a salary of £2,000 per annum.

Herbert, still unmarried but apparently in better health, could now look forward to a proper schooling in the ways of government. Despite the references to him as a coming man, he remained as yet a peripheral figure in politics. Even his speeches, the main source of any reputation he enjoyed, must be kept in perspective. They were all comparatively brief; the longest, on the no confidence motion in January 1840, probably took little more than ten minutes to deliver. Qualitatively too, Herbert's speeches were not the finished article, certainly if mid-1840s critiques of his style as being both verbose and lacking in fluency are anything to go by.[3] At least Herbert was outshining his friend Lord Lincoln, yet to make his maiden speech but sharing his reputation as being amongst the most talented of the new generation of Conservative MPs. Compared to Gladstone, however, who had made roughly seventy speeches by 1841, Herbert was clearly in the shade: he was far better known in the world of high society than high politics. The thirty or so references to him in *The Times* between 1833 and 1841 are overwhelmingly to his having been present at

1 NUL Ne C 11921/1-2, SH to Lincoln, 25 Feb., 5 Mar. 1841; *SWJ*, 8 Mar. 1841.
2 *SWJ*, 30 Aug. 1841; *Morning Post*, 10 Sept. 1841.
3 *Illustrated London News*, 2 Mar. 1844; WSHC 2057/F1/12, unidentified press cutting, July 1846.

prestigious social gatherings, not for any great accomplishment in the House of Commons.

In party political terms too, Herbert remained something of an unknown quantity. Harriet Martineau concluded that he was 'chiefly distinguished for his vindication of the Corn Laws'.[1] Her claim is not without foundation. At the 1835 election Herbert had said that those who called for an end to the Corn Laws 'should kill the bird that laid the golden eggs'.[2] On the hustings in 1841 too, as we have seen, he was unambiguous that the Corn Laws must be retained. Against this, Herbert increasingly spoke the language of moderate Peelite Conservatism and of the need for 'cautious and well-digested reform'. If one looks beyond his professions of what Conservatism meant, however, to consider how he actually voted, one has to conclude that Herbert was decidedly illiberal during the 1830s. For all his talk of wanting to extend religious liberty, he opposed initiatives for greater civil liberties for non-Anglicans, be they Roman Catholics, Dissenters or Jews. He also supported the draconian Poor Law Amendment Act in 1834. And whilst he was willing to concede that some reform of the old municipal corporations was inevitable, he refused to endorse the landmark Municipal Corporations Act of 1835. Herbert also voted against proposals for other constitutional reforms, notably the establishment of ratepayer-elected county boards in 1837, and the secret ballot in both 1838 and 1839. Neither does he appear to have been an enthusiast for the 1839 Rural Police Act which made permissible the introduction of professional county constabularies. But he did vote against a motion to end capital punishment in March 1840. Furthermore, his opposition to direct British intervention in Spain in support of Queen Isabella can be construed as evidence that he was illiberal in foreign policy. Even on slavery, his position was ambiguous. He declared fervently against it during his speech on the sugar duties in May 1841 but he had been silent on the slavery question in 1832 when it was a major election issue.

1 Martineau, *Biographical Sketches*, p. 319.
2 *DWG*, 15 Jan. 1835; *SWJ*, 19 Jan. 1835.

By the standards of the day, the above registers Herbert as a mainstream Tory. What made him most atypical was not his attachment to the Corn Laws, but his High Churchmanship. Herbert's journals for the 1830s abound with descriptions of the churches and cathedrals he had seen, not fields of corn and the price of bread. This was the Herbert who agreed to become a steward for the Salisbury and Wiltshire Society for Christian Knowledge and Propagation of the Gospel in Foreign Parts in 1834. The same year Herbert agreed to present a petition from the clergy of the archdeaconry of Sarum to parliament calling for the defence of the Established Church. Towards the end of the 1837 parliament we find him taking a close interest in the detail of the Ecclesiastical Duties and Revenues Bill.[1] The present and future state of Mother Church was also the subject most likely to bring Herbert to his feet when speaking outside parliament. At the end of October 1838, for example, he appeared at a meeting of the Salisbury Diocesan Church Building Association in Devizes. It was sufficient in itself he told his audience:

> when we see the immense population of this country, to convince us how great an object it is, amidst the busy hum of manual and mechanical and industry, that the voice of religion shall still be heard, to attract our attention from those toils which too much engross us, and form the thoughts of that prosperity, which we seek so diligently in this world, to our prospects of happiness in the next.[2]

Even at the election of July 1841, though Herbert's remarks on the hustings were tailored to freeholders anxious about the Corn Laws, it was the Church which figured most prominently in the speech he made at the celebratory dinner afterwards. Since 1815, he asserted triumphantly, the Established Church had made considerable strides forward: 'the clergy now acted in a different spirit: they were at this day, active, pure and full of zeal in their sacred calling, attending the

---

1 *SWJ*, 23, 30 June 1834; Hansard, 15 June 1840, LIV, cols. 1202-4.
2 *SWJ*, 5 Nov. 1838.

death-bed of the poor, and administering consolation to every one under their charge'.[1]

Rumours of Herbert's incipient liberalism, therefore, were much exaggerated by his nineteenth-century biographers. In 1841 he was a mixture of more notable ingredients, chiefly those of the self-confident, High Church scion of the British aristocracy, infused with its patrician values, and seasoned with a pinch of superciliousness. Had he but known it, his life would soon be two-thirds over. For the moment he was seemingly content to be a young man in no particular hurry.

1 *SWJ*, 12 July 1841.

4
Debatable Progress 1841-1845

Herbert's life as a politician changed gear from September 1841. As Secretary to the Admiralty he was required to attend formal meetings of the full Admiralty Board, usually for three days a week.[1] Since he answered for the Board in parliament, there was a steep learning curve to be overcome: never before had he had to master such a substantial brief. As a junior member of the government, moreover, Herbert could no longer be so unenthusiastic about appearing in the division lobbies. He cast well over a hundred votes each year between 1842 and 1844, more than twice the average for Members as a whole. In these, if he wished to remain in government, the new mantra of loyalty to party would have to supersede the old one of independence. The change in Herbert's habits was no less marked in debate: he had made scarcely a dozen interventions between 1832 and 1841; between 1841 and 1845 he made over seventy. By 1845, with his administration fracturing, Peel was sufficiently impressed by his protégé's progress that he promoted him to the cabinet.

Herbert's Pembroke ancestors had had little to do with Britain's senior service. The exception was the 8th Earl who, on the strength of limited experience at sea, had risen to be Lord High Admiral in 1701.[2] Herbert's serving as First Secretary to the Admiralty Board for more than three years (the best remembered former incumbent of the equivalent position was Samuel Pepys) conferred less exalted status. But

1   PP 1860 (441), VII, pp. 503-4.
2   *ODNB*.

it did provide him with the opportunity to demonstrate administrative acumen and was a springboard from which to advance to higher things in government. Herbert's Admiralty years also introduced him to the policy area with which he would be closely connected for the rest of his life: national defence.

The Admiralty had experienced major restructuring under Sir James Graham, First Lord during Earl Grey's premiership. He fixed the Board of Commissioners, who discharged the duties overseen historically by the Lord High Admiral, at six members: the First Lord, four Naval Lords and one Civil Lord. During Herbert's time as Secretary, the Board comprised the Earl of Haddington as First Lord, Sir George Cockburn, Sir William Gage, Sir George Seymour and the Hon. William Gordon as Sea Lords, and the Hon. Henry Lowry-Corry (who became a good friend of Herbert's) as Civil Lord.[1]

Whilst Herbert, First Secretary from 10 September 1841, served the Board, he also sat at the apex of a clerical establishment. The key figure in this was the permanent Second Secretary. Sir John Barrow had been appointed to the position in 1807: he left it, at the age of 80, in 1845. Herbert, no expert in naval affairs, and with the various other demands of parliament on his time, had little option but to defer to him. Barrow it was therefore, who 'exercised much of the real authority in the running of the department'.[2] There is no reason to believe that the pair did not cooperate amicably: Herbert presented the portrait of Barrow which hangs in Admiralty House to this day. There are no portraits of the Chief Clerk, H.F. Amedroz, or the 37 junior clerks, divided into three classes, who worked under them. But in a typically Peelite minute of 24 October 1842, Herbert recorded with approval that the Board was thenceforth to be guided by considerations of merit when deciding on promotions to vacancies within the various classes. This bureaucracy was responsible for a myriad of tasks including

---

1 Ward, *Graham*, pp. 121-9; Hamilton, *Admiralty*, ch. 4; *British History Online* http://www.british-history.ac.uk/office-holders/vol4/pp1-17, accessed 11 Sept. 2017. Seymour was replaced by William Bowles in May 1844.
2 Hamilton, *Admiralty*, pp. 116-18.

victualling, stores, the fitting out of warships, the protection of trade and fishery, naval education, appointments and pensions.[1]

A few of the many letters and circulars drawn up by the clerks, and signed by Herbert on behalf of the Lords of the Admiralty, appeared in the press. One of the first to do so was Herbert's letter of 15 October 1841 to Messrs Grissell and Peto. They had informed the Board that masons in their employ on a project at Woolwich were on strike, demanding the same remuneration as their counterparts working on Westminster Palace. Their Lordships, via Herbert, peremptorily instructed Messrs Grissell and Peto to settle the dispute themselves.[2] Far more typical was a letter Herbert sent on behalf of the Board informing mariners to steer clear of a reported Russian shipwreck off Aldeburgh; and another to Lloyds of London informing them that the brig, *Respect*, was sinking with its cargo of coal en route from Sunderland to Calais. In June 1843 Herbert received a report, which he forwarded to the Board, arguing the case as to why Holyhead rather than Porthdinllaen would be a better port for use by mail packets with Dublin. Later that month, he issued details of their Lordships' rulings on alterations to the dress uniform worn by Royal Naval officers.[3]

Away from the public gaze Herbert was besieged with requests for patronage. The Reverend G.R. Gleig, for instance, now best known for his popular biography of Wellington, sought and received Herbert's support in his successful attempt to become Chaplain-General of the Forces in 1844. It was the first of several occasions on which their paths would cross.[4] An example of how simple commonsense could ease frictions between navy and army, meanwhile, is provided by Herbert's correspondence on behalf of the Board with the Secretary at War, Sir Henry Hardinge. From 1837 marines were required to serve ten years on board ship in order to qualify for a pension, with each year spent on

1   Partridge, *Military Planning*, pp. 47-8.
2   *The Times*, 18 Oct. 1841.
3   *Morning Advertiser*, 11 Oct. 1841; *The Times*, 22 Nov. 1841, 24 Oct. 1843; *London Gazette*, 30 June 1843.
4   *ODNB*; WSHC 2057/F8/1/M/3, Goulburn to SH, 31 Mar. 1844. For other examples, Surrey History Centre Goulburn Mss., 304/A1/1/14/6-13.

land reckoned at only six months' service. A marine might therefore have to amass twenty years' service to qualify for a pension compared with just ten years for a soldier in the regulars. Understandably, this provoked 'great discontent' amongst marines, 'a practical hardship and an inconvenience to the service'. The terms of service between marines and their army counterparts were duly harmonised.[1]

As the navy's chief representative in the Commons, Herbert was called upon to respond to Members on a range of questions. His answers were usually brief, though since they were often replies to very specific issues, he needed to be on his mettle. Assisting him in being so, as he later acknowledged, was Sir George Cockburn, the First Sea Lord, who sat for Ripon.[2] Topics which arose included whether or not some retiring and long-serving captains would receive enhanced pensions, supposed shortcomings in the mail packet service with the West Indies, and allegations that the navy discriminated against the employment of Irishmen in its selection of officers.[3] Herbert felt obliged to make a more substantial speech in February 1844 defending the Board against the more general charge that it was abusing its powers of patronage.[4]

Herbert also sponsored or spoke on three legislative measures of relevance during his time as First Secretary. Two of these were relatively uncontentious: the 1843 Admiralty Lands Act, which allowed the Crown to acquire lands in order to enlarge the Royal Dockyards; and the 1845 Naval Medical Supplemental Fund Society Act.[5] More problematic was a Merchant Seamen Bill. Some 240,000 men were employed in the mercantile marine; by mid-century 34,000 British ships were transporting £75 million worth of goods. But no less impressive were figures suggesting that one in five of those employed would end their lives at sea, courtesy of the 'wooden coffins' in which

1   WSHC 2057/F8/1/I, Hardinge to SH, 10, 28 Oct. 1841, SH to Hardinge, 7, 9 Oct. 1841.
2   PP 1860 (441), VII, p. 525.
3   Hansard, 7 Mar. 1842, LXI, col. 137; 2 May 1842, XLII, cols. 1381-2; 14 Mar. 1844, LXXIII, col. 1059.
4   Hansard, 24 Feb. 1844, LXXIII, cols. 313-16.
5   Hansard, 24 July 1843, LXX, cols. 1319-21.

they sailed. Herbert might well have reflected as to why there was a need for the Merchant Seamen's Orphan Asylum of which he consented to become president. Instead he co-sponsored a Bill whose declared intent was 'to promote the increase of the number of Seamen, and to afford them all due encouragement and protection'. Merchant seamen, after all, were the obvious pool for the Royal Navy to draw from in time of war.[1] Introduced in the House by Herbert on 5 July 1844, the Bill's main provisions attempted to define more clearly the relationship between masters and seamen, and to maintain a compulsory register of merchant seamen in British ports. Some opponents protested that the measure was being rushed through at the end of the session, others that it smacked of unwarranted interference in labour relations, and a few because it seemed to be weighted in favour of ship owners against seamen. Herbert spoke four times in defence of the proposals before the summer recess.[2] The resulting 1845 Merchant Seaman Act was, in truth, a modest measure, advancing little beyond its predecessor of a decade earlier. Criticism was quickly voiced that it was insufficient. Above all, it did not address the fundamental issues: ship owners being allowed to run vessels that were not seaworthy; and overloading those that were. Merchant seamen would have to wait another generation for Samuel Plimsoll and his eponymous line.[3]

Existing accounts identify Herbert's main achievement at the Admiralty as being the reorganisation of the Royal Naval Schools at Greenwich: 'He found them in a state of indiscipline bordering upon mutiny, and of ignorance below the level of most parochial schools'; by 1845, they 'were second, in general acquirements, to none in England; in professional character, to no naval schools of their class in the world'.[4] However, whilst it was undoubtedly the case that

1 Partridge, *Military Planning*, pp. 30-2.
2 WSHC 2057/F8/L/3; Hansard, 5 July 1844, LXXVI, cols. 445-7; 29 July 1844, LXXVI, col. 1510; 8 Aug. 1844, LXXVI, cols. 1922-3; 9 Aug. 1844, LXXVI, cols. 1994-5.
3 *The Times*, 23 Apr. 1844, 25 Jan. 1845; Jones, *The Plimsoll Sensation*, pp. 10-12, 15-16; WSHC 2057/F8/I/M/2, unidentified press cutting, 25 Jan. 1845.
4 *Fraser's Magazine*, 'Herbert', p. 199. Cf. Stanmore, I, p. 69; *ODNB*.

Herbert supported educational reform at Greenwich, it was a process underway long before he became First Secretary. The original school of 1712 and its junior counterpart, established in 1807, merged to form the Greenwich Royal Hospital Schools (comprising an Upper and Lower School) as early as 1821. It was these that Herbert admitted, in a speech of June 1842, to have been deficient. But this was only months after he entered office; and he was at pains to stress that most problems had already been addressed. The credit for having done so, he bestowed on 'the gentlemen who presided over their education'. The Schools' historian names them as headmasters Edward and John Riddle. Responsibility for naval schools and education was anyway part of the remit of the Fourth Naval Lord, not the First Secretary.[1] Herbert never claimed the credit for reforming the naval schools; he does not deserve it.

Herbert's responsibilities lay elsewhere. Since he was both a political appointee and a member of the Commons, easily the most important of these was to present the annual naval estimates to the House. This was never the most stimulating of occasions. As one ironic commentator put it, the House was treated to 'a catechism from Mr Sidney Herbert upon every conceivable *minutiae* of propulsion, gunnery, and patronage'. One suspects that even Hansard's reporter was losing the will to live in 1844: the official record states simply that 'The Hon. Member explained at some length the various items of the Estimates and the alterations made in them'. Herbert relished the experience as little as his listeners. Twenty years later, he recalled that 'The estimates are so voluminous that one might as well open a dictionary & take a division upon each word'.[2] In fairness, few politicians have mastered the art of rendering statistics interesting. Herbert was endeavouring to do so, moreover, as a member of a government striving to balance the nation's books in wake of the deficits incurred by its predecessor. With 'retrenchment' a popular political buzz word, and with 25 years of relative peace in Europe since

---

1 Hansard, 30 June 1842, LXIV, cols. 835-6; http://www.mariners-l.co.uk/GreenwichRoyal.html accessed 17 Sept. 2017; Partridge, *Military Planning*, p. 47.
2 Hansard, 26 Feb. 1844, LXXIII, cols. 318-19; *The Times*, 27 June 1846.

Waterloo, the estimates had long become an area for close scrutiny. Except for a brief reversal of the trend (occasioned by the Near Eastern crisis of 1839-41) the navy had had to endure a generation and more of cuts.[1]

Herbert's first foray into this straitjacketed world of statistics was made on 4 March 1842. In what was his longest parliamentary speech to date, he explained that in order to ensure that ships performed at peak efficiency, they needed to go to sea fully manned. This had not, apparently, been happening when Melbourne was in office. Herbert anticipated the obvious objection to his proposition – that expenditure would need to increase – by saying that naval personnel would be maintained at existing levels (43,000, including 10,500 marines), but that fewer ships would sail. Pre-empting those who might complain that this represented a weakening of the service, Herbert added that Britain's navy would still compare favourably to that of France or the United States. In a peroration that fully reflected the mood of the time, 'he trusted that feeling of economy which sometimes prevailed so strongly in that House would not lead it to object to an estimate which was certainly large (£6,739,318) at a time when, excepting in India, this country was at peace'. The navy, after all, 'was the great national arm of our strength'. *The Times* judged Herbert's statement to have been 'most conclusive and most satisfactory'.[2]

In truth, neither Herbert nor the navy regarded the situation as satisfactory, but they lacked strong grounds for arguing the case for the estimates to be increased. Retrenchment thus remained the keynote on the two further occasions when Herbert presented them. In 1843 indeed, he was able to inform the House that further savings could be made by dint of reducing the number of men employed by 4,000. The following year he was able to argue that the end of the First Opium War with China allowed for yet further reductions and 'begged to propose [...] that 36,000 Seamen be employed, 10,500

---

1   Jenkins, *Trelawny Diaries*, pp. 126-7, 31 May 1860; Partridge, *Military Planning*, pp. 21-3.
2   Hansard, 4 Mar. 1842, LXI, cols. 69-74; *The Times*, 11 Mar. 1842.

Royal Marines, and 2,000 boys'. It would fall to his successor, amid changing circumstances, to ask the House for an increase in 1845.[1]

More interesting, because less mundane, was Herbert's work away from Admiralty House. He served, for example, on the committee overseeing the construction of Nelson's Column: in May 1843 it met 'to consider whether the Corinthian capital should be gilt or bronzed'.[2] In public, meanwhile, Herbert regularly accompanied members of the Admiralty Board on official visits. In June 1842 he was aboard the steam vessel, *Black Eagle*, with Haddington and Cockburn to watch tests of long range 68-pounder guns. In the autumn, with two of the Lords Commissioners, he went to Devonport for the launch of the 98 gun *Albion*. And Herbert went alone for a two-day visit to Chatham in April 1844 'for the purpose of attending the quarterly examination of the apprentices in their scholastic education, with which he expressed himself much pleased'. He ordered that they receive a holiday in recognition of their achievements.[3]

Equally congenial was Herbert's visit to Portsmouth in August 1844 to check that preparations were in hand for the visit of Prince William (the future Kaiser Wilhelm I) of Prussia.[4] It offered some recompense for the less seemly visit he had made with Lord Lincoln (the latter in his capacity as Commissioner of Woods and Forests) to Greenwich Park on 13 June. The two friends did so in response to protests at the Admiralty's plan to site a vast water tank on Croom's Hill within the park. The location had been chosen because it would serve either Greenwich Hospital or Deptford Dockyard in the event of a fire. Opponents charged that construction of the tank would destroy up to 25 barrows and tumuli. Work was halted pending the visit but Herbert and Lincoln ordered that it be resumed the following day. This 'dexterous but shabby manoeuvre' brought condemnation upon the pair, 'little respect as they have shown for antiquities'.[5] Unintended

1 Hansard, 24 Feb. 1843, LXVI, cols. 1326-30; 26 Feb. 1844, LXXIII, cols. 318-19.
2 *SWJ*, 3 June 1843. Nelson's statue was erected in November 1843.
3 *The Times*, 28 June 1842, 8 Sept. 1842, 1 May 1844.
4 *The Times*, 22 Aug. 1844.
5 *The Times*, 19, 22 June 1844.

light relief of sorts followed in July when Herbert was amongst the official delegation and an estimated 40,000 civilians who gathered at Brighton to witness trials of Captain Samuel Alfred Warner's latest experiment in missile technology. As the projectile hurtled towards the 300-ton *John O'Gaunt*:

> the suspense of all present was painful, the silence was deep and unbroken. A smoke seemed suddenly to envelope the *John O'Gaunt*, her mainmast shot up perpendicular from her deck, no noise save that of the rending of timbers was heard, and on the apparent smoke's clearing away, the smitten ship heeled over to port and sank.[1]

It was something more fundamental than the placing of water tanks and the efficacy of missiles, however, which was changing the face of the navy during the 1840s. Before Herbert took office, the fleet consisted mostly of wooden and unarmoured vessels; a few months after he left it authorisation was granted to convert four of the existing battleships from sail to steam.[2] This was by no means what everybody at the Admiralty wanted. Sir William Symonds, the influential Surveyor of the Navy, had no time for steam power, dismissing it as 'scientific humbug'. Herbert, though, was firmly on the side of the modernisers. Though the evidence is scanty, he seems, unusually for a First Secretary, to have taken a direct interest in ship design; and he supported those who advocated the merits of screw as opposed to paddle propulsion.[3]

This was not mere navel-gazing. During the summer of 1844 French forces became embroiled in Morocco and Tahiti, allegedly maltreating a British consul. It did not help that the former expedition was headed by the Prince de Joinville, a younger son of King Louis Phillipe. Joinville had just published a pamphlet, *Note sur l'étatdes forces navales de la France*. In it he impolitically suggested that recent developments in steam power had conferred sufficient advantages on the French navy that it could realistically contemplate the invasion

---

1 *The Times*, 22 July 1844. Longford, *Wellington*, p. 375.
2 Hamilton, *Naval Rivalry*, pp. 15, 25-7.
3 Hamilton, *Naval Rivalry*, pp. 46-8, 132-3.

of England. War fever broke out on both sides of the Channel. Foreign Secretary Aberdeen, who had spent several years labouring to establish friendly relations with France, objected that the reaction was unwarranted. Others disagreed. Palmerston, his shadow, famously announced in July 1845 that 'The Channel is no longer a barrier'. Doom-monger in chief, however, was Wellington, the Commander-in-Chief. Joinville's pamphlet simply confirmed the Iron Duke's conclusion that steam-powered warships could strike quickly and unannounced.[1]

When questioned in the Commons in 1844 about the alleged ill-preparedness of the British navy, Herbert was defiant:

> the building of new ships had not been neglected and a great addition to our steam navy has been made [...] They found the Navy in an inefficient state – the ships were under-manned, since then the complements throughout the service had been generally increased, which had given perfect satisfaction in the Navy. The steam power had been doubled [...] and they were, in fact, adding between 5,000 and 6,000 horse power annually to the steam force of the Navy [...] there were thirty ships of the line in an efficient state which could be got ready at a moment's notice and every day is adding to the efficiency both of ships and men.[2]

Privately, however, Herbert was only too aware of the truth of the charge. As long ago as July 1842 he had drawn the government's attention to the fact that the Royal Navy did not greatly exceed the French. At the time of his 1844 speech there were only nine capital ships in commission, of which just three were in home waters.[3] He was clearly of Wellington's mind when he wrote to Peel that 'the power to be friendly, of a popular Government representing a hostile nation cannot permanently be relied on'. Herbert's own mind during the summer of

---

1   Partridge, 'Wellington and the Defence of the Realm' in Gash, *Wellington Studies*, pp. 242-3; Muir, *Wellington*, pp. 534-6; Gash, *Peel*, pp. 507-17; Chamberlain, *Aberdeen*, pp. 359-67.
2   Hansard, 22 July 1844, LXXVI, cols. 1238-9.
3   Gash, *Peel*, p. 519; Partridge, *Military Planning*, p. 22-3.

1844 was 'forcibly turned to the means we may have at hand for the defence of the country in the event of sudden hostility'. His private papers contain ample evidence of the fact, including returns of naval officers either actively engaged or on half pay, the results of trials for different sorts of brigs, and notes for speeches.[1]

The fruits of Herbert's cogitations were set out in a lengthy memorandum to Peel in December. In it he identified a number of particular 'evils to be remedied'. The problem of too few steam-powered warships, he contended, could be overcome by a short-term building programme of fifteen vessels a year. A second issue, addressed within the year, was 'the want of a reserve squadron at home to act as a squadron of exercise during peace'. Herbert also favoured the creation of 'harbours of refuge', places where merchant ships could find sanctuary during periods of hostility. His idea enjoyed a certain vogue during the late 1840s, before being deemed impractical. More rudimentary concerns were Herbert's anxieties that the royal dockyards were ill-equipped to service steam vessels, and that the dockyards themselves lacked sufficient fortification. On these points, however, Herbert was exceeding his remit: the dockyards were the responsibility of the Ordnance, not the Admiralty.[2]

By virtue of the detail which he included, the most important section of Herbert's memorandum concerned the navy's command structure. As matters stood, promotion up to the rank of post captain was by selection: the average age of a captain was just 36. Thereafter, by contrast, one's progress up the naval hierarchy was governed by a strict process of seniority. Herbert's researches yielded the disconcerting statistic that 76 of the supposedly 'effective' admirals were over 70. Quite apart from the fact there was not 'a sufficient number of Admirals possessing youth, vigour, and practice to take command of our fleets', there were the added dilemmas that 'there are no officers in the upper ranks young enough to teach [tactics and manoeuvring a fleet] so there are none in the lower ranks who have had the opportunity of learning'. There was great merit, Herbert suggested, in adopting the

1   Stanmore, I, p. 28; WSHC 2057/F8/1/I; WSHC 2057/F8/L/10-11.
2   Stanmore, I, pp. 28-32; Partridge, *Military Planning*, pp. 34-8.

French practice whereby the lower ranks were gained by seniority, and the higher by merit. To catalyse such a far-reaching reform he proposed retiring 300 captains and empowering 'the Admiralty to reward brilliant service by promotion'. Lord Stanley, Secretary for War and the Colonies, thought Herbert's ideas 'bold and judicious'. Those in the service on the other hand, deemed them heretical. Peel, though sending Herbert 'rather a complimentary & satisfactory letter', baulked at the expenditure which implementing the plans would entail.[1] It fell to Russell's Liberal government, encouraged by Herbert, to remove 200 captains in 1847; more followed in 1851. But it would be the mid-1860s, thanks to interventions from the Grim Reaper, before the logjam at the top of the naval command can be said to have been properly broken.[2] Even so, Herbert's role in having initiated the process was an important one. It revealed his willingness to see elements of meritocracy introduced into a revered institution in the name of efficiency. This, at last, was Herbert the Peelite Conservative, perhaps even the nascent mid-Victorian Liberal.

Although Peel had been disinclined to support Herbert's 1844 recommendations with respect to naval officers, he was persuaded that the nation's defences were fragile. The Prime Minister proved true to his word that 'We must make a great naval effort next year'. Early in 1845 a £1 million naval programme was announced; the estimates rose commensurately and the number of sailors peaked at 40,000 in 1846.[3] Herbert was no longer at the Admiralty by then but it is tempting to see this as his achievement. Admiral Sir Charles Napier, Member for Marylebone, the recognised guru on naval affairs in the House, said that 'it was mainly owing to the right hon. gentleman that at last the navy was about to obtain redress'.[4] He exaggerated.

1   Stanmore, I, pp. 30-2; NUL Ne C 11925/1-2, SH to Lincoln, Dec. 1844.
2   Lewis, *The Navy in Transition*, ch. 7; Hansard, 12 June 1851, CXVII, cols. 648-52; PP 1847-8 (555), XXI, pp. 799-804.
3   Parker, *Peel*, III, pp. 196-7, Peel to Stanley, 23 Dec. 1844; Gash, *Peel*, pp. 520-1; Chamberlain, *Aberdeen*, pp. 371-2.
4   *DWG*, 3 Apr. 1845. 31 Mar. 1845. The Hansard version of Napier's speech, 31 Mar. 1845, does not include this sentence.

The big beasts in cabinet as the arguments raged over defence during 1844 were Wellington and Aberdeen. Neither should it be forgotten that Haddington, Herbert's chief, also sat round the cabinet table. He was self-evidently better placed than Herbert to lobby the Prime Minister over issues such as under-manning and the need for more battleships.[1] But from a personal point of view the timing of Herbert's memorandum did him no harm: was it entirely coincidental that within weeks of submitting it he would be moving onwards and upwards in his ministerial career?

Looked at in its entirety, what are we to make of Herbert's period at the Admiralty? We may safely ignore his claim that he had made the country 'inviolable to attack'.[2] But Sir Charles Napier, well-qualified to judge, was generous: 'it was very generally admitted that no man had performed the duties better than he did. He had had a good deal of communication with him, and would bear testimony to the zeal and efficiency he had exhibited while in the Admiralty'.[3] A more balanced assessment might be that Herbert was an enterprising but not exceptional Secretary. The chief importance of his tenure was threefold. First, he had shown himself to be a good Peelite, pursuing the related goals of reform and efficiency. His distinctiveness under that umbrella lay in his refusal to equate efficiency with economy. Exposure to the realities of the naval world demonstrated to him that short-term costs might have to be incurred as part of the price for greater efficiency in the longer term. Second, and more generally, Herbert's Admiralty experiences foreshadowed his time at the War Office, notably in getting him to think about the thorny issues surrounding the selection, promotion and retirement of officers. Most important of all, life at the Admiralty 'converted' Herbert to the cause of national defence. In July 1845, several months after leaving Admiralty House, he was still writing to Peel expressing alarm at the continuing paucity of steam-powered battleships. Those who argued that the problem might be remedied by converting steam-powered merchant ships, he

---

1 Gash, *Peel*, pp. 517-18.
2 *SWJ*, 22 Feb. 1845.
3 *DWG*, 3 Apr. 1845.

cautioned, were misguided: 'a ship is a very large house & is not to be altered in hours or even in days'.¹ Herbert, like others more expert than he, was guilty of exaggerating the impact of steam power on naval warfare. But the Prime Minister was tolerant of his naval Young Turk.

Peel's tolerance of Herbert's chivvying derived partly from the fact that he had only recently promoted him. At the beginning of 1845 Gladstone's resignation from the Board of Trade, the most significant of several departures from the government, had forced him to reshuffle his ministers. Herbert found himself in the cabinet. Some commentators were perplexed. Charles Greville, though conceding that 'Sidney Herbert is a smart young fellow', 'could remember no instance of two men [Lincoln was the other] who had distinguished themselves so little in Parliament being made Cabinet Ministers. Herbert has done very neatly the little he has done [but it] remains to be seen what [he] can do'. Lord Lyndhurst believed Peel advanced them 'in order to have two young pliant men trained in his school, to keep his older and more independent colleagues in check'.² This was unduly cynical. The truth was that Peel continued to hold Herbert in relatively high regard. He told Hardinge that 'Sidney Herbert promises well as a debater', a judgement made at a time when he was only too aware that he lacked debating talent on his front bench.³

The speech which weighed heavily in Peel's mind when deciding how and where to promote Herbert concerned Ireland. After a relatively peaceful interlude, there was a resurgence of organised agitation there following the launch of the National Repeal Association in 1840. It peaked in 1843. Peel responded by banning a monster meeting at Clontarf in October and charged O'Connell with conspiracy. The Opposition in turn tabled a debate on the state of Ireland in February 1844. Conservative ministers, unable to agree a common line, adopted a generally defensive posture.⁴ Not so Herbert, who spoke in what many agreed to be a markedly liberal and enlightened fashion. He appealed

1 WSHC 2057/F4/53, SH to Peel, 3 July 1845.
2 Reeve, *Greville Memoirs*, pt. 2, II, pp. 268, 30 Jan. 1845; Vincent, *Stanley Journals*, p. 94, 24 Dec. 1852.
3 Parker, *Peel*, III, Peel to Hardinge, 1 Mar. 1845; Gash, *Peel*, p. 458.
4 Gash, *Peel*, ch. 12 especially pp. 415-9.

to the House that Ireland should not 'be made the battle field of party', and whilst conceding that Irishmen entertained no 'great enthusiasm in favour of the present Government' voiced his determination to support 'measures [...] calculated to promote [...] tranquillity and welfare'. This, he went on to explain, required that government act impartially between Ireland's Protestant and Catholics. To this end 'in all civil matters there should be the fullest equality between the Protestant and Roman Catholic'. So far as religious matters were concerned, he 'did not think that the Roman Catholics, as a body, looked to the spoliation of the Established Church, as a condition of their tranquillity'. But 'he must frankly state that he entertained the opinion that the Roman Catholic Clergy ought to be endowed by the State'. 'He was not', he concluded:

> so presumptuous as to set himself up as the mouth-piece of the Irish landlords, but he believed he might say for them, as he could on his own behalf, that they were most anxious to co-operate in anything that might tend to the benefit of their common country.[1]

Although Peel disagreed that the State should pay Catholic clergy, Herbert's speech chimed well with his innermost thoughts. Coercive policies would not suffice. They had to be accompanied by measures 'to build up in Catholic Ireland a feeling of confidence in the effectiveness and impartiality of government and the law, and thus reconcile the community to the benefits of the Union and the maintenance of the Anglican Establishment'. Small wonder then, that on 28 January 1845 as part of his reshuffle, Peel invited Herbert to become Chief Secretary for Ireland.[2]

Herbert was underwhelmed. He had already told his sister Mary that 'I have not the slightest intention of going to Ireland'.[3] At most he would take it 'on the condition that it should be temporary, and that at the end of the next session an arrangement should be made for his admission into the Cabinet with some office in England'. Since Peel

1   Hansard, 19 Feb. 1844, LXXII, cols. 1110-16.
2   Adelman, *Peel*, p. 45; WSHC 2057/F4/53, Peel to SH, 28 Jan. 1845.
3   WSHC 2057/F4/50, SH to Lady Bruce, 22 Jan. 1845.

deemed this impractical, the Chief Secretaryship went to Sir Thomas Freemantle instead.[1] Herbert replaced Freemantle as Secretary at War with a seat in the cabinet. He was also sworn in as a member of the Privy Council on 4 February.

Why was Herbert so reluctant to go to Ireland? He was an obvious fit, a substantial landowner and interested in its affairs. Heytesbury, the Lord Lieutenant, was a family friend. The Chief Secretaryship was a more prestigious office than that of Secretary at War. Not a few thought it more than he merited. 'Mr Herbert's success in his present post', wrote *The Times*, 'has been by no means so great as to give him any right to aspire to so arduous and so important a post as that of Irish Secretary'.[2] Herbert did not doubt that he could do the job but he did profess to his sister that he was:

> naturally indolent […] I am not in love with politics. I have thought for myself too much to hold opinions as a partisan does, and I have outgrown personal ambition. I have seen how much vexation and disappointment are inseparable from public life.[3]

But why therefore did Herbert not also turn down the War Office? It is difficult to resist the conclusion that he regarded Ireland as too much of a poisoned chalice. *The Examiner* ruefully observed that Herbert would be relieved not 'to be exposed to the quicksands of Irish politics'. Had he gone to Dublin, of course, he would have been at the sharp end of the government's response to the failure of the Irish potato crop in 1845. Heytesbury was soon writing that it was 'impossible to conceive a more ungrateful task than that of administering the affairs of Ireland'. There was facetiousness, even disdain, in Herbert's quip to Lincoln, who, with no Irish interest, had dutifully agreed to become Chief Secretary in 1846, that he had seen 'no mention of your being shot in the Irish news'.[4] The whole episode is reminiscent of a decade

1   Parker, *Graham*, II, p. 4.
2   *The Times*, 23 Jan. 1845.
3   WSHC 2057/F4/50, SH to Lady Bruce, 22 Jan. 1845.
4   *SWJ*, 8 Feb. 1845; Munsell, *Unfortunate Duke*, p. 78; NUL Ne C 11934, SH to Lincoln, 9 Nov. 1846.

earlier when Herbert had declined a Lordship of the Treasury but had been prepared to accept office at the Board of Control. Herbert could appear self-effacing: he told Graham on joining the cabinet that he doubted that he could be 'immediately of much effective use to the government but I am prepared to work hard & do my best'. He could also protest a sense of *noblesse oblige*. He wrote to his mother at this time that:

> the step I am taking is one which renders escape from politics at any future time more impossible than before. But as we are not born to ease, but to labour in our different conditions, none of us may refuse our burdens, least of all those who are high enough in position to set an example.[1]

But were there not also elements of self-deception or worse in these letters? There were, at this stage of his life at least, limits to Herbert's altruism.

The Chief Secretaryship would also have taken Herbert away from Wilton. Writing from there in January 1845, he reaffirmed his love for the family seat:

> If one had nothing to do but to consult one's own taste and one's own ease, I should be too glad to live down here a domestic life, looking after the people and doing what good I could, in a field which, though narrow, has plenty to be done in it.[2]

As it was, the demands of the Admiralty had resulted in Herbert's being able to spend less time in Wiltshire than he would have liked. He was unable, for example, to attend a grand gathering of Wiltshire's yeomanry cavalry at Devizes in May 1842. Herbert nevertheless remained an enthusiastic captain of the Warminster troop. He 'put them through a variety of movements' in April 1843 before rewarding them with dinner at the town's Bell Inn; and entertained them at Wilton

---

1 BL Add. Mss. 79657, fols. 1-2, SH to JRG, 1 Feb. 1845; WSHC 2057/F4/49, SH to Lady Pembroke, 1 Feb. 1845.
2 WSHC 2057/F4/50, SH to Lady Bruce, 22 Jan. 1845.

the following spring.[1] Herbert also made efforts to attend the quarterly meetings of the South Wiltshire and Warminster Farmers' Club: he was present in November 1842 when 'Croskett's clod-crusher elicited general approbation'.[2] His chief local interest beyond the Wilton estate, however, remained the provision of church accommodation. Though not always able to be present in person he was conspicuous in his support of the Salisbury Diocesan Church Building Association; from 1843 he increased his annual subscription from £5 to £50. A one-off donation of £100 was subscribed for a new church at Westbury in 1843, and £300 was given towards the provision of a chaplain and suitable accommodation at the Salisbury Infirmary.[3]

Another frustrating by-product of Herbert's being at the Admiralty during the early 1840s was the necessity of curtailing his plans for overseas travel. It was more a case, therefore, of travellers descending upon him. Seemingly the whole clan of Woronzow relations (in tandem with the Grand Duke Michael, grandson of Peter the Great) descended on Wilton in October 1843, though not before they had taken a wrong train! Other guests invited to meet them there included Lord Fitzroy Somerset who, in his subsequent incarnation as Lord Raglan, would encounter some of them in the less friendly environment of the Crimea.[4] Convivial gatherings of Herbert and his siblings, meanwhile, continued relatively uninterrupted: all assembled at Clifton Hotwells near Bristol for the end of year festivities in 1842.[5] Neither does government business appear to have impaired Herbert's partiality for the turf. The Secretary of the Admiralty was present at Tattersalls in May 1843 to witness the sale of some of his 'extensive stud'. What remained of it continued to bring him regular success on the track.[6]

Of greatest interest to Herbert's Wiltshire constituents was his position on the Corn Laws. True to his pledge at the 1841 election

1   DWG, 12 May 1842; SWJ, 29 Apr. 1843, 18 May 1844.
2   SWJ, 5 Nov. 1842.
3   SWJ, 19 Nov., 3 Dec. 1842, 28 Jan. 1 Apr. 1843.
4   SWJ, 28 Oct. 1843.
5   SWJ, 21 Jan. 1843.
6   SWJ, 20 May, 1 July 1843.

to uphold them, he opposed Radical motions of 1842 and 1843 demanding their repeal. By then, however, Peel had decided that the prevailing system of protection needed modification. In 1842, as part of his economic package designed to balance the nation's books, the Prime Minister revised the 1828 sliding scale on corn, in practice reducing the level of protection for British farmers whilst attempting to maintain grain prices at a stable level. The change was accepted only grudgingly by the agricultural interest. John Benett, Herbert's parliamentary colleague for South Wiltshire, was one Member who voiced strong reservations; the Duke of Buckingham resigned from the government. Herbert, though he voted for the revised scale, was mindful that it was a sensitive issue: more than once he deemed it expedient to explain to constituents that 'He thought the old law gave too much protection, and indeed unnecessary protection, because it gave no corresponding advantages for the odium which it attached to the agricultural body'.[1]

Free traders, however, exasperated by what they considered to be only modest changes in the Corn Laws, intensified their campaign against them. This included lecture tours by leading lights of the Anti-Corn Law League during 1843 aimed at persuading farmers that the Corn Laws were inimical to their interests. Richard Cobden, addressing a large audience in Salisbury in August, derided Herbert for failing to recognise that it was the Corn Laws which explained why the rich were getting richer and the poor poorer. Herbert would have been more angered, one suspects, to hear that Cobden had said that Salisbury Cathedral would be better used if converted into a factory.[2] Cobden and John Bright, together with the League's president, George Wilson, returned to Salisbury in the autumn to lend their support to the Liberal candidate in a by-election there. The Conservative candidate narrowly prevailed but not before Herbert was accused of interfering and using his local influence on his behalf.[3] The episodes presaged, by proxy, the

1   Moody, *Benett*, pp. 271-2; *SWJ*, 10 Feb. 1844.
2   *SWJ*, 12 Aug. 1843; McCord, *Anti-Corn Law League*, pp. 143-7.
3   *Wiltshire Independent*, 30 Nov. 1843.

famous parliamentary exchange between Cobden and Herbert in the Commons sixteen months later.

In rural Wiltshire, as elsewhere, the agriculturalists' response to the League was to form branches of the Central Agricultural Protection Society (or Anti-League). Herbert was duly present at the Bear Inn in Devizes in February 1844 to support such an initiative. Referring specifically to the recent events in Salisbury, he seconded the verbose motion that the League's doctrines were:

> false in principle, and that their proceedings tend to produce jealousy and evil feeling amongst the several classes of the community, are dangerous to the peace and injurious to the trade and prosperity of the country, and ought to be firmly resisted.

'Never in his life', Herbert went on to say,

> had he advocated any proposition more sincerely or more heartily [...] It had been fully proved that high and low wages followed high and low prices [...] he thought nothing could be worse than constant change and constant meddling with laws, upon the faith of which large investment had been made.

The League's contention that Britain's adopting free trade would be reciprocated in kind, he insisted, was a *non sequitur*: 'they would very much resemble the man who made a present of his valuable horse, and was afterwards obliged to walk home on foot'. What was needed was 'remunerative' wages and 'fair' protection. 'I know there is every disposition on the part of those who hold the reins of power', he concluded, 'to uphold and maintain the laws as they now are'. As proof of his commitment he subscribed £100 to the fledgling society on the spot.[1]

This was the most important speech Herbert had made outside parliament. It was widely reported in the national and provincial press. As one of very few English county Members in government who also

1   *DWG*, 7 Feb. 1844; *SWJ*, 10 Feb. 1844.

sat in the Commons, it marked Herbert out as a leading spokesman for the agricultural interest. Close observers might have cavilled that Herbert's speech was less a defence of the economic case for the Corn Laws ('there was nothing', he joked, 'so elastic as figures') than a plea for social harmony: 'Every year, he regretted to say, classes became more and more separated – because the poor became poorer, and the rich were getting more rich. They should do everything in their power to better the condition of the labourers, and then they would see who their best friends were'.[1] But there were very few, if any, close observers.

Where did Herbert's reputation stand as he prepared to attend his first cabinet meeting? It was a question addressed by the *Illustrated London News* in a profile written soon after his speech in Devizes:

> The name of Sidney Herbert reads as if it would read better in the pages of fashionable novels, than at the foot of a grim Admiralty order for equipping for storm or battle a 'Formidable' or a 'Thunderer'. There are men born in such a position that they seem to inherit that which the greatest talents and most unceasing exertions can never reach, and Mr Sidney Herbert is of the fortunate and privileged number. The office he holds, it is true, is not one of the most important in a political sense; but if he display but ordinary abilities, and if the ascendancy of the Conservative party continue, it will be the stepping-stone to others. Not having the slightest want of office for its rewards, he stands precisely in the position that is most likely to obtain it: almost all the members of the Ministry are rich men. Mr Herbert, however, is one of the most wealthy [...] his age does not exceed thirty-three and himself and Mr Gladstone are almost the youngest members of the Government [...] Mr Herbert has confined himself to speaking on points connected with his office, in which his greatest efforts were only in explaining and proposing the navy estimates. During the present debate on Ireland he has spoken on the general question. He made a much better impression in his speech on this subject than on the Estimates. There the necessity and the anxiety to be accurate as to details impeded his fluency. On this occasion he exhibited very

---

1 *SWJ*, 10 Feb. 1844.

little of embarrassment or hesitation. His opinions, too, were liberal on many points, and his tone conciliating on all [...] Mr Herbert is rather slenderly made; neat and genteel rather than commanding: his voice is not of the strongest, and altogether, though we do not think he is fitted 'the applause of listening senates to command', he may yet take a very creditable position in them [...] He is a decided supporter of the present Corn Laws and at a recent meeting of agriculturists 'came out' very strongly against the League.[1]

The sketch had its limitations. It did not mention the High Church Toryism which had defined Herbert during the 1830s. Herbert was no less a High Churchman in January 1845. But High Churchmanship had not been much needed at the Admiralty. Even if he had not been at the Admiralty, the fact that a Conservative government in office from 1841 contributed to a sense that the Anglican Church did not seem to be in so much danger as it had been in the decade before. It was what Thomas Carlyle had famously dubbed the 'Condition of England Question' which most preoccupied Peel's government. As a member of that government, the Herbert of 1845 was far more the moderate Conservative than the traditional Church and King Tory he threatened to be when he first entered parliament in 1832. As he told Sir James Graham on entering the cabinet, with respect to Peel's reforms effected thus far, 'I go heart & soul with the spirit of the proposed measures which are in complete accordance with the opinions which I have formed for myself'.[2] More fundamentally, Herbert was a Conservative because he believed that the hegemony of the landed order risked being overthrown: by industrialisation and urbanisation (and Ireland) at home; by steamships and France from abroad. It was what had persuaded him, against his inclinations, to play a part in national affairs. As he put it to his sister, 'An aristocracy that does nothing, that takes no part, that will not enter the lists, an aristocracy of ease and quiet and retirement, would be soon upset in this country – and, what is more, it would deserve to be upset'.[3] Like

1 *Illustrated London News*, 2 Mar. 1844.
2 BL Add. Mss. 79657, fols. 1-2, SH to JRG, 1 Feb. 1845.
3 WSHC 2057/F4/50, SH to Lady Bruce, 22 Jan. 1845.

all Conservatives he was soon to discover that upsetting choices had to be made.

5
Treacherous Times 1845-1846

Herbert's name had been linked with the vacant War Office in May 1844. A desire to fill it may have been one reason why he held out against going to Ireland eight months later. When he finally set foot inside it in January 1845, however, Herbert expressed disappointment at finding it 'dry and dull'. On the other hand, as he told his mother, the Dowager Lady Pembroke,

> the Cabinet is, of course, a great step, and gives one at once a view of the whole system of government. With the new responsibility of course comes new labour; for though I shall have much less to do at the War Office than I have here [the Admiralty], I must now work up other general questions for debate.[1]

Herbert's presumptions proved more or less accurate. What he could not foresee were the party political convulsions attendant upon Peel's decision to repeal the Corn Laws. They would propel Herbert close to the centre of one of the great controversies of modern British political history. By the summer of 1846, it was generally accepted that he had emerged as a major political figure. There was fierce disagreement, however, as to how he should be judged. To friends he was a Peelite man of principle who had chosen to put country before

1 *The Times*, 8 May 1844; WSHC 2057/F4/49, SH to Lady Pembroke, 1 Feb. 1845.

party; to foes he was the Tory agriculturalist who had betrayed both his principles and his class.

If he did not already know it, Herbert quickly discovered that the army gloried in a far more complex administrative structure than the navy. In the first place there was Horse Guards, home to the Commander-in-Chief (from 1842, Wellington) appointed directly by the Crown. He was responsible for operations, discipline, promotions and patronage. But he did not control the artillery, engineers, forts or barracks. The remit for these fell to the Master-General of the Ordnance. Both officers tended to be wary of politicians, civilians who interfered with their work as professionals. The politicians countered that the army must be under parliament's control. Theoretically supreme in exercising that control was the Secretary for War and the Colonies. In practice the demands of his portfolio meant that he could rarely 'give the army more than perfunctory attention'. The vacuum was filled in part by the cash-conscious Treasury, responsible anyway for overseeing the Commissariat which supplied the army with food, fuel and transport. Given that his office was responsible for the militia and yeomanry, institutions which might need to coordinate their activities with the army, the Home Secretary too could be influential.[1]

Ensconced at the War Office, the Secretary at War lay further down the pecking order. He was not normally a member of cabinet. His primary responsibilities were to answer to parliament for army finances. Lord Liverpool had aptly dubbed him the 'Finance Minister of the Army'. As such the Secretary at War prepared the annual military estimates, a chore rendering him liable to falling foul of both the Chancellor and the Commons. He was also responsible for preparing the Mutiny Act, the codification of military law (which included the increasingly contentious use of flogging) that had to be renewed annually. The corresponding Articles of War governed army personnel outside the colonies overseas. Beyond that, as Herbert pointed out in 1855,

---

1 Jones, 'The British Army', ch. 3; Partridge, *Military Planning*, pp. 39-43.

he properly has no executive duties except those which of late years he has acquired by his having originated certain improvements and reforms in the army; and being the originator [...] kept them in his own hands to see them effectually carried out.[1]

These included responsibility for military prisons, army pensioners, and schools. The latter, as will be seen, owed something to Herbert's initiatives.

Historically less popular than the navy, the army was an irresistible target for reformers after Waterloo. From an effective strength of nearly 224,000 men in 1815, numbers had fallen to 109,285 by 1835. Thereafter, in response to the First Opium War with China (1839-42) and the fear of war with France, numbers increased. Herbert did not, therefore, as he had at the Admiralty, have to battle against demands for further cuts. The estimates he presented in 1845 were predicated on an army establishment of 138,461 men rising to 148,760 in 1846. Estimates for 1846-7 projected expenditure approaching £13 million. With approximately 10,000 men annually leaving the service, mostly through a mixture of retirement, death and desertion (2,417 deserted in 1846), recruitment was arguably a more pressing problem than finances. Contrary to the popular myth that the army ossified in the decades after Waterloo, minds had been turning to how the institution might be made more appealing, for example by reviewing the terms of enlistment and the code of discipline.[2]

Herbert could hardly avoid such questions during his sixteen months at the War Office but few placed him in the vanguard of reform. In July 1845 he opposed a motion from somebody who was. Captain Brownlow Layard moved that the term of enlistment be reduced from life (in practice usually twenty-one years) to ten years in order 'to procure a better class of recruits, diminish desertion, and thus add to the efficiency of the Service'. On the matter of desertions at least, Herbert had grounds for his opposition. He was correct in pointing out that desertions tended to occur during the early years of

1 PP 1854-5 (247), IX, p. 166.
2 Spiers, *Army and Society*, pp. 35-7, 74; Strachan, *Wellington's Legacy*, pp. 50, 182-4; Hansard, 4 Apr. 1845, LXXIX, cols. 213-15.

service; Layard's proposal would have little practical impact.[1] Herbert emerges as similarly conservative from a debate of July 1845. It was prompted by a report in the *Morning Chronicle* that two men in the Guards at Windsor had each received a hundred lashes for refusing to strip naked with the rest of their company prior to being examined by a surgeon. 'It appeared that for some time past', as the report phrased it, that 'many of the soldiers were affected with a certain disease, which, if suffered to continue, must have been attended with serious results'. Herbert did not deny that the proceedings appeared harsh. But he was insistent that the two unfortunates had been treated correctly, given the substantive point that they were guilty of disobeying an order.[2]

Yet Herbert should not be dismissed out of hand as a martinet. As he said in July 1845, 'He did not mean to assert that the system now in practice in the management of the British soldier was perfect; on the contrary every effort should be made to improve it'.[3] His chief contribution in this respect was in the field of education. Sir Henry Hardinge, Herbert's predecessor but one at the War Office, had asked the Reverend G.R. Gleig, recently appointed Chaplain-General, to report on the state of regimental schools. Gleig's report of September 1844 reached the unsurprising conclusion that they were generally poor (the masters, 'being chiefly sergeants of the old school', were 'as ignorant as they are drunken'), redeemed only in the few instances where a regimental commander took a direct interest in the school. Gleig recommended that higher and more consistent standards might be obtained by establishing a Normal School, one where students and putative masters would be taught side by side, at the Royal Military Asylum in Chelsea.[4] It fell to Herbert to decide the next moves forward. He called for further information and included himself on the committee charged with finding it. Plans for the Normal School thereafter proceeded apace. There would be four

1 Hansard, 1 July 1845, LXXXI, cols. 1398-1412; Strachan, *Wellington's Legacy*, pp. 70-5.
2 Hansard, 18 July 1845, LXXXII, cols. 674-7.
3 Hansard, 1 July 1845, LXXXI, col. 1408.
4 Jones, 'The British Army', pp. 227-8; TNA WO 43/84, 'Report on Regimental Schools and the Training of Schoolmasters', 25 Sept. 1844.

companies of boys comprising a Model School. They would follow a practically-based curriculum which included tactics, military drawing, surveying and fortifications. Their masters were to receive half a crown daily rising to three shillings, their authority clarified by ranking them next to regimental sergeant majors. Wellington accepted Herbert's recommendations in June 1846. The Normal School opened in April 1847; its first teacher graduated in April 1849.[1]

Herbert would subsequently claim that the above was his plan and that he had risked impinging upon the authority of Horse Guards to advance it.[2] Whilst he was right on the latter point (Wellington could simply have vetoed the proposals), he exaggerated on the former. Hardinge clearly laid the groundwork and Gleig deserves the credit for much of the spadework; he became Inspector-General of Military Schools in 1847. But Herbert was Gleig's essential ally as an onward Christian soldier. The two men shared a passion for religious instruction and the stocking of regimental libraries. Ten thousand volumes were added in 1846-7; £2,000 was voted to provide more the following year. A better educated, and presumably more moral army, the pair reasoned, would be better disciplined, appeal to a better class of recruit, and thus in time become more popular with the general public. Herbert was praised by Fox Maule, his successor at the War Office, for 'a plan which did him infinite credit'. The more meaningful compliment was the Reformers' announcement that they would extend his initiatives.[3]

The most tangible proof of Herbert's concern for men already enlisted was the Royal Warrant issued on 19 December 1845.[4] It brought an end to the practice of deducting four pence a day from the pay of men who were in hospital. Another carrot dispensed by the man who was content to defend the stick of corporal punishment was the changes made to the regulations for good conduct. Existing regulations stipulated that men could earn up to four marks (and an

1 TNA WO 43/84, SH to Fox Maule, 13 Dec. 1846; Strachan, *Wellington's Legacy*, pp. 88-96.
2 PP 1860 (441), VII, p. 505.
3 Hansard, 1 Mar. 1847, XC, col. 652.
4 *The Times*, 7 Jan. 1846.

extra penny a day's pay) after seven, fourteen, twenty-one and twenty-eight years of service respectively. Herbert's system introduced six good conduct marks, one attainable for every five years' service. Within a year no fewer than 9,253 men were beneficiaries of his restructuring.[1]

Another area in which Herbert pushed for change was in the awarding of commissions. In 1849, 338 of 461 commissions were purchased; only 24 went to non-commissioned officers. Horse Guards inclined to the view that this was 24 too many: whatever the military merits of such men, they often lacked the financial means considered necessary to sustain the ranks of captain and major. Herbert attempted to mitigate this objection by providing £100 for NCOs commissioned in the infantry and £150 for those commissioned in the cavalry. These sums, it has to be admitted, were too little to make any real impact. So was the fund of £2,000 from which sergeants might grant annuities of £20 and issue medals to men 'for meritorious service'; it was exhausted by August 1847. Further, in face of objections from Wellington, Herbert's proposal to give £25 to deserving NCOs when they retired was abandoned altogether.[2] But Herbert had given notice, as he had at the Admiralty, that he was willing to admit greater meritocracy into the officer cadre. On this issue his relatively liberal stance would several times bring him into conflict with the military hierarchy as his career progressed.

Herbert certainly felt that enough had been done for the ordinary soldier to warrant a defiant response to Layard's call for further reform in July 1845. He told the House that:

> great care had been taken of the moral culture of the army. Regimental schools had been established – care had been taken to suit the food, the hours, and the clothing, to the climate in which the regiment was stationed – the system of reliefs had been improved – libraries for the men had been collected, and five-courts and similar recreations provided for them. Very material changes had been made, and the

---

1   Jones, 'The British Army', p. 229.
2   Strachan, *Wellington's Legacy*, pp. 99-101; Jones, 'The British Army', pp. 229-30.

result of all was, that the comfort and well-being of the soldiers were more effectually secured. In the same way the system of increased pay for good conduct had had a most excellent effect; and he believed that there were now 12,000 men receiving increased pay for good conduct, though the good conduct warrant had been but a short time in operation. He might also mention the advantages which had resulted from the practice of investing the money of soldiers in savings banks [...] It was by carrying out the system already adopted [...] that he relied for making the service popular with the men.[1]

Looking back in 1853 the *United Service Gazette*, concurred. Herbert, it wrote, deserved plaudits for his 'liberality of principle, strong common sense, purity of character and official aptitude'. He had 'introduced more beneficial measures than any other secretary in five times the number of years'.[2]

Far and away Herbert's biggest concern as Secretary at War, though, was the one which he brought with him from the Admiralty: how best Britain could defend herself in the event of attempted invasion by France. Wellington's preference was to increase the size of the army by 100,000. With Peel having identified the navy as the priority, this was never remotely likely. Herbert reflected more fully on the reasons why:

> England has always been jealous of standing armies. In their long struggles for freedom, the people have found how important it is that they, as well as the Sovereign, should have a hand on the hilt of the sword of state [...] A large home military force maintained irrespective of foreign enemies or foreign apprehensions, imbued with a thoroughly military spirit, and animated by a devotion to their colours, in which the sense of citizenship is altogether lost, is what we never have seen in this country, and probably never will.[3]

---

1 Hansard, 1 July 1845, LXXXI, cols. 1406-9.
2 *The United Service Gazette*, 1 Jan. 1853.
3 Herbert, 'The Sanitary Condition of the Army', *Westminster Review*, XV, (1859), p. 52.

But one can understand his and the Duke's anxiety. The bulk of the army was on service overseas, some 30,000 in India alone. There were only 56,000 troops available in the UK in 1845; and 20,000 of those were stationed in Ireland. France could boast an army of approximately 500,000 men at the same date.[1]

In face of these realities, those charged with providing for the nation's security had to trust to the navy whilst considering alternatives for augmenting the auxiliary land forces. Of these, the one with which Herbert was most familiar, being a member, was the yeomanry cavalry. As he knew, however, it was really only a local force for maintaining public order, concentrated predominantly in rural areas, and simply too small (about 14,000 men) to be of much use. Volunteer battalions might bring forth greater numbers, but they would be untrained and patriotism was too variable a phenomenon to be relied upon.[2] A better option was army pensioners. They would be well-trained, many only in their forties and fifties. Parliament had already passed the Enrolled Pensioners Act in 1843 to authorise their use in the wake of domestic unrest. Herbert was at first bullish as to their potential. He told Graham in August 1845 that up to 44,000 might be available in the event of an emergency and thus 'quite capable of being made a considerable adjunct to our means of defence in case of invasion'. But he was being woefully over-optimistic. Wellington put the figure at 19,000; parliamentary returns for 1847-8 reveal that just 8,720 had been enrolled.[3]

By a process of elimination, this left only the militia. Militiamen had been used as a supplement to the regular army since the seventeenth century and played an important defensive role during the Napoleonic Wars. Central government determined the size of the force to be raised and allocated quotas to counties. County magistrates then oversaw the work of parish officials in drawing up a list of those liable to serve for a term of seven years, essentially able-bodied males

---

1   Partridge, *Military Planning*, pp.66-71; WSHC 2057/F8/L/6.
2   Spiers, *Army and Society*, pp. 79-80.
3   BL Add. Mss. 79657, fols. 3-8, SH to JRG, 27 June, 5 Aug. 1845; WSHC 2057/F8/I/M/14, SH to JRG, 14 Aug. 1845; Mather, *Public Order*, pp. 150-3.

between 18 and 45. If there were insufficient volunteers, a ballot was held to fill the requisite quota. Once enrolled, militia regiments might be assembled for 28 days' annual training; in wartime they could be placed on permanent duty. As well as being the principal home-based adjunct to the regular army, moreover, the militia was also its obvious feeder school. Nobody could realistically claim that militia regiments were the equal of regulars. All were part time amateurs; those balloted were often reluctant conscripts. But the militia commended itself as an institution to many Englishmen. It was comparatively cheap; 'constitutional', in that it was controlled by the Home Office; and officered by the local landed. Herbert was well aware that several of his Pembroke ancestors had commanded the Wiltshire militia. The problem was that, another victim of post-war retrenchment, militia regiments had not been embodied for training since 1825, and no ballot had been held since 1830. Herbert estimated that the ballot alone would cost £35,000 to administer; 28 days' training and exercise up to £150,000.[1]

Even so, Herbert was enthused into action by Peel's request in the summer that he examine the feasibility of rejuvenating the militia. This entailed working closely for the first time alongside the Home Secretary, Sir James Graham. Graham, who like Herbert was tall, but balding and nearly twenty years older, hailed from Netherby in Cumberland. A member of the committee which had drafted the Reform Bill, church issues drew him into the Conservative camp, to the point where he was now Peel's safest pair of administrative hands. The two men struck up an immediate rapport. There was an easy familiarity in Herbert's inviting him to Wilton in the autumn to assist in 'destroying some of the game wh is so noxious to agriculture'.[2] Though their politics diverged somewhat in the early 1850s, Graham was Herbert's closest political friend by the time that decade ended.

For the present, both men agreed that it was worth reviving the militia if only 'to habituate the present generation to this legal call

---

1   Partridge, *Military Planning*, pp. 120-6; BL Add. Mss. 79657, fols. 13-18, SH to JRG, 14 Aug. 1845.
2   BL Add. Mss. 79657, fols. 23-4, SH to JRG, 8 Nov. 1845.

on them for military service for the protection of our native shores'. Herbert instructed his permanent officials to produce memoranda setting out what needed to be done.[1] His papers for the period overflow with answers to queries made and advice offered, both solicited and otherwise. Lord Fitzroy Somerset, for instance, referred 'My dear Sidney' to the 1808 Militia Act. The Duke of Richmond, meanwhile, recommended that notices about arrangements for training should not be placed on church doors: non-churchgoers had, in his recollection, used their being so as an excuse for not having seen them. There are also Lord Howick's notes on a failed Militia Bill in 1837; and a letter from Gladstone lobbying for borough treasurers to be added to the groups exempted from the militia ballot.[2]

By early September Graham was informing Lord Stanley, Secretary for War and the Colonies, that 'Sidney Herbert and I have been considering the Militia system together, and the means of internal defence in the event of sudden invasion'. Graham retained formal control of the exercise but it was increasingly Herbert who undertook the detailed work required. Proceeding 'steadily but quietly' (they were aware that the revived militia ran the risk of provoking both the French and those liable to serve in it), the two men made plans to equip at least 30,000 men.[3] They also worked on the draft of the new Militia Bill that would be required to give those plans effect. Herbert was particularly insistent, in face of recommendations to the contrary, that they must retain the unpopular ballot. His line was endorsed by both Wellington and Palmerston: volunteers were more than usually likely to be thin on the ground 'when wages are high and labour

---

1   Parker, *Graham*, II, pp. 16-17, JRG to Peel, 16 Aug. 1845; WSHC 2057/8/1/M/17, 18; WSHC 2057/8/1/O.
2   WSHC 2057/8/1/M/15, Fitzroy Somerset to SH, 17 Aug. 1845; WSHC 2057/8/1/M/16, Richmond to SH, 18 Aug. 1845; WSHC 2057/F8/1/E; 2057/8/1/N/7, WEG to SH, 5 Feb. 1846.
3   Parker, *Graham*, II, p. 17, JRG to Stanley, 6, 9 Sept. 1845; BL Add. Mss. 79657, fols. 19-22, SH to JRG, 4 Nov. 1845.

scarce'.[1] He adopted a similarly robust approach to the argument that regiments need only be embodied for training if there was prospect of an imminent invasion: Herbert wrote to Graham in November saying that the time was ripe to make public 'the intentions of the Government, and desiring me to take the necessary steps to enable the Government to call out the Militia next spring'.[2] Reservations about the risks of arming the lower orders aside, nobody in government was more effusive than Herbert about the militia as the solution to the country's deficiencies in military manpower:

> There is no doubt that there is risk attending the arming of the manufacturing population, or rather the giving them military knowledge (for so long as they wear a red coat and have the Mutiny Act over their heads I am not much afraid of their carrying a musket [*sic*]). Our danger will begin when their time of service shall be out, and they retain their military knowledge, but lose military control. But the advantage of security against foreign attacks must be weighed against the evil of the increased organisation of domestic disturbance.
>
> When danger is apprehended from abroad, you want masses of men. Our standing army abroad is little more than a police force. An increase to it of ten or twenty thousand men in case of invasion would be as nothing. A greater number you could not procure; we have no compulsory enlistment, and to raise ten or twelve thousand recruits per annum to keep up the supply for our Army as it now stands is as much as we can do. Even if we could raise fifty thousand or more men, the jealousy would be great and the expense enormous.
>
> Our militia gives you at once, and at one-fourth of the cost of recruiting in the Line, a force of any amount, which can, if not wanted for immediate use, be maintained by annual training in a state next to efficiency at one-twelfth of the cost of regular troops. When embodied, the Militia becomes a regular army. In discipline, in drill,

1 WSHC 2057/8/1/M/30, Wellington to JRG, 1 Nov. 1845; WSHC 2057/8/1/M/9, memorandum from Colonel Wood, Aug. 1845; BL Add. Mss. 79657, fols. 19-22, SH to JRG, 4 Nov. 1845.
2 *The Times*, 13 Dec. 1845; BL Add. Mss. 79657, fols. 19-22, SH to JRG, 4 Nov. 1845.

in pay, in arms, they are identical. The officers are drawn from the same classes, so are the men; whatever difference there may be is in favour of the Militia.¹

But even as Herbert wrote, Peel's government was in crisis over the Corn Laws. Although he informed the Commons on 2 February 1846 that 'it was the intention of the Government to introduce a Bill to amend and consolidate the different Militia Acts' with the possibility of ordering the militia out for training later in the year, the moment was lost. Legislation on the militia would have to wait until 1852.² Herbert's statement therefore marks the end of his first period as Secretary at War.

Herbert had rightly told his mother, however, that cabinet ministers had to do more than run their offices. An early example of this came in February 1845 when, in his longest speech to date, he mounted a vigorous defence of a beleaguered Graham. The Home Secretary had invoked the legitimate powers of his office in 1842 and 1843 to intercept letters sent by Chartist and Anti-Corn League leaders suspected of fomenting disorder. Graham had gone further in 1844 when acceding to the Foreign Office request that the same liberty be taken with respect to the Italian nationalist, Giuseppe Mazzini, living in exile in London.³ When knowledge of what had been going on became public, there was a furore. It was spearheaded by the Radical MP, Thomas Slingsby Duncombe, who demanded an inquiry. Graham was exonerated. Duncombe, one of those whose letters had been opened, refused to be placated. He revived the debate on 19 February. Herbert agreed 'that it is a grave thing that the correspondence of the country should be tampered with; that private family secrets should be known'. But he rounded on Duncombe by pointing out that Graham had been cleared and accusing him of taking:

> an opportunity to strike a man with his hands tied – what a generous – what a chivalrous proceeding! [...] nothing but a personal and a – I

1   BL Add. Mss. 79657, fols. 33-6, SH to JRG, 4 Dec. 1845.
2   Hansard, 2 Feb. 1846, LXXXIII, cols. 426-7.
3   Ward, *Graham*, pp. 209-11; Mather, *Public Order*, pp. 218-25.

was going to say "cowardly," but I will not – nothing but a personal and an invidious persecution.

For good measure he accused Liberals who supported Duncombe, knowing full well that Liberal Home Secretaries had used the same power during the 1830s, of hypocritical partisanship.[1] The bruised Home Secretary survived. In the process Herbert had reminded Members that his language could come close to being un-parliamentary.

It was a more emollient Herbert who joined in the inevitable debates about Ireland. Apart from a fleeting visit in 1844 he does not seem to have been there since 1841 but as a paternal and pragmatic Irish landlord he had continued to take an interest in its affairs. O'Connell, in his own way, agreed. He attacked Herbert in 1841 for his 'malignant feelings towards the people of Ireland', and for 'always distinguish[ing] himself by making most virulent attacks upon the Catholic clergy of Ireland'.[2] The reality was somewhat different. Herbert contributed to the founding of St John the Baptist Blackrock Catholic Church, County Dublin, in 1842. More generally,

> Having always held it to be his duty as a landlord to assist in the maintenance of chapels and schools for the Roman Catholic population; so, on the same principle, he had thought it his duty, however it might expose him to calumny, to have advances made for the purpose of endowment in each parish of his estates.[3]

By 1843 at the latest, he had concluded that it was in the interest of the State, not least out of self-interest, to support Ireland's Catholic priests. As he said in his notable speech on Ireland in 1844:

> As matters stood many Catholic clergy felt no option but to support agitation because their income derived from their congregations [...] he was anxious to see them placed in a situation above the necessity

---

1 Hansard, 20 Feb. 1845, LXXVII, cols. 886-93. Mather, *Public Order*, p. 243, appendix 2.
2 *Dublin Monitor*, 29 Sept. 1841.
3 Hansard, 14 April 1845, LXXIX, col. 671.

of taking part in political agitation [...] The Roman Catholic religion was one so attached to order, that it had often been accused of being unfriendly to liberty. Such being the case he could conceive nothing worse than to see the clergy of a monarchical religion deriving their stipends from political agitation. He wished to see the ranks of the Roman Catholic Clergy filled from a higher order of men.[1]

Herbert was in no doubt, therefore, where he stood on the more limited proposal from the government in the spring of 1845 to increase the grant to Maynooth College, set up in County Kildare in 1795, to train Catholic priests. Peel recommended raising State assistance from £9,000 to £26,000 per annum. But what he and Herbert considered modest and sensible unleashed a furious backlash, not only from Protestant Nonconformists but also from Low Church and even Broad Church members of the Conservative party. The latter accused their leaders of betraying the Established Church, endowing the Roman Catholic Church, and taking a step that would lead inexorably to the end of the Union.[2]

In a major speech of 14 April, Herbert attempted to inject some perspective into the debate. No new principle was involved, he reasoned 'if, for the last fifty years, you had annually expended a grant for the support of that religion, the mere arithmetical operation of multiplying that sum by three was no alteration of the principle whatever'. The issue was, as he had pointed out in 1844:

> that the Irish people were necessarily, for their temporal as well as their spiritual guidance, cast upon the priesthood of the country. If that was the case, and if it existed in no other country as it did in Ireland, he would ask them whether it was not the duty of the State to see that these teachers of the people should themselves receive a liberal and enlightened education, through which alone they might reach the hearts of the people? [...] He was not one who would expect peace and civilization at once to spring up as under the wand of an

---

1 Hansard, 19 Feb. 1844, LXXII, cols. 1113-14.
2 Stewart, *Conservative Party*, pp. 190-5.

enchanter to cure all the evils of pursuing a policy in Ireland which he thought ought long ago to have been changed. A new generation must first spring up with new sentiments and opinions. All bad laws long leave their effects behind them – good laws do not immediately produce their fruits. He did, however, anticipate much good from this measure, though it might be in the distance of time; and he had been anxious to address the House because the measure was in strict accordance with what he always thought should be the policy adopted in Ireland.[1]

Herbert spoke again on the question ten days later, and was present in the aye lobby for the Third Reading on 21 May.[2] The government secured a thumping majority of 133. But the majority consisted of Liberals and Peelites. Conservative Members as a whole had divided against the Third Reading by 149 votes to 148. The fissure between rival visions of Conservatism had been laid bare.[3]

The political heat generated by the Maynooth Bill – the Commons received over 10,000 petitions against it – was in part a reflection of the contemporary angst within the Church of England. Anglicans had been able to mask their differences during the 1830s when confronted by what they regarded as an unholy alliance of Reformers intent on undermining them. By the mid-1840s, however, Low and Broad Church clergy, plus an anti-Catholic laity, were becoming increasingly anxious at the progress of Tractarianism. The latter centred on the theological outpouring emanating chiefly from members of Oxford University, most of whom Herbert had encountered in his days as an undergraduate. John Henry Newman's famous Tract 90, published in 1841, provoked fury in contending that the 39 Articles were not seriously at variance with Roman Catholic teaching. Similarly, though now less well-known, the Reverend William George Ward's *Ideal of a Christian Church*, published in 1844, maintained that he could be an Anglican without renouncing any tenet of Catholic doctrine. Ward, who had matriculated at Christ Church

1 Hansard, 14 Apr. 1845, LXXIX, cols. 666-71.
2 Hansard, 24 Apr. 1845, LXXIX, cols. 1305-9.
3 Stewart, *Conservative Party*, pp. 192-4.

in 1830 before progressing to a Fellowship at Balliol in 1834, was amongst those known to Herbert. When, sensationally, both Ward and Newman converted to Catholicism in 1845, Herbert, like prominent High Churchmen everywhere, was bound to come under suspicion of being at least a closet fellow traveller.[1] Herbert's undisguised sympathy for Roman Catholicism stood in stark contrast to his barely disguised disdain at what he deemed to be the theological intransigence of Protestant Nonconformists. The latter was exemplified in his not entirely accurate comment that the main opposition to Maynooth came from 'the great Dissenting interest'. Herbert's defiant wish that he wanted 'to partake of any unpopularity' that might attach itself to Conservatives who supported the Maynooth Bill would be granted on several occasions in the years which followed.[2]

It was Herbert's stance on the Corn Laws, however, which ensured that he received his share of opprobrium. He had reiterated his commitment to upholding the status quo following his unopposed return for South Wiltshire on being appointed Secretary at War in February 1845: 'he did not think that protection was one bit larger than it ought to be [...] no one could say that protection was too large, looking at the burdens on agriculture'.[3] Such was the background to Herbert's celebrated clash in the Commons with Richard Cobden less than a month later. On 13 March, in a speech characterised by Herbert as 'an engine through which he would blow up agricultural protection', Cobden called for a committee to investigate the supposed deleterious impact of the Corn Laws upon the rural classes. According to the more colourful accounts, a discomfited Peel tore up his prepared notes, turned to Herbert and said, 'you must answer this for I cannot'. That detail is probably apocryphal: it was popularised by John Morley over sixty years later in his life of Cobden.[4] Newspaper accounts at the time did not report it: such a theatrical moment would surely not have

1 Yates, 'Oxford Movement', pp. 12-15; Gash, *Aristocracy and People*, pp. 231-2.
2 Hansard, 14 Apr. 1845, LXXIX, cols. 667, 669.
3 *SWJ*, 15, 22 Feb. 1845.
4 *DWG*, 21 Aug. 1845; Hansard, 13 Mar. 1845, LXXVIII, cols. 785-881; Morley, *Cobden*, I, p. 342; Gash, *Peel*, pp. 470-1.

gone unnoticed. Neither was it mentioned by Disraeli, Peel's nemesis, present in the Chamber, and who four days later would have found it irresistible ammunition during one of his most famous attacks on the Prime Minister. Peel could easily have rebutted the case for the committee for which Cobden was calling (exactly what Herbert proceeded to do); he was not required to argue the case for protection. Neither was there any possibility that Cobden's motion would be carried. It failed by 213 votes to 121.

Truth should not always get in the way of a good story. In this instance, however, it has obscured the fact that Cobden's motion was less important for what Peel did not say than for what Herbert did.[1] His speech started predictably enough. A committee, he contended, like several others on a similar question since 1815, would resolve nothing. On 'the evidence of my eyes' travelling through Wiltshire and Ireland, he dissented 'very materially' from Cobden's contention that protection disincentivised farmers from embracing modern methods. There followed what would be remembered as a political *faux pas*. Herbert said that:

> Whatever might be his (Mr. S. Herbert's) partiality for agriculturists, he must confess that, as a body they possessed very delicate nerves, and were extremely susceptible of alarm [...] he must add further, as the representative of an agricultural constituency, that it would be distasteful to the agriculturists to come whining to Parliament at every period of temporary distress.[2]

The reference to agriculturalists 'whining' subjected Herbert to an outpouring of obloquy in the protectionist press. The *Farmer's Journal* fumed that 'such an undeserved and gratuitous insult was never before passed on any body of men'.[3] One suspects that the writer had not read Herbert's speech, or at least not in context. Herbert had not used the word 'whining' in the derogatory way in which those who took exception to it professed. On the contrary, the point that he

1 Hansard, 13 Mar. 1845, LXXVIII, cols. 810-20.
2 Hansard, 13 Mar. 1845, LXXVIII, cols. 815, 818.
3 *Wiltshire Independent*, 20 Mar., 1845.

was trying to make was a complimentary one, that rather than come to parliament demanding more protection 'in adverse circumstances, such as failure of crop, and the like, they [agriculturalists] would meet them manfully and put their shoulder to the wheel'.¹ As he explained at a meeting of Wiltshire farmers, he had been 'totally misrepresented [...] his expression could be twisted into a charge that they were doing the very thing I said they would not do'. His infelicity was just part of the political game. Herbert accepted with commendable stoicism that 'he must take the rough with the smooth; and if he is not going to do that he had best go home at once'. His critics, he knew, were not to be denied their moment of schadenfreude.²

It was Benjamin Disraeli who made the greatest capital from Herbert's perceived lapse. The two men had met socially since at least 1840. Herbert was known to have spoken favourably of Disraeli's 1839 verse drama, *Count Alarcos*, a piece regarded as unsuitable reading for those with delicate sensibilities.³ But it is easy to see how Disraeli, with his Jewish heritage, entering parliament at the fourth attempt in 1837 at the age of 33 and ambitious for office, should come to hold the patrician Herbert, with his effortless entrée into politics and government, in contempt. By 1845, in Disraeli's view, Herbert had become the lackey of a prime minister who, with his liberal policies, was betraying his party. On 17 March 1845 it was Herbert's fate to be the 'valet' in one of Disraeli's most memorable perorations:

> The right hon. Gentleman being compelled to interfere, sends down his valet, who says in the genteelest manner, 'We can have no whining here'. And that, Sir, is exactly the case of the great agricultural interest – that beauty which everybody wooed, and one deluded [...] a Conservative Government is an Organised Hypocrisy.⁴

---

1   Hansard, 13 Mar. 1845, LXXVIII, col. 818; Gash, *Peel*, p. 471.
2   *DWG*, 21 Aug. 1845; *The Times*, 30 Aug. 1845 for Cobden's letter of 25 Aug. ridiculing SH's attempt at explanation.
3   *Dublin Morning Register*, 12 Feb. 1840; Ridley, *Disraeli*, pp. 220-32.
4   Hansard, 17 Mar. 1845, LXXVIII, col. 1028; Blake, *Disraeli*, p. 187.

Disraeli's jibe marked the start of a personal antipathy with Herbert, one with important political consequences that would end only with Herbert's death.

Stanmore, who disingenuously ignored the brouhaha over 'whining', argued that Herbert's speech of 13 March was chiefly important for intimations that he was becoming a free trader. He points to Herbert's saying 'that he would not have joined the Government, in however subordinate a capacity, if his right hon. Friend at the head of affairs had not, in his statement made on the dissolution of the last Parliament, declared his intention to revise the existing Corn Law'.[1] Herbert may well have said this to MPs in 1845 but it is not what he told his constituents in 1841. Then, he had been unambiguous in defence of the Corn Laws. It was only after 1842 that Herbert spoke in favour of their being revised – by which time he was only stating government policy. Surely Herbert's more important remark in his speech of March 1845 was the emphatic one that he believed free trade in corn to have gone far enough: 'The Government did not deny that there was a certain amount of protecting duty in favour of agriculture; but they did not express any intention of altering it, but the contrary'.[2] Herbert, it is important to appreciate, was still regarded as a popular standard bearer for the agricultural interest as parliament neared the summer recess. This is understandable. From the spring of 1845, he was the only member of the cabinet, apart from Lord Lincoln, who sat for an English county. In June 1845 he reminded the House that since agriculturalists bore the brunt of tithes, highway rates, and poor rates, the latter 'a great burden on the land', they remained entitled to protection.[3] And lest anybody still be in any doubt as to where he stood, he told the South Wiltshire and Warminster Farmers' Club on 15 August that 'I do not partake in those alarms he [John Benett MP] appears to entertain, that we are going to have a free trade in corn […] my interest in agriculture is unchanged'.[4]

---

1   Stanmore, I, pp. 42-3; Hansard, 13 Mar. 1845, LXXVIII, col. 818.
2   Hansard, 13 Mar. 1845, LXXVIII, col. 819.
3   Hansard, 3 June 1845, LXXX, cols. 1410-13.
4   *DWG*, 21 Aug. 1845.

Alarm bells of a different type, however, would soon force the Corn Laws to the forefront of public attention. The potato blight which spread across much of Western Europe from late summer threatened catastrophe in Ireland: potatoes were the staple foodstuff of the peasant population. At the beginning of November Peel recommended to his cabinet that the Corn Laws should be suspended in order to facilitate the import of cheap grain.[1] It has been suggested that Peel had told Herbert in March that he intended to repeal the Corn Laws when occasion allowed. Given Herbert's speeches down to mid-August, this seems unlikely. More plausible is J.W. Croker's belief that Peel intimated his inclinations to his trusted junior lieutenant in August or September.[2] Either way, Herbert was in no doubt by the autumn that he would support his chief. Proof of this is the lengthy memorandum he presented to cabinet colleagues on 2 November:

> When pits are opened, potatoes harvested as sound are now found to be diseased: in some cases they are no better than masses of putrid slime [...] a sufficient loss has been experienced to pinch the labourer considerably and force him to consume a much larger quantity of bread than usual, while the price, of course, is already very much risen [...] I believe therefore, that we are entering in Ireland on one year's famine, and through the United Kingdom on two years' scarcity, if not more [...] I need not here call attention to the peculiar evils attending the use of the potato as the principal article of food. It is obvious that, being the cheapest kind of food a population entirely dependent upon it are forced, when it fails, to look, when most incapable of purchasing, to the dearer kinds of food which, in their more prosperous days are, from their cost, beyond their reach. The Irish must, therefore, to a greater degree, pass from a potato to a grain diet. The demand thus created will be enormous, for it will greatly exceed the precautions in the way of sowing additional grain [...] and

---

1 Gash, *Peel*, ch. 15.
2 Blake, *Disraeli*, p. 187; Jennings, *Croker Papers*, III, pp. 91-2.

thus the failure of the potato crop is starvation. But the people must not starve, and the Government must feed them.¹

Impassioned though this was, at a crucial cabinet meeting on 6 November, only Aberdeen and Graham joined Herbert in lending Peel their unreserved support. Ministers dispersed for a few days whilst further information about the scale of the crisis was assessed. Herbert went down to Wilton. Whilst there, he began to doubt that things really were as bad as he had been given to understand. The potato crop on the Wilton estate was no more than ten per cent down; the latest letters from Ireland painted a less dystopic picture than previously. Back in London, he concurred in the decision reached in cabinet on 19 November that parliament should be prorogued until 16 December.² Outsiders could only speculate. *The Times* reported erroneously that Herbert had 'protested against all change whatever' and was, along with Wellington and Stanley, the chief obstacle to some modification of the Corn Laws being agreed.³

The crisis was unhelpfully complicated by Russell, now leader of the Liberals. On 22 November he published the so-called *Edinburgh Letter* announcing his conversion to the total repeal (as opposed to temporary suspension) of the Corn Laws. This meant, as Herbert appreciated, that the government would now be seen as reacting to, rather than controlling events, what he called 'a timid plagiarism by bewildered men [...] Lord John Russell has seized the moment of inaction on the part of the Government to seize on the very position which we ought to have occupied'.⁴ Recovering from a severe bilious attack, and surveying the political scene at the end of November, Herbert could not see how the cabinet, let alone the Conservative party, could agree a path forward. 'My opinion', he told Lincoln, 'is that the government is a dying one & that it is more useful to the

1   WSHC 2057/F8/1/M/31.
2   *The Times*, 12, 20 Nov. 1845; BL Add. Mss. 79657, fols. 25-6, SH to JRG, 18 Nov. 1845; Gash, *Peel*, pp. 542-3.
3   *The Times*, 27 Nov. 1845.
4   Stanmore, I, pp. 50-4, undated memorandum.

country to take precautions to secure food'. His conclusion that 'Our difficulty is great' was a serious understatement.[1]

Herbert himself traditionally figured at the centre of the next and 'truly sensational development'. On 4 December *The Times* dropped the bombshell that the 'decision of the Cabinet is no longer a secret': it had been decided that the Corn Laws must go. Herbert was later said to be the source for the scoop.[2] The origin of that claim, however, is unclear; no such allegation appears on the contemporary charge sheet against him over the Corn Laws. That inveterate political gossip, Charles Greville, was in no doubt that the leak was attributable to Lord Aberdeen. A friend of John Thadeus Delane, newly appointed editor of *The Times*, Aberdeen, with the connivance of Peel, had let it be known where the Prime Minister's intentions lay. It was not intended, however, that the newspaper should report the story so soon. Stanmore, Aberdeen's son, who had no reason to disparage his father's memory, consistently confirmed the truth of this version of events in later life. It was as much a case of cock-up as conspiracy.[3]

The most colourful version of Herbert's alleged actions in 1845, however, suggests that his behaviour was less Machiavellian than naïve. Whilst dining with Mrs Caroline Norton, 'perfectly infatuated with her beauty and cleverness', he had been indiscreet with cabinet secrets. Mrs Norton promptly went to *The Times* and traded the information for £500:

> Sidney Herbert at once knew that he had been betrayed and that he had betrayed his chief. He went and told him all. Sir Robert Peel shook him warmly by the hand, and ended the interview with the words: 'You must try to cheer up and forget this business as readily as I shall'.[4]

---

1   NUL Ne C 11926, SH to Lincoln, 29 Nov. 1845.
2   *The Times*, 4 Dec. 1845; Brighton, *Original Spin*, pp. 89-90.
3   Reeve, *Greville Memoirs*, pt. 2, II, pp. 309-14, 5 Dec. 1845; *St James's Gazette*, 12 Dec. 1895; Stanmore, I, pp. 61-3.
4   *St James's Gazette*, 6 Dec. 1895, citing the first edition of the autobiography of Sir William Gregory.

The story as thus relayed strains all credibility. Peel would never have been so forgiving; Mrs Norton could have saved herself the journey to Fleet Street by asking Herbert for money direct. The implausibility of the tale is reinforced by its provenance. It is taken from the autobiography of Sir William Gregory which appeared nearly fifty years later in 1894. Gregory, an Irish MP, certainly knew Herbert, but not well. His colourful mind was probably moved to embroider the version of events which had appeared in George Meredith's 1885 novel, *Diana of the Crossways*. Where Meredith got his information from, or whether what he wrote was pure fiction, remains unknown.

But a whiff of suspicion remains. Delane later claimed that he had had two sources for his scoop. If that were so, Herbert is by far the most likely candidate as the second informant. He was privy to Peel's thinking on the Corn Laws, shared his convictions, and was deeply frustrated by cabinet inaction. His later life, most famously during the Crimean period, demonstrates that he regarded it as perfectly legitimate to use the press in pursuance of his ends. Whatever the truth, the leak catalysed the fall of Peel's government. Following the cabinet meeting of 5 December, which remained deadlocked on the Corn Laws, Peel concluded that ministers should resign. Herbert agreed: 'A good oar should be pulled by every man in the boat'. For the next fortnight Russell was handed the 'poisoned chalice'. But he found it impossible to form a stable government. Lord Howick, for example, told Herbert on 17 December during a congenial evening in the library of the Travellers Club, that he could not serve if Palmerston insisted on having the Foreign Office. Herbert needed little persuading of Howick's conviction that Palmerston 'was a dangerous man'. Russell duly surrendered the Queen's commission; a reconstituted Conservative cabinet resumed office on 20 December.[1]

Remarkable as it might seem, Herbert was still being held up as a bulwark of protectionism. Sir John Tyrrell, the unreconstructed Tory Member for North Essex, assured listeners in Chelmsford on 12 December that Herbert was one of four cabinet members who could

---

1 *The Times*, 9, 15, 16, 18 Dec. 1845; Gash, *Peel*, pp. 549-63; WSHC 2057/F4/54.

be relied upon as staunch friends of the agriculturalists. Four days later, the Earl of Chichester toasted Herbert at the meeting of the Lewes Fat Stock Show and declared that he 'was looked to as the agricultural leader in the House of Commons'.[1] In reality, Herbert was now part of Peel's inner circle. He was present at endless meetings to formulate a Repeal package in time for the opening of parliament on 22 January. Curiously, it was the leading French weekly newspaper, the *Journal des débats,* which was amongst the first to draw attention to the fact that Herbert 'has hitherto been erroneously classed among his [Peel's] opponents'.[2]

An appreciation of this misperception is essential to understanding the special wrath that was reserved for Herbert when Peel presented his free trade proposals to the House on 27 January. Although Peel outlined what Prince Albert called 'an immense scheme', designed to compensate agriculturalists, attention focused on the proposition that duties on corn would be phased out entirely by 1849. Over a hundred Members spoke during the twelve nights of debate which took place from 9 February. For Herbert, there was no chance of his views becoming lost in the crowd: it was his lot to be the main government spokesman on the very first evening. At least this gave him an early opportunity of answering the charge levelled by the Earl of March (son of the Duke of Richmond) that he had changed his mind over protection.[3] In doing so he was necessarily defensive. He did not deny that after 'much doubt [...] reluctantly, slowly, I changed my opinions'. But he was unapologetic. The failure of the Irish potato crop had introduced 'different circumstances, which no man by possibility could have contemplated'. In face of them, the 1842 sliding scale governing the price of corn had 'signally failed'. He conceded that repealing the Corn Laws would mean that agriculturalists 'must incur some temporary sacrifice' but he was adamant that they would escape ruin. Not for the first time he exhorted agriculturalists to embrace new

---

1   *The Times*, 18 Dec. 1845.
2   *The Times*, 26 Dec. 1845, 2, 3, 5, 7, 12, 14, 21, 22 Jan. 1846.
3   Hansard, 27 Jan. 1846, LXXXIII, cols. 310-14.

and efficient methods, to embark 'upon what is called "the system of high farming."'[1]

Herbert's speech would be remembered, though, for its loftier themes. He painted a near messianic vision of how repealing the Corn Laws would reconcile the old landed interest with rising manufacturing ones:

> Hon. Members must recollect that great changes have taken place in the last fifty years in the social constitution of this country; that the manufacturing power has increased to an enormous degree. You may dislike the effect of it – you may think it congregates together great masses of men – that you have less security for their morality and welfare; but depend upon it, it is a power you cannot check nor control; it has become a permanent element in our society; it has great wealth, and offers great employment; it is a source of that commerce which has maintained our colonial empire, and given us the dominion we possess throughout the world; it is now, as it has always been, the great source of our maritime power, and you must also recollect that if you intend to maintain this great Empire, and think, as I do, that it is possible to carry its free institutions, and temperate liberties, and reformed faith to other parts of the globe, it is by these humble means, these manufactures, these woollens, and linens, that under Providence you are enabled to do it; it is by extending your commerce that you are able to penetrate into every part of the world, to civilise, and to teach. You must recollect, too, that men who give you these benefits – who contribute so largely to our prosperity – are entitled also to a full share of the advantages of the State [...] I wish to see the two interests of agriculture and manufacture united. If they have been separated, it has been by the fault of legislation, it is not a fault of their own; but I wish to see those two knitted together.

For all that this is redolent of liberalism, Herbert would rarely make a more conservative speech. He made no secret of the fact that

---

1 Gash, *Peel*, pp. 569-70, 577-81; Hansard, 9 Feb. 1845, LXXXIII, cols. 621-34.

for a parliament dominated by the landed interest to repeal the Corn Laws was less an act of altruism than one of self-interest essential to its very survival:

> I say, now is the time to concede with honour, when there is no appearance that your concession is extorted by violence [...] If you do not now yield to reason [...] some day force may be added; and then you will yield, not as now, with honour, but with loss of station, influence, and character [...] You have men of all classes, of all shades, and of all colours, and engaged in all domestic pursuits, beginning to think that one part of the community has a benefit over another, and at the expense of another. Then, if we are to stand upon such ground as that, we stand upon a mine, upon a rotten footing, and we cannot maintain it [...] it has been said, that Corn Laws are part of our Constitution. Sir, if I am right in thinking that they impose a burden on one part of the community for the benefit of another, then I say they are contrary to the whole spirit of our Constitution. I am not one of those who wish to see the Constitution of this country rendered more democratic than it is. I cannot think that the public mind wishes it to be more democratic than it is [...] I have no faith in Governments guided by uncontrolled popular passions. I have no wish to see the aristocratic element weakened in our Constitution [...] I should lament, moreover, to see the class to which you and I belong; to which by birth, by habit, by prejudice if you will, I am attached; and which I consider to have one of the noblest spheres of usefulness that exists in private life in any country in the world – I mean the class of English country gentlemen – debased in any way, or lose its natural influence [...] I believe the measures we propose will be for the interest of all classes of the community.

As a statement of the case for moderate Conservatism, of the need for reform in order to preserve, Peel could hardly have put it better. Herbert was pleased with his efforts. Hours later he wrote to Lincoln that 'I gave the Country Gentlemen a class last night. It was well received by the House'.¹

The judgement was premature; Protectionist Conservatives were not to be swayed. Only a day later, a disillusioned Herbert was reporting to his friend that:

> Nothing could be more hostile than the House last night. They almost mobbed Graham. It is clear to me that the breach between us & our friends is irreconcilable. They evidently put the worst construction on our <u>motives</u> as well as our policy & our position under such circumstances cannot in my opinion be held with advantage to the country. The moment we have passed this measure our power of usefulness & our task will be at an end & the sooner the whole thing is broken up the better.²

In the House, the Earl of March renewed his charge of treachery against Herbert. He was joined by an improbable ally in William Smith O'Brien, the Irish Nationalist Member for County Limerick, who would, ironically, be convicted of treason for his part in the Young Ireland Rising of 1848.³ Outside parliament, Herbert and his speech drew praise and abuse in roughly equal measure. John Eklees, speaking at a meeting of the labouring class in Gosport, lauded it as one 'which did great honour to his [Herbert's] head and heart'. By contrast, a letter from 'A deluded member of the Salisbury Association for the Protection of Agriculture' regarded Herbert's 'betrayal' as 'a lesson in political tergiversation unparalleled in modern times'. Most prominent of all was the 2,000 word piece in *The Times*.⁴ Its vitriolic opening lines, however implausible the charges, convey well the flavour of the whole:

---

1 NUL Ne C 11928, SH to Lincoln, 10 Feb. 1846.
2 NUL Ne C 11929, SH to Lincoln, 11 Feb. 1846.
3 Hansard, 10 Feb. 1846, LXXXIII, cols. 644-57; 16 Mar. 1846, LXXXIII, cols. 965-72.
4 *DWG*, 19 Feb. 1846; *The Times*, 11, 20 Feb. 1846.

Mr Sidney Herbert, after all, is the arch traitor of the plot. He is the prime mover of all the mischief. It is he who has corrupted Sir R. Peel, intimidated the Duke, ousted Lord Stanley [who had resigned from the government], and converted all the rest [...] So complete a structure of opinions, such a magazine of arguments, such confidence in his cause, and so dexterous an application of facts, indicate him a long practised man, a free trader to the backbone, a disciple from his youth up of ADAM SMITH and the other economical doctors.

Herbert would not have been human had he not fallen prey to the passions about which he complained. Lord Malmesbury, his childhood friend and briefly Wilton's MP, was shocked by the strength of Herbert's feelings when they met at Lady Palmerston's after a night out at the opera:

Mr Sidney Herbert was there, and came up to me in a state of great excitement, saying that my conduct in leaving Peel was unworthy a gentleman, that the whole Protectionist party were a set of fools, and Lord Stanley the greatest fool among us, and that Peel was delighted at having got rid of us & c. In short, he said everything that was most obnoxious. If he had not been in such a frantic passion I should probably not have been able to keep my temper, but there was something so absurd in his unprovoked attack that I retained perfect command over myself. It was certainly very extraordinary, as I had not spoken to him that evening, or seen him since he came to London, and had given him no provocation whatever. He is generally careful of what he says; in fact, he carries caution to that degree that he is famous for it [...] This shows the violence of party feeling at present, as Sidney Herbert and I have always been like brothers.[1]

The violent party feeling, it needs to be remembered, existed principally inside the Conservative party. Only a third of them were prepared to follow the Prime Minister. But there was never any

---

1 Malmesbury, *Memoirs*, I, pp. 169-70, 15 Mar. 1846.

doubt that the combined strength of the Peelites and a united Liberal party would see the Corn Importation Bill through the Commons. The Second Reading was carried on 27 March by 302 votes to 214. Herbert then went down to Wilton to see his mother, returning to London on 27 April. He made a final, but unremarkable, contribution to the Corn Law debate on 8 May, a week before the Third Reading.[1]

Herbert's view was that the government should resign as soon as the Corn Laws were repealed.[2] Revengeful Protectionists ensured that his wish was granted. The occasion was the Irish Crimes Bill, introduced in March in response to the upsurge in violent crime which accompanied the potato famine. A sombre Herbert informed the House that there had been 552 murders. He proceeded to paint a lurid picture of some of the recent atrocities, 'of women attacked, of fire-arms discharged into poor men's cottages, of old ladies attacked as they came home from church in broad day'. Herbert implored Members to set aside their differences: 'he never would assist in making Ireland again the battle-field of party'.[3] Unhappy Irish and Liberal Members demurred, declaring the measure to be unnecessarily coercive. Ordinarily, this would not have mattered: the Conservative majority would have seen it on to the statute book. Protectionists, however, were determined to have their pound of flesh, even though it meant opposing a Bill whose principles they approved. Apprised of what was afoot, Herbert gave vent to his fury. He denounced Lord George Bentinck, the Protectionist leader, and his followers as men prepared to countenance outrages in Ireland because they 'hate more the men who at present hold the reins of Government'. Unmoved, 125 Protectionists joined with Liberal and Irish Members to defeat the Second Reading by 292 to 219 on 25 June.[4] The ministry resigned four days later. In what were virtually his final words of the parliament, a defiant Herbert could lay claim only to the moral high ground:

1   *The Times*, 11, 28 Apr. 1846; Hansard, 8 May 1846, LXXXVI, cols. 281-8.
2   NUL Ne C, 11929, SH to Lincoln, 11 Feb. 1846.
3   Hansard, 3 Apr. 1846, LXXXV, cols. 536-47; 8 June 1846, LXXXVII, cols. 184-9.
4   Hansard, 8 June 1846, LXXXVII, col. 186; Gash, *Peel*, pp. 593-601.

I for one, at least, shall deeply regret to see power placed in the hands of those who seem to be incapable of understanding that a public man may have higher than mere party objects, and that he may be ready to sacrifice even party support for the purpose of ensuring the success of measures, necessary, in his opinion, for promoting the happiness and prosperity of the country.[1]

In what was a remarkably objective article for the time, one writer judged Herbert to have emerged with an enhanced reputation from the scrapes and stresses of 1845-6. This, a few caveats aside, he attributed to Herbert's maturing as a speaker:

Mr Sidney Herbert is a good and fluent speaker. Without aiming at any flowers of rhetoric or straining to speak for effect, he had a great command of language; and this circumstance sometimes renders him diffuse. When he shall have enjoyed the benefit of a longer experience of the House, there can be no doubt that he will prove an able debater and a powerful adjunct to the Ministry. His manner is calm and tranquil; his mode of delivering it somewhat monotonous; but his voice is good and clear; and he enunciates in such a manner that not a word of what he says is lost. He possesses talent – for upon the Corn Laws and the Protection of Life (Ireland) Bill, – on which latter measure Sir Robert Peel's ministry was defeated, – he evidenced an intimate acquaintance with the matter on which he was frequently called upon to speak. Ready with argument – prompt to reply – and perfectly lucid in his manner of dealing with a subject, he is endowed with all the requisites to form a sterling debater, so soon as he shall have learnt how to condense his ideas and shake off the fault of verbosity to which we have before alluded.[2]

Even the author of the violent article against Herbert in *The Times* had observed that Herbert's speech of 9 February 1846 gave notice that 'His life's great puzzle is solved by free trade. His tongue is at last untied'. No longer need there be 'a suspicion of the smothered

1   Hansard, 8 June 1846, LXXXVII, col. 189.
2   WSHC 2057/F1/12, unidentified press cutting, July 1846.

volcano'. It was not so very long after that Peel stated 'his belief that Sidney Herbert or Gladstone would one day be premier'.¹

---

1   *The Times*, 11 Feb. 1846; Morley, *Gladstone*, I, p. 374

6
Halcyon Days 1846-1850

The four or five years which followed Herbert's departure from the War Office in 1846 were the happiest of his adult life. Yet he was far from idle. In local government he attended routine meetings of petty and quarter sessions. As acting head of the Wilton estate, he devoted time to the provision of labourers' cottages, model farms and a new parish church. As an Irish landowner, he financed public works and church building in the wake of the Great Famine. As a Christian philanthropist, he attracted nationwide attention when he espoused the cause of female emigration. All these initiatives can be said, to some degree, to have been labours of love. Even a mandatory period of training and exercise with his yeomanry troop in cold and windy weather near Heytesbury in 1849 did not entirely dampen his bonhomie.[1] More unequivocally pleasurable were trips abroad and the time spent indulging his preferences for leisure. At a summer fete in Wilton in 1849, it was reported that 'Mr Herbert mingled in all the sports, and took the lead in all the rustic revels, with as complete an *abandon*, and as hearty a sense of enjoyment, as the merriest reveller of them all'.[2] Above all, however, his joy during this period derived from being a devoted husband and proud father.

This picture of a carefree existence was exemplified in the four month visit Herbert made to the Scottish Highlands from August

1   WSHC 2057/F4/51, SH to EH, 5 Nov. 1849.
2   *SWJ*, 28 July 1849.

1848.¹ The letters he sent whilst there reveal a warm and impish character, one possessed of the artist's eye for topographical detail, the journalist's nose for gossip, and the novelist's antennae for the absurdities of humanity. At Blackmount, in Argyll and Bute, he stayed in a house where 'the walls [are] so treacherously thin that everybody is in full possession of his neighbour's opinion of him'. At Tyninghame in East Lothian he attended church 'where we had the Presbyterian service, and a very good sermon, though I am not quite sure which was the prayer and which the sermon'. There was also a Herbert frustrated by his inability to bag a deer, but half-tempted to compensate for it by shooting a man with a speech impediment.² Unsurprisingly, he took the opportunity to return to the Highlands in 1849 and again in 1850.³

Of course, life could never be one long unbroken idyll. Politics were bound to impinge. Economically, the period was a difficult one for many of his Wiltshire and Irish tenants. His friend Lord Lincoln experienced domestic unhappiness. Herbert's personal life too was not entirely devoid of a whiff of scandal. The latter was as nothing, though, compared to the vexations Herbert experienced on account of his half-brother. Following the seemingly harmonious interlude of the 1830s, Robert Pembroke's life aroused considerable public interest in the 1840s. It was only too clear that the 12th Earl of Pembroke was managing to dig himself into a deep pit of shame. Dressed in a white hat with a black band, he was regularly to be seen in the company of George Wombwell, an eccentric character whose travelling menagerie comprised fifteen wagons and a brass band. The unlikely pair frequented the gambling dens and tableaux shows of Paris: Pembroke was reported to be disappointed if the female artistes wore even a shred of clothing. Whilst ogling, he was spending: his account book for 1847 includes bills of £653 from a carpet maker, £2,252 from a coachmaker, £3,466 from an upholsterer, £4,182 from an ironmonger, and £6,018

1   *Freeman's Journal*, 2 Dec. 1848.
2   WSHC 2057/F4/51, SH to EH, especially letters of 2, 4, 5, 14, 15, 30 Oct. 1848.
3   Bodleian MS Eng. Lett. C. 657, fols. 31-2, EH to Manning, 7 Aug. 1849; *Freeman's Journal*, 21 Aug. 1849, 17 Sept. 1850.

from a silversmith.[1] But it was the prurient humour bordering upon the lubricious which was most damaging to his reputation. Between 1840 and 1846 he sired three children with a mistress, Alexina Sophie Gallot, thirty years his junior.[2] Worse, even before she was displaced in his affections, was the 'truly diabolical & revolting affair' which he began with an eighteen-year old French opera girl, Marie Schöeffer. The inevitable ribaldry ensued:

> Scheffer's [*sic*] the girl of the opera stage,
> Who the greatest attraction carries,
> For she could not 'draw' here, but's able to draw
> The Earl of Pembroke to Paris.

Although not great poetry, it had the merit of being essentially true. The couple set up permanent home in the *Place Vendôme* where she presented him with two sons and two daughters.[3] Why, one wit asked, was the Earl spending more than £8,000 furnishing one living room in his luxurious Paris apartment when, 'notwithstanding this lavish disbursement, his lordship's bed-room is the apartment he anticipates will afford him the greatest amount of pleasure'. The characterisation of Robert in 1845 as the modern day Sardanapalus (the mythical, self-indulgent and decadent king of Assyria who perished in an orgy of destruction) was as apt as it was erudite.[4] Herbert was all too aware of the potential damage to his own reputation of being linked by association with Robert in the public mind. At the February 1845

---

1   WSHC 2057/A6/61.
2   WSHC 2057/D5/14, for probate, birth certificates. The children were Robert (b. 9 Dec. 1840), Sidney (b. 14 Jan. 1842), and Ida (c. 1846). Gallot was born in London in 1821.
3   WSHC 2057/D5/14, probate, birth certificates. The children were Henriette (1844-1910), Henri Georges (1845-1900), Henri Adolphus (b. 2 Nov. 1848), and Marie Jeanne (1855-1904). There are various spellings of Schöeffer. The one used here is that adopted in Pembroke's will.
4   WSHC 2057/F1/12 for various, mostly undated, press cuttings.

South Wiltshire by-election, for example, one of the first victory toasts was to 'Lord Pembroke and Sidney Herbert'.[1]

Even without Robert, however, Herbert's own bachelor status could not but arouse interest and speculation. In 1842 Princess Dorothea Lieven wrote from her Paris salon, known as 'the observation post of Europe', that she had received reports that the Hon. Emily de Flahault may have made a 'conquest' of Herbert. 'It would', she opined, 'be an excellent thing, but is there any truth in the rumour?'[2] As it turned out, there was not: the following year the Hon. Emily married Lord Shelburne, widower of Herbert's sister Georgiana.

By then, in any case, Herbert's name was starting to become linked with that of Mrs Caroline Norton. Born Caroline Sheridan, she was granddaughter of the playwright, Richard Brinsley Sheridan. Vivacious, quick-witted, and with a growing literary reputation, she had married a dull barrister, George Norton. The inevitable affairs followed. A jealous and impecunious Norton retaliated with physical violence, and by denying her access to their three sons. In 1836 he created a sensation when he brought a case of criminal conversation against her and the Prime Minister, Lord Melbourne, suing for £10,000 in damages for adultery. His case was laughed out of court; it is said to have inspired Dickens' classic scene of Bardell v. Pickwick in *The Pickwick Papers*. But mud sticks. Even if only in the confines of his private journal, Herbert delighted in recording that 'The town [was] full of the Norton v. Melbourne story'; wags were referring to Melbourne's ministry as 'the Crim-Connell administration'.[3] Over the next decade, however, it was Herbert himself who would come to feature in the innuendo directed towards Mrs Norton and her alleged paramours. For all that she was an injured party, it was fact that Mrs Norton had had affairs and that she was still married. Whilst not mad,

1 *SWJ*, 22 Feb. 1845.
2 Sudley, *Lieven-Palmerston Correspondence*, pp. 223-5, Lieven to Lady Palmerston, 21 Feb. 1842.
3 Atkinson, *Norton*, chs. 3-4; WSHC 2057/F5/15, journal entry, Apr. 1836. 'Conversation', in the old legal sense of the term used here, means sexual intercourse.

some contemporaries deemed her bad, and many others as dangerous to know.

Herbert certainly knew Mrs Norton socially by 1841. He was probably introduced to her by their mutual friend, Lord Lincoln.[1] It was between 1844 and 1846 however, that the 'rumours swirled about them like spun sugar'. In the summer of 1844 Herbert and Caroline were spotted walking along the beach on the Isle of Wight; soon afterwards, they were spied together on the yacht, *Fanny*, in the Solent. At the end of the year Herbert was deeply concerned when he learnt that Mrs Norton was suffering from 'spasmodic shiverings & fainting fits' and 'much more ill than from her letter to me I had at all expected'. Well before then, claims Norton's latest biographer, 'many were convinced they were lovers', an opinion most writers have endorsed.[2] During 1845, Norton's 'new special friend' was a frequent visitor to 3 Chesterfield Street, the property she leased in London's Mayfair. The Earl of Malmesbury found nothing remarkable in the fact that he found Herbert and Caroline all day together on one occasion in March 1846.[3]

What should one make of all this? Both Norton and Herbert were alluring to members of the opposite sex. There were clearly letters between them which have not survived. That they conducted some sort of affair is incontrovertible. We can reasonably presume that she was in love with Herbert, not least because she could identify in him gentlemanly virtues that were sadly lacking in her own husband. She was also palpably devastated, 'a rose shut out by thorny briars', when she learned that he was to marry in 1846.[4] For his part, Herbert clearly entertained deep feelings for her, though whether they were born of lust, compassion, or both, is impossible to fathom. What is certain is that he was the most prominent of several men (Dickens and the travel writer Alexander William Kinglake were others) who

1 WSHC 2057/F4/52, Norton to EH, 22 Oct. 1864.
2 NUL Ne C 11923, 11924/1-2, SH to Lincoln, 20 Dec. 1844, 1 Jan. 1845; Atkinson, *Norton*, pp. 314-15.
3 Perkins, *Norton*, p. 181; Atkinson, *Norton*, pp. 314-15, 318, 327; Malmesbury, *Memoirs*, I, pp. 169-70, 15 Mar. 1846.
4 Atkinson, *Norton*, pp. 327-8.

were prepared to lend their names to the cause of rehabilitating her in society.¹ If only because of Herbert's strong disapproval of his own half-brother's various liaisons, however, and his reputation for moral rectitude, it is improbable that his relationship with Mrs Norton was ever carnal. His letter to Lincoln about her at the end of 1844 reads like that from a close friend. Like Gladstone, who was soon to embark on his famous missionary work in attempting to 'rescue' some of the fallen women of London's underworld, Herbert may reasonably stand accused of a certain naiveté: the greater charge of sexual impropriety is, as it was, best left to the gossips.

Somewhat quixotically, Mrs Norton promised never again to cross Herbert's path once he was married.² In the first instance her evasion took the form of a self-imposed exile in County Down. But it was brief and the promise was never kept. Herbert happily agreed to publish her *Letters to the Mob* in the *Morning Chronicle* after he became its co-proprietor in 1848.³ In addition, he could hardly fail to notice the unseemly and very public feud which broke out between the Nortons in the early 1850s over unpaid allowances following the couple's formal separation in 1848. Herbert was subsequently one of three people who lent Caroline a thousand guineas in the later 1850s to enable her to buy her Mayfair home outright.⁴ She carried a flame for Herbert down to his death and beyond. A letter she sent to Lady Herbert in 1864 speaks of 'the deepest interest which memory can impress on the human heart'. The words in her narrative poem, *The Lady of Garaye*, written very shortly after Herbert's death, were unquestionably heartfelt:⁵

1 Atkinson, *Norton*, pp. 318-19, 327-8.
2 Acland, *Norton*, pp. 170-1.
3 Perkins, *Norton*, pp. 189-90.
4 Atkinson, *Norton*, p. 399.
5 WSHC 2057/F8/52, Norton to EH, 22 Oct. 1864; Norton, *The Lady of Garaye*, p. 123. Norton continued to write and campaign for the rest of her life, notably for women's property rights. She played a part in securing the Matrimonial Causes Act of 1857. Freed by her husband's death in 1875, she married her long-term friend and support, Sir William Stirling Maxwell in March 1877. She died three-and-a-half months later.

Even as I write, before me seem to rise,
Like stars in darkness, well remembered eyes
Whose light but lately shone on earth's endeavour,
Now vanished from this troubled world for ever.
Oh! missed and mourned by many, – I being one, –
HERBERT [...]

By then, however, over fifteen years had passed since the news, announced in July 1846, that Herbert was to marry Elizabeth A'Court. Elizabeth, twelve years younger than Herbert, was born in July 1822. She was the only surviving daughter of General Charles Ashe A'Court, who saw active service during the Napoleonic Wars; he was subsequently better known as an Assistant Poor Law Commissioner. A younger brother of the diplomat Lord Heytesbury, the family's Wiltshire seat of Heytesbury House was largely at the General's disposal.[1] Just fifteen miles from Wilton, the A'Courts and Herberts boasted a long tradition of 'intimacy'. Lady Emma Herbert recalled fondly 'all the kindnesses we have all received from them from the time we were quite little toddlers'. Herbert, they viewed 'always as a sort of child of theirs'. Herbert, for his part, regarded the A'Courts as 'real good friends & delightful people'. More pertinently for his political career, the General had 'worked with the utmost energy to secure [his] first election for the county'.[2] It was during a visit to Heytesbury during the campaign that the ten-year-old Elizabeth confided to her journal 'when looking out of the schoolroom window as he was riding away [...] when I am a Woman, I will marry that man and no other!' In the short term, however, the most newsworthy story about the ties between the two families was how the young MP and General A'Court had driven over from Wilton to Salisbury together on the Dowager Lady Pembroke's Russian sleigh.[3]

1 *The Times*, 20 Apr. 1861; *ODNB*.
2 WSHC 2057/F5/15, journal entry, July 1832; WSHC 2057/F4/50, Lady E. Herbert to SH, July 1846; Stanmore, I, p. 71.
3 WSHC 2057/F4/52, Hildegard to EH, 17 July 1846; *SWJ*, 2 Jan. 1837. Catherine Woronzow's sleigh can still be seen at Wilton.

It was helpful for Herbert and Elizabeth's future relationship that the A'Courts inherited Amington Hall in Staffordshire.[1] This facilitated their becoming friendly with Peel who lived just five miles distant. Elizabeth, who spent a good deal of time at Amington as a teenager, recorded that Sir Robert 'took a fancy to me as a Pupil', employed her as a secretary, and imparted any 'political training' that she had received. Herbert would have encountered the maturing woman on his various visits to Drayton. She, in turn, must have been including him when she wrote that 'I had always lived with and been treated as the equal and companion of clever men'. It was probably whilst staying with Peel that Herbert rode over from Drayton to Amington for the purpose of proposing to her.[2]

All this would seem to dispose of the story that it was some of Herbert's friends and relations, concerned about the potential scandal of his relationship with Mrs Norton, who pressured him into marrying Elizabeth; that he never really loved her and proposed only reluctantly.[3] There is no contemporary evidence for this. Rather the contrary. In an unusual outpouring of emotion, he wrote to his eldest sister following the announcement of his engagement that:

> I pray that I may make the happiness of this dear child who has given herself to me [...] I love her with all my heart & strength and she is so pure & good I look with a sort of awe & fear on the deep responsibility I have undertaken [...] You will love Lizzy more and more as you know her more.

Herbert had fallen in love of his own volition with a girl from a family with whom he had fond and regular acquaintance. He had seen Elizabeth blossom from a girl into an acknowledged society beauty, one who shared his High Church convictions. Owing to her quick-wittedness, friends called her 'Lady Lightning': she evinced an

---

1 The A'Courts inherited Amington (and added the Repington name) from Edward Repington, a cousin, in 1837.
2 HLPP GC/HE/105, EH to Pam, 16 Oct. 1861; Herbert, *How I Came Home*, pp. 3, 12; Stanmore, I, pp. 77-8.
3 Atkinson, *Mrs Norton*, p. 328.

intelligent interest in politics and readily acted as his amanuensis.¹ What was there not to love? Elizabeth, for her part, was initially in some awe of her new spouse. She was full of self-doubt that she could provide sufficient stimulus for his brilliance. Her confessor retorted that 'Your business is not to make your husband's home <u>brilliant</u>, but <u>blessed</u>'. She did, and the awe quickly evaporated. To each other they were, and remained, 'My darling Sid' and 'My Dearest Heart'.²

The news that Herbert and Elizabeth had become engaged took their friends and families almost completely by surprise. Of his sisters, Emma wrote to him that he was a 'naughty Boy with your tiresome mystery'. Elizabeth alone professed that 'I have been rather expecting it of late,' adding proprietorially that she had once suggested that the pair would make a good match. The other sisters united in their enthusiasm for their brother's choice of bride. They also reassured Miss A'Court that Herbert 'has always been, what he is, the most warm-hearted & affectionate & <u>Comfy</u> of Brothers'.³ Outside the family, Wellington and Peel signalled their delight: the latter could think of no announcement that had given him more pleasure. Only Lord Lincoln expressed mock concern for Elizabeth. In a teasing but nevertheless revealing letter of congratulation, he concluded:

> As an intimate and old friend of yours I can hardly avow myself unacquainted with your Pride, though I never had the honour of being introduced to Miss A'Court and therefore I hope she will forgive the impertinence of offering her through you my earnest wishes for her welfare.⁴

---

1 WSHC 2057/F4/50, SH to Lady E. Herbert, 15 July 1846; Bostridge, *Nightingale*, p. 117. The suggestion that SH could have written this whilst more or less simultaneously conducting an affair with Caroline Norton beggars belief.
2 Herbert, *How I Came Home*, p. 5.
3 WSHC 2057/F4/50, Lady Bruce to SH, 18 July 1846, Lady de Vesci, nd, July 1846.
4 WSHC 2057/F4/53, Lincoln to SH, 10 July 1846; WSHC 2057/F4/53, Peel to SH, 18 July 1846.

In 'the presence of a select family circle', the wedding took place on 12 August at St George's Church in Hanover Square. The wedding night was spent with the Ailesburys at Tottenham Park. It was from there that Mrs Elizabeth Herbert wrote to her mother-in-law the following morning. She thanked the Dowager Lady Pembroke for the 'overpowering love & tenderness with which you have received me as your child'. Elizabeth informed her too of 'our inexpressible happiness – tho' of this I find it hard to speak', and that she and Herbert had read 'our "Good Book" together before we went to bed & again this morning'.[1] Down at Wilton, meanwhile, 400 tradesman and workers had marked the wedding day by attending a dinner in the cloisters of Wilton House. A loaf of bread, a pound of meat, and a pint of strong beer was distributed 'to every man, woman, and child of the humble class in Wilton'. Two days of celebration followed, the highlights of which included a brass band in Wilton grounds, a grand procession, sporting contests and fireworks.[2]

The happy couple approached the town on 27 August. Three hundred tenants rode out to meet them. On reaching the entrance to Wilton House, the Herberts were 'preceded by young females, dressed in white, wearing chaplets of white roses, strewing flowers, to the gates of the Abbey'.[3] 'Darling Sid' addressed the crowd, many of whom were shedding tears of joy: 'how beautifully & simply he spoke his little speech', noted Elizabeth, 'when we had to step near the Gate: and how deeply the love with which he is looked upon by all the people here'. When at last she and her husband were able to snatch some privacy, 'we went out into the Garden & to the Palladian Bridge & there darling Sid, who was much moved, took both my hands & said to me – "you see how good these people are to me, darling. Will you help me to try more to deserve their love?"' Marriage, it would seem, agreed with Sidney Herbert, for 'he is grown quite fat in this last month'.[4]

A year passed before the Herberts left England, on 20 August 1847, for what was effectively an extended eight-month honeymoon.

1   WSHC 2057/F4/49, EH to Lady Pembroke, 13 Aug. 1846.
2   *SWJ*, 15 Aug. 1846.
3   *SWJ*, 29 Aug. 1846.
4   WSHC 2057/F4/49, EH to Lady Pembroke, nd, Sept. 1846.

They passed the first weeks in the Rhineland spa towns of Kreuznach and Ems, but quickly longed for the treasures of the Italian states.[1] By way of Venice, where they saw Titian's *Assumption of the Virgin* ('a magnificent composition' judged Herbert) they reached the Eternal City on 24 November.[2]

It was during the last week of November that the Herberts first met Florence Nightingale. Frances, her mother, was daughter of William Smith, supporter of worthy causes, in particular the abolition of slavery. Her father, William Shore, born into a Yorkshire banking family, had inherited a fortune in Derbyshire. Part of this had been used to establish a new family base at Embley Park in Hampshire, only fifteen miles from Wilton. Although the two families therefore knew of each other, they moved in different political, social and religious circles. Whilst the Herberts were Anglican-Tories of ancient aristocratic lineage, the Nightingales were nouveau riche advanced Liberals with a Unitarian heritage.[3] When she met the Herberts, Florence, the Nightingales' second daughter, was a headstrong 27 year-old. Increasingly desperate to enlist in God's service under the banner of nursing, she had been despatched to the Continent by her despairing parents in the care of Charles and Selina Bracebridge. It was the Bracebridges, already friends of the Herberts, who provided the link whose consequences would be profound.

Over the next three months, the travellers were in regular contact, whether visiting churches and galleries, walking excursions or nights at the opera.[4] Florence and Elizabeth quickly established a rapport: they were barely two years apart in age. The former wrote home that 'Mrs Herbert is the sunbeam of Rome'. She was a little more ambivalent about Herbert, awed as much as charmed by the recently-ousted cabinet minister ten years her senior. 'Mr H. is a most brilliant companion' but he could also be wearing: 'Mr Herbert's

---

1   WSHC 2057/F4/49, SH to Lady Pembroke, 19 Sept. 1847.
2   WSHC 2057/F4/49, SH to Lady Pembroke, 22 Dec. 1847; *Dublin Evening Mail*, 9 Aug., 1 Nov., 17 Dec. 1847.
3   Bostridge, *Nightingale*, chapters 1-5, *passim*.
4   *CWFN*, VII, pp. 124-6, 132-3.

wit and spirits are no intermittent spring'.[1] As for Herbert's first impressions of Nightingale, it was reported that he 'quite appreciates her and talks of her forever'. But this was Mrs Bracebridge's verdict, and one written for the edification of Florence's mother, the socially-aspiring Frances Nightingale.[2] Whilst there is no doubt, as Florence would recall, that it was 'a time pregnant to me of all my future life', imagination and nostalgia have probably conspired to make this iconic meeting more memorable than it actually was. Three months later, when the Herberts were in Sicily, Elizabeth was longing to hear from the 'the dear Bracebridges'. There was no mention of their travelling companion.[3]

Early in the New Year, Nightingale, the Bracebridges and the Herberts were amongst those who were granted an audience with Pope Pius IX. Although Herbert thought that 'Nothing could be better than the tone and language of his views on Ireland', he did not share the opinion of many that the Pontiff was especially progressive in his outlook: 'you are all gone mad about the Pope, calling him the "Great Reformer."'[4] Herbert saw him more as a man who reacted to, or was the prisoner of events, not as somebody who fashioned them. When, therefore, Pius bowed to popular pressure and granted a constitution in mid-March, Herbert was 'sorry the Pope didn't do what he all along intended until it was apparently forced from him by popular demonstration'. It was not how a good Peelite would have proceeded: by dithering, the Pope's actions now appeared as 'a defeat & humiliation to him'.[5]

In his prognostication that Pope Pius would ultimately prove to have feet of clay when it came to supporting liberal and nationalist causes, Herbert proved prescient. In the early months of 1848,

---

1 *CWFN*, VII, pp. 139-47, 166-71, FN to her family 12 Dec. 1847, FN to Dr Fowler, 24 Dec. 1847.
2 *CWFN*, VII, pp. 100-1, Bracebridge to W. Nightingale, nd, Dec. 1847.
3 Bodleian MS Eng. Lett. C. 657, fols. 14-17, EH to Manning, 13 Mar. 1848; Bostridge, *Nightingale*, pp. 115-7.
4 WSHC 2057/F4/49, SH to Lady Pembroke, nd, Sept. 1847.
5 Bodleian MS Eng. Lett. C. 657, fols. 6-11, EH to Manning, 22 Feb. 1848.

however, reform in the Papal States did serve as the trigger for a series of popular uprisings which swept across Europe. As Herbert noted as early as mid-February:

> We could not have been here at a more interesting moment, whilst all this fermentation is going on and mighty changes are brewing, for it is the capital of the religious world still, and her changes will affect to a wonderful degree the state of every other country, even of those not in communion with her.[1]

The truth of Herbert's prediction was amply borne out by the letters which he and Elizabeth penned over the coming weeks. Seemingly unperturbed by what was going on around them, they mixed accounts of sightseeing expeditions with tales of revolutionary fervour. On 22 February, for example, Elizabeth detailed 'a delicious expedition' to the eleventh-century Benedictine convent of La Trinita della Cava, six miles north-west of Salerno. In Salerno itself, despite 'the look of intense wretchedness & starvation of the poor people about there', they witnessed processions and an illumination in celebration of King Ferdinand II's having granted them a constitution. It proved to be something of a busman's holiday for her husband: 'The English fleet arrived here yesterday to Sid's great delight'.[2] He was anything but delighted when Elizabeth became trapped beneath their overturned carriage. After Herbert's death, Mrs Norton wrote to Elizabeth about 'his description of his attempt to lift the weight off you; "her life, – her life you know, – and I am not strong enough to save it."'[3]

Just over a fortnight later the Herberts crossed the Straits of Messina to Palermo, 'the prettiest little bay in the world'. Herbert informed his 'Mamsey' that 'we have been seeing the beautiful things here, ancient churches etc'.[4] The Dowager Lady Pembroke was spared the graphic detail contained in his wife's letter to Manning describing

---

1 WSHC 2057/F4/49, SH to Lady Pembroke, nd, Feb. 1848.
2 Bodleian MS Eng. Lett. C. 657, fols. 6-11, EH to Manning, 22 Feb. 1848.
3 WSHC 2057/F4/54, Norton to EH, nd, 1860s.
4 WSHC 2057/F4/49, SH to Lady Pembroke, 11 Mar. 1848.

how men had been parading around the town with pistols and tricolour flags: 'The Palace is a heap of ruins but they have spared the beautiful chapel with its glorious mosaics'. Those leading the rising, Elizabeth decided, 'wouldn't look well in Downing Street'. One reminded her of 'a fat comfortable grocer or linen draper'. Another, an erstwhile bandit turned chief of police, had dealt with the inconvenience that a price was on his head by decapitating a corpse and presenting its head as his own. One presumes that Elizabeth was more appalled than impressed by a ruse which meant that he 'actually pocketed the money for his own Head!' Rejoicing in 'the glorious French news' (King Louis Phillipe had abdicated on 24 February), Elizabeth impishly enquired if revolution had yet crossed the Channel and 'whether Queen Victoria is sharing Louis Phillipe's retirement at Twickenham'.[1]

By mid-April, via Rome, Florence, Pisa, Turin and Genoa, the Herberts were ready to return to England. They were in London by 21 April. Herbert waxed lyrical to his mother that 'No one can tell how charming Liz has been in our tour, and how completely sufficient we are to one another […] in everything she is a comfort and assistance'. Elizabeth likewise wrote of the joy they had shared abroad where they had the luxury 'of companionship with each other, so rarely enjoyed at home'.[2]

But where exactly was home? Pembroke House in Whitehall had been vacated soon after the death of Herbert's father. Pembroke Lodge, where Herbert was born, had reverted to the Crown in 1831 and was granted to Lord John Russell in 1847. During his early parliamentary career Herbert had stayed at his mother's London address, 1 Grafton Street, in Mayfair. In 1846 he took a lease on 5 Carlton Gardens; it was here, therefore, that the young couple spent their early years together in the capital. One cannot resist the mischievous speculation that it was the reputation of the neighbours which persuaded them to look elsewhere: the Palmerstons lived at number four, the Gladstones at

1   Bodleian MS Eng. Lett. C. 657, fols. 14-17, EH to Manning, 13 Mar. 1848.
2   WSHC 2057/F4/49, SH to Lady Pembroke, 19 Sept. 1847; Bodleian MS Eng. Lett. C. 657, fols. 18-24, EH to Manning, 3, 9 Apr. 1848; *Freeman's Journal*, 22 Apr. 1848.

number six. Whatever the reason, in 1851 the Herberts moved to the four storey mansion recently completed by Thomas Cubitt in a prime location at the northern corner of Belgrave Square. Incorporating several marble fixtures presumably acquired during their time in Italy, number forty-nine would provide the base for much of their work over the coming decade.[1] It was the arcadia that was Wilton, however, that Herbert at least, continued to regard as his true home. He did not conceal his frustration at how parliamentary affairs all too often prevented him from being there, the more so if Elizabeth was already in Wiltshire. In July 1849, apologising to her for an unexpected delay in coming home, he explained that he had been detained by a debate on shipping that was 'duller than ditch water'. He might have consoled himself with the thought that matters would have been far worse without the advent of the railways: from March 1847, travelling from Salisbury station at 8 a.m. via Bishopstoke, he could be in Belgrave Square shortly after 11 a.m.[2]

Nothing puts the fact of the Herberts' marital bliss into better perspective, however, than the domestic woes of Herbert's friend, Lord Lincoln. Lincoln's wife, after several affairs, separations and attempted reconciliations, had left him for good in August 1848. As Herbert put it, perhaps a little harshly, 'He took her for worse as well as for better, and worse he has found her'. Consequently, for all that he respected the sanctity of the marriage vow, Herbert became 'convinced that the return of lady L to her home would end in the utter ruin of their children'.[3] In a move calculated to mitigate the chances of that happening, he and Elizabeth readily agreed to take care of Lincoln's three youngest children at Wilton for the winter of 1848-9. Lincoln, meanwhile, sailed to North Africa on his yacht to reflect on his misfortunes. On returning to collect his charges he found himself struggling for words:

1   The house has been the official residence of the Argentinean ambassador since 1936.
2   WSHC 2057/F4/51, SH to EH, 3 July 1849; BL Add. Mss. 50134, fols. 192-3, SH to Balfour, 11 Aug. 1857.
3   BL Add. Mss. 44210, fols. 22-5, SH to WEG, 16 Nov. 1849.

I was quite unable yesterday to say all – or even half – of what I felt for your and Sidney's kindness to me and mine. My lot in this life has had its share of sorrows but the steadiness and strength of a few friendships present the bright spots in my existence and have almost alone enabled me to bear life against a continuity of misery which would otherwise have been far too grievous to bear.[1]

The presence of the various Lincoln siblings at Wilton – his Oxford friend had sired five children by 1845 – may have given Herbert cause for reflection. According to Nightingale in 1848, Elizabeth was ill-informed as to the mechanics of human reproduction, 'owing to her having been brought up without the knowledge by which even a hen lays eggs'.[2] The real cause of her early difficulties when it came to child bearing, however, was biological. Elizabeth suffered at least two miscarriages before, following a five-and-a-half hour labour, she finally gave birth to a daughter, Mary, on 21 May 1849. A son and heir, George Robert, was born on 6 July 1850.[3]

Some of the anxieties inseparable from the joys of parenting soon followed. Generally at such moments it was Herbert who reassured Elizabeth, telling her for example, in July 1849, not to 'fret about baby who will do better any day I trust'.[4] Only a month after the birth of his son, however, it was 'Dear Sidney' who 'suffered very much', talking through his anxieties with Elizabeth, as well as praying with her, that the infant George would grow up without a period 'of folly in early manhood'. This was, presumably, a fear informed by his half-brother's example, not his own. When George almost immediately afterwards fell dangerously ill, as Elizabeth ruefully recognised, 'it seemed as if

---

1 WSHC 2057/F4/49, SH to Lady Pembroke, nd, Sept. 1847; WSHC 2057/F4/53, Lincoln to EH, 31 Jan. 1849; Munsell, *Unfortunate Duke*, ch. 6. The Lincolns went through a public and painful divorce in 1850.
2 *CWFN*, VIII, p. 653.
3 Bodleian MS Eng. Lett. C. 657, fols. 29-30, SH to Manning, 21 May 1849.
4 WSHC, 2057/F4/51, SH to EH, 2 July 1849.

our prayers were being answered in a way we dreamt not of'.[1] George recovered, only for Mary to hover between life and death a fortnight later. Herbert, on being told the news, 'burst into tears'.[2] But Mary too rallied. Sibling reinforcements were thereafter regularly forthcoming in the persons of Elizabeth (30 July 1851), for whose birth Nightingale was present as midwife, Sidney (20 February 1853), William Reginald (21 May 1854), Michael (25 June 1857) and Constance (24 April 1859).

His immediate dependants aside, Herbert also needed to consider the wider Wilton family in his role as de facto 'administrator and virtual master of the Pembroke estates'.[3] It was a challenge he relished, not least because of his very real interest in agricultural questions. Herbert was an assiduous reader of agricultural journals. Through these, he could speak authoritatively about such matters as the quality of the harvest in Scotland and the north as compared with the south. He also had a nuanced appreciation of the practical effect of variables, most obviously the weather, something which accounts for his exasperation with the theoretical blanket approach of both free traders and protectionists. Above all Herbert was an apostle of high farming, that is to say, in favour of following the best and newest methods and practices. As he put it, 'If there was any depression in agriculture arising from the influence of seasons or from other causes, then the best remedy, in his view of the case, would be a vigorous outlay of capital on the land, with a view to its further improvement'.[4] Hence his support for the 1847 Drainage of Land Bill that would enable agriculturalists 'to improve their lands by means of loans from the State'. Hence too his accepting the need to legislate on the contentious question of tenant right: insecurity of tenure was a major impediment to tenants being prepared to invest capital in long term improvement schemes on their farms. During debates on the Landlord

1   Bodleian MS Eng. Lett. C. 657, fols. 48-50, EH to Manning, 19 Aug. 1850.
2   Bodleian MS Eng. Lett. C. 657, fols. 51-3, EH to Manning, 2 Sept. 1850.
3   Stanmore, I, p. 38.
4   Hansard, 13 Mar. 1845, LXXVIII, cols. 810-20.

and Tenant Bill of 1850, therefore, Herbert called for tenants to be compensated for any improvements they had made when ending a tenancy, and a law which 'ought not to prevent landlords from making bargains with their tenants, which were necessary for the improvement of the soil'.[1]

It thus comes as no surprise to discover that Herbert was both a modern high farming and a traditionally paternalist landlord. With agriculture experiencing its worst depression in thirty years, he granted rent abatements of 10% in 1848 and 15% in 1849. But he required tenants to use the sums thus saved to them to be spent on artificial manures with a view to boosting crop output and thereby offsetting the fall in agricultural prices. Herbert was also prepared to loan money to his tenants for the purpose of improvements such as drainage.[2] More novel was his introduction of a 'produce rent' at Wilton. This, it was hoped, would be more sensitive to changing market conditions than fixed money rents. Under the new system, rents were to be calculated according to the cost of key foodstuffs. Thus, a tenant's rent might be calculated as being the aggregate cost of so many pounds of meat together with so many bushels of corn. To safeguard the tenant further, it was stipulated that maximum rents could not exceed pre-1846 levels or, as a minute a few months after Herbert's death put it, that 'the landlord does not go beyond the fair rent, it being considered that all profit above that should belong to the tenant'.[3] James Caird, the Scottish agricultural writer, when visiting Wiltshire at mid-century, endorsed the sagacity of Herbert's initiatives: 'On the Corn farms a reduction of rent is considered indispensable, or a conversion of money into produce-rents [...] The idea of a return to protection appears to be abandoned'.[4]

Most innovative of all were the handful of model farms Herbert established. The first was the 200-acre holding known as Wilton

1   Hansard, 10 Mar. 1847, XC, col. 1125; 1 May 1850, CX, cols. 1064-5; 12 June 1850, CXI, col. 1123.
2   Thompson, *English Landed Society*, pp. 234, 238-9; *SWJ*, 1 Jan. 1848, 2 June 1849.
3   Thompson, *English Landed Society*, pp. 240-3.
4   Caird, *English Agriculture in 1850-51*, pp. 79-87.

House Farm. Before Herbert assumed control in 1846, it was denuded of buildings and notorious for encompassing land that was sometimes too wet to work. Three years later, it was employing twenty men, boasted a manager's house, and:

> stabling for six horses [...] opposite to it is a block of buildings which comprise boxes for twelve beasts, manure houses and tanks, pig yard and pig rooms for crushing, cutting and storing corn and chaff [...] all these are built in a substantial manner with stone and slate [...] the homestead is everything a farmer could wish.

Critics mocked the 'model mutton' that Herbert's farmers sent to Salisbury market but they could not deny that their achievement was impressive.[1]

Wilton's labourers too, excited Herbert's concern. From 1847 he had turned his attention to the subject of their accommodation. On his orders, 'a number of neat, brick-built, slate-covered, four room cottages, with convenient and necessary outbuildings', were constructed in South Newton. Each had 'a garden of not less than half an acre of good land, the whole let at less rent than is usually charged around for the most miserable and unhealthy thatched and mud-walled hovels'. The cottages were available, in the first instance, to those of good character with large families. Seed crop was provided for their first year. Herbert hoped that this would enable them to sell enough produce to cover their rent and fatten a pig for the coming year. During 1848 and 1849, Herbert extended the cottage-building scheme to Chilhampton, Quidhampton and Wishford, three other villages on the Wilton estate. Unmarried labourers, meanwhile, were invited to take advantage of a model lodging house in the middle of Wilton. Here they would be provided with an 'ample but plain' diet from a housekeeper. They would also have access to a library, and the occasional lecture from a curate, all for 4s 4d a week. Regardless of whether or not they found themselves in one of these model homes,

1   *SWJ*, 3 Nov., 22 Dec. 1849.

no labourer on the Wilton estate earned less than 10 shillings a week; some received as much as 12 shillings.[1]

There was, however, a downside to Herbert's munificence. As the *Morning Chronicle* pointed out in March 1849, 'Some of the large farmers complain greatly of this, asserting that it makes the labourer too independent, as they now refuse to work for the wages hitherto paid them, viz, 6s to 8s per week'. The following October there was a strike by labourers in the villages of Wishford, South Newton and Stoford (all of them part of the Wilton estate) in response to farmers who tried to mitigate the impact of falling prices by cutting labourers' weekly wages to six or seven shillings. Up to sixty labourers were reported to have met with Herbert at Wilton. He, 'having listened to their simple, unvarnished tale,' promised that his land steward would try to persuade the farmers to restore previous wage levels, 'and if either of them should lose employment by the peaceful course which they had adopted, he would give such persons employment in the park'.[2] This was doubtless all very commendable but Herbert, whose frustration with the conservatism of farmers was unconcealed, could afford to shoulder the burdens of agricultural depression far more readily than they. The Wilton estate's income from rental in 1859-60 was £45,168.[3]

The Herberts' popularity at Wilton, and for several miles around, was nevertheless genuine. It stemmed from the commitment they made on the Palladian bridge following their wedding to be deserving of the love of their community. They soon began what Elizabeth called their charity of *le plat du bon Jesu*. This involved plating some of the food uneaten at dinner, perhaps 'the wing of a chicken or pheasant, or a cutlet with some nice vegetables; a slice of pudding, or pie or fruit', and taking it to the home of a sick labourer.[4] Both Herbert and Elizabeth became increasingly convinced of the need for education, and not just of the elementary kind. Elizabeth set up a girls' school within the grounds of Wilton Park which pupils attended until they were fifteen. Herbert set up an industrial school for boys. The eldest

1 *SWJ*, 8 Jan. 1848, 21 Apr. 1849, 29 Nov. 1852.
2 *Morning Chronicle*, 19 Mar. 1849; *The Times*, 3 Nov. 1849.
3 WSHC 2057/D5/14.
4 BL Add. Mss. 49270, fol. 143.

amongst them were provided with plots of land supervised by a bailiff: in addition to the 'three R's' they would be furnished with the practical skills which would make them useful to farmers.[1] The town's poor were bought blankets with the money donated by visitors who were granted access to view the treasures of Wilton House on Wednesdays and Fridays. James Smith, who produced an overview of the town in 1851, reported Herbert as saying that 'in his opinion the Proprietor of an estate like Wilton should consider himself as holding its treasures in trust, as it were, for the benefit of his neighbours'.[2] Neither did he neglect his neighbours' leisure. In 1851 Herbert paid for 400 people from Wilton (including 120 carpet workers and all children on the Wilton estate) to travel by train to visit the Great Exhibition at the Crystal Palace.[3] Those forty or so persons who formed part of his immediate household were looked after down to the grave, and indeed beyond. Elizabeth recalled that on one occasion Herbert had temporarily abandoned his parliamentary duties to return to Wilton to hold the hand of a dying woman who had lived and worked in the house for 60 years. She was laid to rest in the plot reserved in the parish graveyard for former household servants. Herbert took it upon himself to design the various tombs and crosses.[4]

Herbert's greatest acts of bounty, however, were bestowed on local churches. Churches in at least ten parishes on the Wilton estate were restored with additional funds provided for their maintenance.[5] By far his grandest initiative in this regard was the one undertaken with his mother in Wilton itself. In July 1839 it was announced that Herbert and the Dowager Countess would provide Wilton with a new parish church. Work proper began in the spring of 1841.[6] By the time the new church of St Mary and St Nicholas was consecrated on 9

1 HLPP GC/HE 105, EH to Pam, 16 Oct. 1861; BL Add. Mss. 49270, fol. 144.
2 Smith, *Wilton and its Associations*, p. 222.
3 *The Times*, 11 Sept. 1851.
4 BL Add. Mss 49270, fol. 143.
5 *Fraser's Magazine*, 'Herbert', p. 211.
6 *SWJ*, 29 July 1839, 31 May 1841.

October 1845, mother and son had lavished well over £60,000 on their grand design.¹

Today Thomas Henry Wyatt and David Brandon are feted as the architects of St Mary and St Nicholas; contemporaries were in no doubt that the decisive input came from their paymasters. The Dowager, for example, was responsible for the decision to build the church on a north–south alignment in the Russian manner as opposed to the east–west alignment usual with most Anglican churches. But it was Herbert who was responsible for the 'minute details' of the design, and also for procuring most of the various pieces which constituted what has recently been described as the church's 'stately' interior. Based, it is said, on two churches which he had seen at Toscanello during his earlier travels in Italy, the result was one of the first churches in England built in the Lombardic Romanesque style.²

Herbert's eclectic mix for the church's interior included two-thousand-year-old black columns from a Roman temple, a Baroque font, thirteenth-century mosaic columns from a Roman shrine (previously part of Horace Walpole's garden chapel at Strawberry Hill and acquired by Herbert at auction), and doors fashioned in part from Flemish Renaissance panels. The crowning glory, however, remains the medieval stained glass, including some from the abbey of St Denis and La Sainte-Chapelle in Paris – courtesy of the entrepreneurial iconoclasts of the French Revolution.³ Well over two years after the church was consecrated, Herbert remained alive to the possibility of further additions: in February 1848, during his extended honeymoon tour, he wrote from Naples that he was 'hard at work at the Pavement Plans having just obtained the church measurements from England'.⁴

The Anglican-Tory press fawned in admiration at Herbert's munificence. Others took a different view. This was partly a question

1 Stanmore, I, pp. 99-100; *SWJ*, 11 Oct. 1845.
2 Stanmore, I, pp. 99-100; Jenkins, *England's Thousand Best Churches*, p. 739.
3 Jenkins, *Best Churches*, p. 739; *Victoria County History*, VI, pp. 29-31; *SWJ*, 28 Mar. 1846.
4 Bodleian MS Eng. Lett. C. 657, fols. 6-11, SH to Manning, 22 Feb. 1848.

of aesthetics. An editorial in the *Wiltshire Independent* bemoaned 'a want of that harmony and consistency of design, which characterises purer styles'. Politically-motivated critics, meanwhile, charged that it was a 'frolic', unnecessary and a waste of money at a time when labourers were struggling to make ends meet, or that it was part of 'a crusade against Dissenters'.[1] More personal was the complainant who protested that many locals had been unable to secure tickets to attend the consecration because the Herberts had distributed so many to their friends. It must be considered doubtful that many cared: Herbert distributed 1,700 tickets to the supposedly disappointed, entitling them to a celebratory meal of bread, beef, plum pudding and beer. The further criticism lodged against him, 'that the edifice was built less for prayer than for pride', was manifestly unfair. Herbert had refused the suggestion that his name be recorded as being the founder of the church. Instead he had inscribed above the main door a verse from First Chronicles: 'All things come from Thee and of thine own have we given Thee'.[2]

The widespread interest aroused by Wilton's new church inevitably revived speculation as to the nature of Herbert's religious beliefs: Newman, ironically, converted to Rome the same day that the church was consecrated. But it was the 'Puseyite tendencies that are attributed to Mr Herbert', insisted one correspondent, that gave cause for alarm to good Protestants. The chief grounds for the warning were reports that the Bishop of Salisbury had vetoed Herbert's plans for several sacred paintings and a stone altar incorporating mosaics.[3] Herbert made no comment. For such light as can be shed on his religious outlook at this time we are mostly reliant on Elizabeth. She was unashamedly a friend of the Oxford Movement. After an upbringing in an 'utterly and entirely distasteful' Anglican Church, with its 'intolerably dry sermons', it had provided her with 'my

---

1 *Wiltshire Independent*, 16 Oct. 1845.
2 *Wiltshire Independent*, 16 Oct. 1845; BL Add. Mss. 49270, fol. 143.
3 *Wiltshire Independent*, 16 Oct. 1845; Mozley, *Reminiscences*, p. 161. The name of Edward Bouverie Pusey, Regius Professor of Hebrew at Oxford, had become a popular label of abuse aimed at presumed supporters of Tractarianism.

first view of real religion'. Newman, in her view, simply 'carried our principles to their legitimate conclusion'.[1] She did not however, even after hundreds of discussions on theological topics during their early life together, claim that Herbert agreed with her. He did, though, she recalled, often refer to the 'curse of the Reformation'. It had, in his opinion, destroyed more than it had reformed. One's religion, he often told her, was partly a question of temperament: his had always been High Church. But even more, he contended, one's religion was the result of 'geographical accident'. In the latter judgement he pointed to himself as an example: had he been brought up in Russia, he would almost certainly have been an Orthodox Christian.[2]

Elizabeth Herbert's comments are particularly suggestive with respect to the period of her extended honeymoon. She claims that Herbert introduced her to Newman in Rome. Her further claims that Manning, then Archdeacon of Chichester, accompanied them to Italy, and that he was Herbert's 'oldest school and college friend' are untrue, but they certainly met Manning in Rome and were on intimate terms. Anxious that she might be unable to produce children, all three of them 'joined in the novena (prayers for nine days asking for the intercession of the Virgin Mary) said by the nuns of the Sacred Heart at Rome on their behalf'. Herbert may have been induced to do this because some of the nuns were, apparently, his cousins but Elizabeth adds that 'we used often to go Benedictine or early Mass'.[3] None of this, of course, makes Herbert a Roman Catholic: he was lukewarm at best about the papacy. But Elizabeth had fair grounds for stating that 'He had no prejudice whatever against the Catholic Church'. He had, after all, said in his Maynooth speech of 1845 that nineteenth-century Catholicism was not something to be feared. A liberal Herbert sympathetic to much in the Catholic faith chose to look at its similarities with Anglicanism, not its differences. As he put

---

1 Herbert, *How I Came Home*, pp. 1-3.
2 Herbert, *How I Came Home*, pp. 8-9.
3 Herbert, *How I Came Home*, pp. 5-9.

it, 'He respected the Roman Catholics, not because they were Roman Catholics, but because they were fellow-Christians'.[1]

Details of what went on during the Herbert's honeymoon were clearly best kept out of the public domain. It was bad enough that 'some treat his endowment of two Popish priests in Ireland as evidence of a lingering attachment towards the scarlet lady of Babylon'.[2] Had his critic but known it, the truth was that Herbert was dividing £200 a year between three Irish Roman Catholic priests: £90 to the Reverend J. Ennis, of Booterstown, £90 to the Reverend V. Finn, of Irishtown, and £20 to the Reverend A. Roche, of Bray, County Wicklow.[3] The remuneration of two or three priests, however, was incidental to the great challenge facing Ireland from the summer of 1845. A third of the potato crop was lost; in 1846 three-quarters of the crop failed. Although there was a relative improvement in 1847, a further third was lost in 1849. The resulting Great Famine of 1846-9 cost over a million lives. Over two million Irish emigrated in the decade from 1845. Attempting to mitigate the impact of the Famine was not the Russell government's finest hour. Some £7 million was spent, principally on maize, soup kitchens and public works. This was woefully insufficient. But a Conservative government would have done no more. Contemporary political culture was instinctively opposed to state interference, whilst a Protestant mind-set inclined some to see the disaster as heaven sent. Only 'an authoritarian state committed to the welfare of the poor at all costs', it has been observed, 'could have alleviated suffering and death much more effectively'.[4]

We have already seen that the failure of the Irish potato crop played a major part in Herbert's conversion to the cause of free trade; his memorandum of December 1845 stating that 'the people must not starve, and the Government must feed them' could not have been more emphatic.[5] Herbert's comments sprang from his humanitarianism

1   BL Add. Mss. 49270, fol. 149; Hansard, 14 Apr. 1845, LXXIX, col. 670.
2   *Wiltshire Independent*, 16 Oct. 1845.
3   *Dublin Weekly Nation*, 1 May 1847.
4   Hoppen, *Mid-Victorian Generation*, pp. 564-71.
5   WSHC 2057/F8/1/M/31; Stanmore, I, pp. 44-7.

and his assessment of the data to hand. There was subsequently, however, the hint of a suggestion that he came to a more Providential explanation for the scale of the human catastrophe which followed. The prospectus he wrote for the Female Emigration Fund in 1849 reminded Englishmen 'of the great and grievous affliction which, by the providence of God, they have just escaped'.[1] He was no clearer than anybody else as to how the will of the Almighty might have been thwarted.

Herbert was almost deafeningly silent in his public comments regarding Ireland's plight. In office he had made several major speeches pontificating on Irish affairs. In stark contrast he made barely a handful of references to Ireland during the 1847 parliament. Exceptions were brief interventions on the Poor Relief (Ireland) Bill, the Dublin Consolidation Improvement Waterworks and Sewers Bill, and the Dublin Corporation Waterworks Bill. He was also accused of having used 'every species of interference' to emasculate several versions of a Dublin Improvement Bill. But such matters were hardly consequential in the grand scheme of things.[2] His only explicit public comment about the horrors of the Irish famine was made at the 1847 South Wiltshire election when he asked those who condemned his supporting the repeal of the Corn Laws whether they had heard of Skibbereen 'in Ireland, where the people had perished in great numbers from famine and pestilence, and where Christian men unburied have been devoured by dogs?'[3] But Herbert said nothing to suggest that he dissented from the actions – or inactions – of the Russell government's response to the Irish crisis. Perhaps there were limits to his sympathy? Elizabeth related how her husband took umbrage in 1847 after reading Giaocchino Ventura's pamphlet, *Breve notizia dell' attuale Carestia in Irlanda*. In it, the Sicilian Padre depicted graphic scenes of starving Irish peasants juxtaposed alongside a lassitudinous British government. Herbert objected that the pamphlet 'is infamously written'. It was

1 *Morning Chronicle*, 13 Dec. 1849.
2 *Freeman's Journal*, 15 Apr. 1847, 14 Mar. 1849; Hansard, 19 Mar. 1847, XCI, col. 229; 27 Feb. 1849, CII, col. 1315; 2 Mar. 1849, CIII, col. 89.
3 *SWJ*, 7 Aug. 1847.

left for Elizabeth to add that Ventura 'can't resist a hit at us & poor Ireland'.[1]

In Herbert's defence it is only fair to point out that even at the height of the Famine his estates were reckoned to be 'amongst the most flourishing in Ireland'. Even today he is remembered 'as one of the few decent Irish landlords' from that time.[2] He was never accused of having evicted tenants, yet over 100,000 Irish were evicted in 1849 alone. To some extent Herbert's situation in Ireland was fortuitous: the areas worst hit by the disaster were the agricultural counties of the west and south; Herbert was doubtless grateful that many of his tenants, living in the environs of Dublin, were not directly engaged in agriculture. But he deserves credit for his evident concern for their plight. When he and Elizabeth first visited Mount Merrion together in October 1846 he received an address thanking him for his efforts on behalf of free trade. He replied to his tenants on 9 October that:

> The poorer population of this immediate neighbourhood, though not generally engaged in agriculture, and therefore not suffering directly by the loss of crops, must still be most seriously affected by the enhanced price of all articles of food; and I shall consider it my duty to provide employment wherever it is possible, by which our poorer neighbours may be enabled to earn the means of subsistence; and with that view I have given directions for the commencement of works in different parts of my property.[3]

Herbert the paternalist landlord fully understood that he had a duty to those dependent on him. Like most, though, it was a duty which he sought to discharge by providing work, not handouts. The detail fell to his agent, Cornelius Sullivan. Money was forthcoming to support projects in the environs of Dublin. Some went to labourers removing a hill at Drummartin; more was disbursed on workers

1 Bodleian MS Eng. Lett. C. 657, fols. 6-11, EH to Manning, 22 Feb. 1848.
2 *Dublin Evening Mail*, 13 Aug. 1848; http://humphrysfamilytree.com/Herbert/lea.html, accessed 5 Dec. 2017.
3 *Freeman's Journal*, 5 Oct. 1846; *Dublin Evening Mail*, 21 Oct. 1846.

employed to fill a hollow at Ballinteer. These were just two of many proto-Keynesian examples of digging holes to fill them.[1] Herbert also financed the construction of sewers, sluices, river embankments, and a sea wall along Sandymount Strand. Much of his Irish land was susceptible to flooding; it made sense to continue a programme which began before the Famine and continued after it.[2] In Dublin itself he was responsible for improvements around Lincoln Place. And though the beneficiaries were necessarily few in number, he was lauded for ordering taboret furniture 'of the most superb and chaste description', from Messrs Atkinson and Co. for his home in Belgrave Square.[3]

So far as the Irish Famine was concerned, therefore, Herbert's actions spoke louder than his words. Letters he wrote to Elizabeth during a second short visit in October 1849, and a third in the spring of 1850, make absolutely no reference to it. In 1849 his chief items of news were that the church nearing completion at Sandymount was 'very pretty', and that 'The Ringsend school house looks very imposing'. His biggest concern was that the congregation in the cathedral seemed more like an 'audience' because they 'coolly left their seats when the anthem began to crowd round the singers'.[4] In March 1850 he was chiefly impressed by Doe Castle at Sheephaven Bay in County Donegal. A long description and a highly competent sketch of the castle accompanied his verdict that it was somewhere that 'very little would do a great deal with'.[5] Perhaps he was sparing Elizabeth the detail of the poverty which he must surely have witnessed? But even in a letter to Gladstone shortly after returning from his trip in October 1849 Herbert's tone was strangely detached. He reported tersely that he had 'found everyone disheartened at seeing all the old sores breaking out again, with the new evils of famine and poor law superadded'.[6] A

1 *Dublin Evening Mail*, 2 Nov. 1846.
2 *Dublin Evening Mail*, 10 Dec. 1849; *Freeman's Journal*, 19 Nov.1852; Stanmore, I, pp. 98-9.
3 *Freeman's Journal*, 16 Nov. 1846, 8 Aug. 1851.
4 WSHC 2057/F4/51, SH to EH, 13, 15 Oct. 1849.
5 *Freeman's Journal*, 8 Apr. 1850; WSHC 2057/F4/51, SH to EH, 29 Mar. 1850.
6 BL Add. Mss. 44210, fols. 18-19, SH to WEG, 29 Oct. 1849.

year later he was decidedly upbeat in his assessment, telling Graham after his month's visit that he was 'greatly encouraged by all I heard and saw. All speak cheerfully of the future. Indeed it seems the most happy and contented country in Europe just now. There is certainly far less grumbling than here'.[1]

It is difficult to resist the conclusion that Herbert's lasting contribution to Ireland during these years was two churches. His 1849 letter to Elizabeth had mentioned the church at Sandymount. Herbert had given land for the site together with £1,500 in 1844. Construction began in the summer of 1846; an inscription stone (and time capsule) was laid on Elizabeth Herbert's behalf by Cornelius Sullivan's granddaughter in May 1848. St John's Church was finally consecrated in 1850. In total Herbert had expended £7,000 on it; Elizabeth added the present of an organ.[2] The same year Herbert gave a four-acre site for a new Catholic church at Irishtown. The foundation stone of St Mary's, Star of the Sea, Sandymount, was laid in May 1851; it was consecrated in August 1853.[3]

Elizabeth Herbert saw the completed church at Sandymount when she accompanied her husband to Ireland in October 1850. It was the most public of Herbert's four visits in as many years. The highlight was a visit to inspect the two schools he maintained at Ringsend. Flags, it was reported, 'projected from, or surmounted every house, and the [main] street was lined with dense crowds of the people'. Nearly 500 boys and girls from the two schools assembled to meet their patrons. It was because of the Herberts' munificence, the Reverend O'Connell reminded those present, that even the poorest were enabled to tear down the walls of ignorance, they having been provided with 'ample means of acquiring a due sense of the principles of moral and social ethics'. Herbert replied briefly and unimaginatively by exhorting the pupils 'to persevere in their educational studies'.[4] His visit, like his previous ones, underscored his belief that Ireland's ills were to be cured

1 BL Add. Mss. 79657, fols. 55-61, SH to JRG, 30 Nov. 1850.
2 *Saunders's News-letter*, 2 July 1846; *Dublin Evening Mail*, 24 May 1848; *SWJ*, 6 Apr. 1850, 25 May 1851.
3 *Freeman's Journal*, 8 May, 18 Oct. 1850, 9 May 1851.
4 *Freeman's Journal*, 31 Oct. 1850.

by promoting religious tolerance, not least through education. This, as he acknowledged, would take decades. It was of cold comfort to those struggling for the necessaries of life in the here and now.

None of the above, however, not even the Famine, can really be said to have altered prevailing opinions in Ireland towards Herbert. To critics he remained one of the 64 'aristocratic' landlords who between them drew over £6.5 million per annum in rent; William Smith O'Brien, one of the more militant Irish Members, happily denounced him in the House as an absentee.[1] John O'Connell, son of Daniel, carried on what had evidently become a family tradition: at a Dublin ratepayers' meeting in 1847 he admonished Herbert for taking £45,000 per annum from Ireland tax free.[2] A few months later he would have been able to add that it never occurred to Herbert to postpone or even curtail his extended honeymoon as the Famine reached its zenith. It is also true that although Herbert spent more time in Ireland between 1846 and 1850 than he would during any other four year period of his life, he spent far more time shooting and fishing in the Scottish Highlands.

Herbert does not seem to have been amongst those MPs who looked to emigration as an answer to Ireland's problems. This is a little odd since he was soon to become involved with three groups dedicated to promoting it. The first of these was the Canterbury Association. Set up in London in March 1848 by Edward Gibbon Wakefield and John Robert Godley, Herbert became a founder member. He found himself in congenial company. Many of its 84 members were Conservative High Churchmen. They included 8 Oriel men and 34 MPs. Those he knew well included Peel's erstwhile Chancellor of the Exchequer, Henry Goulburn, Lord Lincoln, Lord Ashley (from 1851 Earl of Shaftesbury), and the Reverend George Gleig. Presided over by John Sumner, Archbishop of Canterbury, the Association's objective was to establish a colony in New Zealand's South Island. Funds were provided to assist emigrants subject to their providing character references from

---

1 *Dublin Weekly Nation*, 11 Apr. 1846, 4 Mar. 1848; Hansard, 18 Mar. 1847, XCI, cols. 159-66.
2 *Freeman's Journal*, 21 Apr. 1847.

a clergyman. Before the Association wound up its affairs in 1853, 28 ships had carried 3,500 settlers to Canterbury Province centred on the future city of Christchurch.[1]

More important still in fuelling Herbert's interest in emigration was the work of Caroline Chisholm. From lowly Northamptonshire origins, Chisholm had come to public attention after providing homes and jobs for over 10,000 female emigrants to Australia during the early 1840s. Following her return to Britain in 1846, she continued to proselytise the cause. In 1849 she founded the Family Loan and Colonisation Society. This new initiative provided individual loans to cover half the cost of emigration; the money had to be repaid after two years. Herbert's name is to be found at the head of the list of the society's subscribers (with £200) in 1850; in June 1853 he agreed to succeed Shaftesbury as chairman of its central committee.[2] Under the Society's auspices some 3,000 people had emigrated by the time that Chisholm – unfairly caricatured by Dickens as Mrs Jellyby in *Bleak House* – returned to Australia in 1854.

At the end of 1849, however, Herbert had determined upon his own emigration initiative. His motives were a mix of the moral, religious, paternal and humanitarian. In public he could be positively messianic about the subject:

> the sea is the empire and the home of Englishmen; and it is by bridging the sea, and spreading in countries beyond the sea our English freedoms and free institutions – aye, and our English pure religion too, that we hope ultimately not only to ameliorate the condition of ourselves in this little island but also to benefit the condition of the whole human race throughout the world.[3]

Privately, he admitted also to being moved by the less high-minded concerns deriving from his abiding fear of social and political upheaval. As he explained to Manning at the end of November 1849,

---

1 Blain, *The Canterbury Association*.
2 WSHC 2057/F8/VIII/27, Chisholm to SH, 20 Aug., 19 Sept. 1850; *Australian Dictionary of National Biography*; *The Times*, 5 Aug. 1850.
3 *SWJ*, 17 July 1852.

a combination of too much capital and too large a population was 'producing fearful effects'. Raising money for the destitute would be of little avail: it would simply be 'lost in this abyss of poverty'. It was necessary, therefore, to address the root of the problem:

> The state of the poor I mean industrious poor in this Country makes me almost despair in spite of my sanguine disposition but people will not look the matter in the face. There are seeds of communism & revolution such as no country not even France possesses within herself [...] nothing but a vast emigration can save us.[1]

The timing of Herbert's letter was significant. Over the previous months, the *Morning Chronicle*, of which he had become part-proprietor, had carried a series of articles on London's labouring poor. They were written by the journalist and social researcher, Henry Mayhew. Herbert was sufficiently interested that, invited by Lord Ashley to accompany him, he attended a meeting of an estimated 1,200 slopworkers in Shadwell in the East End on 3 December.[2] Clearly both moved and inspired, Herbert addressed a long letter to the *Morning Chronicle* the next day. In addressing the afflictions of poverty, he suggested, special priority should be given to London's needlewomen. There were, according to his information, over 33,000 of them (28,500 of whom were aged under 20) attempting to subsist on pay between 2½d and 4¼d a day. Bearing in mind the wider demographic consideration that the 1841 census showed there to be 320,000 more women than men – Herbert speculated that it was nearer 500,000 as he wrote – there was little prospect that their circumstances would improve. In South Australia, by contrast, the most recent data showed there to be 17,000 men and 13,000 women. The gender imbalance In New South Wales was even greater with 83,000 men to 41,000 women. Herbert proposed 'to abate this double evil' by creating a fund to facilitate female emigration.[3]

---

1 Bodleian MS Eng. Lett. C. 657, fols. 41-5, SH to Manning, 24 Nov. 1849.
2 HL Shaftesbury Diaries, 4 Dec. 1849; *Morning Chronicle*, 4 Dec. 1849.
3 *Morning Chronicle*, 5 Dec. 1849.

In its way, Herbert's letter was as talismanic as the one which he addressed to Florence Nightingale five years later. Ashley's surprise at the response evoked by it bordered upon envy: 'Sidney Herbert is "born with a silver spoon"; he writes a single letter, and obtains, by ten minutes' work, an amount of public confidence that I have missed after the toil of twenty years. A grand Committee will be formed, and vast sums will be collected – how much more than I could have done!' Good God-fearing Evangelical that he was, Ashley was quick to add 'but I therein do rejoice, yea, & will rejoice. God knows that I will labour for his fame and for the cause'.[1] He happily agreed to serve under Herbert on the management committee. Other luminaries included the Prime Minister and the bishops of London and Oxford.

Herbert worked indefatigably over the next few weeks, not least in turning promises of money into hard cash. In what was effectively the prospectus for the Fund, he ventured 'to remind the nation of the great and grievous affliction which, by the providence of God, they have just escaped, and [urged] upon them the great duty of showing their gratitude to their Divine Benefactor by assisting the most helpless and needy of His creatures'.[2] Herbert's solicitations met with a mixed response. Queen Victoria and Prince Albert matched his own contribution of £500. Lord John Russell, much to his delight, though a political opponent, subscribed £100. Lord Stanley by contrast, Protectionist leader in the Lords, did not: 'you have to deal with men & women, & not with machines [...] A thousand other difficulties start up at every step in the conduct of any plan of Emigration'.[3] Some of Herbert's closest political friends were similarly sceptical. Peel voiced his 'misgivings as to the ultimate effect of your plan on the condition of the class which it is most kindly and benevolently intended to benefit'. A private initiative, he felt, could not succeed; he declined to contribute.[4] Lord Aberdeen was similarly unpersuaded:

1   HL Shaftesbury Diaries, 8 Dec. 1849; Finlayson, *Shaftesbury*, pp. 273-6.
2   *Morning Chronicle*, 13 Dec. 1849.
3   WSHC 2057/F4/51, SH to EH, 20 Dec. 1849; LRO 920 DER/14/178/2, Stanley to SH, 9 Dec. 1849.
4   WSHC 2057/F4/53, Peel to SH, 7 Dec. 1849, 15 Jan. 1850.

'I cannot say that I have any great faith in your emigration scheme'. But as he did 'not make these observations with the view of saving my money' (unlike Peel and Stanley, he was not a Lancastrian), he donated £100.[1] More discouraging than either of these political heavyweights, however, was Lincoln. He wrote from Cairo that 'nothing really effective can be done till the social and political condition of the colonies themselves is improved – emigration will continue a "mere shovelling out of paupers."'[2]

Undaunted, Herbert engrossed himself in the work of his pet scheme. He was ex officio chair of the finance, home, shipping, corresponding and selection committees; he also presided over an executive coordinating committee every Friday.[3] In irreverent style, he described to Elizabeth on 10 December how he had just endured a meeting with a stuttering Mr Heathcote and a coughing colonel amidst a yellow fog. Two days later, he apologised to her that an impending meeting of the selection committee prevented him from returning to Wilton. His frustration was compounded by the fact that it was 'a cold day & such hard work'. A week later, he was reporting that he and the committee were in urgent need of a house of probation, a cook and a matron.[4] Number 76 Hatton Gardens was promptly leased from the Society for Improving the Condition of the Labouring Classes, and a Mrs Batkin installed as matron. Herbert was well aware that 'The character of the emigration will be judged in the Colony from the first sample, and they must be most carefully selected'.[5] Raw data suggests that they were: 20% (102 of 509) of those who applied to the Fund in 1850 were rejected. Moreover, some of those who were successful stayed at Hatton Garden for extended periods until they were skilled in the ways of housemaids and servants, their most likely employ when they reached the colonies.[6]

1 WSHC 2057/F4/53, Aberdeen to SH, 29 Dec. 1849.
2 WSHC 2057/F4/53, Lincoln to SH, 31 Jan. 1850.
3 WSHC 2057/F8/VIII/8.
4 WSHC 2057/F4/51, SH to EH, 10, 12, 13, 19, 20 Dec. 1849.
5 Stanmore, I, pp. 113-16, SH to WEG, 18 Dec. 1849.
6 *Morning Chronicle*, 17 Apr. 1851; Jupp, *The Australian People*, p. 41.

The Times was amongst those who welcomed Herbert's plans for the fairer sex: 'They will not be missed from Great Britain, but they will be a sensible addition to the society of New South Wales and Australia'. Had its editor read Herbert's strictures about the necessity for women of good character, it would not have been necessary to issue the caveat that it was important to avoid sending 'sluts and slatterns, flirts and fine ladies, dawdlers and do-nothings, the awkward, ill-tempered, and intractable'.[1] But the newspaper was right to say that 'Mr Sidney Herbert's benevolent scheme seems to be rather variously received'. There was a flurry of practical questions: who would ensure that the voyage out would be decent and comfortable; what machinery existed to deal with emigrants when they arrived? More fundamentally, did women, however destitute, really want to sever 'the tie which binds even the poorest classes to the home of their birth'?[2] The most common objection, however, as Herbert noted, was the cynical defeatist one that his efforts would be akin to casting a tiny pebble into the vast pond of poverty. Disraeli was predictably dismissive, writing on New Year's Day 1850 that:

> I think Sidney Herbert is in a pretty scrape; 85,000 needlewomen to be deported at 15s a-piece (his own estimate) would take upwards of £600,000. He should have subscribed at least one year's income as an example, and if he succeeds in his object, which is impossible, he will do no good.[3]

Herbert's riposte, albeit in a letter addressed to Gladstone, was robustly optimistic: 'because we cannot do everything, are we to do nothing? If, again, we can dig a channel, the water will flow through it ultimately without help of ours. We may be pioneers for public opinion and ultimately for government assistance.'[4]

As Disraeli well knew, however, the most damaging grounds for objection, in terms of Herbert's reputation anyway, were political. Was

---

1   *The Times*, 2 Jan. 1850.
2   *The Times*, 4 Jan., 18 Feb., 16 Mar. 1850.
3   Malmesbury, *Memoirs*, I, pp. 255-6.
4   Stanmore, I, pp. 113-16, SH to WEG, 18 Dec. 1849.

not poverty (though hardly very obviously that of female needle workers in London) exacerbated by the free trade principles which Herbert now espoused? Protectionists certainly professed it to be so. Typical was the Marquis of Granby, then co-leader of the Protectionists in the Commons, who attacked Herbert at a meeting of the Leicestershire Agricultural Society. Herbert's emigration scheme, he contended, was inimical to the very idea of free trade:

> It interfered with the rights of capital, and with the labour market [was it not odd that] whilst Mr Sidney Herbert sees their distress, and that it is open to competition, and that one remedy is to diminish the demand for employment, he should not see the more natural and more just means of relieving their distress, by increasing the employment and preventing the competition of foreigners.[1]

Granby's hypothesising that Herbert was at last coming to his senses about the reality of free trade was not, of course, true. On the contrary, the animosity stoked up by Protectionists over the Female Emigration Fund underlined just how difficult it remained for Herbert to contemplate returning to the main body of the Conservative party. Emigration even raised its head as an election issue in Wiltshire politics. Richard Long, Herbert's opponent in 1852, mocked him for wanting to export 'to the colonies those who had been reduced to abject poverty by foreign competition at home'.[2]

Politics aside, Herbert's scheme enjoyed early success. Nearly £19,000 had been subscribed by the end of January 1850. The first party of 39 emigrants left London on board the *Culloden* on 25 February. Nine more vessels followed that year, carrying some 371 women in total. Continued publicity was assured by Herbert's endeavouring to be present in person for each departure. Often accompanied by Elizabeth, a zealous philanthropist in her own right, he would deliver a valedictory message. Each woman was then issued with a farewell missive exhorting her to be charitable and hardworking;

---

1   *The Times*, 7 Jan. 1850.
2   *SWJ*, 12 Jan. 1850.

they were even provided with addressed envelopes in the hope that they would apprise him of their progress.[1] In one particular case Herbert was reported to have interceded on behalf of a 34-year-old 'accomplished needlewoman' 'of rather attractive appearance'. She had been confined to Hanwell lunatic asylum following several failed suicide attempts: her 'affections and heart had been betrayed'. When she told magistrates that she wished to emigrate, Herbert personally paid for her passage to Sydney. She was one of the 409 emigrants on the ten ships (seven bound for Australia, one each to Canada, Tasmania and Cape Colony) to sail out of London in 1850.[2] At the close of that year Herbert was the dedicatee of *Meloides*, a collection of poems and songs, the profit from which would go to the Fund. Sadly, not much: the *Morning Chronicle* judged that the anonymous author's 'work would seem to be his *debut* in the department of literature'.[3]

Few emigrants' stories evoked pathos in the manner of Herbert's anonymous and heartbroken 34-year old detailed above. Henry Mayhew's investigations, published in book form in 1851 as *London Labour and the London Poor* suggested links between needlewomen and prostitution. Herbert, on the basis of less research, was unpersuaded. He believed that needlewomen were 'young women of all classes who have been driven to live on that occupation exclusively as a last resource'. In fact, such detail as is available shows that the majority of those who emigrated were not needlewomen at all. Needlewomen comprised just 79 of the 409 who emigrated under Herbert's scheme in 1850; they were outnumbered by the 169 who described themselves as domestic servants. There were also three teachers, three governesses, and a further sixteen from a more genteel background who had fallen on hard times. Given that most emigrants did end up in domestic service, the latter may well have been amongst those whom the receiving authorities in New South Wales categorised as unsuitable.[4] The more important fact is that virtually all those who emigrated soon

1 *The Times*, 30 Jan., 18 Feb., 22 July, 1850; *Freeman's Journal*, 6 Apr. 1850.
2 *The Times*, 28 Feb. 1851.
3 *Morning Chronicle*, 26 Dec. 1850.
4 WSHC 2057/F8/VIII/16; *Morning Chronicle*, 17 Apr. 1851.

seem to have found employment: the 65 women who reached Adelaide on board the *Duke of Portland* on 2 August all had jobs within four days, with wages ranging between £8 and £30 per annum.[1]

Relatively little can be said of Herbert's brainchild beyond 1850. This reflects the fact that it peaked very quickly. Ten ships sailed between March and June 1851, but they included only 19 women travelling under the auspices of the Female Emigration Fund. This must cast in doubt the accuracy of the *Morning Chronicle's* claim, in June 1853, that the Fund had by then expended £26,000 in providing passage for 1,200 women.[2] At any event, June 1853 was a pivotal moment. Herbert announced that, in face of better employment prospects for labouring women at home, there had been a dwindling in the number of applications for emigration. Consequently he would change tack. Henceforth, he sought to attract 'lower middle class and educated women of some gentility', not 'untaught paupers', still less 'matrimonial necessities of Australia'. In confirmation of Herbert's intent, it was resolved at a committee meeting of 10 June that future activities would be limited to providing ships and subsidies: free passage would end but might be secured for £22 as compared with the market rate of £32. Forty women were reported to be ready to embark for Sydney on this basis by July. Thereafter all reference to the work of the Fund ceases. Most probably it simply merged with Caroline Chisholm's Family Loan and Colonisation Society. Herbert was now, after all, chairman of its committee. It was not quite his final contribution to the cause. Following his death it was reported that 300 Spitalfields weavers and their families had emigrated to Queensland thanks to the balance on the 'Sidney Herbert Fund'.[3]

Herbert's Female Emigration Fund was only ever conceived of as a temporary private initiative. It was more successful than similar groups, such as the Highland and Island Emigration Society, but less successful than Chisholm's Family Loan and Colonisation Society. The latter benefitted as its name suggests, from aspiring to assist entire

1 *The Times*, 18, 20 Nov. 1850.
2 WSHC 2057/F8/VIII/16; *Morning Chronicle*, 11 June1853.
3 *SWJ*, 29 Jan., 11 June, 13 Aug. 1853; *The Times*, 3 Nov. 1862; Stanmore, I, pp. 119-20.

families possessed of the financial wherewithal to repay the cost of their passage.[1] But Chisholm's society apart, Herbert's enterprise has been judged 'one of the most fashionable charities on the London scene', and that 'its favourable publicity contributed to the changing image of emigration'. For all that Disraeli saw fit to scoff, Herbert had used his wealth, contacts and industry to transform several thousand lives.[2]

His efforts have not been forgotten, as a grateful descendant of one of the needlewomen on a pilgrimage to Wilton House in 2018 was happy to testify to the author. Herbert would have been humbled. 'The temptation to neglect public duties becomes very strong when one is happy in one's nest', he had told his mother in 1847, 'and every day one feels more strongly how very short life is, and with all exertion how miserably small is the amount of usefulness to others which even the best men can produce'.[3] He was in similarly reflective mood on his birthday five years later: 'I think scarcely any one has ever had so many advantages & blessings as I have & I pray to make more effective use of them'.[4] The vicissitudes of national party politics were soon to present him with the opportunity to be able to do so.

---

1 Jupp, *The Australian People*, p. 41; Richards, *Britannia's Children*, pp. 138-40.
2 Hammerton, *Emigrant Gentlewomen*, ch. 4.
3 WSHC 2057/F4/49, SH to Lady Pembroke, 19 Sept. 1847.
4 WSHC 2057/F4/49, SH to Lady Pembroke, 16 Sept. 1852.

7
Progressive Conservative 1850-1852

Relieved of the burdens of office, and happily diverted elsewhere, Herbert was conspicuous by his absence from the House of Commons for much of the later 1840s. Owing to his extended honeymoon, he cast no votes at all there between 17 July 1847 and 17 May 1848. From about 1850, however, he became an increasingly important figure in the unfolding political drama, playing a part in the downfall of two ministries before returning to office at the end of 1852.

The greatest uncertainty in British politics during the 1847 parliament was what would happen to the Peelites. They were the hundred or so MPs, including Herbert, who had split from the main body of the Conservative party in 1846. Looking back from the vantage point of the later 1850s, Herbert took the view that his having become a Liberal had been inevitable. This was to be wise after the event: he was still paying his ten guinea annual subscription to the Tory Carlton Club until at least 1857.[1] It is true that there was logic in the Peelites moving in a liberal direction: free trade, after all, was the defining liberal issue of the day. But Liberals and High Churchmen such as Herbert, Gladstone and Newcastle were improbable bedfellows. The Peelites might instead have maintained their independence, as what

1 WSHC 2057/F4/53, SH to Aberdeen, 12 Apr. 1857; WSHC 2057/A6/63.

Peel dubbed 'a party of observation'. In a hung parliament, this gave them influence disproportionate to their numbers. There was much that Herbert, inclined to be critical of many of those regarded by others as his political betters, found congenial about this scenario. As a long term option, however, especially for talented younger Peelites harbouring ambitions of real power, the idea was obviously less attractive: Peel's disinclination to seek office had an inevitably fissiparous tendency amongst his followers. Arguably the most likely option of all, therefore, was for Conservatives to reunite. From the Peelite perspective, however, this could only be seriously contemplated if Derby and Disraeli, who emerged as the leaders of the Protectionists, could be persuaded to drop their commitment to restore some form of Corn Law.[1]

Even before the Corn Laws were repealed, Herbert made it clear that he hoped to be part of a reunited Conservative party: 'notwithstanding the obloquy and abuse which have been heaped upon us, I cannot forget that they have long been my friends, politically and privately'. But the feeling was not mutual. As the *Morning Herald* pointed out:

> The country party will offer no opposition to the reconstruction of the Conservative party, provided only that Sir Robert Peel, Sir James Graham, Lord Aberdeen, Mr Sidney Herbert, and Lord Lincoln are excluded from the amnesty. These five ex-minsters constituted, as is now ascertained, an interior Cabinet [...] which kept its projects as secret from the other members of the ostensible cabinet as from the world outside.

Herbert later conceded that there would need to be a period of 'necessary political ostracism' before his desired reunion could be effected.[2]

1   Edward, Lord Stanley, succeeded as 14th Earl of Derby in 1851. To avoid confusion he is referred to hereafter as Derby. Disraeli was de facto leader in the Commons from about 1848, though only recognised so in fact from 1852.
2   Hansard, 8 May 1846, LXXXVI, col. 286; 5 Apr. 1852, CXX, col. 709; *Morning Herald*, 4 July 1846.

Since Liberals and Peelites agreed about free trade, it made sense for Lord John Russell to attempt to recruit Peelites to the Liberal ministry he formed in June 1846. Herbert, Lincoln and Dalhousie received invitations to that effect on 1 July. They declined, citing 'the double ground of public duty and of private honour'. The triumvirate were well aware that acceptance meant being swamped by Liberals and policies which they might find unpalatable. Peel, who was not averse to his acolytes being approached, agreed that Russell's offer represented a dubious career move. So long as Peel was alive, Herbert was never likely to dissent from his advice on a question of such magnitude.[1] Newspapers revived rumours that Whigs and Peelites were about to coalesce in the spring of 1847 – Herbert's name was linked variously with the Board of Control, the Admiralty, and Ireland – but any such talk remained premature.[2]

Herbert's record towards the end of the 1841 parliament suggests an understandable disillusionment with party politics. He was present for just 22 divisions in the year after he left office. If he rose to his feet, it was to speak briefly about an issue on which he could now claim some authority. His first speech of 1847, for example, addressed the question of corporal punishment in the navy. Whilst accepting that 'checks upon the exercise of the power of flogging ought to exist', he defended the practice as 'the only means of maintaining a discipline necessary for the safety of a vessel during its lonely transit across the Atlantic or other oceans, many miles apart from land and the civil authorities'.[3] In March he spoke at the committee stage of the Army Service Bill. In an attempt to boost the number of recruits, the Liberal government proposed supplementing enlistment for life with a form of short service. It was an idea Herbert had opposed when Secretary at War. He rejected it again now, articulating fears he had hitherto confined to his private correspondence:

---

1   WSHC 2057/F4/53, Russell to SH, 1 July 1846; SH to Russell, 2 July 1846.
2   *SWJ*, 15 May 1847.
3   Hansard, 9 Feb. 1847, LXXXIX, cols. 1066-7.

they might produce such a state of things by a legislative measure of this kind, that a very large proportion of the population should have passed through the ranks of the Army, and thus have obtained a knowledge of military discipline and habits [...] popular commotions were rendered more dangerous by those who had been discharged from the Army.[1]

Herbert's warning was to no avail: the Bill became law in June. Henceforth recruits signed on for ten years in the infantry or twelve in the cavalry, engineers and artillery.[2] But he had confirmed his status as the Peelites' leading spokesman on military and naval affairs. He reinforced it further as a member of the select committees on the militia estimates, and for army and ordnance expenditure.[3]

In August 1847, before he was free to depart with Elizabeth for Europe, Herbert had to face his constituents. Members who had been elected in 1841 pledging to uphold the Corn Laws could reasonably expect retribution. The Protectionist *Devizes and Wiltshire Gazette* had demanded that he should resign in 1846; three groans had been given for him at a meeting of the Wiltshire Agricultural Protection Society.[4] But Herbert took defiant pride in the Peel ministry's record. It had been his 'bounden duty to allow no preconceived opinions I might have entertained under very different circumstances to prevent my advocating immediate measures to avert so great a calamity as that the people should perish for want of food'.[5] A week later he was able to write to Peel:

> My election has taken place without so much as a threat of opposition. About four hundred horsemen, <u>mostly farmers</u>, accompanied me to the hustings, and scarcely an angry word was heard [...] I think you will be glad to hear of the result of an election in a purely agricultural

---

1 Hansard, 30 Mar. 1847, XCI, cols. 659-63.
2 Jones, 'The British Army', pp. 246-8, 257-63.
3 PP 1849 (499), IX; 1850 (530), XIII.
4 *DWG*, 12 Feb. 1846.
5 *SWJ*, 31, 7 Aug. 1847; *DWG*, 12 Aug. 1847.

constituency, which was expected by the Protectionists to take signal vengeance upon a member of your Government.[1]

The latter sentiment was more an attempt to boost his chief's morale than a statement of the truth. Herbert's victory was another for his acres. And had there been a contest, he would have been saved by South Wiltshire's Liberal free traders, specifically Lord Radnor's acres. Failing that, there was the borough seat at Wilton. Here, the incumbent Member (Herbert's nephew, Viscount Somerton) faced the ticklish dilemma that his Protectionist father was threatening to disown him for having followed Uncle Sidney in voting for the Repeal of the Corn Laws. Since, if only to oblige his father, he was one of the Peelites now inclined to reunite with the main body of the Conservative party, Somerton offered Herbert his resignation. Herbert answered by telling Somerton 'that nothing would content him but my remaining seated'.[2] This was calculated generosity on Herbert's part: allowing a Conservative to remain at Wilton when he could have installed a free trader was an unspoken quid pro quo for his being allowed to remain undisturbed for the county. Both Herbert and Peel knew that the election as a whole had not gone well for the Peelites. Their numbers in the House were reduced from roughly 120 to somewhere between 80 and 90. Herbert was an increasingly endangered species: only six Peelites were returned for English counties.[3]

Herbert returned from his honeymoon as unenthusiastic for the Commons as he was before he went. He was silent throughout 1848 apart from an important speech of 6 July concerning the electoral system. The young Herbert who had denounced the Reform Bill as revolutionary now admitted:

> that there was much that was bad in the system, and that it would be possible for a wise and practical hand – with time and consideration – to effect great improvements, without risking the institutions which it was the desire of all wise men to maintain unimpaired.

1 Parker, *Peel*, III, p. 488, SH to Peel, 5 Aug. 1847.
2 HRO 21M57/3A1/1, memorandum of 16 May 1846.
3 Conacher, *Peelites*, pp. 28-32.

The particular shortcoming he identified was that 'the representation was not sufficiently varied'. It could be remedied by extending the franchise in some constituencies to give 'the working classes a feeling that they were directly represented'. Paradoxically, his motivation for advocating this was anti-democratic:

> it diminished the tendency, on the part of the people, to what was termed hero worship – the devotion to some demagogue who had hitherto been an object of admiration to the people, and who had spoken to them of the wonderful things he would effect when he should be sent to Parliament. By the admission of men to Parliament who were more upon a level with the working classes, it would induce the working classes themselves not to pay so much attention to the delusive promises that were held out to them.[1]

These were conservative sentiments. But they were not those of the Conservative party, most of whose Members were adamant against the need to modify the 1832 Reform Act. As such, though Radicals envisaged a much greater measure of Reform, Herbert's speech was one signpost, at least, that pointed him in a liberal direction.

Of greater practical consequence in 1848 was Herbert's becoming part of the coterie which purchased the *Morning Chronicle*. Although *The Times* was often favourably disposed towards the Peelites, Peel's followers lacked the outright control of a title which would guarantee them a supportive voice amongst the Fourth Estate. Under the ownership of Sir John Easthope, the *Morning Chronicle* had most recently been a vehicle for Palmerston; in February 1848 Herbert was one of those who took over the controls.[2]

The precise details of the transaction are cloaked in obscurity. Since Herbert was still abroad when the deal for the *Morning Chronicle* was struck, the claim that he was chiefly responsible for it is unlikely. Lord Lincoln was probably chief negotiator. But Herbert was his main financial accomplice. The two men appointed J.D. Cooke as

---

1 Hansard, 6 July 1848, C, cols. 213-17.
2 Conacher, *Peelites*, pp. 47-8.

editor.¹ By the late spring of 1848, the *Morning Chronicle* had become staunchly anti-Protectionist in its stance; thereafter it remained a thorn in Protectionists' flesh. Lord Clarendon believed that Herbert, 'Lincoln and Co. are writing articles in the *Chronicle* that will never be forgiven'. The most unforgiving were written when Derby formed a minority Protectionist ministry in 1852. Malmesbury, his Foreign Secretary, confessed to being bewildered and hurt by 'the most bitter and disparaging articles' written against him by Herbert and Lincoln, 'both of whom have been for years my most intimate and "familiar friends", and I confess their anonymous and treacherous warfare gives me great pain'.² Comments such as these suggest that Herbert's and Lincoln's journalistic assaults on their erstwhile friends and colleagues have been an underestimated factor amongst those which militated against the reunion of Conservatives.

But the *Morning Chronicle* was also prepared to be critical of the Whigs: as a later reporter remembered, 'it was extremely clever, and delighted many of its readers by attacking everybody all round'. In July 1848, for example, it accused ministers of 'an irresolution, a self-contradiction, and an aptitude for bungling, which would suffice to explain any imaginable amount of failure'.³ Such unflattering remarks imparted a spin to the notion of 'a party of observation' of which Peel did not approve. His priority was to keep the Whigs in office. For Herbert and Lincoln that principle was apparently becoming less sacrosanct. The ministry's collapse, after all, might presage a coalition of moderates: Peel, for all his disclaimers, would be the most obvious man to lead it.⁴ After a Liberal-Peelite coalition was finally formed in 1852, Graham was prompted to remark that the *Morning Chronicle* 'is written with great ability and has done the Government good service on many trying occasions'.⁵ It was also of use to Herbert as a vehicle

1 Munsell, *Unfortunate Duke*, pp. 99-106.
2 Munsell, *Unfortunate Duke*, p. 103; Malmesbury, *Memoirs*, I, pp. 316-17; Hawkins, *Derby*, II, pp. 32-4. *Morning Chronicle*, 4 Mar., 12, 19 Apr., 4 May 1852.
3 *The Times*, 4 Feb. 1884; *Morning Chronicle*, 18 July 1848.
4 Stewart, *Politics of Protection*, p. 163; Conacher, *Peelites*, pp. 47-8.
5 WSHC 2057/F4/59, JRG to SH, 29 Oct. 1853.

through which he could publicise his efforts on behalf of female emigration; and, to a lesser extent, his experiments in high farming. But overall it proved a disastrous investment. When the paper was sold in 1854 Herbert was rumoured to have lost £116,000.[1]

So far as Herbert's record in the division lobbies in 1848 and 1849 is concerned, he was far from being neutral between the two main parties. But the key votes in which he took part also illustrate the increasingly centrifugal proclivities of the Peelites. In February 1848, for example, he was one of 29 Peelites who supported the Second Reading of the government's Jewish Disabilities Bill; 43 others did not share his liberal outlook on the question. In June 1848, however, he was one of the Peelites who refused to follow his leader in supporting Russell's plan for compensating owners of West Indian sugar plantations.[2] But siding against the government, still less his political guru, was untypical. When, in March 1849, Disraeli moved a resolution for a committee to consider the burdens of local taxation on land, Herbert spoke and voted against it. In similar vein he was one of the 52 Peelites who defeated Disraeli's call for a select committee on the state of the nation in December. In between whiles, Herbert followed Peel in supporting the government (the Peelites, however, divided only 45 to 33 in favour) in voting for the repeal of the Navigation Acts, the key legislative measure of 1849.[3]

One widely-reported attempt to formalise cooperation between Whigs and Peelites followed the death of Lord Auckland in January 1849. Russell was inclined to offer Auckland's office as First Lord of the Admiralty to Herbert. Palmerston was discouraging: 'My impression as to Sidney Herbert is that he and others of the Peel Party look to forming a Govt. of their own upon the ruins of yours; and that neither he nor any of the others will come out singly to be merged in your cabinet'. Undeterred, Russell approached other Peelites, in particular Sir James Graham. His overtures proved abortive but they have been interpreted as possibly narrowing the gap between the two sides, a

---

1   *The Times*, 4 Feb. 1884; Blain, *Canterbury Association*, pp. 42-3.
2   Conacher, *Peelites*, pp. 49-51.
3   Conacher, *Peelites*, pp. 52, 56; Hansard, 15 Mar. 1849, CIII, cols. 805-9.

harbinger of future coalition. If so, it was not how Herbert saw it. Very probably at his instigation, Russell's manoeuvrings were denounced in the *Morning Chronicle*.[1]

A year later, not much had changed. Herbert's underlying preference remained for Conservatives to reunite. He wrote to Malmesbury, his closest friend amongst the Protectionists: 'I wish I could foresee with any confidence the time when this fiscal question [tariffs] shall be no bar to our cooperation on social and political matters which are far more important to the vitality of this country'. But he could not. He wrote to Lincoln just a few days later that 'The Protectionists are hotter & more noisy than they have been yet & talk very big. On the whole I think their agitation has failed, but an election at this moment wd regain them the English counties.' It would consequently be necessary to continue the increasingly unsatisfactory period of 'political drift'.[2] In February 1850, therefore, Herbert was one of 58 Peelites who found himself backing the government in face of an amendment to the Address moved by Disraeli blaming free trade for the distress in agriculture. He was more amenable to Disraeli's nuanced suggestion later that month that agriculture be assisted by relieving it of some of the burdens (principally the poor rates) of local taxation. Mindful of his constituents' privations, Herbert was one of the 56 Peelites who supported him. It required the 32 Peelites who sided with ministers in opposing Disraeli to negative the motion by 272 votes to 252.[3]

The political kaleidoscope was shaken, temporarily anyway, by Palmerston. Leading Peelites were as one in condemning what they regarded as his provocative and heavy-handed approach to foreign affairs. In the summer of 1850, they were not alone in thinking that he had finally placed himself beyond the pale. The Foreign Secretary had decided to defend the claims of Don Pacifico, a Portuguese Jew who, by

1 HLPP GC/RU/241/2, Pam to Russell, 5 Jan. 1849; *Morning Chronicle*, 16 Jan. 1849.
2 Malmesbury, *Memoirs*, I, p. 190, SH to Malmesbury, 6 Jan. 1850; NUL Ne C 11940, SH to Lincoln, 17 Jan. 1850; WSHC 2057/F4/53, Lincoln to SH, 31 Jan. 1850.
3 Hawkins, *Derby*, I, pp. 373-4.

dint of having been born in Gibraltar, could claim British citizenship. At best a 'businessman' of doubtful probity, Pacifico maintained that property of his had been destroyed during an anti-Semitic riot in Athens. Palmerston demanded compensation and ordered the navy to blockade the Greek capital to ensure that it was paid.[1]

Peelites and Protectionists for once joined ranks in condemnation of a brazen act of gunboat diplomacy. Herbert was a principal speaker in the debate on the motion as to whether the conduct of the Foreign Secretary met with the approval of the House. Leaving the merits of Pacifico's case to others, Herbert damned 'the noble Lord's system of interference [...] it is with shame that I see the foreign affairs of this country conducted in this attorney-like spirit'. He called on the House to:

> Mark with your reprobation that policy which not only by its sentiments and its objects, but also by its tone, has tended to lower the public character of this country, and to produce alienation from, and an aversion to, the British people and the British name.

It was, contemporaries agreed, 'one of the ablest speeches which he ever delivered'.[2] But he was trumped by Palmerston's *civis romanus sum* speech, his famous plea for upholding the right of the ordinary British citizen. Though 67 Peelites responded to Herbert's cry for censure, the Foreign Secretary survived the vote against him by 310 to 264.

The following day Peel was thrown from his horse; he died, in great pain, on 2 July. Herbert relayed the news to Manning:

> He died with great firmness and Christian resignation [...] there is something in its suddenness wh. makes it the more awful [a feeling that] a great statesman was passing away and that each had an interest in a life which had been lavishly devoted to the service of the nation.

Yet for Herbert personally, it was something worse:

---

1   Brown, *Palmerston*, pp. 318-24.
2   Hansard, 27 June 1850, CXII, cols. 520-34; *SWJ*, 3 Aug. 1861.

I have lost much more than a political leader for in no matter of any deep interest or difficulty to myself have I not consulted him & received the full attention & concerned judgement as a father might have given to a son.

It was a Herbert 'visibly affected by the sad scene', who was present in the church gallery at Market Drayton for Peel's funeral a week later.[1]

Peel's death punctuated a year more generally notable for two controversies over religion. The first of these concerned the Reverend George Gorham. In 1847 Henry Phillpotts, the Bishop of Exeter, had refused to institute Gorham to a parish in Devon, judging his views on baptism to be too Calvinistic. Gorham appealed to a judicial committee of the Privy Council. When it found in his favour, on 9 March 1850, High Churchmen expostulated that a secular court was ruling on doctrinal affairs. Herbert described it as a 'crisis'.[2] His wife would recall 'discussions' generated by the judgement which took place at 49 Belgrave Square. Manning, who took the lead in the protests which followed, must have been amongst those present. Herbert, she maintained, was prominent in assisting him. This was untrue. He resisted Gladstone's solicitation to sign a letter from prominent laymen addressed to Bishop Blomfield of London on the matter. When the letter appeared in *The Times* on 23 March, Herbert's name was not one of the twenty MPs amongst the 63 signatories.[3] Not that he was unconcerned. The failure of Blomfield, in June, to get the House of Lords to agree to a Bill making bishops the court of appeal on doctrinal matters, was the moment when several prominent High Churchmen concluded that they could not remain within the Anglican Communion. When Henry Manning, an increasingly close friend in recent years, went over to Rome on 6 April 1851, Herbert's reputation was bound to be affected, even if only by association.

1   Bodleian MS Eng. Lett. C. 657 fols. 46-7, SH to Manning, 4 July 1850; *The Times*, 10 July 1850; *SWJ*, 13 July 1850.
2   Stanmore, I, p. 127, SH to EH, 31 Mar. 1850; Chadwick, *Victorian Church*, I, pp. 250-71.
3   Herbert, *How I Came Home*, pp. 6-7; WSHC 2057/F4/60, WEG to SH, 19, 21 Mar. 1850; *The Times*, 28 Mar. 1850.

Disraeli, who was gossiping in December 1850 that Herbert was 'very fervent, acting under the influence of Archdeacon Manning,' could now report that since Manning was regarded as his 'spiritual adviser', 'S. Herbert is looked upon with a very suspicious eye'.[1] Even Elizabeth appreciated that it was 'an intimacy which might be prejudicial to my husband in his present position'. By mutual agreement, Herbert and Manning agreed to break off all communication.[2]

By April 1851, however, an atavistic outpouring of anti-Catholicism had been provoked by the so-called Papal Aggression. In this controversy Herbert, regardless of the risk to his reputation, refused to be silent. The unedifying episode began in September 1850 when Pius IX announced the restoration of a Catholic episcopacy in England for the first time since the Reformation. Lord John Russell wrote a letter to the Bishop of Durham condemning it. Spontaneous meetings across the nation to the same effect made retaliatory measures irresistible. Herbert's view was that the question was 'of greater importance in a social and religious point of view than any event which has taken place during my life'.[3] Of the impropriety of the papal initiative he was in no doubt: 'I look upon this act of the Pope's as a dangerous religious movement', he wrote, 'to be met by counter-movement, in the ways of increased exertion and activity, each for themselves, among all Protestant churches, by legitimate argument and discussion'. But he did not share the widespread belief that a legislative response was required: 'I have never had faith in combatting religious opinions with Acts of Parliament'. Such an Act would, in any case, contravene his support for the principle of religious liberty. The law as it stood 'allows the full and undiluted exercise of his religion however false or absurd in any way or to any extent, which each man seems best'. Such liberal views put him on a crash course with many Peelites, even more parliamentarians, and most of his constituents.[4]

---

1   Monypenny and Buckle, *Disraeli*, III, pp. 272-4, 302-3, Disraeli to Derby, 7 Dec. 1850, Disraeli to Lady Londonderry, 20 Apr. 1851.
2   Purcell, *Manning*, I, p. 622, Manning to SH, 7 Apr. 1851; Herbert, *How I Came Home*, pp. 7, 9.
3   *SWJ*, 7 Dec. 1850.
4   BL Add. Mss. 79657, fols. 55-61, SH to JRG, 30 Nov. 1850.

Wiltshire's County Meeting to agree a response to the Pope's initiative took place in Devizes on 6 December. Recognising that 'As member for my county I cannot but attend a public county meeting', his conscience allowed him to move the first resolution condemning the Pope's action as an invasion of the royal prerogative. His listeners were delighted when he referred to 'the arrogant blasphemy of that document which assigned to a fallible man the interpretation of the judgement of the Creator [...] It had no more value than if it had been a state document from China'. The rest of Herbert's speech, however, was devoid of the Protestant demagoguery which the assembled freeholders wanted to hear. He was heckled when he insisted that 'every English subject should enjoy all political privileges, and the full exercise of his religion, whatever that may be'. Legislative penalties for what he thought were 'small disabilities' would be un-Christian acts of persecution. Gladstone, on reading an account of the meeting, wryly observed that 'you endeavoured to give a Christian turn to these proceedings – no easy matter'.[1]

The subsequent Ecclesiastical Titles Bill, prohibiting anybody from outside the Anglican Church from using an episcopal title in Britain, was introduced on 7 February 1851. Debate over it dominated the parliamentary session. Whilst Members from both main parties fell over themselves to endorse it, Herbert remained consistent in his opposition. He was one of only 63 Members (most were Irish Catholics) who objected to its coming to the floor. On 18 March, during the debate on the Second Reading, he made what was, at 7,500 words, the longest speech of his career to date. In it he deprecated the Bill as 'precipitate legislation', 'fatal to the best interests of the country', 'embracing as it did the great question of toleration, and being one on which the possibility of governing one-third of the subjects of the Crown must ultimately depend'.[2] Alongside 19 other Peelites (71 voted the other way) he was amongst the minority of 95 who opposed the 438 Members who passed the Second Reading a week later.

1 *SWJ*, 7 Dec. 1850; BL Add. Mss. 79657, fols. 62-5, SH to JRG, 4 Dec. 1850; Stanmore, I, pp. 136-7, WEG to SH, 25 Jan. 1851.
2 Hansard, 18 Mar. 1851, CXV, cols. 164-82.

Seldom has a measure generated more heat than light. Herbert was right to predict its inefficacy; Gladstone had it repealed in 1871. However, it is easy to see why Herbert should have incurred the charge that he was an apologist for the Pope, somebody who might easily join the trickle of High Churchmen who were going over to Rome. Religious innuendo, after all, had followed him for nearly two decades. Even the Crown would seek assurances that Herbert was 'sound' on religion.[1] Much suggests that he was. For all his alleged sympathies for the early Oxford Movement, Herbert was writing to Graham in 1850 of 'Puseyite tom-fooleries' and that 'Tractarianism has had its day. The extremes to which they have lately gone have alienated all the rational men, and they have failed.' At the 1852 election, he was dismissive of taunts that he was both a Puseyite and a Papist: 'I have as firm an attachment to our Protestant faith as anyone alive [...] I differ with my whole heart from those erroneous doctrines by which, I think, their [the Catholic] Church is corrupted'.[2]

Forty years later, though, Elizabeth Herbert would paint a different picture of this period. She maintained that Herbert agonised over which religious road to take, that his leanings towards Catholicism were narrowly outweighed by his calculations as a Peelite pragmatist (between 1850 and 1878, only one peer, the Earl of Abingdon in 1858, announced his conversion to Catholicism). He supposedly told her that:

> he always maintained that as long as the Anglican Church does not force us to believe anything contrary to Catholic truth, we are bound to remain in her communion in spite of her many heretical teachers [...] and that as everything Romanist was looked upon with such distrust and aversion in England, all hope of doing good, or of influencing others and being of use in one's generation, depended on our staying where we were and making the best of it.[3]

1   Bodleian MS Eng. Lett. C. 657 fols. 24-30, SH to Manning, 23 Jan., 21 May 1849; Conacher, *Peelites*, p. 96.
2   *SWJ*, 17 July 1852; BL Add. Mss. 79657, fols. 55-65, SH to JRG, 30 Nov., 4 Dec. 1850.
3   Herbert, *How I Came Home*, p. 9.

Elizabeth insisted that juxtaposed with this short-term realism, her husband spoke of a long-term ideal. He 'was only deterred from following them [Manning and others] by his hope for what was then called "Corporate Union", that is, the merging of minor differences and the return of the Church of England to the old Faith'. Since he believed that this goal would be set back if all those inclining towards Catholicism around mid-century were to convert, he was one of those who hung back from doing so, judging 'that it was better to struggle on and wait'.[1]

Mrs Herbert knew that she would be thought guilty of interpreting her husband's religion through the prism of her own conversion to Catholicism in 1865. The fact that she makes much of the Gorham episode but says nothing about Papal Aggression is obvious bias. Though one would fall short of accusing her of inventing the words she attributed to Herbert, she surely did distort the reality of where he stood in 1850. It is suggestive too that she admits to his insisting on ending their many debates about theological questions from this time onwards. There is no third party evidence that he was talking the language of 'corporate union' in 1850; that notion anyway was not destined to enjoy much of a vogue until the Malines Conversations of the 1920s. Herbert, as he had told Elizabeth a few years before, increasingly appreciated that he owed his religious heritage to an accident of geography. He was an Anglo-Catholic and, as he aged, one more inclined to toleration of those who were not. He found the anti-Catholicism of his countrymen unseemly; hence his distaste for partisan Protestants of all shades. As a landowner in Ireland he had regard for its Catholic clergy and saw them as a vital conduit if better social relations were to be established there. But he had no time for a Papacy that fuelled the religious divide as it had in 1850. A single sentence from a long letter he wrote to Peel from Naples in 1848 is as revealing as any of where he saw himself: 'They [the Holy See] cannot believe that statesmen are ready to accept the religions of different portions of the people, and govern without reference to them, and try to promote peace between them'. Perhaps that was why Nightingale

1   BL Add. Mss. 49270, fol. 148.

told Manning in 1852 that she believed Herbert to be a pantheist, somebody who saw God in everything.[1]

Herbert's talk of toleration in religion, as he had made clear at the County Meeting, was not incompatible with his fervent desire to advance the Established Church. In the wake of the furore over ecclesiastical titles he seized the opportunity to advocate what might be styled Anglican aggression. His objectives were to combat not just 'the progress of erroneous and unscriptural doctrine' but what he perceived to be the larger and more worrying evil of religious ignorance. He, 'and those with whom he acted, had distinct and clear ideas how the Church of England ought to be reformed, and how her ministrations and her pure scriptural doctrines ought to be carried not only into every cottage, but into every cellar, court, and alley in the great cities of this country'. Those ideas included:

> a great extension of the Episcopate, for the purpose of giving to the bishops the power of really exercising episcopal functions, instead of making them isolated beings, of a rank so high, on the one hand, that their clergy could not approach them, or, on the other, of giving them so much work that their clergy could not see them.[2]

Herbert was also adamant that cathedral chapters had to be revitalised. In a pamphlet of 1849 he had written that the cathedral canon too often merited his reputation as 'an indefensible sinecurist', somebody who had forgotten that 'The parish of the Cathedral is not the Close, but the Diocese'. Failings might be overcome, he recommended, by reviving cathedral schools, establishing divinity colleges and prohibiting non-residence. In language which was unmistakably that of the Peelite High Churchman, he said that 'if Chapters are to be retained, they must be made defensible – that is, efficient'.[3]

---

1   Parker, *Peel*, III, pp. 493-5, SH to Peel, 3 Mar. 1848; *CWFN*, III, p. 257, FN to Manning, 19 Aug. 1852.
2   Hansard, 1 July 1851, CXVIII, col. 85.
3   WSHC 2057/F4/51, SH to EH, 28 Feb., 2 Mar. 1849; Stanmore, I, pp. 100-7.

The case which Herbert argued loudest and longest, however, was his familiar one that more churches needed to be built. Even before the Wiltshire County Meeting, he had met with Lord Harrowby (an acknowledged stalwart of Anglicanism) and others to discuss 'a church extension move as a fruit of this wordy excitement'.[1] The result was an address presented by the Archbishop of Canterbury to the Queen on 14 April 1851. To meet its objective that there should be 'no sheep without a fold, nor any flock without a shepherd,' it had been determined that over £2 million was needed to build 600 churches and provide emoluments for the attendant clergy. Herbert, who was one of 59 MPs to sign the address, agreed to serve on the committee for the purpose. 'I believe that the Church of England', he enthused to Graham, 'has that within herself which will always override both Papacy and infidelity in this country'.[2] He matched words with action by sending £500 for a new church to the Bishop of Salisbury. The funds were destined not for the lost souls of Manchester or Bradford but the ungodly denizens of Fisherton on the western edge of the city.[3]

Herbert erred in implying that the Anglican Church had been guilty of inertia. New bishoprics had recently been created for Ripon and Manchester; parish boundaries were being re-drawn to take account of changing population patterns. Over 2,000 new churches had been built in the twenty years before 1851, notably in the new industrial districts. Further, he was out of line with mainstream thinking about cathedral chapters. The 1840 Ecclesiastical Duties and Revenues Act had abolished hundreds of non-resident cathedral appointments: the engine of religious reform was clearly going to be the Ecclesiastical Commission set up by Peel in 1835. But Herbert was right, amid the clamour of anti-Catholicism, to inject a dose of perspective. In the famous religious census of March 1851 Catholics constituted only 1.4% of churchgoers. Far more salient facts were that whilst Anglicans and Nonconformists shared the remainder of the congregations between them in roughly equal numbers, over half

1   BL Add. Mss. 79657, fols. 62-5, SH to JRG, 4 Dec. 1850.
2   *Morning Chronicle*, 24 Apr. 1851; BL Add. Mss. 79657, fols. 55-61, SH to JRG, 30 Nov. 1850.
3   *SWJ*, 16 Aug. 1851; *The Times*, 8 Apr., 21 Aug. 1851.

the population attended no service at all. The level of attendance was worst amongst the industrial and manufacturing working class in the larger urban areas. The religious ignorance of which Herbert spoke was a reality.[1]

A desire to make the nation more godly does much to explain Herbert's interest in education during the 1847 parliament. He had already manifested concern for the subject through attention to schools on his Irish and Wiltshire estates. Herbert also took pride in having overseen educational reform whilst Secretary at War: 'a spirit of thought and providence in the Army was beginning to exist'. Likewise, his plans for cathedral chapters sought 'to apply them to the purposes for which they were originally created – namely, the diffusion of religious and secular education throughout the country'.[2] Not least of the attractions for him of the scheme launched in 1851 to build 600 new churches, was the commitment to provide 200,000 school places as well. The churches themselves, by his logic, after all, were glorified classrooms.

Regardless of motivation, all this placed Herbert well ahead of many contemporaries on education. There was no state provision for elementary education before he entered parliament. Insofar as it existed at all, it was largely the work of two voluntary bodies. These were the National Society, composed of Anglicans; and the British and Foreign School Society, whose supporters included both Anglicans and Nonconformists. Only from 1833 did the State provide financial aid in the shape of an annual grant of £20,000. This was increased to £30,000 in 1839. When Russell proposed raising it further to £100,000 in 1847 Herbert lent the suggestion his warm support. In fact, he went further in expressing the hope:

> that when they came to deal with the question as it affected the Roman Catholics, hon. Members would not revert to party feelings, and that those who acted in a spirit of toleration towards the Roman Catholics

---

1 Evans, *Forging of the Modern State*, pp. 237-44, 426-7; Hoppen, *Mid-Victorian Generation*, ch. 12.
2 Hansard, 1 Mar. 1847, XC, col. 655; 1 July 1851, CXVIII, col. 85.

would not be considered as unfaithful members of their own Church, but that they would agree to extend to all sects all the light which, if they believed in the truth of their own principles, would be the best means of propagating what they thought to be truth.

Russell was amenable but judged, correctly, that the House was not.[1]

Two years later Herbert confirmed his reputation as both a defender of religious liberty and advocate of religious instruction. He welcomed the fact that it fell to Nonconformists (being the majority congregations there) to counter 'irreligion and infidelity' in St Pancras:

> He (Mr. Herbert) would be most happy if the numbers [of Nonconformists] were larger than they were; they would not then, perhaps, hear such lamentable accounts of the spiritual destitution of the people. They had lately heard of the case of some boys who had expressed their astonishment at the things which were taught them – not dogmas of theology or catechisms, but it was said that their exclamation was, 'We have never heard of such a strange thing as the doctrine of the immortality of the soul'. It was a lamentable thing, that in a Christian country there should be persons living who were ignorant whether the soul would exist in a future state or not, who were ignorant of the doctrine of the redemption, and knew not that there was any salvation for them.[2]

Where Herbert drew the line became predictably clear in May 1851. William John Fox, a Unitarian minister turned Rationalist who advocated freer divorce (a combination taxing even Herbert's ideas of Christian tolerance), proposed a motion for free secular schools run by elected committees. Herbert protested that education:

> must be not only secular but likewise religious [...] He contended that no system of education could be successful which was not founded on the full development of the religious system of each religious denomination [...] Whatever religious education was to be got by the

1 Hansard, 26 Apr. 1847, XCI, cols. 1398-9; Conacher, *Peelites*, p. 27.
2 Hansard, 1 Mar. 1849, CIII, cols. 43-4.

children of the poor man, was to be got at the school, and the school only [...] If they excluded all religious instruction from the school, they would virtually deprive the children of the poor of all chance of being grounded in the simplest elements of Christianity.[1]

In a thinly attended House, Fox's motion was defeated by 139 votes to 49.

Diversion of sorts from religious questions during the 1851 session was provided by Herbert's agreeing to chair the Select Committee on the Passengers' Act. One can understand why the role appealed to him: the Acts mostly concerned the transit of emigrants. Between late May and the end of July Herbert presided at sixteen sessions of the committee. The report which he penned, containing recommendations for action, was completed on 2 August. Parliament responded by passing a consolidatory Passengers' Act on 30 June 1852. It laid down a list of provisions with which all passengers should be supplied, the medicines which each vessel should carry, and the number of lifeboats. The further instruction that no spirits should be sold on board bears the obvious impress of Herbert. From the other side of the world the Act was judged to be of 'a very parental as well as of a very stringent character, and it appears well calculated to diminish the chances of accident, disease, and discomfort which passengers in these days of fitful emigration are but too frequently exposed'.[2]

Religious controversy, education, and the comforts of emigrants could not ultimately distract from the fact that the Peelites needed to take stock of where they stood in the wake of their hero's demise. Of Peel's senior lieutenants, Aberdeen, the cultivated but diffident former Foreign Secretary, was his obvious successor; but he was content to pursue a life of quiet detachment in the Lords. Graham, meanwhile, the Peelites' elder statesman in the Commons, was the cause of increasing anxiety amongst Herbert and others on account of his growing predilection for Russell and Liberalism. With Lincoln succeeding his father in the Lords as 5th Duke of Newcastle in January

---

1 Hansard, 22 May 1851, CXVI, cols. 1293-6.
2 PP 1851 (632), XIX; *South Australian Register*, 17 Jan. 1853.

1851, the onus to lead the Peelites in the Lower House perforce devolved upon Herbert and Gladstone. As the latter remembered it, 'Mr Sidney Herbert and I took pains to bring them together, in the recognised modes'.[1]

But where would they lead them? The unexpected necessity of addressing this question arose on 20 February when Russell resigned after his government was defeated on a motion calling for an extension of the franchise. Both Derby and Russell approached the Peelites with a view to forming some sort of coalition. Herbert's first reaction was that the country needed 'a solid & strong government' to end the uncertainty.[2] But since he was decidedly against joining Derby he was happy to concur with Newcastle's recommendation that they should be 'discreet and obdurate to all entreaties or offers from either side'. As the Wiltshire press observed, perhaps informed by Herbert himself, the Peelites for the moment were as much anti-Russell on Papal Aggression as they were anti-Derby on protection. Russell was forced to resume office at the head of what was clearly a weakened ministry.[3]

Put another way, the Peelite leaders had concluded that even without Peel, their strength lay in what Newcastle referred to immodestly as being 'superior'.[4] On balance this meant propping up a Liberal government which more than ever needed their support. They had no chance of preventing the passage of the Ecclesiastical Titles Bill but they could veto the accession to office of a Conservative party under Derby still officially committed to protection. Herbert was consequently amongst the 39 Peelites whose support enabled Russell's government to survive Disraeli's motion on agricultural distress by just 14 votes on 13 February. Having hosted 'a small family party of Peelites to discuss the Budget' he was one of fifty-three of them who

---

1 Brooke and Sorensen, *Gladstone*, pp. 264-5.
2 BL Add. Mss. 79657, fols. 67-8, SH to JRG, 24 Feb. 1851.
3 WSHC 2057/F4/53, Newcastle to SH, 23 Feb. 1851; Reeve, *Greville Memoirs*, pt. 2, III, p. 384, 25 Feb. 1851; *The Times*, 28 Feb., 1, 3 Mar. 1851; *SWJ*, 1 Mar. 1851; Conacher, *Peelites*, pp. 80-3.
4 WSHC 2057/F4/53, Newcastle to SH, 23 Feb. 1851.

helped to reject a Protectionist amendment to it by 278 votes to 230 on 7 April.[1]

But there were limits to Herbert's patience. As the summer recess approached he made clear his lack of confidence in the government's economic strategy: 'a better Budget might easily have been made'. In particular he was unhappy with the Treasury's wish to renew income tax for three years. As he reminded Members it should not become:

> a permanent source of revenue [...] It was imposed distinctly as a temporary tax, for the purpose of effecting certain changes in the fiscal system of the country, and to cover the deficiency which in the course of that purpose would certainly be incurred [...] its inequalities are not so great as those of many other taxes; but they are by far the most visible [...] Another and a paramount objection to the income tax is, that it engenders an immense amount of fraud, and success leads to further experiments, until it reaches an ingenuity of evasion which defies any of the scrutinies which fiscal provisions can impose.[2]

Herbert did not on this occasion translate his protest into a vote against ministers: he was well aware that in the absence of their having a plan to raise revenues that would compensate for the loss of income tax, the Protectionist argument for import duties was waiting in the wings. But he did join Gladstone as one of four Peelites who supported Disraeli's financial resolutions against Russell's government at the end of June.[3]

This ongoing scenario, of Peelites exercising a sort of power but not being in office, was no way to run a country. It was also wearing for the Peelites themselves: Greville thought that 'the party is so scattered that it can hardly be called a party'. Gladstone had already reached a similar conclusion. He suggested to Newcastle and Herbert that if

---

1   Conacher, *Peelites*, pp. 79-88; NUL Ne C 12558/1-3, Newcastle to SH, 19 Feb. 1851.
2   Hansard, 2 May 1851, CXVI, cols. 464-9. Introduced by Peel for three years in 1842, parliament had agreed to renew income tax in 1845 and 1848.
3   Hansard, 30 June 1851, CXVII, cols. 1416-40; Conacher, *Peelites*, pp. 88-9.

Aberdeen refused to 'seize the reins', they should formally elect a leader from amongst themselves for the 1851-2 session. Herbert baulked at such a novel idea, by implication preferring an unofficial leadership whereby the three of them could meet as friends who enjoyed a frank exchange of views.[1] Whilst they were still cogitating, matters were given an unexpected twist in December 1851 when Russell sacked his Foreign Secretary. Palmerston's crime was to have precipitately endorsed Louis Napoleon's coup against the Second Republic: the President was on course to becoming Emperor Napoleon III. Russell, forced to reshuffle his cabinet, made fresh overtures to the Peelites. He met Newcastle on 30 December but their encounter did not go well. Newcastle informed Herbert (whose name was already being rumoured as a replacement for Fox Maule as Secretary at War) not to expect any invitation from the Prime Minister. Herbert was anyway disinclined to accept any offer of office. He (or Elizabeth) wrote on the reverse of Newcastle's letter that it concerned 'the proposed amalgamation'.[2] This rather suggests that he viewed the initiative as one that was inviting him and his friends to surrender their separate identity as a party – the very thing they had just agreed to maintain. In truth, the triumvirate of Herbert, Gladstone and Newcastle had come to be regarded as something of an awkward squad. Greville described them a few days later as 'High Churchmen of a deep colour, which makes it difficult to mix them up with any other party'.[3]

In retrospect these weeks were chiefly important for Herbert in helping to redefine his relationship with Palmerston.[4] Herbert's chief objection to the latter was his style of diplomacy. Removed from the Foreign Office, Herbert could make common cause with him over proposals for the militia. As has been seen, Herbert had been instrumental in plans to revive the militia as Peel's Secretary at War. The Corn Law crisis, an easing of tensions with France, and the advent

1 WSHC 2057/F4/53, Newcastle to SH, 27 Oct. 1851; Reeve, *Greville Memoirs*, pt. 2, III, p. 440, 11 Jan. 1852.
2 WSHC 2057/F4/53, Newcastle to SH, 30 Dec. 1851; *SWJ*, 29 Nov. 1851.
3 Reeve, *Greville Memoirs*, pt. 2, III, p. 440, 11 Jan. 1852.
4 Stanmore, I, p. 147.

of a Liberal government intent on holding down expenditure, had pushed the subject down the political agenda. Palmerston, however, had been a persistent voice in government arguing the necessity for a reformed militia. The case finally received a favourable hearing in the wake of Louis Napoleon's coup, an event which revived both Frenchmen's dreams of *La Gloire* and Englishmen's fears of invasion. Russell introduced a Militia Bill on 16 February 1852.[1]

Palmerston agreed with Herbert that the government's proposals were insufficient. Russell was proposing only a local militia. As Herbert explained:

> the local militia could not be removed out of their respective counties, except in case of invasion, or under the immediate apprehension of invasion, while the general militia could be moved at any time, without any such condition, on the notification of any such apprehension. The local militia, therefore, was less efficient than the general, and, therefore, less fit to be a model.[2]

Whilst Russell, as Herbert pointed out in a second speech, was prepared to give ground over wording, he would not concede the substantive point. The government lost the division of 20 February on Palmerston's amendment to the Militia Bill by 136 votes to 125. Russell took umbrage and resigned.

The episode is remembered, in Palmerton's famous characterisation of it, as his 'tit for tat with Johnny Russell'. But Herbert's part in it, as the Peelites' chief spokesman on military affairs, should not be underestimated. Had the nine Peelites who followed him into the anti-government lobby voted the other way, Russell would have survived.[3] For most of the rest of the year, however, Palmerston chose to sit next to Herbert below the gangway on the Opposition benches. He told Disraeli that though he did not 'act in concert' with Herbert, he was 'an old personal friend'. This was stretching the point

1 Partridge, *Military Planning*, pp. 128-33.
2 Hansard, 16 Feb. 1852, CXIX, cols. 587-9; Partridge, *Military Planning*, p. 133.
3 Hansard, 20 Feb. 1852, CXIX, cols. 869-70; Conacher, *Peelites*, p. 97.

– Palmerston was 26 years older than Herbert; the friendship was with his father – but his moving closer to Herbert in 1852, both politically and physically, was an important portent for Herbert's future.[1]

Russell was succeeded in Downing Street by Lord Derby as head of a minority Protectionist government. To discuss the position they should adopt towards it, Herbert gave a dinner for the leading Peelites in Belgrave Square on 26 February. As Gladstone recorded it:

> we set to immediately after Mrs Herbert left the room and discussed the matter till half past eleven. Sidney Herbert threw off by declaring our position to be that of men who only differed on free trade and as such that they should sit below the gangway on the government's side [...] Thus he made his start freely enough but the opinion he had stated he did not rigorously or toughly sustain in our ensuing debate.[2]

Perhaps, as host, Herbert did not think it right that he should dominate the debate. But letters written shortly afterwards make clear what he wanted: that Derby should ditch protection and call an election that would allow Peelites and moderate Protectionist Conservatives to come together. The latter should therefore be afforded 'any facility & any bridge to cross over without a taunt or a reproach'.[3] There existed, Herbert believed, 'the materials, both in men and in measures, for a sound and practical Government, if the men do not get so bespattered in this transition from Protection to Free Trade opinions'. As he expounded in greater detail to Gladstone:

> What the country wants is a progressive Conservative Government, heartily for Free Trade, willing to apply still further the principles of reduction to all taxes of an elastic character, which will regain the amount of their produce by increased consumption consequent upon

---

1 Benson and Esher, *Letters of Queen Victoria*, II, pp. 402-3, Derby to Victoria, 25 Nov. 1852.
2 Brooke and Sorensen, *Gladstone*, p. 109.
3 WSHC 2057/F4/51, SH to EH, 21 Mar. 1852.

diminished duty, not opposed to Parliamentary Reform, though stout against mere democratic infusion.[1]

The problem was, as Herbert recognised, that 'anxious as the Govt are to throw over Protection they will, I have no doubts, have a strong body of supporters determined if possible to keep them to it'. For this reason, he agreed with Gladstone and Aberdeen that 'the matter is too crude and too difficult and important for anticipating any conclusion and that our clear line of duty is independence until the question of Protection shall be settled'.[2]

Herbert was distracted at this juncture by unwelcome domestic news from Paris: Robert Pembroke's predilection for high living had been interrupted by a cocktail of bronchitis, blisters and other ailments. It was such 'a hopeless state of illness' that Herbert's elevation to the House of Lords as 13th Earl was considered imminent.[3] Summoned by electric telegraph, Herbert and his sister, Catherine, Dowager Countess of Dunmore, set off for the French capital. For over a week Robert hovered between life and death, so ill that in his more lucid moments he promised to start attending church as proof of his determination to lead a better life. It was, reported Herbert, 'a very painful state of things', with 'madam' [Marie Schöeffer] 'there more continuously in order to keep us away'. But the crisis passed and the half-brothers parted. They had got on amicably enough: Herbert was even introduced to the Earl's three children.[4]

With Robert out of danger, Herbert had time (an unwelcome visit to an eminent American dentist excepted) for more agreeable diversions. 'I am enerveille [sic] with the beauty of the Town', he related in one of his daily updates to Elizabeth, 'far exceeding that of any town I ever saw [...] the gaiety & brilliancy of the streets is very striking'. He visited the Louvre twice. Herbert was also at the Tuileries

1   BL Add. Mss. 44210, fols. 44-6, SH to WEG, 30 Mar. 1852.
2   WSHC 2057/F4/51, SH to EH, 21 Mar. 1852; Brooke and Sorensen, *Gladstone*, p. 119.
3   WSHC 2057/F4/51, SH to EH, 19 Mar. 1852; *Freeman's Journal*, 23 Mar. 1852.
4   WSHC 2057/F4/51, SH to EH, 19, 20, 21, 30 Mar. 1852.

to witness Louis Napoleon's opening the *Corps Législatif* and Senate. 'One has the feeling that it is history', he recorded, 'though not history of a very high class, or giving any precedents that will be useful to mankind except as warnings'.¹

When Herbert returned to England and parliament, he and Gladstone had a new balancing act to perform. Instead of having to persuade their supporters to buttress a Liberal ministry on key votes, they now had to restrain those who would have been happy to throw in their lot with Derby's government before an election. As Herbert put it in somewhat apocalyptic tones to Elizabeth, 'the necessity of maintaining a strong body of independent Liberal-Conservatives to contest and overthrow the ultra-Tory element and tendencies of the present Government is more than ever necessary for the safety of the country'. In an attempt to maintain some sense of the Peelites' identity as a third party, he and Gladstone organised political and social gatherings of their increasingly restless troops: Belgrave Square was the venue for a dinner to 22 MPs, the 'fag end of the Peel Party', in May.² At least they no longer had to worry about Graham. He made a speech at Carlisle on 24 March, announcing that 'the wanderer had returned' and that he would stand as a free trader in tandem with a Radical at the next election. Herbert was typically caustic on hearing the news, dismissing Graham as 'a strange mixture with great ability & considerable experience & considerable foresight as to what is to occur but none as to how he ought to behave'.³

So long as Derby made no attempt to re-impose protective duties, Herbert was perfectly prepared to support his government. The best example of this was provided in March when Spencer Walpole, the Home Secretary, introduced a revised version of the Whigs' Militia Bill. In proposing to establish a militia of 80,000 men, this came close to matching Herbert's ambition for the institution. 'They had proclaimed through the mouths of two Governments', he told the House, 'the necessity of defence, and, having so done, if they now

1 WSHC 2057/F4/51, SH to EH, 25, 29 Mar. 1852.
2 WSHC 2057/F4/51, SH to EH, 22 Mar. 1852; BL Add. Mss. 44210, fols. 47-8, EH to WEG, 15 May 1852.
3 Ward, *Graham*, p. 257; WSHC 2057/F4/51, SH to EH, 31 Mar. 1852.

fell back without making an attempt to remedy the evils they had themselves not only admitted but proclaimed, they would be guilty of treason to the welfare of the State'. In a bravura performance, he proceeded to regale his listeners with a history of the militia, and to spell out in detail the necessity for rejuvenating it.[1] Most Peelites joined with him in helping to secure the Bill a comfortable majority on its Second Reading. In an unforced compliment it was, of all people, Disraeli, who informed the Queen that next to Walpole it was Herbert who had 'made their greatest efforts' and been 'distinguished' in their speeches. Herbert, Disraeli added, was 'singularly happy in his treatment of a subject of which he was master'.[2] The Bill became law on 7 June.

Herbert had grounds to be aggrieved, therefore, when less than a week following his speech ministers accused him of factious opposition. His lengthy rebuttal gave voice to sentiments hitherto confided in private. The speech can be interpreted (perhaps Herbert consciously intended it to be so) as his own updated version of a Tamworth Manifesto. Conservatives across the floor from him were exhorted to draw a line under their Protectionist past and to make common cause for the future:

> My object is to see the country well governed, and to see sound principles prevail. If there is a bridge to be built, and I could contribute an arch to it, to enable you to escape by a frank avowal of free-trade principles from the dilemma in which you are placed, I would cheerfully add that arch [...] I say that, wishing to see sound progressive Conservatism prevail in the Government of this country, I do look upon it as a great misfortune that a large party, comprising many men of public as well as private virtues, should identify itself with a cause which is hateful to the people [...] the Government having taken the course which it has on the subject of protection, the

---

1 Hansard, 26 Apr. 1852, CXX, cols. 1158-67; BL Add. Mss. 79657, fols. 71-8, SH to JRG, 24 Apr. 1852; Partridge, *Military Planning*, pp. 133-4.

2 Benson and Esher, *Letters of Queen Victoria*, II, p. 471, Disraeli to the Queen, 26 Apr. 1852.

only way in which this question can be permanently or satisfactorily settled is by an appeal to the country, and I wish to see that appeal come to as soon as the public business will admit.[1]

Herbert's wish was granted when parliament was dissolved on 1 July. The election that followed was a quiet affair: Derby went to the country as much searching for a policy as presenting one for its approval.[2] For Herbert personally, though, the campaign was anything but quiet. He was embroiled in controversy in three constituencies, demonstrating once again a preparedness to dirty his hands in the grubby process of electioneering.

The first of the three constituencies was County Dublin where Herbert was rumoured as a possible candidate. His 'enormous' influence there, allied to the certain support he would receive from Catholics, Whig and moderate Protestant voters, was said to make his return inevitable.[3] He did not stand but he was, to the inevitable fury of some, reported to be backing two Catholic candidates.[4] This was untrue: he urged Conservatives and Liberals to share the representation. But this, in effect, meant that he was endorsing the more popular of the two Liberal candidates, the diplomat Augustus Craven. Craven was both a Catholic and, allegedly, a member of the Catholic Defence Association set up to defend the rights of Catholic tenant farmers.[5] Whilst Protestant Tory landlords looked on askance, Herbert insisted, 'as one having a large interest in the peace and well-being of County Dublin', that he had a legitimate right to interfere in the election as he saw fit. In the event, two Conservative candidates were returned with a comfortable majority.[6]

There was never any doubt, by contrast, that Herbert's wishes would prevail at Wilton. Even so, the events there were remarkable. Herbert's nephew, Viscount Somerton, announced that he was

1 Hansard, 5 Apr. 1852, CXX, cols. 707-10.
2 Stewart, *Conservative Party*, pp. 244-5.
3 *The Times*, 9 Mar. 1852.
4 *The Times*, 8 July 1852.
5 *The Spectator*, 4 Apr. 1891.
6 *Freeman's Journal*, 6, 12 July 1852.

standing down. This was probably at Herbert's insistence since the two were at odds over both protection and the Ecclesiastical Titles Act. Herbert's nominee as Somerton's successor was Charles A'Court, his brother-in-law. A body of disgruntled farmers responded by putting up a London lawyer, Jeremiah Greene, to oppose him. Greene pulled no punches. He attacked Herbert at the nomination as a 'mighty man' who had changed course. A'Court was a stooge, who, if elected:

> would faithfully represent Mr Sidney Herbert's opinions [...] he came to tell them that their borough was no longer to be handed down with the silver spoons and the other heirlooms of the house of Pembroke [...] that it was to be free, that it was to be raised from the dust, and never more to be oppressed.[1]

Greene received just 26 votes against the 125 cast for A'Court. But this represented Wilton's first polled contest since 1710. Even in his own political backyard, Herbert was far from universally popular.

The greater challenge was to Herbert's South Wiltshire seat. He had already been taunted with cries of 'whining' and 'turn him out' as he struggled to gain a hearing at a County Meeting on distress in March 1849. In 1850 there were concerted efforts by Protectionists to register new voters. Protestant hackles, as we have seen, were then raised by the stance Herbert had taken on the Ecclesiastical Titles Bill in 1851. By May 1851 Protectionists had secured a formidable candidate in Richard Penruddocke Long, scion of a Wiltshire family whose ancestors had sat for the county centuries before the parvenu Herberts had even arrived there.[2] It could have been worse. Long was laid low with illness in Spain during the campaign, whilst the retirement of the elderly John Benett, Herbert's parliamentary colleague since 1832, opened the door to Long and Herbert sharing the representation without a contest. Their agents were reported to have reached an understanding to that effect. If so, Herbert now risked overplaying his hand. William Wyndham threw his hat into the ring as a free trade Conservative; his

1 *SWJ*, 10 July 1852.
2 *SWJ*, 31 Mar. 1849, 5 Jan. 1850; *DWG*, 29 July 1852

candidacy was widely believed to have been orchestrated by Herbert.[1] Wyndham denied that he came forward 'under his [Herbert's] wing', but he may have been protesting too much. The two men were friends; Wyndham had nominated Herbert at the 1845 by-election. Herbert stood accused of opportunism and 'duplicity' in the contest which followed. In the event he was returned with Wyndham ahead of Long by just 248 votes. It had, as he admitted, been a close run thing: 'the great mass of the tenants voted against me, and amongst them those connected with the property with which, by near relationship, I am connected'.[2] His victory left a sour taste in the mouth.

For all that Herbert's activities during the 1852 election were dubious, the general election as a whole generated more heat than light; Aberdeen may have inadvertently touched a nerve when he told Herbert that the electorate had been too morally obtuse to see 'political shuffling and dishonesty in its true light'.[3] Gladstone estimated that 26 'pure' Peelites were returned of the 40 or so who had sat in the 1847 parliament. More importantly, Derby, though he had increased his support by about 20 seats to approximately 300, was still nearly 30 seats short of an outright majority. It was easier to say what the electorate had not voted for than what it had. On the former point there was broad agreement that it had not voted for the Corn Laws.[4]

Disraeli for one believed that the election provided sufficient mandate for Derby to announce the abandonment of protection. His preferred course of action was that Derby should attempt to enlist Palmerston to their colours and 'that when Palmerston has joined, Gladstone and Herbert will follow'.[5] James Wilson, owner of the *Economist*, who had been returned as a Liberal for Westbury in Wiltshire at the election, did not share this perception. He reported to Russell that 'the treatment' meted out to 'Mr Sidney Herbert here from the supporters of Ld Derby will show them [the Peelites] that

1 *The Times*, 1 July 1852; *DWG*, 15, 22 July 1852; *SWJ*, 17 July 1852.
2 *SWJ*, 17, 24 July 1852; *DWG*, 22 July 1852; Hansard, 14 June 1853, CXXVIII, cols. 183-93.
3 WSHC 2057/F4/53, Aberdeen to SH, 26 Oct. 1852.
4 Stewart, *Conservative Party*, pp. 254-7.
5 Vincent, *Stanley Journals*, pp. 74-5, 12 July 1852.

they can never join his government'. Following a lengthy conversation with Herbert, Wilson had formed the opinion that Herbert 'seemed more than ever alienated from the present Government'.[1] Russell was sufficiently encouraged by this news that he asked Graham 'to ascertain whether Gladstone and Herbert would act with the Whigs, & whether the two could act with the Radicals'.[2] Neither would. Never one to under-estimate his own abilities, Russell responded with another offer, made through Lord Aberdeen: could the latter 'ascertain whether Mr Gladstone and Mr Sidney Herbert would be disposed with you and the D. of Newcastle to concert with the Whigs the course to be adopted when Parlt. meets'.[3]

There was a distinct feeling here, with parliament not scheduled to meet until November, of going round in circles. Herbert, for one, would write in late October that 'We appear to me to meet this Session, so far as combination is concerned, exactly as we parted in July last'.[4] In the interim he had taken himself off to the continent, stopping off briefly in Paris to catch up with a revitalised Robert Pembroke before continuing on to Germany.[5] His aspiration that the road to a progressive Conservative government would have been cleared by Derby and Disraeli declaring against protection *before* the election had not been realised. Clearly dispirited about the state of politics, Herbert complained that:

> The 'little man' [his irreverent name for Russell], seems to me never to have understood the nature or amount of the change effected by his own reform bill [...] Lord John is not aware how sick the country is of the Whigs & of himself, nor how much they fear the Radicals.

But Derby's government was at least as bad, hypocritical in the extreme if it was now intending to announce an end to its commitment to protection as an opportunistic response to the election result.

---

1 Conacher, *Peelites*, pp. 124, 204.
2 Parker, *Graham*, II, p. 166, Russell to JRG, 19 July 1852.
3 BL Add. Mss. 43066, fols. 87-90, Russell to Aberdeen, 21 July 1852.
4 BL Add. Mss. 43197, fols. 101-10, SH to Aberdeen, 22 Oct. 1852.
5 *SWJ*, 7 Aug. 1852.

Herbert feared that this would prove to be either an act of political self-immolation, or worse, if successful, consolidate Disraeli's position in government: 'He has a great sagacity & no scruple, & his preference, insofar as he had any for any set of opinions, has no doubt always been in favour of Free Trade'.[1] It was far better, in Herbert's opinion, to enjoy his time abroad, return in time for the autumn session, and then judge the Derby government on the basis of what it proposed to do.

Soon after arriving home in September, Herbert was invited to Broadlands, Palmerston's seat in Hampshire. He had not been there for many years. Reporting on the visit to Gladstone, Herbert described his host in predictably ungracious terms: 'Palmerston like all the septuagenarians is in a hurry and being of sanguine disposition he believes in all those castles in the air which he builds'.[2] The particular castle to which Herbert alluded was Palmerston's notion that the Marquis of Lansdowne might be persuaded to take the premiership as the Whig most likely to persuade moderate Liberals and Peelites to serve together. Herbert peremptorily scotched the idea on grounds of age: Lansdowne, who was 71, had been Chancellor of the Exchequer as long ago as 1806. His time abroad had reinforced him in the view that the Peelites should remain independent. Whilst he was happy, therefore, to see Derby's government given 'plenty of rope', Herbert believed that entering into a formal coalition to defeat it would be construed as factious: 'Strangers cannot suddenly swear an eternal friendship'.[3]

Strangers could, however, unite in mourning the Duke of Wellington who died on 14 September. Herbert heard the news whilst journeying in Wales the following day. His reaction was typical of his countrymen: 'a gap is created by the absence of this great name [...] certainly he was the noblest citizen England ever had, and his memory & example will still form the character of many who come after him'.[4] But Herbert's own relationship with Wellington was a curious one. Forty years his junior, he knew him only as a politician. Had

1 BL Add. Mss. 44210, fols. 49-52, SH to WEG, 11 Aug. 1852.
2 BL Add. Mss. 44210, fols. 59-64, SH to WEG, 21 Oct. 1852.
3 BL Add. Mss. 43197, fols. 101-10, SH to Aberdeen, 22 Oct. 1852.
4 WSHC 2057/F4/49, SH to Lady Pembroke, 16 Sept. 1852.

the rumours that Lady Mary Herbert was about to become engaged to Wellington's second son, Lord Charles Wellesley, proved true, he would have become his nephew by marriage.[1] Though he first entered parliament as the Duke's avowed supporter, invoked his name on the hustings and eulogised his leadership in the Lords, the two were never close. There is virtually no surviving correspondence between them; Wellington seems never to have stayed at Wilton. And whilst they sat in cabinet together and cared passionately about national defence, the Duke evidently harboured suspicions about the young civilian's predisposition to reform his beloved British army. On the other hand, when Herbert and Elizabeth became engaged, 'The Duke had been saying the kindest & prettiest things to Lord Heytesbury about you both'.[2] Elizabeth Herbert was subsequently a visitor to the elderly Duke's favourite summer retreat of Walmer Castle: he had a penchant for young, intelligent, politically-aware females.

Herbert reserved his hero-worship for Peel but he respected Wellington and was in London for his State funeral at St Paul's on 18 November. Considerably more than a million people witnessed the grand procession which accompanied the huge iron carriage bearing the Duke's coffin to the cathedral. The masses loved it. Herbert the High Churchman, as he admitted to his brother-in-law, found it mostly repugnant:

> We had all been anticipating some dire misfortunes & accident from the press of people coming from all over the country to see the funeral, to my mind the whole thing is most 'painful' as it replaces dignities 'with a mere show' and is treated as a junket rather than as the most solemn & mournful occasion the Country has ever seen.[3]

Obsequies completed, attentions turned at last to the working out of the summer's election result. The Queen's Speech of 11 November had been ambiguous on the question of free trade: it qualified an admission that the industrial classes were now better off with the

1   WSHC 2057/F1/12, unidentified press cutting of 1832.
2   WSHC 2057/F4/50, Lady Clanwilliam to SH, nd, July 1846.
3   HRO 21M57/5/13, SH to Normanton, 15 Nov. 1852.

observation that agriculture had suffered. Herbert was amongst those 'much dissatisfied and disappointed' by what he heard. In response to the speech, C.P. Villiers, a Radical, moved an amendment, on 23 November, asserting that free trade had been 'wise, just and beneficial'. Herbert, who had met with fellow Peelites at Aberdeen's five days before, was amongst those who thought that this went too far. Various versions exist as to the detail of what happened next but Herbert was closely involved. A counter-amendment was formulated, to be presented by Palmerston. Gladstone's recollection was that 'he did this at the express request of S. Herbert and mine, and we carried the amendment to him at his house'. Palmerston moved the amendment on 25 November. It asserted that trade had improved since parliament had 'established the principle of unrestricted competition, and abolished taxes imposed for protection'; and called on the legislature to consider future proposals 'consistent with those principles'.[1]

The government's fate hung on the four day debate which followed. Herbert spoke on 26 November.[2] His speech consisted of an all-out assault on a government which, in his judgement, had preached protection but now, dishonourably, wished to claim that it had not. He would therefore vote for Palmerston's amendment 'as the last and crowning act of a great controversy', one that would finally vindicate Peel's actions. Not that the latter was necessary:

> the memory of Sir Robert Peel requires no vindication – his memory is embalmed in the grateful recollections of the people of this country; and I say, if ever retribution is wanted – for it is not words that humiliate, but deeds – if a man wants to see humiliation –- which, God knows, is always a painful sight – he need but look there [pointing to the Treasury bench].

If this was not already personal enough, Herbert then proceeded to excoriate Disraeli for his opportunism:

---

1   Brooke and Sorensen, *Gladstone*, p. 128; Morley, *Gladstone*, I, p. 433; Conacher, *Peelites*, pp. 149-57.
2   Hansard, 26 Nov. 1852, CXXIII, cols. 602-12.

For my part, I acquit the right hon. Gentleman the Chancellor of the Exchequer, as far as his own convictions are concerned, of the charge of having ever been a protectionist. I never for one moment thought he believed in the least degree in protection. I do not accuse him of having forgotten what he said or what he believed in those years. I only accuse him of having forgotten now what he then wished it to appear that he believed.

Contemporaries were shocked by Herbert's vitriol. *Fraser's Magazine* judged it 'the sole outburst of indignant anger which his admirable temper ever allowed him within the walls of Parliament: when with kindling eye and quivering frame, and outstretched arm, he launched at Mr Disraeli, fairly cowering on the Treasury bench'.[1] Peel's whining valet had, in this debate at least, played the part of his late master's political rottweiler. Palmerston's amendment was carried by a clear majority; protection was damned by 468 votes to 53.

Herbert's speech is best remembered now as the one in which he exhibited an unseemly anti-Semitism.[2] Whilst not seeking to exonerate him completely, it is only fair to see his remarks in context. In the first place, the full sentence needs to be read, not just the offending final phrase: 'I recollect an observation made by a witty contemporaneous writer, to the effect that all religious sects in free countries succeeded in making converts except the Jews; and he asked rather quaintly how it could be expected that any man would become a convert to a faith, the profession of which must begin with a surgical operation?'[3] Herbert, in other words, was paraphrasing (or so he claimed), not coining, a quip of his own devising. How Members received it was not recorded; it was the reference to the humiliated government front bench that most remembered. Nobody, it might be noted, had taken him to task for an equally blatant anti-Semitic remark in an 1845 speech when he said that soldiers who were paid prize money 'might either be robbed of it by the Jews, or be induced to spend it in debauchery'. Most would probably have been more amused than offended had

1 *Fraser's Magazine*, 'Herbert', p. 208.
2 Blake, *Disraeli*, pp. 336-7
3 Hansard, 26 Nov. 1852, CXXIII, col. 610.

they seen Herbert's comment about Disraeli in a letter to Lincoln in 1847: 'I dare say [he] has a portrait of Pontius Pilate in his dressing room'.[1] Herbert was simply voicing a contemporary stereotype: plenty of Disraeli's supporters spoke of him in uncomplimentary terms as 'the Jew'. In Herbert's case it was his deep-seated personal animus for Disraeli, more than any racial prejudice, which informed his speech in November 1852. Herbert, it should be remembered, was one of a relatively small minority of Members (for example one of forty-four on 21 July 1845) who had supported various versions of the Jewish Disabilities Removal Bill since at least 1845.

Remarkably, for all its personal and political bile, Herbert's speech had not entirely ruled him out of the government's calculations for a stay of execution. When Gladstone met Derby at a party the next evening, they found it politic to agree that Herbert's speech probably 'went beyond his intention'.[2] Derby was intimating to Malmesbury, on 28 November, that he was still considering the possibility of finding room for Herbert at the cabinet table alongside Palmerston and Gladstone.[3] But Herbert had surely cast his die. In any event, the debate which began on 3 December when Disraeli presented his budget to the House proved terminal. With Herbert and most of the remaining Peelites filing into the 'no' lobby, it was defeated in the Commons by 305 votes to 286. Derby resigned on 17 December. Aberdeen accepted the Queen's commission to replace him.

The claim that Herbert played a pivotal role in taking the Peelites into coalition, or 'fusion', with the Liberals, and that without him 'considerable evils, in all probability, must have ensued', is exaggerated.[4] But he was certainly involved. The day after Aberdeen accepted the Queen's commission, Herbert invited Gladstone and Newcastle, amongst others, to Belgrave Square. Over dinner they made up their differences with another guest, Graham, who had been frozen out of their counsels since the spring because of his Carlisle speech.

1 Hansard, 1 July 1845, LXXXI, col. 1409; NUL Ne C 11939, SH to Lincoln, 9 Apr. 1847.
2 Morley, *Gladstone*, I, pp. 434-5.
3 Malmesbury, *Memoirs*, I, pp. 368-9, 24, 25, 28 Nov. 1852.
4 *Fraser's Magazine*, 'Herbert', p. 204.

Palmerston, another vital player in the drama, chose to let it be known, via Herbert, that he would head the opposition in the Commons 'if not included in the pending arrangement'. Aberdeen himself several times turned to Herbert for advice during the delicate negotiations which took place down to the end of December. On Christmas Eve, for example, 'afraid there is some new difficulty', Herbert summoned Gladstone to join Aberdeen and himself in Belgrave Square, in an attempt to resolve it.[1]

Commentators reasonably took it for granted that Herbert would be happy to be part of the new coalition government.[2] In public Herbert agreed that he and his friends 'had been long enough in a state of isolation'. It was:

> an excellent situation to occupy if you wish to criticise other men's measures, but except as criticism, I know of little good that you can do in such a situation. It is like the fable of the bundle of sticks. Separate them, and they are easily broken; tie them together, and they acquire strength and consistency.[3]

In private though, Herbert dreaded the thought of a return to government. Christmas Day in consequence was 'the dreariest one I ever passed [...] I confess I am out of all heart [...] one cannot tell at any moment what the next hour will bring'.[4] Aberdeen contemplated putting him at the Admiralty, possibly at the same time raising him to the Lords as debating ballast. In the end Herbert accepted the offer of his old office as Secretary at War. He was at Aberdeen's on Boxing Day as part of the inner circle convened to discuss junior appointments.[5]

Herbert's preferred scenario in the years between 1846 and 1852 had been for Conservatives to reunite as a re-branded progressive party. He was by, inclination, a liberal Conservative. Almost by

---

1 Conacher, *Aberdeen*, p. 13; Parker, *Graham*, II, pp. 192-3; BL Add. Mss. 44210, fols. 67-8, SH to WEG, 24 Dec. 1852.
2 *The Times*, 24 Dec. 1852.
3 *SWJ*, 15 Jan. 1853.
4 BL Add. Mss. 44210, fols. 68-9, SH to WEG, 25 Dec. 1852.
5 Conacher, *Aberdeen*, pp. 21, 24, 29.

default, at the end of 1852 he found himself cast as a conservative Liberal. In terms of policy, the key determinants for Herbert in this process were economics and religion. Conservative reunion was impossible for Peelites whilst protection remained the official policy of the party led by Derby and Disraeli. But church questions impeded what would otherwise have seemed Herbert's obvious road to the Liberal party. Religious questions, after all, not economic ones, had brought Herbert into politics. The Tory party was the natural home of High Churchmen. It is true that Herbert had become repulsed by the religious bigotry and intolerance of some sections of the Conservative party, but he viewed some parties to the Reformer alliance of the 1830s as enemies of the Church. This was far less of an issue by the 1840s but the Liberal party which preached civil liberty had also introduced the Ecclesiastical Titles Bill which he abhorred. This could at least be rationalised as an aberration. It was not an insuperable obstacle to allying with the Liberals in the same way that the Corn Laws was one preventing his forging new alliances with the Conservatives.

Herbert's decision to join Aberdeen's coalition, however, was as much about personalities as policies. Above all, he was determined to act in concert with Aberdeen, Gladstone and Newcastle. If Aberdeen advocated in December 1852 that Peelites should coalesce with Liberals, so be it: at least there was some safety in numbers. And it sugared the pill immeasurably that Aberdeen was to be Prime Minister. Towards Palmerston, Herbert's former animosities had mellowed. He still thought him 'very conservative' with a 'readiness to believe whatever he wishes'.[1] But these were not disqualifications to serving with him, especially as Palmerston was to be Home, not Foreign Secretary. Russell, 'whose general conduct in the House had inspired him [Herbert] with feelings of respect' in 1848, was another matter. By 1852 Herbert was more his acerbic self when he wrote that 'The country does not hold that the only business of a statesman out of office is to get in again, which I suspect is Lord John's creed'.[2] The

---

1 BL Add. Mss. 43197, fols. 101-10, SH to Aberdeen, 22 Oct. 1852.
2 Hansard, 6 July 1848, C, col. 217; BL Add. Mss. 43197, fols. 101-10, SH to Aberdeen, 22 Oct. 1852.

two must have looked odd standing together: Russell at less than five feet, four inches tall; Herbert's slender frame making him appear more than his six feet. But at least Herbert could stomach sitting with him in cabinet as Foreign Secretary.

The same was not true of Disraeli; Herbert could never forget or forgive his treatment of Peel. And since Derby (about whom Herbert had no obvious strong feelings) would not abandon Disraeli, serving alongside him, even if protection had been abandoned, would never have been easy. Richard Cobden had it right in October 1852 when he wrote that 'so long as Disraeli continues at the head of the Tory party, I do not see how Gladstone, S Herbert, & the rest of Peels followers can ever rejoin them'.[1] The individual who decided to sit Disraeli between Herbert and Gladstone at a Royal Academy dinner in 1850 was either unbelievably politically ignorant – 'they seemed to have made somewhat of a blunder', wrote the meat in that improbable sandwich – or possessed of a malicious sense of mischief.[2]

Herbert reflected to his mother on New Year's Day 1853 that 'Everything has certainly turned out very differently from what I had expected a few weeks ago'. Even now he blamed Disraeli: 'I think the Jew was determined at all events to make a union impossible [...] and not to risk his ascendancy in his [i.e. Derby's] Cabinet which seems to have been complete'.[3] This was palpably unfair. Was Herbert himself not partly to blame? The verbal assault he delivered on 26 November against his putative allies had surely destroyed some of the bridges he had talked about building only months before. And was he not also guilty, a failing common amongst the Peelite leaders, of exhibiting an undue sense of superiority? Why, after all, should a parliamentary party of 300 Members submit to the entreaties of 40 or so erstwhile traitors and abandon their *raison d'être* as Protectionists? Herbert's use of the phrase 'There is joy over every sinner that repenteth', in a speech

---

1 Howe, *Cobden Letters*, II, pp. 429-30, Cobden to G. Wilson, 4 Oct. 1852.
2 Monypenny and Buckle, *Disraeli*, III, p. 250, Disraeli to Sarah Disraeli, 13 May 1850.
3 WSHC 2057/F4/49, SH to Lady Pembroke, 1 Jan. 1853.

of April 1852 urging them to do just that, was more than a touch sanctimonious.[1]

But Herbert was not in the best of tempers at the start of 1853. Over the previous six years he had been taunted with accusations of betraying his party, repeatedly of 'whining', and frequently of being an apologist for the Pope. Even his philanthropic acts of building churches and heading the Female Emigration Fund had attracted criticism. Duty had now called him to join a government whose sympathies did not especially accord with his own, and which anyway might be short lived. In many respects he had been well suited to his role of the previous half-decade, essentially one of looking down from the political fence on the shortcomings of others. It was, therefore, he told his mother in his New Year's Day letter, commiserations, not congratulations, that she should be sending him:

> I hope the new Government may do good service. We shall be fired into by both extremes, and it will be anything but pleasant. I felt it was my duty to help in any way I could, and if we fail, at any rate, as the old Duke [Wellington] used to say "we shall have done our best."
>
> I wonder sometimes how any one can engage on public life; and yet the willingness of men of fortune and station to undertake the labour and the cares, and face the abuse, is what maintains this nation. Still, sometimes, when I look at little George, I think, "When you grow up, if you want something to do, sweep a crossing, but don't go into Parliament."[2]

---

1 Hansard, 5 Apr. 1852, CXX, col. 709.
2 WSHC 2057/F4/49, SH to Lady Pembroke, 1 Jan. 1853.

8
Crimean Prelude 1852-1854

'England does not love coalitions', observed Disraeli, when Derby's government fell in December 1852. The fact that Aberdeen's ministry survived for barely two years suggests that he had a point. It was never a strong administration, relying as it did on the support of Irish Members for a majority in the Commons. Aberdeen could never feel entirely secure: the votes of his 50 fellow Peelites would have been of little avail without those of the 270 Liberals with whom they coalesced. Even half the cabinet over which Aberdeen presided was made up of Whigs. But it was the fortunes of war that would sweep it away: in its first eighteen months in office, Aberdeen's administration has been judged to have presided over a 'substantial' package of reforms.[1] Herbert contributed his fair share to these achievements and not just those at the War Office. In consequence his reputation continued on an upward trajectory whilst, at the same time, his outlook in domestic affairs moved notably further in a liberal direction. More realistic than most in his stance on foreign affairs, it was little fault of his that Herbert found himself in what seemed like a political cul-de-sac by the summer of 1854.

Herbert's first action on returning to office, however, sprang from his High Church convictions. He wrote to Aberdeen on Christmas Day, concerned that the Prime Minister had recommended Edward Strutt to be Chancellor of the Duchy of Lancaster. Strutt was, Herbert believed, a Socinian, that is to say somebody who rejected the

1 Chamberlain, *Aberdeen*, p. 468.

doctrine of the Trinity. This was objectionable in itself but the more so since the Chancellor had some church patronage at his disposal. Herbert felt sufficiently emboldened to suggest alternative names for the office. Aberdeen ignored them.[1] There remained limits both to Herbert's liberalism on religious affairs and the degree to which Aberdeen was prepared to be influenced by his young High Church minister. However, Herbert and Gladstone, in face of criticism, did lobby successfully to get the High Church Walter Kerr Hamilton appointed to the vacant see of Salisbury in May 1854.[2]

Resisting measures which he deemed damaging to the Church, for instance the 1853 Union of Benefices Bill, and the 1853 Episcopal and Capitular Estates Bill, remained a salient feature of Herbert's record in the Commons.[3] He remained even more conspicuous in his support of initiatives which increased church accommodation. In Wiltshire such occasions remained the ones at which he was most likely to be seen in public, for example the re-opening of Amesbury Church, and the consecration of the new church in Fisherton, Salisbury, towards whose building he had contributed £500.[4] In parliament, in July 1854, he made a substantial speech in support of the Church Building Acts Amendment Bill. This provided for the demolition of churches where there were too many, with any resulting revenues being used to erect new churches in places where there were too few. Observing, with mock irony, that he might now be considered a Utilitarian, Herbert instanced the example of Bethnal Green where:

> there were plenty of parishioners but no congregation – and even when a congregation was collected a great difficulty was experienced in inducing them to behave in church with ordinary decency and decorum. They had never been to church before, and they therefore did not know what they were to do when they got there. During the service the whole place was filled with a buzz of conversation; in

1 WSHC 2057/F4/53, SH to Aberdeen, 25 Dec. 1852.
2 *SWJ*, 25 Mar. 1854; *DWG*, 27 Apr. 1854.
3 Hansard, 2 Mar. 1853, CXXIV, cols. 886-8; 3 Aug. 1853, CXXIX, cols. 1218-20.
4 *SWJ*, 29 Jan., 10 Dec. 1853.

addition the congregation employed themselves in cracking nuts, and every day after the service was concluded, orange-peel and nut-shells were swept out by basketsful [...] and as regarded the question of dealing with consecrated buildings he would beg to point out that the people were not for the churches, but the churches for the people.[1]

Irish affairs, by contrast, proved relatively untaxing for Herbert during this period. They were most prominently in the news during the spring of 1853 when, in his capacity as Secretary at War, he was criticised for endorsing the recommendation that the number of military pensioners at Kilmainham Hospital be reduced. Herbert's motivation, it was alleged, was 'the love of centralisation which characterises the Red-tapism of the Whig Peelite school of administrative talent'.[2] Herbert protested that he was merely continuing a policy put in train by his two predecessors. Unpersuaded, Irish Members combined to defeat the government on the question on 12 April.[3]

Less contentious was a visit to Mount Merrion in October 1853. An enjoyable day at the Great Industrial Exhibition in Dublin was tempered by the less happy duty of attending the funeral of his land agent, Major Fairfield. The lucrative vacancy was filled by Herbert's brother-in-law, Charles A'Court.[4] This blatant piece of nepotism aside, Herbert's reputation for being a good landlord remained intact: later that year the press related the instance of how a reporter 'when travelling some time through Ireland [...] asked, "What sort of character his landlord, Mr Sidney Herbert, bore?" and we marked the reply – "Wisha, yer honour, he's just a rale prince, and may he live all the days of his life, and when they are over, may life begin again!"'[5] The compliment was indirectly underscored by Herbert's shock at what he saw of Ireland during a visit to County Mayo in 1854. He wrote to Gladstone that 'after an excursion to a country as wild as anything in

---

1 Hansard, 6 July 1854, CXXXIV, cols. 1260-3.
2 *Dublin Evening Post*, 10 Mar. 1853; *DWG*, 21 Apr. 1853.
3 Hansard, 12 Apr. 1853, CXXV, cols. 1065-8; Conacher, *Aberdeen*, p. 125.
4 *SWJ*, 22, 29 Oct. 1853; *Dublin Evening Post*, 15, 25 Oct. 1853.
5 *SWJ*, 10 Sept. 1853.

the Falkland Islands!' where roofless houses testified to homes from which poverty-struck families had been evicted by their landlords:

> It looks like a country over wh. war has passed. Of that population some are in America, some in the workhouses, a vast portion died at the roadside & yet there has been no outrage. What a singular mixture these people are.[1]

Back in England, Herbert sat in a cabinet that comprised six Whigs, six Peelites and a Radical. He sat relatively low in the pecking order. Russell occupied the Foreign Office; Palmerston was at the Home Office. Gladstone, promoted to the Exchequer, confirmed his reputation as the most precocious of the younger Peelites. Graham, next to Aberdeen, the senior Peelite, became First Lord of the Admiralty. Lincoln, since 1851 in the Lords as Newcastle, became Secretary for War and the Colonies. He had overtaken Herbert in the cabinet hierarchy. Herbert, as Secretary at War, was only ahead of the Duke of Argyll, who had been appointed Lord Privy Seal.

It is easy to forget that these ministers had come together in opposition to the Conservatives' budget of December 1852, and that they coalesced in pursuit of a programme of progressive reform. At the South Wiltshire by-election necessitated by his return to office, Herbert made clear his awareness of both points. In a widely reported address he afforded his audience a less than riveting dissection of Disraeli's budget speech before spelling out his hopes the new government would extend free trade, and bolster education. Economic prosperity and education, he maintained, contributed to 'the advancing morality and intelligence of the people'. And since it was imperative to maintain 'continued harmony' between the nation's institutions, it followed that Parliamentary Reform merited serious consideration. It was the most liberal speech of his career thus far.[2]

One of the first proposals put before the House, in March 1853, was the Jewish Disabilities Bill. Herbert had been conspicuously absent

---

1 BL Add. Mss. 44210, fols. 145-6, SH to WEG, 19 Aug. 1854.
2 *SWJ*, 15 Jan. 1853.

from the division lobbies when three previous versions of the measure, in 1848, 1849 and 1851, had passed the Commons only to fail in the Lords. Now, in denouncing sectarianism, he made one of the strongest speeches in its favour:

> this House must reflect their different opinions, or it is not an accurate representation of the country [...] the great truth which, after all our changes of constitution, has now became an axiom is, that no British-born subject should be excluded from his political rights on account of his religion.[1]

The Bill met the same fate as its predecessors. Herbert's votes for it, though, marked further mileposts on his journey in support of the cause of religious liberty.

The government's main priority in 1853 was the budget. Gladstone devised an ambitious plan to abolish income tax by 1860. However, in the short term he argued the paradox that income tax would have to rise: it would make good the shortfall in revenue which would result from his reducing tariffs in furthering the government's commitment to extend free trade. Herbert presumably acted as a sounding bound for these ideas when he and Mrs Gladstone visited Wilton for a few days between late March and early April. During the inevitable excursions to Stonehenge and Salisbury Cathedral which ensued, Herbert may well have argued his preference for a reduction in income tax from 5d in 1854 to 3d by 1860, even though Newcastle considered the latter 'a sum hardly worth collecting'.[2] What is certain is that Herbert was one of four ministers who voiced objections to the detail of Gladstone's proposals at the cabinet meeting of 12 April. His particular objection on that occasion was to Gladstone's wish to extend the joys of income tax to Ireland. Herbert persisted in his opposition; Gladstone compromised. There were no hard feelings. After his celebrated budget speech of 18 April, lasting four-and-three-

---

[1] Hansard, 11 Mar. 1853, CXXV, cols. 104-8; Conacher, *Aberdeen*, pp. 103-5.
[2] *SWJ*, 2 Apr. 1853; NUL Ne C 12558/1-3, Newcastle to SH, 19 Feb. 1851; Shannon, *Gladstone. Peel's Inheritor*, p. 268.

quarter hours, was over, he invited the Herberts to come 'home with us and [we] had soup and negus'.[1]

Herbert played an even more prominent part in the arguments which took place about the future government of India. He formed part of a cabinet committee charged with reviewing the role of the East India Company, whose charter was due to be renewed. Arguments about the question overspilled into the full cabinet; they continued at a dinner given to ministers by the Herberts in Belgrave Square on 25 May. Herbert's opinion was that India should be governed by a single authority, though he advised delaying a final decision until 1854. He was confounded on both points. The 1853 India Act retained the dual (that is to say Crown and Company) system of government. But Herbert did welcome the provision which introduced competitive exams for the Indian civil service.[2] In November, as a good Peelite convinced of the efficiency which would be born of meritocracy, he also welcomed the recommendation contained in the famous Northcote-Trevelyan report that competitive examinations be introduced for sections of the home civil service.[3]

Proposals to reform the University of Oxford saw Herbert voice his opinions more publicly. In 1845 he was one of thirty-three alumni who signed a letter to heads of houses. It accused them of failing to make adequate educational provision 'in proportion to the growing population of the country, its increasing empire or deepening responsibilities'.[4] A commission on Oxbridge reform had subsequently been established in 1850. The Aberdeen government introduced a Bill, for Oxford only, in March 1854. Herbert joined the debate at the committee stage in response to the Radical MP, James Heywood, who moved an amendment abolishing the requirement for students to subscribe to the 39 Articles on matriculating. Heywood's intention was

---

1   Brooke and Sorensen, *Gladstone*, pp. 136, 138, 142; Chamberlain, *Aberdeen*, pp. 457-9; Morley, *Gladstone*, I, p. 468.
2   Brooke and Sorensen, *Gladstone*, pp. 145-6; Conacher, *Aberdeen*, pp. 81-4.
3   Chamberlain, *Aberdeen*, p. 462.
4   BL Add. Mss. 44210, fols. 14-15, SH to WEG, 2 Aug. 1845; PP 1854 (90), X, pp. 470-1.

to open up Oxford to Nonconformists. Herbert opposed Heywood's proposal, raising memories of his maiden speech of 1834. But the grounds for Herbert's opposition in 1854 were tactical: he believed that the Bill so amended would have less chance of passage through the House of Lords. To the principle of Heywood's amendment, civil and religious liberty, he lent his full support:

> the maintenance of this exclusion was no longer either politic or necessary, whilst, with regard to the interests of that large class, the Dissenters, whom Parliament was bound to consider, he felt that their exclusion from these institutions, at the same time that it did not add to their stability, was a grievance and a natural ground of complaint.[1]

In the event Heywood's amendment was passed and the Oxford University Act received the Royal Assent in August. By establishing a Hebdomadal Council, a more representative body to regulate the University's governance, the measure inaugurated what has been called 'a quiet revolution in Oxford life'.[2]

Herbert was anything but a revolutionary when it came to the secret ballot. In June 1853 he made the main speech against the annual Radical motion calling for it to be introduced.[3] The motion was defeated by 232 votes to 172. He was more of an evolutionist, however, when it came to the electoral system, a dangerously divisive question for Aberdeen's government in 1853-4. As Herbert had made clear at the South Wiltshire by-election, he favoured a moderate instalment of Reform. He was not, therefore, so alarmed as some of his cabinet colleagues when Lord John Russell, the government's standard bearer on the question, put forward a Bill that proposed taking 70 seats from the smaller boroughs and redistributing them to places where population growth was most pronounced. Herbert, with Wilton surely in mind, expressed doubt that Russell had properly identified his target. The Bill, he said,

---

1 Hansard, 22 June 1854, CXXXIV, cols. 518-22.
2 Conacher, *Aberdeen*, pp. 334-44; Chamberlain, *Aberdeen*, pp. 461-2.
3 Hansard, 14 June 1853, CXXVIII, cols. 183-93.

tends rather to the diminution of rotten than of corrupt boroughs. When there is nomination, there is of course no corruption for there is no struggle. The popular demand is for the suppression of corrupt boroughs but that is merely an impossibility and nomination boroughs are no longer maintainable as a part of the constitution & as they were argued before the Reform Bill.

Herbert also voiced concern over Russell's criterion for redistribution. More seats, he felt, should be given to 'learning or learned professions' whilst many, though ostensibly going to county seats, he found on close inspection to be earmarked for 'rather an aggregate of towns than counties in the ordinary sense'. Herbert's views were similarly nuanced on the question of who should vote. Russell proposed new £20 county and £6 borough voting qualifications.[1] Herbert's suggestion, on the basis that it demonstrated thrift and responsibility, was to enfranchise those with money in savings accounts. This was a good example of his preference for 'inequalities & varieties in the suffrage because the society to be represented is composed of unequal and various materials'. In general terms, however, he thought Russell's scheme 'for an extension & a considerable one', about right. But his motivation, unlike Russell's, was unashamedly conservative: a desire to put the issue to bed for a generation and more: 'If we open this question it ought to be so dealt with as to be closed'.[2]

Russell introduced his Bill in the Commons on 13 February. A fortnight later, in face of opposition, and with war against Russia looming, he decided against proceeding further until after Easter. Herbert wrote him a long letter agreeing that this was the correct decision: 'The people are so possessed by the gambling excitement of the chances of war that they will listen to nothing else [...] The country cannot entertain two such subjects as war & reform simultaneously. Its capacity for excitement is not large enough'.[3] Herbert likewise concurred with the line agreed in cabinet on 3 March that there

---

1   Prest, *Russell*, pp. 361-2.
2   BL Add. Mss. 44210, fols. 112-15, SH to WEG, 1 Jan. 1854.
3   TNA 30/12/11/C, fols. 797-802, SH to Russell, 28 Feb. 1854; Conacher, *Aberdeen*, pp. 298-9.

should be a further delay until at least the end of April. But this was too much for Russell. He informed Herbert of his belief that war (declared on 28 March) would be used as a pretext for dropping the Reform Bill altogether. His inclination was to resign, a step that would almost certainly have spelt the end of the government.[1] That he did not owed much to Herbert's smoothing of his prickly colleague's ego. On 11 April, in what has been described as 'a special effort to break the impasse', Herbert wrote Russell a long letter in which he employed a range of arguments: that a Reform Bill at that moment would go down to defeat, that its doing so would set back the cause for the future, that Russell had a duty to stay in the government at a time of national emergency, and that the country would not forgive him if he did not. For the future he dangled the carrot that the Reform Bill could be reintroduced early in February 1855.[2]

Russell signified his intention to remain in office by return. He utilised some of Herbert's arguments when he explained to the House why the Reform Bill would be postponed.[3] Speaking in the same debate, Herbert could reasonably claim that honour had been satisfied. He assuaged Russell's disappointment further by flattery: Herbert hoped that he 'may finish that great work of Parliamentary reform with which his name, his honour, and his fame will be indissolubly connected'. Ignoring the obvious untruth of his opening assertion, Herbert also provided fresh proof of how far his stance on Reform had changed over the course of his generation in politics:

> I have never feared Parliamentary reform; I have seen the growing intelligence and power of the working classes. I have long seen the true conservation that exists in extending to them that Parliamentary power which they are capable of exercising. I wish to see the basis of our representative system enlarged. I wish to see those who are without, and who may be enemies, taken into the citadel and converted into

---

1 WSHC 2057/F4/53, Russell to SH, 31 Mar. 1854; Chamberlain, *Aberdeen*, p. 468.
2 TNA 30/22/11C, fols. 955-8, SH to Russell, 11 Apr. 1854.
3 WSHC 2057/F4/53, Russell to SH, 11 Apr. 1854; Hansard, 11 Apr. 1854, CXXXII, cols. 836-44.

defenders. My opinions in favour of Parliamentary reform, so far from being weakened, are strengthened.[1]

Herbert's contributions to the legislative successes of Aberdeen's government have been under-appreciated. The fact that his speeches in the Commons during this period, filling 35 columns in Hansard, ranks him only the sixth most active cabinet member, is a crude yardstick by which to judge his performance.[2] He also spoke, for example, on 19 days during 1853, and 33 days during 1854. Measured by his presence in the division lobbies, the years 1853 (177 votes) and 1854 (149 votes) were easily the busiest of his parliamentary career: this level of attendance was roughly twice the average for Members as a whole. Of greater significance, Herbert embraced liberal causes during this period far more than he ever had before. And how is one to quantify the value of his emollient temperament in a government whose leader was in a weak parliamentary position whilst having to manage some strong and difficult cabinet colleagues? In October 1853 Prince Albert, no mean judge, intimated to Aberdeen that Herbert was one of the younger Peelites who had impressed the Court by the abilities which he had displayed since coming into office.[3] Herbert, it might be noted, was now often mentioned in the press as having dined with members of the royal family. Further proof of the esteem in which he was held in high places was his presence as one of a select group at the private chapel in Buckingham Palace for the baptism of Prince Leopold, Victoria and Albert's eighth child, in June 1853.[4]

The most widely reported assessment of Herbert in these years, hardly uncritical, yet indicative of his rising stock, appeared in the *Athenaeum* in September 1853:

1   Hansard, 11 Apr. 1854, CXXXII, cols. 868-70; *SWJ*, 15 Apr. 1854. Russell had been a member of the committee which devised the Great Reform Bill.
2   Conacher, *Aberdeen*, p. 118, n. 3.
3   Conacher, *Aberdeen*, pp. 128-9.
4   *Dublin Evening Post*, 30 June 1853.

We have heard from more than one source that there was no member of the old aristocracy of England for whom the late Sir Robert Peel entertained as much respect as Mr Sidney Herbert. How often have we ourselves seen, in the chill morning dawn, the late statesman, after some great party debate, walk slowly across Palace Yard, the erect collar of his surtout up to his ears, leaning on Mr Sidney Herbert [...] No doubt he wants *vivida vis animi*, [vigour of mind and body] and is too much at home in the salon. He is too sentimental to be sturdy in debate, too aesthetical to be vigorous in action. He cannot generalise his views with the inductive logic and laconic felicity of Lord John Russell, – he cannot intimidate a long row of clamorous adversaries, like Mr Disraeli, with a frown and an invective, – he never could bully a troublesome opponent, while affecting merely banter, like Lord Palmerston, – nor can he guide the understanding, in the mazes of subtle argument, with the ingenuity of Mr Gladstone. But he can bring to whatever party he joins the weight of a great English name [...] An Aristocracy, if fertile in example of virtue, might bid defiance to the leveller; and if nobility is to bear a part in our mixed Constitution, the character of its leading members must be of incalculable importance. So, inheriting a renowned name, himself illustrating it by high personal qualities, and stamped with the decisive attribution of Peel, – Mr Sidney Herbert may challenge even hostile criticism to impeach his claims to a seat in the Cabinet.[1]

Herbert's main claim to a cabinet seat was his record as Secretary at War. One of the first demands on his time, at least, was enjoyable: hosting a reception at his Belgrave Square home. It was attended by a thousand guests headed by the Queen's cousin, the Duke of Cambridge.[2] The daily routine for those who worked in the War Office was less leisurely. Some 1,069,371 letters were received there in 1852, nearly three times as many as had been received in the mid-1830s. The number of clerks, meanwhile, had increased only from 50 to 85. Herbert could hardly be accused of exaggeration when

---

1   *SWJ*, 24 Sept. 1853.
2   *SWJ*, 30 Apr. 1853.

he wrote that 'the war office has discharged a good deal of additional business during the last years without any additional advantages'.[1] But when Herbert pressed for more clerks to cope with the yet greater burdens imposed on his department by the 1852 Militia Act ('The raising of 80,000 militia is I can assure you no small affair as a matter of detail'), Gladstone's Treasury was prepared to countenance the appointment of only temporary clerks. Herbert regarded this as an 'ineffective substitute'. It would be far from the last or biggest clash between the two friends.

Starved of funds, Herbert had to manage as best he could. He introduced examinations for junior clerks. When vacancies for promotion occurred, he spoke to the head of the relevant department and sought their recommendation. His guiding principle was that advancement must be by merit: 'I have always adhered to it most rigidly'. Despite this, administrative processes during his stewardship appear to have remained cumbrous. Junior clerks would prepare memoranda, forwarding them up through a hierarchy of more senior clerks. Numerous emendations and suggestions littered the documents which finally came before Herbert's eyes.[2]

Herbert's biggest concern, however, was the familiar one he outlined to the House eight months before resuming office: 'the Navy was only the first line of defence, and if it were broken through, we ought to consider what was best to be done to compensate for that disaster'. In an ideal world the answer remained to increase the size of the army. He dismissed as 'a very false impression' claims from Radical Members that there were already 130,000 men who could be called upon in the event of invasion. The official figures for the number of infantry and cavalry under arms was 101,937. But many of these were overseas, in Ireland or on home garrison duty. Herbert estimated that there were no more than 45,000 regulars who could be deployed against an invader. To supplement them, in an auxiliary capacity, there were just 14,000 volunteer yeomanry (Herbert remained active as

---

1   BL Add. Mss. 44210, fols. 87-94, SH to WEG, 23 Mar., 14 Apr. 1853.
2   PP 1854-5 (247), IX, p. 199; Jones, 'The British Army', pp. 292-3.

captain of his Wiltshire troop) and 9,000 army pensioners.[1] But the former remained no more than an amateur mounted police force; the latter, though better, 'would not', Herbert insisted, 'give us a force at all commensurate for the purposes of defence with that which had been given by the militia'.[2]

It was the militia, therefore, to which Herbert looked as part remedy for his problem. As we have seen, events had overtaken Herbert's hopes of reviving the institution in 1846, but his return to office coincided with the implementation of the 1852 Militia Act of which he had been a prominent supporter. After a generation in abeyance, there were inevitable teething problems which he assisted in seeking to resolve. Fishermen, he ruled, would be better enrolled as naval or coastal than militia volunteers.[3] Far more problematic was the discouraging state of affairs in Northumberland as relayed to him by Lord Grey: there were insufficient qualified men to oversee training; gentlemen completely unversed in military affairs were refusing to accept commissions beneath the rank of captain; only 400 of 1,200 rank and file had ever had any sort of training. Worse, 279 had taken the bounty given to volunteers and then failed to appear for training, 'chiefly the very worst inhabitants of Newcastle, habitual thieves & vagabonds with a very large proportion of Irish tramps'. But this was more colourful than representative. Herbert's considered view was that 'Upon the whole, tho' necessarily attended with much difficulty at the outset the calling out of the militia has been very successful'. He was able to report to the House that 62,000 men had been enrolled in militia regiments by August 1853. The exercise had demonstrated that 'the military spirit is by no means extinct in the population' and that the 'recruit can be converted into a soldier in a far less time than the theory of the army allows'.[4]

---

1 Hansard, 26 Apr. 1852, CII, cols. 1158-67; *SWJ*, 14 May 1853; Jones, 'The British Army', p. 316; Strachan, *Wellington's Legacy*, pp. 203-11.
2 Hansard, 25 Feb. 1853, CXXV, cols. 657-8.
3 PGL GRE/B109/10, fol. 16, SH to Grey, 29 July 1853.
4 PGL GRE/B109/10, fols. 3-5, 10-15, Grey to SH, 6 July, 1 Aug. 1853; Hansard, 8 Aug. 1853, CXXIX, cols. 1470-1.

More enthusiastic than most about the possibilities for the militia, Herbert was also more alive than most to the potential of the nation's rapidly developing rail network. In 1832 there were just 166 miles of track in Britain; by 1850 there were 6,000. Herbert provided clear evidence that he appreciated the positive implications this had for national defence when he appeared as a witness before the Select Committee on the Devon and Dorset Railway Bill on 22 June 1853. In a lengthy testimony, he revealed a detailed knowledge of which stations were already connected to which, those towns which were served by broad or narrow gauge lines (or both), and the advantages to communication conferred by the electric telegraph. But mastering such detail was necessary if he was to make his case that Portsmouth, Exeter and Plymouth should be connected, both to improve the defence of the south coast and link its major arsenals.[1]

Even so, as Herbert pointed out, the various auxiliary forces, still less railways, did not constitute a properly integrated reserve force for the army. Russell suggested to him that remedy lay in raising a force of 25,000 new regulars, and using them to replace men who had already served as regulars for more than seven years, the latter then forming a reserve.[2] Herbert, together with Hardinge (now Commander-in-Chief), refined the idea. They proposed that pensions be offered to regulars with more than 10 years' service on condition that they agree to serve in reserve battalions for periods of either 11 or 22 years. The great drawback with both this and Russell's scheme, as Herbert knew full well, was that implementing it would deprive regiments of many of their best troops. As he told the House in February 1853, 'The men of ten years' service and upwards formed the real strength of the Army, from their length of service, experience, and habits of attachment to their standards [...] the House would be surprised to find how few they were'. Raising 25,000 new men for the regular army would also

1 PP 1852-3, (705), pp. 107-16.
2 Strachan, *Wellington's Legacy*, p. 217.

severely impact upon the pool of men available for the militia. For the moment, at least, the plans for a reserve were shelved.[1]

In the battle for manpower, therefore, Herbert had to acknowledge defeat. Presenting the military estimates for 1853-4, he asked for a sum of £6,025,016 to maintain a cavalry and infantry force of 102,283. This was only marginally more than Beresford, his Conservative predecessor, had asked for the previous year. Making a virtue of necessity he went on to point out that his request was £132,766 lower than the one granted in 1835 ('which was always taken as the pattern year of economy'), when 21,000 fewer men were being maintained.[2] In fairness Herbert's failure to get what he really wanted was preordained. He never spoke a truer word than when he said that 'through every government and every Parliament we have always had the same stereotyped system of economy in military affairs'.[3]

On the strength of the above evidence, it would be easy to dismiss Herbert's record at the War Office as bereft of achievement. Such a judgement would fit well with the popular narrative of the Crimean War as a catalogue of disasters fought by an army unchanged since 1815. But it would be wrong. We have already seen that Herbert earned a reputation as a reformer during his first stint at the War Office. More recent scholarly studies, even though they afford Herbert little of the credit, have concluded that army reform was a reality in the decades after Waterloo. In terms of personnel, the prospects for reform at the end of 1852 had rarely been more encouraging. The Reverend George Gleig, with whom Herbert had cooperated fruitfully on army school reform in 1845-6, was still Chaplain-General of the Forces, and Inspector-General of Military Schools. Lord Fiztroy Somerset, who became Lord Raglan in October 1852, and who had long enjoyed cordial relations with Herbert, had been appointed Master-General of the Ordnance in September. Most important of all, Sir Henry

---

1   Hansard, 25 Feb. 1853, CXXIV, cols. 657-8; Strachan, *Wellington's Legacy*, pp. 217-18. Herbert did, however, return to it in 1859 when Secretary for War.
2   Hansard, 25 Feb. 1853, CXXIV, cols. 670-92; Jones, 'The Army', pp. 315-16.
3   Gash, *Pillars of Government*, p. 49.

Hardinge, who had been Secretary at War (1841-4), was now Lord Hardinge and had succeeded Wellington as Commander-in-Chief. Like Herbert, popular and pragmatic, the two men 'shared a close personal friendship and regard for Peel'.[1]

Herbert was soon able to give fresh substance to the established perception that he was the soldiers' friend. His 1845 proposal to grant £150 towards the cost of outfitting to cavalrymen who had risen from the ranks to gain commissions (£100 to those who had done so in the infantry) was finally implemented in January 1853. The military estimates for 1853-4 included £2,000 to allow for an increase in good conduct awards for non-commissioned officers.[2] On 6 June 1854, having chivvied Hardinge to get it done, Herbert signed a warrant abolishing off-reckonings. These were deductions made from a soldier's pay which went to his colonel, ostensibly for providing him with his uniform. Herbert regarded the practice as inefficient and, though he did not say so, open to abuse: Prince Albert earned notoriety when it was revealed that he had made £1,840 profit from clothing the Grenadier Guards. By contrast, Herbert earned praise for a reform 'which he and his friends may well be proud of'.[3] Some of Herbert's initiatives, motivated by an over-zealous desire to economise, received less ringing endorsement. This was particularly so of the royal warrant, issued in February 1854, announcing that soldiers should be issued with 'best seconds bread' to reduce expenditure 'in dear seasons at home'. Herbert's defence that 'the same kind of bread was frequently used by the aristocratic classes on account of its exceedingly wholesome and nutritious quality', was ill-received.[4] And whilst the decision by Horse Guards to cut the amount of gold lace used in officers' uniforms provoked no widespread outcry from those who wore them, Herbert had to issue a reply to a petition from London's gold and silver lace

1 Strachan, *Wellington's Legacy*, pp. 37-8.
2 *SWJ*, 29 Jan. 1853; Hansard, 25 Feb. 1853, CXXIV, col. 672.
3 BL Add. Mss. 46448, fols. 10-21, SH to Hardinge, nd, May 1854; Hardinge to SH, 15 May 1854; *The Times*, 27 Feb. 1854; Hansard, 31 July 1854, CXXXV, cols. 1056-7.
4 PP 1854 (169), XIX, p. 530; Hansard, 25 Feb. 1853, CXXIV, cols. 669-70.

weavers in which he attempted to reassure them that their livelihoods were not thereby threatened.¹

It might be considered doubtful that any of the above made the army a more effective fighting force. Not so the creation of training camps. Though the credit for this has gone largely to Hardinge, Herbert had previously suggested the idea to Wellington only to be told that the nation would not stand for war games in peacetime. Aware, however, that the patriotic stirrings occasioned by the Great Duke's passing created a favourable climate, Herbert included a figure of £7,000 for a training camp in the estimates for 1853-4. As he explained:

> we had been in the habit of using our Army far too much as a police force in aid of the civil magistrates, spreading it for this purpose in separate detachments all over the country, so that the men had had no opportunities for field practice, or scarcely a chance of seeing two regiments brigaded together, with a view to the acquisition of a knowledge of manoeuvres on anything like a large scale [...] A very small sum would suffice to provide a station where there could be ball practice with the Minié rifle; non-commissioned officers, and a certain proportion of men from each regiment, would there be enabled to acquire the practice of rifle firing at various distances, and, with this practice thoroughly attained, would then return to their respective regiments, and communicate that scientific practice to their comrades; the whole Army would thus by degrees be brought into one system of effective firing.²

The practical outcome was that over 16,000 men took part in field exercises at Chobham during the summer of 1853. They proved to be a popular public spectacle. By May 1854 nearly £100,000 had been spent on acquiring 4,000 acres of Aldershot Common as a permanent training base.³

1 *SWJ*, 2 Sept 1854.
2 Hansard, 25 Feb. 1853, CXXIV, cols. 679-80.
3 Jones, 'The British Army', pp. 287-90; Strachan, *Wellington's Legacy*, pp. 166-70; Stanmore, I, pp. 177-8.

Herbert warrants credit too for making the financial case for placing 'in the hands of our soldiers a weapon lighter, and equally efficient, in every respect, with the Minié rifle'. This was the Enfield Pattern 1853 rifle-musket, which superseded the percussion muskets with which infantrymen had been issued in the 1830s. A leading authority on such matters judges this 'the most important single change in tactics in the British army until the appearance of heavy field artillery following the Boer war'. The switch was accompanied by Hardinge and Herbert's successful push to establish a musketry school at Hythe to raise shooting standards.[1]

Education, however, remained the facet of army reform with which Herbert was most commonly associated. His earlier scheme for Normal Schools had been endorsed and extended by his successors. He took it further still in 1854. The existing system, by which army schoolmasters were remunerated by a small stipend supplemented by fees, was superseded by one according to which:

> there should be three fixed rates of pay, into which the fees should be merged applicable to three classes of schoolmasters [...] promotion from one class to another should be by merit, and by merit alone [...] the hope of appreciation and reward would be in this, as in other professions, the very best stimulus to exertion [...] I hope that it will also improve the somewhat anomalous position of the regimental schoolmaster, who is at present considered neither fish, flesh, nor fowl.[2]

In his second period at the War Office, however, Herbert chose to focus more on the provision of an appropriate military education for junior officers. He had first raised the issue in parliament in March 1847.[3] Progress of sorts had been made when Wellington agreed to a general order requiring all those who entered Sandhurst to sit an exam,

---

1 Hansard, 25 Feb. 1853, CXXIV, col. 680; 24 Feb. 1854, CXXX, col. 1289; Stanmore, I, pp. 176-7; Strachan, *Wellington's Legacy*, pp. 42-3.
2 Hansard, 24 Feb. 1854, CXXX, cols. 1284-5; Jones, 'The Army', pp. 273-5.
3 Hansard, 1 Mar. 1847, XC, cols. 654-5.

with further such ordeals for those promoted to a higher rank. Herbert's opinion was that the entrance examination encouraged cramming. It was 'too limited [...] because certain text books only are required to be studied'. His preference was for 'a fair liberal education to be examined in what it is stated that he had learned [...] making that the test of his fitness as regarded sufficiency of instruction'. He conveyed similar sentiments to Hardinge in a memorandum of January 1854, adding that the syllabus should be controlled by an independent examination board.[1] It was for those who aspired to promotion that:

> [you] want a professional examination; you want to know that, in addition to a fair gentlemanly education, your officer has applied his mind to mathematical and strategetical studies, to such studies as will render him efficient as an officer.

In pursuit of this end, Gleig drew up a syllabus which included military drawing, surveying and fortifications. Herbert approved but added military history and strategy. Hardinge and the government endorsed his proposals; parliament voted £2,000 to start implementing them in the military estimates for 1854-5. The start of fighting in the Crimea, however, threw the scheme into temporary limbo.[2]

A related issue identified by Herbert and Gleig was the lack of a general staff. The army in 1852 could reasonably be characterised as a collection of semi-autonomous regiments: the Staff School established at High Wycombe during the Napoleonic Wars had moved to Sandhurst where it languished as the 'Senior Branch'. Herbert took up Gleig's suggestion that those candidates who had distinguished themselves in their captaincy exams at Sandhurst be offered further study with a view to employment on a revivified staff. The first Chief of Staff was appointed in 1855, though as with Herbert's plans for the education of junior officers, the outbreak of war rendered the scheme incomplete. Even so, taken together these reforms meant that 'almost

---

1   Hansard, 24 Feb. 1854, CXXX, cols. 1285-6; Strachan, *Wellington's Legacy*, pp. 130, 135.
2   Hansard, 24 Feb. 1854, CXXX, cols. 1286-7; Strachan, *Wellington's Legacy*, p. 139.

as much was done or planned for the higher education of the army in 1853 and 1854 as was to be carried through for the next half-century'.[1]

In seeking to lay the foundations for a new cadre of better trained officers, Herbert was inevitably concerned (mirroring the anxiety he had shown when Secretary to the Admiralty) at the logjam which existed amongst the higher ranks. It was a startling statistic that half the colonels in the army in 1846 had joined the service in the previous century. Herbert calculated that whereas nearly all general officers in 1815 were in their thirties (Wellington had just turned 46 by Waterloo), the average age of major-generals in 1854 was 65, lieutenant-generals older still. As he put it, with wry understatement, there is 'reason to think' that the efficiency of the army 'is impaired by the advanced age of the great majority of officers now in the upper ranks'.[2] Herbert was the driving force in securing the appointment of a royal commission to examine the question. Its remit was to devise an accelerated system for promotion that would produce younger generals on a more meritocratic basis.

The Royal Commission on Promotion in the Army was issued on 25 February 1854. Herbert chaired the body of eleven commissioners in the work which followed. It was a wearisome task. He hounded departments for statistics; the Ordnance provided data that was inaccurate.[3] In early June, at the eleventh hour, he received objections from Sir Hew Ross, one of his commissioners, 'an excellent soldier & a very worthy man but he is not quick in apprehension & it took him some days to find out that he differed from the report to wh. he had agreed'.[4] Herbert was unable to sign his 28 page report until 17 June. Two days later, 'to my great surprise', he received further protests, this time from Lieutenant-General Earl Cathcart and Lieutenant-General Sir John Burgoyne, 'inveighing against any infraction of the principle of seniority'. Refusing to be intimidated by 'an unfair proceeding on

---

1   Strachan, *Wellington's Legacy*, pp. 154-5, 171-2; Jones, 'The British Army', pp. 299-300.
2   PP 1854 (1802), XIX, p. 833.
3   BL Add. Mss. 46448, fols. 6-9, SH to Ramsay, 8, 9 May 1854.
4   PGL GRE/B109/10, fols. 17-19, SH to Earl Grey, 6 June 1854.

their part', Herbert consented only to submitting their protests as an appendix.¹

Herbert's report called for 'immediate and effective measures'. These included the proposals that all lieutenant-colonels with three years' experience should be advanced to full colonel and then, by seniority, up to the rank of major-general. The key recommendation, however, was that when it came to full generals, 'the fittest officer that can be found for the particular duty should be selected, without reference to seniority'. In a further attempt to ease the unseemly number of those holding high rank, the report suggested ending brevet appointments (honourary appointments and promotions), and improving retirement provision to encourage those on half pay to leave the service.² Gladstone baulked at the £18,850 which would be required as payments in compensation but he was overruled.³ A royal warrant of 6 October made the recommendations effective. Herbert called them, modestly, 'a step in the right direction'; later, seemingly immodestly, as 'greater changes in the system of promotion than had previously been made during the present century'. But he was right: they have been judged 'reforms of the first magnitude'.⁴

Although Herbert did not claim a monopoly of the credit, he also took pride in what he judged to be the qualitative improvements made to the lot of the ordinary soldier by 1854. Sixty masters and sixteen assistant masters from the Normal School were employed with army units. There were 150 barrack libraries housing 118,000 volumes available to nearly 16,000 subscribers. The number of soldiers with savings accounts (an initiative begun in 1844) was 10,723 with deposits totalling £124,000. Herbert adduced as further proof of more sober habits a probable decline in drunkenness and a definite reduction in the use of corporal punishment: 206 cases in 1851 compared with 879

---

1   PGL GRE/B109/10, fols. 20-1, SH to Earl Grey, 20 June 1854, SH to Ross, 20 June 1854.
2   PP 1854 (1802), XIX.
3   BL Add. Mss. 44210, fols. 127-8, SH to WEG, 5 June 1854; WSHC 2057/F4/60, SH to WEG, 18 June 1854.
4   Hansard, 1 Mar. 1855, CXXXVI, col. 2156; 4 Mar. 1856, CXL, col. 1846; Strachan, *Wellington's Legacy*, pp. 43, 117-21.

in 1838.¹ The expeditionary force which left British shores in 1854 would have fared worse than it did without the reforms which Herbert and others had helped to bring about. There was much truth in his statement of 2 March 1854 that:

> It is a larger British force than that which the Duke of Wellington took with him to Portugal, or than he had with him at Waterloo; and it has been fitted out with greater attention to efficiency and to health than any that ever previously left our shores. This was done in an unprecedented short time; and all who have seen the troops will admit that an army never went forth in a higher state of efficiency both in the personnel and the matériel.²

Herbert's speech is a necessary reminder that the reforms he oversaw were being made as Britain drifted towards the conflict now remembered as the Crimean War. Its short term origins can be traced to Napoleon III's demand that French Roman Catholic monks be restored as the principal custodians of the Holy Places in Bethlehem and Jerusalem. The Ottoman Sultan, Abdul I, within whose empire they lay, appeared amenable to doing so. But Czar Nicholas I reacted, in May 1853, by asserting the rights of the Greek Orthodox monks who had supplanted their French counterparts. Nicholas added the further demand that he be recognised as protector of the ten million Christians living in the Turkish Empire. The Sultan compromised on the first point (the dispute over the Holy Places was effectively resolved thereby) but refused the second. Nicholas responded by threatening the Turkish provinces of Moldavia and Wallachia, part of present day Romania.³

Britain had little love for Turkey. The Ottoman regime was deemed to be backward; the mistreatment of its Christian population well-known. But these considerations were trumped by fears that the

---

1 Hansard, 25 Feb. 1853, CXXIV, cols. 674-9; 24 Feb. 1854, CXXX, cols. 1283-9.
2 Hansard, 2 Mar. 1854, CXXXI, col. 244; Strachan, *Wellington's Legacy*, pp. 267-71.
3 Chamberlain, *'Pax Britannica?'*, pp. 102-5.

European balance of power would be upset if the 'sick man of Europe' finally shuffled off his mortal coil. Russia would be only too ready to expand into the Balkans. Furthermore, control of the Bosphorus and Dardanelles Straits would allow her ships uninterrupted access to the Mediterranean from the Black Sea. Herbert was therefore expressing a commonplace when he wrote that:

> We must have a power at the Bosphorus holding the keys of the Mediterranean from the east, which shall not be Russia, and we cannot allow Russia to encroach upon or undermine the Power which is there necessary for us. We are not bound by treaty to interfere in this quarrel; but we are bound by our own interests, and by European interests, not to allow Turkey to be overborne.[1]

But Aberdeen's government was divided as to how these objectives might be achieved. Cabinet hawks, notably Russell and Palmerston, fortified by a Russophobic British public, insisted that only the threat of belligerence would deter the Russian Bear. Aberdeen, with his long schooling in diplomacy, inclined to negotiation. Herbert, given years of personal and political attachment to Aberdeen, and his disdain for the Palmerstonian approach to foreign affairs, agreed with him. On 4 June he was amongst the minority in cabinet when Aberdeen was forced into agreeing that Britain send a fleet to Besika Bay outside the Dardanelles to make rendezvous with her French ally. Undeterred, the Czar ordered the occupation of Moldavia and Wallachia at the end of July.[2]

In an attempt to resolve the crisis, Austria convened a conference. On 1 August, representatives from France, Britain and Prussia agreed the Vienna Note. This proposed that the Sultan respect existing treaty obligations to Russia, so far as the Orthodox Church was concerned; and that the consent of both France and Russia be secured before any alterations be made. Herbert warmly supported the initiative.[3] But whilst the Russians were disposed to acquiesce in

---

1 WSHC 2057/F4/53, SH to Clarendon, 7 Oct. 1853.
2 Chamberlain, *Aberdeen*, p. 482.
3 Stanmore, I, p. 201.

it, the Turks, increasingly confident that Britain and France would not abandon them, rejected it on 20 August. Russia's position was then muddied in September by the unhelpful revelation that its Chancellor, Count Nesselrode, interpreted the Note to imply that the Czar had, after all, been vested with the right to regard himself as the protector of all Balkan Christians. Palmerston wrote to Herbert that the situation 'seems as you say to be unsatisfactory'. One clear consequence was that British public opinion became more anti-Russian. The *Morning Chronicle*, for example, still part-owned by Herbert, urged the government to be more resolute in defence of Turkey.[1]

Herbert, more level-headed than the public, did not welcome the escalation of the crisis which followed Turkey's declaring war on Russia on 4 October. Like others he suspected, albeit incorrectly, that Turkey's resolve derived chiefly from Lord Stratford de Redcliffe, the influential British ambassador at Constantinople. He agreed with Graham that 'Europe cannot be involved in war on account of the phrases of a Note, and for the sake of a word-mongering and disappointed diplomatist'.[2] He set great store, therefore, by news that the Czar had told the Austrian Emperor at Olmütz that he sought only to restore the status quo. Such temperate language was the only straw at which he could clutch in a letter sent to Elizabeth from the War Office on 6 October:

> I cannot say that I think anything else looks better. The public seem to think that there is nothing to do but declare war against Russia, just when she is yielding the point in dispute, and back the Turk, just when he acts contrary to our advice; and this without any guarantee on our part and without any English or European interest at stake, if the question of the Note be adjusted as I think it would be, or rather would have been, if the Turks could have been kept quiet. I believe they, the Turks, expect to take Petersburg before Christmas![3]

1   WSHC 2057/F4/61, Pam to SH, 21 Sept. 1853; Conacher, *Aberdeen*, pp. 186-7.
2   WSHC 2057/F4/59, JRG to SH, 15 Sept. 1853.
3   Chamberlain, *Aberdeen*, p. 486; WSHC 2057/F4/51, SH to EH, 6 Oct. 1853.

A divided cabinet met the next day to agree its next move. Herbert was one of those 'active and energetic for peace'. In a decision which satisfied neither doves nor hawks it was agreed that the fleet should wait in the Bosphorus, poised to enter the Black Sea if Russian forces attacked the Turkish coast or crossed the Danube.[1] It was testimony to the strength of Herbert's feelings on the matter, that having apologised to Clarendon for 'adding a sheet of paper to the quantity' the Foreign Secretary already had to read, he proceeded to write him a long letter restating the case for Britain's avoiding war. The Ottoman Empire, he argued, would not survive a war; 'her Constitution will not stand blood-letting'. Thus Britain, even though Turkey had declared war against Russia, 'should hold our own, and not allow the fanaticism and folly of the rabble at Constantinople to supersede the decisions of the Cabinets of Paris and London'. Rather, Britain should press for 'the most effectual' means for peace. By this he meant not the Vienna Note, 'now so blown upon [...] that it is hopeless to press it further', but the noises emanating from the Czar at Olmütz. Turkey meanwhile should be warned against escalating hostilities further. The balance of power, self-interest and national honour all dictated, Herbert admitted, that Britain would not desert Turkey if it came to the crunch, but he still hoped that diplomacy might prevail:

> The Russians have been throughout in the wrong but it is not our interest to keep them there [...] On the contrary, if we get Russia out of a scrape, we get Turkey and ourselves out of one likewise.[2]

Herbert's letter may have eased his conscience but it achieved little else. A further cabinet meeting on 8 October found only Aberdeen prepared to agree with him in taking the meeting at Olmütz seriously. The fleet was authorised to move towards Constantinople; it entered the Dardanelles on 17 October. Resigned to the fact that he could do little more for the moment, Herbert set off amid 'stormy weather' for Ireland. Graham provided him with a more or less daily update

---

1 Brown, *Palmerston*, pp. 366-7; Chamberlain, *Aberdeen*, p. 488.
2 WSHC 2057/F4/53, SH to Clarendon, 7 Oct. 1853. Clarendon had succeeded Russell as Foreign Secretary on 21 February.

on developments and promised to telegraph if Aberdeen convened an unexpected cabinet.[1] Back in England the following month, it was Herbert who was doing the updating. In more optimistic spirits he informed Gladstone that the cabinet meeting of 26 November had endorsed an Anglo-French proposal for a fresh diplomatic initiative: 'it defines the limit and cause of our interference, namely the preservation of the status quo, and it tells the belligerents plainly that they are fighting for nothing, which may greatly cool their ardour'.[2] Within hours of Herbert's writing this letter, events took a decisive turn: on 30 November Russian warships sunk part of the Turkish fleet in the Black Sea at Sinope. Cabinet hawks, bolstered by the ever growing strength of public opinion, now held the whip hand. Herbert admitted privately to Gladstone that 'I have little hope now of a pacific result'. The cabinet agreed that the fleet should enter the Black Sea. It did so as one with its French ally on 3 January.[3]

The mood of MPs was decidedly Russophobic when parliament met in February. Ministers faced censure for what was deemed their insufficiently robust response over the previous months. Herbert spoke on the second night of the debate.[4] His speech was a stout defence of a government which he characterised as having been:

> placed between two fires. We are told by one party in the House that we have arrived tardily at the right place, but that we took the wrong road to it; we are told by another that we took the right road at first, but that now we have arrived at the wrong place.

He reminded those who accused ministers of having been supine that Britain, 'as a Protestant nation, had nothing to do with a quarrel

---

1   Chamberlain, *Aberdeen*, p. 488; BL Add. Mss. 44210, fols. 97-8, SH to WEG, 27 Oct. 1853; WSHC 2057/F4/59, JRG to SH, 15 Oct. 1853.
2   BL Add. Mss. 44210, fols. 102-5, SH to WEG, 29 Nov. 1853; Conacher, *Aberdeen*, p. 213.
3   BL Add. Mss. 44210, fols. 106-10, SH to WEG, 28 Dec. 1853; Chamberlain, *'Pax Britannica?'*, pp. 106-8.
4   Hansard, 20 Feb. 1854, CXXX, cols. 988-95.

which originated in the ignorance and fanaticism of two different sets of monks at Jerusalem':

> I believe if we had pursued what has been called a more vigorous course last summer – I believe if we had plunged the country into war, we should have justly been called to account for having precipitated a calamity which might have been averted – at any rate for not having exhausted every means which could be thought of to ward off from the civilised world a calamity so great.

But he was even more severe towards those few pacific MPs, principally Cobdenite Radicals, who insisted that Britain had nothing at stake in the quarrel: 'if there be a country which, above all other countries, has an interest in maintaining the security of nations, it must be that which, like England, is engaged in commerce all over the world'. Britain was not supporting the Sultan 'out of a romantic feeling and sympathy for Turkey and her institutions', but 'for the purpose of keeping up the balance of the Powers of Europe and resisting the encroachment of Russia'.[1]

The government survived; an ultimatum that Russia withdraw from the occupied provinces and order its fleet to return to Sebastopol was issued, and rejected. War was declared on 28 March. Herbert was one of eighteen privy councillors present at Buckingham Palace on 29 March to authorise the general order for 'reprisals against Russia'.[2] He had been consistent throughout in maintaining that the balance of power was the key issue at stake for Britain. Patently no pacifist, he was, equally, no warmonger. His preference for a negotiated settlement of this particular round of the Eastern Question, however, was, as he reluctantly conceded from October 1853 onwards, increasingly unlikely.

Some critics have suggested that Herbert might have done more to prevent war by arguing the case for peace more stridently in cabinet. It is difficult to see, though, how he and other doves

---

1 Conacher, *Aberdeen*, pp. 278-80.
2 PP 1854 (1762), LXXII, p. 213.

could have prevailed against more senior and hawkish figures such as Russell, Palmerston, Lansdowne and Clarendon. Aberdeen, after all, failed in the same objective: agreeing only to an incremental increase on the pressure exerted on Russia during 1853 was the most that the peace party could realistically achieve if the government were to hold together.[1] A more serious charge was that Herbert's being half-Russian 'imposed on him a degree of reticence which he would not otherwise have shown in combatting the apprehensions expressed with regard to the designs of Russia, or in demonstrating the impolicy of lending an unqualified support to Turkey'.[2] Herbert was certainly happy to flaunt his connections with England's putative enemy. As late as September 1853, he was playing host to the Grand Duchess Maria, daughter of Czar Nicholas I, an avid art collector who evidently appreciated the treasures Wilton House had to offer. She was accompanied by a gaggle of Russian counts and Herbert's Woronzow relations: their visit attracted widespread notice in the press.[3] Two months earlier, a satirical piece in *The Press* ridiculed Herbert for failing to roll his R's sufficiently. His uncle, Prince Michael Woronzow, recently retired as Commander-in-Chief and Viceroy of the Caucasus, was reported to have suggested that Herbert might overcome his impediment by daily repetition of 'God save the Emperor of Russia'.[4]

The reality could hardly have been more different. Baron Nikolay Pavlovich, diplomat and friend of the Woronzows, had accused Herbert, in a private letter of November 1853, of belonging to a government 'bullying us' for no purpose 'unless you mean to adopt the Mohametan creed and are anxious therefore to fight for the blessed shrine at Mecca!' Herbert wrote a stout defence of Britain's position in reply. His loyalty and patriotism were as pure as that of any English gentleman. It is revealing that, as war fever grew, his name was not listed by alarmist newspapers, alongside those of Lord Aberdeen and Prince Albert, as being an enemy agent who should be sent to the

1   Conacher, *Aberdeen*, p. 199.
2   Stanmore, I, p. 181.
3   *SWJ*, 24 Sept. 1853.
4   *DWG*, 21 July 1853.

Tower of London!¹ What Herbert's Russian blood and connections did perhaps do was to provide him with a more realistic appreciation than most Englishmen of what war with Russia might entail. Early in October 1853 he told Clarendon that there would be 'eventualities which no man can pretend, foresee or limit'.² He repeated the point to Gladstone at the end of December, adding that 'except destroying the two Russian fleets if we can get at them, I do not know what we can do against Russia'. On land, he believed his uncle, Prince Michael, to be 'the most enlightened and able man in Russia, and I believe the army of the Caucasus to be one of the finest armies in the world'. More generally, he continued:

> the Russian power has been so underrated of late, and the Turkish so unduly magnified, that, once engaged in a struggle which will be far more severe than this wayward unreflecting public choose now to think, there will be great reaction, and those warlike gentlemen will begin to abuse us for not having done enough to preserve peace.³

In equally prescient language, in February 1854, Herbert cautioned the Commons that Russia was no pushover, rather 'a most powerful country [...] if you are going to engage in a mortal struggle, you must make your preparations in proportion to your estimation of your antagonist'.⁴

By the early spring, however, Herbert was sharing his cabinet colleagues' alarm that Russia would seize Constantinople. With the arrival of British and French forces at Gallipoli and Scutari in May, this fear was eliminated. Thoughts turned instead to employing the troops alongside Turkish contingents to expel the Russians from Moldavia and Wallachia. To this end they were re-embarked for Varna on the Black Sea coast. Had these facts constituted the sum total of public knowledge about what was happening 3,000 miles away, the political

---

1   Struve, 'An Anglo-Russia Medley', *California Slavic Studies*, V (1970), pp. 120-5; Stanmore, I, p. 218.
2   WSHC 2057/F4/53, SH to Clarendon, 7 Oct. 1853.
3   BL Add. Mss. 44210, fols. 106-10, SH to WEG, 28 Dec. 1853.
4   Hansard, 20 Feb. 1854, CXXX, cols. 992-3.

waters in Britain might have run smoothly. But Lord Hardinge, in his wisdom, had sanctioned the journalist William Howard Russell's sailing with the expeditionary force. Russell's reports, which appeared in *The Times* (boasting a daily circulation of 40,000), impacted adversely on the public mood in ways similar to those Herbert had feared. The picture Russell painted was one of men suffering needless hardships, victims of a bureaucracy operating what masqueraded as a system.[1]

Herbert was called upon to answer charges inspired by Russell's reports as early as the end of April. Specifically, it was alleged that the government had made inadequate preparations for the troops landed at Gallipoli. Whilst not disputing that language, local customs and prejudices had generated difficulties, Herbert was robust in his denial: reconnaissance missions (employing local language speakers) had been carried out in mid-February, the Turks had proved cooperative, medical supplies had been despatched, the men's quarters were good. 'We must recollect', he concluded:

> what is the nature of the duties of the correspondent for a newspaper here in London. I apprehend that the business of a correspondent of a newspaper is to do that which, I must say, they do with singular skill and success, to give graphic pictures of everything that is done, thought, and said, and to convey to the people of England a general impression of the scene of operations; but it is not his business to sift reports, to ascertain whether every rumour is well founded, when he is engaged in presenting amusing pictures to the readers of a newspaper.[2]

In private, though, Herbert was only too aware that shortcomings existed. Almost a year before the expeditionary was despatched, he had voiced concerns that the machinery 'fit for larger operations, or capable of sudden expansion, is not being maintained', and that in the event of war 'they would then require an organisation for which

---

1   Spiers, *Army and Society*, pp. 98-100.
2   Hansard, 28 Apr. 1854, CXXXII, cols. 999-1003.

they had no preparation'.[1] And alive to the truth that the men of the expeditionary force were burdened by unnecessary punctilio, he wrote to its commanding officer, his friend Lord Raglan. The army's dress code, Herbert suggested, might be relaxed: tight tunics and tall shakos did not strike him as the best apparel for the hot climate; perhaps the men might also be excused from shaving every day? Raglan sent a dismissive 'let us appear as Englishmen' in reply.[2]

Far and away Herbert's greatest complaint, however, concerned Britain's lack of manpower. In his view, the country had spent years making inadequate preparations against a possible French invasion: how on earth was it to wage unexpected offensive operations with France against a major European state? Two months before war was formally declared, in conference with Newcastle and Clarendon, Herbert asserted that:

> *if* we were to go to war with such a country as Russia which makes nothing of raising a hundred thousand men [...] it would be ridiculous for us to propose raising 10,000 men, and that the effect upon our neighbours the French would be much better if we proposed raising 30,000 or 35,000.[3]

The following month, aware that the public was baying for a war it did not wish to pay for, Herbert emphasised that the estimates he was presenting to the House for 1854-5 were only 'an estimate formed in time of peace'. He asked for £6,287,486 to maintain an army of 112,997 men. This represented a 4.36% increase in money terms, and a 10.47% increase in manpower compared with his figures for 1853-4. Excepting 1848, the figures were higher than for any year since 1815. But as Herbert pointed out, critics could more reasonably ask why he was asking for so little as so much.[4]

1 Strachan, *Wellington's Legacy*, p. 240; Hansard, 25 Feb. 1853, CXXIV, cols. 669-70.
2 Figes, *Crimea*, pp. 180-1, Raglan to SH, 15 May 1854.
3 Maxwell, *Clarendon*, II, p. 39, 22 Jan. 1854.
4 Hansard, 24 Feb. 1854, CXXX, cols. 1283-92; Jones, 'The British Army' pp. 315-16.

With war a reality, and illness taking its toll on the expeditionary force – Hardinge reckoned on a hundred casualties per month in a battalion of 800 – the need to do something even to maintain troop numbers became acute. The obvious remedy was to send regulars from home. But given that 25,000 men had already been earmarked for the East with a further 5,000 or so to follow, this would leave home forces 'ineffective' 'for some time to come'. Herbert was particularly concerned for the security of the dockyards: the admirals and generals at Portsmouth and Plymouth were 'crying out for more men'. Herbert suggested, therefore, that it might be expedient to embody up to eight regiments of militia 'from counties where labour is cheap'.[1] Aberdeen agreed; he informed the Queen that 15,000 militia were to be embodied. The initiative was followed by a warrant, signed by Herbert, offering militiamen a ten shilling bounty if they volunteered for the regulars. This, he hoped, would help provide the 14,799 additional men he asked for in revised army estimates on 5 May. By June the number of embodied militia exceeded 30,000. Many did then progress to the army; others were able to relieve pressure on the regulars when they assumed home duties in July.[2] To make them a more flexible force, a supplementary Militia Act was rushed through parliament. This empowered the Secretary for War and the Colonies, 'in time of war', to deploy militia regiments anywhere within the country, not just, as had been the case, in their own county. Taken together, and bolstered by the withdrawal of some regulars from foreign stations, these measures facilitated the despatch of 33,586 officers and men to the East by the end of August. Nearly 27,000 would be landed in the Crimea before the first major engagement in September.[3] Herbert deserves some credit for his part in this under-appreciated achievement.

The public's attention in the early summer, however, refused to be diverted from stories that the army was being mismanaged. Contemporary estimates that the number of departments responsible for administering its affairs ranged from five to fourteen appeared to tell

1 HLPP GC/HE/44, SH to Pam, 26 Apr. 1854.
2 Beckett, *Britain's Part-Time Soldiers*, pp. 152-3; Hansard, 5 May 1854, CXXXII, cols. 1375-9; Strachan, *Wellington's Legacy*, pp. 220-1.
3 Conacher, *Aberdeen*, p. 505.

their own story. Herbert agreed. He had written to Aberdeen in 1852 that there were 'great confusions' and numerous examples of 'blunders between departments arising simply from not knowing what the other is doing'. A weekly two-hour meeting of heads of department, he mooted, would 'rectify what is amiss to a great degree'.[1] He appears to have practised what he preached:

> Since I have been in office [...] it has been the custom for the Master General of the Ordnance, the Inspector General of Fortifications, the First Lord of the Admiralty, the Commander-in-Chief, and myself, to meet periodically at the War Office, and go carefully through all the different changes which were being made with regard to our home defences. Whenever we had colonial questions of a like character to consider, we did the same in conjunction with the Colonial Secretary. And so everything has gone on harmoniously, and, I trust, efficiently.[2]

For all that this may have been true in peace time, though, it was far from being the popular perception of how the army was being run in 1854. In February 1854 *The Times* had taken up the issue of army governance as part of its campaign for administrative reform. Joseph Hume, the Radical, raised it in the Commons on 2 March.[3] Centralisation and rationalisation were demanded, in particular the creation of a new Secretary of State for War with far-reaching powers over Horse Guards, the Ordnance and such other officers and departments as survived a restructuring. Herbert made a lengthy, and sometimes contradictory, speech in reply: he was not averse to some merging of Horse Guards with the Ordnance or ending the anomaly whereby the Treasury was responsible for the Commissariat; but he was adamant that the existing departments had cooperated well in recent years, and the new Secretary of State for War would be overwhelmed by 'the vast increase of duties' apportioned to him. Above all, he was emphatic that:

1 Sweetman, *War and Administration*, p. 8; WSHC 2057/F4/53, SH to Aberdeen, 28 Dec. 1852.
2 Hansard, 2 Mar. 1854, CXXXI, cols. 242-3.
3 *The Times*, 27 Feb. 1854; Hansard, 2 Mar. 1854, CXXXI, cols. 223-60.

you ought to proceed step by step. The process should be gradual. But at this moment I do not believe you could undertake a more rash experiment than when you are about to enter upon a serious contest, and when you will have the greatest pressure upon your machinery from being engaged in a very hot war.[1]

By May at the latest, in face of the failings being endured by the expeditionary force, Herbert had been forced to modify his position. He now accepted the case for the office of Secretary for War and the Colonies to be broken in two. But he argued passionately for the new Secretary for War to be vested with limited rather than omnipotent powers: 'What you most want is, not so much the consolidation of the different departments, but one supervising authority, with a view to make all of them act in harmonious combination'.[2] Russell was his chief opponent in cabinet. He represented a Whig tradition that aspired to greater civilian and parliamentary control over an institution which Liberals believed to be autocratic and Tory. Had Herbert not been in cabinet to object, it is likely that his own office of Secretary at War would have been abolished as part of a series of more thoroughgoing reforms. Instead, it was confirmed, on 12 June, that there were to be separate Secretaries of State for War and the Colonies. Questions regarding the streamlining of army departments and the parameters of potentially competing authorities were left to another day.[3]

The immediate question to be answered was who would become Secretary for War. Had Newcastle, as the incumbent Secretary of State for War and the Colonies, opted for the Colonies, logic pointed to Herbert taking the War portfolio. But Newcastle, even though Aberdeen was inclined to favour Herbert, wanted War for himself. It was a close call. Whilst some 'highly competent judges' thought Newcastle 'a man of larger grasp of mind and more statesmanlike character than Mr Herbert', Herbert was felt to have the edge when

---

1 Hansard, 2 Mar. 1854, CXXXI, cols. 233-45.
2 Hansard, 17 July 1854, CXXXV, col. 335.
3 Conacher, *Aberdeen*, pp. 394-413.

it came to judging men and inspiring colleagues.[1] What it did mean, with Sir George Grey having been appointed to the Colonial Office, was that Herbert found himself in a sort of limbo: what need was there for a Secretary *at* War now that there was a Secretary *for* War? Herbert accepted, at the very least, the logic that the latter should not be a member of the cabinet.

Herbert took what has been called the 'emasculation' of his office with surprisingly good grace.[2] On 17 July, 180 of the government's supporters met in Downing Street to hear some of its leading figures outline their thoughts on recent events. When Herbert spoke he acknowledged that 'The office he held was now one of reduced dignity, and he might for that reason have given it up without reproach'. But the Prime Minister had judged it in the national interest for him to remain in government, and on that basis he was prepared to do so. Herbert's speech, Aberdeen reported to the Queen, had made 'a very good impression'.[3] Later that day, in a speech to the House, Herbert put a more positive spin on his position, if only to justify his own existence:

> The duties of the Secretary at War are duties delegated to him by the Treasury [...] financially speaking, the existence of the office of Secretary at War is vital to the cause of economy and efficiency in the administration of the Army [...] the control which the Secretary at War has over the expenditure of the Army, under the Commander in Chief, ought to be extended to the expenditure which is now under the Master General of the Ordnance [...] I think that some additional duties might be imposed upon him, such as moving the Commissariat Estimates [...] I should be inclined to say, therefore, retain the office of Secretary at War as a finance officer [...] my services might be of great value to assist not only in promoting the efficiency of the Army, but also in assisting the Government in arranging in a final and satisfactory manner the various duties of the War Department [...] I

---

1   Stanmore, I, p. 224; Chamberlain, *Aberdeen*, pp. 510-11; Southgate, *The Most English Minister*, p. 352.
2   Strachan, *Wellington's Legacy*, p. 42.
3   *Dublin Evening Post*, 20 July 1854; Conacher, *Aberdeen*, p. 359.

hope that the result will be, that we shall shortly be able to lay upon the table of the House a detailed plan of the entire change.[1]

More pressing matters supervened. On 17 June, Herbert had submitted a memorandum to the cabinet. It proceeded from the premise that 'I see no security for future peace unless Sebastopol [the Russian fortress and naval base in the Crimea judged to threaten Turkish security] is destroyed'. Since Russia 'will treat any such proposal much as we should a proposal to destroy Portsmouth', offensive operations were inevitable. 'I agree with Ld Palmerston that if it be not done this year, it will not be possible next'.[2] Herbert was thenceforth indefatigable in pursuit of this end. In mid-July he was one of the cabinet ministers accused of trying to stifle criticism of the government's conduct of the war. On 25 July, in what Gladstone called an excellent speech, Herbert extolled what the expeditionary force had already achieved. It helped head off an attempt by some MPs to prolong the parliamentary session with a view to further scrutinising the administration. Herbert was not happy when early August brought rumours that hostilities might be ended following the news that Russian forces had quit Moldavia and Wallachia.[3] But there was little prospect of that: government had instructed Raglan that, unless he felt that the chances of doing so were minimal, he should use the forces at his disposal to destroy Sebastopol.

Even so, Herbert did not relax. He was at the War Office for most of the summer, excepting his 'practice was to go into the country invariable for the Sunday, and for the Saturday or Monday, when possible'. When in town he was in constant communication with Newcastle, and claimed to have seen all his correspondence. Earl Granville, Lord President of the Council, holidaying in Carlsbad, wrote that besides Aberdeen and Newcastle, Herbert was the only man 'fit to be in the government'.[4] Only after parliament was prorogued on 14 August was he able to seize two short breaks. The first consisted of

1   Hansard, 17 July 1854, CXXXV, cols. 338-40.
2   HLPP CAB 73/1-2, memorandum of 17 June 1854.
3   *DWG*, 20 July 1854; Hansard, 25 July, CXXXV, cols. 716-28; Conacher, *Aberdeen*, p. 433.
4   WSHC 2057/F4/53, Granville to SH, 7 Sept. 1854.

a week in which he squeezed in visits to both Broadstairs and Ireland. In late August he stayed with the Queen at Osborne House on the Isle of Wight before spending a few days at Wilton.[1] Whilst there, he presided over meetings of the local scientific society and played host to the annual fete in Wilton's grounds given to nearly 500 children from local schools. Herbert, it was reported, looked relaxed as 'Secretary-at-*Peace*'.[2] Appearances were deceptive. On 14 September over 60,000 men (27,000 British, 28,000 French and 7,000 Turkish) came ashore 25 miles north of Sebastopol at the ominously named Calamita Bay.

1 PP 1854-5 (247), IX, p. 193; NUL Ne C 12241/1-2, EH to Newcastle, 29 Apr. 1855; *Dublin Evening Post*, 3 Aug., 2 Sept. 1854.
2 *SWJ*, 2 Sept. 1854.

Map 1. The Black Sea

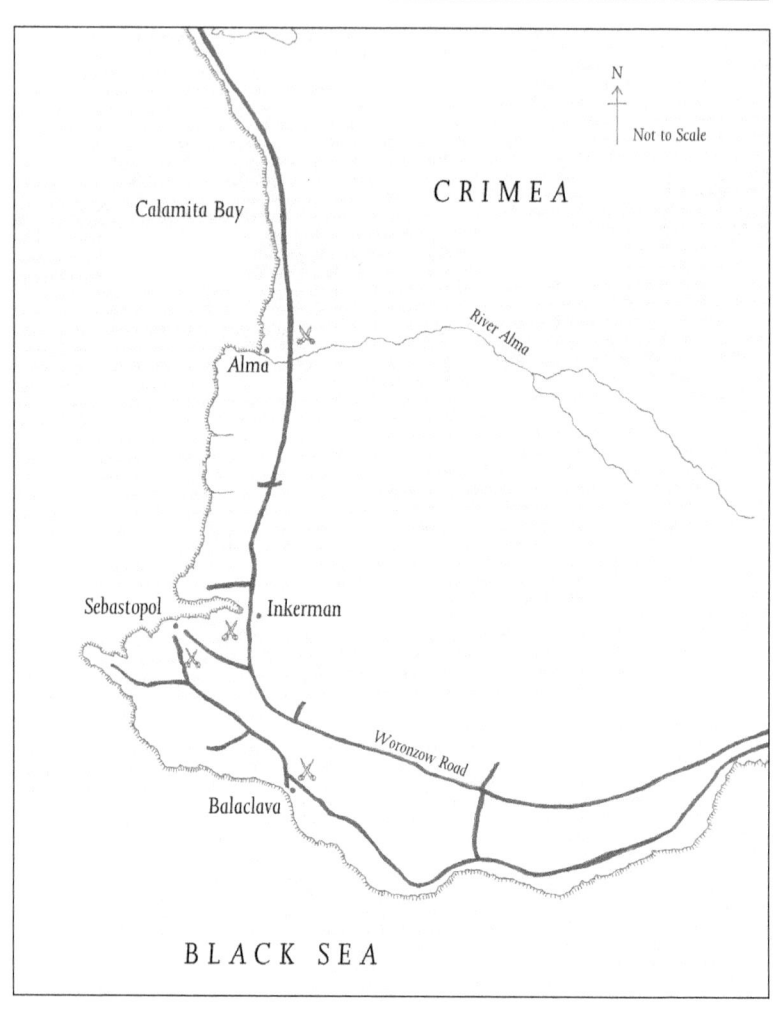

Map 2. The Crimean Campaign

Fig 1 George Augustus, 11th Earl of Pembroke, 1821, by William Owen

Fig 2 Catherine Woronzow, Countess of Pembroke, 1810 by Sir Thomas Lawrence

Fig 3 Pembroke Lodge, c. 1780, Herbert's birthplace

Fig 4 Simon Woronzow beating his secretary at chess. Sketch by Herbert of his maternal grandfather, c. 1825

Fig 5 South front of Wilton House with the Palladian Bridge across the River Nadder, c. 1830

Fig 6 Mount Merrion, Herbert's Irish seat, c. 1820

Fig 7 Robert, 12th Earl of Pembroke, Herbert's half-brother, 1837, engraving by W. Hall after the portrait by A.E. Chalon

Fig 8 William Ewart Gladstone, 1847

Fig 9 Henry Pelham Clinton, Earl of Lincoln and 5th Duke of Newcastle, Illustrated London News, 22 Dec. 1860

Fig 10 The Duke of Wellington and Sir Robert Peel, 1844

Fig 11 Sidney Herbert by Sir Francis Grant, 1847

Fig 12 Lithograph of Elizabeth Herbert by Richard Lane after the painting by James Rannie Swinton, 1850

Fig 13 Photograph labelled by Elizabeth Herbert as 'Sidney's Own Room' at Wilton, 1850s

Fig 14 49 Belgrave Square, Herbert's main London residence, now the home of the Argentinean ambassador

above: Fig 15 Elizabeth Herbert with Lady Mary and Hon. George Herbert by Robert Thorburn, 1853. Herbert paid Thorburn £165. Malmesbury noted society gossip that 'she has had herself and two children painted as a Holy Family.'

right: Fig 16 Leaflet issued in Elizabeth Herbert's name appealing for clothes on behalf of the Female Emigration Fund, 1850

left: Fig 17 John Howard Harris, 3rd Earl of Malmesbury

above: Fig 18 Henry John Temple, 3rd Viscount Palmerston

Fig 19 George Hamilton Gordon, 4th Earl of Aberdeen

Fig 20 Sir James Graham

Fig 21 Lord John, 1st Earl Russell

Fig 22 Edward Geoffrey Stanley, 14th Earl of Derby

Fig 23 Benjamin Disraeli

Fig 24 The Aberdeen Cabinet, Illustrated London News, *8 Jan. 1853. Herbert is bottom right*

Fig 25 Florence Nightingale, c. 1856

Fig 26 George Frederick Robinson, Earl de Grey and Ripon

Fig 27 St Mary and St Nicholas' Church, Wilton

Fig 28 St John's Church, Sandymount

Fig 29 St Mary's, Star of the Sea, Sandymount

Fig 30 St John's Church, Bemerton

Fig 31 Herbert, late 1850s

Fig 32 Elizabeth, Lady Herbert, photograph by William Walker and sons, 1863

Fig 33 T.H. Wyatt's memorial of Herbert in Wilton Church

Fig 34 Carlo Marochetti's statue of Herbert unveiled in Salisbury's Market Square, Illustrated London News, 11 July 1863

Fig 35 J.H. Foley's statue of Herbert in its original location in front of the War Office

Fig 36 Nightingale visits the Herbert Hospital at Woolwich, bronze bas relief below Foley's statue of Herbert

Fig 37 Casting of an Armstrong gun at Woolwich, bronze bas relief below Foley's statue of Herbert

Fig 38 Men from London volunteer rifle corps, bronze bas relief below Foley's statue of Herbert

Fig 39 Foley's statue of Herbert, now alongside Nightingale in Waterloo Place

Fig 40 Marochetti's statue today, lost and forlorn, overlooking the bowling green in Salisbury's Victoria Park

Fig 41 Sidney Herbert, from the drawing by George Richmond, 1847

9
Crimean Controversies 1854-1855

Herbert, like most, shared the assumption that Sebastopol would fall at an early date: 'I think the expectation was that it would be a *coup de main*'.[1] The government consequently gave little thought to the logistics of sustaining an army through the Crimean winter. Hardships were inevitable. The resultant popular clamour, especially at the inadequacy of hospital provision, was unprecedented. Parliament demanded scapegoats: Aberdeen's ministry resigned in January 1855. Herbert could not but be dragged into the various controversies which erupted. As Secretary at War he was heavily involved in efforts to keep the army up to strength. In what he considered to be an unofficial capacity, he also attempted to mitigate some of the shortcomings. Famously, he invited Florence Nightingale to head a party of nurses to Scutari. By February 1855, however, he had resigned, not once but twice, and his political prospects looked decidedly doubtful.

King Cholera had landed with the expeditionary force at Calalmita Bay on 14 September. In a letter to Newcastle, Herbert referred to reports which 'are awful especially on the score of health'. But this was tempered by optimism that the army had reached the River Alma north of Sebastopol and that 'If so they will have been fighting on the 21st & we shall hear any hour'.[2] Herbert was right.

1   PP 1854-5 (247), IX, p. 167.
2   NUL Ne C 11821/1-3, SH to Newcastle, 20 Sept. 1855.

Russian forces were driven back by Anglo-Franco-Turkish troops in what he described as 'a battle memorable, not only for the valour displayed by the allied forces, but for the fact that it was the first occasion in modern history on which French and English soldiers had fought together'.[1] Newcastle went further: 'I now am convinced that Sebastopol has really fallen'. He invited his friend to join a royal commission. It led to what became known as the Patriotic Fund to provide monies for widows and orphans.[2]

Newcastle's optimism was misplaced. The Allied commanders decided against an immediate assault on Sebastopol, opting instead for a flank march in order to besiege it. Herbert's first reaction was to see this as an opportunity lost, though he later conceded that there was 'a general feeling that flesh and blood must not again be led against batteries'.[3] Raglan, meanwhile, had chosen the small port of Balaclava as his supply base. His advance position included the Causeway Heights. It was here, on 25 October, that Russian forces attacked. Turkish soldiers in the first line were pushed back. So eventually were the Russians, but not before the Light Brigade charged into immortality. Herbert wrote and spoke of the Battle of Balaclava in Tennysonian terms. Although 'the rascally Turks took to their heels at the first sight of the enemy', it was 'also a day to which we may look with pride – for I believe there is not an Englishman who would not feel proud of being the countryman of but one of those heroes'. He took serious exception to the Member who described the charge as 'a melancholy disaster'.[4] Herbert did not deem it politic to mention that the engagement had resulted in Russia's gaining control of the Woronzow Road, named for his maternal family, and the army's main artery of communication with Balaclava.

The third action in what Herbert deemed to be a successful start to the campaign took place on 5 November. British forces were

1   Hansard, 12 Dec. 1854, CXXXVI, col. 98.
2   WSHC 2057/F4/53, Newcastle to SH, 2 letters of 30 Sept. 1854; David, *Victoria's Wars*, p. 218.
3   Stanmore, I, pp. 318-35, memorandum of 9 Jan. 1855.
4   HLPP GC/HE/55, SH to Pam, 5 Nov. 1854; Hansard, 12 Dec. 1854, CXXXVI, col. 98; 29 Jan. 1855, CXXXVI, cols. 1118-19.

attacked five miles east of Sebastopol along Inkerman Ridge. Aided in large part by the French, to a lesser extent by thick fog and the rifles for whose introduction Herbert had pressed, the Czar's army failed to break through. Ignoring the contribution of Napoleon III's men, Herbert enthused to Palmerston about 'what a wonderful battle is this of the Inkerman'. He perpetuated the myth that it represented a purely British triumph when he told the House: 'On that occasion 8,000 of our countrymen, who were alone engaged, well and bravely sustained the honour of old England'.[1]

But the mood in old England was changing. Newcastle wrote to Herbert that 'The private letters are beginning to be unpleasant'.[2] A great storm on 14 November wrought havoc amongst the supply ships moored outside Balaclava harbour. The 21 vessels lost included the steamship, *Prince*, whose cargo included 40,000 winter uniforms; and the *Resolute*, which was carrying 10 million rounds of ammunition. Consigned likewise to the deep was nearly 500 tons of corn, 160 tons of biscuits, 34 tons of salted meat, 33 tons of rice, 8,000 gallons of rum, and over 350 tons of hay, the latter equivalent to 20 days' worth of vital forage.[3] Herbert wrote without exaggeration to Raglan of the 'disasters you have had at sea'. To his parliamentary colleagues he reflected in solemn terms that 'when we talk of commanding the seas, we are apt to be rebuked by Him at whose breath the stormy wind arises, and we are visited by the terrible calamity which befell our transports a short time ago'.[4]

'Calamity' was a word Herbert employed without exaggeration. The storm was an important catalyst which transformed the drama of war into a crisis for survival. Another was the onset of the Russian winter. The expeditionary force had to endure it with poor rations, inappropriate clothing, inadequate accommodation and wretched medical provision. Following the loss of the Woronzow Road,

1 HLPP GC/HE/45, SH to Pam, 22 Nov. 1854; Hansard, 12 Dec. 1854, CXXXVI, col. 98.
2 WSHC 2057/F4/53, Newcastle to SH, 7 Nov. 1854.
3 Figes, *Crimea*, pp. 278-80; Stanmore, I, pp. 277-83.
4 WSHC 2057 F4/63, SH to Raglan, 8 Dec. 1854; Hansard, 26 Jan. 1855, CXXXVI, col. 989.

materials for the front had to be transported fourteen kilometres uphill. Our 'only communication', noted Herbert, was 'by a metal road [more accurately a trackway] between the camp and Balaclava, the basis of our whole operations'. He was guilty of euphemism when he recorded that 'the Government at home and the allied commanders abroad underrated the difficulties they had to encounter, and were not sufficiently aware of the great resources which our enemy would have at his command'. They found themselves 'a minority besieging a majority'.[1]

Herbert's official powers for responding to this situation were imprecisely defined and certainly limited. As he wryly observed, he had 'exercised more authority' at the War Office in 1845; one result of Newcastle's incarnation as Secretary for War in June 1854 had been 'to diminish the powers of the Secretary at War'.[2] In theory his role was now confined to financial oversight of the Commander-in-Chief at Horse Guards. Before 1854, as we have seen, this meant fighting an uphill battle to maintain troop numbers and expenditure in a public and political climate determined to limit both. But Herbert was never going to content himself in wartime as a passive spectator wielding a financial rubber stamp. As casualties from death and disease mounted, he was more alive than most in government to the necessity of finding reinforcements. Only a modest 4,000 had been sent out by the end of October; the number of reported sick that month was 11,236.[3] Herbert therefore shared Russell's concern ('The little man is uneasy') when the two of them met at Windsor, that 'our position may become critical', in particular if Balaclava were to fall. A week later he confided to Graham that 'I do not like the accounts of the siege – the safety of our army depends on reinforcements'.[4] This, he knew full well, would not be easy: 'England has not usually been very successful at the commencement of her wars for the reason, that she does not in time of peace maintain an army large enough to be capable of lasting as well

1 Stanmore, I, pp. 318-25, memorandum of 9 Jan. 1855.
2 PP 1854-5 (247), IX, pp. 165, 194.
3 Conacher, *Aberdeen*, pp. 504-5.
4 BL Add. Mss. 44210, fols. 157-60, SH to WEG, 3 Nov. 1854; BL Add. Mss. 79657, fols. 82-4, SH to JRG, 6 Nov. 1854.

as sudden extension'. 'Our army is exhausted', he concluded in a stark memorandum for the cabinet, 'and we have a new army to create'.[1]

One obvious expedient, Herbert agreed with Newcastle, would be to continue the policy, begun in the summer, of transferring regulars from postings overseas. But this was to redeploy an existing army, not furnish a new one.[2] Herbert entertained some hopes that the latter might be facilitated by a flood of volunteers, especially after heroic tales of derring-do reached home. 'The spirit of the country is up', he informed Palmerston, 'and they are determined that Lord Raglan shall be supported'.[3] But volunteers, as he had pointed out in the past, were an unreliable source of manpower. The groundswell of national pride engendered by victories at the Alma and Inkerman, he later admitted, was punctured from later November by press reports detailing the privations to which the ordinary soldier had become exposed. Such accounts were 'a very great discouragement, and did a very great deal of harm'.[4] To offset the damage, Herbert urged cabinet colleagues to sanction a more judicious use of bounties. Such dividends, he pointed out, would be otiose at harvest time when agricultural workers were unlikely to be tempted; and superfluous at a moment of military triumph, such as the Alma, when patriotism was enough. But as the memory of that fillip to recruitment faded, the prospect of an attractive bounty (Herbert recommended that the sums offered be left to the discretion of the Secretary at War to determine) might prove decisive in the mind of the putative redcoat. The pool of potential recruits, meanwhile, was made bigger by raising the upper age limit from twenty-five to 'thirty, and even to thirty-five years, in the case of men who have served', and by lowering the minimum height requirement from five feet, six inches to five feet, four inches.[5] Herbert took pride in pointing out that civilian volunteers were coming forward at the

1 PP 1854-5 (247), IX, appendix 11 to Fourth Report, pp. 339-41, memoranda of 23, 27 Nov. 1854.
2 WSHC 2057/F4/53, Newcastle to SH, 7 Nov. 1854.
3 HLPP GC/HE/45, SH to Pam, 22 Nov. 1854.
4 PP 1854-5 (247), IX, p. 195.
5 Conacher, *Aberdeen*, p. 515; Hansard, 20 Dec. 1854, CXXXVI, col. 661.

rate of a thousand men a week during November. They helped make it possible to despatch 7,000 additional men to Raglan before the month was out.[1]

Herbert nevertheless estimated that another 10,000 men would be needed in the near future. Further reform of the militia, he believed, offered the best prospect of finding them. As late as the summer, he had still been thinking of that institution primarily as an adjunct to home defences in the event of invasion. With the French now an ally, that scenario could reasonably be discounted: 'our object, at this moment', he wrote, 'is not the efficiency of the militia but the recruiting of the army'. This would be far more effective, he contended, if more militia regiments were embodied for service: 'the military spirit thus awakened, they would come in bodies, which they would not do from their homes'.[2]

The three memoranda which Herbert wrote for the cabinet during November indicate how swiftly his mind was moving. On 6 November, he reported that only eighteen militia regiments were then embodied (about 12,000 men). Subject to the Militia Act being amended to allow them to serve abroad, Herbert recommended that nine of these be sent to the Mediterranean. This would allow the regulars there to be redeployed to the Crimea.[3] He also recommended that recruiting sergeants from the regulars be attached to all militia regiments at home until a quarter of their strength had signed up for the regulars. A bounty of £3 per man would be offered. This was more than was offered to ordinary volunteers but justifiable on the basis that, already having received training, militiamen would be more useful to the army.[4]

It chimed well with Herbert's intentions that Palmerston was in Paris for part of November. In his absence, Herbert was delegated the

---

1   PP 1854-5 (247), IX, pp. 194-5; Conacher, *Aberdeen*, pp. 504-5.
2   PP 1854-5 (247), IX, appendix 11 to Fourth Report, pp. 335-8, memorandum of 6 Nov. 1854.
3   Hansard, 13 Dec. 1854, CXXXVI, cols. 244-5.
4   PP 1854-5 (247), IX, appendix 11 to Fourth Report, pp. 335-8, memorandum of 6 Nov. 1854.

Home Secretary's authority for calling out militia regiments.[1] Quick to use it, Herbert was able to report, in a second memorandum to cabinet on 23 November, that nine more militia regiments had been ordered to embody. He also recommended that any other regiments of reasonable strength be similarly instructed. This meant, however, that more men would be embodied than there was barrack space available. To obviate this problem, Herbert insisted that the excess be billeted on publicans. The latter were to receive up to 2d per day per man in recompense.[2] Four days later, in his third memorandum, Herbert informed the cabinet that 61 militia regiments were now in the process of being embodied. He also suggested that the maximum from each that might be recruited to the regulars be raised from a quarter to a third.[3] It was largely by dint of Herbert's efforts that 12,265 militiamen had transferred to the regular army by the end of the year.

Another initiative in which Herbert was prominent was the Foreign Enlistment Bill. This made provision for up to 10,000 men to be recruited for the army from abroad. Objections were raised that the measure was unconstitutional, immoral, and would dilute the efficiency of the British army by introducing foreigners into its ranks.[4] Herbert gave the soothsayers short shrift. The King's German Legion, he reminded the House, had fought with distinction at Waterloo, and that had once been 'looked upon quite in the same way as the foreign legion now proposed, and the terms scum of the earth, mercenaries, hired assassins, & c., were applied to them then as they now were'.[5] The reality, he told his critics, was that many home recruits were little better than untrained boys: 'they may apply a very simple test on this point, by observing, now that the troops are allowed to wear moustaches, how many among the militia succeed in doing so, and I think they will

---

1 HLPP GC/HE/54, SH to Pam, 16 Nov. 1854; PP 1854-5 (247), IX, pp. 194-5.
2 PP 1854-5 (247), IX, appendix 11 to Fourth Report, pp. 339-40, memorandum of 23 Nov. 1854.
3 PP 1854-5 (247), IX, appendix 11 to Fourth Report, pp. 340-1, memorandum of 27 Nov. 1854.
4 Conacher, *Aberdeen*, pp. 512-14.
5 Hansard, 21 Dec. 1854, CXXXVI, col. 785.

then be satisfied as to their age'.[1] In the present emergency, the House should 'exercise […] common sense, and if we see the means of getting assistance – if we see the means of obtaining ready-trained troops – in God's name let us do it, and not talk about precedents'.[2] Herbert made over a dozen interventions in three days as the Bill was rushed through the Commons. On 21 December, indeed, 'the questions came so quickly that he could not answer them at once'.[3] The measure passed with comfortable majorities but proved disappointing. A month later Herbert admitted that it had not been possible to raise even a single battalion.[4]

Taking a wider view of the manpower problem in late November, Herbert reminded his colleagues that 'The army of the East has been created by discounting the future. Every regiment at home, or within reach, has been robbed to complete it'. More quickly than most, he also recognised that 'Clearly the war with Russia will not be the affair of a year'. The initiatives he had been instrumental in putting in place to provide reinforcements, therefore, would avail little 'unless they are followed by further constant and large supplies of men'.[5] He promised to lay proposals before the cabinet for a systematic, longer term approach to the problem within a few days.

The proposals were duly presented and approved on 1 December. They emanated from a committee composed of Herbert, Newcastle, Hardinge and the Prince Consort. Forty-four army regiments were to be expanded from twelve to sixteen companies. Eight of the companies in each regiment would be placed on immediate active service; four would be kept in England where they would receive drill instruction. The remaining four would be sent to Malta and Gibraltar where they would form a reserve of up to 16,000 men undergoing advanced training and rifle practice. From here, they could be transferred by steamer to the war zone. Herbert and the committee estimated that

1   Hansard, 20 Dec. 1854, CXXXVI, col. 662.
2   Hansard, 19 Dec. 1854, CXXXVI, cols. 555-67.
3   Hansard, 21 Dec. 1854, CXXXVI, cols. 776-7.
4   WSHC 2057/F4/53, SH to Newcastle, 8 Jan. 1855.
5   PP 1854-5 (247), IX, appendix 11 to Fourth Report, pp. 340-1, memorandum of 27 Nov. 1854.

20,000 new men would be needed to effect the scheme.[1] But he would be out of office before it had a chance to reach fruition.

Herbert has reasonably been credited with being more alive to the problem of recruiting than any other member of the cabinet. It was his most substantial, though not his best remembered, contribution to the war effort. He took some pride in announcing to the House on 12 December that almost 55,000 men had either been (or were about to be) sent to the Crimea. Even so, he had been running to stand still. British forces remained overstretched and overworked: some 23,076 reported sick in January 1855.[2] The truth was that there was no swift or easy way to achieve a vast expansion of the army through traditional mechanisms. But even some form of mass conscription could not have produced sufficient trained men in the timescale required. A satisfactory solution, as he had already grudgingly intimated, would not be reached 'till arrangements are made with the French to relieve our men of some of the duty'.[3] Napoleon III obliged: the number of French troops in the Crimea had shot up from 45,000 in October 1854 to 78,000 by mid-January 1855.

The British public, however, was concerned less with quantitative than qualitative matters, the consequence of newspaper reports which dwelt upon the sufferings, born of alleged mismanagement, which the ordinary solider had to endure. As late as mid-October 1854 Herbert had taken a relatively relaxed view of the Fourth Estate; he answered a suggestion that some thought should be given to the adverse impact of publishing casualty lists with the emphatic response that 'I think the War office had better as hitherto publish the list of the killed & wounded men'.[4] By December, however, Herbert's tone was much altered. He complained that journalists 'are a reckless race, and the long habit of newsgathering and publishing in any way and at any price altogether dulls their sense of right and wrong'. 'The violence and abuse of *The Times*', he informed Raglan, 'has, I think, inspired great

1 PP 1854-5 (247), IX, pp. 191, 195; Conacher, *Aberdeen*, p. 509.
2 Conacher, *Aberdeen*, p. 505; Hansard, 12 Dec 1854, CXXXVI, cols. 136-7.
3 Stanmore, I, pp. 310-11, SH to Estcourt, 12 Dec. 1854.
4 BL Add. Mss. 46448, fols. 29-30, SH to Ramsay, 15 Oct. 1854.

disgust, but still these attacks, daily repeated, tell'. He was therefore in full agreement with Newcastle that editors should be asked to 'exclude all objectionable information'.[1] Raglan, reasonably refusing to be distracted from purely military considerations, shared the view of Lord Grey that Herbert and Newcastle 'have the common fault of always looking for newspaper popularity'.[2] But they had a point: a weak government and a parliament increasingly susceptible to popular pressure were not matters that could be ignored if the war were to be prosecuted to a successful conclusion.

Herbert never denied that the army was experiencing hardships. But he was apt to downplay them in public. Speaking in Salisbury in February 1855 he professed still to believe that 'the regimental system of the English army is as near perfection as any human institution can be'. A month earlier, addressing an audience in Knightsbridge at a meeting in aid of the Patriotic Fund, he was at pains to emphasise the improvements that had been made in recent years to the army, 'the condition of which he believed was unexampled in the history of this or of any other nation!'[3] His private view of what was really happening was founded on a unique range of sources. The most senior was Raglan, a friend and visitor to Wilton for over a decade. His letters were complemented by those from Brigadier-General James Bucknall Bucknall Estcourt, Adjutant General, and the man responsible for army discipline. Estcourt hailed from a Gloucestershire family with whom the Herberts were on familiar terms.[4] Both men could unbutton themselves when writing to him. Estcourt in particular sent him a series of long and detailed letters often as graphic as anything contained in W.H. Russell's despatches for *The Times*. In December 1854, for example, he wrote of how 'The oxen begin to die on the road. The provisions are robbed, or the guard is kept out all night, the weather pouring. Diarrhoea, dysentery, and vexations; ill-humour and disorganisation'.[5]

1   WSHC 2057/F4/63, SH to Raglan, 8 Dec. 1854.
2   Sweetman, *Raglan*, p. 271.
3   *SWJ*, 9 Dec. 1854, 17 Feb. 1855.
4   *ODNB*.
5   WSHC 2057/F4/63, Estcourt to SH, 8 Dec. 1854.

In addition, Herbert 'got a great deal from non-official sources'. Best known of these was Florence Nightingale: 'she corresponded with me at my request, to inform me of all those details, she being a very intimate friend'.[1] Her travelling companions, also his friends, Charles and Selina Bracebridge, added further to the picture. So too did the Hon. Sydney Godolphin Osborne. Well-known for his 'lay sermons', a series of controversial articles which had appeared in *The Times* over the previous decade, Osborne went out to Scutari armed with a letter of introduction from Herbert.[2] He published the bestselling *Scutari and its Hospitals* on his return to England in 1855. Osborne was joined at the end of 1854 by the Hon. Josceline Percy, Conservative MP for Launceston. Herbert wanted his friend's input as a supposed expert on hospitals but also as a proxy for instilling his mantra that 'There are two things which must not be thought of when real good is to be obtained, namely trouble and expense [...] Promptitude, which is everything in a hospital, must not be sacrificed to the forms'.[3] He also suggested that Percy might like to oversee a party of nurses, though rather undersold his invitation by adding that 'It is a heavy & not an agreeable task to take charge of this large number of females thro' a long and trying voyage to a strange land'.[4]

Suitably provided with the witnesses to assure himself that shortcomings existed, Herbert impressed upon Newcastle that 'If there is anything I can do or relieve you of, I will do it with pleasure'. It was in this guise, one which Herbert characterised as that of 'a volunteer', that he 'undertook, with a view to relieve the Duke of Newcastle, to do a good deal which properly it was not the business of my office to do; but I did it as his assistant, by delegation from him'.[5] Several months of unremitting labour ensued. 'Herbert strained himself morning, noon, and night', Gladstone would recall, 'to invent wants for the army, and

1 PP 1854-5 (247), IX, pp. 176-7.
2 *ODNB*.
3 WSHC 2057/F4/64, SH to Percy, 30 Nov. 1854.
4 WSHC 2057/F4/64, SH to Percy, 30 Nov. 1854. This was the party of nurses headed by Mary Stanley.
5 WSHC 2057/F4/53, SH to Newcastle, 8 Jan. 1855; PP 1854-5 (247), IX, pp. 167, 194.

according to his best judgement or conjecture to supply them'. Neither did weekends at Wilton signify a rest, as a list of documents required to be brought down to him by George Ramsay, Herbert's hard-pressed secretary, testifies.[1] There is space here to convey only a flavour of the sort of problem with which Herbert was confronted. One letter he received contained detail of failings over the despatch of beds. 'The last mail from Scutari', Herbert fumed, 'announces that the iron beds are arrived, I believe in the <u>Manilla</u>, but that the legs were put into another ship and sent on to Balaclava (I believe in the <u>Jura</u>)'. This was, he continued, 'the natural result of the different Departments who are to cooperate all working in ignorance of what the other is doing'. Judging from the amount of ink he spilt on it, few stories of incompetence angered him more.[2]

One area of particular concern for Herbert was the Commissariat, responsible for the army's food, fodder, tents, and land transport. Well before the conflict started, Herbert had highlighted the incongruity of such prerequisites for the army being provided by a civilian department under Treasury control. By December 1854 he was writing to Estcourt that:

> I hear disastrous stories of ships arriving at Balaklava and leaving it without discharging their cargo – finding no one to take charge of it. Newcastle is sending out men from the docks here to assist, supposing that the Commissariat must be short-handed; and if they are, they never write to say so, nor to ask for what they want. Lord Raglan ought to put a very active, energetic, and intelligent officer as commandant at Balaklava, for on good management there depends the safety and comfort of your Army.[3]

1   Morley, *Gladstone*, I, pp. 651-2, memorandum of 17 Sept. 1897; BL Add. Mss. 46448, fols. 47-8, SH to Ramsay, 5 Nov. 1854.
2   WSHC 2057/F4/53, SH to Newcastle, 8 Jan. 1855; BL Add. Mss. 79657, fols. 94-7, SH to JRG, 7 Jan. 1855.
3   Stanmore, I, pp. 310-11, SH to Estcourt, 12 Dec. 1854.

Herbert's assessment of the Commissary-General, William Filder, as a man with a 'great want of energy and resource', was one of the more favourable testimonials bestowed on the latter.[1]

Another department for which Herbert evinced low regard was the Ordnance, responsible in particular for rifles, swords, ammunition, greatcoats and boots. In 1854, only 50,000 of the 90,000 rifles requested for the army reached their destination; there were likewise complaints about rusty weapons, and boots and tents that leaked. Part of the problem was that the Ordnance contracted for a good deal of its materials with an eye more to price than quality. Though Herbert maintained in public that most stories about substandard boots were ill-founded, he wrote privately of his expectation that the Ordnance will 'trounce the villainous contractors who supplied the bad boots'.[2]

Herbert also became more directly involved in Ordnance affairs, especially in matters pertaining to clothing in which he assisted 'to the best of my power'. On 8 November he demanded a report on the merits of sheepskin over its rivals ('all skins end by breeding vermin'); in the same letter he related to his secretary that he expected 2,000 pairs of boots to be ready any day.[3] With respect to the last named items, 'I was constantly at the Ordnance urging and hastening those proceedings; I had always the pattern of everything sent out to me'. He even insisted on having one of the stoutest Grenadier Guardsmen at hand to be sent to him:

> and I made him try the boots on; and I imagine if a guardsman of considerable size and height could be comfortable and easy in them,

---

1 WSHC 2057/F4/63, SH to Raglan, 5 Mar. 1855. In June 1854 the Commissariat had been transferred to Newcastle as Secretary for War, but it was the end of the year before the switchover was effected in practice.
2 PP 1854-5 (247), IX, p. 188; WSHC 2057/F4/63, SH to Estcourt, 26 Feb. 1855.
3 PP 1854-5 (247), IX, p. 187; BL Add. Mss. 46448, fol. 57, SH to Ramsay, 8 Nov. 1854.

they would be quite large enough, even with two or three pairs of stockings, for a small man.[1]

Herbert also encouraged the public to donate 'Fur boots or shoes, woollen or flannel Jerseys, wash leather drawers, woollen hose, stockings, gloves or mitts and flannel dresses for the hospitals'. Socks and mittens in particular he welcomed, 'inasmuch as it gratifies the donors [and] will also give them pleasure as showing the warmth of feeling entertained towards your [Raglan's] Army here at home'. Queen Victoria, no less, headed the army of volunteer knitters.[2]

It was not just officialdom which found itself subjected to Herbert's intrusions. His friend, Sir James Graham, First Lord of the Admiralty, was a regular recipient of his missives. Would it be possible, Herbert asked, to loan French ships lying idle at Toulon to transport more cavalry? Failing that, 'we have small battalions we could send, & small battalions are better than none'. And what about the possibility of pressing the Queen's yacht into service?[3] Revealing a fondness for the potential of esoteric gadgetry, Herbert also forwarded Graham a proposal from Isambard Kingdom Brunel for what the engineer called a floating gun carriage, adding that 'He is wild in his love of novelties, but very ingenious'.[4] Herbert it was too, along with Palmerston and Clarendon, who urged a lukewarm First Lord to avail himself of Napoleon III's offer of 8,000 troops provided that the British arrange their transport. Mr Samuel Cunard was able to oblige.[5] Herbert even dared to ask his political boss, Newcastle, 'what progress you have made with the baggage train'. In what could easily be construed as a patronising tone, Herbert also suggested that Newcastle might make better use of cabinet meetings as an opportunity to brief colleagues:

1 PP 1854-5 (247), IX, p. 188.
2 *Dublin Evening Post*, 12 Dec. 1854; WSHC 2057/F4/63, SH to Raglan, 8 Dec. 1854.
3 BL Add. Mss. 79657, fols. 89-90, 92-93, SH to JRG, 19 Nov., 4 Dec. 1854.
4 BL Add. Mss. 79657, fols. 82-4, SH to JRG, 6 Nov. 1854.
5 Conacher, *Aberdeen*, pp. 506-7.

'People to be carried with you must be kept au courant of what is being done, and made parties to it by giving their assent'.[1]

Herbert even dared to chivvy the military hierarchy. Raglan would be well advised, his friend suggested, to appoint a sanitary officer to every division in order to 'keep the camp clear of offal and excrement, etc'. Herbert also bemoaned 'the absence of detailed information from yourself': the cabinet sometimes had no option but to derive information from other sources, even, heaven forfend, French ones!.[2] Less endearing, behind his friend's back, Herbert vouchsafed to Estcourt the need to 'supply for Lord Raglan that which his age prevents his obtaining for himself – namely, suggestions which an ocular acquaintance with all details can alone inspire'. Ten days later Estcourt himself was one of the intended targets (the other was Richard Airey, the Quartermaster-General) when Raglan was offered Herbert's opinion that 'I fear you are not well served as regards the two chief officers on your staff'.[3]

Even the latter examples, however, have paled in the popular memory compared with Herbert's initiatives to improve hospital and nursing provision. The Army Medical Department, set up in 1810, had functioned tolerably well in peacetime. But it proved unequal to the challenge of providing and sustaining the large general hospitals the war necessitated. Any supplies the Department required were furnished by the Purveyor but, following its abolition in 1830, that office was revived only in April 1853. It hardly augured well that whilst the Purveyor-General turned to the Ordnance for materials, his money to pay for them came via the Commissariat and thus ultimately from the cash-conscious Treasury. Equally perplexing, Dr Andrew Smith, Director-General of the Army Medical Department, professed himself unclear as to which of five different authorities he was responsible. He and Herbert were at best wary of each other: they clashed openly

---

1   WSHC 2057/F4/53, SH to Newcastle, 8 Jan. 1855.
2   WSHC 2057/F4/63, SH to Raglan, 8 Dec. 1854, 5 Mar. 1855.
3   WSHC 2057/F4/63, SH to Raglan, 12, 22 Dec. 1854.

in January 1855 when Smith resisted Herbert's proposals to employ civilian surgeons in military hospitals.[1]

Herbert had demonstrated concern for medical provision in the army before hostilities commenced. In February 1854, following inquiries instituted by him at Paris and Vienna, he announced the introduction of lectures in military surgery at London, Dublin and Glasgow. Two years previously, in a private capacity, he had donated £20 to the Queen's College in Birmingham, to help provide for medical scholarships.[2] Six months before war was declared, he wrote to Graham 'that the invalided soldier is well entitled to kinder and more generous treatment on his passage home than he now receives'.[3] So far as the specific question of employing female nurses in military hospitals was concerned, Newcastle recalled that Herbert had touted the idea before the army set sail. Unsurprisingly, 'the general opinion of military men was adverse to their employment'. Even in civilian life, it will be remembered, female nursing was held in low regard, associated in the popular mind with the drunken and socially-dubious Sairey Gamp, immortalised in the pages of *Martin Chuzzlewit*.[4] Army nursing was left to male orderlies, assisted, when occasion demanded, by the walking wounded.

During the autumn of 1854, however, the need for something more to be done became only too apparent. There was a base hospital at Balaclava, but the general hospitals, converted Turkish military quarters, were 300 miles distant at Scutari, opposite Constantinople. No ambulance corps or dedicated hospital ships existed to facilitate transfers there. And although between them the Barrack Hospital and the General Hospital could accommodate 4,000 patients, they were notable less for their size than their insalubrity: the Barrack Hospital sat perched over a blocked sewer. One modern authority has blamed Herbert for having chosen these sites; the instruction was, in fact,

---

1   Strachan, *Wellington's Legacy*, pp. 241-5; Stanmore, I, pp. 398-400, SH to Smith, 19, 23 Jan. 1855.
2   Hansard, 24 Feb. 1853, CXXX, cols. 1287-8; *The Times*, 13 June 1851.
3   WSHC 2057/F4/59, JRG to SH, 15 Oct. 1853.
4   Goldie, *Nightingale*, p. 22.

issued by Newcastle.¹ It does not much matter. The substantive point was that they were self-evidently ill-fitted for purpose. As casualties streamed in from the Battle of Balaclava, the hospitals, already under-supplied, were hopelessly overwhelmed. One witness described to Herbert scenes of 'four miles of beds and not 18 inches apart'. A month later, the same writer added that 'The vermin might, if they had but "unity of purpose" carry off the four miles of beds on their backs, and march with them into the War Office and Horse Guards'.²

Herbert's correspondent was Florence Nightingale. Like many, she had been moved by reports of what British servicemen were having to endure in the East, notably by Thomas Chenery's account of the suffering wounded which appeared in *The Times* on 12 October. Why, asked 'A Sufferer by the Present War' two days later, did Britain, unlike France, have no 'sisters of charity'? Answering rhetoric with action, Nightingale wrote to Elizabeth Herbert on 14 October. She informed her that Lady Maria Forester, the philanthropic Evangelical daughter of the Earl of Roden, was willing to provide £200 if Nightingale would head a 'small private expedition of nurses' with a view to being 'of use to the wounded wretches'.³ Sidney Herbert famously trumped Forester. In a letter of 15 October he invited Nightingale to head a party of nurses to the East at the government's expense.

Nightingale's ties with the Herberts (she was closer to Elizabeth before the war) had developed significantly since their first meeting in Rome in 1847. Her first invitation to Wilton was received in April 1848. She shared their interest in convalescent homes: the Herberts had established one at Charmouth in Dorset, staffed by a German Protestant sisterhood, for the benefit of those living on the Wilton estate. Elizabeth allowed her to deputise as teacher in the school house in Wilton Park.⁴ In the summer of 1851 the Herberts sought her out at Kaiserwerth en route from Hornburg in Germany for advice on the appointment of a deaconess. Elizabeth Herbert's influence as a

1   *CWFN*, I, p. 29.
2   Stanmore, I, pp. 347-8, FN to SH, 14 Nov. 1854; Sweetman, *Raglan*, p. 269, FN to SH, 31 Dec. 1854.
3   BL Add. Mss. 43396, fol. 11, FN to EH, 14 Oct. 1854.
4   Bostridge, *Nightingale*, pp. 119-23; Stanmore, I, pp. 97-8.

member of the governing body of the Institute for the Care of Sick Gentlewomen in Upper Harley Street was probably decisive in securing Nightingale's appointment as its Superintendent in April 1853.[1] A year later, she wrote to Nightingale for 'some authentic information on the subject of the nurses [at St Barts], their bad pay and worse lodgings [in order that Herbert] could get the evil more or less remedied, and public attention, at any rate, turned that way'.[2]

An awareness that such connections existed has generated debate as to whether Herbert's letter of 15 October was serendipitous or pre-arranged.[3] We can at least be certain that no conniving took place in the 72 hours before his invitation was issued: following 'a confounded archaeological meeting' in Wilton, on 11 October, the Herberts had gone to Bournemouth for a few days.[4] What is intriguing, however, is the possibility that from there Herbert wrote the anonymous letter which appeared in *The Times* on 14 October, effectively an open invitation for would-be nurses to volunteer their services. He was, after all, one who was 'A Sufferer by the Present War', and somebody who, from his experiment at Charmouth, had experience of religious sisterhoods. He may, in other words, have been teeing up the shot which he hit the next day. Such a move would certainly be of a piece with his clearly documented actions, so far as the press is concerned, over the next few days.

Herbert, it is clear, had decided some time before mid-October that he was going to send a party of nurses to the East. He was no less decided that he wanted Nightingale to head it. His letter of 15 October notes that 'I have been several times on the point of asking you hypothetically if, supposing the attempt were made, you wd. undertake to direct it'. He was, after all, stating a literal truth in his much quoted line that 'There is but one person in England that I know of, who would be capable of, organising & superintending such a scheme'.[5] But the basis for his knowledge was relatively slender. Nightingale had presided

---

1 *CWFN*, I, pp. 123, 127, 304-5.
2 *CWFN*, XIII, p. 59, EH to FN, 29 May 1854.
3 Smith, *Nightingale*, pp. 26-7; Bostridge, *Nightingale*, p. 206.
4 BL Add. Mss. 46448, fols. 24-8, SH to Ramsay, 5, 11 Oct. 1854.
5 Goldie, *Nightingale*, pp. 23-5, SH to FN, 15 Oct. 1854.

at Harley Street for just fourteen months, responsible for genteel ladies occupying 27 beds. By no stretch of the imagination was this Scutari. It was thus partly to forestall opposition to his desire that Nightingale should head the nursing party that Herbert now acted so swiftly. He secured the Cabinet's approval for his initiative on 18 October; he was surely also the answer to the ostensible mystery of how a lithographed copy of his 15 October letter, supposedly distributed only to friends, found its way into the newspapers as early as 19 October.[1] A letter under his own name, sent to the editor of the *Morning Chronicle* on 21 October, informed its readers that other offers to go to the East would be regretfully declined. The same letter outlined details of Nightingale's remit. To dissuade other persons 'going straight off to Constantinople for nothing', Herbert wrote an article for his secretary to send to the editor of the *Globe* saying that it had come from 'a gentleman in the midland counties'.[2] The means to Herbert's ends were surely justified by subsequent events. Nightingale's biographer generously concedes that he deserves 'full credit' for the aspiration expressed in his 15 October letter that 'an enormous amount of good will be done, now, & to persons deserving everything at our hands, & a prejudice will have been broken through, & a precedent established wh. will multiply the good to all time'. Gladstone had a point when he wrote a year later that 'I wish some one of the thousand who in prose justly celebrate Miss Nightingale would say a single word for the man of routine who devised and projected her going – Sidney Herbert'.[3]

Drawing upon their earlier work with the Female Emigration Fund, the Herberts (Elizabeth, it must be admitted, more than Herbert) were central to what followed. Advertisements were placed for would-be nurses to accompany Nightingale. Formal interviews followed at 49 Belgrave Square. They were conducted by Elizabeth, Selina Bracebridge, Mary Stanley (another nursing friend of the

1   Dossey, *Nightingale*, p. 117.
2   *Morning Chronicle*, 24 Oct. 1854; BL Add. Mss. 46448, fols. 31-4, SH to Ramsay, 22 Oct. 1854.
3   Bostridge, *Nightingale*, p. 207; Reid, *Monckton Milnes*, WEG to Milnes, 15 Oct. 1855.

Herberts), and Nightingale's sister, Parthenope.[1] Herbert, meanwhile, was active in making arrangements for the passage out. He instructed his secretary to make contact with a Mr Forster 'as he could tell her [Nightingale] a great deal about the locality wh. might be useful to her'. First class cabins were procured on the *Vectis*. On 20 October, Herbert addressed the full ensemble of 38 nurses in his Belgrave Square dining room before they set off for Southampton the next day.[2]

One might have expected that Nightingale and her entourage departed amid universal goodwill. Such was not the case. Recent writers have focused on the particular case of the creole (Jamaican-Scot) Mary Seacole. Seacole tried, but failed, to see Herbert at the War Office in an attempt to join the nursing party. She did succeed in gaining admission to Belgrave Square where she was interviewed (but rejected) by a lady, most likely Selina Bracebridge. Seacole ascribed her being spurned to her skin colour. Doubtless this was a bar, but so was her age and social background. In any event, none of these criteria were the root of the contemporary controversy. It was instead the familiar one of religion.[3]

The trigger was the publication of Herbert's letter of 15 October which, *inter alia*, had alluded to Lady Maria Forester. An earlier offer from Forester to head a party of nurses to the East had been rejected by Herbert; Nightingale's offer, though Forester's credentials were arguably stronger, had been accepted. Some Protestant commentators ascribed this turn of events to Lady Maria's well-known Evangelicalism compared to Nightingale, 'a lady with a retinue of Puseyites and Papists'.[4] The insinuation that Nightingale herself was at least a closet Catholic was ludicrous: her family's religious heritage was Unitarian; Elizabeth Herbert categorised her, not unreasonably, as broadly Low Church.[5] But the bigots had been let loose and old charges were

1   Bostridge, *Nightingale*, pp. 207-9.
2   BL Add. Mss. 46448, fols. 41-2, SH to Ramsay, 24 Oct. 1854; Cook, Nightingale, I, pp. 159-60.
3   Robinson, *Mary Seacole*, pp. 88-90; Salih, *Wonderful Adventures of Mrs Seacole in Many Lands*, pp. xxviii, 71-4.
4   *London Daily News*, 3 Nov. 1854; *Stroud Journal*, 11 Nov. 1854.
5   *Cork Examiner*, 10 Jan. 1855 for EH's letter of 9 Dec. 1854.

revived. 'A Protestant Churchman' wrote of 'the Anglo-Catholic ladies at the War Office' and the Herberts as 'Anglo-Catholic dissenters'. 'The pervert Mr Manning', the correspondent added, 'is said to be constantly at the War-office'. Herbert specifically was accused of spoiling his otherwise laudable experiment in nursing by 'the eccentric influence of that passion for sentimental crotchets by which he is so singularly characterised [...] seldom did the official mind commit a more offensive blunder'.[1]

The flames of the religious controversy were fanned by the undeniable fact that 10 of the 38 nurses despatched to the East with Nightingale were Catholics, a fact compounded by the presence of 15 more Catholics in a second party of 48 nurses sent out under Mary Stanley (herself a very recent convert to Catholicism) in December. It was a trend about which Nightingale herself expressed reservations to Herbert: 'The proportion of R. Catholics, which is already making an outcry, you have increased to 25 in 84'.[2] But the Herberts were fully alive to, indeed they had anticipated, such a commotion. Elizabeth Herbert, for example, wrote to Gladstone about the awkwardness of Mary Stanley's being on the interviewing panel. She seems to have adopted Charles Bracebridge's suggestion (he and his wife were both Low Church) that Herbert insist on Elizabeth's seeing prospective applicants with her jointly.[3] Herbert himself had been unambiguous in his instructions to Nightingale of 20 October prohibiting nurses 'without any reference to religious creed to make use of their position in the Hospitals to tamper with or disturb the religious opinions of the patients of any denomination whatever'. His critics, however, chose to overlook the reality that the pool of suitable nurses outside the Catholic sisterhoods was extremely limited. They also ignored the inconvenient truth that up to a third of the troops in the Crimea were themselves Catholics.[4] Herbert, however, was well aware of it and was

1 *Morning Chronicle*, 18 Jan. 1855; *Belfast Commercial Chronicle*, 24 Jan. 1855.
2 BL Add. Mss. 43393, fol. 34, FN to SH, 15 Dec. 1854; *Cork Examiner*, 10 Jan. 1855; Dossey, *Nightingale*, p. 116.
3 BL Add. Mss. 44212, fols. 19-22, EH to WEG, 23 Nov. 1854.
4 TNA WO 43/963, fol. 251.

determined to provide religious succour (he ordered the appointment of additional chaplains to accompany troop ships) in due proportion. At the beginning of 1855, 12 Protestant chaplains, 4 Presbyterian ministers and 8 Catholic priests were available to minister to the spiritual needs of the army.[1] It is difficult, in face of the efforts that she and her husband were making, not to concur with Elizabeth Herbert in lamenting 'these most uncharitable and sectarian attacks'.[2]

Nightingale's work at Scutari would, in short order, become the stuff of legend. The image of the Lady with the Lamp, and the words of Henry Wadsworth Longfellow's 'Santa Filomena' provided a heartening alternative narrative to the prevailing one of ineptitude and mismanagement. The British public could reasonably be forgiven, therefore, for not knowing that the Nightingale with whom Herbert corresponded was less than a saint. Like Herbert himself, she could be bitingly acerbic on paper, prone also to 'colourful hyperbole'.[3] This, to be fair, was born of legitimate frustration. She penned few lines more memorable than, when in replying to a Herbert letter of March 1856, she wrote that 'It is written from Belgrave Square. I write from a Crimean Hut. The point of sight is different'.[4] The riposte in itself, however (Herbert was out of office by then), reveals part of the function that Herbert performed for her, that of safety valve. Her friend was a sounding board to whom, and even against whom, she knew that she could vent her spleen. It is inconceivable that anybody else in his place at the War Office would have been so tolerant and understanding. She was particularly incensed at Herbert's decision to send a second party of nurses to the East (as with the first, he addressed them in Belgrave Square before their departure) in December 1854. Nightingale regarded it as a breach of an agreement that he would only do so at her request. She threatened to resign in favour of Mary Stanley.[5] In Herbert's defence, it might be pointed out that there

---

1   BL Add. Mss. 46448, fols. 35-6, SH to Hardinge, 23 Oct. 1854; *Morning Chronicle*, 18 Jan.1855.
2   *Cork Examiner*, 10 Jan. 1855 for EH's letter of 9 Dec. 1854.
3   Sweetman, *War and Administration*, p. 2.
4   BL Add. Mss. 43393, fol. 224, FN to SH, 3 Apr. 1856.
5   BL Add. Mss. 43393, fol. 34, FN to SH, 15 Dec. 1854.

was no such undertaking in his official instructions to Nightingale; the offending reference was contained in his letter to the *Morning Chronicle* of 21 October. The episode smacks of one where the tail was attempting to wag the dog. Why, in his capacity as Secretary at War, should Herbert not rule that more nurses were necessary? The situation in the hospitals, after all, was worsening: the number of patients rose from 3,200 in November 1854 to 13,600 by the end of February 1855. Eighty-six nurses hardly seems like a case of overstaffing. Herbert nevertheless acknowledged that he had been at fault in a letter which assisted in dissuading Nightingale from quitting her post. His biographer, Lord Stanmore, was given to understand that it was 'one of the most beautiful letters ever written'. For whatever reason, Nightingale could not provide it when Stanmore asked to see it forty years later. She probably consigned it to the flames when she sorted her papers shortly after Herbert's death.[1]

When equanimity prevailed, Nightingale knew full well that Herbert was lending her the full weight of his support. When she grumbled that she would like greater notice from the Commander-in-Chief as to how many wounded to prepare for ('our notice comes in the shape of a steamer with the patients'), Herbert promised to mention it to Raglan.[2] This was yet another example of the chivvying, specifically with regard to medical matters, which characterised Herbert's working practice during the war. Raglan, whose grasp of the medical realities Herbert thought less than convincing, was told to bear in mind that in administering hospitals the size of those at Scutari, 'it is really twenty or thirty hospitals concentrated'.[3] In light of reports of 'the entire failure of the system of hospital orderlies' (untrained males who undertook most of the military nursing then provided), Herbert wrote to Dr Andrew Smith on Christmas Eve 1854 urging that the Army Medical Department should look to create a dedicated establishment: 'There is no necessity for their now being soldiers any more than there

---

1   WSHC 2057/F4/52, Stanmore to EH, 11 Nov. 1901; Stanmore, I, p. 372.
2   WSHC 2057/F4/63, SH to Raglan, 5 Mar. 1855.
3   WSHC 2057/F4/63, SH to Raglan, 22 Dec. 1854.

is for the purveyors and the commissariat being soldiers'.[1] A particular target of Herbert's criticism was the elderly Purveyor-General, Thomas Wreford, a parsimonious jobsworth. 'It seems impossible to make him understand', he fulminated, 'that the job of a purveyor is to purvey'. He attempted to circumvent Wreford's shortcomings by despatching six new clerks to assist him. But Wreford remained 'incompetent', and Herbert was frustrated that the Commandant at Scutari failed to remove him.[2] Successive commandants were in turn subjected to Herbert's strictures. He thought that Major Charles Sillery, in post when Nightingale arrived, was unequal to the demands of managing an establishment in excess of 6,000 people. The unfortunate major, it is generally agreed, lacked sufficient rank to deal with the myriad problems confronting him.[3] But Brigadier-General Lord William Paulet, appointed to succeed him in January 1855, he judged little better. Had Paulet, Herbert demanded to know, procured a steamer for transferring provisions? Had the pier been rebuilt in stone ('Wood only got knocked to pieces by every surf'.)? Had hospitals been properly ventilated? Paulet, Herbert insisted, must see all these things with his own eyes. Having done so, he must then send him precise information as to how matters stood; thereafter a weekly progress report would suffice.[4]

Just how much difference did Herbert make to remedy the evils of the hospitals during this period? Nightingale, no sycophant, was generous in her assessment early in February 1854 that 'Your orders have produced an essential difference – & all hands are called to work'. Only a fortnight later, however, she qualified this with the observation that 'You have done all you could, but the Personnel is wanting here to carry out your intentions'.[5] She wrote, moreover, just as the mortality

1   Stanmore, I, p. 366, SH to Smith, 24 Dec. 1854; Goldie, *Nightingale*, p. 117.
2   WSHC 2057/F4/43, SH to Paulet, 26 Feb. 1855; Stanmore, I, pp. 412-16, SH to FN, 5 Mar. 1855.
3   Conacher, *Aberdeen*, pp. 480-2; WSHC 2057/F4/63, SH to Paulet, 18 Jan. 1855.
4   WSHC 2057/F4/63, SH to Paulet, 18 Jan. 1855.
5   BL Add. Mss. 43393, fols. 131, 173, FN to SH, 5, 22 Feb. 1855.

rate in the hospitals was peaking: 52% of those admitted that month did not survive. Even Nightingale subsequently agreed that the turning point, so far as mortality rates were concerned, dated from the spring of 1855, thanks to fewer admissions, improving weather, and the arrival at Scutari of a sanitary commission endowed with effective power to right wrongs. But Herbert had played his part over the preceding four months in helping, as Nightingale put it, to 'pull it through'.[1]

Herbert's approach more generally during this critical period brings to mind that of Winston Churchill (the 3rd Duke of Marlborough was their common ancestor) nearly a century later. During the Second World War, Churchill famously utilised red labels bearing the legend 'Action this Day'. Whether Herbert's similarity of style translated into substance is another matter. He lacked the authority that would have come with being Prime Minister. Gladstone, however, told Herbert that 'You have sent out everything except common sense'; Goulburn thought that he had been 'one of the most if not the most efficient member of the government'.[2] Lord Granville, taking stock as Herbert was leaving office, told Elizabeth that 'I was surprised at the universal appreciation of the work done by your husband'.[3] Conversely, Herbert's scattergun approach might be said to have added to the very confusion which he was attempting to reduce. There is also plenty of evidence that his chivvying bred resentment. Nightingale relayed to him the news that 'Your name is [...] continually used as a bugbear'.[4] Even a friend such as Sir James Graham was clearly irked by Herbert's irresistible urge to interfere. To Herbert's complaint, in November 1854, that the Admiralty needed to transport more men, Graham retorted that 3,000 men had been despatched to Raglan over the previous fortnight, with 2,000 more ready to follow them within the next ten days. Furthermore, Graham was 'entirely opposed' to the idea of depriving the Queen of her boat, a notion he dismissed

---

1   BL Add. Mss. 43396, fols. 35-8, FN to EH, 11 July 1855; Bostridge, *Nightingale*, pp. 247-50.
2   Stanmore, I, pp. 313-4, 460, WEG to SH, 14 Jan. 1855; WSHC 2057/F4/52, Goulburn to EH, 29 June 1855.
3   WSHC 2057/F4/53, Granville to EH, 23 Jan. 1855.
4   Stanmore, I, p. 361.

as a gimmick, merely 'for effect'.¹ Raglan, meanwhile, was as close to incensed as his congenial temperament would allow, by Herbert's presumption in recommending that he dismiss his senior subordinates. On balance Herbert's badgering probably did more good than harm: 'anyone can indirectly assist', he pleaded to Estcourt.² But it was a phrase which expressed a dictum, not one which defined a system.

Would Herbert, therefore, have made a better War Minister than Newcastle? Lord Grey told his brother in December 1854 that neither man was fit 'for taking a lead in so weighty a business as the conduct of a war'.³ But he was no friend of either. Grey aside, the general consensus is in favour of Herbert. Granville spoke for many when he wrote that 'The best man connected with the Department appears to be Sidney Herbert. He is by far the best judge of men, is practical, unegotistical, and without official nonsense'. Even Gladstone, one of Newcastle's best friends, considered the latter 'ill for the war office, as he was no administrator'.⁴ There were rumours in January 1855 that Aberdeen 'wishes to appoint Herbert in his place'. Most contemporaries, and historians since, however, have agreed that this would have been a mistake. As Aberdeen's son put it, 'It must, under existing circumstances, be Palmerston. Not that Herbert would not fill the office better, but because if a change is made, this is the only one that will give real confidence.' Palmerston's appointment, in other words, was favoured on the grounds that style was then more important than substance: he was popularly depicted as a puckish John Bull; Herbert's slender frame and elegance were all too easily equated with a certain delicacy. Image apart, however, it is worth noting that Herbert's qualifications to fill the office were regarded as being at least as strong as Palmerston's.⁵ In truth, though, neither man would have been able to hold back the flood of problems with which he would have been inundated. For the sake of both Herbert's and Palmerston's

1   BL Add. Mss. 79657, fols. 85-6, 91, JRG to SH, 7 Nov., 4 Dec. 1854.
2   WSHC 2057/F4/63, Raglan to SH, 23 Jan. 1855; Stanmore, I, pp. 310-11, SH to Estcourt, 12 Dec. 1854.
3   Sweetman, *Raglan*, p. 271.
4   Morley, *Gladstone*, I, pp. 651-2, memorandum of 17 Sept. 1897.
5   Conacher, *Aberdeen*, pp. 532-3, 551-2.

subsequent reputations, the fall of Aberdeen before he could appoint either as War Minister, was a blessing in disguise.

Speculation that a cabinet reshuffle was imminent at this time had much to do with Lord John Russell. Fuelled by personal ambition, he shared the growing popular view that the war needed to be prosecuted with greater vigour. Persuaded that he was the man to instil it, he proffered Aberdeen the unsolicited advice, in November 1854, that the office of Secretary at War should be abolished. Herbert, he suggested, might become Paymaster General. The office of Secretary for War, meanwhile, should be vested in a member of the Commons, a clear swipe at Newcastle who was in the Lords. Aberdeen took exception, responding, so far as the Secretary at War was concerned, that Herbert was 'deservedly popular and likely to find favour'. The correspondence between Prime Minister and Foreign Secretary continued, and was made known to the full cabinet early in December. Herbert was understandably nonplussed. But his place was secure. Palmerston argued that the Secretary at War needed to be retained; Lansdowne felt that there was no need to disturb Newcastle given that a man 'so able and so popular as Sidney Herbert' could answer for him in the Commons.[1] For a few more weeks, at least, the status quo prevailed.

Ministers did agree, however, in face of mounting criticism, to the early recall of parliament. Following the Queen's Speech on 12 December, it fell to Herbert, as spokesman for the army in the Commons, to respond to the charge that it had hitherto achieved nothing in the East. He did so in a lengthy speech detailing the progress of the expeditionary force since March. The 'country has ample cause to congratulate itself', Herbert concluded, 'on the important results that have already been attained, as well as the splendid success of our arms'. Members were asked to join him in sending a clear message to the Czar:

> Let us show him that we will send any number of men that may be necessary – men such as scaled the heights of the Alma, dashed through

---

1   Conacher, *Aberdeen*, pp. 493-503.

his ranks at Balaklava, and defeated his battalions against such fearful odds at Inkerman. I hope the House, by its unanimity, will be worthy of the people of England. The pride of all England is in arms.[1]

Lord Richard Cavendish wrote to Elizabeth Herbert to congratulate her on her husband's 'splendid speech'; John Murray published it, priced one shilling. Disraeli, by contrast, ridiculed it as an exercise in attempting to bamboozle the House with statistics.[2] Herbert was not, of course, blinded by his own spin. Privately, he had just expressed the view to Raglan that if Sebastopol did not fall within two months, it would probably not be taken at all. Three weeks later, in a memorandum for the cabinet, he even raised the spectre of an ignominious evacuation, 'a fearful alternative to contemplate [...] It is useless, however, to shut our eyes to the possibility of the necessity'.[3]

The House adjourned for a month on 23 December. During the recess, Herbert thought a great deal about how those in government charged with running the war might cooperate more effectively. Both he and Palmerston wrote to Newcastle urging him to institute regular meetings of the military departments, ideally extending the invitation to a Lord of the Admiralty as well. Newcastle duly convened a meeting on 3 January. He was joined by the Secretary at War, the Commander-in-Chief, the Lieutenant-General of the Ordnance, and the Clerk of the Ordnance.[4] Herbert regarded this as insufficient. Five days later he was writing to Newcastle again with the exhortation that: 'We have a storm brewing against the working of the military departments, and if we intend to outlive it we must make vigorous use of the fortnight between this and the meeting of Parliament'.[5] His vision as to how

---

1 Hansard, 12 Dec. 1854, CXXXVI, cols. 92-102, 197-215.
2 WSHC 2057/F4/52, Cavendish to EH, 15 Dec. 1854; *Morning Chronicle*, 19 Dec. 1854; Hansard, 12 Dec. 1854, CXXXVI, cols. 197-215.
3 WSHC 2057/F4/63, SH to Raglan, 8 Dec. 1854; Stanmore, I, pp. 318-25, memorandum of 9 Jan. 1855.
4 Conacher, *Aberdeen*, p. 521.
5 WSHC 2057/F4/53, SH to Newcastle, 8 Jan. 1855.

business might be better transacted was subsequently spelt out to all Members:

> You want some person to conduct the finance of the army, another for the provisioning of the army, another for the arming of the army, and again, the commander-in-chief to maintain and conduct the business of the army; these are the persons who in my opinion should form a Board, over which the Secretary of State, the chief Minister for the War Department, should preside, and from whom the others should receive instructions, and to whom they should make the suggestions they might have to offer respecting the carrying out of his recommendations, and to whom they should report the progress made in carrying out his will.[1]

What was effectively a War Committee along those lines met on 10, 17 and 20 January. According to Herbert:

> The object of this was that they should understand the object of the orders that were given, and should be enabled to combine all the means in their power to attain a common object. Unless that be done, there can be no unity of action. Minutes were taken at these meetings, copies of which were sent to the principal Members of the Government. At every fresh meeting the minutes of the last were read, and reports were made as to the progress of the works going forward under the administration.[2]

Herbert sought to have the committee's existence formally recognised by an Order in Council following the cabinet meeting of 20 January. The possible fly in the ointment, as he was aware, was Russell. The fact that Russell was one of those who would receive the committee's minutes would, he hoped, suffice to win his support: 'The amour propre of Lord John is satisfied, and his foibles enlisted in favour

---

1 Hansard, 26 Jan. 1855, CXXXVI, cols. 993-4.
2 Hansard, 26 Jan. 1855, CXXXVI, col. 994; Sweetman, *War and Administration*, pp. 121-3.

of instead of against the public service'.[1] Herbert was wrong. Russell had drawn up his own proposals for the reorganisation of military departments at the end of December: he submitted them to Aberdeen on 22 January. Graham informed Herbert that, with rival proposals in the air, 'I am afraid that discussions in the Cabinet, as matters now stand, will not improve the chances of a wise and dispassionate decision [...] We must, however, pass thro' this ordeal, if Lord John desire it'.[2]

The obdurate Lord John did not desire it. When parliament reassembled on 23 January, John Arthur Roebuck, the fiercely patriotic Member for Sheffield, gave notice that he would bring forward a motion 'for a Select Committee to inquire into the condition of our army before Sebastopol, and into the conduct of those departments of the Government whose duty it has been to minister to the wants of that army'. Russell, professing that he could not in conscience oppose such a motion, resigned that evening. A 'Government already weak has received a heavy blow', judged Herbert.[3] By the time that Roebuck moved his motion on 26 January, Lord Lonsdale was being more emphatic. Ministers, he wrote, must be turned out 'on account of their incapacity and their negligence [...] do not suppose that the only men fit for office are Newcastle and Sidney Herbert'.[4]

It fell to Herbert, in a scenario analogous to that of Neville Chamberlain in May 1940, to lead the government's response to Roebuck's censure.[5] Facing a hostile House, Herbert's task was made the more difficult by Roebuck's labouring under 'physical infirmity', in consequence of which he had been unable to say very little in support of his motion. This, as Herbert pointed out in his opening remarks, presented something of a dilemma, 'inasmuch as there has been no charge made, no case substantiated, or even attempted to be substantiated, to which I might apply myself to answer'. In such circumstances, he protested, he could add little to the exhaustive

1   WSHC 2057/F4/53, SH to Newcastle, 8 Jan. 1855.
2   BL Add. Mss. 79657, fols. 100-1, JRG to SH, 22 Jan. 1855; Prest, *Russell*, p. 368.
3   Hansard, 28 Jan. 1855, CXXXVI, col. 1000; Prest, *Russell*, pp. 370-1.
4   Jennings, *Croker Papers*, III, p. 325, Lonsdale to Croker, 29 Jan. 1855.
5   Hansard, 26 Jan. 1855, CXXXVI, cols. 982-1002.

review of the war which he had provided in his speech of 12 December. Adopting a more offensive tone, he then declared it nonsense to call for an inquiry whilst the war still raged:

> If you intend to carry this motion, you intend to paralyse the action of the Government at home and of the army abroad, for it is impossible for a Commander in Chief and his officers to act freely when they know that there is a jury sitting on their every action, and that there are witnesses whom they have not the means of answering misrepresenting their conduct.

Moreover, it was not the role of the legislature to aggregate to itself executive responsibilities:

> I do not want a precedent to be set for transferring to Committees upstairs the functions and prerogatives of the Crown, and I wish the Executive to be respected by this House, as well as to see it respect the decisions of the House. Each has its own peculiar functions, and neither can encroach upon the other without danger to the State.

But if the House did insist on having its way, the government would not dodge the bullet:

> [Ministers] are determined to take upon themselves the whole responsibility [...] it is not in the power of the Government, at this distance and without the information that is requisite, and it would be a cowardly and discreditable thing without they were certain of what they were saying or doing, to attempt to throw the blame on men who are absent.

The speech had lasted for perhaps an hour. Palmerston informed the Queen that Herbert had 'acquitted himself with great ability'.[1] Another source, albeit with exaggeration, characterised it as 'pregnant with demonstration that he had worthily conceived the duties of a

---

1 Benson and Esher, *Letters of Queen Victoria*, III, pp. 96-7, Pam to Victoria, 26 Jan 1855.

Prime Minister'.¹ Yet it was in vain. Roebuck's motion was carried in the early hours of 30 January by the overwhelming margin of 305 votes to 148. The government resigned later that day.

Herbert characterised the ministerial crisis of the next few days as 'a great public emergency, and a case of a singularly exceptional character'. His inclination was for Aberdeen to head a new coalition; failing that, a ministry headed by Lansdowne. Aberdeen ruled out the former; old age ruled out the latter. With Russell's recent conduct having conspired to place him in low regard, the most plausible candidates were Derby and Palmerston.²

Queen Victoria's preference was for Derby: the Conservative leader duly received her commission to form a ministry. Acknowledging that it would need to be broad-based, he approached Palmerston. Lord Stanley, Derby's son, was optimistic that 'after a little hesitation' Palmerston would agree to become Leader of the House 'bringing with him Gladstone and Herbert'. There were rumours in the press that Herbert was to be Secretary for War. Such speculation was misplaced. Malmesbury's understanding was that up to 80 Conservatives had threatened to abandon Derby if Herbert and Gladstone were enlisted.³ The threat was never put to the test. When Palmerston called on Herbert at the War Office at three o'clock on 31 January he 'seemed to be disinclined'. He protested that it was unclear where Derby stood on the war. But there was also a good deal of personal calculation in Herbert's reasoning. Joining Derby would be construed as 'a volte face so rapid and so damaging that no public character could stand it'. And there remained his ongoing objection to serving alongside Disraeli, who knew 'no principle but that of seizing and making capital of the popular feeling of the moment'. Thus Herbert remained obdurate when Gladstone, who was not averse to Derby's offer, joined

---

1   *Fraser's Magazine*, 'Herbert', p. 206.
2   WSHC 2057/F4/53, SH to Aberdeen, 5 Feb. 1855; Brooke and Sorensen, *Gladstone*, pp. 164-6, memorandum of 6 Feb. 1855.
3   Vincent, *Stanley Journals*, p. 130, 30 Jan. 1855; *Morning Chronicle*, 1 Feb. 1855; Malmesbury, *Memoirs*, II, pp. 56-7, 3 Feb. 1857.

the conversation that evening.¹ Palmerston had no option but to report to Derby that his recruiting mission had proved fruitless. As a matter of courtesy, Herbert and Gladstone wrote separately to the Conservative leader, politely declining office, 'but thought it well to send off nothing till after dinner, and we went to Grillon's where we had a small but merry party'. Herbert, noted Gladstone, was 'even beyond himself amusing'.²

Derby accepted that he would not be able to form a sustainable ministry; the task of trying to do so now fell to Palmerston. On 4 February, in the briefest of notes, he asked Herbert: 'will you take the Home Department?'³ For all that this represented a considerable advance up the ministerial ladder, Herbert resisted acting precipitately. He met with Aberdeen and Graham that day in an attempt to agree a common Peelite response. At home that night, he wrote a long letter to Gladstone, as much to clarify his own thoughts as anything else:

> I am very much disturbed about our position. There are some occasions in which the acceptance of office carries with it in vulgar estimation a certain amount of suspicion, and the refusal is held to be a prima facie case of virtue. In the present instance it is exactly the contrary, and the national instinct is right. Any […] who now hold aloof on a great public emergency, and who, unable to form a Government themselves, refuse their aid to any of those who with their assistance could do it, will be held to be intriguing for their own ends. My instinct tells me that this is a moment when we ought to be helping, not obstructing […]
>
> I cannot see on what public grounds we can refuse to continue cooperation, under circumstances of great difficulty to which we have ourselves contributed, to men who show this readiness to continue to act with us […] My personal feelings are certainly in favour of entire abstinence from office […] But I am not the less bound, so long as I

---

1   Brooke and Sorensen, *Gladstone*, pp. 183-7, memorandum of 21 Feb. 1855; WSHC 2057/F4/53, SH to Aberdeen, 5 Feb. 1855.
2   HLPP GC/DE/76, Pam to Derby, 31 Jan. 1855; D/16, diary entry, 31 Jan. 1855; Morley, *Gladstone*, I, pp. 526-7.
3   WSHC 2057/F4/61, Pam to SH, 4 Feb. 1855.

can remain in public life, and if I do so remain, to do my utmost for what seems to me the public welfare.

There remained, however, the problematic question of the putative premier:

> Palmerston without us [...] may be, and I think will be, very dangerous [...] he would give a war impetus to our foreign policy which would be the greatest public calamity [...] It is possible that by joining him we may keep him in a right course, and he can afford to make peace on easier terms than almost any one else, if he can be got to do it. It is of course possible that we may fail [...] But if we stand aloof, we must say why; and if we state that we are for peace, or for a peace which he is not for, then we divide England into two camps, and encourage the Emperor of Russia to trade on our divisions and to hold out for terms far less favourable than those now under discussion even in their largest interpretation. In this way we should do immeasurable mischief. We should protract the contest and render certain a result less favourable to England. [...] In short, I look upon our position as most critical.[1]

A two-hour meeting of leading Peelites was held at Graham's the next morning; their host was 'confined by operation for carbuncle and by gout'. Gladstone recalled Herbert to have been 'full of doubts and fears', a perception not necessarily inconsistent with Argyll's observation that 'Herbert was as decided as it was his nature to be in favour of joining Palmerston'.[2] Opinion more generally was divided. Argyll agreed with Herbert; Gladstone and Graham disagreed; all sought a lead from Aberdeen. When the outgoing Prime Minister joined them, he recommended their joining Palmerston, even though he was disinclined to support Palmerston himself. The latter point appeared to be decisive until 'Herbert ventured faintly to recommend his [Herbert] joining the Palmerston Cabinet'. But he did not press the suggestion. Instead he accompanied Gladstone home, from where

1   WSHC 2057/F4/60, SH to WEG, 4 Feb. 1855.
2   HLPP D/16, diary entries, 5, 6 Feb. 1855; Argyll, *Memoirs*, I, p. 526.

both men sent letters to Palmerston declining office. Yet even now, Herbert agonised. On returning from Gladstone's to Belgrave Square he confided that 'I am not yet clear as to what I ought to do. But with the opinions I entertain I feel that I am in a thoroughly false position'. Gladstone replied at midnight that Herbert was free to join Palmerston if he really wanted to, and that he 'should not to be prevented by any personal feeling from altering your mind [...] But pray go to bed'.[1]

This was good advice – and peremptorily ignored. Even at that moment, Herbert was writing to Aberdeen. Herbert urged him to return to office under Palmerston, not least because this would enable him to have a clear conscience in doing likewise, and Peelite honour would be preserved.[2] But Aberdeen was implacable. Correctly identifying Herbert's chief objection to serving under Palmerston as 'the apprehension that he will pursue a warlike policy beyond reasonable bounds', Aberdeen ventured the opinion that this would not happen so long as Herbert and his friends 'rely on the weight of your own character and opinions in the Cabinet'. Peelite refusal to serve, he added, echoing the point made by Herbert himself in his letter to Gladstone of the previous day, would be politically damaging: 'The public feeling will be strongly pronounced against you, and you will greatly suffer in reputation, if you persevere at such a moment as this in refusing to continue in the Cabinet'.[3]

Aberdeen put the case in person when the Peelites reconvened the following morning. The critical change, however, was his agreeing to give any Palmerston government in which they served his independent support. 'To Herbert of course', as Gladstone noted, 'it was a simple release from a difficulty'. But so it was for all of them. With the promise of Peelite support thus obtained, Palmerston was at last able to form his ministry on 6 February. Though the view of many, such as Lord Canning, was that Herbert would end up at the Home Office, Gladstone knew his friend's mind better in writing to the incoming Prime Minister that he 'was sure that S. Herbert would

---

1 BL Add. Mss. 44210, fols. 165-8, SH to WEG, 5 Feb. 1855; Stanmore, I, p. 259, WEG to SH, 5 Feb. 1855.
2 WSHC 2057/F4/53, SH to Aberdeen, 5 Feb. 1855.
3 WSHC 2057/F4/53, Aberdeen to SH, 6 Feb. 1855.

greatly prefer the colonies to the Home Office'. Palmerston was happy to oblige.[1] Thus the ministerial crisis of February 1855, akin to those of December 1916 and May 1940, seemed to have been brought to an end. Herbert's part in it was substantial. Had he not held out against Palmerston and Gladstone, he might well have become part of a Conservative-dominated coalition under Derby. Had he not cavilled at the Peelite meeting of 5 February and stayed up into the early hours of 6 February, Palmerston might in turn have failed to form a ministry. What then?

Herbert's immediate concern, however, was not 'what if?' but 'what now?' First, there was the formality of his return for South Wiltshire following his appointment to the Colonial Office. There was some discernible coldness in the air. In sub-zero temperatures, on 15 February, he answered catcalls of 'Who sent out green coffee?' and 'Where's the army?' by responding that the army:

> has had to undergo hardships and privations which have been borne with a heroism almost unexampled, but which may be and must be attributed to causes that require a searching investigation (cheers) in order that a proper remedy should be applied, and that the blame, if blame there be, should fall upon the right shoulders. (Cheers). It behoves the Government to lose no time in instituting this investigation.[2]

In view of what would follow over the next week or so, his remarks would be construed as having given a hostage to fortune.

Herbert's constituents would have been disconcerted had they known that he spoke 'with feelings of strong disinclination' when the question of how to respond to Roebuck's motion for a committee of inquiry was discussed in cabinet the next day.[3] In private, Herbert's

1   Brooke and Sorensen, *Gladstone*, pp. 164-6, memorandum of 6 Feb. 1855; NUL MS Os C 593, Canning to Denison, 6 Feb. 1855; WSHC 2057/F4/61, Pam to SH, 7 Feb. 1855.
2   *SWJ*, 17 Feb. 1855.
3   Brooke and Sorensen, *Gladstone*, p. 179, memorandum of 17 Feb. 1855.

view was that the nature and timing of such an inquiry was 'for every purpose of investigation – i.e. every good purpose – a sham'.[1] Being 'on the sick list', he was not present to press his objections at the cabinet meeting of 20 February. By then, he took 'it for granted that the Government will decide to allow the nomination of the Committee or some nomination of the Committee without limitation as to powers,' and that in consequence he, Graham and Gladstone 'shall find ourselves in a position of considerable difficulty'.[2] They resigned the next day.

In a speech explaining his resignation to the House on 23 February, Herbert's argument was that Roebuck's motion had constituted a vote of no confidence in Aberdeen's government. The motion being passed, and the government having fallen, 'its work is done'. This interpretation of events, he insisted, was one Palmerston had shared, and the basis on which he had agreed to join his government. That the House still persisted in its desire for an inquiry, he attributed solely to the weight of popular pressure on Members to press for one. Such pressure, he asserted, was born of misinformation transmitted via the newspapers. As such, he believed that he had a duty to resist demands for an inquiry. He thought that the legislature should support the executive by doing likewise:

> I think it is necessary it should be supported, and with the single object in view of giving stability to the Government and strength to the country in a moment of great difficulty, and of seeking the promotion of the public welfare. Sir, you will not have a strong Government by having in it strong men who take a weak course. You must have strong men taking a strong course. They must not at the first moment throw down the reins, and act contrary to the opinions which they strongly expressed only a fortnight ago, because the House at the moment happens to demand it. The Government, to be a strong Government,

---

1   BL Add. Mss. 44210, fol. 171, SH to WEG, 20 Feb. 1855.
2   Brooke and Sorensen, *Gladstone*, p. 180; BL Add. Mss. 44210, fols. 169-70, SH to WEG, 20 Feb. 1855.

must be something more than the mere reflex of the caprices of a large popular assembly.

This, as Herbert acknowledged, was a restatement of Peel's conception of parliamentary government. The contrast with what he conceived to be Palmerston's weak leadership of an unsupportive Commons could hardly have been starker. Insisting that he was 'no deserter', Herbert resumed his seat.[1]

Herbert's conduct received some plaudits. Granville thought he was 'one of the very few of the present cabinet whose character will stand much higher than two years ago in public estimation'. The *Morning Chronicle* judged that his resignation statement had 'most triumphantly repelled the suspicion of crotchetiness'; the *Worcestershire Chronicle* that he had demonstrated 'stubborn conscientiousness'.[2] One could even make the argument that he had been motivated by altruism. As he said himself, remaining in government whilst his conduct in the former government was being investigated might serve to weaken the Palmerston ministry, 'for though in civil life we hold that a man is to be considered innocent until he is proved guilty, that is not so with respect to an Administration'. 'It was clear to me', he wrote subsequently to Raglan, 'that the sacrifice was not complete or satisfactory so long as I remained in office'.[3]

But these were minority viewpoints. Responding to Herbert's resignation statement, James Milnes Gaskell, Conservative Member for Wenlock, spoke for many in expressing 'feelings of very great surprise' at his arguments.[4] Roebuck's motion had received overwhelming parliamentary support. It was naïve beyond belief to presume that Palmerston could resist it even if he had wanted to (Herbert admitted, albeit privately, that this was always the probable outcome). And whilst Herbert might maintain that everybody knew that it was really

---

1   Hansard, 23 Feb. 1855, CXXXVI, cols. 1762-72.
2   WSHC 2057/F4/53, Granville to EH, 23 Jan. 1855; *Morning Chronicle*, 21, 25 Feb. 1855; *Worcestershire Chronicle*, 28 Feb. 1855.
3   Hansard, 23 Feb. 1855, CXXXVI, cols. 1763-4; WSHC 2057/F4/63, SH to Raglan, 5 Mar. 1855.
4   Hansard, 23 Feb. 1855, CXXXVI, cols. 1772-3.

a confidence motion, its wording had called unambiguously for an inquiry; an inquiry which he had agreed was a necessity at the South Wiltshire by-election only a week before. *The Times* judged that alongside Graham's and Gladstone's rationale for resigning, Herbert's was 'the least defensible and the most absurd'.[1]

Others were not nearly so charitable. Palmerston ascribed the Peelite resignations to their being opposed to the war. Sarah Disraeli called them 'selfish intriguers'.[2] The simpler truth is that they should never have agreed to join Palmerston in the first place, something that, deep down, Herbert probably realised as soon as he was in the government.[3] He had agonised over joining it – he meant it when he told Raglan afterwards that 'I have lived in a turmoil of doubts and difficulties and "crisis"'[4] – yet of the three of them, he had been the most amenable to the idea of resuming office. He, Graham and Gladstone had never quite been of one mind on the question except that they should act together. Clarendon, the Whig Foreign Secretary, was thus closer than most in his assessment of events when he wrote that Gladstone had resigned on a quirk, Graham from fear and Herbert from 'sentiment', that is to say out of loyalty to his two friends.[5] One resignation from the cabinet might have been regarded as unfortunate; two looked like carelessness. Herbert's first resignation had been forced upon him by the doctrine of collective cabinet responsibility; it could be regarded as honourable. The second was a matter of personal responsibility; it was judged as factious. Palmerston, who less than three weeks before, could not form a government without the key Peelites, could now survive without them.

Herbert and his friends thus found their careers in jeopardy. The war had damaged their reputation as competent and efficient administrators; their resignations had left them politically isolated. Had Gladstone stayed at the Exchequer and Herbert taken the Home

1   BL Add. Mss. 44210, fol. 171, SH to WEG, 20 Feb. 1855.
2   Ridley, *Palmerston*, p. 436; Monypenny and Buckle, *Disraeli*, III, p. 568, S. Disraeli to S. Disraeli, 21 Feb. 1855.
3   BL Add. Mss. 44210, fols. 169-70, SH to WEG, 20 Feb. 1855.
4   WSHC 2057/F4/63, SH to Raglan, 5 Mar. 1855.
5   Maxwell, *Clarendon*, II, p. 69.

Office, little stood in the way of Newcastle's prediction that 'we should grow into the natural leaders of the Liberal party'.[1] Instead, Sir Charles Wood was left bemoaning that 'we have come to an end of that fusion of all the liberal bodies which has been a public object for years'.[2] Herbert stood more or less reviled, the very scenario which he had warned against in his letter to Gladstone of 4 February. Even in Wilton, at the end of March, it was acknowledged, in euphemistic terms, that Herbert was experiencing some temporary loss of popularity.[3]

To Herbert's sudden fall from grace must be added increasing anxieties as to the state of his health. On New Year's Eve 1854, in a cryptic fragment to his secretary, he noted that 'I am being doctored in the "opiate concoction"'.[4] Illness had caused him to miss the important cabinet meeting of 20 February 1855; his resignation statement was prefaced by an apology for enforced brevity 'on account of physical inability to address the House at any great length at the present moment'. Most telling of all, was his confiding to Gladstone that 'I have been for some time so unwell that I am conscious that without rest I run great risk for the future'.[5] Hence the observation in Harriet Martineau's essay that Herbert took leave of office 'manifestly ill; and he retired from his work under a depression as deep perhaps as his nature permitted'. Richard Cobden was at once more blunt and less sympathetic, writing to his wife that 'Gladstone, Graham & Sidney Herbert have taken their seats below the gangway next to where Bright & I sit; but I don't know what we shall do with them'.

1 Brooke and Sorensen, *Gladstone*, pp. 172-5, memorandum of 6 February 1855.
2 Stanmore, I, pp. 266-8, Wood to SH, Feb. 1855
3 *SWJ*, 31 Mar. 1855.
4 BL Add. Mss. 46448, fol. 65, SH to Ramsay, 31 Dec. 1854.
5 Hansard, 23 Jan. 1855, CXXXVI, col. 1762; WSHC 2057/F4/60, SH to WEG, 4 Feb. 1855.

10
Confronting Obloquy
1855-1857

Self-inflicted ostracism was not a course to be embarked upon lightly. Herbert's political stock, accrued incrementally over a generation, had fallen precipitately when he resigned for the second time within a month in February 1855. Restitution of sorts would be provided by his renewed prominence in the cause of army reform, and by his efforts to secure a legacy for the work of Florence Nightingale. So too, there were compensating diversions to be enjoyed as a young father: Elizabeth had borne him a fifth child in five years in May 1855. But the political landscape looked distinctly less fecund. Herbert faced the imminent prospect of being summoned before a parliamentary committee of inquiry; the war, to which he was increasingly opposed, continued. Even in Wiltshire his proverbial popularity, as the 1857 election would show, was called into question. In the face of such challenges, Herbert maintained an outward show of defiant equanimity. He told his critics in the House that he would not compromise his opinions: 'I would sooner lie under any amount of obloquy, however injurious, trusting to time to justify us, as it eventually will'.[1]

The Select Committee of Inquiry into the State of the Army before Sebastopol began its work on 5 March. By 15 May, its 12 members had asked over 20,000 questions of 57 witnesses. Herbert followed proceedings closely via the newspapers. Dr Andrew Smith's

1   Hansard, 19 July 1855, CXXXIX, col. 1145.

evidence, heard on 22 March, excited his disapproval. Given the frictions evident between him and the Director-General of the Army Medical Department over the previous months, this was no surprise.[1] What did come as an unpleasant shock was the testimony from his friend, the Duke of Newcastle. It was not that the erstwhile Secretary of State for War criticised Herbert; rather that he simply did not mention him at all. Elizabeth complained that it was an omission which 'has, of course, been commented upon by friends as well as enemies'. She gave full vent to her fury, writing:

> to tell you [Newcastle] how deeply hurt I feel that in the one opportunity you had in your evidence before the committee of doing justice to Sidney's indefatigable exertions in the War Office you not only omitted all mention of him but implied that you were left alone & unassisted in carrying on the business of the war during the whole Summer; the facts of the case being, that except for one week in August & 5 days in September Sidney never was absent from the War Office.[2]

This was, her rebarbative 'I need not remind you of the past' included, a typical example of Elizabeth as Herbert's devoted and protective wife. Newcastle, protesting that that no letter had ever caused him 'so much pain & astonishment', reassured her that 'I am deeply grateful to him for the assistance which he gave me on every occasion when he cd render it, & for the generous spirit in wh he always acted towards me'. His motive for not having referred to Herbert in his testimony, he insisted, 'was to assume to myself the whole might of obloquy wh. attached to the conduct of the War, & our respective positions in Feby last proved that in this respect at least I was successful'.[3] Mollified to a degree, Elizabeth accepted the Duke's protestations.

Herbert did not appear before the committee until 9 May. His testimony took most of the day. Roebuck, 'old tear 'em' as the chairman was known, opened the questioning. He wanted 'to ascertain exactly

---

1   NUL Ne C 18459, SH to Newcastle, 22 Apr. 1855.
2   NUL Ne C 12241/1-2, EH to Newcastle, 29 Apr. 1855.
3   NUL Ne C 12445/1-2, Newcastle to EH, 1 May 1855.

the part of the proceedings over which you had control, and that part over which you had not control'. Herbert's response was that as Secretary at War he had 'no executive duties except those of late years which he has acquired by his having originated certain improvements and reforms in the army'. Thus, when questioned about transport arrangements he answered that 'The Secretary-at-War never had any authority over the Commissariat'. Similarly, he pointed out that provision of clothing was the remit of the Ordnance. Responsibility for preparing the hospitals at Scutari, he admitted, was his but only insofar as he had a general financial oversight over them. And whilst it was true that he was involved in the setting up of an additional hospital at Smyrna, at the time he left office, 'all those things were rather for his [Newcastle's] decision than mine'. To the charge, towards the end of his testimony, that 'you were rather more than the mere Secretary-at-War', Herbert offered the familiar refrain that 'mine is an entirely financial department'. 'I was a volunteer; I was assisting the Duke of Newcastle, and so far mine was an anomalous position'.[1]

Occasionally Herbert allowed himself to be more expansive in his testimony. He was laudably protective of those who had worked under him. Of his clerks, he asserted that 'I made great demands on their time, and I lengthened the officer hours, but they never murmured or objected'. But he refused to comment on other departments except to observe that 'they had not that intercommunication amongst themselves' to work properly together. This was, as we have seen, a considerable understatement of his true feelings on the subject.[2] Neither could he be induced to blame individuals. To Roebuck's question of who the war 'has shown us to be incompetent', Herbert demurred that 'That is a matter upon which I ought not to be called upon to give of opinion'. And unlike many of those questioned, he was also reluctant to blame the system. Whilst conceding that it 'has not been expansive enough for war', Herbert denied the popular supposition that it was necessarily moribund:

---

1 PP 1854-5 (247), IX, especially pp. 166-7, 184-5, 193-4.
2 PP 1854-5 (247), IX, pp. 198-9.

I do not believe that the difference between one system and another is nearly so great as between one man and another. If you have good men, they will work a bad system; but the best system will not work well with inferior men; but the men must know their business, and have experience in it.[1]

Neither did Herbert shrink from taking the offensive against his interrogators. Armed with a handful of letters to substantiate his claims, he drew attention to personal initiatives which he had taken: 'I was very much dissatisfied with the state of things, and I did not think it was a moment to be stickling upon mere questions of official form; I thought that my interference by letters would have the effect of pushing on the service more rapidly'.[2] Hence, when he learnt of a shortage of supplies and stores at Scutari, he entered into a 'correspondence of some length with the principal medical officer, and the purveyor there, urging upon them, in every possible way, to exert themselves' to get what was required.[3] To the reasonable question of whether his 'adding to the complication of its administration in any way was a serious evil in itself', Herbert was adamant in his response that 'I think any complication is an evil, and it is only on occasions of emergency that you are justified in departing from the ordinary rule: this, I think, was one'.[4] Above all, mindful of his self-defined financial role as Secretary at War, he was at considerable pains to emphasise that he had written 'a great many' letters to officials saying 'that though the checking of expenditure was the most essential of their duties in peace, yet that in war questions of pounds shillings and pence could not be put in competition with human life'.[5]

Truth be told, Herbert was not subjected to the most gruelling of ordeals. He was not pursued on the question of whether his numerous unofficial interventions were counterproductive, an area on which he was clearly vulnerable. He was not questioned at all about his role in

1   PP 1854-5 (247), IX, pp. 198-9.
2   PP 1854-5 (247), IX, p. 175.
3   PP 1854-5 (247), IX, p. 169.
4   PP 1854-5 (247), IX, p. 187.
5   PP 1854-5 (247), IX, p. 170.

raising reinforcements for the army, the field in which he had been most active. Moreover, not all committee members started from Roebuck's hostile premise that 'though I had no authority in the management of the war, I was supposed to have'.[1] Serving alongside Roebuck were General Jonathan Peel, son of Herbert's political godfather, and Captain John Neilson Gladstone, brother of William, and MP for Devizes in Herbert's Wiltshire. Herbert had little to fear from them. He could also expect empathy, if not outright sympathy, from Edward Ellice, a former Secretary at War, and Sir John Pakington, who would precede him as Secretary for War. *The Times*, on scrutinising these and other names nominated to the committee, condemned it as an exercise in jobbery well before its job of taking evidence had even begun.[2]

There was nevertheless a consensus that Herbert had delivered his testimony with modesty, good temper and candour.[3] The sharpest criticisms were levelled by Lieutenant-General Sir William Napier. But they were of a recondite nature. As author of a celebrated multi-volume history of the Peninsular War, Napier objected to Herbert's inference that the deficiencies and problems evident in preparations made for the Crimea were not so very different from those in Spain and Portugal a generation before.[4] A more measured critique appeared in *The Times*. Whilst noting that it would be 'very ungracious' to condemn his efforts as a self-styled volunteer, Herbert:

> instead of discharging one system of duties of equal and uniform obligation, for neglecting which he might have been impeached, was engaged in a variety of transactions, some officious, some extra-official, and some anti-official – in fact, dividing themselves into half-a-dozen distinct categories.[5]

He had succeeded, in other words, in highlighting the shortcomings of an aristocratically-controlled military administration.

1 Stanmore, I, pp. 326-30, SH to Raglan, 5 Mar. 1855.
2 *The Times*, 23 Apr. 1855.
3 *DWG*, 10 May 1855.
4 *Inverness Courier*, 17 May 1855.
5 *The Times*, 10 May 1855.

The verdict that mattered was published on 18 June. It was remarkably anodyne. Roebuck's committee not only accepted Herbert's line but more or less adopted his language in endorsing it. 'Mr Sidney Herbert', it concluded, 'as Secretary-at-War, had no power to originate anything; but from praiseworthy motives, and with a view to relieve the Duke of Newcastle, he undertook to do a good deal which was not the business of his Office'. And whilst it was true that, from a financial perspective, 'some regulations were still enforced, suited to a time of peace but inapplicable to a period of war, and operating unjustly on the soldiers who had been wounded or afflicted with sickness in the Crimea', this was despite, not because of Herbert. The letters which he had sent to Lord Paulet and Dr Smith, which he submitted in support of his testimony, showed that 'expenditure was [...] encouraged'. The report also credited Herbert for having taken the initiative in trying to rationalise the organisation of the War Office in January 1855.[1]

The wider verdict from the committee, though, was more critical in tone: Britain's army, it judged, had lacked adequate care from mid-November 1854. Most damning, in this respect, were the words added by virtue of Roebuck's casting vote as committee chairman, namely that Aberdeen's government had 'hoped and expected that the expedition would be immediately successful, and, as they did not see the possibility of a protracted struggle, they made no preparation for a winter campaign'.[2] Roebuck duly gave notice that he would move a censure motion in the House. Herbert was not immediately concerned. For several days past, he and Elizabeth had been in the Scottish Highlands, 'advised by his medical attendant to abstain from all public business for a time in order to recruit his health'.[3] It proved to be a suitably rejuvenating experience: 'early rising, mountain air, and complete rest, with the enjoyment of magnificent scenery and excellent sport', he reported, 'would set up anybody'. Informed by both Graham and Gladstone that Roebuck's motion was delayed, the news was 'not unwelcome, as after long intervals of drought and spate

1 PP 1854-5 (247), IX, pp. 371-2.
2 Spiers, *Army and Society*, pp. 111-12.
3 *SWJ*, 16 June 1855.

the river is just getting into order, and I had got five fish out of it in the course of the day'. To the regret of countless more fish, the Herberts' return home was delayed until the second week of July.[1]

Roebuck's motion finally came on for debate on 17 July. Herbert was one of five Members in the Commons (the others were Palmerston, Russell, Graham and Gladstone) who, by dint of their posts in the Aberdeen government, were especially singled out for censure. A week earlier, Herbert had made clear to Gladstone that he intended meeting Roebuck's charges of incompetence head on, to 'throw dirt on the Committee, their leading questions, their acceptance of gossip and hearsay evidence'.[2] He now proved true to his word. The inquiry, he mocked, had been 'a half investigation'. Its members 'must either have acquitted men for want of sufficient evidence, or they must have condemned men on a guess that there was evidence behind which would have condemned them had it been brought forward'. Worse, they had 'left imputations by insinuations rather than by open attack, upon absent men who have never been heard, and who, in one or two cases, I grieve to say, never can be heard'. How, having not seen government intelligence, could they 'say that the expedition to the Crimea was undertaken with inadequate information'? The report, Herbert continued, in believing 'the gossip of the camp, picked up by men who do not understand the facts', had exaggerated the sufferings of the army. It had 'forgotten the great and eminent successes and triumphs which have been accomplished by that army'. Choosing to ignore that 'there are some small acts of injustice personal to myself in the Report of the Committee', Herbert proceeded to refute in considerable detail, as he was well placed to do, the 'rather serious' charge that there had been no adequate reserve force. He ended with a promise and a plea: 'If while endeavouring to serve the public I failed, I failed, at any rate, with this consolation, that I did my utmost to succeed [...] when a Minister's character is impugned he is entitled to ask a clear and distinct verdict from the House of Commons'.[3]

1   BL Add. Mss. 79657, fols. 111-21, SH to JRG, 30 June, 8 July 1855; St Deniol's GG 2099, WEG to SH, 2 July 1855.
2   BL Add. Mss. 44210, fols. 193-8, SH to WEG, 9 July 1855.
3   Hansard, 19 July 1855, CXXXIX, cols. 1132-50.

That verdict was already more or less decided. It owed little to Herbert's speech and much to Roebuck's inept performance in moving his motion. 'No man', Roebuck had said of Herbert,

> could have been more intent than that right hon. Gentleman had always been upon the honour of his country, and on performing the duties of his office. I do not mean to say that he did not often do wrong. I think he did; but then I draw the distinction between him and other Members of the Administration, that he was conscientiously endeavouring to perform his duty and was always at his post, and his kindliness of spirit was always pervading the office to which he belonged.[1]

To many, Roebuck appeared to want it both ways. How could he speak in exculpatory language of Herbert whilst moving a resolution to censure all members of the cabinet equally? The episode threatened to degenerate into a farce. A less critical motion, moved by General Peel, insisting that the government had every right to send an expeditionary force but had made errors of judgement in doing so, was passed by 289 votes to 182. As Herbert had pointed out in his resignation statement of 23 February, both the House and the country had had their pound of flesh when Aberdeen's government resigned in January.[2]

The search for villains nevertheless persisted. In January 1856 Sir John McNeill and Colonel Alexander Tulloch published their findings 'into the arrangement and management of the Commissariat Department'. In doing so, they pointed fingers of blame not only at Commissary-General Filder, but also Lords Lucan and Cardigan of Balaclava fame, General Sir Richard Airey and Colonel the Hon. Alexander Gordon, respectively Quartermaster-General and Deputy Quartermaster-General. Herbert welcomed the report, tactfully going so far as to recommend it as a model to Nightingale whose tendencies he judged to be the opposite of those he described:

1   Hansard, 17 July 1855, CXXXIX, cols. 964-5.
2   Conacher, *Crimea*, pp. 66-75; Hansard, 23 Feb. 1855, CXXXVI, cols. 1762-72.

There is not a hard word in it, nor an epithet, not an accusation, scarcely an animadversion, but this sobriety of tone has arrested the attention & conquered the confidence of the public & they have made the necessary inferences & pretty broad ones too.[1]

Alleging that the accusations had been levelled on the basis of a dodgy dossier, however, those named by McNeill and Tulloch judged otherwise. Parliament acquiesced in their demand that soldiers should be tried by military, not civilian, authorities. Herbert was exasperated: 'The danger was that it should be, or if it is not, that it should look like a Commission to try the Commissioners instead of a Court to try the officers'. Concerned that the issue was rumbling on, to the detriment of both the landed order and the army, he therefore cautioned Palmerston that:

> the Court must be so composed and the proceedings so conducted as to inspire confidence in the public both as regards its competency and its impartiality. A court of general officers is a tribunal to which in a case like this, where the authorities at the Horse Guards and the War Department are in a certain sense parties, a good deal of public suspicion will necessarily attach.[2]

A Board comprising seven General Officers largely exonerated the plaintiffs in July.[3] Popular outrage to the effect that there had been a whitewash duly erupted. It was Herbert who tried to find some middle ground. Insisting, more or less correctly, that McNeill's and Tulloch's report 'except in one single sentence, and then only by implication, brings no charge against any one', he praised their work as 'a mine of information upon which, no doubt, many important changes in our military administration will be founded'. Palmerston seized with alacrity Herbert's suggestion that its authors therefore 'receive some

---

1 Goldie, *Nightingale*, pp. 217-19, SH to FN, 6 Mar. 1856.
2 WSHC 2057/F4/61, SH to Pam, 25, 28 Feb. 1856; BL Add. Mss. 79657, fols. 102-4, SH to JRG, 22 Feb. 1855.
3 Spiers, *Army and Society*, pp. 113-15.

suitable acknowledgment for the services they had rendered'.[1] McNeill became a privy councillor; Tulloch received a K.C.B. To Herbert's credit, a messy compromise of sorts was thereby effected.

As to whether the Roebuck committee's verdict on Herbert's record during 1854-5 was the right one, opinion has inevitably been divided. Some absolved him from blame entirely. Whilst affairs were at their lowest ebb, General Estcourt made the unsolicited comment in a letter from the war zone that:

> I have only to say in respect to your office that you have either adopted the suggestions I have ventured to make, or you have (as in most cases you have) <u>anticipated</u> them. Therefore no stones will be thrown from this Army on your department.[2]

Gladstone, reviewing the Crimean episode at the time of Herbert's death, judged that 'whoever was wrong, whoever was responsible, the thing most of all certain is that <u>he</u> was not and that he not only did far more than position required but all that it made possible'. Nearly forty years later Gladstone remained insistent that Herbert had been 'abused for his good deeds'.[3] Alexander William Kinglake, meanwhile, journalist, politician, and author of a voluminous history of the conflict, had nothing to say about Herbert's role save that:

> his personal qualities ensuring him great weight with his colleagues, he proved able to render excellent service in the business of the war [...] If only for the frank, courageous, and unswerving support that he gave to Miss Nightingale's great enterprise, his memory would be dear to the country.[4]

---

1   Hansard, 19 Feb. 1857, CXLIV, col. 925; 12 Mar. 1857, CXLIV, cols. 2239-42.
2   Stanmore, I, pp. 299-300, Estcourt to SH, 27 Jan. 185.
3   WSHC 2057/F4/60, WEG to Charles A'Court, 4 Aug. 1861; Morley, *Gladstone*, I, pp. 651-2, memorandum of 17 Sept. 1897.
4   Kinglake, *Crimea*, VII, p. 400, n. 3.

At the other extreme, there were those who accused Herbert (with Gladstone and Graham) of having behaved factiously in deciding to quit the government in February 1855. Herbert himself privately acknowledged that the decision had been a mistake.[1] But the further charge, that in resigning from the government, the three friends weakened the counsels for peace, and thus inadvertently prolonged the conflict, is something of a *non sequitur*. Given the strength of popular opinion in favour of the war, a line shared by most in the cabinet and especially by Palmerston, it is difficult to see just how any such counsels could have prevailed. Arguably the best assessment of Herbert's culpability or otherwise, therefore, was his own:

> I was connected by my official position with one of the War Departments; and was, therefore, though in a secondary degree, implicated in the censure which has been passed by the House upon the management of those departments; and, although by all constitutional theory every man who forms part of any Cabinet is equally as responsible with his colleagues for whatever may have been done by that Cabinet, yet, at the same time, our common sense teaches us that those who are the most nearly allied to the departments the operations of which have been condemned, do, in fact, bear a heavier weight of responsibility, are more liable to censure, and are, therefore, bound to endeavour to stand more clearly before this House.[2]

Theoretically, in other words, Herbert bore little responsibility for what had gone wrong. In practice, however, his official position as Secretary at War, and his unofficial position as a self-appointed general factotum to Newcastle, rendered him more culpable than most who served in the Aberdeen coalition. The war did, therefore, fairly damage Herbert's reputation. What was unfair was that the blame was magnified by the failure of the layman to appreciate the distinction which existed between the Secretary *at* War and the Secretary *for* War. This, Gladstone reasonably believed, was in no small measure

1 WSHC 2057/F4/53, SH to Aberdeen, 12 Apr. 1857.
2 Hansard, 23 Feb. 1855, CXXXVI, col. 1762.

responsible for 'those vials of wrath to which his office exposed him in the eyes especially of the uninformed'.[1] Damaging also for Herbert's standing was the tendency for many to apportion blame on the basis of personalities, not systems. Herbert, modern historians would agree, was a medium-sized cog in a wheel which was not turning very effectively. As one more perceptive contemporary commentator wryly observed, 'The British army has often been successful *in spite* of its administration'.[2]

One of Herbert's fundamental objections to the Roebuck inquiry was its timing: the committee sat when the war was far from done. The death of Czar Nicholas on 2 March was regarded by many, including Herbert ('I think it must ultimately tend to peace') as a possible catalyst for an end to hostilities. Alexander II, the new Czar, made an encouraging move in agreeing to resume talks to that end in Vienna. Britain's war aims, agreed when Herbert was in office, had been outlined in December 1854. They were that the integrity of Moldavia and Wallachia be guaranteed, that Russia abandon its claim to exercise a protectorate over Ottoman Christians, free navigation of the Danube, and some revision of the 1841 Straits Convention which had closed the Black Sea to warships in peacetime. By the spring of 1855, however, Palmerston was looking for more: that Russia cede Bessarabia at the mouth of the Danube, and agree to a complete neutralisation of the Black Sea.[3] There was also the general presumption that Sebastopol must fall before military honour could be said to have been satisfied. Herbert thought the demand for Bessarabia unfair, the neutralisation of the Black Sea problematic, and the fall of Sebastopol improbable. He was disposed to see a peace settlement brokered on the basis of the original proposals.

Palmerston dampened hopes that peace was imminent when he told the Commons on 23 April that Czar Alexander would not give sufficient ground on the Black Sea question. Thomas Milner Gibson, a prominent member of the Manchester School (free traders who

1 Morley, *Gladstone*, I, pp. 651-2, memorandum of 17 Sept. 1897.
2 *Fraser's Magazine*, 'Herbert', p. 201.
3 Chamberlain, *'Pax Britanica'?*, pp. 109-10.

advocated a pacific approach to international affairs), responded to him by giving notice of a motion deploring the government's failure to effect a compromise that would have delivered an honourable peace. Aberdeen, Graham, Gladstone and Cardwell (the latter a Liverpool merchant's son who had served as Peelite President of the Board of Trade under Aberdeen) agreed to lend Milner Gibson their support. An angry Herbert, who had been absent from their deliberations, judged that his friends were pursuing 'an ill-advised course'. They would lose their 'influence for peace, when the real occasion arises, if we make ourselves its advocates in company with those who have already injured the cause by their fanaticism'. It was, he argued, a case of realpolitik: Palmerston would be unmoved, public opinion would not stomach a compromise; the Russians, believing the British to be divided, would themselves be less inclined to make concessions. 'There is', Herbert concluded, 'every risk of protracting the war indefinitely'.[1]

Rising from his seat on 21 May, in an attempt to forestall the events he feared, Herbert asked the Prime Minister:

> Does the noble Lord consider or not that the different modes of solution are exhausted, or does he consider it, and does Austria still consider it, to be her task to look for means of accommodation, and is the conference completely dissolved, or is it in a such a state that any of its members may make any new propositions to the allied Powers?[2]

The two men had patently colluded. Palmerston duly assured the House, with less than complete honesty, that the Vienna talks had not yet failed. The hoped-for corollary, that Milner Gibson would not press his motion, ensued. It was an inglorious affair. Gladstone in particular objected to a want of principle in Herbert's method of proceeding: with childlike petulance he temporarily vacated his seat beside him in the House. In a letter attempting to build bridges, Herbert pointed out that:

---

1 Stanmore, I, pp. 424-6, SH to WEG, 17 May 1855.
2 Hansard, 21 May 1855, CXXXVIII, col. 836; Conacher, *Crimea*, pp. 48-9.

We two have had a quarrel for the first time in our lives [...] I was annoyed and hurt at the arrangement made with Milner Gibson in my absence. I have no liking for the Manchester school or the men of whom it is composed, and I was not pleased to find myself, through others, but without my own consent, committed to a cooperation which is called a coalition [...] for the purposes of peace these are the very men we ought to avoid [...] We want an honourable peace. They want peace honourable or not.[1]

Gladstone was magnanimous in reply: 'the question will be as if it had never been'.[2] But it had, and as Herbert had feared, it proved damaging. With Gladstone adopting a strong moral stance for peace in his public utterances at this time, critics were only too ready to tar both him and Herbert with the brush of pacifism. Henry Goulburn wrote to Elizabeth Herbert of Gladstone's 'perverseness', that 'Cela est bien beau mais ce n'est pas la politique'. Herbert put it to Gladstone in plain English when he told him 'that the British were a race of flesh and blood, and not a congress of professors of moral philosophy'.[3]

Disraeli described Herbert's charade of 21 May as 'more convenient than honourable'.[4] He gave notice of a resolution censuring the government for 'ambiguous language and uncertain conduct'. The ensuing debate spilled on into the early hours of 9 June. Disraeli's motion (Herbert was one of thirty-one Peelites supporting a counter amendment) was easily defeated. But the debate gave Members the chance to say where they stood on the war. Herbert insisted that he was neither Palmerstonian nor pacifist. Rather he identified with those who did not see:

that there is anything inconsistent or dishonourable in those who were advocates for war to attain certain objects, when they think those

1   BL Add. Mss. 44210, fols. 175-8, SH to WEG, 27 May 1855.
2   WSHC 2057/F4/60, WEG to SH, 30 May 1855.
3   WSHC 2057/F4/52, Goulburn to EH, 29 June 1855. Argyll, *Memoirs*, I, pp. 555-7; Magnus, *Gladstone*, p. 122
4   Hansard, 21 May 1855, CXXXVIII, col. 842; Hawkins, *Derby*, II, pp. 115-16; Conacher, *Crimea*, pp. 50-6.

objects have been gained, to become the advocates of a peace as a natural consequence [...] The objects of the war have been successfully attained, and that this gives us a golden opportunity of bringing the war to a termination [...] I admit that I long for successes, and I believe that successes will bring us nearer to peace; I think, undoubtedly, that success facilitates immensely the acquirement of an honourable peace, but it must be borne in mind that there are dangers imminent – the want of water in the Crimea, and a climate which Europeans seldom encounter without loss of health or life.[1]

Another example of the 'dangers' impeding a peace settlement befell the British army as early as 18 June; a failed Allied attack on Sebastopol was accompanied by heavy losses. Herbert's conclusion was that public opinion would demand revenge, leaving Palmerston 'to go on playing double or quits. In that opinion there is not much sign of change yet, but the question "what are we fighting for?" will soon be asked by the innumerable families whose sons are daily risking and losing their lives in this now undefined quarrel'.[2] Ten days later, his mood was not lightened by the news that Raglan had succumbed to a combination of dysentery and depression. Apparently forgetting that he had only lately been amongst those critical of his old friend, Herbert lamented 'dear Ld Fitzroy's death. I cannot say how painful it is'.[3]

Following the debate on Roebuck's motion in July, the Herberts set off to Bad Kissingen in Bavaria for a 'season of rest and cure'.[4] But Herbert's mind was never allowed to wander far from the war. Newcastle, who had taken himself off to the Crimea to see things for himself, wrote him a long letter replete with forebodings for the next winter.[5] It came as a surprise to Herbert, therefore, to learn that largely through French force of arms, Sebastopol had fallen on 9 September. He was jubilant at the news: 'the taking of Sebastopol will give us for

1 Hansard, 7 June 1855, CXXXVIII, cols. 1560-82.
2 BL Add. Mss. 79657, fols. 111-16, SH to JRG, 30 June 1855.
3 WSHC 2057/F4/50, SH to Lady Clanwilliam, 4 July 1855.
4 WSHC 2057/F4/52, Goulburn to EH, 29 June 1855.
5 NUL Ne C 12559, Newcastle to SH, 23 July 1855.

many years great security in India, where the prestige of force goes for so much, and where the Orientals watched this struggle as one for Asiatic supremacy between Russia and ourselves'.[1] In the short term it also offered 'a better chance of peace than we have yet had'. On returning to England, he told Granville that the Peelites 'would support Dizzy if he went for peace'.[2]

To Gladstone, however, Herbert gave the impression that he wanted the military advantage to be pressed further. There was, Herbert assured him, no contradiction in his position:

> People make peace either because they think it right or because they think it prudent, or because they cannot help it. After a defeat, if they think the disaster recoverable, they think it neither right nor prudent, and if they make peace at all it is because they think the disaster is not recoverable, and they will only make their position worse by going on. The Russians have now had all the mortification of defeat. The feeling while fresh of course indisposes to peace. But the more in number are their disasters the less will be the prospect of recovering them. A certain amount of time still remains available for operations in the field – some is gone since I wrote. This should be made vigorous use of, and the worse the material position of the Russians when the campaign closes the more the chance of peace after the winter shall have given time for reflection.[3]

Well aware that Herbert had more stomach for war than his Peelite friends, Palmerston now attempted to re-enlist Herbert under his banner. He was encouraged by the 'strong impression' given by Herbert to Sir Charles Wood, First Lord of the Admiralty, over dinner that he 'would be willing to separate himself from Mr Gladstone

---

1   BL Add. Mss 44210, fols. 205-8, SH to WEG, 27 Sept. 1855.
2   Maxwell, *Clarendon*, II, pp. 94-5, Granville to Clarendon, 18 Sept. 1855; BL Add. Mss. 44210, fols. 205-8, SH to WEG, 27 Sept. 1855.
3   WSHC 2057/F4/60, WEG to SH, 1 Oct. 1855; BL Add. Mss. 44210, fols. 209-12, SH to WEG, 7 Oct. 1855.

and Sir James Graham and the Peace Party, and to join the present Government'.[1] 'Mr Herbert', Palmerston informed the Queen:

> is the most promising man of his standing in the House of Commons, and is personally very popular in that House; he is a good and an improving speaker, and his accession to the Government would add a good Speaker to the Treasury Bench, and take away a good speaker from ranks that may become hostile.

'The difference between him and the Government', Palmerston assured Her Majesty, 'is not as to the necessity of prosecuting the war with vigour, but as to the conditions of peace with which he would be satisfied'.[2]

The Prime Minister, to some degree at least, misjudged his man. Palmerston may have raised his estimation of Herbert, but the sentiment was not reciprocated. 'Palmerston has a good deal of Irish braggadocio about him', he told Aberdeen.[3] Herbert nevertheless travelled over to Broadlands by afternoon train on 11 November. In the hour-and-a-quarter's conversation which followed, Palmerston complimented Herbert on the initiatives he had made to improve the efficiency of the army before war broke out, and offered him the vacant Colonial Office. Herbert politely declined. Acceptance, he explained, would lead to the accusation that he was swallowing his opinions for the sake of place. His memorandum of the meeting suggests that he was not being completely ingenuous. Palmerston had no blueprint for peace, he gauged, 'except for what you could ask and how much you could get'. Further, he believed that Palmerston's hands were tied politically by the perception that his popularity in the country stemmed from his 'supposed war-at-all price leanings'. The most that Herbert could promise was that when the next chance to end the war presented itself, 'I would support his peace with all the means I possess, provided he made it, and would not look too closely at his terms; but

---

1 BL Add. Mss. 43197, fol. 144, SH to Aberdeen, 30 Nov. 1855.
2 Benson and Esher, *Letters of Queen Victoria*, III, pp. 189-91, Pam to Victoria, 10, 11 Nov. 1855.
3 Stanmore, II, pp. 8-12, SH to Aberdeen, 13 Nov. 1855.

if the opportunity were lost through his proposing terms which in my opinion rendered peace impossible, my support would be at an end'. On this basis the two of them 'Parted very good friends. I dined with him and came home by 9 o'clock train'.[1]

Having declined office, Herbert turned his mind to the 'great question' of how he and his friends should act in the new session 'if we intend to influence public opinion in favour of peace'. Herbert was still pondering it nearly two months later: on 11 January he invited Newcastle, Gladstone and Graham to meet with him to discuss 'the course to be taken & the language to be held', in an ideal world agreeing 'unity of action without a sacrifice of opinion and principle'.[2] Just five days later, however, under pressure from an ultimatum from Austria, Czar Alexander finally accepted the Four Points. Napoleon III, anxious to bring the war to an end, was in the mood to talk. With four times more French troops in the field than the British, even Palmerston had to dance to the Emperor's tune. Discussions began in Paris on 25 February; a peace treaty was signed on 30 March. Russia formally agreed to respect the integrity of the Danubian Principalities, abandon its claim to a protectorate over Ottoman Christians, ceded southern Bessarabia at the mouth of the Danube to Moldavia, and accepted that the Black Sea should be closed to all warships whilst Turkey was at peace.[3]

The Commons responded in May by passing a resolution expressing joy that an honourable peace had been secured. Speaking in the debate, Herbert welcomed the outcome:

> To carry on the war for the purpose of obtaining great military successes would be an offence against the laws of God and of man [...] No man can deny with justice that, looking at the treaty as a whole, we have not attained the main objects of the war [...] I think, in short, that the terms of the peace are fully commensurate with the success of our arms.

---

1 WSHC 2057/F4/61, SH's memorandum of 11 Nov. 1855.
2 NUL Ne C 12552, SH to Newcastle, 11 Jan. 1856.
3 Conacher, *Crimea*, chs 6-7.

But he continued in a vein that was more critical than most who spoke. Terms similar to those obtained, he insisted, might have been gained in autumn 1854. The army would then have been spared the ravages of the winter. It was also 'a great error' not to have reached a compromise peace at Vienna in the spring of 1855. And given that 'our military operations having deteriorated in their direction and management after the capture of Sebastopol, we should have been entitled to demand better terms immediately upon that event than at any subsequent period'.[1]

Hindsight is a wonderful thing. Herbert was not the clairvoyant that some of his sentiments suggested. Before the war he was, by his own admission, guilty of overestimating the strength of the Russian military machine: 'The Russians made a fine defence, and the whole campaign reflects immense credit on the Army actually engaged, but shows far less formidable resources on the part of Russia than I had supposed them to possess'.[2] He also underrated the French, failing to anticipate that they would take Sebastopol in September 1855. And in December 1855 he was prophesying to Lord Stanley that Russia would not agree terms: 'Nothing will make peace so impossible as a repetition of abortive negotiations'. With no obvious end to the conflict in sight, he thought Britain would have to brace itself for at least another year of war.[3]

On one fundamental point, however, Herbert was prescient, the conundrum of the Black Sea. As he told Gladstone three months before the Treaty of Paris was concluded:

> I do not understand the machinery by which the neutralisation is to be made effective in war as well as peace. I suppose there must be a solemn European compact and guarantee by which the Black Sea must be removed from the map. Unless this can be done effectually it will be no settlement at all because the want of security to Russia will force her to evade the Treaty, and the evasion will either be repressed

1 Conacher, *Crimea*, pp. 214-17; Hansard, 6 May 1856, CXLII, cols. 35-46.
2 BL Add. Mss. 44210, fols. 205-8, SH to WEG, 27 Sept. 1855.
3 LRO 920 DER/15/43/16/55, fol. 6, SH to Stanley, 28 Dec. 1855.

or it will not. If it be, there will be another war; if it be not, there will have been no settlement as the result of the present war.[1]

Herbert was correct. In October 1870 Russia took advantage of the Franco-Prussian War to refute the Black Sea clauses of the Treaty of Paris. The British government, then headed by Gladstone, could do little other than join with the other European powers in signing the March 1871 Treaty of London, recognising what Russia had done.

One reason, so far as the war was concerned, why Herbert's counsels were less effective than they might have been, was his Russian blood. Whilst in government the fact had attracted relatively little attention; out of office it quickly became a stick with which to beat him. Following his first resignation, the *Exeter Flying Post* accused him of having tried to 'obstruct the way [of the government] and favour the designs of the Czar'.[2] Worse was to follow. Herbert could not hide his anger in the House at Roebuck's charge that his second resignation was an act of disloyalty, an aspersion heightened by the observation that the war effort seemed to go better when the half-Russian was no longer part of its direction.[3] And shortly after the war ended, Lady Palmerston, with undisguised malice, wrote that Lady Elcho had 'met Sidney Herbert on the train and never saw anybody look so disappointed as he does at the Peace news, evidently quite disturbed by it'. Herbert's countenance, Lady Palmerston believed, was chiefly to be explained by his realisation that the Treaty of Paris would destroy 'the power and prestige of Russia which is so dear to every Russian and therefore I have no doubt in the same way to this half Russian'.[4] Even Malmesbury, a lifelong friend, suggested to Herbert in December 1855 that 'you have naturally a bias for the Russians'.[5]

In his reply to Malmesbury, Herbert was indignant at such a suggestion. He reasonably pointed out that had he been sympathetic

---

1 BL Add. Mss. 44210, fols. 229-35, SH to WEG, 9 Jan. 1856.
2 *Exeter Flying Post*, 31 Jan. 1855.
3 Hansard, 7 June 1855, CXXXVIII, cols. 1565-6.
4 Lever, *Lady Palmerston*, pp. 348-9, Lady Palmerston to Pam, 20 June 1856.
5 WSHC 2057/F4/52, Malmesbury to SH, 6 Dec. 1855.

to the enemy, 'I could not have been a member of Lord Aberdeen's Government'. 'Every country', he continued,

> situated as Russia is will encroach on its neighbours if not prevented. Her relations with Circassia, Georgia, Persia, are the same as ours with Rangoon, Scinde, the Sikhs, and Oude. The stronger and more civilised necessarily absorb the weaker and more barbarous [...] we in Europe will not allow the process of absorption to go on [...] The Russians are just as great fools as other people, but they encroach as we encroach in India, Africa, and everywhere because they can't help it. We, however, have an interest in preventing her, and by a combination of circumstances we have the power. We have rightly and justly availed ourselves of it [...] I must correct one opinion of yours namely, that I hold that a Russian is better for us than a French alliance, and that it arises from my having a natural bias in favour of Russia. Now, I have no bias in favour of Russia, but on the contrary, arising from the natural bias of my mind, am in favour of a liberal policy [...] I mean that the Russian system and politics are the opposite of ours, and do by their intervention arrest the progress of good government in Europe.[1]

There can be absolutely no doubting Herbert's patriotism, even if, as the above extract illustrates, it was of a more cerebral nature than that of most of his fellow countrymen. But he was occasionally happy to indulge a more atavistic variety. In October 1855, for example, he invited the Reverend Sidney Godolphin Osborne to Wilton to celebrate the anniversary of the town's library and reading room. The walls of the room were bedecked with images of the Alma, Balaclava and Inkerman. Addressing an audience of 500, Osborne, just returned from the Crimea, digressed from his homily on the merits of literary pursuits to produce various trophies of war. They included a Russian sabre, picked up at Inkerman and, more improbably, a pair of Prince Menshikov's boots.[2] A willingness to chair such gatherings, however,

1 Stanmore, II, pp. 17-20, SH to Malmesbury, 8 Dec. 1855.
2 *SWJ*, 13 Oct. 1855. Prince Alexander Menshikov (1787-1869) had commanded Russian forces in the Crimea until February 1855.

was perfectly compatible with Herbert's taking pride in his Russian kith and kin. He was especially fond of his uncle, Prince Michael Woronzow. There were rumours that he intended meeting him on a visit to Holland in the summer of 1854. Given the international picture at that moment, it was, if true, a decidedly impolitic idea. But Herbert did spend 'a happy week' with him in July 1856.[1] Nephew and uncle would not meet again: Woronzow died on 6 November. Reflecting on his life, Herbert was careful to distinguish between a man he came close to venerating, and a regime he despised: Woronzow had been 'one of the foremost of public men in Europe a proud soldier a skilful administrator and a model of integrity & virtue in a corrupt court and a corrupt country'.[2] In wartime, the distinction Herbert drew was far too nuanced for the British public to appreciate.

The British public did recognise, however, that although the war could be depicted as a triumph of British arms, there was plenty of scope for reform of its army. Herbert, as we have seen, had been active in that realm well before hostilities commenced. Palmerston, in tandem with the new Secretary for War, Lord Panmure, carried reform further in 1855. The Ordnance Department was abolished: its responsibilities for the discipline of the Royal Engineers and Royal Artillery were transferred to Horse Guards, its civil duties to the War Office. The latter also assumed responsibility for the militia from the Home Office. A new Land Transport Corps (subsequently known as the Military Train) was created, similar in design to an idea that had been floated by Herbert in January. And with Palmerston opting not to appoint a Secretary at War, Herbert proved to be the last occupant of the office.[3] But public opinion was less concerned with structures than people. By virtue of the fact that the realities of war had been brought home to it as never before, the ordinary soldier was now perceived of as a popular hero. As such, he deserved to be saved, not just from the enemy, but also from his officers. For the latter, on the basis of their perceived incompetence in the Crimea, had become targets for

---

1 WSHC 2057/F4/71, EH to Hon. G. Herbert, 1 July 1856.
2 BL Add. Mss. 79658, fols. 9-14, SH to JRG, 14 Dec. 1856.
3 Sweetman, *War and Administration*, pp. 54-6, 70-3.

popular opprobrium. Two particular themes emerged through which improvements were deemed attainable: reforming the system by which officers joined the army; and better education. Although out of office, Herbert, already familiar with such questions, would be prominently involved in both.

Since 1815, approximately three-quarters of the army's officers had entered the service by purchasing a commission. Between 1851 and 1853, for instance, 963 (78.4%) of the 1,229 who entered the service had done so in this way. More often than not, they were the sons of landed gentlemen. As a report of which Herbert was the co-signatory put it, purchase of commissions:

> is said to restrict the number of those from whom officers in the first instance can be obtained; it deadens the feelings of emulation and the eagerness to acquire military knowledge, and it renders men eligible for the highest command without taking any security that they are fitted for such a position.[1]

Before the war, Herbert had said little on the matter in public. This changed when, on 1 March 1855, Viscount Goderich and Lieutenant-General Sir George de Lacy Evans (the latter recently invalided from the Crimea) tabled a motion against what they perceived to be the pernicious effects of the purchase system. The question was, Herbert contended in response, partly a matter of perspective. Eighty-eight 'men who had handled the plough or the shuttle' had received commissions in the past year. This made the army, of all the supposed aristocratic professions, 'the most democratic, for the greatest number of men of low station through this profession find their way to the higher ranks'. From this proposition, Herbert proceeded to mount a defence of his class. Aristocrats had risen to the apex of the social pyramid for a reason. The principle of promotion on merit was perfectly reasonable but 'you must not handicap them, and make the race more difficult for them than it is for any other class

---

1 PP 1857 [2267], XVIII, pp. 24, 33; Spiers, *Army and Society*, pp. 10-22.

of the community. There ought to be perfect equality here'. Officers, after all, were required to set their men:

> an example in many ways that require superior talent when the men are under great difficulties and discouragements. That fearlessness under responsibility which assists the officer who has been accustomed to it from his birth upwards does not always assist the officer who rises from the ranks, and it is therefore nothing more than a reasonable expectation that the liberally educated man, on a general average, will make a better officer than a man who has risen from the ranks.[1]

The motion was defeated by 158 votes to 114. But Evans was not the sort of man who believed that losing a battle meant losing the war. He crossed swords with Herbert again when he called for a select committee on purchase in March 1856. Herbert urged caution, but he did indicate the sort of reform he would be prepared to countenance:

> I have always been a warm advocate of selection where you have good opportunity of knowing the qualifications of your men [...] I have great doubts whether captains ought to be allowed to become colonels merely by seniority combined with purchase, or by seniority at all [...] I should be very glad to see purchase put an end to in every rank above that of captain.[2]

To such possible ends, Herbert proposed that the best way of proceeding was by a royal commission comprising 'military officers and civilians'.[3] Panmure, Secretary for War, agreed. On 10 May 1856, both Herbert and Evans were named as members of a commission under the Duke of Somerset.

Herbert, ordered to seek restorative cures abroad in the summer of 1856, was the least active member of the commission. But he was present for three of the four meetings which concluded its hearings in 1857. Herbert was also amongst the six commissioners who endorsed

1 Hansard, 1 Mar. 1855, CXXXVI, cols. 2148-61.
2 Hansard, 4 Mar. 1856, CXL, cols. 1843-4.
3 Hansard, 4 Mar. 1856, CXL, cols. 1845-6.

the report (the other four opposed it) which followed in August. The vote was close because the royal commission had not kicked the issue of purchase into the long grass as many, Panmure included, had hoped. Purchase, the report concluded, had its merits: it allowed for accelerated promotion and was a safeguard against the exercise of favouritism by more senior officers. Abolishing it outright, moreover, 'would not be favourably received' by the existing cadre of officers.[1] Some modifications, though, were recommended. In particular, the ability to purchase regimental commands should be abolished. Instead, lieutenant-colonels should be selected on merit from the pool of majors. The government was unimpressed. With officers performing well under prevailing arrangements in suppressing the Indian Mutiny, which had begun in May 1857, the report was shelved.[2]

Herbert would be instrumental in reviving the purchase issue when he returned to office in 1859. His more immediate concern was education. The need to do something, in his view, was more pressing than it had been before war broke out: Britain was spending just £1,300 per annum on military education; Austria £127,000.[3] Unlike many, Herbert saw no paradox in defending purchase whilst advocating instruction:

> It is just because we have purchase that we the more require examination [...] The evils of purchase of course are, that many young men enter the army without intending to make it their profession [...] we want to correct that evil by infusing a spirit of emulation into the minds of our young men, and by creating an incentive to military study, with a view to its adoption as a regular profession.[4]

In May 1856 Herbert told Gladstone that he had received letters from officers asking him to raise the subject of military instruction in the House.[5] On 5 June, in a speech which exceeded 9,000 words in the

1 PP 1857 [2267], XVIII, pp. 25, 30.
2 PP 1857 [2267], XVIII, pp. 32-3; Spiers, *Army and Society*, pp. 145-8.
3 Spiers, *Army and Society*, p. 152.
4 Hansard, 5 June 1856, CXLII, col. 1000.
5 BL Add. Mss. 44210, fols. 252-5, SH to WEG, 16 May 1856.

columns of Hansard, he duly set out how his grand vision for officer education would work. Would-be officers should be encouraged to go to Sandhurst: 'I would propose that no one should be admitted into the army who had not passed the examination at Sandhurst, or, at all events, an examination equal to it'. Sandhurst should provide a two-year course with an emphasis on practical affairs. A new school for cavalry officers should be set up at Maidstone. A separate staff college should be revived, perhaps at Farnham. Candidates for the latter must first have had three years' experience: 'one in the infantry, one in the cavalry, and one in the artillery'. And for those already in the army seeking promotion (to facilitate which, Herbert envisaged every division having a military instructor attached to it), he proposed appointing three examiners to appraise candidates. These would be sufficient for the thousand or so commissions he expected to fall vacant in a typical year.[1]

Lord Brougham, the veteran Reformer who had championed Queen Caroline in 1820 and been Lord Chancellor at the time of the Reform Bill, wrote to congratulate Herbert. He had made an 'admirable & most useful speech', even if it was 'Too technical' for many Members.[2] Within days, the speech had become more readily available when it was re-published as a pamphlet. Herbert's object was laudable ('We want to inoculate the whole army with a more professional spirit') but the modern reader cannot but be struck by the conservatism of the sentiments which he uttered. When Herbert spoke of equality of opportunity, what he meant was equality of opportunity for those who had attended public school. They would be men possessed of academic potential and an aptitude for military affairs, but also, crucially, men inscribed with the hallmarks of gentility. Herbert was adamant that he had 'seen men of very high rank to whom no amount of politeness could induce me to apply the term "gentleman."' He was equally insistent that 'I have seen men of very humble station whose natural liberality of mind has fairly entitled them to that appellation'. But he

1   Hansard, 5 June 1856, CXLII, cols. 980-1001.
2   WSHC 2057/F4/52, Brougham to SH, 7 Aug. 1856.

also conceded that the practical effect of what he was proposing would militate against all but the occasional genius rising from the ranks.[1]

In the Britain of 1856, Herbert's views on the fitness of gentlemen to command still garnered widespread support. His view that they should be better educated, meanwhile, was beginning to gain traction. A select committee on Sandhurst had reported in 1855. Herbert had not served on it, but he would have been gratified to discover that it decided to include his educational reform proposals of 1854 as an appendix.[2] Panmure (Herbert rightly believed him to be opposed to the detail of his ideas) had responded by appointing his own committee to advise on the best way forward.[3] The Duke of Cambridge, who had succeeded Hardinge at Horse Guards in July 1856, was sympathetic to the cause of military education. Prince Albert was favourably disposed to the idea of a staff college. Herbert was even given reason to think that he would be asked to adjudicate between rival proposals for reform emanating from the War Office and Horse Guards.[4] He was not, but in the febrile atmosphere which Herbert had helped to engender, a Council of Military Education, under the Commander-in-Chief but subject to War Office control, was established in April 1857. It was a lot less than Herbert had been calling for. Nevertheless, given that he was out of office and had so recently been out of public favour, Herbert's attempts to catalyse army reform from the backbenches had not been made in vain.[5]

An initiative which yielded Herbert more tangible success was the Nightingale Fund. The famous image of Florence carrying a lighted candle in a ward at Scutari, which appeared in the *Illustrated London News* on 24 February 1855, had consummated her status as national heroine. It served also to galvanise minds as to how best her efforts might be rewarded. 'There broke out in different parts of the country', as Herbert later put it, 'a feeling of immediate and

1 Hansard, 1 Mar. 1855, CXXXVI, cols. 2148-61.
2 PP 1854-5 (317), XII, appendix 5.
3 BL Add. Mss. 79658, fols. 15-22, SH to JRG, 27 Jan. 1857.
4 BL Add. Mss. 44210, fols. 260-1, SH to WEG, 20 June 1856.
5 Spiers, *Army and Society*, pp. 150-3.

spontaneous expression of public gratitude'.[1] Nobody before the summer of 1855, however, had canalised those sentiments with a view to doing something concrete. One of those who had tried, albeit unsuccessfully, was the lady who wrote to Elizabeth Herbert in July as 'H'. 'H' was Anna Maria Hall, an Irish novelist whose many philanthropic projects included helping to found what became the Royal Brompton Hospital. Mrs Herbert was able to reply to Hall that her sentiments had been anticipated, and that an account would soon be opened at Coutts Bank in the name of the 'Nightingale Hospital Fund'. She and her husband had 'felt it was right to give appropriate direction to this generous feeling'.[2]

Well aware that Nightingale would scorn a reward of the 'teapot and bracelet' variety, the Herberts had indeed set to work.[3] They concluded that a training school for nurses, something which they knew Nightingale had long contemplated, would be an apt commemoration of her efforts. The Halls were enlisted in the enterprise. Anna's husband, Samuel Carter Hall, was an unlikely ally, an Irish journalist who later became chairman of the British National Association of Spiritualists. Many reckoned him to be the model for the unctuous Mr Pecksniff in *Martin Chuzzlewit*. How Herbert perceived him – Hall was suitably obsequious towards Herbert – is unrecorded, but Hall appears to have been a willing workhorse. In August 1855, for example, Herbert instructed Hall that 'a Fund circular be prepared to be sent to 300 banking houses' soliciting their support.[4] On 29 September, Herbert himself wrote an ill-judged letter to Nightingale requesting that she outline her plans for the training school to be built from the money raised: she was of course far too preoccupied to give the question serious thought. More satisfying were the missives he despatched to the great and the good asking that they allow their names to be added to a provisional committee. One found its way to

1 *The Times*, 25 Jan. 1856.
2 *SWJ*, 26 Aug. 1855; *The Times*, 25 Jan. 1856.
3 Cook, *Nightingale*, I, p. 268.
4 LMA A/NFC/29/1, SH to Hall, Aug. 1855; Baly, *Nursing Legacy*, p. 8.

the Duke of Newcastle in Paris; he was one of 70 who responded in the affirmative.[1]

Herbert chaired the first meeting of the Nightingale Fund committee on 8 November. Four proposals were adopted: to hold a public meeting to recognise Nightingale's work, 'to establish a permanent institution for the training, sustenance and protection of nurses', to launch a public subscription for the same, and to agree that Nightingale herself should have the last word in directing the project.[2] The public meeting took place in Willis's Rooms, off St James's Square, on 29 November. An estimated 1,250 people attended with the Duke of Cambridge in the chair. In seconding the fourth resolution, Herbert made a speech which Nightingale's mother reported 'delighted every one'. If only because he read a letter from a soldier relating how Nightingale walked through the wards of Scutari and that 'we could kiss her shadow as it fell, and lay our heads on the pillow again content' he succeeded in adding an unforgettable image to the legend of the Lady with the Lamp.[3]

For Herbert, confirmed alongside Hall as joint secretary of the Fund's permanent committee, the real work of fundraising now began in earnest. Nightingale made it clear that, in her absence, she trusted and deferred to Herbert's judgement on all matters related to it. What followed was arguably 'the first national appeal in Britain aimed at all classes' of society.[4] By the end of 1855, Herbert had written publicity articles, attended innumerable committee meetings, and assisted in sending out 20,000 circulars to clergy, mayors, and other civic dignitaries. From Reading railway station, on 27 December, waiting for the connection that would transport him to yet another fundraiser, he wrote to Hall 'to send you the note Lord Monteagle required in order for Coutts to finalise exchequer bills'.[5] One of his own circulars,

1 NUL Ne C 12560, Newcastle to SH, 4 Dec. 1855.
2 Baly, *Nursing Legacy*, pp. 8-9.
3 *The Times*, 30 Nov. 1855; Cook, *Nightingale*, I, pp. 269-70.
4 BL Add. Mss. 43393, fol. 209, FN to SH, 6 Jan. 1856; Baly, *Nursing Legacy*, p. 17.
5 LMA A/NFC/29/1/52, SH to Hall, 22 Jan. 1856; Baly, *Nursing Legacy*, p. 14.

he informed Lord Stanley with unconcealed pride, was bringing in nearly £200 a day, all part of 'a steady daily influx of money'.[1] But 'steady' was not 'spectacular'. As the Fund's historian has said, such success as the Fund had owed much to 'hard work and anxiety on the part of the Committee as the letters which passed almost daily between the two secretaries testify'.[2] Not least of Herbert's contributions were his suggestions, often accompanied by chivvying and cajoling (shades of the Secretary at War of a year previously), as to where meetings might be held and who would speak. 'Monckton Milnes would be good on resolutions' for Oxford or Leeds, he mused, 'but what about Gladstone?'[3] Similarly, he pestered Lord Stanley to rouse the North, perhaps in Liverpool but certainly in Manchester where the mayor, James Watts, was apparently doing nothing to convene a meeting. In the end Herbert wrote to Watts direct. He suggested too, that John Bright, more often than not a political opponent, be approached to lend the weight of his oratory and prestige when the hoped-for meeting finally took place there.[4]

At the outset of the fundraising campaign, an optimistic Herbert had informed the Prime Minister that Nightingale's 'prestige is great & she has lived down the religious prejudices & suspicions by wh. she was at first assailed'.[5] Sadly, this did not prove to be the case. Nightingale was accused of belonging to all manner of religious persuasions; in consequence the Fund was seen as a vehicle for extending their various pernicious doctrines. Herbert rightly dismissed such attacks as 'silly', but was mindful of their potential damage. Hence he was the moving force behind an anonymous article in *The Times* (no surprise there) denying that the Fund had links to any particular denomination. One reason he was keen for Anglican bishops to speak at meetings was 'to counteract the charge of Socinianism that has been levelled at

---

1   LRO 920 DER15/43/16/55, fol. 4, SH to Stanley, 18 Dec. 1855.
2   Baly, *Nursing Legacy*, p. 13.
3   Baly, *Nursing Legacy*, p. 13.
4   LRO 920 DER15/43/16/55, fols. 5-6, 10, SH to Stanley, 23, 28 Dec. 1855, 27 Jan.1856.
5   WSHC 2057/F4/61, SH to Pam, 17 Oct. 1855.

Miss Nightingale and the charge of Romanism by Dr Cummings, the Presbyterian'.[1]

Predictably, Herbert himself became a target for innuendo: 'I am supposed to have High Church leanings and a Low Church certificate would not be much value'.[2] Angered too by allegations that the Fund was managing the paradoxical feat of doing both too little and too much, he agreed to speak in person at the meeting which mayor Watts finally convened in Manchester on 17 January. The Fund, Herbert insisted (with the war still raging), had not been launched prematurely. Trained nurses were essential: those he had seen at first hand in Salisbury knew 'no more about nursing in hospital than about conic sections'. Further, as regards the training school, 'nothing sectarian of any kind is intended in the plans we have to submit'. After all, those nurses in the Crimea 'did not think to show their Christianity by quarrelling among themselves as to the different paths to Heaven'. Their chief was, 'to use the slang term of the day "the right women in the right place."' For all that Herbert's speech was well-received, the meeting as a whole, he thought, had been marred by bigotry.[3]

The news that Herbert was to speak in Manchester prompted several other invitations for him to address meetings in northern venues. On reflection he declined: 'tho it is well to go to a place like Manchester wh is a capital in itself a round of towns wd be too Barnum-like a proceeding'.[4] He did, however, agree to speak at the town hall in Oxford on 23 January. Having left the moving of the resolutions to luminaries of the University, he spoke in sentiments similar to those he had uttered in Manchester. His only substantive addition was to deny that a training school was better organised locally than nationally. With a due nod to those alongside him on the platform he noted that 'We want a university for nurses, to which all may have access,

1 LMA A/NFC/29/1/39, SH to Hall, 25 Nov. 1856; Baly, *Nursing Legacy*, pp. 14-15. Dr John Cumming (1807-1881), was a Scottish clergyman known for his virulently anti-Catholic lectures.
2 Baly, *Nursing Legacy*, pp. 14-15.
3 *The Times*, 18 Jan. 1856; Baly, *Nursing Legacy*, p. 14.
4 LRO 920 DER15/43/16/55, fol. 7, SH to Stanley, 4 Jan. 1856. The allusion is to Phineas Taylor Barnum, the American showman.

and which shall be beneficial to the whole community'. The Oxford meeting at least, he concluded, had been a good one.[1]

Herbert's tireless efforts on behalf of the Fund either side of the New Year were made, as he knew full well, at a personal cost: whilst he laboured, his mother was dying. The Dowager Lady Pembroke died in London on 27 March 1856, aged 71. Few knew, he confided to Newcastle, 'the warmth & strength of her affections'.[2] In a long letter to Michael Woronzow, her brother, Herbert described in detail the final weeks of the mother who had led 'a pure and holy life'.[3] Elizabeth Herbert was in no doubt that the bonds were mutual: 'There was no part of his character more striking than his love for his Mother – to see them together, she so proud of him, he so tender and careful of, and yet so reverential towards her'.[4] Still extant is the small envelope which Herbert labelled 'Dearest Mammy's Hair'. Over 700 locals paid their respects to Wilton's patroness of nearly half a century when Herbert admitted them to the hall of Wilton House on 2 April. A family funeral, in the church which they had lovingly created together, followed.[5] Presumably a consequence of the war with her motherland (the ink on the Treaty of Paris had then barely dried), there was scarcely a mention of her passing in the press.

The Nightingale Fund, meanwhile, continued to grow. It was finally wound up on 20 June 1856. Some £44,037 had been contributed, a sum equivalent to roughly £4 million in the early twenty-first century. By the time a deed of trust for the Fund was signed on 20 June 1857, it had risen to £48,000, just shy of the £50,000 which Herbert had mooted to Palmerston as the target back in October 1855.[6] Herbert was one of five trustees appointed to oversee its use for the 'training, sustenance and protection of nurses and hospital attendants'.

---

1 *The Times*, 25 Jan. 1856; LRO 920 DER15/43/16/55, fol. 10, SH to Stanley, 27 Jan. 1856.
2 NUL Ne C 11922/1-2, SH to Lincoln, 5 Mar. 1841.
3 Stanmore, II, pp. 35-8, SH to Michael Woronzow, 28 Mar. 1856.
4 WSHC 2057/F6/98, 'Account of Sidney Herbert', p. 39.
5 *SWJ*, 5 Apr. 1856.
6 WSHC 2057/F4/61, SH to Pam, 17 Oct. 1855.

Achieving this end, however, would prove problematic. For Nightingale it was never a pressing priority. Neither was she initially clear in her own mind as to how the scheme should proceed; certainly she had no intention of heading any training school in person. Writing to Herbert on 23 March 1858, she asked to be disassociated from the project. Herbert immediately turned her letter to his advantage. He replied to her on 26 March, urging her to reconsider; she relented in her reply of the following day. To Nightingale's surprise – 'I had no idea, till I saw Mrs. Herbert yesterday that you would think it necessary to put the correspondence in the "Times"' – Herbert then passed their exchange to the press. Thus was the project given the necessary fresh impetus.[1] Having poured cold water on Herbert's suggestion that the training school be established at King's College, Nightingale finally opted for St Thomas's Hospital in Southwark in May 1859. Herbert was one of the five man sub-committee set up to negotiate the terms under which her wish would become a reality. Following yet more tortuous discussions, the Nightingale Training School finally opened its doors on 24 June 1860. There were sufficient monies left over to help support a training school for midwives at King's College from October 1861. By then Herbert had been dead for over two months but he, as much as anybody, deserves credit for a scheme which he helped to originate, sustain, and bring to fruition.[2]

Whilst Herbert's industry on behalf of the Nightingale Fund may have done much to restore his reputation out of doors, his position in parliament after February 1855 was more precarious. Set-piece speeches such as that on army education enhanced his status as an orator but his record in the division lobbies was abysmal. Following his exit from the Colonial Office, Herbert voted only eleven times in 1855 and only fifteen times during the whole of 1856. The Peelites, meanwhile, were held in widespread contempt. Herbert acknowledged that the decline in their influence stemmed partly from his, Gladstone's

1 WSHC 2057/F4/66, FN to SH, 23, 27 Mar. 1858; BL Add. Mss. 43395, fols. 29-33, SH to FN, 26 Mar. 1858, FN to SH, 27 Mar. 1858; *SWJ*, 3 Apr. 1858.
2 Goldie, *Nightingale*, pp. 184-5; Baly, *Nursing Legacy*, ch. 2; Bostridge, *Nightingale*, pp. 364-9, 428-31.

and Graham's having resigned in February 1855, and their having opposed the war when it was still popular with the public.[1] But the Peelites – more broadly defined as the 45 Members who had been elected in 1852 – were hamstrung by the absence of an issue around which they could rally. As Herbert put it to Malmesbury early in 1857, 'They are much divided and on almost every question lately submitted to the House of Commons, they have voted in different lobbies'.[2]

So far as the limited evidence of his own votes is concerned, Herbert was yet to cast his stone decisively in favour of one of the two main party groupings. During 1855-6, he appeared twelve times in the division lobbies with Palmerston, but seven times with Disraeli. More revealing of what might be called a friendly disposition towards Palmerston's ministry, was his decision to sit on the government side of the House below the gangway. This was, Herbert thought, 'more significant of one's own view of one's party position and intentions, than any profession of faith, oral or written'.[3] Speculation nevertheless persisted. In April 1856 there were 'strong rumours', in wake of a 'flurry' of interviews, that Herbert and Graham were about to re-join Palmerston, with Herbert replacing Panmure at the War Office.[4] But at the same time, Herbert, Graham, Gladstone and Cardwell, agreeing that they 'rather eschewed acting as a party', were meeting to discuss their preferred scenario for an alternative government. Their subsequent conclusion that Clarendon, a moderate Whig, should become Prime Minister with the Peelites controlling the major spending and financial departments suggests that the gathering was more akin to a parlour game than a war council. Sir William Heathcote, a staunch Tory who sat with Gladstone for Oxford University, gave voice to what many thought when he told Gladstone that he was 'under the impression

---

1   WSHC 2057/F4/53, SH to Aberdeen, 12 Apr. 1857.
2   Stanmore, II, p. 78, SH to Malmesbury, 6 Mar. 1857; Hawkins, *Parliament*, pp. 38-44.
3   WSHC 2057/F4/53, SH to Aberdeen, 12 Apr. 1857.
4   *SWJ*, 19 Apr. 1856.

that Herbert from health or otherwise might not be looking to office at the present moment'.[1]

Heathcote was right. Herbert, though in better health than twelve months previously, followed his doctor's recommendation (on the proviso that he resist the temptation to eat the wild strawberries) to take a 'short recess' at Carlsbad. He spent a congenial two months abroad. Returning to Wilton in mid-August 1856, he found a welcome invitation from Speaker Denison to join him in the Scottish Highlands, and another asking him to become involved with plans for the new National Portrait Gallery.[2] The bait of hook and line lured him to Ireland for a month to mid-September; he spent a further week there in October via a stay with Gladstone at Hawarden. When he returned to Wilton in late October, it was for 'a long sojourn', something that had not been the case for several years past. There was time, therefore, to attend to the banalities of petty and quarter sessions, to assemble with his troop of yeomanry cavalry, and for sport with the celebrated Tedworth Hunt. A traditional family Christmas and New Year gathering at Tottenham House, as guest of the Ailesburys, was the perfect culmination to a period of six months of relative calm.[3]

Surveying the political scene in the autumn of 1856, Herbert had been struck by the absence of any particular issue exciting the public. This was mirrored at Westminster by 'the existence of two parties, each offering to do the same thing, but one claiming to do it better than the other'. Given the sharp political divisions of the 1830s and 1840s this was, he thought, 'by no means an unmixed evil as regards the country', even if in the House it meant that 'each man can afford to kick and cuff or desert the Government on his own account and then talk to his constituency of his independence'.[4] Put another way, it meant that an individual Member's allegiances remained as likely to be determined by personalities as issues.

1 Brooke and Sorensen, *Gladstone*, pp. 199-204, memorandum of 17 Apr. 1856.
2 WSHC 2057/F4/52, Denison to SH, 29 July 1856; WSHC 2057/F4/53, Cornewall Lewis to SH, 11 Aug. 1856; *SWJ*, 23 Aug. 1856.
3 *SWJ*, 25 Oct., 1 Nov. 1856, 10 Jan. 1857.
4 BL Add. Mss. 44210, fols. 268-71, SH to WEG, 26 Oct. 1856.

So far as Herbert was concerned, Derby's view, in 1856, was that Herbert had 'personal leanings to some members of the present government'.¹ He had a point. Herbert's house guests at Wilton that autumn included Sir Charles Wood and Earl Granville, respectively First Lord of the Admiralty and Lord President of the Council. In a five-and-a-half hour shoot, the three of them bagged 150 pheasants, 164 hares and 199 rabbits, a rate of slaughter to rival anything in the Crimea.² But Wood and Granville were not yet political hotshots. For those who could reasonably aspire to be Prime Minister in the immediate future, Herbert continued to have little personal regard. Of the Conservatives' leaders, he shared Graham's view that 'The Jew and the jockey [Derby's sobriquet was the consequence of his well-known predilection for the Turf] are still in bad odour, and when it comes to the point, this nation will not be governed by them'.³ On the Liberal side, with Russell's star having waned, this left only Palmerston. Yet Herbert had described him only recently as a man 'able to make three speeches with scarcely an idea in one of them'.⁴ Palmerston was thus Herbert's lesser of evils. But he was one whose septuagenarian status gave Herbert grounds for the encouraging presumption that his unique brand was nearing the end of its shelf life:

> Palmerston is an exceptional Prime Minister. We never shall again see an old-fashioned ultra-Tory leading the Liberal party, and this exceptional state of things cannot last very long, looking at the age of the man and the ordinary temper of the men on whose support he must ultimately rely.⁵

Herbert looked forward, therefore, to the day of 'that Moderate Liberal party which I think must govern this country'.⁶ In the meantime, he would face 'the impotent lassitude of neutrality'. 'I try to console

1 Brooke and Sorensen, *Gladstone*, pp. 199-204, 213-14.
2 *SWJ*, 22 Nov., 13 Dec. 1856.
3 WSHC 2057/F4/59, JRG to SH, 29 Jan. 1857.
4 BL Add. Mss. 44210, fols. 272-5, SH to WEG, 10 Nov. 1856.
5 BL Add. Mss. 79658, fols. 25-30, SH to JRG, 15 Mar. 1857.
6 WSHC 2057/F4/53, SH to Aberdeen, 12 Apr. 1857.

myself', he told Gladstone, 'with the idea that I shall occupy myself out of the House with commissions, and leave Parliamentary discussions and tactics to those who have better heart for them'.[1] Club-land, as the year turned, remained awash with gossip to the contrary: renewed rumours that Herbert was about to succeed Panmure at the War Office competed with those that he would become President of the Board of Trade in a Derby ministry.[2]

Politics were no clearer following Herbert's 'long sitting' about 'our position' with Aberdeen at Wilton in January 1857. Whilst Herbert thought Palmerston relatively secure in office, Graham's view was that Russell would soon replace him as Liberal leader, and Gladstone's that the Liberals would be turned out in favour of the Conservatives. The two major parliamentary divisions in the early part of the year, meanwhile, served to underscore the continuing division within Peelite ranks. Herbert, Graham and Gladstone were amongst eleven Peelites who, on 23 February, supported Disraeli's resolutions calling for the abolition of income tax by 1860. But eleven more voted against them and helped the government to a comfortable majority of eighty.[3] Four days earlier, the maths had been closer but even more confused. The annual Radical motion for an equalisation of the borough and county franchises failed by just 192 votes to 179: Graham was one of eight Peelites in the minority; Herbert and Gladstone with the majority. Though not intending to, Herbert felt constrained to speak in the debate, if only to explain why he was going into the opposite lobby from Graham: 'Society is not uniform', he told the House, 'and an uniform franchise will never fairly and completely represent the variety of classes into which society is divided'.[4]

The Reform question would have remained centre stage had it not been for events 6,000 miles away in China. In October 1856 the Chinese authorities had arrested the crew of the lorcha *Arrow*, men

1   Stanmore, II, pp. 65-6, JRG to SH, 16 Dec. 1856; BL Add. Mss. 44210, fols. 312-19, SH to WEG, 13 Apr. 1857.
2   *SWJ*, 6 Dec. 1856, 10 Jan. 1857.
3   Shannon, *Gladstone. Peel's Inheritor*, p. 329; Hawkins, *Parliament*, p. 58.
4   Hansard, 19 Feb. 1857, CXLIV, cols. 859-61; WSHC 2057/F4/53, SH to Aberdeen, 12 Apr. 1857.

whom Herbert characterised as 'Chinese, picked up from the very refuse and scum of the population along the Canton river'. Historians have been more politically correct than Herbert in their phraseology, but few have dissented from the general thrust of his remarks. The vessel was probably being used to carry opium but it had a (lapsed) registration at the British colony of Hong Kong. When its governor, Sir John Bowring, failed to secure the release of the crew together with an apology from the Chinese government, he ordered the bombardment of Canton. The Prime Minister endorsed Bowring's actions. His critics in the House responded by lining up behind Richard Cobden's motion condemning them.[1]

Herbert made a long speech in the ensuing debate on 2 March. He objected 'to the bombardment of a populous city and the shedding of innocent blood'. The Chinese were 'a most precocious and extraordinary people, and do possess an extraordinary degree of refinement'. And even if was the case that the 'Cantonese are a set of blackguards', 'surely, it is not logical to say that every town with a blackguard population may be justly subjected to a bombardment'. Were Britons, by the same token, 'fairly represented by the rabble of Shoreditch and Wapping'? The Prime Minister's decision to support Bowring's act of bellicosity, he concluded, was morally wrong and could not but damage Britain's standing:

> I know what is the public opinion of England throughout Europe; I am not anxious that we should go on piling up year after year fresh offences against that public opinion, until some day we may reap the consequence to our detriment. Above all, I confess I see with the deepest sorrow force exercised with so little mercy, upon a pretext so transparent – I will not say so transparently fraudulent – in a manner so destructive to the character of this country for truth, justice, faith, and mercy.[2]

---

1   Hawkins, *Parliament*, pp. 58-62.
2   Hansard, 2 Mar. 1857, CXLIV, cols. 1668-80.

It was all very reminiscent of Herbert's speech on China in 1840 and his role in the Don Pacifico affair of 1850. Except that the outcome was different. Cobden's motion was passed by 263 votes to 247. Palmerston, rather than resign, called an election.

The 1857 South Wiltshire election required Herbert to walk a political tightrope. Palmerston's stance was hugely popular with the public; Herbert prominently opposed to it. There were even rumours that he would join the Conservatives over the issue.[1] Malmesbury, at Derby's behest, saw Herbert on 6 March, to suggest 'that we should not take a hostile part towards each other's candidates [South Wiltshire Conservatives were running Lord Henry Thynne, son of the Marquis of Bath] so that, no personal enmities being made, there should be less difficulty in the two parties acting together, should circumstances make it advisable'. This, though, was presuming too much. Herbert received his old friend 'in a very unfriendly and even uncivil manner'.[2] Partly to dampen speculation that he was about to become a Conservative, Herbert was at pains to emphasise his independence of parties in his election address of 13 March. He did, however, promise to support 'liberal, but moderate and enlightened, legislation'. This he later itemised as including reform of the law, reform of church rates, and an extension of the franchise to graduates, those who paid 40 shillings in direct taxes or who had £50 in a savings bank account.[3] Even so, he confided to Elizabeth that 'all his most influential supporters are dissatisfied at the course he has taken', something, she thought, 'has mortified & I think, disheartened him'. Her own view was that if a strong Palmerstonian Liberal candidate entered the field 'Sidney would run a bad chance and meet with the fate of the Church in Laodicea'.[4]

---

1 Malmesbury, *Memoirs*, II, pp. 56-7, 3 Feb. 1857; *DWG*, 12 Mar. 1857; WSHC 2057/F4/53, JRG to Somerset, 19 Mar. 1857.
2 Stanmore, II, p. 78, SH to Malmesbury, 6 Mar. 1857; Malmesbury, *Memoirs*, II, pp. 63-4
3 *SWJ*, 28 Mar., 4 Apr. 1857.
4 BL Add. Mss. 44212, fol. 37, EH to WEG, 7 Mar. 1857. The early Christian community of Laodicea in Asia Minor was said to have come to grief in consequence of its sense of pride and self-sufficiency.

But Herbert responded astutely. To mitigate the possibility that he would have to face a challenge from two Palmerstonian Liberals, he made it clear that the family interest would not be used to dislodge Sir Edmund Antrobus from Wilton borough, even though Antrobus had supported Palmerston over the Canton motion. Elizabeth Herbert predicted that 'that fact will pull him through!!'[1] To make that prediction safer still, Herbert sent explanatory letters to political friends who had been aggrieved by his votes in support of Disraeli's resolutions on finance and against Palmerston on Canton. These initiatives, taken in conjunction with a series of well received speeches around the constituency, convinced him that he had 'no fear whatever for the result, and every day is strengthening me'.[2] Even so, a boisterous crowd of 3,000 gathered in Salisbury for the nomination. Greeted by heckles of 'Send him to Rooshia', one of Thynne's two proposers denounced Herbert as 'clever, weak, and vacillating [...] by turns the friend and opponent of all parties'; the other as a man who had deserted Palmerston 'when the soldiers were lying in heaps in the Crimea'.[3] There must have been a measure of relief when Herbert's 1,517 votes placed him at the head of the poll.

Herbert welcomed the general election results as a whole (367 Liberals, 260 Conservatives), seeing them as a triumph for moderate Liberals who would 'keep the Government in order'. Paradoxically, he also welcomed an outcome where 'what the world called Peelites are extinct'.[4] Whilst this was something of an exaggeration – the best modern assessment puts their numbers as having fallen from 45 to 27 – it was true that the Peelites would have to abandon any pretence of being able to hold the balance of power in the new parliament. Herbert found this liberating. It would allow him to 'take my place where my opinions and predilections alike keep me – namely, on

---

1 BL Add. Mss. 44212, fols. 38-40, EH to WEG, 9 Mar. 1857.
2 BL Add. Mss. 79658, fols. 25-30, SH to JRG, 15 Mar. 1857; BL Add. Mss. 44210, fols. 302-5, SH to WEG, 18 Mar. 1857.
3 *SWJ*, 4 Apr. 1857.
4 BL Add. Mss. 44210, fols. 302-5, SH to WEG, 18 Mar. 1857; WSHC 2057/F4/53, SH to Aberdeen, 12 Apr. 1857.

the Liberal side of the House'.[1] Count Paul Strzelecki, who became a close friend and collaborator of Herbert in his final years, welcomed the 'honest conviction, & leaning, which you have long entertained to the party of progress & liberal principles'.[2] There was, perhaps, a degree of post hoc rationalisation here. Herbert endorsed it when he told Aberdeen on 12 April that his (and the Peelites) fusion with the Liberals had really taken place in 1852. But this was neither the interpretation shared by Gladstone, nor one which the various turns of the political kaleidoscope since 1852 rendered inevitable. It is revealing that Herbert felt it necessary to write to his wife, his greatest confidante, protesting that 'I have, ever since I joined Lord Aberdeen's Government, considered myself a member of the Liberal party, and certainly have never had the least intention of leaving it'.[3] The gist of Herbert's claim was nevertheless true. Graham defined it best and most succinctly when he wrote that 'his principles & feelings are strongly in favour of the Liberal Party, altho' he cannot recognise Ld Palmerston as its legitimate organ'.[4]

For this reason, though now prepared and preferring to describe himself as a Liberal, Herbert still resisted sitting with the government. He also believed that a parting of the ways was imminent: Gladstone, he presumed, would cross the floor to sit with the Conservatives. Thus Herbert declared himself averse to Gladstone, Graham and himself continuing to sit together below the gangway on the government side of the House. Their doing so, he feared, would be construed by the political world as meaning that they were still in concert as a party.[5] Both Gladstone and Graham assured Herbert that he was overthinking the case, that they should wait on events to determine such details, not seek to anticipate them. For good measure, Aberdeen offered his two

1   BL Add. Mss. 44210, fols. 302-5, SH to WEG, 18 Mar. 1857.
2   WSHC 2057/F4/52, Strzelecki to SH, 23 Mar. 1857.
3   Stanmore, II, p. 81, SH to EH, 18 Mar. 1857.
4   WSHC 2057/F4/53, JRG to Somerset, 19 Mar. 1857.
5   BL Add. Mss. 44210, fols. 312-19, SH to WEG, 13 Apr. 1857.

pennies' worth 'that you sit together, not as Peelites, but as friends'.[1] Herbert's sensitivity and anxiety on the point is odd, to be explained, perhaps, by the fact that he had been suffering from rheumatic fever since the election. In the event he deferred to his two friends. Thus Graham's ironic letter of 27 April that 'with regard to "the great Seat Question", I shall be happy to compound for having you as my next neighbour, even tho' the Gang Way be interposed between us'.[2] In the event Herbert would have little time for the Commons: the warrant for an army sanitary commission, which he was to chair, was issued on 5 May.

1   BL Add. Mss. 79658, fols. 37-40, JRG to SH, 15 Apr. 1857; WSHC 2057/F4/53, Aberdeen to SH, 18 Apr. 1857; Stanmore, II, pp. 96-8, WEG to SH, 17 Apr. 1857.
2   WSHC 2057/F4/59, JRG to SH, 27 Apr. 1857.

11
Allied Reformers 1857-1859

The two years before Herbert returned to the War Office in June 1859 are best known for his chairing the royal commission 'to inquire into the regulations affecting the sanitary condition of the army, the organisation of military hospitals, and the treatment of the sick and wounded'. By dint of the superfluity of Nightingale biographies, her perspective on these matters is well-known. In such accounts Herbert tends to be relegated to the status of mouthpiece, forever at her beck and call. From Herbert's perspective, the world looked somewhat different. He was the central figure in transacting the formal work of the commission between May and August 1857. His report spawned four sub-commissions, all of which he chaired. The consequences were more work and a great deal of travelling. The Indian Mutiny, which began in May 1857, would contribute to his remit being extended still further. In his wider domestic life he had ongoing responsibilities as father, head of an estate, and local patron. As a senior Member of Parliament, he was a significant player in the making and unmaking of governments. Arguably most important of all, in 1859 he was prominent in the machinations which led to the formation of the modern Liberal party. All of this coincided – as frequent reference to it in his correspondence testifies – with a downward spiral in his health.

It was the health of the British army which occupied public attention at the end of the Crimean War. Of the 97,800 men who fought in the conflict, 4,500 had died as the result of enemy action, but 17,600 from disease and exposure. Nightingale's fear, however, even before returning to England in August 1856, was that 'in six months all these sufferings will be forgotten'.[1] Herbert was her obvious and indispensable ally in ensuring that they were not. He had invited her, on resigning in February 1855, 'to write to me for anything you want [...] I will do everything I can'. She had taken him at his word: 'you will be listened to at home as much as if you were in office'. In November 1855, for example, she was asking him to lobby for extra diets.[2]

Herbert and Nightingale's partnership is one of the most famous in British history. The fact is apt to obscure significant differences between them. Two in particular might be borne in mind. First, Nightingale was what modern political scientists call a pressure group campaigner. She benefitted from possessing several of the ingredients judged necessary for success: a clear objective, a sympathetic public opinion, and money. She was rightly tunnel-visioned. But she was also essentially an outsider, not least in being a woman. Herbert, by contrast, was a pragmatic statesman, a patrician insider, both socially and politically. For all that sanitary reform was important, it was never his exclusive concern, quite often not even his primary one. But he could open doors. A second difference between Herbert and Nightingale lay in what motivated them. Nightingale was on a God-inspired mission. As she put it, 'I stand at the altar of the murdered men and whilst I live I fight their cause'. For her, the reform of army sanitary conditions was an end in itself. Herbert, whilst moved by his Christian humanity, was energised more by the prosaic considerations which stemmed from his love of country. He stood amongst the foremost of Britain's politicians whose minds were exercised by questions affecting her security. Whilst he lived, he was no less determined than Nightingale to fight his cause. Reform of army sanitary conditions, desirable in itself, was also a means to further that end.

---

1 Sweetman, *War and Administration*, p. 130.
2 Stanmore, I, pp. 412-16, SH to FN, 5 Mar. 1856; BL Add. Mss. 43396, fol. 40, FN to EH, 17 Nov. 1855.

Herbert was fishing in Ireland when Nightingale saw English waters. They met for the first time in nearly two years at Atherstone Hall, the Warwickshire home of Charles and Selina Bracebridge, early in September 1856. Whilst Nightingale overflowed with ideas for the amelioration of military hospitals, Herbert was wary.[1] This was not, as Nightingale thought, that he was lukewarm about change; rather that his mind dwelt more on the practicalities of overcoming conservatism in the War Office. It was, after all, in the hands of Lord Panmure, 'The Bison', a 'name that fitted both physical demeanour and his habit of mind [...] four square and menacing, in the doorway of reform'.[2] Nightingale, to her enormous credit, was not to be diverted. Asking Herbert to join her for 'a combined attack upon the Bison' – 'I hope you will (like a Cid) stand up for the cause of the poor oppressed army hospitals, which I assure you have not won a step of the ground yet by the experience of the war' – she sallied forth alone to Scotland. In October, Panmure agreed in principle that a royal commission might be set up with Herbert as chairman.[3]

At first glance, Herbert's reply to Panmure's offer of the chair appears unenthusiastic. 'My faith in Commissions', it began, 'is rather shaken [...] a Commission may [...] get rid of the necessity for immediate action, and hang up the subject till public feeling or expectation has died away'. Alternatively, reactionary forces in the Army Medical Department might proffer evidence 'tending to establish that our present system is perfect', in the event of which eventuality 'we shall have done much harm'. But Herbert's diffidence was calculated; he was seeking to maximise prospects for the commission's success. Hence his insistence was that 'the instructions should be such that there shall be no part of our rules and regulations and system in any branch of the Army which bears on the sanitary condition of our troops which shall not be open to the investigation of the Commission'. His aim was nothing less than to 'lay the foundation for its utmost future

1 *CWFN*, XII, FN to Lefroy, 7 Sept. 1856.
2 Strachey, *Eminent Victorians*, p. 145; BL Add. Mss. 43393, fols. 239-41, 244-5, SH to FN, 9 Sept., 3 Oct. 1856.
3 WSHC 2057/F4/66, FN to SH, 28 Sept., 31 Oct. 1856; Bostridge, *Nightingale*, pp. 307-9.

improvement, with a view to render impossible, so far as human means can, the recurrence of the sufferings and the evils we have undergone'.[1]

To further this end, Herbert and Nightingale devoted much energy either side of New Year to securing the appointment of commissioners who would be sympathetic to their quest. Herbert came up from Wilton on 15 December, partly in an attempt to kick start the process. He was not especially successful: 'I spent the day in rushing from Lincoln's Inn at one end to Queen's Gate at the other, where a nephew of mine is laid up with an eye destroyed by a shot. I have never heard a word from Panmure'. Three weeks later, he was 'beginning to wonder what is to become of our commission'.[2] Nightingale shared his frustration, even going so far as to suggest that he might renounce the chair. She also thought that threatening to publish her own account of the evils she had witnessed might galvanise the Secretary for War into action.[3] Herbert wisely disregarded the former idea and cautioned against the latter: it risked 'reprisals' in the shape of stories detailing shortcomings in the performance of some of the nurses under her charge. Perhaps Panmure failed to issue the commission, he speculated facetiously, because he had gout 'in the hands and this explains his not writing'.[4]

Progress towards establishing a royal commission, though slow, was not as bad as Herbert insinuated. On the question of who would sit with him the auguries were good. Conceding that he would have to hold his nose at the inclusion of Dr Andrew Smith, Director-General of the Army Medical Department, the other names agreed represented a series of lesser or greater victories. Heading the list was the army sanitarian, Dr John Sutherland who, 'despite his deafness', Herbert thought 'an invaluable man with a great gift of organisation'.[5] Surgeon Dr Ranald Martin, an expert on tropical medicine and Inspector-General of Hospitals, was a personal friend.

1   WSHC 2057/F8/IV/B/23, SH to Panmure, 22 Nov. 1856.
2   BL Add. Mss. 43393, fols. 261-6, SH to FN, 17 Dec. 1856; BL Add. Mss. 43394, fol. 1, SH to FN, 6 Jan. 1857.
3   WSHC 2057/F4/66, FN to SH, 7, 10 Feb. 1857.
4   Cook, *Nightingale*, I, p. 335.
5   LRO 920 DER15/43/16/55, fol. 12, SH to Stanley, 11 Dec. 1860.

So too was the examining lawyer, Sir Thomas Phillips.[1] And Herbert had been particularly insistent that his fellow commissioners include Dr Thomas Alexander ('the ablest and most effective man with our Army'), even though it meant summoning him back from his recent posting to Canada.[2] The remaining members of the commission were General Henry Storks, who had impressed Nightingale following his appointment as Commandant at Scutari, Sir James Clark, the Queen's physician, and Augustus Stafford MP, like Herbert, a member of the Canterbury Association. Dr Thomas Graham Balfour, surgeon to the Royal Military Asylum at Chelsea (and later Surgeon-General) was designated secretary.

By the start of March 1857, the chief concern was as much Herbert's health as Panmure's backsliding. Nightingale lamented that 'Mr Herbert is ill and probably going abroad – which will put off the "commission" we were going to have with him as chairman'. She rued their not having started preliminary work when parliament was in recess. Furthermore, to do so now would mean Herbert having to juggle it 'amid the multiplicity of subjects afforded by the Parliamentary session'. As if telepathically, Herbert reassured her that 'I still think that with help I shall be able to manage the commission. It is not labour that tries people, it is excitement.'[3] Unconvinced, Nightingale wrote again in April asking if 'you are better and not changing your plans for your health's sake'. 'From several speeches you have made in the House of Commons', she pleaded:

> you have assumed and still occupy in the opinion of the country the solitary position of 'Reformer of the Army' [...] Pray write to me <u>by return of post</u> and tell me what you mean to say to Panmure, and what I am to say to him, that we may be in the same story.[4]

1   Dossey, *Nightingale*, p. 196.
2   WSHC 2057/F8/IV/B/23, SH to Panmure, 22 Nov. 1856; Stanmore, II, p. 122, SH to Panmure, 12 Feb. 1857.
3   WSHC 2057/F4/66, FN to SH, 13 Feb. 1857; *CWFN*, XIV, pp. 498-500, FN to McNeill, 1 Mar. 1857; BL Add. Mss. 43394, fol. 23, SH to FN, 2 Mar. 1857.
4   WSHC 2057/F4/66, FN to SH, 10, 25 Apr. 1857.

Nightingale need not have worried: affairs thereafter were concluded swiftly. Having secured his return for South Wiltshire, Herbert came up from Wilton on Thursday 30 April, 'reaching London at dawn. I go from the station to Lincoln['s Inn] (I am engaged in an Irish law suit) and shall then wend my way westward and will call in [at] Burlington Street'. Final details were thrashed out in a face to face meeting with Panmure the next day. 'I hope these additions will serve us,' reported Herbert, 'I think it ought to make a good working committee'. The conscientious Member then made a rapid return to Wiltshire for the weekend: 'we have an annual cattle fair at Wilton one of the largest in England it takes place tomorrow'. The royal warrant establishing the commission was finally issued on 5 May.[1]

If the previous month's toing and froing gives some indication of the pressures on a man in less than rude health, it was as nothing compared to the work which Herbert undertook as chairman of the commission over the next three months. It is true that Nightingale advised him on such matters as who to summon as witnesses, in which order to call them, and possible lines of questioning, but Herbert was far from being her proxy.[2] The man who had chaired the 1854 Royal Commission on Promotions, appeared before Roebuck's 1855 select committee of inquiry as a witness, and served on the 1856-7 royal commission examining the buying and selling of commissions in the army, needed no coaching in the practicalities of committee work. Where Nightingale's help was invaluable, by dint of her research into mortality rates and the like, was in serving as a reservoir of knowledge. Herbert could turn to her, for example, asking for a comparison between the mortality rates for sailors and marines, knowing that he would receive a prompt and evidence-based response.[3] He happily acknowledged her importance to him. 'I never intend to tell you', he wrote, as the work of the commission drew to a close, 'how much I owe you for all your help during the last three months, for I should never be

---

1 BL Add. Mss. 43394, fols. 29-35, SH to FN, 26, 28 Apr., 2 May 1857; Cook, *Nightingale*, I, p. 354.
2 Bostridge, *Nightingale*, pp. 319-21; WSHC 2057/F4/65.
3 Cook, *Nightingale*, I, pp. 356-7; WSHC 2057/F4/65, FN to SH, nd, 1857.

able to make you understand how helpless my ignorance would have been among the Medical Philistines. God bless you.' But it helped that Herbert was endowed with what Nightingale called 'extreme quickness of perception'.[1] Reduced to its essentials, Nightingale played the role of solicitor providing the brief; Herbert the barrister.

To be fair, Nightingale never claimed to be the fount of all wisdom. She turned to Herbert, for example, for information concerning rates of remuneration for those working in the Army Medical Department. And summoned to a meeting with the Duke of Cambridge, on 9 July, she wrote, 'I want to ask you if he asks me any questions, what I had better say, and what leave unsaid'.[2] Herbert was equally aware of his own limitations. Dr Balfour, as secretary to the commission, found himself bombarded with letters from Herbert demanding facts and figures. Dr Alexander too, unsurprising given the fuss that Herbert had made in having him recalled from Canada, was somebody he wanted 'very much to talk matters over with'.[3] Replicating the practice he had adopted at the War Office in 1854-5, Herbert was also happy to draw on the expertise of 'unofficial' advisers. Why not take advantage of Dr John McNeill's volunteering himself as a sounding board: McNeill, after all, had been sent to the Crimea in 1855 to report on the workings of the Commissariat. None of this is to gainsay the centrality of the Herbert-Nightingale relationship; merely to point out that both they and it were more broadly collaborative than the Nightingale legend would have it. Nightingale herself, even as the commission neared the end of its labours, was well aware that Herbert's ear was not hers alone. She wrote urgently to McNeill about 'the conclusions I want to impress upon Mr Herbert', a comment

---

1 BL Add. Mss. 43395, fol. 126, SH to FN, 7 Aug. 1857; Cook, *Nightingale*, I, p. 366, FN to McNeill, 15 Nov. 1857.
2 BL Add. Mss. 43394, fols. 89-90, FN to SH, 5 July 1857.
3 Stanmore, II, pp. 126-30, SH to McNeill, 18 May 1857; BL Add. Mss. 43394, fol. 29, SH to FN, 26 Apr. 1857.

implying that his mind was open to others.[1] In later life, she nearly always referred to the commission as Sidney Herbert's commission.[2]

Herbert opened the commission on Wednesday 13 May. He planned to meet Mondays, Wednesdays and Fridays for so long as was deemed necessary.[3] Dr Andrew Smith, Director-General of the Army Medical Department, himself a member of the commission, was the first witness called. What might be termed his case for the defence was supplemented by the testimony of Sir John Hall, Inspector-General of Hospitals during the war: 'among the chief causes of evil he puts idleness', wrote Herbert contemptuously.[4] Smith and Hall would be more than outflanked by witnesses known by Herbert to be more sympathetic to the cause of sanitary reform. These were headed by fellow commissioners, Doctors Sutherland, Martin and Balfour. Besides them, there were Dr McNeill and Colonel Alexander Tulloch (co-author of the report on the Commissariat praised by Herbert), and Dr William Farr, statistician with the General Register Office. Nearly fifty witnesses would be called in total. They ranged from the celebrated engineer, Colonel Sir Joshua Jebb, to the actuary Francis Neison, and Samuel Gaskell, a Commissioner-in-Lunacy.

As the commission laboured – 'We are at work on facts, so far as they can be got, and very rare they seem to be' – wrote Herbert on 18 May, he proved himself to be an active chairman.[5] He took the lead, to choose but three from many possible examples, in examining Sir Benjamin Brodie on army medical officers (15 May), Major-General Mansel on rations (12 June), and Dr Henry Mapleton of the 15th Hussars on the nature of ventilation in French hospitals (15 June). This was the more necessary in Herbert's view because, with the exceptions of Sutherland and Alexander, he judged his colleagues 'heavy in hand'.[6] What they thought of him is less clear. But Nightingale was in

1 *CWFN*, XIV, p. 516, FN to McNeill, 27 June 1857.
2 For example, *CWFN*, IX, pp. 457-9, FN to Sir H. Verney, 19 Sept. 1863.
3 *SWJ*, 6 June 1857.
4 BL Add. Mss. 43394, fols. 71-6, SH to FN, 23 June 1857.
5 Stanmore, II, pp. 126-30, SH to McNeill, 18 May 1857.
6 WSHC 2057/F4/68, FN to SH, 1 Jan. 1859.

no doubt that 'His very manner engaged the most sulky and the most recalcitrant of witnesses. He never made an enemy or a quarrel in the Commission. He used to say, "There takes two to be a quarrel, and I won't be one."'[1]

Probably Herbert's most important work during these busy weeks, however, was discharged away from the public gaze. 'Dr Balfour', he informed Nightingale at the height of proceedings, 'is coming to me between 10 & 11 and I will come on to you afterwards. It is very little use examining people without first seeing them, you do not know what they can tell you & they do not know what you want to get out'.[2] A week later, he was anxious for Nightingale to meet Sir Thomas Phillips, his fellow commissioner 'and "talk him over" with me on 2 or 3 points'. On 30 June, Herbert asked Nightingale to 'come at 4: as I want to be at Neison's at 5 on my way to the House'.[3] In his Belgrave Square home, quite apart from the unwelcome distraction of the theft of Elizabeth's jewellery (the police, it was reported, were 'at sea'), there were a myriad of other tasks to be performed: papers to be read, statistics to be scrutinised, printers to be seen, and a parliamentary election committee to be avoided.[4] The latter objective was not achieved: 'I have been shut up in the House the last two days', bemoaned a frustrated Herbert on 5 July.[5] Such respite as he got proved something of a busman's holiday. On 19 May, he inspected Chatham Dockyard; he found it 'dirty stuffy cramped unwholesome in every sense'. Towards the end of June, though reported to be unwell, he spent three days inspecting the barracks at Dover. Even then, the wider business of the commission was never far from his mind: he asked Dr Balfour to publish a letter on lighting by a Mr Whitfield, to send him more statistics, and to report on a meeting with Dr Sutherland.[6]

1   Cook, *Nightingale*, I, p. 358.
2   BL Add. Mss. 43394, fols. 47-50, SH to FN, nd, 1857. Balfour appeared as a witness on 17 July.
3   BL Add. Mss. 43394, fols. 62, 79, SH to FN, 5, 30 June 1857.
4   *SWJ*, 6 June 1857.
5   BL Add. Mss. 43394, fols. 87, 91-2, SH to FN, 5, 7 July 1857.
6   BL Add. Mss. 43394, fols. 42, 77, SH to FN, 19 May, 28 June 1857; BL Add. Mss. 50134, fols. 171-4, SH to Balfour, 26, 28 June 1857.

The most delicate of Herbert's behind the scenes tasks concerned Nightingale herself; she was as qualified as anybody to be a witness. But aside from the fact that it would have been unusual for a woman to be called (not, however, an argument Herbert used), there was a risk in her propensity to be forthright. She was quite prepared to risk the controversy which would have resulted from her pointing out that death rates in the East had been highest in her hospital at Scutari, bad news that Herbert thought best left buried in the morass of statistics and appendices. He resolved the conundrum with a mix of tact and flattery. Declaring his '"repugnance" to your being examined viva voce', but admitting that 'I know that your evidence would fortify our proceedings and hasten the adoption of our recommendations', he asked her to submit written evidence. Not without some grumbling Nightingale acquiesced.[1] But she cheered up when Herbert wrote, not perhaps entirely ethically, 'Cd you send me this morning the list of questions (without the answers) which I am to put to you'. She restricted herself to 89, eliciting replies that ran to 35 pages.[2]

Herbert had been too unwell to hold the meetings of the commission scheduled for 27 May, 26 June, and the week of 1 July. But he was back in the chair when it met for the twenty-fifth and final time on 20 July. In total, some 9,981 questions were asked; in the process, much previously unseen official correspondence was unearthed. Transcripts of the proceedings and associated appendices would be published in two volumes amounting to nearly a thousand pages. The commission, Herbert concluded, had 'made wonderful progress' and 'worked admirably'.[3] Delane, editor of *The Times*, thought it 'one of

---

1 BL Add. Mss. 43394, fols. 100-2, SH to FN, 8 July 1857; BL Add. Mss. 50134, fols. 204-5, SH to Balfour, 11 Oct. 1857; Bostridge, *Nightingale*, pp. 318-19.
2 BL Add. Mss. 43394, fol. 112, SH to FN, 20 July 1857; *CWFN*, XIV, pp. 889-90. Nightingale was able to give full vent to her spleen in her confidential *Notes on the Health of the British Army*. This ran to 853 pages.
3 BL Add. Mss. 43394, fol. 119, SH to FN, 20 July 1857.

the most important and interesting documents ever published in a blue cover [...] How can a man like you get ill?'[1]

There remained the formidable job of writing the report. Nightingale's claim that 'Sidney Herbert wrote the whole report himself' is untrue. He was assisted by an inner circle, whose key figures were Sutherland (who 'got up the evidence'), Farr, and, above all, Nightingale herself.[2] 'Dear Miss Nightingale', he wrote to her impishly on 12 July, 'I shd like to have a cabinet council with you today'. Three days later she responded by returning him a working draft of the report with the comment 'I agree and more than agree with it'.[3] Their dialogue would continue for another three weeks. At last, on 7 August, he was able to write that the job was done. The report, judged one early commentator, was 'a masterly condensation of a minute, laborious, and effective inquiry'.[4]

The report ran to well over 30,000 words. It included subsections on subjects ranging from barracks and encampments, to cooking, clothing, field hospitals and military hospitals. But the crucial sections were those concerning the rates and causes of mortality in the army. The former it transpired, the more shocking because the ordinary soldier was reckoned to be a fit young male, was over twice as high as that for the civilian population as a whole. In explaining this, Herbert 'assigned' four causes: night duty; want of exercise and suitable employment; intemperate and debauched habits; and overcrowding in barracks. The evils of the latter were compounded by inadequate ventilation and the 'nuisances' arising from latrines and defective sewerage.

In expanding upon the relative importance of the causes, Herbert's report was emphatic that 'the last is the one to which the chief blame should be attached'.[5] To combat it, his central recommendation was that four sub-commissions should be established. Of these, the

1 BL Add. Mss. 43394, fol. 290, Delane to SH, 6 July 1858.
2 *CWFN*, XIV, p. 1037, FN to Frederick, 22 July 1891.
3 BL Add. Mss. 43394, fols. 103-4, SH to FN, 12 July 1857; WSHC 2057/F4/66, FN to EH, 15 July 1857.
4 *Fraser's Magazine*, 'Herbert', pp. 201-2.
5 PP 1857-8 (2318), XXXIV, pp. 8-19.

key one would be charged with placing army barracks and hospitals in sanitary order. The other three would seek to establish an army medical school, create an army medical statistics department, and restructure the Army Medical Department, the latter to include a revision of army hospital regulations and the preparation of a warrant for the promotion of army medical officers.[1]

The demands of the royal commission left Herbert little time or inclination to bother himself much with other parliamentary matters. He was present for only eleven divisions between the spring general election and the August summer recess. Herbert was anyway right in his prediction that the new parliament would not differ greatly from its predecessor; he resisted Graham's tease that he should join 'honest reformers' like himself and Russell to present the country with a new Reform Bill.[2] On the half dozen occasions when Herbert spoke in the Chamber between May and July, it was army-related affairs which brought him to his feet. As a reformer, he welcomed proposals to build a permanent barracks at Aldershot, whilst viewing with dismay 'a tendency to revert to economy' in the military estimates.[3] A more substantial speech was made, in between meetings of the royal commission, on 9 June. In it, Herbert took up a chorus being sung by several of Nightingale's parliamentary friends in complaining about the design and siting of Britain's first general military hospital at Netley, on the shore of Southampton Water. 'I am informed', Herbert told the House, 'that Southampton Water lies upon a bed of peat, with a coating of mud, not so deep but that the salt water percolates through the mud to the peat, and there generates sulphuretted hydrogen gas'. His protest was seemingly in vain: Queen Victoria had laid the foundation stone, at the site identified by his old antagonist, Dr Andrew Smith, in May 1856.[4]

There was no time to lay the report of the royal commission before parliament prior to the summer recess; Members were in any

1   PP 1857-8 (2318), XXXIV, pp. 83-4; *CWFN*, IX, p. 13.
2   BL Add. Mss. 79658, fols. 41-4, SH to JRG, 26 Apr. 1857.
3   Hansard, 5 June 1857, CXLV, cols. 1259-61.
4   Hansard, 9 June 1857, CXLV, cols. 1280-2; Bostridge, *Nightingale*, pp. 335-6. The Royal Victoria Hospital opened in 1863.

case focused on news of events 5,000 miles away in India where rebellion had broken out. But Herbert was determined to strike whilst the iron was hot. Informing Panmure, on 7 August, that 'the Commission on the Sanitary State of the Army has now closed its labours', he added that 'I will gladly help you in any way I can, either by serving on these subcommissions, or by drawing up, or helping to draw up, regulations, or both'.[1] He came away from a meeting with Panmure on 14 August under the impression that the Secretary of State would act promptly and favourably on his recommendations. At last he could allow himself a break: 'I leave town with a lighter heart after seeing Panmure', he told Nightingale, 'I think we have no predisposition against us but the contrary. Now am I going to lead an animal life for a month, get up early, pursue your animal, catch him, eat him, and go to sleep.'[2] For once, neither contemporaries nor historians made snide remarks about Herbert's entitlement to a fishing holiday in Ireland. Via Mount Merrion to Delphi in County Mayo, Herbert reported to Balfour, he had found himself in 'a magnificent country of sea, lake and mountain'.[3]

Evidently having taken a copy of the royal commission's report with him, fishing afforded Herbert time to re-read and contemplate it at greater leisure: he was 'more than ever struck with the necessity of dwelling much more in detail on it'. The reason he wrote to Balfour was not to gloat about his surroundings but to tell him to send an amended version of the report to Panmure, and to ruminate about who would be the best persons to sit on the sub-commissions.[4] But it was family affairs that threatened to spoil his vacation. News reached England that Octavia Spinelli, his half-brother's long-estranged wife, had died in Naples on 31 July. Robert Pembroke was free to seek a countess, or as Elizabeth Herbert put it on learning of Spinelli's passing, 'how soon to be replaced we do not know, but there is no doubt <u>by whom</u>'. Her

---

1   Stanmore, II, p. 130, Herbert to Panmure, 7 Aug. 1857.
2   Cook, *Nightingale*, I, p. 364; BL Add. Mss. 43394, fols. 135-7, SH to FN, 14 Aug. 1857; BL Add. Mss. 50134, fols. 194-5, SH to Balfour, 14 Aug. 1857.
3   BL Add. Mss. 50134, fols. 196-7, SH to Balfour, 19 Aug. 1857.
4   BL Add. Mss. 50134, fols. 196-9, SH to Balfour, 19, 22 Aug. 1857.

reference was, of course, to the 12th Earl's long-term mistress, Marie Schöeffer. Elizabeth's gall concealed a real fear that if Marie married Robert, the Earl and Countess would want to leave Paris and take up the ancestral reins at Wilton. If so, she and Herbert would simply have to accept the fact 'that we have loved the dear old place too much'. In the event her anxieties proved baseless. Robert was content to continue his domestic arrangements as they were.[1] He was not always the pagan dissolute that Elizabeth, sometimes unfairly, imagined. A note from him addressed to Lord Grey, which has recently come to light, requests that his name be added 'to the Church subscription list for £50'. Only months earlier, he had provided the land and subscribed £200 for a new church at Bemerton, close to Wilton House. He also corresponded amicably with Herbert at this time over the loan of pictures from Wilton's impressive art collection for a major exhibition in Manchester.[2] The supposed devil incarnate was at least hedging his bets.

Herbert, who to his credit, did not entirely share his wife and siblings' view of the 12th Earl, returned from holiday amid rumours that he was to succeed Robert Vernon Smith as President of the Board of Control.[3] Political reality was that the Bison (to mix a metaphor) had not changed his spots. Having set off to hunt in the Scottish Highlands before Herbert went to Ireland, 'Pan [was] still shooting', Herbert complained to Nightingale, at the end of September. 'It is to me unconscionable. In future you must defend the Bison, for I won't.'[4] She, of course, would do no such thing, and battle was re-joined as they sought action on the issue of the sub-commissions. They briefly met their quarry on 1 October, only for Herbert to have to leave town to catch up with Woronzow relations in Manchester. From there he wrote that 'if Panmure has done nothing about them there will be

1 BL Add. Mss. 44212, fols. 48-54, EH to WEG, 30 Aug. 1857.
2 *SWJ*, 25 Oct. 1856, 15 Dec. 1860. Pembroke's note to Grey, 30 Apr. 1859, appeared on the ebay auction site in Aug. 2018.
3 *SWJ*, 5 Sept. 1857.
4 Cook, *Nightingale*, I, pp. 363, 365.

a great delay to get a sanction at the Treasury and the immediate expedition on barracks'.[1]

Unconvinced that Panmure would do anything, Herbert appealed direct to the Prime Minister:

> There must be something radically wrong when soldiers at home [...] at the healthiest and strongest period of life, offer an amount of mortality exceeding that of the most notoriously unhealthy trades and double that of ordinary civil life. If you add to this the number of men invalided and who die out of the Army, though killed by it, and who instead of counting as soldiers in the comparison with civil life actually go to swell the mortality of the latter, the excess becomes positively frightful [...] With an Army raised by volunteering the country cannot afford to let men die in this way, even were there no other motive for doing our utmost to secure health and life to them. I cannot undertake to say that we have fathomed the depth of the evil, that we know all its causes, or have suggested all the remedies, but we know some causes and have urged some remedies, and I am very anxious to commence their trial without loss of time.[2]

The letter, plus another meeting between Herbert and Panmure on 10 October, bore fruit: Herbert was able to inform Nightingale on 11 October that the War Office had issued instructions for the sub-commissions on army medical statistics and barrack inspections.[3] What he jokingly referred to as the Cabal, consisting of himself, Nightingale, 'Alexander and Sutherland, and sometimes Martin and Farr', could now meet regularly to wage the next phase in the war against insalubrity.

A month later, Herbert was informing Panmure that 'All our Sub-Commissions or Committees are at work, and with more or less

1 BL Add. Mss. 43394, fol. 159, SH to FN, 4 Oct. 1857.
2 WSHC 2057/F4/61, SH to Pam, 6 Oct. 1857.
3 BL Add. Mss. 50134, fols. 202-3, SH to Balfour, 9 Oct. 1857; BL Add. Mss. 43394, fol. 162, SH to FN, 11 Oct. 1857.

advanced progress'.[1] In truth, the progress was uneven. The one on the creation of an army medical statistics department proved uncontentious. Consisting of Herbert, Tulloch and Farr, it presented its report in June 1858. Advances towards establishing an Army Medical School, however, were inhibited by yet more procrastinating from Panmure. The Secretary for War failed to appoint any of Herbert's nominees for professorships, prompting him to complain that he would not do so 'even if the Angel Gabriel had offered himself, St Michael and all angels to fill the different chairs'.[2] The reorganisation of the Army Medical Department provoked even greater opposition: the War Office did not take kindly to any vestige of outside interference in its affairs. Panmure went so far as to try and rescind the offending sub-commission. Only Herbert, it is agreed, kept it in being.[3] Herbert's priority, however, was to begin the practical business of inspecting barracks and military hospitals. As he had said in his letter to Palmerston, 'The barrack inspection ought to begin immediately. The days are shortening, and the weather in which immediate alteration can be effected is passing away'.[4] First on his list were those in London.

Over a Christmas and New Year break spent at Wilton, Herbert might reasonably have taken some satisfaction in what he had accomplished in little over six months.[5] Instead he fell ill, with what he described as a 'neuralgic headache and tic in the temple and jaw'. To combat it, he experimented with a concoction dubbed Christchurch Remedy:

> It smells and tastes of chloroform and camphor and is applied by saturating a bit of cotton and putting it up the nostril and [...] inhaling it so as to draw the liquid well out the cavities above [...]

---

1 Stanmore, II, pp. 136-7, SH to Panmure, 11 Nov. 1857; Cook, *Nightingale*, I, pp. 365-6.
2 Cook, *Nightingale*, I, p. 378.
3 PP 1861 (366), XXXVII; Bostridge, *Nightingale*, pp. 343-5.
4 WSHC 2057/F4/61, SH to Pam, 6 Oct. 1857.
5 BL Add. Mss. 43394, fols. 195, 199, 219-22, SH to FN, 30 Nov., 2, 27 Dec. 1857.

if you take too much of it you may make yourself sick as I found yesterday when I tried it.

He would have been better advised to restrict the treatment to the 'several glasses of brandy' which accompanied it.

Nightingale's view was that inspecting barracks in cold weather, Herbert's plan for early 1858, was unlikely to aid his recovery.[1] He ignored her. Leaving Wilton with Elizabeth on 11 January, 'We went to Charmouth [the convalescent home they had established] in company with 7 patients and established them there'. He then met Dr Sutherland and Captain Francis Galton, his fellow commissioners on the barracks and hospitals sub-commission, to inspect buildings in Hampshire. Two days later he was reporting that:

> We went thro the Portsmouth Barrack Hospital [...] there is no attempt at ventilation whatever, except in back to back wards, there are small openings from one to the other [...] The hospital is very poor. It had 3 stories each very low in homage to the fiction that Portsmouth is defensible by its fortifications.

Back at Wilton by the weekend, Herbert had to admit that Nightingale had been right: 'I am going to bed for an hour being knocked up'.[2] For the next fortnight, a metaphorical sore plagued him in the shape of Netley Hospital, whose building he had been unable to prevent. Herbert was 'more dissatisfied than ever about Netley', buoyed only by Palmerston's concession that it fell within the purview of his sub-commission. 'Nevertheless', he told Nightingale, 'we are not asked to make any suggestion tending to abandonment or alteration of destination, but only to say how, given the site and the foundations, it can be improved'. The best he could hope for was that 'Netley can be altered so as in some degree to diminish the cost of administration'.[3]

1 BL Add. Mss. 43396, fol. 54, FN to EH, 7 Jan. 1858; BL Add. Mss. 50134, fols. 256-7, SH to Balfour, 10 Jan. 1858.
2 BL Add. Mss. 43394, fols. 223-8, 236, 240-3, SH to FN, 2, 13, 16 Jan. 1858.
3 BL Add. Mss. 43394, fols. 244-7, 258, SH to FN, 21, 30 Jan. 1858.

Herbert had planned on going to France at the beginning of February with a view to inspecting barracks in Paris. Continuing 'neuralgic affections' prevented it; he was 'fairly broken down'. Unfolding events would probably have stopped him going in any case.[1] On 14 January, Napoleon III had survived bombs thrown by Italian nationalists, but the explosions killed 8 people and injured over 150. The ringleader, Felice Orsini, it transpired, had been living in England, had assembled his devices in Birmingham, and travelled to Paris on a British passport. He and his leading accomplices were guillotined. French Anglophobes, meanwhile, were condemning England as 'a den of conspiracy'; Count Alexandre Walewski, the French Foreign Minister (an illegitimate son of Napoleon I), demanded that the British government take action to ensure the security of its ally.[2] Palmerston responded, on 9 February, with a Conspiracy to Murder Bill, proposing to increase penalties for putative terrorists found on British soil. The First Reading passed comfortably by 299 votes to 99. In a strong speech during the debate, Herbert decried the attack as a 'fearful and diabolical crime'. But he also urged caution: 'when resident in England [Orsini may] have harboured some idea of the crime. That is very possible. It is said that the grenades were made in England. But were they made with our connivance?' As he explained to Gladstone, 'we should not refuse to do right if it be right on the ground that we are asked to do it by a foreign country; but we must be sure that it is right, safe, and effectual'. For once, he was pleased with his speech. It had been received 'very favourably', certainly by comparison with Palmerston's which he thought 'very feeble and disheartened'.[3] The Prime Minister, of all people, was deemed to be truckling to the Gallic cockerel. As the vote on the Second Reading approached on 19 February, Herbert was spotted as part of an 'ominous gathering of

---

1   BL Add. Mss. 50134, fol. 261, SH to Balfour, 30 Jan. 1858; BL Add. Mss. 43394, fol. 262, SH to FN, 2 Feb. 1858.
2   Hawkins, *Parliament*, pp. 96-106.
3   Hansard, 9 Feb. 1858, CXLVIII, cols. 1063-9; BL Add. Mss.44211, fols. 1-2, SH to WEG, 10 Feb. 1858.

leading Peelites [...] in eager confabulation'.[1] Palmerston lost the vote and resigned.

Next evening, Herbert entertained Gladstone and Graham in Belgrave Square. They 'sat till 12.30 a.m. but did not talk quite through the crisis'. The following morning, Gladstone received a summons from Derby to join the minority Conservative government which he was attempting to form. Despite the open recriminations between Conservatives and Herbert at the South Wilshire election in 1857, Derby was more than happy to broaden his invitation: 'I would willingly include Sidney Herbert in this offer; but I fear he is too intimately associated with John Russell to make it possible for him to accept'. Derby, whilst wrong that Herbert was close to Russell, was correct in his general presumption. Herbert had pinned his political colours too firmly to the Liberal mast for him to be able to make the necessary volte face. He joined Gladstone and Graham at Aberdeen's where the four of them deliberated over the wording of Gladstone's reply. Having despatched his letter declining office, Gladstone left Aberdeen's accompanied by Herbert just before 6 p.m.: 'We separated for the evening', recalled Gladstone, 'with the fervent wish that in public life we might never part'.[2] As in 1852, Derby made his government without the senior Peelites.

The Orsini affair was unfortunate for army reformers as well as Palmerston. Herbert had spent months tweaking, correcting, indexing and generally perfecting the findings of the army sanitary commission. When it was finally published, he aspired to harness the weight of public opinion to 'carry our remedies'. Instead, publication coincided with the public's being diverted by Orsini. Press coverage of the royal commission's findings was consequently relatively muted.[3] Early spring was equally dispiriting. What Herbert described as 'a sort of pleurisy wh. kept me to my bed' prevented him from attending the Commons for the first fortnight of March. He informed Nightingale ironically that he had just spent two days idling in bed 'instead of minding my

1 Jenkins, *Trelawny Diaries*, p. 22, 16 Feb. 1858.
2 Morley, *Gladstone*, I, pp. 576-7, Derby to WEG, 21 Feb. 1858.
3 BL Add. Mss. 50134, fols. 245-7, 254-5, SH to Balfour, 26 Dec. 1857, 6 Jan. 1858; *The Times*, 6 Feb. 1858; *SWJ*, 20 Feb. 1858.

business in London'. But 'I really am not ill', he was quick to add, 'only washy and weak, while I always recover wonderfully'.[1] He was at least well enough, by late March, to chair a lecture on sanitary reform by Dr Guy of King's College at the United Services Institute; then departing for Dunmore Park, in Stirlingshire, for a fortnight with his sister Catherine.[2] If his intention had been a restorative cure, it did not succeed. A renewed bout of illness meant that he was unable to attend the 'battle of church rates' in the Commons on 21 April. It is unlikely that he was able to play much part in the deliberations of the Royal Commission on Promotion and Retirement in the Higher Ranks of the Army to which he had been appointed the same month.[3] Certainly one must regard as fanciful the commentator who spied Herbert in the Chamber 'eminently handsome, with his bright cold smile and subtlety of aspect [...] the Jesuit of the world, ambitious, artful, and always on the watch for making his rapier thrusts'.[4] Taken to task by Argyll at this time for 'the severity of your Pamphobiacal symptoms', Herbert's reply reveals him aspiring to a less colourful role:

> What I wish is that disagreements should cease. I look forward to a gloomy future. I had rather make no contrasts between the faults of possible Prime Ministers. There is too much material of that kind to make it either difficult or pleasant [...] It will require cautious steering on the part of those who prefer the interest of the country to the interest of the party to prevent mischief being done between them all [...] I, though wearied and disquieted with politics and politicians, would contribute what I can to this desirable, but, I fear, unattainable object.[5]

1 BL Add. Mss. 50134, fols. 274-5, SH to Balfour, 16 Mar. 1858; BL Add. Mss. 43393, fols. 9-12, 19, SH to FN, 16, 18 Mar. 1858.
2 *SWJ*, 27 Mar. 1857; NUL Ne C 12554/1-2, SH to Newcastle, 27 Mar. 1858.
3 WSHC 2057/F4/59, JRG to EH, 21 Apr. 1858; PP 1857-8 [2418], XIX.
4 Morley, *Gladstone*, I, pp. 582-3, citing *Press*, 7 Apr. 1858.
5 Stanmore, II, pp. 110-12, Argyll to SH, 8 Mar. 1858; Argyll, *Autobiography*, II, pp. 121-2, SH to Argyll, 15 Mar. 1858.

Progress of sorts was made in May when Herbert was able to complete and submit reports on London's barracks and military hospitals. He also made a point of cultivating General Jonathan Peel (son of Sir Robert) who had replaced Panmure at the War Office. The process had begun in February when Peel had promised to make no appointment nor 'to take any step in regard to the Medical Department or sanitary matters till he has conferred with me'.[1] On 10 May Herbert went out of his way in the House to say that 'He had every confidence that his right hon. and gallant Friend (General Peel) would, when the whole facts were before him, deal with the question of barrack accommodation in a proper spirit'.[2] Herbert was well aware that next day, because he and Nightingale were behind it, Lord Ebrington was to move resolutions, chief of which was 'That the long-continued excessive mortality of the British Army has been mainly caused by the bad sanitary condition of their barrack accommodation'.[3] Herbert, having weighed into the debate with an impassioned declaration that 'cubic space was a question of bricks and mortar, and they could give it to-morrow morning if they liked to put their hands in their pockets', could not but have noticed that Peel gave the motion his general approval.[4] And he effected a major coup in June when ill-health forced Dr Andrew Smith to retire as Director-General of the Army Medical Department. On the basis of seniority, Smith ought to have been succeeded by another of the army reformers' chief antagonists, Sir John Hall. Following intense lobbying from Herbert, however (Nightingale said that he lay awake all night worrying about it), Peel was persuaded to appoint Dr Thomas Alexander.[5]

Herbert's initiatives were possibly one reason which prompted Derby to make fresh approaches to the Peelites when he reshuffled his government at the end of May. As previously, the conduit was Gladstone. 'Gladstone wishes to join', reported Graham, 'and to carry

1 BL Add. Mss. 43394, fols. 305-6, SH to FN, 27 Feb. 1858.
2 Hansard, 10 May 1858, CL, cols. 396-7
3 Hansard, 11 May 1858, CL, cols. 473-95.
4 Hansard, 11 May 1858, CL, cols. 489-92.
5 Cook, *Nightingale*, I, pp. 378-9.

with him Herbert and his most intimate friends'.[1] Spencer Walpole, the Home Secretary, who was acting as the go-between for the Conservatives, put the view of most party members, however, when he said that 'they were under the impression that Herbert entertained strong personal feelings towards Disraeli'. Graham chose to put it in less personal terms but did not disagree. He advised Gladstone that Herbert:

> has taken his decision and will act with the Whigs, in opposition to Lord Derby's government. Feelings and influences, which it is vain to counteract, lead him irreversibly in that direction. The struggle has made him unhappy: and it must now be considered an established fact, that his part is taken.[2]

The Royal Commission on Promotion and Retirement, chaired by Cambridge but of which Herbert had been a member, reported in July. It recommended 'adhesion to the principle which animated the recommendations of the Commission of 1854', that is to say, that one over which Herbert had laboured as chairman.[3] In the knowledge of this happy outcome, Herbert and Elizabeth left Wilton for Germany. They would not return until September, when Herbert, much restored in health, reported that 'I have great faith in suitable waters. I got great good from mine, though it may not last long'.[4] Whilst abroad, he had received a letter from Nightingale about India. It did not come as a surprise. Herbert had been taking a close interest in Indian affairs for more than a year. 'This Indian news sits like lead upon me', he had said of the Cawnpore Massacre, in which 200 British women and children had perished on 15 July 1857. At the end of 1857, with less fatal consequences, he had had no objection on hearing that his sons were staging mock battles at Wilton re-enacting the relief of the siege

---

1   Hawkins, *Derby*, II, p. 179.
2   BL Add. Mss. 44164, fols. 165-72, JRG to WEG, 25 May 1858; Brooke and Sorensen, *Gladstone*, p. 224.
3   PP 1857-8 [2418], XIX, p. 263.
4   *SWJ*, 17 July 1858; BL Add. Mss. 79658, fols. 55-9, SH to JRG, 8 Oct. 1858.

of Lucknow.[1] And shortly before leaving for Germany, in a speech at Warminster, with the Mutiny now effectively over, Herbert had told his audience that he shared 'a determination that, come what might, the British Empire should be maintained in its fullest integrity'.[2] Unsurprisingly, therefore, he had been active in the House as the Government of India Bill made its way through parliament in 1858. This ended East India Company rule, substituting for it a Secretary of State in London and a Viceroy in Calcutta. For policing purposes, the Mutiny also demanded that Britain despatch more troops: before 1857 roughly 40,000 were garrisoned there, a figure that rose to 65,000 during the 1860s. Herbert was fully alive to the conundrum thus created: 'how could a European army be kept in the climate of India without creating such a drain on the mother country as to endanger our defensive power at home'.[3]

Nightingale, who had been developing her own interest in India, had no doubt that she could resolve the conundrum. She calculated that death rates amongst soldiers in India were 69 per 1,000, six times those for the civil population at home. Since 60 of those, she contended, were victims of poor sanitation (barrack room floors, for example, were regularly varnished with cow dung), there was a preventable loss to the Treasury of £388,000 per annum, quite apart from the more important saving of lives. Herbert had to persuade her not to visit India in person.[4] He had not been able to prevent her sending him a copy of Joseph Ewart's *Colonization in India*. Presumably intended as holiday reading (she despatched it on Christmas Eve 1857), her pithy summation was that it showed 'that men may live in India as well as they live in England, if people will set about it, but that nobody has set about it'. Herbert had responded, in March 1858, by volunteering to Lord Stanley, Secretary for the Colonies (and soon to become the

1 BL Add. Mss. 43394, fols. 101-4, SH to FN, nd, July 1857; BL Add. Mss 44212, fols. 55-8, EH to WEG, 10 Dec. 1857. Lucknow had been relieved in November.
2 *SWJ*, 29 May 1858.
3 PGL GRE/B109/10, fol. 28, SH to Grey, 21 Jan. 1860; Spiers, *Army and Society*, pp. 121, 135-8.
4 *CWFN*, IX, pp. 506-7, Walker to FN, 3 Jan. 1865.

first Secretary of State for India), his willingness to extend his work inspecting army barracks to include colonial ones.[1] Nightingale pushed for more. In a letter of 4 August, echoing the one Herbert had sent to her in October 1854, she wrote to Stanley urging the creation of an Indian sanitary commission and that 'I know no man [...] who could preside over such a commission but Mr Herbert'.[2] In a not entirely ingenuous letter the same day, she assured Herbert 'that I have not been so good as to offer your services to Lord Stanley [but] with any other chairman, he will bring together a great mass of blunders instead of information'. She did at least acknowledge (the Herberts were in Salzburg at the time) that 'Mrs Herbert will say that I give you the best possible reason for not coming back to England'.[3]

Herbert did return to England, resigned to the fact that he would head an Indian sanitary commission. A flattering invitation from Stanley to do so ('much will depend on your acceptance', he wrote) arrived in April 1859. Coinciding as this did, with a general election campaign, the timing was unfortunate but Herbert's enthusiasm was by now fired. 'I am ready to begin', he told Nightingale on 14 April. 'I have no contest and could run up to town twice a week without difficulty. If a contest should arise, I can but adjourn for a few days. There must too, I should think, be some preliminary work in getting at documents, maps, etc'.[4]

Herbert formally accepted Stanley's offer on 4 May. There followed the predictable wrangle over the names of those who would sit alongside him.[5] Several proved familiar: Sutherland, Martin and Alexander had served with him on the 1857 royal commission. Equally well-known to him was the statistician, Dr William Farr. To join them, Herbert touted the merits of the liberal philosopher, John Stuart

1   WSHC 2057/F4/66, FN to SH, 24 Dec.1857; LRO 920 DER 15/7/95, fol. 1, SH to Stanley, 12 Mar. 1858.
2   *CWFN*, IX, pp. 53-6, FN to Stanley, 4 Aug. 1858.
3   WSHC 2057/F4/67, FN to SH, 4, 19 Aug.1858.
4   LRO 920 DER/15/8/108, fol. 3, Stanley to SH, 18 April 1859; *CWFN*, IX, p. 78, SH to FN, 14 Apr. 1859.
5   LRO 920 DER 15/7/95, fols. 3-10 for SH's letters to Stanley, 1-23 May; LRO 920 DER/15/8/108, fols. 1-11 for Stanley's replies.

Mill ('a most intelligent but very odd man', thought Nightingale), but Mill's longstanding connection with the East India Company effectively debarred him.¹ The vacant positions were eventually filled by Sir Robert Hussey Vivian and Sir Proby Cautley, two members of the newly created Council of India, and Colonel Edward Greathed, an 'officer of acknowledged Indian experience'.² The warrant for a royal commission 'to inquire into, and report upon, the measures which it may be expedient to take for maintaining and improving the health of all ranks of Her Majesty's army serving in India' was issued on 31 May. Herbert was convinced, as head of 'a good working body' that 'we can scarcely fail to effect some good'.³

Herbert's more immediate priority in the autumn of 1858, before Indian matters began to interpose, was to continue the work of inspecting barracks within the United Kingdom. He had already visited at least twenty in London and ten in Hampshire. Arrangements were put in place to travel to Limerick for several days' inspection in late September. This was to be followed by a trip to Haddo House in Aberdeenshire for what he presumed would be a valedictory meeting ('he will not be long among us') with Lord Aberdeen.⁴ The ever unpredictable Grim Reaper scuppered both plans by striking far closer to home. Lady Elizabeth Clanwilliam, Herbert's eldest sister, died unexpectedly 'at a little wayside inn on Loch Etive' on 20 September. Herbert admitted to it being 'a terrible shock', the more so since he and his siblings agreed that, of all of them, she was 'loved the best'. It was a sombre family gathering that laid her to rest at Wilton.⁵

1   WSHC 2057/F4/68, FN to SH, 1 Jan. 1859.
2   BL Add. Mss. 43395, fol. 185, SH to FN, 12 May 1859.
3   *London Gazette*, 31 May 1859; LRO 920 DER 15/7/95, fol. 4, SH to Stanley, 3 May 1859; LRO 920 DER 15/7/95, fols. 8, 10, letters from SH to Stanley, 18, 23 May 1859.
4   *Dublin Evening Post*, 18 Sept. 1858; BL Add. Mss. 79658, fols. 55-9, SH to JRG, 8 Oct. 1858.
5   BL Add. Mss. 43395, fol. 74, SH to FN, 26 Sept. 1858; *SWJ*, 2 Oct. 1858.

Grief was still raw a month later when Herbert spoke at the opening of the Warminster Athenaeum.[1] It was the sort of occasion normally warranting a few column inches in a provincial newspaper. Herbert's speech of 28 October instead attracted more attention than any other he made outdoors, not only across the nation but the Channel too. From the *Revue des Deux Mondes*, threatened with closure by the French censors, there was approval.[2] Herbert had contrasted English liberties with the increasingly authoritarian regime of Napoleon III:

> Instead of having in the chair [in Warminster] a neighbouring landowner, you would have had the Prefect of the district probably in full uniform and with a cocked hat on, and you would have had throughout the proceedings the consciousness that you must be careful what language you used and topics you broached, or you might probably very suddenly have the opportunity of testing upon your constitution the effect of the warm climate of Cayenne.

Edward Baines, by contrast, Nonconformist editor of the *Leeds Mercury*, and another of the speakers at Warminster, took exception to what he perceived to be Herbert's ridiculing of reading rooms as a potential seedbed for budding geniuses. 'Who is it', Herbert had asked, in recommending the novels of Scott and Kingsley, 'that will sit down after a hard day's work [...] and will attempt to refresh his mind by taking an abstruse work on conic sections, or by entering into a learned philosophical argument on metaphysics'. It was Herbert's remarks on newspapers, however, that provoked comment in the British press. All newspapers, he suggested, were 'contemporary history. They are not always accurate, but I fear they are not the less history for that [...] the man who shuts his eyes to the contemporaneous history of a newspaper, is a man unfit to deal with the practical exigencies of society'. *The Times* objected, not so much to the former point as to Herbert's follow-on one that it would be better if articles did not appear anonymously, that if readers knew a piece came from the pen

---

1 *SWJ*, 30 Oct. 1858.
2 *SWJ*, 27 Nov. 1858.

of a man of substance, it would carry more weight. Herbert, a man with innumerable advantages over the lowly journalist, complained *The Thunderer*, one with 'the possibility of being one day a Premier', 'knows [...] that it is just the anonymous character of the Press that has secured its independence'.[1] The coverage afforded Herbert's words was clearly disproportionate to their importance. Perhaps it was simply a quiet news week?

With parliament not due to meet until February 1859, Herbert was able to throw off his autumn travails by re-immersing himself in the work of inspecting barracks and hospitals. He was in Exeter at the end of November. December found him in Dublin, where, as usual, he was painstaking in his approach:

> The Royal Sanitary Commissioners, with their president, Mr. Sidney Herbert, the late Minister for War, concluded their inspection of the garrison of Dublin on Tuesday, with the barracks in Ship-street, where they were entertained at luncheon by Colonel Buchanan and the officers of the Lanarkshire Regiment. They then proceeded to the Royal College of Surgeons to see the Military Surgery Museum [...] but went through the dissecting-rooms and remained in them for some time. Mr. Herbert made many inquiries as to the supply of subjects for dissection, and said he was gratified at the earnestness with which the students seemed to engage in their work, and the large number prosecuting anatomy.[2]

Formal reports on the basis of these and other visits duly followed. As Herbert's biographer wrote, 'The proof sheets of the draft Reports are covered with emendations in his handwriting'. But he was wrong if he thought that Herbert's signature on the cavalry barracks at Chichester, dated 23 March 1859, represented the end of his involvement with the process.[3] Although political developments in May derailed Herbert's plans to join Sutherland and Galton in Scotland, he had been with them to inspect barracks in Ireland at

1 *The Times*, 29 October 1858.
2 *Dublin Evening Post*, 16 Dec. 1858.
3 Stanmore, II, pp. 162-3.

Newry, Dundalk, Drogheda, and Armagh.[1] Nightingale recalled that the commanding officers of barracks 'complained that he went "so much into detail."' A modern authority puts it less euphemistically: 'Herbert had to travel throughout the country, physically inspecting barracks and dealing with uncooperative and sometimes insolent commanding officers'.[2] But it was worth it. Panmure's instructions had given him a wide remit, in particular the power, so long as it did not exceed £100, 'to direct the immediate execution of such works as may appear to you to be necessary for the ventilation, warming, lighting, draining and sewering of, and the securing a sufficient supply of good water for, such hospitals and barracks'.[3] It amounted to no more than a start; the sums required to make the alterations Herbert recommended in his reports ran to many thousands of pounds. But the money, initially at least, was forthcoming. In 1859, £756,000 was spent on barracks compared to £233,000 in 1854. To Herbert's labours, therefore, must principally be ascribed the fact that the death rate of the army at home fell from 17 per thousand in 1855 to 9.95 per thousand in 1860.[4]

There remained the danger, as the Herberts and Nightingale were acutely aware, that the question of army sanitary reform would fade from the public mind. Hence what Nightingale's biographer refers to as the 'curious' collection of letters and memoranda 'showing how industriously they set to work to pull wires in the press'.[5] The start of 1859, they agreed, would be a good moment, via well-placed articles, to run a new campaign of publicity. Several names being discounted, Herbert took upon himself the responsibility for writing a piece for the *Westminster Review*, 'the flagship of Radical freethinking'. The resulting essay of nearly 20,000 words, 'The Sanitary Condition of the Army', which appeared in the number for January 1859, made a

1 WSHC 2057/F4/68, FN to SH, 7 May 1859; *SWJ*, 21 May 1859.
2 BL Add. Mss. 43396, fols. 110-19, FN to EH, 17 Jan. 1861; Spiers, *Army and Society*, p. 160.
3 PP 1861 [2817], XXXVI, pp. 7-8.
4 Smith, *Nightingale*, p. 97.
5 Cook, *Nightingale*, 1, pp. 377-8.

considerable impact.[1] It was immediately reissued as a pamphlet and remains easily obtainable.

Understandably keen to add it to their armoury, Nightingale biographers hail the essay as essentially hers, one that was completed only as a result of her having chivvied the dilatory Herbert.[2] This is unfair. Herbert was living a gruellingly peripatetic existence at this time. In the period before the article appeared he wrote letters dated variously from Dunmore (9 November), Tamworth (14 November), London (19 November), Wilton (21 November), Exeter (29 November), and London again (7 December). In other words he had travelled roughly 750 miles in a month in the public service. He then went inspecting barracks in Dublin before returning to Wilton for Christmas.

More pertinently still, the article itself is unmistakably Herbert's. It begins with refrains familiar from his time at the War Office in the 1840s: that 'England has always been jealous of standing armies', that 'we do not like expenditure, because we do not like taxes'. There follows a trademark side-swipe at Palmerston, that British forces might be the instrument 'of a captious, arrogant, meddlesome, "spirited" foreign policy, which diverts public attention from domestic reforms for which, may be, the minister had no stomach'. Only then do we get a brief resumé of the work of the royal commission.[3] By contrast, a quarter of the article is devoted to rebutting claims made in a recent paper by the actuary, Dr Neison, that overcrowding and poor ventilation did not result in higher mortality. It was a matter about which Herbert felt strongly. A propos the royal commission, he had met Neison in 1857, complaining afterwards that 'his determination to believe that non-ventilation produces no bad effects on human health or life is a nuisance and it seems to me from very insufficient data'.[4] He had told the House that:

1 'The Sanitary Condition of the Army', *Westminster Review*, XV (1859), pp. 52-98.
2 For example Bostridge, *Nightingale*, p. 341.
3 'Sanitary Condition', pp. 52-61.
4 'Sanitary Condition', pp. 61-71; BL Add. Mss. 43394, fols. 71-6, SH to FN, 23 June 1857.

If it were the case that cubic space was immaterial, no man had been done greater injustice to than Shah Soojah Dowlah, who killed a number of people by putting them in the Black Hole at Calcutta. It was not a bad room, but it was overcrowded. According, however, to the theory of space being immaterial, and exercise everything, if he had only put a treadwheel in with them so that they might have had plenty of exercise the people confined in it would have turned out perfectly healthy the next morning.[1]

Sidney Herbert could get very aeriated about ventilation.

In drawing his article towards its close, Herbert outlined the work of his sub-commissions. But his concluding remarks went beyond them. Without the greater professionalisation of the army through the better education of its officers, he insisted, the benefits of the royal commission would be 'neutralised or lost'. At present, the officer 'finds himself able to get drunk without being flogged, and possibly to smoke without being sick – he is apt to assert his claim to manhood by imitating its vices, and to look down upon a man who neither drinks, nor hunts, nor rides races, as a sorry creature'. There was a need equally, to overcome 'the cumbrous consolidation of the War Office'. Without reform, Herbert concluded, another Crimean-style disaster was inevitable; with reform 'neither envy of our prosperity, nor hatred of our freedom, will induce any nation to risk aggression or court a contest with us'. Following the example he had recommended in his recent speech at Warminster, in an attempt to add weight to the arguments the article contained, Herbert then added his initials at the end. The article was emphatically not Nightingale's. Rather it was a synthesis of some of the strands of Herbert's thoughts on army matters as they had evolved since the early 1840s.

There is, however, by way of a postscript, one unseemly revelation that does not reflect well on Herbert. In 1858, 'Uncle Sidney' received a letter from his 'affectionate nephew', the seventeen-year-old Charles Murray, 7th Earl of Dunmore.[2] Whilst staying with his Woronzow

1   Hansard, 11 May 1858, CL, cols. 489-92.
2   WSHC 2057/F4/50, Dunmore to SH, nd, 1858/9.

relations, Dunmore had made an extensive tour of the principle battle sites in the Crimea. What he saw appalled him: gravestones chipped and crumbling, grave markers fast becoming indistinct. 'Nobody', he wrote, 'takes the slightest care of them'. Far worse, however, were the scenes which confronted Dunmore at Sebastopol. There were bones piled up to thirty feet high, half of which at least he estimated to be those of British soldiers. Their fate was not to be laid with dignity in a grand ossuary, but instead to suffer the ignominy bestowed on them by a Mr Edwards 'who sends them to England for manure'. Dunmore was understandably incensed: 'Now is this the way that our brave soldiers who perished in defence of their country are to be treated? Instead of sleeping quietly (at least under the turf if they had no tomb) on the field of battle where they fell [they are] to be carted about in England as manure!' 'Russian rascals', he added, were even then exhuming more bodies with a view to adding to the profits to be had from human fertiliser. Dunmore intended that Uncle Sidney would pass the information to his friend Malmesbury, the Foreign Secretary. There is no evidence that he did, or if he did, that Malmesbury took any action.[1]

Herbert's continuing rapport with Malmesbury was one reason why he had no great desire to see an end to the Derby ministry. But his reasoning was also pragmatic: 'It [was] a great mistake to take office before your opponents had made blunders enough to efface the memory of one's own', allied to which he saw no prospect 'of the formation of an efficient party, let alone government, out of the chaos on the opposition benches'.[2] The chief topic of political conversation in Peelite circles as 1858 drew to a close was the meaning of Gladstone's quixotic decision, in November, to accept Derby's offer to visit the Ionian Islands as Lord High Commissioner Extraordinary. Herbert confessed to finding it 'unintelligible', unless it was to presage his formal union with the Conservatives. Whatever Gladstone's

1   Bones of Waterloo dead, as indeed of earlier conflicts, had suffered similar indignity, but I am unaware of any other reference to the practice being continued in the aftermath of the Crimean War.
2   TNA 30/29/18/6, fol. 65, SH to Granville, 31 Aug. 1858; BL Add. Mss. 79658, fols. 66-73, SH to JRG, 10 Jan. 1859.

reasoning, 'He really is not safe to go about out of Lord Aberdeen's room'.[1]

It was Russell, Palmerston's career widely presumed to be over, who took the lead in seeking to revive Liberal fortunes. Over New Year, he 'intimated to me [Graham] a desire that you [Herbert], Lewis, and I should form a little coterie around him for the purpose of concert on questions of Reform and of Finance'. Graham, pointing out that Herbert 'could not be regarded as an <u>ardent</u> reformer', declined.[2] Herbert concurred, pointing out, so far as Reform was concerned, that 'It is very difficult to find any one very keen for it, the tide of discussion of late having set strongly against it'. Rather than continue the debate by correspondence, Graham accepted Herbert's invitation to come to Wilton at the end of January where the two could 'talk over the black future before we have to deal with it'.[3]

By the time Sir James arrived in Wiltshire, Herbert was convinced that Derby's government would introduce a Reform Bill, not least because Bright, who had been making speeches calling for a large extension of the franchise since October, 'has thoroughly frightened the country'.[4] He was right. Disraeli, seeking to retain the political initiative, proposed a Reform Bill. Its chief features included lowering the occupancy franchise in counties to £10 (the same as in boroughs), and prohibiting borough freeholders (those with freeholds less than the £10 value which qualified them to vote in their borough but possessed of the 40 shilling property which qualified them for a county vote) from voting in counties.

Herbert objected for a number of reasons. In the first place, the Bill was blatantly partisan: borough freeholders were regarded as predominantly Liberal and as such a threat to Tory hegemony in county constituencies. Second, Herbert remained opposed to equalising the borough and county franchise: 'I am an advocate for

1 BL Add. Mss. 79658, fols. 73-5, SH to JRG, 19 Jan. 1859.
2 WSHC 2057/F4/59, JRG to SH, 9 Jan. 1859. Sir George Cornewall Lewis had been Chancellor of the Exchequer 1855-8.
3 WSHC 2057/F4/59, JRG to SH, 9 Jan. 1859; BL Add. Mss. 79658, fols. 66-73, SH to JRG, 10 Jan. 1859.
4 BL Add. Mss. 44211, fols. 28-31, SH to WEG, 28 Jan. 1859.

maintaining a marked difference', he reminded Russell on 9 March.¹ His fundamental objection, however, was to the Conservatives proposing a Reform Bill at all. Reform was one of the litmus tests which made him a Liberal. Could one be both a Conservative and a Reformer without dire consequences? He complained to Argyll that:

> the present people seem inclined to outbid the Liberal party – a course which will be justly fatal to themselves, and, what is more important, will be fatal to the country too. Whatever they propose our friends must cap. If Derby goes for universal suffrage, Palmerston or Johnny will produce the women and children.²

How then to proceed? Russell, a torch bearer of Reform, advocated a full frontal assault on the Conservative Bill. He drafted a resolution to that effect. Herbert and Graham counselled a more oblique approach, confining the resolution to specifics: deploring the proposed disenfranchisement of borough freeholders, whilst failing to extend the franchise sufficiently. On the latter detail, Herbert suggested that Russell's reference to 'the great body of the working classes' was impolitic. If 'industrious classes' was substituted, would-be moderate supporters of his resolution were less likely to be scared off. Russell agreed.³

Debate on the Reform Bill restored Herbert to prominence in the House. Excepting interventions on the army estimates and a speech opposing a Bill to abolish church rates ('Sidney Herbert poured out some milk and water – drawing nice distinctions and refinements', noted Sir John Trelawny), he had not spoken there since July 1858.⁴ On 22 March 1859, however, he delivered a lengthy speech in which he voiced his anxieties over Reform in a tone of calculated reasonableness:

---

1 WSHC 2057/F4/53, SH to Russell, 9, 10 Mar. 1859.
2 Argyll, *Autobiography*, II, pp. 121-2, SH to Argyll, 15 Mar. 1858.
3 WSHC 2057/F4/53, SH to Russell, 10 Mar. 1859.
4 Jenkins, *Trelawny Diaries*, pp. 72-3, 15 Mar. 1859; Hansard, 15 Mar. 1859, CLIII, cols. 189-91.

I am no democratic Reformer [...] I occupy a middle position – a position which I believe is occupied by the great mass of the people of this country, who are attached to our ancient institutions, who look upon them as sacred traditions handed down to them from their ancestors, and which it is their duty to maintain inviolate [...] Elections, and hustings, and polls are necessary to our constitution, but they are only to be considered as the means of obtaining a certain result; they are not the end itself. The first end is to bring the best men into this House; the second, the importance of which I do not undervalue, is, that the mass of the population should have the sense of contributing to the common welfare.[1]

Aberdeen, who asked Elizabeth whether she had heard her husband's speech, delighted in informing her that it had elicited many favourable reports.[2] Russell's resolution, as modified by Herbert, was carried as an amendment to the Reform Bill by 330 votes to 291. Derby appealed to the country.

Herbert's return for South Wiltshire proved to be a straightforward affair. He spoke for all parties when he wrote of his wish to avoid a contest which would 'involve me in all the trouble and expense which I wish to save myself'.[3] When, therefore, William Wyndham, returned with Herbert in the contested elections of 1852 and 1857, announced his retirement, the Conservatives brought forward just one candidate, Lord Henry Thynne. With neither side opting to field a second candidate, the representation could be shared without the necessity of going to a poll. At the nomination, Herbert reiterated his opposition to the Conservatives' Reform Bill. It provided, he explained in the apposite surroundings of Salisbury's Market Square, 'only the garnish of the dish, without the dish itself [...] it gave us the carrots and greens, but altogether omitted the round of beef'.[4]

Relief at the outcome of the election, though for different reasons, was expressed by Tory clergymen around Salisbury. They had

1   Hansard, 22 Mar. 1859, CLIII, cols. 581-98.
2   WSHC 2057/F4/53, Aberdeen to EH, 23 Mar. 1859.
3   Stanmore, II, p. 177, SH to WEG, 10 Apr. 1859.
4   *SWJ*, 9 Apr. 1859.

'the audacity to tell [Elizabeth] how glad they are there is to be no county contest, as they couldn't have voted for my husband this time, after his article had appeared in the "Westminster Review."' Their view was echoed by 'a droll little Tanner', who declared that 'Herbert was a Papist last time & an Atheist this! I wonder how we manage to live with such a neighbour!'[1] Neither clergy, nor tanner, one may safely presume, had actually read Herbert's article. Herbert made no attempt to set them right. He was more concerned with Elizabeth, heavily pregnant when parliament was dissolved on 18 April. Their seventh child, Lady Constance, was born on 24 April. 'Thank God my dear wife is safe thro' her trial', he wrote to tell Nightingale, 'a fine, fat dark-haired baby girl came into the world; we cannot be thankful enough for this short labour'.[2]

The spring election led to Palmerston forming a Liberal government in June. This was an outcome which few foresaw. The Conservatives after all, had increased their number of seats from 260 to 306. Herbert himself, as we have seen, was presuming on starting work as chairman of the royal commission on Indian sanitary reform. True, Derby was in a minority but the 325 Liberals and 23 Peelites ranged against him were a heterogeneous mass: it was a fanciful pundit who pictured a scenario in which Russell would be Prime Minister from the Lords with Herbert installed as Leader of the House.[3] Forming any Liberal administration was contingent upon agreeing a formula to end the internecine squabbles of the past. By June, however, it had been. Herbert can be argued to have made three important contributions to the process: by attempting to smooth the reconciliation of Palmerston and Russell; by easing Gladstone's passage into the fold; and by insisting on grounding new-found Liberal unity on broad and open foundations in opposition to those whose instinct was to act privately in a clique.

The first moves in this final political chess game of the 1850s were made by Russell. He agreed with Palmerston that a motion of

1   BL Add. Mss. 43396, fols. 61-2, EH to FN, 17 Apr. 1859.
2   BL Add. Mss. 43395, fol. 169, SH to FN, 25 Apr. 1859.
3   Hawkins, *Parliament*, p. 227

no confidence should be moved against the Conservatives as soon as the new parliament met. Russell also identified Herbert as 'a possible interpreter of the mind of Mr Gladstone', if that formidable loose cannon was to be wooed into joining a successor ministry.[1] On 16 May, therefore, Russell asked Herbert for his thoughts, both as to the motion of no confidence and Gladstone's likely intentions, adding that 'I should like to see Graham, you, Gladstone, and Milner Gibson members of any new Cabinet'. Herbert was broadly positive in reply: 'if there be a good prospect of a fair cooperation among the Liberal party, the present Government ought to be put an end to'. But he was unconvinced that the mathematics pointed to that outcome. The certainty that 300 Conservative Members 'will run together like a Pack of Hounds' meant that if Derby could garner support from some Radical and Irish Members, he might well survive. Thus Herbert counselled a three-point plan of campaign: 'The establishment of an union among the mass of the Liberal party', 'A clear understanding as to Reform i.e. as to the borough franchise', and 'A certainty that the proposed motion can be carried'. Russell forwarded Herbert's letter to Palmerston, and offered to come down to Wilton to discuss matters further.[2] Unbeknown to Russell, the Herberts were simultaneously exhorting Gladstone to visit Wilton: 'surely there never was a moment', Elizabeth pleaded with him, 'when Disunion would be more fatal'. Gladstone, for the moment, was unpersuaded.[3]

Privately, Herbert confessed to being 'very gloomy', believing that the 'little man' was letting ambition run ahead of him. Russell, it seemed clear, was intent on being king pin in any Liberal government, even imagining a scenario in which he would serve under Palmerston, provided that the latter was emasculated by being elevated to the Lords.

---

1   HLPP GC/GR/LE/116, Cornwall Lewis to Pam, 16 May 1859; WSHC 2057/F4/53, Wood to SH, 24 May 1859; Fitzmaurice, *Granville*, II, p. 327.
2   WSHC 2057/F4/53, Russell to SH, 16, 19 May 1859; HLPP GC/HE/48, SH to Russell, 17 May 1859.
3   BL Add. Mss. 44211, fols. 47-50, SH to WEG, 17 May 1859; BL Add. Mss. 44212, fol. 63, EH to WEG, 17 May 1859; BL Add. Mss. 44211, fols. 56-9, WEG to SH, 18 May 1859.

Russell assured Herbert, that following a meeting with Palmerston at Pembroke Lodge (Herbert's birthplace) on 20 May, the two were in perfect accord.¹ Herbert simply could not believe that the 'little man' and Palmerston were 'wondrously agreed!' He wrote to the latter for his take on the meeting. Palmerston confirmed that they were agreed as to tactics and policy but less so as to people. Russell had been vague as to the place he sought for himself in any government; Palmerston made it clear that he was not inclined to go to the Lords, even if Prime Minister.²

The drama now relocated to Wilton, where Herbert greeted Russell on 25 May.³ Whatever Russell's objectives for the meeting, Herbert was clear about his: Russell must accept that he might not become Premier, and state publicly that he would be prepared to serve unconditionally under Palmerston. In the course of two long conversations, Herbert endeavoured to impress on his house guest:

> that the man who forgets himself the most will be the best remembered by the country, and I told him very unmistakably that neither he nor Palmerston can form a Government without the other, and that Palmerston, Prime Minister, would have a far better chance than he, Lord John, would in that position.⁴

Unhappy at the turn events had taken, the watching Lady Russell brought a peremptory end to proceedings by declaring her wish to go home: she refused Herbert's offer to take her to the station in order that Lord John might remain. The disgruntled spouse had no option but to go with her, muttering that the talks and any supposed agreements *would not do*. The 'little man', Herbert told Granville, 'is in a very unsettled state of mind'.⁵

1   WSHC 2057/F4/53, Russell to SH, 21 May 1859.
2   BL Add. Mss. 44211, fols. 62-3, SH to WEG, 22 May 1859; WSHC 2057/F4/61, Pam to SH, 24 May 1859.
3   WSHC 2057/F4/53, Russell to SH, 23 May 1859.
4   Fitzmaurice, *Granville*, I, pp. 327-9, SH to Granville, 27 May 1859.
5   Hawkins, *Parliament*, pp. 244-6, citing Cornewall Lewis's diary. Cornewall Lewis had also been at Wilton during Russell's visit.

Keeping Gladstone abreast of developments, Herbert was by now even more sure about what needed to happen:

> I urge on all that, if any move is to be made, a meeting of the whole Liberal party should be held, and we should have it out with them. Palmerston, I understand, objects on the ground that they will say disagreeable things, and ask awkward questions. Of course they will, and if they have not the opportunity in a dining-room, they will do it in the House of Commons. Unless the men who are to turn out the present Government are prepared to support the Government that is to follow, it is folly to make any hostile move; but, before such a meeting is called, the two leaders must have come to this understanding that both are willing to serve the Queen together, and in such mutual relation as she may herself think best. If they do not do this, the party will not be satisfied, nor will the leaders have any security till they have had a frank explanation with the party. This said Liberal party consists of men who think for themselves, and when they don't, think they do, and their independent habits of thought and action must be considered. They must be made parties to, and responsible for, the course to be taken, by previously being taken into council. They won't blindly follow a course concocted by some half-dozen gentlemen in a library.[1]

Under pressure from Herbert, as well as Granville, Wood and Cornewall Lewis, Palmerston and Russell finally agreed to participate in the sort of meeting that Herbert envisaged. Even so, it was, as Herbert confided to Elizabeth, a high risk strategy: 'People seem very doubtful about the proceeding to be taken, and feel, not without truth, that it is a desperate undertaking, requiring much more hearty co-operation and goodwill than we all possess'. But at least, if unsuccessful, the initiative would have demonstrated that a stable Liberal government was not viable.[2] A sanguine Herbert added his name, one of nine

---

1   BL Add. Mss. 44211, fols. 64-9, SH to WEG, 28 May 1859.
2   WSHC 2057/F4/51, SH to EH, 3, 4 June 1859; Hawkins, *Parliament*, pp. 249-51.

covering a broad spectrum of liberal opinion, 'to the requisition' of 4 June 'for the purpose of uniting the Liberal party'.¹

The famous gathering of 6 June at Willis's Rooms spawned numerous reports. For immediacy and colour, however, no account surpassed that from Herbert in a letter to Elizabeth:

> I am just returned in a state of liquefaction from Willis's Rooms. There were about 280 members present, which is thought very large, as the Irish members are not yet come over in any number. Pam. first got upon the raised dais, and when he helped Johnny up by the hand there was a droll burst of cheering. Pam. spoke shortly and well, described the challenge in the Queen's dissolution speech, alluded to the failures of the Government in legislation, and the danger of their involving us in a war, said that he and Johnny were at one (great cheering). Then there was a pause, and a call for Lord John, who spoke in the same sense, and said if the vote succeeded it was necessary to look forward, and if the Queen sent for Pam., he, Johnny, would cheerfully co-operate with him in the formation of a Government broad basis, etc. and then Pam. whispered to him, and he added as much for Pam. Then calls for Bright, who spoke in a for him decent manner enough; said the differences had been in the party as well as the leaders, and the fault of the leaders. Wanted some clearer assurance about war, but upon the whole promised co-operation. Pam. gave the clearer assurance, and I got up: said I also came from below the gangway (here comes Edward, who says it is post time). I preached union, and said I did not mind if we were beat, as if we are a minority we should know our place and watch, but also support the Government in all national matters [...] So the proposition was put and carried amidst loud cheers, and Lord Hartington and Mr. Hanbury are to move and second the identical amendment which Peel carried against Lord Melbourne in 1841. On the whole it was very successful, no one objecting who was not expected to do so, and others concurring who had not been reckoned on.²

1 *Morning Advertiser*, 7 June 1859; *The Irishman*, 11 June 1859.
2 WSHC 2057/F4/51, SH to EH, 6 June 1859.

Still intoxicated with success, Herbert was present when the no confidence motion was moved the next day. He spoke near the close of the debate on 10 June. Accusing the government, in dissolving parliament, of 'a declaration of war to the knife against the Liberal party', he proceeded to ridicule it: 'I confess when I am asked to give my confidence to the Government, I am at a loss to know what it is I am to confide to them'. The ministry had been consistent only in being hypocritical, supporting measures, such as the abolition of the property qualification for MPs, which it had previously opposed. 'I may in the heat of discussion', Herbert conceded, to those who accused him in turn of being hypocritical in now allying with Palmerston, 'have said some things which in cooler moments I might have thought far stronger than were required', but 'a more honourable, more truthful, and I need not add more agreeable, colleague than the noble Viscount it would be impossible to find'.[1] Disraeli, who knew full well that Herbert had often been trenchant in his criticisms of the man who now stood on the threshold of 10 Downing Street, would sneer at Herbert as one of those 'who have signed the vouchers for the reconciled sections'. But Herbert's contribution to the debate was well-received: Sir John Trelawny, fan neither of Herbert nor his oratory, judged it 'the best speech of the evening'.[2] The motion was carried by 323 votes 310 and the government resigned.

Attentions immediately turned to the minutiae of cabinet making. Herbert had declared at Willis's Rooms that he 'had no wish to be a member of' a Liberal government, a piece of self-denial that fooled nobody. As his kinsman the Earl of Carnarvon observed, Herbert's return to office was 'long expected'.[3] Far more doubtful was what Gladstone would do. Given virtual carte blanche by Palmerston as to portfolio, Gladstone answered the question by becoming Chancellor of the Exchequer. He would always claim that he did so because of his sympathies for the cause of Italian nationalism, something he believed Liberals more likely to support than Conservatives. Like Herbert,

1 Hansard, 10 June 1859, CLIV, cols. 318-35.
2 Monypenny and Buckle, *Disraeli*, IV, p. 245; Jenkins, *Trelawny Diaries*, p. 84, 10 June 1859.
3 *The Irishman*, 11 June 1859; Hawkins, *Parliament*, p. 261.

however, going into the spring election Gladstone had endorsed the Conservative government's policy of neutrality on the Italian question. He also possessed the happy knack, as Herbert later put it, that 'he can deceive himself to almost any extent when it accords with his wishes'.[1] Personalities played more of a part in Gladstone's calculations than he was wont to admit. And no personality figured more in his mind than Herbert. Herbert had kept Gladstone abreast of developments within the Liberal camp since the election, showing him key correspondence as well as opening his own political heart to him. True, whilst the Conservatives remained in office, Gladstone remained obdurate to Herbert's entreaties to make common cause.[2] Herbert thought he had managed to persuade him at the start of June, relaying to Elizabeth that 'He is evidently now anxious to see them [the Conservatives] upset, and ready to join a Government to succeed them!' Elizabeth was consequently angry that Gladstone refused to accompany her husband to the meeting at Willis's Rooms; she took him severely to task for his omission.[3] With the news that Herbert was re-entering office following hard on the heels of Derby's demise, however, Gladstone faced a stark choice. If he wanted to give substance to the aspiration expressed only a year before that they should never part in public life, it was a case of now or never. This being so, Italy became the bridge that allowed Gladstone to cross from the political wilderness to be with his friend in government.

So far as Herbert's portfolio was concerned, he was summoned to Cambridge House, Palmerston's London home, on 13 June and offered the War Office. In deference to pressure from Elizabeth and Sir James Graham, he floated the possibility 'that I should go to the Lords if I found the work too much, together with the House of Commons; and I even offered (in homage to advice) to go there now if convenient to the Government'. Palmerston declared this 'to be highly inconvenient, spoke of the great battle to be fought under

1 BL Add. Mss. 79658, SH to JRG, 12 Apr. 1860; Shannon, *Gladstone. Peel's Inheritor*, pp. 378-82.
2 WSHC 2057/F4/60, WEG to SH, 29 May 1859.
3 WSHC 2057/F4/51, SH to EH, 3, 4 June 1859; Aldous, *The Lion and the Unicorn*, p. 116.

great difficulties in the Commons, and [...] begged me at any rate to try the Commons with the Office'. Herbert agreed.¹ But that was not quite the end of the matter. Sir Charles Wood's diary for 16 June records that Herbert, 'vain enough to believe anything', had hoped to succeed Lytton at the Colonial Office. This may well explain the vague reference in Herbert's letter of 18 June to Graham that he had seen Palmerston and 'tried again for the higher office, but clearly he is hampered by engagements to others'.² Not for the first time, Herbert's altruism conflicted with a sense of his due worth.

Herbert's long-held hopes to see the formation of a broad-based, moderate Liberal administration were otherwise satisfied. With Gladstone, he helped persuade Palmerston to bring Newcastle in from the political cold as Colonial Secretary. Cardwell, partly in response to Herbert's lobbying, was advanced to the cabinet as Chief Secretary for Ireland. His only caveat was 'I fear we must run the risk of the three Dukes'. He seems entirely to have missed the irony of his comment, made as it was by one of the five peers or sons of peers, not to mention the brother of a duke and three baronets in a cabinet of fourteen.³

---

1   BL Add. Mss. 79658, fol. 80-7, SH to JRG, 14 June 1859. One can dismiss as exaggerated Elizabeth's version of events that Palmerston had said 'that he could not form a Government without Sidney's assistance in the Commons'. See WSHC 2057/F6/98, 'Account of Sidney Herbert', pp. 1-2.
2   BL Add. Mss. 79658, fols. 88-9, SH to JRG, 18 June 1859; Hawkins, *Parliament*, p. 262.
3   BL Add. Mss. 79658, fols. 80-7, SH to JRG, 14 June 1859; Hawkins, *Parliament*, pp. 259-65. The three dukes were Argyll, Newcastle and Somerset.

12
Cumulative Burdens 1859-1861

Chlodwig, Prince of Hohenlohe-Schillingsfürst, later Chancellor of Germany, who met Herbert in June 1859, described him as 'a very vivacious man, who gesticulated a great deal'. The latter observation, perhaps, is explained by the fact that Herbert was so busy that summer. He had work from the ongoing sub-commissions on sanitary reform to attend to. Just before the general election of May, he had been appointed to an important parliamentary select committee on military organisation. There was also the prospect of chairing a new royal commission on the state of the British army in India to consider. If he had remained on the backbenches these burdens could have been offset by absenting himself from the Commons. With the summer recess approaching he could have contemplated a lengthy period in a spa town on the continent. Instead, Herbert's return to goverment heralded an eighteen month period during which he had never been busier. In addition to the commitments itemised above, Herbert assisted in overseeing preparations for a war 5,000 miles away, confronted the headache of a possible French invasion, and partially reorganised the War Office. He also became one of the government's senior spokesmen in parliament. 'And so', Elizabeth recorded, 'the life of overwork began'. As early as mid-June, Herbert was wont to quote the chilling dictum that 'Every day that I keep the War Office with the House of Commons is one day taken off my life'.[1]

1   WSHC 2057/F6/98, 'Account of Sidney Herbert', pp. 1-2; BL Add. Mss. 43396, fols. 65-6, EH to FN, 16 June 1859.

One of the first questions to be decided was whether Herbert would continue as chairman of the Indian sanitary commission. 'Mr Herbert told me', confided a concerned Nightingale, 'that if he were secretary of state for war, he would turn over this India matter to Lord Stanley [...] I believe the sanitary salvation of India depends upon Mr Herbert doing it'.[1] For the moment she persuaded him to stay on. By August, however, and again in October, 'overdone as I am with a heavy Department with an immense amount [of] business', Herbert was imploring Stanley to take his place.[2] Stanley did eventually agree to take the chair in December – 1860! Thus eighteen months elapsed during which the commission's members met on only three occasions.[3] Their report would not appear until May 1863. It would have been better all-round if Herbert had insisted on surrendering the chair in June 1859.

Not least of Herbert's new responsibilities was his playing a more active part in the life of the Commons. In the four years since he left office in 1855, he had spoken on only 60 days. By contrast, during the 37 days on which the House sat before the session ended on 13 August 1859, Herbert made over 50 interventions. Only half a dozen of these were significant speeches, but even the briefest answer to a question about some recondite War Office matter required that he master his departmental brief. Herbert was no less mindful that he was one of only seven members of the cabinet who sat in the Commons. Apart from Palmerston, Russell, Gladstone and Cornewall Lewis, the major office holders, he was its most senior and, measured by frequency of interventions, its most active member.

Departmental responsibilities, sadly, did not end with the parliamentary recess. Elizabeth avowed that Herbert worked 'literally day and night' at the War Office, a routine made the more detestable

1 *CWFN*, IX, p. 93, FN to McNeill, 11 June 1859.
2 LRO 920 DER/15/7/252/9, Wood to Stanley, 24 Aug. 1859; LRO 920 DER15/7/95, SH to Stanley, 9 Oct. 1859; LRO 920 DER15/8/108, Stanley to SH, 20 Oct. 1859.
3 WSHC 2057/F4/68, FN to EH, 5 Dec. 1860; LRO 920 DER15/43/16/55, SH to Stanley, 8, 11 Dec. 1860; BL Add. Mss. 43395, fol. 271, SH to FN, 11 Dec. 1860.

by the fact that 'The heat was intense and the smell of the Thames most offensive'. She tried to lighten his burdens by taking on more work herself as his de facto private secretary. Welcome relief for both was provided by Nightingale's invitations to dine with her most weekends at West Hill Lodge, the property she had leased in Highgate Rise. Better still, Lord Granville gave the Herberts the run of his farm at Golders Green on the Finchley Road. There were also occasional excursions further afield, including a visit to the Queen at Osborne in July. Elizabeth would, in retrospect, judge the summer of 1859 to have been 'a very happy one'.[1]

All the same, the relative repose of the autumn was surely happier. One can sense the relief in Elizabeth's letter of 1 September that 'We go to Wilton tonight for two weeks'. A house party there at the end of the month was graced by Her Imperial Highness the Grand Duchess Marie Nikolaevna, sister of Alexander II, accompanied by the unfortunately named Count Wankoff. The Duke of Cambridge joined them for a shoot which bagged 68 hares and 83 brace of birds.[2] November and War Office work necessitated Herbert's return to London: 'To return into this choking atmosphere during these fogs is certainly most unwise', he acknowledged. But he managed to be more upbeat in a letter to Graham:

> My office as it is now conjoined is a handfull. Except when there is a Cabinet I spend over seven hours a day there besides work in the morning & in the evening at home [...] I never was better in health in my life, but I keep early hours & take an hour's jollys every day.[3]

As the year drew to a close Herbert even foreswore the pleasures of Wilton, save for a few days over Christmas to 'give our usual Xmas Trees, Choir Supper, Servants Ball, etc'. He played charades with his

---

1   SWJ, 30 July 1859; WSHC 2057/F6/98, 'Account of Sidney Herbert', pp. 2-3.
2   BL Add. Mss. 43395, fol. 200, EH to FN, 1 Sept. 1859; SWJ, 1 Oct. 1859.
3   BL Add. Mss. 79658, fols. 94-9, SH to JRG, 13 Nov. 1859.

children 'as if he had no work and no cares'.[1] But all too soon the War Office beckoned again.

Herbert's appointment to the War Office had been greeted with ambivalence by the press. The *London Daily News* was fairly typical in observing that:

> The stubborn resistance encountered by Ministers in getting their own objects achieved in their own offices is the great trouble; and the main point about MR SIDNEY HERBERT is to see whether he, with his clear and full knowledge of what ought to be done, can get it done. [...] He can plead no excuse of imperfect preparation on his own part; and we have a right to expect perfect work.[2]

From a reformers' perspective, some of the auguries were discouraging. There were, for example, no significant new initiatives on military education. Worse, in defending the use of the lash in the army in February 1860, Herbert raised eyebrows when asserting that 'Our English nature is a strong nature and a turbulent nature, and in all ages and among all classes has required a stronger code than nations of a quieter and more pliable disposition'. Sir John Trelawny reckoned this as 'an unfortunate passage, which elicited a burst of derisive shouts'.[3]

On the matter of buying and selling commissions, at least, Herbert still favoured reform. He risked the ire of the Duke of Cambridge, Commander-in-Chief, when he wrote that 'I have always believed that if the scandals and abuses which beset the Purchase System could be removed, much of the Feeling against the system itself would die out'.[4] To this end, Herbert drew up a 'most confidential' memorandum in which he developed the views which he had endorsed as a member of the 1857 royal commission on the subject. Purchase of commissions for the ranks of lieutenant-colonel (the current going rate was £6,175) and above, he argued, should be abolished; they

1 WSHC 2057/F6/98, 'Account of Sidney Herbert', pp. 2-3.
2 *London Daily News*, 27 June 1859.
3 Hansard, 16 Feb. 1860, CLVI, col. 1182; Jenkins, *Trelawny Diaries*, pp. 100-1, 16 Feb. 1860.
4 Spiers, *Army and Society*, pp. 148-9.

could be phased out within a decade. Palmerston advised him that his recommendations were unlikely to pass the Commons as they stood.¹ Prince Albert expressed 'great alarm' about Herbert's proposed 'transferring the patronage of the army above the rank of Major from the Queen to the House of Commons – a change striking at the root of the prerogative of the Crown'. The Queen, unamused, told Herbert direct that she would not approve.² Herbert persisted nevertheless, rehearsing the outline of his scheme, on 6 March, in a debate on a motion from Sir George de Lacy Evans to abolish purchase outright. Trelawny judged Herbert's speech that of a man who had studied his subject and that 'he produced the impression that he was doing his best for the Army'.³ The mood of the House, however, was for the status quo – Evans' motion was overwhelmed by 213 votes to 59 – and Herbert had to accept that he was ahead of his time.

There was progress, albeit prosaic, for the rank and file. A School of Practical Cookery was set up at Aldershot; a new set of regulations was issued to define the duties of purveyors. In barracks, there were attempts to improve day rooms, to make them places where the men could read, write and 'play innocent games', sufficient inducements it was hoped, to divert them from the 'demoralising dram-shop'.⁴ Most reforms of this ilk derived from the four sub-commissions which Herbert was chairing before returning to the War Office. The first annual statistical report on the state of the army ('upon a proper statistical organisation depends all future progress of the army', Herbert had told Nightingale) was issued in March 1861. Nightingale's view was that it enabled 'the exact state of health, of every regiment and station to be ascertained, and any unusual amount of disease, *with its removable causes*, to be brought at once to the cognizance of the

---

1   TNA WO 33/9, memorandum of 23 Feb. 1860; WSHC 2057/F4/61, Pam to SH, 5 Mar. 1860.
2   WSHC 2057/F4/55, Albert to SH, 3 Feb. 1860; Victoria to SH, 3 Feb. 1860.
3   HL PP/GC/HE/62, SH to Pam, 5 Mar. 1860; Hansard, 6 Mar. 1860, CLVII, cols. 47-59; Jenkins, *Trelawny Diaries*, pp. 106-7, 6 Mar. 1860.
4   Nightingale, *Army Sanitary Administration*, pp. 5, 7, 9-10.

authorities'.[1] The new department soon enjoyed a reputation as one of the most reliable in Europe.

The reorganisation of the Army Medical Department, given earlier opposition, proved to be more straightforward than was feared. Three officers were placed under the Director-General: one to oversee sanitary questions, one for other medical matters, and one to head the new statistical department. Together they comprised a council: the Secretary of State was to be kept fully appraised of its deliberations.[2] Of greater practical importance, a new code of regulations for the sanitary service of the army was issued. Hitherto, it transpired, the department's remit was confined to sickness, not health. The duties required of army medical officers, therefore, were clarified. Commanding officers, unless they could show good reason, were required to give effect to their recommendations. The new code also included regulations for regimental and general hospitals, the latter in wartime having been 'fatal examples of how to kill, not to cure'.[3] In facilitating these initiatives, it had helped immeasurably that Herbert could draw upon Nightingale; also that he had persuaded Peel to appoint his favourite doctor, Thomas Alexander, to be Director-General in 1858. Herbert was profoundly upset at the news of Alexander's untimely death early in 1860: 'The public loses an excellent administrator in whom his profession had the greatest confidence [...] He was one of the honestest men I ever knew'.[4]

Moves towards establishing an Army Medical School were less successful. Arguments over the academic status (lecturers or professors) and background of its staff (military or civilian) had raged until Herbert was able to pull rank on the question in 1859. Fort Pitt at Chatham finally opened its doors on 2 October 1860. Herbert addressed the first cohort of 43 students in person. Presumably he was as aghast as anybody that when they ventured inside they discovered

1 WSHC 2057/F4/66, FN to SH, 12 Oct. 1857; PP 1861 (366), XXXVII; Nightingale, *Army Sanitary Administration*, p. 6;
2 PP 1860 (441), VII, p. 562.
3 Nightingale, *Army Sanitary Administration*, pp. 5-6.
4 BL Add. Mss.43395, fols. 244-5, SH to H. Bonham Carter, 1 Feb. 1860.

that the establishment was still to be properly fitted out. That done, the students and their successors were to receive a four-month programme in subjects such as gunshot wounds, tropical disease and sanitation.[1] A bullish Herbert told parliament in 1861 that:

> The army surgeon now is in a very different position from what he was when Sir Benjamin Brodie [an early-nineteenth-century pioneer into researching bone disease] recommended his pupils never to go into the army. For a long time in our service the medical profession was not much regarded, but now we have the best skill which can be found; all the best men are coming to us.[2]

Sadly this was not so. The pay and status of army medics compared unfavourably with that enjoyed by their counterparts in civilian life. Real advance lay a generation away. The School, however, flourished following its relocation to Netley in 1863.[3]

Herbert's place on the barrack and hospital sub-commission, meanwhile, had been filled by W.H. Burrell. By spring 1861, the commissioners had visited 162 barracks and 114 hospitals, roughly two-thirds of the whole.[4] Nightingale's evaluation of their achievements could hardly have been more glowing. They had:

> combined ventilation and warming [...] Drainage has been introduced or improved. Water supply has been extended, baths introduced [...] and the lavatory arrangements generally improved. The barrack kitchens have been completely remodelled: the wasteful cooking apparatus [...] has been replaced by improved and economical cooking ranges [...] man may now have the change of cookery required for health, instead of the eternal soup and boiled beef. Gas has been introduced [...] instead of the couple of 'dips' [...] which only made the barrack room look darker still, and by the light of which it was impossible for the men to read, or to pursue any occupation except

1 PP 1861 (2853), XXXVII, pp. 380-3; Stanmore, II, pp. 364-8.
2 Hansard, 21 June 1861, CLXIII, cols. 1400-2.
3 Bostridge, *Nightingale*, pp. 345-6.
4 The 81 barracks and 53 hospitals yet to be visited were mostly small.

smoking [...] more cubic space for both sick and well, and greater facilities for administration and discipline.[1]

Much, in fact, remained to be done. Piped water had only been made available in a third of all barracks, and barely a fifth of the hospitals; latrines had replaced cess pits and privies in fewer than half of the former. Finance, as ever, was the chief impediment to progress. Estimates for structural repairs and alterations, which peaked at £726,841 for 1859-60, would fall back to £313,112 by 1864-5. Not for the last time, Gladstone stymied Herbert's ambitions. He insisted that the money raised from the sale of the most insanitary barracks should go to Treasury coffers and not, as Herbert proposed, be applied direct to barrack improvements. Even so, the death rate of the army at home had fallen to 8.86 per thousand by 1865, more or less the rate for the civilian population. Nightingale insisted that Herbert had been 'head and centre' in all this work, that he deserved to 'be remembered chiefly as the first war minister who ever seriously set himself the task of saving life'.[2]

Arguably the greatest challenge facing Herbert as he entered the War Office was the Office itself. He had complained in June 1858 that it 'wants a thorough recasting'. His predecessor, Panmure, had addressed that conundrum 'by the simple process of never attempting to do it'. Herbert was ambivalent about the prospects for himself: 'in certain branches of administration I believe that I can be of use, but I do not disguise from myself the severity of the task nor the probability of my proving unequal to it'.[3] Friends at least were encouraging: Graham thought that 'Under Sidney's mild influence the Duke of Cambridge may be guided into the wisest courses'; Nightingale was emphatic that 'he is the only man who could do it'.[4]

1 Nightingale, *Army Sanitary Administration*, p. 4.
2 Spiers, *Army and Society*, pp. 160-1; Nightingale, *Army Sanitary Administration*, pp. 7, 10-11.
3 Cook, *Nightingale*, I, pp. 380, 387.
4 WSHC 2057/F4/59, JRG to EH, 18 Nov. 1859; BL Add. Mss. 43396, fols. 63-4, FN to EH, 15 June 1859.

Supposedly well-placed observers, such as Malmesbury, were convinced that Herbert's key objective was 'to abolish the place of Commander-in-Chief, and to put the army under the House of Commons [...] Nothing will dissuade him from the plan'. Malmesbury was misinformed: Herbert had opposed a motion proposing as much in June 1858.[1] He was emphatic that the relationship between the Secretary of State and the Commander-in-Chief was perfectly satisfactory; further, that it made no difference that the Duke of Cambridge was of royal blood. But Herbert was also clear that although he was bound to seek professional advice from the Commander-in-Chief, it was 'a constitutional necessity' that he retained 'full power to enforce his own opinion, if he be satisfied that it is the right one'.[2] Happily, he had never found this to be necessary. His approach to questions where it looked like their respective jurisdictions might be pitted against each other was to interpose between officials and seek out the Commander-in-Chief in person.[3]

The wider debate as to how the War Office might better function was part of the remit for the Select Committee on Military Organisation established in 1859.[4] Herbert took the chair when it met for the first time on 18 March. He persuaded Graham to take his place on entering government, but he was sufficiently convinced of the committee's importance that he opted to remain an ordinary member.[5] Over the coming year or so, he attended virtually all of its meetings. His evidence as a witness before the committee, given on 25 May and 1 June 1860, constitutes his fullest and wide-ranging set of reflections on matters military.[6]

Asked by the committee to set out his ideas for reform, Herbert responded with alacrity. The broad outlines had not really changed in nearly a decade. He was wary of further consolidating military

1 Malmesbury, *Memoirs*, II, p. 217, 16 Feb. 1860; Hansard, 1 June 1858, CL, cols. 1348-52.
2 PP 1860 (441), VII, pp. 506, 556-7.
3 PP 1860 (441), VII, p. 559.
4 PP 1860 (441), VII.
5 BL Add. Mss. 79658, fols. 90-3, SH to JRG, 28 June 1859.
6 PP 1860 (441), VII, pp. 503-73.

departments, convinced that the process had already been taken too far. His favourite exemplar was the abolition of the office of Master-General of the Ordnance in 1855, 'which deprived ministers of a source of professional advice'. As he pointed out, his current departmental heads, with one or two exceptions, were civilians.[1] For the future, therefore, he aspired 'to bring the Horse Guards more into the War Office; I think there is a very considerable want of military advice in the War Office'. In an ideal world, reflecting wistfully on his time as Secretary to the Admiralty, when he had Sir George Cockburn (First Sea Lord) to turn to, the Secretary of State for War would also have a professional soldier to assist him in the Commons. Answers to Members on professional and technical questions would carry far more authority if they came from someone who had held high command – as opposed to a minister all too obviously 'crammed' to respond to them.[2]

Herbert developed his themes in more detailed proposals for the reorganisation of the War Office. The Secretary of State should be assisted by the Parliamentary Under-Secretary, two Permanent Secretaries (one of whom should be a military officer), and an Assistant Secretary for military correspondence. The existing office of Inspector-General of Fortifications, a senior officer from the Royal Engineers, should be complemented by creating a new office of Director of Matériel. The latter should be a senior artillery officer who would be responsible for overseeing military factories and stores, chiefly those at Woolwich, Enfield and Waltham Abbey. Another military officer, styled Director of Supplies, should oversee the Commissariat and other non-'warlike' stores. The existing offices of Director-General of the Army Medical Department, Storekeeper-General and Commissary-in-Chief should be retained, and a new Inspector for the Militia and Volunteers added. An Accountant-General, meanwhile, should control finances.[3]

As to how the War Office should function, Herbert remained adamant that the various departments had acted too independently

---

1   PP 1860 (441), VII, pp. 524, 560; Hansard, 1 June 1858, CL, cols. 1348-52.
2   PP 1860 (441), VII, p. 525.
3   PP 1860 (441), VII, pp. 22, 572.

in the past. His own modus operandi since 1859, he explained, had been to convene weekly advisory boards, usually on a Saturday. This was consistent with his credo 'that men cannot co-operate unless they communicate', and that conference was more conducive to better decision making than correspondence. He advocated, therefore, both the extension and formalising of his practice except that, in order to emphasise that the meetings were advisory, they should be designated Councils, not Boards. The Council, he suggested, might comprise the Secretary of State, Commander-in-Chief, the various Secretaries, the Inspector-General of Fortifications, the Director of Matériel, and the Director of Supplies.[1] 'On the whole', concluded the select committee's members in July 1860, Herbert's recommendations were theirs. His scheme had 'the merit of reducing change to the minimum, while it promises an increase of real efficiency'. Barring a few details it was duly adopted.[2]

Assessments of what was actually accomplished have been less than fulsome. Nobody was more scathing than Florence Nightingale. 'No man in my day', she scorned, 'has thrown away so noble a game as Sidney Herbert with all the winning cards in his hands'. She thought the failure to remove 'that worthless profligate' Sir Benjamin Hawes, the Permanent Secretary, 'the most fatal error Sidney Herbert ever committed'.[3] Herbert apparently stood condemned out of his own mouth. He told her in June 1861, that 'The real truth is I do not understand it. I have not the bump of system in me.' This, as the above detail makes clear, was patent nonsense; they were the words of a dying man. Herbert had thought more about systems than most people; his views, by dint of his experience, were treated with considerable deference. But Nightingale had a point in her unspoken premise that War Office reform under Herbert was limited. The standard modern work on the subject doubts that the reformed system 'could have withstood the strains of a major military effort'. Moreover, the

1 PP 1860 (441), VII, pp. 22, 559-60.
2 PP 1860 (441), VII, p. 22; Partridge, *Military Planning*, pp. 59-60.
3 Smith, *Nightingale*, pp. 102-3; *CWFN*, I, pp. 252-4, FN to W. Nightingale, 24 May 1862; BL Add. Mss. 43395, fols. 306-9, memorandum, c. 9 June 1861.

fact that the reforms had emanated from such authoritative sources (besides Herbert, the select committee had included Palmerston, Russell and Graham) made it unlikely that any more would follow in the foreseeable future. The limitations were in part the consequence of Herbert's instincts. The mantra, 'I believe more in good men than in good systems', was one which he clung to more or less throughout his life. In this instance it was reinforced by pragmatism. The real obstructions to more root and branch reform were not the unfortunate Hawes, with whom he had no great issue, but the military lobby in parliament, the Duke of Cambridge, Prince Albert and Queen Victoria. Sir James Graham, who chaired the select committee, was simply admitting reality when he wrote that 'Some great state necessity or some Iron hand can alone break thro' trammels'.[1]

Herbert was never, in any case, allowed the luxury to make administrative reform his top priority. Much time was necessarily taken up with preparing for a real war, one that would, amongst other things, put his army sanitary reforms to the test. This was the Second China, or Opium, War. It had begun, as we have seen, when Chinese authorities arrested the crew of the *Arrow* in 1856. Herbert had condemned the subsequent bombardment of Canton in 1857 but was silent as Anglo-French forces took the city in December (the French sought compensation for the murder of a Catholic missionary) before advancing to Tientsin, just 30 miles south of Peking in May 1858. The July 1858 Treaty of Tientsin required the Chinese to pay £5 million compensation, open 11 new ports to foreign traders, allow entry to Christian missionaries, and accept a permanent ambassador in Peking.[2] Sir James Graham put it well when he told Herbert that 'we want this strange People to trade and not to fight with us; our course is to teach them to fight and not to trade'. Herbert was similarly unconvinced that the war was over. He told the House in February

---

1 BL Add. Mss. 43395, fol. 302, SH to FN, 7 June 1861; Partridge, *Military Planning*, pp. 59-60.
2 David, *Victoria's Wars*, pp. 361-4.

1859 that 'to me it seems a treaty of peace with a casus belli in every clause'.¹

The Chinese duly reneged on the treaty. In June 1859, an attempt to enforce its terms came to grief at the Battle of Taku Forts, 35 miles south-east of Tientsin on the Po Hai River. By the time these details were established in England, Herbert was at the War Office. In a letter of 13 September he begged to inform Palmerston that there was 'very bad news from China and the renewal of the war has come sooner than I expected'.² But he was in no doubt as to the necessary course of action: 'the deplorable mishap at the mouth of the Peiho makes retaliation unavoidable'. This, he confidently assured his audience at a Friendly Society meeting in Salisbury a few days later, would be swiftly accomplished.³

Privately, Herbert was far less bullish. As matters stood, there was a 'poor force' of just 1,300 men at Hong Kong under Major General Sir C.T. van Straubenzee, in Herbert's view 'not a first rate man'. A less than encouraging Straubenzee advised Herbert that 15,000 men would be needed for a successful operation, and that failure 'would be ruin to our prestige and interest in China'.⁴ Herbert had to balance these considerations against the fear, considered shortly, that France might be planning an invasion of Britain. For this reason he did not want to send more men than absolutely necessary to China; he confided to Palmerston his aversion to 'sending even a couple of batteries away from home in the present precarious state of European politics'.⁵ Matters were further complicated when the French made clear their determination to be part of any China expedition. But what exactly was the objective? Outright humiliation of Emperor Hsien Feng might 'upset the whole concern by still further destroying the

---

1   WSHC 2057/F4/59, JRG to EH, 15 June 1859; Hansard, 25 Feb. 1859, CLII, cols. 930-2.
2   HLPP GC/HE/51, SH to Pam, 12 Sept. 1859.
3   *SWJ*, 24 Sept. 1859; WSHC 2057/F8/V/B/192a, SH to Grant, 26 Nov. 1859.
4   HLPP GC/HE/51, SH to Pam, 12 Sept. 1859; TNA WO 33/8, Straubenzee to SH, 9 Oct. 1859.
5   WSHC 2057/F4/61, SH to Pam, 7 Oct. 1859.

prestige of the present dynasty, and so plunging the country into a state of anarchy which would be fatal to our trade, the prosecution of which is the object of all our proceedings'.[1]

Small wonder then, that Palmerston was content to delegate preparations for the expedition to Herbert. Liaising with the India Office and Lord Canning, the Governor-General in Calcutta, he secured the despatch of troops from India to reinforce those in Hong Kong. In tandem with Russell, the Foreign Secretary, he established an understanding with the French. Lieutenant-General Sir James Hope Grant, a Scotsman blessed with diplomatic skills, was identified as a suitable commander.[2] In conveying Grant news of his appointment, and plagued by memories of what had happened in the Crimea, Herbert was at pains to spell out the objectives as well as the potential pitfalls of what lay ahead:

> Our object in going to China is to trade [...] I trust that the reduction of the forts at the mouth of the [Po Hai] river, and if that, though successful as an operation, should fail to bring them to terms an advance up the Peiho to Tientsin, would enable us to dictate a peace to the Chinese Emperor [...] Our object is to get our peace ratified without being obliged to have recourse to an advance on Pekin itself [...] the Chinese capital is so situated that it is, first, from ice, and secondly, from the N.E. monsoon, almost unattackable till the beginning of May, and the great heats of June and July are almost as powerful for its defence [...] Add to this that the Government are most anxious, whether from China or from India, to effect a greater concentration of our troops in England as soon as possible. An early termination of our Chinese 'difficulty' is, therefore, most desirable [...] Our Allies probably have different views. They have no great commercial interests at stake. The good-will of the Chinese, or the stability of the Chinese Empire, is not important to them; but [...] I

---

1   WSHC 2057/F4/61, SH to Pam, 7 Oct. 1859.
2   PP 1861 (423), XIII, p. 333; WSHC 2057/F4/53, Russell to SH, 11, 24 Oct., 21 Nov. 1859; HLPP GC/HE/60, SH to Pam, 24 Dec. 1859. Hope Grant was brother of Sir Francis, the artist who twice painted Herbert.

need scarcely impress on you the necessity of a most open, cordial, and conciliatory bearing towards the commanders of the French forces. Although the two Governments are on perfectly friendly terms, it is impossible to deny that there exists between the two nations a jealous and uneasy feeling.[1]

Palmerston concluded that Herbert's arrangements were 'very good & provide for everything'.[2]

Events did not unfold exactly as Herbert desired. The number of British and Indian troops deployed for the expedition, 'around 14,000 in round numbers', was more, and thus commensurately more expensive, than he considered necessary.[3] They began the process of disembarkation at Beitang, 10 miles north of the Taku forts, on 1 August, later than he wanted. But the subsequent advance proved remarkably successful. The Taku forts were successfully assaulted on 21 August; the river route to Peking laid open. When the Chinese refused to make terms, the Allied commanders felt that they had little option but to use the discretion vested in them (albeit contrary to Herbert's advice) to advance on the capital. Peking was surrendered on 13 October. The one real stain on the operation, even if the French were the principal offenders, was the looting and burning of the Summer Palace. It was an outrage about which, for all his love of the arts, Herbert made no comment. One may doubt whether this was because his wife's share of the booty was a llama presented to her by Grant. Peace treaties, essentially confirming the terms agreed in 1858, were concluded on 24 October.[4]

Several weeks' communication away, Herbert had done his best to support the expedition. Publicly, this consisted chiefly in making brief, but frequent, replies to questions in the Commons. It also fell to him to justify the expense of a venture that was exciting little popular

1 WSHC 2057/F8/V/B/192a, SH to Grant, 26 Nov. 1859; TNA 30/22/25/58, fols. 223-6, SH to Russell, 27 Nov. 1859.
2 WSHC 2057/F4/61, Pam to SH, 27 Dec. 1859.
3 BL Mss. Eur. F699/1/1/1/2/38, SH to Canning, 3 May 1860; Hansard, 7 May 1860, CLVIII, cols. 753-4. French forces numbered 6,500.
4 WSHC 2057/E4/15; David, *Victoria's Wars*, pp. 371-84, 391-9.

interest. In July 1860 he asked the House to sanction expenditure of £3.8 million.¹ Privately, his main concern was to pre-empt the need to find a second Florence Nightingale. He told Grant in June that 'We are building hospital huts here to send out to the Cape; they will leave in August. Their plan is excellent, and you have no healthier place to which you could send your sick for recovery'.² The very day that peace was being concluded, he chivvied the commander in a manner familiar to those who had heard from him during the Crimean campaign:

> One thing has made me rather anxious – namely, the postponement of sending for warm winter clothing, I think for the purpose of ascertaining whether it can be got in China. I trust you may winter south, but if not you will have a fearful climate to contend with. At Bombay a great supply of sheepskin clothing can, I understand, be obtained. No doubt in China the same skins and furs can be got, but can they be got by an enemy? However, I have no doubt you will have thought of all this.³

Herbert's anxieties proved groundless. According to Nightingale, the death rate amongst British forces was only 3 per 100 per year. In stark contrast, some 61 per 100 had perished in the first seven months in Russia. The figures for numbers hospitalised were even more impressive: Nightingale estimated that 'the "constantly sick" in hospital were about the same as at home'.⁴ Herbert took understandable pride in announcing in February 1861 that:

> we have had no failures in the Civil Department of the expedition. It had an excellent Commissariat [...] it had an excellent Medical Staff; and for the first time an attempt has been made to introduce the system of appointing a medical officer for purely preventive and sanitary purposes. I am informed that the greatest success has attended the operations of this system. Not only has there been more attention

1   Hansard, 12 July 1860, CLIX, cols. 1812-20.
2   WSHC 2057/F8/V/B/192u, SH to Grant, 10 June 1860.
3   WSHC 2057/F8/V/B/192ii, SH to Grant, 24 Oct. 1860.
4   Nightingale, *Army Sanitary Administration*, p. 8.

to prevention, at all times better than cure, but it has diffused the same spirit of care among the officers, and certainly the greatest success did attend the operations in a sanitary point of view.[1]

It helped of course that the campaign had been short, that casualties were light, and borne by an expeditionary force that was less than half the size of that despatched to the Crimea. But posterity has rightly endorsed Herbert's verdict: medical arrangements 'were almost beyond reproach'.[2]

Further proof that Herbert and others were satisfied with operational matters in China was the switch of focus to financial considerations.[3] Although forces were being withdrawn from China by November 1860, some were pledged to remain there until the Chinese government had paid a £3 million war indemnity. By April 1861 Herbert was concerned that the point would soon be reached when the cost of the occupation would exceed that of the indemnity.[4] His caveat proved myopic. As early as 1864, British exports to China (mostly, it must be admitted, opium) were worth £100,000. Herbert had therefore offered a more rounded evaluation of the expedition three months before when he reported to Grant that:

> The public here are, I think, very pleased with the way everything has been done in China – firmness, temper, skill, success [...] a first-rate general, a capital staff, an excellent commissariat, and a good medical department are four things the English public are especially pleased to see, and the more so when all are got together.[5]

1 Hansard, 14 Feb. 1861, CLXI, col. 374.
2 Selby, 'The Third China War, 1860' in Bond, *Victorian Military Campaigns*, pp. 82-3. Some historians, such as Selby, see the war of 1856-60 as two conflicts, the 1858 Treaty of Tientsin marking the divide between them.
3 BL Add. Mss. Eur. F699/1/1/1/2/39, SH to Canning, 21 July 1860.
4 TNA 30/22/25/65, fols. 247-53, SH to Russell, 7 Apr. 1861.
5 WSHC 2057/F8/V/B/192ss, SH to Grant, 10 Jan. 1861.

Military historians have concurred in the verdict that the China war was a model of its kind.

Important though the China war was, Herbert could never entirely isolate it from his wider concerns about international affairs. 'I do not myself see how peace is now possible', he had told Gladstone in January 1859, 'Europe is passing from a state of terror to one of wrath, and I suppose we shall have some years of blood and waste and crime, of which, before it is ended, we shall have our share'.[1] He was alluding, in particular, to what became known as the third Anglo-French war scare. Anglo-French relations had plummeted rapidly from their Crimean high. The Orsini affair was partly to blame; events in Italy even more so. War between Austria and Piedmont, the latter backed by France, broke out in April 1859. Herbert regarded French involvement 'under the mask of liberty', as 'a flagitious crime'.[2] It risked upsetting the European power balance, perhaps even foreshadowed the creation of a new Napoleonic empire. Hence his sentiment that 'I shd like the Italians to thrash the Austrians and the Austrians to thrash the French, but I fear it will be altogether the other way'.[3] He was not so very far wrong. Piedmontese and French armies defeated the Austrians at Magenta and Solferino in June; France would annex the provinces of Savoy and Nice in March 1860. The previous November, the French had launched the ironclad, *Gloire*. With its breech-loading rifled cannon, it was the world's most powerful warship. The French were also developing the port of Cherbourg. Of what possible purpose could this be, if not to prepare for an invasion of England?[4]

Herbert's prescription for the nation's security, which he outlined in July 1859, was a building programme concentrated on the fortifications of 'those great ports and arsenals in which we have all our materials of war'. To convince sceptics 'that the Government are not about to ask for the immediate outlay of immense sums without a thorough consideration of the plans to be carried into effect', Herbert

---

1 BL Add. Mss. 44211, fols. 36-8, SH to WEG, 19 Jan. 1859.
2 WSHC 2057/F4/59, JRG to SH, 9 Jan. 1859; BL Add. Mss. 79658, fols. 66-73, SH to JRG, 10 Jan. 1859.
3 BL Add. Mss. 43395, fol. 164, SH to FN, 17 Apr. 1859.
4 Beckett, *Britain's Part-Time Soldiers*, pp. 164-5.

issued instructions for a royal commission 'to consider the Defences of the United Kingdom'.[1] He also, for 'a particular purpose', asked for copies of despatches received at the Foreign Office detailing the rise of Anglophobia in France. That purpose was a lurid memorandum which he laid before the cabinet towards the end of 1859:

> Our insular security as such is lost. No mere preponderance of our fleet in the Channel can insure perfect safety [...] Neither adverse winds nor adverse currents can prevent a fleet putting to sea in a dark night [...] The passage by sea cannot be mined, and has no known terminus [...] we put an undue trust in our first line of defence, which may constantly be evaded, if not broken through, and [...] putting that blind confidence in it, we neglect the second [fortifications] which must resist aggression on our own shores [...] A Bonaparte has seized on the throne of France [...] we have to deal with a man who has himself proclaimed his readiness to make war for an idea. He clearly has no horror of war, nor any scruple in making it.[2]

Somewhat ineluctably, Herbert turned also to the question of manpower. War Office figures told him that the strength of UK regular forces was 57,708 at the start of 1859; France, by comparison, had approximately 400,000 men under arms. Given that the public remained averse to 'a vast war army in time of peace', he pondered, not for the first time, how 'to keep up such a force as can be easily strengthened in the case of an emergency'.[3] One measure, which he pushed through, was the 1859 Reserve Forces Bill. Those who had served between ten and twenty-one years with the regulars were offered incentives, including a £4 bounty, if they agreed to volunteer for a reserve. This was hardly enticing: only 300 of a possible 4,125 had volunteered by 1862; the scheme was scrapped in 1867. Another possibility was to bring home some of the garrisons in Canada, Australia

---

1 WSHC 2057/F4/55, SH to Prince Albert, 21 July 1859; Hansard, 29 July 1859, CLV, cols. 692-700.
2 Bodleian Ms. Eng. Lett. C. 4004, fols. 41-2, SH to Wodehouse, 28 Nov. 1859; Stanmore, II, pp. 211-20.
3 TNA WO 33/8, p. 567; Hansard, 5 Aug. 1859, CLV, cols. 1075-6.

and New Zealand. But this could hardly be effected overnight. It also presumed relative peace in those territories.[1] By default, therefore, Herbert mounted his trusted hobby horse, the militia.

Palmerston had proposed disembodying the militia at the end of the Crimean War, though the policy was only gradually implemented: at the beginning of 1859, some 19,545 militiamen remained embodied.[2] Herbert was in principle committed to further disembodiment, but changes on the international scene, 'necessarily very uncertain [...] retarded in the present instance by the requirements of India, and to the demand upon our regular force caused by the recent unfortunate calamity in China', persuaded him that the timescale must be revised.[3] By the end of March 1860, only days after France gained Nice and Savoy, he was palpably alarmed:

> The last few weeks have seen many rapid changes in the prospects of Europe [...] No one can tell what the next day may bring forth [...] a new point of departure now exists, which make it necessary to be on the watch for any indications of a coming storm [...] We have to deal with a man very uncertain in his conduct, wielding an immense power, and acting on his decision, when it is made, with great rapidity and vigour [...] If we have a rupture with France, there is a risk that we may have to bear the brunt of it alone.

The 'responsibility on myself', he confessed to Palmerston, 'is a heavy one, and I should fail in my duty if I acquiesced now in a proceeding namely, the reduction of our force which though practicable a few weeks ago, seems to me in the present state of affairs so imprudent as not to be justifiable'.[4]

Gladstone, not Palmerston, was the man who needed persuading. The Chancellor of the Exchequer was, in his own way, every bit as formidable as a French ironclad. Elizabeth Herbert,

---

1 Bond, 'Prelude to the Cardwell Reforms', pp. 231-2; Stanmore, II, pp. 217-18, memorandum of Nov. 1859.
2 TNA WO 33/8, p. 568.
3 Hansard, 3 Feb. 1860, CLVI, cols. 530-2.
4 HLPP GC/HE/63, SH to Pam, 27 Mar. 1860.

in puckish mood, captured the dilemma when sending Florence Nightingale the riddle: 'Why is Gladstone like a lobster? Because he is so good, but he disagrees with everybody'.[1] More pointedly, Aberdeen was reported to have said that Herbert and Gladstone 'would never go on together'; and so it seemed.[2] The battle between the two began in November 1859. Herbert provoked the opening salvoes when he informally communicated to Gladstone the essence of his imminent memorandum for cabinet on the necessity for increased defence expenditure. Gladstone sent two unconscionably long replies: the first queried the detail in Herbert's financial projections; the 'second barrel' questioned the fundamental premise that France had evil designs. Herbert was guilty of hyperbole, Gladstone complained, in writing that:

> We have to do with a godless people who look on war as a game open to all without responsibility or sin; and there is a man at the head of them who combines the qualities of a gambler and a fatalist.[3]

'The scheme imputed to France', Gladstone protested, 'is not merely wrong, not merely wild and wicked, it is diabolical'.

Herbert and Gladstone's stand-off over the size of the militia estimates in the early spring of 1860 need to be seen within this context, as a sideshow which was part of a bigger battle. Matters came to a head at the start of April. Teetering on the brink of resignation, Graham (Herbert's chief political sage in his last years) cautioned Herbert against doing anything precipitate.[4] A cabinet meeting on 3 April suggested a compromise: the estimates would not be increased but the process of disembodying the militia should be halted, at least

---

1 Cook, *Nightingale*, I, p. 388.
2 Shannon, *Gladstone. Peel's Inheritor*, p. 413.
3 Morley, *Gladstone*, II, p. 43, SH to WEG, 23 Nov. 1859; Stanmore, II, pp. 221-35, WEG to SH, 27, 28 Nov. 1859.
4 When Graham died, Lady Herbert wrote that 'He was our truest friend and counsellor. Whenever Sidney was ever in any doubt or difficulty, he always said, "I will go and consult Graham."' See Parker, *Graham*, II, pp. 442-3, EH to Mrs Baring, 28 Oct. 1861.

until the autumn. At a meeting with Graham next day, however, Herbert was resolved not to give ground.[1] On 6 April, therefore, averring that he could not make 'bricks without straw', Herbert sent what was effectively a letter of resignation. 'I quite admit', he told Palmerston,

> that I may be in error in the opinion I have formed, but I am thoroughly in earnest in holding it. Holding it, I am asked to propose either what I believe to be an insufficient force, or what I know to be an insufficient Estimate [...] If this be so, and the Cabinet adhere to this decision, I must explicitly say that I cannot do either. I feel that the best and indeed only course I can take under the circumstances I have described is to retire from it at once.[2]

Retreating to Wilton, Herbert received letters simultaneously from Gladstone and Graham, the former urging restraint, the latter endorsing his stand.[3] Palmerston went down to Wilton on 11 April. 'He said my going would relieve him from no difficulty', recounted Herbert, 'because no possible War Minister would take any other course'. But Herbert remained immovable: 'I feel that my own character for truth and straightforwardness are very much at stake'. Palmerston, Herbert told Gladstone, 'must decide the question; I cannot pretend to impose my will or my opinion on the Cabinet, but my own course is clear'.[4] Palmerston did decide – in Herbert's favour. Injecting some welcome perspective into the dispute between his two recalcitrant ministers, he told Gladstone on 12 April that 'We must not part with him for so small a sum. He is by far the best administrator of Army Matters I have ever known'. The sum in question, approaching

---

1   BL Add. Mss. 79658, fols. 105-8, SH to JRG, 1 Apr. 1860, JRG to SH, 2 Apr. 1860; WSHC 2057/F4/59, memorandum of 4 Apr. 1860.
2   HLPP GC/HE/66, SH to Pam, 6 Apr. 1860.
3   Stanmore, II, pp. 252-3, WEG to SH, 10 Apr. 1860; BL Add. Mss. 79658, fols. 109-10, JRG to SH, 10 Apr. 1860.
4   WSHC 2057/F4/61, Pam to SH, 11 Apr. 1860; BL Add. Mss. 79658, fols. 111-12, SH to JRG, 12 Apr. 1860; BL Add. Mss. 44211, fols. 186-91, SH to WEG, 12 Apr. 1860.

£150,000, sufficient to keep the militia embodied for the coming year, was agreed by cabinet on 24 April. For once the Iron Chancellor agreed to bend.[1]

Herbert thus survived to address the question of how the militia might be reformed so as to become a large and efficient body that could be called out in the event of an emergency.[2] In March 1859 the Royal Commission appointed to enquire into the Establishment, Organisation, Government and Direction of the Militia had concluded that there was much to be done.[3] For 1859 the quota for the militia provided for approximately 110,000 men to be enrolled. The nominal roll for the disembodied militia, however, was only 74,899, and of these only 44,340 had turned up for training. There were a staggering 30,557 absentees. Herbert, who euphemistically regarded the royal commission's report as 'a disappointing document', admitted that putting the force in order 'will be a hard nut to crack'.[4]

The Secretary of State's nutcrackers were employed in various ways. Smaller battalions were amalgamated, quartermasters and hospital sergeants appointed, adjutants' pay increased, privates equipped with rifles, and provision made for instructing them in musketry. In February 1860 Herbert introduced a ten shilling a year bonus on top of the existing bounty to those who agreed to re-enlist when their initial five year term was up.[5] A problem which particularly vexed him, since he been instrumental in creating it, was having allowed the army to recruit directly from militia regiments during the Crimean War. The initiative had borne fruit: approximately three-quarters (30,000) of those recruited to the regulars had come from the militia. But the price of achieving this objective had been to deplete the militia both quantitively and qualitatively. If the institution was to be rejuvenated, that policy had to be ended. As Herbert told his cabinet colleague Sir George Grey, 'In the Russian war the emergency justified

1 Southgate, *The Most English Minister*, pp. 474-5; HLPP GC/HE/68, SH to Pam, 13 Apr. 1860; Stanmore, II, p. 266.
2 Stanmore, II, pp. 211-20, memorandum of Nov. 1859.
3 PP 1859 [2533], IX.
4 PGL GRE/B109/10, fol. 23, SH to Grey, 20 July 1859.
5 Beckett, *Britain's Part-Time Soldiers*, p. 155.

the course taken. There was a sudden want of men abroad, no danger of attack at home. Now we want to be strong at home & the militia should be the reserve & not the nursery for the army'.[1] From June 1860, therefore, Herbert prohibited militiamen volunteering for the army directly from their regiments. The same month Herbert steered the Militia (Ballot) Act onto the statute book. This proposed uniting regiments in maritime counties in order to create militia artillery corps, and allowing counties to build accommodation for the permanent staff. Militia quotas for Scotland and Ireland would be raised (that for England had already been raised from 80,000 to 120,000) such that the government would be able to call upon 120,000 men in peacetime and up to 180,000 in the event of war.[2]

The green shoots of recovery, Herbert assured the House in June 1860, were already discernible. Returns down to 1 June indicated that 48,569 men had turned out for training. Anecdotal evidence pointed to a qualitative improvement too. Magistrates were telling him that:

> the men formerly brought before them by the militia sergeants were of a very indifferent class, and in some cases spoke a dialect which was not that of the county in which they were enlisting, while the same gentlemen now say that there is a great difference in the men brought before them, and that they evidently belong to the county, and that in many instances their residences are known and their characters ascertained.[3]

Truth be told, the nut Herbert was trying to crack remained relatively obdurate to his blows. In putting forward his 1860 Bill, he admitted that 'Its purpose is very humble; it attempts but little. It does not essay re-organization'. Despite Herbert's stated aim 'to keep the Militia in a disembodied state, and to give them the confidence and assurance that they shall remain so except in cases of great emergency', the institution simply was not popular.[4] Volunteer rifle corps, as will be seen below,

---

1 PGL GRE/B109/10, fols. 26-7, SH to Grey, 1 Sept. 1859.
2 Hansard, 26 June 1860, CLIX, cols. 1030-45.
3 Hansard, 26 June 1860, CLIX, col. 1037.
4 Hansard, 26 June 1860, CLIX, cols. 1042-5.

were the fad of the moment – and they denuded the militia still further of putative recruits.

Arguments over the militia were not the staple diet of most people's political fare during the first half of 1860. The latest battle in the war to abolish church rates had seen a Bill to that effect pass the Commons in February. 'If the Lords are wise', opined Herbert, 'they will take advantage of this reflux to pass a compromise on very liberal terms; but Lords are not always wiser than other men'.[1] Their Lordships were not; the Bill failed. The conduct of the Upper House proved even more questionable in May. Peers defied the convention that they did not interfere with money Bills when they vetoed Gladstone's proposal to abolish paper duties, a tax long emotive with Radicals as a tax (via newspapers) on knowledge. 'Herbert advised resignation, opposed any other course', a view tempered more by the burdens of office and declining health than the issue per se. From a purely financial point of view, he thought that 'no sane man' would give up a 'permanent revenue' like paper duties. Gladstone, whose sanity was apparently not in doubt, was not to be dissuaded, though he had to wait another year to get his way.[2] Less dogged was Russell, who had made a Reform Bill a pre-condition of his joining the government. Herbert had written a memorandum on the subject in August 1859; Granville read it 'with the same interest as a novel. I like it better than Adam Bede'.[3] Although waxing less lyrical, Herbert approved of Russell's 1860 Reform Bill which provided for a £6 rental qualification in borough and £10 in county seats. 'I think I see daylight for the Reform Bill', he ventured to Graham in April. 'Lord John's sensible and moderate speeches have inspired the hope of passing the Bill without much modification. He is reasonable about it, and sees the hopelessness of passing any but a very cautious and moderate measure'.[4] The more typical response to Reform, though, was indifference; Russell abandoned his initiative in June.

1 BL Add. Mss. 79658, fols. 118-21, SH to JRG, 28 Apr. 1860.
2 Morley, *Gladstone*, II, p. 33.
3 WSHC 2057/F4/53, Granville to SH, 20 Aug. 1859. George Eliot's novel had appeared earlier that year.
4 BL Add. Mss. 79658, fols. 118-21, SH to JRG, 28 Apr. 1860.

Indifference to Reform was largely the consequence of the ongoing war scare. As Tennyson helpfully expressed it in *The War*:

> Let your reforms for a moment go,
> Look to your butts and take good aims.
> Better a rotten borough or so,
> Than a rotten fleet or a city in flames![1]

The Poet Laureate failed to mention, however, that the government's focus was fortifications, not butts. In a draft report of December 1859, the Royal Commission on National Defences had endorsed Herbert's claim that vast expenditure would be required if the nation wanted adequate safeguard. Thus armed, Herbert presented a confidential memorandum to cabinet on 13 December, amplifying what he had said in November:

> Our Navy must be our first and greatest defence but our Navy is not safe while we leave the dockyards, which produce that Navy and maintain it, exposed, in case of war, to constant risk of destruction [...] Without the means of reproducing a fleet we cannot survive a defeat, nor scarcely even a victory [...] Till these Works are completed [...] the public, conscious of the insecurity of the great reproductive establishments on which our Navy depends for its efficiency, and apprehensive of the ambition of our neighbours, will be subject to alarms and excitements which tend to provoke the very evils and dangers which they fear.

The necessary improvements to Portsmouth, Plymouth, Pembroke, Sheerness, Cork and Dover would require an estimated £11.85 million over 4 years.[2]

Cabinet had agreed the principles of Herbert's memorandum by February 1860. Herbert thereafter verified some of its details with the Inspector-General of Fortifications, Sir John Burgoyne.

---

1 Lines 15-18.
2 TNA WO 33/8; Partridge, *Military Planning*, pp. 100-10.

Adopting a familiar tactic, he also encouraged Burgoyne to write an article, popularising the case for the fortifications programme, for the *Westminster Review*.¹ The familiar obstacle, of course, lived in 11 Downing Street. Herbert was immediately assailed with objections from Gladstone, eliciting the riposte that 'I had anticipated all your fractions'. To his wife, Gladstone therefore announced a different tack: 'Herbert's military plans are the grand trouble. I am going to dine early with him'.²

No gastronomic delights would divert Herbert from his course. The argument was, in truth, more one between Gladstone and Palmerston than himself. In such a showdown the Prime Minister made it clear that 'it would be better to lose Mr. Gladstone than to run the risk of losing Portsmouth or Plymouth'.³ The Chancellor would not easily be mollified, notwithstanding the fact that two meetings at the War Office, attended by Palmerston, Herbert and others, concluded that the sums required might be reduced to £8.7 million. Gladstone's fall-back position was that all funds for the fortifications should come directly out of income tax, rather than, as Herbert and Palmerston preferred, from loans.⁴ In anticipation that his caveat would be overruled, Gladstone absented himself from the cabinet meeting of 21 July which resolved to ask parliament to approve the first instalment of £2 million in order that works could begin immediately. It is by no means clear what Gladstone meant by the 'good news' which Herbert conveyed to him that evening.⁵

Herbert spent 22 July with Palmerston and Cornwall Lewis. Between them, they finalised details for the following day's debate over resolutions which became the basis for the Fortification Loan Bill. Palmerston led the debate of 23 July, followed by Herbert who

1 Wrottesley, *Burgoyne*, II, pp. 398-401.
2 BL Add. Mss. 44211, fols. 130-8, WEG to SH, 19, 21 Dec. 1859, SH to WEG, 27 Dec. 1859; Shannon, *Gladstone. Peel's Inheritor*, pp. 401-2.
3 Stanmore, II, pp. 285-6.
4 BL Add. Mss. 44211, fols. 208-11, SH to WEG, 25 May 1860.
5 Partridge, *Military Planning*, pp. 110-11; Morley, *Gladstone*, II, p. 47, n. 2.

boasted that once the building programme was complete, 'nothing less but enormous preparation, attended necessarily with due notice, should be able to produce a force that could make an impression of a permanent nature upon it'.[1] He spoke in similar vein several more times – at considerable length on 2 August – as the Bill made its way through the House.[2] His old friend Newcastle, on an official tour to Canada with the Prince of Wales, wrote on 15 August wondering if the Fortifications Bill 'has been carried & G still in!'[3] Herbert could reply affirmatively: Gladstone had not resigned and the Bill had been carried by 227 votes two days previously.

Herbert could reasonably claim to have won another round in his battle with the Chancellor. The longer verdict of history has tended to judge Gladstone the winner on points.[4] The main charge against Herbert was that he was crying wolf. Gladstone dubbed him 'the captain-general of alarmists'.[5] Cobden elaborated that:

> the English people have gone mad [...] the willing victims of as great a hoax as any in our history [...] I blame those in high places, who, knowing better, (or who ought to know better) still lend themselves to the delusion – It is persons of the high authority of Mr Sidney Herbert, Lord Clarendon & C who give substance to the vague alarms of even rational people.[6]

Herbert, Cobden concluded, was 'hopelessly committed for fortifications & other abominations'.[7]

Extrapolating from this basis, one might suggest that the fortifications now popularly remembered as 'Palmerston's Follies' should also be known as 'Herbert's Asininities'. Nothing in public life moved Herbert more than fears for his country's security. Justifying

---

1 Hansard, 23 July 1860, CLX, cols. 35-43.
2 Hansard, 2 Aug. 1860, CLX, cols. 495-506.
3 NUL Ne C 12562, Newcastle to SH, 15 Aug. 1860.
4 Matthew, *Gladstone*, pp. 111-12.
5 Shannon, *Gladstone. Peel's Inheritor*, p. 413.
6 Howe, *Cobden Letters*, IV, pp. 5-6, Cobden to WEG, 12 Jan. 1860.
7 Howe, *Cobden Letters*, IV, p. 71, Cobden to Bright, 22 June 1860.

the fortifications programme to the House in August 1860, he said that:

> We ought in our foreign relations to show an appreciation of the rights and feelings of other nations, and if all countries were to do the same there would no longer be any danger of war. But, knowing that such conduct upon our part is not in itself an immunity from danger, we must not only comport ourselves in a manner pacific and moderate towards other nations, but we must likewise deprive other nations of the temptation to attack us which is offered by great wealth and concomitant vulnerability.[1]

As Herbert's words implied, Cobden's and Gladstone's idealistic approach to foreign affairs, of an international order guaranteed by free trade, was a dangerous one. Gladstone's memorandum to the cabinet, of 24 May 1860, in which he described the fortifications as 'dangers to liberty', was reasonably dismissed by Palmerston as 'absurd & nonsensical'.[2] Napoleon III did appear to be increasingly inclined to foreign adventures, even if history has demonstrated that he had no blueprint. French public opinion, as the Orsini episode confirmed, could quickly become Anglophobic. And Herbert knew from past experience that Britons were loath to pay for large standing armies, that the country lacked a truly efficient reserve force, and that the voluntary spirit of its citizen soldiery was more effervescent than durable. Fortifications, in more than one sense, might fairly be viewed as more substantial.

The devil lay in the detail. Even if plans for the fortifications programme had progressed at their optimum speed, they would have taken four years to come to fruition. On this basis, it would have made sense for a genuinely opportunist Napoleon III to launch a preemptive strike: the fortifications would have encouraged the very thing which they were intended to deter. In the event, only £1 million had been spent on the programme by July 1862. Parliamentary opposition

---

1 Hansard, 2 Aug. 1860, CLX, col. 503.
2 Shannon, *Gladstone. Peel's Inheritor*, pp. 417-18.

to the project grew. Some portions were only executed by 1880; a few never. From a technical point of view, it has been questioned whether the guns mounted at the various forts would have been sufficient to pierce the armour of an ironclad. Moreover, a large French invasion force could have opted to attempt landings on the relatively lightly defended east coast, in which event the defence of London would have been rendered problematic. As Herbert confessed in July 1859, 'I am afraid it is impossible to attempt to fortify as against an enemy every portion of the whole coast'.[1] He could but plump for what appeared to be the best option and trust to Providence.

Another option, popular with many of Herbert's contemporaries, was the Volunteer Force. Some volunteer corps had existed during the Napoleonic Wars; governments since then had allowed them to fall into desuetude. Critics had objected that, not being subject to the full military code, volunteers were little more than an ill-disciplined rabble. The popular mood of the late 1850s was not so dismissive. Tennyson's *The War*, published in May 1859, with its exhortation to 'Form! form! 'Riflemen form!' caught that mood well.[2] The Volunteer Force which it spawned was remarkable. Herbert, it must be admitted, belonged to the ranks of the sceptical. 'My view', he told Lord Tweeddale,

> is to keep up a fair standing Army, with a disembodied Militia behind it, and an auxiliary force of Volunteers, composed of men who will do the work <u>for the liking of it, and maintain themselves</u>. But the two first, one with a ten year and the other with a five-year engagement, are the really dependable force.[3]

Partly for this reason, Herbert entrusted much of the work which devolved upon the War Office in response to the volunteer movement

---

1 Hansard, 25 July 1859, CLIV, col. 405; Partridge, *Military Defence*, pp. 113-16.
2 Cunningham, *Volunteer Force*, ch. 1; Beckett, *Britain's Part-Time Soldiers*, ch. 6.
3 WSHC 2057/F8/V/B/323, SH to Tweeddale, 24 Feb. 1860.

to his Under-Secretary, de Grey.¹ But this should not detract from the fact that he was quite prepared to take the lead in attempting to fashion the volunteers into something durable and useful.

It was General Peel, Herbert's predecessor at the War Office, who issued the circular of 12 May 1859 authorising Lords Lieutenant to raise volunteer corps under the 1804 Yeomanry and Volunteers Consolidation Act. Corps were required to assemble for drill 24 times a year and could be called out in the event of an expected or actual invasion when they might 'hang with the most telling effect upon the flanks and communication of a hostile army'.² The initial intention, as Herbert had intimated to Tweeddale, was that each rifleman would bear the expense of his uniform, arms and ammunition. It was presumed that corps would in consequence be drawn chiefly from the urban middle class: a sum of £10 was reckoned necessary to cover essential costs. Herbert conceptualised them as 'a class of persons who never enter the regular army or militia, but who from their education and intelligence are eminently qualified to make the very best marksmen'.³ The appeal of the volunteers lay variously in the imagined glamour of becoming a rifleman and the boon of being spared the draconian discipline experienced by regulars. As Herbert said, 'If we had asked the Volunteer Corps to arm and clothe themselves, and pay for their own drill and musket instruction, and done nothing for them in return but put them under military law, the effect would have been discouraging in the extreme'.⁴ Even so, what the government did not foresee was just how popular Peel's circular would prove. Offers from 133 corps had been accepted by the end of 1859. Herbert later reflected that:

> When he first went into office there were about 20 papers a week on this subject on which it was necessary to give a decision, while the number of papers received last week was 620 – the number disposed of 621, and the number of letters written 467. There had never been such an enormous amount of business undertaken for the first time

1   Hansard, 6 Feb. 1860, CLVI, cols. 724-5.
2   WSRO Goodwood Mss. 2/9/1837, fol. 889.
3   Hansard, 13 Aug. 1859, CLV, col. 1424.
4   Hansard, 5 July 1859, CLIV, col. 696.

and conducted with so little complaint as this connected with the Volunteer Department.[1]

Herbert made clear his priority, with respect to this unexpected rush of enthusiasm to become volunteers, in a speech of 5 July 1859.[2] 'We must have some influence over them,' he asserted, 'and unless there is some equity in the dealings between us, we cannot expect them to pay due deference to the military authorities'. The first instalment of that 'equity' had been announced four days earlier when the government promised to supply 25 Enfield rifles per hundred men. In a circular of 13 July, Herbert reminded volunteer corps that provision of those rifles was conditional on their being kept safe, that corps should be liable to periodic inspection, and that they might be deployed anywhere within Britain in the event of being called out. To improve efficiency, instruction would be provided by members of the permanent staff of the militia. Military efficiency might also be facilitated, Herbert insisted, in an attempt to nip the tendency to do so in the bud, if officers were unelected: 'I cannot recognise the principle of the election of their officers by any body possessing, in any sense, a military organisation'.[3]

Even so, Herbert stood accused more than once in 1859 of being backward in his support of volunteer rifles corps. This was unfair. On 14 October, he had issued a circular promising to make short bayonets available, and that 200 live and 60 blank rounds of ammunition per man could be had at cost price.[4] Herbert's difficulty was that he lacked the resources to be able to achieve his stated objective of extending his control over the movement. To de Grey he bewailed the paucity of short carbines available for distribution to volunteer artillerymen. As the cost of the support that he was providing neared £1 million,

1   Hansard, 6 Feb. 1860, CLVI, cols. 724-5.
2   Hansard, 5 July 1859, CLIV, cols. 695-8.
3   WSRO Goodwood Mss. 2/9/1837, fol. 908; Cunningham, *Volunteer Force*, pp. 26, 52.
4   WSRO Goodwood Mss. 2/9/1837, fol. 941; *SWJ*, 22 Oct. 1859.

he confessed that he did 'not know how it is all to be done'.[1] And Herbert's actions in Wiltshire alone proffered sufficient reply to the charge that he was lukewarm. In August 1859 he subscribed £20 to support the Salisbury Rifles, just the ninth corps to be raised in England. He commended its progress at a Friendly Society meeting in September, and was present in the city's Market Square (subscribing a further £10) to witness its first full dress parade in November. The following year he invited the corps, now 70 strong, to Wilton.[2] No surprise was expressed, therefore, when it had been announced, in November 1859, that Herbert was to become the first president of the National Rifle Association. Its key objective was 'the encouragement of Volunteer Rifle Corps'.[3] Sir James Graham judged that Herbert's 'judicious and satisfactory' efforts were encouraging: 'I think that the tree is planted and will take root and spread. I cannot say that we shall be safe under its branches but it may give some cover in the storm'.[4]

The cover was extended during 1860. Some 578 new corps were raised that year; in consequence Herbert had to increase the number of clerks in the War Office from five to fifteen. Herbert's circulars, meanwhile, maintained his drive to impose greater uniformity, and thus efficiency. In January, the government agreed to supply all rifles and appointed an Inspector-General of Volunteers. A circular of 18 February issued what it was hoped would be definitive instructions 'to make each man a thorough and efficient light infantry soldier,' an aspiration towards which further impetus was given by appointing paid adjutants and authorising a battalion structure.[5] Speaking in Warminster, Herbert proclaimed that 'I have never looked upon a labour more as a labour of love than that connected with the organisation of this enormous and powerful armed force which is

1   BL Add. Mss. 43533, fols. 42-5, 56-7, SH to de Grey, 30 Oct., 14 Nov. 1859.
2   *SWJ*, 20 Aug., 24 Sept., 5 Nov. 1859, 2 June 1860.
3   *SWJ*, 19 Nov. 1859.
4   WSHC 2057/F4/59, JRG to SH, 15 Nov. 1859.
5   Beckett, *Britain's Part-Time Soldiers*, p. 168.

growing up, as it were, by enchantment around', now numbering, he estimated, 120,000.[1] To doubters in the Commons he observed that:

> It is singular how the conduct of the Volunteers has disappointed the prophecies that were made about them. It was said that they would never attain any great proficiency, as they would never submit to the drudgery of drill, but I think they have proved their willingness to submit to drill, and to do everything in their power which is calculated to render them effective soldiers. They have fully shown that they are not mere holiday soldiers, but under great disadvantages they have applied themselves steadily to the duties which they have taken upon themselves.[2]

What many presumed would be a matchless spectacle was the review of 21,000 volunteers in Hyde Park on 23 June. Herbert attended with Queen Victoria. He described it as 'one of the greatest and most imposing which has taken place in the Metropolis for years'.[3] But it was topped on 7 August when he accompanied the Queen to witness (as did an estimated 300,000 others) the review of 20,000 volunteers in Edinburgh. Herbert wrote to Elizabeth that:

> Every crag and ruin is covered with people and tents. It is wonderfully beautiful. The number of Highland Volunteers in kilts adds eminently to the nationality of the whole throng, and the others all have sprigs of heather in their caps [...] Every five minutes there passes a band or a battalion, and I run to the window to look at them.[4]

Any notion that Herbert felt that the volunteers had overcome their teething problems, however, can be discounted. He agreed with the Member who, in June 1860, thought 'that we ought not to take the Volunteers into too great account in estimating the force of the

---

1 *SWJ*, 2 June 1860.
2 Hansard, 22 June 1860, CLIX, col. 877.
3 *Morning Advertiser*, 25 June 1860; Hansard, 26 June 1860, CLIX. col. 1041.
4 WSHC 2057/F4/51, SH to EH, 7 Aug. 1860; *SWJ*, 11 Aug. 1860.

country'.[1] Herbert never divested himself of the suspicion that more than a few volunteers regarded their corps as little more than a bourgeois club, that some riflemen were prima donnas. Why otherwise did he issue a circular in March 1860 ordering that the practice of wearing silk sashes over uniforms be discontinued? Another circular, in May, prohibited any volunteer from wearing gold lace and stipulated that only NCOs could wear swords off duty.[2] He agreed with those who greeted news that several volunteer rifle corps had suggested going to Paris to show off their accomplishments that it was an initiative more likely to encourage than to deter an invasion.

Denied their chance to show off in the French capital, the volunteers continued to flourish during the last months of Herbert's life. Some 747 corps containing 161,239 men had been formed by 1861, a figure easily exceeding that for home-based regulars.[3] But they continued to give him irritations. In particular, far too few were coming forward for artillery corps. 'A Volunteer Artillery Corps', Herbert told MPs, 'is not merely an auxiliary; it becomes a substitute for the Royal Artillery, which can be employed better and more effectually in the field'.[4] The problem was that the would-be volunteer saw rifle corps as being more glamorous. Herbert could do nothing about this. But he could, and did, quash the suggestion of November 1860 that working men's corps be allowed to form. He would have taken the same view, he told critics, if it had been proposed to form a corps consisting entirely of peers' sons.[5]

Herbert was right to argue that the volunteers needed early and continuing coordination from above. His opinions were grounded on two previous stints at the War Office, insights gleaned from the country's senior soldiers over many years, and his long service as a different type of volunteer in the Wiltshire yeomanry cavalry. It is difficult, therefore, to dissent from his judgement that the volunteers would have proved of limited military worth had a French invasion

1 Hansard, 22 June 1860, CLIX, col. 877.
2 *SWJ*, 17 Mar., 19 May 1860.
3 Beckett, *Britain's Part-Time Soldiers*, p. 168.
4 Hansard, 5 July 1859, CLIV, cols. 697-8.
5 *SWJ*, 10 Nov. 1860.

taken place during the summer of 1860, the moment when he and others most expected it. Given the luxury of time, he was quite prepared to admit

> that if the training of these volunteers is regulated by a well detailed system which will insure a preliminary preparation before practice is allowed to take place [...] in a few years a most important reserve [...] will be at all times available, and afford a most valuable and permanent addition to our national defences.[1]

His hypothesis was never put to the ultimate test but volunteers would survive in modified form until the Territorial and Reserve Forces Act of 1907.

With hindsight, Elizabeth would pinpoint Herbert's reviewing the volunteers in Edinburgh, in August 1860, as the moment that 'he first began to feel how his health had given way'. Although he had warned Palmerston in April 'that I doubt whether I can get through the session' – Granville judged that he had 'lost ground' – Herbert survived the parliamentary session of 1860 surprisingly well.[2] He spoke on 70 of the 145 days when the Commons was sitting, making the first of his 213 interventions in debate on 26 January, and the last on 17 August. In the four months from April to July, he often worked until two or three in the morning 'with irregular food, and little or no sleep'. This punishing schedule was bound to take its toll eventually. In early August, Elizabeth recorded, he 'spoke of fatigue', even of being 'unable to walk'. Speaker Denison did not need tell Herbert that 'The work of the War Dept in the last session was frightful, laborious, and trying to the last degree'.[3]

---

1   Hansard, 13 Aug. 1859, CLV, col. 1424; Bond, 'Prelude to the Cardwell Reforms', p. 232.
2   HLPP GC/HE/66, SH to Pam, 6 Apr. 1860; Fitzmaurice, *Granville*, II, pp. 385-7, Granville to Canning, 26 July 1860.
3   WSHC 2057/F6/98, 'Account of Sidney Herbert', pp. 5-6; WSHC 2057/F4/54, Denison to SH, 5 Jan. 1861.

In late August, Herbert returned to Scotland, this time with Elizabeth, for what was meant to be a relaxing tour of the Highlands.[1] However, his congenial regime of salmon fishing and hunting also exacted a price. Whilst out deer stalking on 10 September, Herbert caught a cold from 'lying on the damp grass', and was laid low for a week. Elizabeth confided to her 'darling Chickies' that she was 'very anxious and unhappy'.[2] Herbert rallied sufficiently to be able to enjoy three days with his former chief at Haddo House: it was 'a great pleasure for him to see dear Lord Aberdeen in his own home'. They would not meet again; Aberdeen died on 21 December. The journey home was punctuated by a stay with Graham at Netherby in Cumberland, and another at Studley Park near Ripon to confer with de Grey. Reaching London on 29 September, at the end of 'a damp and sunless summer', Elizabeth regretted that they had not gone to Germany 'which used to set him up so marvellously in previous years'.[3]

There followed 'an <u>intensely</u> cold autumn and winter, with deep snow and incessant rain'. October, spent mostly at Wilton, allowed time for shooting but could not disguise the fact that Herbert was 'ailing [...] very quickly tired and occasionally depressed about himself'. In mid-November, therefore, Elizabeth took it upon herself to seek advice. Dr Henry Bence Jones, the distinguished physician, cautioned her against the idea of taking Herbert to winter in Italy or Egypt, but recommended that he leave the Commons. Elizabeth's preference, that her husband quit office as well, he thought likely to do more harm than good.[4] Contrary, and unsolicited, advice came from a familiar quarter. Florence Nightingale, considering Bence Jones 'too chemical' a doctor, assured Elizabeth that Herbert's 'disease is more functional than organic'; a month's break would suffice to restore him.[5]

---

1 *SWJ*, 11, 25 Aug. 1860.
2 BL Add. Mss. 59671, fols. 48-9, EH to her children, 17 Sept. 1860.
3 WSHC 2057/F6/98, 'Account of Sidney Herbert', pp. 6-8; BL Add. Mss. 59671, fols. 48-9, EH to her children, 17 Sept. 1860.
4 WSHC 2057/F6/98, 'Account of Sidney Herbert', pp. 8-10.
5 BL Add. Mss. 43396, fols. 89-96, FN to EH, 5 Dec. 1860; WSHC 2057/F4/68, FN to SH, 8 Dec. 1860, FN to EH, 27 Dec. 1860.

Counselled by Graham, that Herbert's 'life, & happiness, and health, are, in my estimation, worth the whole of the government put together', Elizabeth determined to force the issue.[1] She saw Palmerston on 1 December. By mid-December he had acquiesced in the suggestion that Herbert should go to the Lords.[2] Ironically, Herbert then enjoyed a better month (he 'slept like a top'), travelling several times between Belgrave Square and Wilton. Part of 10 December was spent out hunting with his ten-year-old son, George: 'We had a lovely bright day & a good run'. Three days later, he attended the consecration of the new church of St John in Bemerton, two miles from Wilton.[3] On Christmas Day all mention of his health was prohibited. A reflective Herbert spent part of it with Elizabeth, visiting 'dear Betsey's grave', and talking about his 'mammy', 'and when we came home [he] kissed me long and tenderly'. En famille, the Herberts joined the Ailesburys at Tottenham House for New Year.[4]

Herbert spent the evening of New Year's Day 'with a very heavy heart' composing a farewell address to his constituents. He thanked them for the 'solemn trust' he had enjoyed for nearly three decades. Elizabeth confirmed that it had proved 'a terrible wrench to him'.[5] From a practical point of view, Herbert's objective was 'to make a safe arrangement for the county'.[6] In pursuit of this end, he had denied rumours that he was about to quit the Commons when the Conservative, Lord Ashburton, confronted him about the same at Wilton the week before. Thomas Grove, the man identified by Herbert as his Liberal successor, was not so discreet: 'either he or Grove has told a lie, and I do not think it was Grove,' wrote Lord Bath. Bath was also right that Grove would not garner support from 'moderate persons who have hitherto supported Herbert strongly but they have done this

1 BL Add. Mss. 79658, fols. 124-5, JRG to EH, 11 Dec. 1860.
2 HLPP GC/HE/68, EH to Pam, 2 Dec. 1860.
3 WSHC 2057/F6/98, 'Account of Sidney Herbert', p. 10; BL Add. Mss. 43395, fol. 271, SH to FN, 11 Dec. 1860; *SWJ*, 15 Dec. 1860.
4 WSHC 2057/F6/98, 'Account of Sidney Herbert', p. 11. Betsey was his late sister, Elizabeth, Lady Clanwilliam.
5 HRO 21M57/2A1/5/18, EH to Normanton, 2 Jan. 1861.
6 HLPP GC/HE/76, SH to Pam, 9 Dec. 1860.

to some extent on personal grounds & traditional respect contrary to their own convictions [...] Herbert's pot for the peerage has [...] boiled over'.¹ The Conservatives took the seat unopposed. Blind to the reality of his own popularity, Herbert's usually acute antennae, so far as Wiltshire politics was concerned, had failed him.

The other question for decision over the festive period was Herbert's title. His first preference was for Lord Herbert of Wilton. As a matter of courtesy he wrote to his half-brother, outlining his intention of 'adding some place or property of my own to distinguish the title from his barony'. Robert Pembroke demurred: 'The wicked Earl has very unfairly deprived you of that [name] of Wilton', wrote a bemused Palmerston.² Herbert settled on Lea instead. It was, he explained to the Prime Minister, 'a farm near Malmesbury which I inherited from Lord Fitzwilliam together with my Irish property'. Thus did 'Darling Sid' act 'in compliance with Robert's wishes'.³ Sidney Herbert became Baron Herbert of Lea in the County of Wiltshire on 15 January.

Cornewall Lewis spoke for most Liberals when he told Palmerston that Herbert 'will be a severe loss to the House of Commons'.⁴ Lord Granville simultaneously assured Herbert that 'you will be an immense addition to us [...] you will find our parliamentary work perfect child's play after the Commons'.⁵ Granville was right. Herbert would speak only a handful of times in the Upper House. His maiden speech of 14 February, on the China war, was praised by Derby for its great ability. Herbert, who confessed to Elizabeth that he missed the buzz of the Commons, likened the experience to 'addressing sheeted tombstones by torchlight'.⁶

1   LRO 920 DER/14/164/11a/3, Bath to Derby, 22 Dec. 1860.
2   HLPP GC/HE 81, SH to Pam, 26 Dec. 1860; WSHC 2057/F4/61, Pam to SH, 25 Dec. 1860.
3   HLPP GC/HE 82, SH to Pam, 28 Dec. 1860; HRO 21M57/2A1/5/18, EH to Normanton, 2 Jan. 1861.
4   HLPP GC/LE/138, Cornewall Lewis to Pam, 4 Jan. 1861.
5   WSHC 2057/F4/53, Granville to SH, 4 Jan. 1861.
6   Hansard, 14 Feb. 1861, CLXI, cols. 375-7; WSHC 2057/F6/98, 'Account of Sidney Herbert', p. 12.

The demands on Herbert's health were not so trivial. Throughout January he was 'very poorly' and lost a stone in weight. 'The report is', recorded Lord Stanley, 'that Herbert's health is seriously affected: that he has an incurable, though slow, disease of the kidneys'. Even Nightingale was now persuaded.[1] Herbert was probably suffering from acute or chronic nephritis, an inflammatory disease of the kidneys. Known to contemporaries as Bright's disease (the physician Richard Bright had first described its signs and indicators as recently as 1827), symptoms included the swelling of body tissues caused by a loss of protein in the urine. Since diabetics were more susceptible than most to contracting Bright's disease, Herbert might also have been suffering with what a modern medical practitioner would diagnose as diabetic nephropathy. In face of this worsening picture, the piteous response was to find an airy house out of town. Lady Herbert's thoughts turned first to Wimbledon, then Hampstead. A solicitous Prime Minister put Brocket Hall, his wife's Hertfordshire property, at their disposal.[2] In the end the Herberts accepted Lord Dufferin's offer of his villa in Highgate. Since his son George was in Paris for two months with a tutor, Herbert endeavoured to spend part of each day riding with his daughters, Mary and Maud.[3]

Improvements to Herbert's domestic arrangements notwithstanding, he found the burdens of office 'heavier than ever'.[4] His mailbag during the spring of 1861 included letters from Russell about the possible need to despatch troops to Mexico, perhaps also to Canada. Newcastle, at the Colonial Office was sure about the latter point. He would also write to Herbert about troop and fortification matters in China, Hong Kong, Ceylon and South Africa.[5] Worse, as

1 Vincent, *Stanley Journals*, p. 166, 10 Feb. 1861; *CWFN*, IX, p. 105, FN to Farr, 9 Jan. 1861.
2 BL Add. Mss. 59671, fols. 50-1, 54-5, EH to M. Herbert, 31 Jan., 7 Feb. 1861; WSHC 2057/F4/61, Pam to SH, 5 July 1861.
3 WSHC 2057/F6/98, 'Account of Sidney Herbert', pp. 12-13.
4 HLPP GC/HE 90, SH to Pam, 18 Jan. 1861.
5 Stanmore, II, pp. 427-32; WSHC 2057/F4/61, Pam to SH, 22 May 1861; St Deniol's GG 2969, fols. 53-6, SH to Newcastle, 2 Apr., 14 May 1861.

the deadlines for the estimates and the budget approached, there was the unedifying prospect of renewed hostilities with Gladstone. The Chancellor, who characterised their clash as a 'deadly struggle', noted after cabinet on 25 January that 'Herbert has told me today with a simplicity and absence of egotism, which one could not but remark in his graceful character, the nature of his complaint'.[1] The detail of the complaint, which unfolded over the coming weeks, was that Herbert wanted to increase spending on the militia from £529,129 to £753,875. Gladstone, muttering generally about the 'inflated state of our Establishment', had understood from earlier cabinets that the cost 'was not to be materially varied'.[2] Differences were to some extent resolved when the Gladstones came down to Wilton over Easter for what turned out to be 'a very pleasant visit'. Whether the conversation turned to pennies as the two men rode over to view the Chapter House in Salisbury Cathedral goes unrecorded. It is hard to think that it did not when they joined the local meet on 1 April, Easter Monday.[3]

Through all these travails, Lady Herbert remained unswerving in her self-appointed role as her husband's shield and protector. She asked 'Dearest' Nightingale if 'you could thro' Miss Martineau or any one else, issue a friendly article in the "Daily News". The hostile tone of that paper towards him for this last year has astonished & vexed me'.[4] Diverted temporarily from her task by her father's death on 19 April, Lady Herbert briefly vouchsafed responsibility for Herbert to his sister, Mary Ailesbury. The latter was shocked to discover how far he had deteriorated: Herbert now preferred to sleep in a downstairs study room in Belgrave Square rather than face the ordeal of the stairs.[5] During May, by which time Lady Herbert had returned, Herbert

---

1 Morley, *Gladstone*, II, p. 93.
2 BL Add. Mss. 44211, fols. 267-70, SH to WEG, 11 Mar. 1861; WEG to SH, 13 Mar. 1861.
3 WSHC 2057/F6/98, 'Account of Sidney Herbert', p. 13; Shannon, *Gladstone. Peel's Inheritor*, p. 435.
4 BL Add. Mss. 43396, fols. 103-9, EH to FN, 1, 3, Jan. 1861.
5 WSHC 2057/F6/98, 'Account of Sidney Herbert', p. 14.

appeared a little better. The couple were able to spend a happy Whitsun at Wilton together with their children.[1]

Respite was brief. In order to avoid the strain of regular visits to Wiltshire, most of June was spent at Lord Granville's farm in Golders Green. Herbert confided to Nightingale at the start of the month that:

> I feel that I am not doing justice to the War Office or myself. On days when the morning is spent on a sofa drinking gulps of brandy till I am fit to crawl down to the Office, I am not very energetic when I get there.[2]

Lady Herbert confirmed as much: 'He began now to suffer terribly and constantly from thirst – and used to keep a stone in his mouth to get rid of the excessive dryness and parching'. Yet she still clung to the idea that her husband might remain in government, albeit 'without any office at all'. The unlikelihood of that became all too evident when, having reached Wilton on 29 June tolerably well, Herbert was struck by a 'violent attack of pain and sickness – a kind of pleurisy […] a fixed look in his eyes – also a yellow shade about the face'. Herbert, with a mix of black humour and self-denial, blamed the various medicines Bence Jones had been prescribing him.[3]

Herbert's doctors nevertheless saw no immediate reason to despair of his life. Dr Williams, the family physician, inclined to attribute Herbert's ailments to gout, 'and said that "a good fit of it" might cure him'.[4] Dr Jones was reported to have said that he saw no reason why Herbert should not live for another decade. Both doctors agreed that a period abroad would help. An initial stay of three weeks at Spa was arranged; there were longer term plans to take a house in Nice for the coming winter. Informing Palmerston of his departure, Herbert expressed his 'great faith in the effect of entire rest and absence from worry'. But though he said that he intended being home by mid-

---

1 WSHC 2057/F6/98, 'Account of Sidney Herbert', p. 15.
2 BL Add. Mss. 43395, fol. 302, SH to FN, 7 June 1861.
3 WSHC 2057/F6/98, 'Account of Sidney Herbert', pp. 12-17; HLPP GC/HE 101, EH to Pam, 15 June 1861.
4 WSHC 2057/F6/98, 'Account of Sidney Herbert', p. 17.

August, he sent the Prime Minister an undated letter of resignation – just in case.¹ Palmerston was amongst those to whom he bid adieu on 9 July. Others included Lord Derby, the Duke of Cambridge and Sir James Graham. The latter, himself gravely ill, was 'very much overcome'. En route to London Bridge there was a brief detour to see Florence Nightingale in Mayfair's South Street.²

Early signs that the trip would prove restorative were encouraging. In Brussels, on 12 July, Herbert ate his first hot food in several weeks. Reaching Spa the next day he was well enough to go out riding. On 21 July, his wife's birthday, Herbert surprised her with the gift of a white muslin gown and matching earrings. Her happiness was severely tempered, however, by the fact that Herbert's symptoms had returned with a vengeance four days before. They decided to return home.³ It was a decision which Palmerston had anticipated: 'Those foreign watering places if they do not decidedly agree with People, do harm instead of good'. Dunmore and Ailesbury relations were at Dover to meet them on 28 July.⁴

Now the inescapable truth that Herbert was near death could not be denied, his 'whole heart was set on getting Home'. That meant leaving Belgrave Square, where he had gone from Dover, for Wilton, 'the place he loved best in the world'.⁵ The journey was made on 31 July. Unbeknown to Herbert, the tormented soul that was Gladstone had informed Lady Herbert that 'I shall go and see him from a distance as he quits his threshold'. Asking that she convey his love to her husband, he asked also 'what I know is needless, to forgive me if I have ever torn his tender spirit'. The Chancellor followed their carriage all the

---

1   HLPP GC/HE 95, SH to Pam, 4 July 1861; WSHC 2057/F4/61, SH to Pam, 16 July 1861. Herbert resigned on 21 July.
2   WSHC 2057/F6/98, 'Account of Sidney Herbert', p. 21; BL Add. Mss. 59671, fols. 65-6, EH to M. Herbert, 11 July 1861.
3   WSHC 2057/F6/98, 'Account of Sidney Herbert', pp. 22-6; BL Add. Mss. 59671, fols. 65-6, EH to M. Herbert, 11 July 1861.
4   WSHC 2057/F4/61, Pam to SH, 24 July 1861; BL Add. Mss. 43996, fols. 147-50, Lady Dunmore to FN, 4 Aug. 1861.
5   Parker, *Graham*, II, A'Court Repington to JRG, 3 Aug. 1861.

way to the station.¹ Safely ensconced at Wilton, the evening lesson was from Hebrews. The penultimate verse, it transpired, was: 'And to whom sware he that they should not enter into his rest, but to them that believed not?' Herbert repeated it before turning to Elizabeth and telling her that 'It is such a <u>very</u> good book tonight, my darling'.²

Herbert was taken out next morning, Thursday 1 August, to the Italianate garden fashioned by his mother. That evening he thanked Elizabeth for 'the intense happiness of our married life,' and apologised for the 'heavy burden' she would have to shoulder in 'the bringing up of all our little ones'. This was followed by heart-wrenching goodbyes, in particular to his heir George, 'to whom he spoke gravely and earnestly about his great responsibilities'. Having taken Communion, Herbert passed a relatively peaceful night, waking only to declare that 'I have had a life of great happiness. A short one, perhaps, but an active one. I have not done all I wished – but I have tried to do my best'. Next morning, in less exalted terms, he observed that 'This is a long business [...] It is not an easy operation to die'. Experiencing some pain at 11.15 a.m., Dr Williams administered him some brandy as a palliative. Herbert died a few minutes later. 'I closed his dear eyes', recorded Lady Herbert, 'and he was at Rest'.³

1 WSHC 2057/F4/60, WEG to EH, 31 July 1861.
2 WSHC 2057/F6/98, 'Account of Sidney Herbert', pp. 36-7; Hebrews, chapter 3, verse 18.
3 WSHC 2057/F6/98, 'Account of Sidney Herbert', pp. 39-49; Parker, *Graham*, II, pp. 413-14, A'Court Repington to JRG, 3 Aug. 1861.

Afterwards
El Cid? Relocating Herbert

'You need not fear for him: his fame will take care of itself'.[1] Benjamin Jowett's prediction, made in 1865, as to whether, and how, Herbert would be remembered, rings decidedly hollow today. Consider the fate of the two statues raised in Herbert's memory. The first, which once took pride of place in Salisbury's Market Square, now stands forlorn in a park on the city's outskirts. The second, which stood in front of the War Office, survived fewer than fifty years before being repositioned beside a statue of Florence Nightingale in Waterloo Place. Nightingale remains iconic. Herbert's life, by contrast, is largely forgotten, not least because it has been obscured by the dazzle from a lamp which he, ironically, had helped to light.

Three people in particular had been determined not to leave Herbert to the vagaries of posterity. They almost vied with each other in their grief. Florence Nightingale had cancelled the newspapers to avoid having to read the obituaries. She asked the committee established to decide how to honour Herbert:

> to accept my small contribution to my dear master because all that is mine is his. And I believe he would rather have spread my earnings [...] on other of his objects than on his memorial [...] £30 seems so

---

1   Quinn and Prest, *Nightingale*, p. 49, Jowett to FN, 10 Mar. 1865.

small a sum to give when God has taken away the opportunity of giving my life's work.[1]

William Gladstone, meanwhile, was visited by Robert Phillimore the day after Herbert's death. 'His eyes', Phillimore recalled, 'filled with tears all the time he spoke to me in a broken voice about his departed friend'. Five years later Gladstone confessed that it remained 'difficult to speak of Herbert'.[2] But it was Lady Herbert, 'quite stunned with the sorrow', who proved the most inconsolable. Having taken several locks of her husband's hair as a keepsake, she returned to his body three days after he died to cut off most that remained. 'My Darling's Hair, all safely preserved in paper', can still be seen.[3] In what was tantamount to an undeclared war between Lady Herbert and Nightingale to be the principal torchbearer of Herbert's memory (Gladstone stayed relatively aloof), Lady Herbert just about triumphed in life. But Nightingale quickly prevailed in death. She nevertheless spoke for all three of them when she had written to Herbert in 1857 that 'You have always been our "Cid" – the true chivalrous sort – which is to be the defender of what is weak and ugly and dirty and undefended, rather than of what is beautiful and artistic'.[4]

The first response of others to the news of Herbert's passing was to focus on the virtues of his character. His sister Catherine wrote that 'To the very last he had the same charm, that dear winning smile, that almost playful pretty way of saying everything'. Malmesbury confided to his diary how much he would miss 'the excellence of his disposition and generous character'.[5] Gladstone particularly approved

---

1 *CWFN*, I, pp. 327-8, FN to Lady Verney, 7 Aug. 1861; Wilton House Mss., FN to Strzelecki, 18 Dec. 1861.
2 Morley, *Gladstone*, II, p. 88; Aldous, *The Lion and the Unicorn*, pp. 140-1.
3 Parker, *Graham*, II, pp. 413-14, A'Court Repington to JRG, 3 Aug. 1861.
4 BL Add. Mss. 43394, fols. 190-3, FN to SH, 26 Nov. 1857.
5 BL Add. Mss. 43396, fols. 147-50, Lady Dunmore to FN, 4 Aug. 1861; Malmesbury, *Memoirs*, II, p. 257, 3 Aug. 1861.

of the obituary in *The Times*. It had captured the 'vivacity about his wonderful social powers and charms'. Herbert was:

> unsparing of himself in the discharge of those social observances which men usually bend to the convenience or humour of the moment. With great manliness of character there was curiously intermingled an extraordinary desire to please. He studied and strove to please, and heightened by all the arts of style the natural attractiveness of his character. He had in his favour every social advantage – high birth, a great estate, a happy home, a handsome person, irresistible manners, many accomplishments, a ready address. He made the most of all this so that his good nature seemed to be always overflowing, his frankness to be almost unbounded, and his power of pleasing to be always undivided. So he won upon all comers, and won most upon those who knew him best. Men would give up to Sidney Herbert what they would grant to no one else. He inspired no jealousy; for his superiority was less the result of brilliant parts than from that indefinable charm from which there is no appeal.[1]

The beauty of Herbert's character explains why some chose to frame their tributes in poetic form. Thomas Sotheron Estcourt, Member for North Wiltshire, wrote in his *Lines on the Death of Lord Herbert* of 'The playful Wit: the rich inventive Thought'. In her more crafted *The Lady of La Garaye*, Caroline Norton reflected how:

> all thy life thy single hope and aim
> Was to do good, – not make thyself a name

But it was Lady Herbert's decision to expose her raw emotion to public gaze that most catches the eye:

> *On the Death of Lord Herbert*
> To all this gold and green of Summer's wealth

---

1   WSHC 2057/F4/60, WEG to Charles A'Court, 4 Aug. 1861; *The Times*, 3 Aug. 1861.

Mapping the country; —all this life and health
Of the full west wind o'er the quivering copse
And corn and clover: – these with garden crops
Round humble dwellings, beautified by him: -
    This early harvest-stir in farmsteads trim
Wide sown by him o'er his ancestral land; -
Dead, dead to all he fostered, wrought, or planned,
Within one curtained room apart he lies,
Quench'd the light fountains in those kindly eyes,
Frozen the pressure of that ready hand.
    From all the daily sheavings of high thought
Into the garners of Fulfilment brought;—
From all the glorious pangs of Freedom's birth,
And the fresh instincts throbbing through the earth; —
From all the crowding annals of the years,—
The generous stress and striving of his peers,—
The widening ends for his loved land revealed; —
From all that Time has yet to ask or yield;—
That brave heart, pulseless in the deep earth's breast,
That agile brain, muffled in dreamless rest,
That gifted tongue, must lie, shut in and sealed.
    With all that Brotherhood who learnt to cast
Life's pleasure by ere yet its bloom was past;
And grasp the thorns of a self-spending toil, —
The Patriot's labour on a stubborn soil, —
The Champion's ebbing wound in other's strife, —
The Martyr's smiling holocaust of life; —
With all these great Inheritors, he reaps
His meed of double life, the love and fame
In which a grateful Land enshrines his name;
While his clear spirit bathes Wisdom's deeps,
And up the widening spheres of Goodness sweeps,
And plucks the immortal fruit of each pure aim.[1]

---

1   *SWJ*, 10 Aug., 28 Sept. 1861; Norton, *The Lady of La Garaye*, lines 122-4.

As condolence letters flooded in – Queen Victoria wrote in person – arrangements for the obsequies were put in train.[1] Herbert had delineated the essentials himself: 'there will only be members of the family, and the simplest funeral – a walking one, his own labourers carrying him to his last resting-place in his own church'.[2] Lady Herbert varied them a little. In recognition that they had accompanied the Herberts on their recent trip to Spa, she welcomed Count Strzelecki and Admiral Gawen to join them. Invitations were also despatched to de Grey, Gladstone, Newcastle and Graham. Gravely ill, Graham ignored his medical advisers and 'decided me at once to attend the funeral'. His hope had been that Herbert would take charge of his papers as 'guardian' of his 'posthumous fame'. Graham died on 25 October.[3]

The funeral took place on Friday 9 August. Herbert's body, 'placed in a cedar shell' within a lead coffin, left Wilton House for the final time at 12.30 p.m. Lady Herbert, accompanied by five of her children, led the main party of 58 mourners. They were followed by members of the household. Outside Wilton's main gates they were joined by civic dignitaries, tenants, tradesmen and townspeople. All were respectfully observed by a substantial crowd from contiguous parishes and beyond. Lady Herbert was greatly affected to hear that one artillery soldier had come all the way from Aldershot.[4] Once the service was concluded, the coffin was lowered into the family vault. Relatives and friends then entered 'the narrow house in which he had been laid' to read the simple inscription:

SIDNEY HERBERT
Founder of this Church
Died 2 August, 1861

---

1 WSHC 2057/F4/55, Queen Victoria to EH, 4 Aug. 1861.
2 Parker, *Graham*, II, pp. 413-14, A'Court Repington to JRG, 3 Aug. 1861.
3 Parker, *Graham*, II, pp. 413-14, 442, 458.
4 BL Add. Mss. 43396, fols. 160-1, EH to FN, 18 Aug. 1861; *CWFN*, V, pp. 434-5, WEG to FN, 10 Aug. 1861; *SWG*, 10 Aug. 1861.

Herbert's will, dated 10 July 1858, was proved on 21 November. It appointed his brothers-in-law, Charles A'Court Repington and Viscount de Vesci, as trustees. Wilton Church received £1,000 for its upkeep; Salisbury Infirmary £300. Legacies of £50 or £100 each were bequeathed to seven close relatives and friends. Those who had been in his service for at least a decade were granted an extra year's pay. The entire residue of the estate was left to Lady Herbert. Probate for personal effects was granted for £160,000, approximately £10 million at current prices. The inventory of effects at Wilton included 772 bottles of sherry, 866 bottles of port, over 250 bottles of wine, and 28 hogsheads of strong beer.[1]

Arguably the key sentence in the will was that 'Lady Herbert is appointed Sole Guardian of the persons and estates of his children'. Nothing had been more poignant at Herbert's funeral than the sight of five children, aged between five and twelve, following their father's coffin. Herbert's 'greatest pleasure', his widow affirmed, had been to play the role of doting father. When at home, no matter how busy, 'he would break off from his letters to make a bunny on the wall for his Baby, or to do a drawing for his boys, or go down to their school room at tea time and tell them funny stories'.[2] She exaggerated – Herbert was often an absent and overworked father during the 1850s, and the few letters to his children that survive are mostly in Elizabeth's hand – but he would hardly have been human had he not delighted in his young brood. Something of this was caught by Sir John Young during Herbert's visit to Scotland in July 1860. Young 'never saw such a perfect father as Sidney is to his children, he makes his boy quite his friend'.[3]

The boy was his eldest son, George, on whom Herbert conferred his own childhood sobriquet of 'Boysey'. For his seventh birthday, Herbert sent George a ship, more welcome surely than the autograph of the Duke of Cambridge which accompanied it. Six weeks before he

---

1 WSHC 2057/D5/13; *SWJ*, 30 Nov. 1861.
2 WSHC 2057/F6/98, 'Account of Sidney Herbert', pp. 19-20.
3 WSHC 2057/F6/98, 'Account of Sidney Herbert', p. 6.

died, Herbert responded to George's request for a toy sword to mark his eleventh birthday that he was too old for one. A real sword which had belonged to the 11th Earl of Pembroke served as a more than acceptable substitute.[1] 'Boysey' succeeded as 13th Earl of Pembroke in 1862. He was appointed Under-Secretary for War by Disraeli in 1874, a turn of events whose improbability did not escape the Prime Minister's attention. Sadly, his constitution proved even weaker than his father's; he died without male issue in 1895, aged 44.[2] Herbert's second son, Sidney, thereupon became the 14th Earl. 'Little bright Sid', as his father dubbed him, had previously sat as a Conservative for the family borough of Wilton. Herbert, who had often referred to the toddler as 'the future MP', had delighted in keeping all his summonses for cabinet meetings, 'pretending they were for him'. He would have been less than delighted had he known that Sidney would later serve as secretary to the national memorial fund set up to commemorate Disraeli.[3]

William Reginald, Herbert's third son, was saddled with the less flattering sobriquets of 'Brownie' and 'Sir Reginald Fat Pig'; the redoubtable Gladstone was his godfather. As a sixteen-year-old midshipman, the Hon. Reginald was one of nearly 500 people who drowned when HMS *Captain* capsized in September 1870. Caroline Norton and Cardinal Manning were amongst those who sent letters of condolence to Lady Herbert.[4] Herbert's youngest son, Michael ('Minga'), was the one reckoned to be most like his father. He entered the diplomatic service and was appointed ambassador to Washington in 1903.

Of Herbert's three daughters, Lady Herbert judged that it was his firstborn, Mary ('Molly'), that he loved best. She married Friedrich von Hügel, the modernist theologian. The youngest, Constance

1 WSHC 2057/F4/71, EH to George Herbert, 1 July 1856; BL Add. Mss.59671, fols. 42-3, 46-7, 56-7, EH to George Herbert, 3 July 1859, 18 June 1861; SH to George Herbert, 9 Aug. 1859.
2 Monypenny and Buckle, *Disraeli*, V, p. 296.
3 BL Add. Mss. 44212, fols. 152-3, EH to WEG, 20 June 1868; *The Times*, 27 May 1881.
4 WSHC 2057/F4/52, Manning to SH, 20 Sept. 1870.

Gwladys ('Papa's Duck'), married the 2nd Marquis of Ripon, son of Herbert's former Under-Secretary for War, Earl de Grey. A noted patroness of the arts, she was the dedicatee of her friend Oscar Wilde's play, *A Woman Of No Importance*. Elizabeth Maud, Herbert's other daughter, variously 'his little Softie' and 'little fat Maudie', overcame family opposition to marry a relatively impecunious composer of few prospects named Hubert Parry.[1] In an attempt to prevent the match, Lady Herbert had sent Maud a nineteen page letter detailing her objections, not least of which was that Maud would never had dared to contemplate it were her father still alive.[2]

Herbert had made it clear that he wanted his wife and children to spend as much time as possible at Wilton after his death. This was subject, of course, to the 12th Earl's continued munificence. There was a belief amongst Herbert's sisters that it would end with their brother's demise. It may be speculation to this effect to which Herbert was referring in a letter exhorting them to abandon 'low' thoughts and that 'poor Robert' 'meant to do what was nice and right'. The truth or otherwise of the Earl's intentions was anyway rendered irrelevant when he died on 25 April 1862.[3] Robert Pembroke was buried in *Père Lachaise* cemetery in Paris. Maligned beyond the grave, Nightingale complained that 'The old scamp left £100,000 to that woman [his mistress Marie Schöeffer] at Paris', adding preposterously that Lady Herbert would be left with hardly a farthing to pay her debts, and that 'It is not quite certain yet whether Wilton falls into chancery'.[4]

Family problems did arise, but they sprang from another source of which Herbert was well aware: his wife's religiosity. Ostensibly for the benefit of their health, Lady Herbert took the children to Rome with her in November 1861. Her choice of destination rang alarm bells. It was only because she was afraid of how Herbert's family would react to her doing so, that she had not converted to Catholicism in

1 BL Add. Mss. 59671, fols. 11-12, 44-5, Lady M. Herbert to SH, nd, EH to Lady E. Herbert, 29 July 1859.
2 'The Prince and the Composer', broadcast on BBC 4, 18 Nov. 2018.
3 WSHC 2057/F6/98, 'Account of Sidney Herbert', pp. 41, 45; *The Times*, 26 April 1862.
4 *CWFN*, I, pp. 252-4, FN to W. Nightingale, 24 May 1862.

the wake of his death. Rumours that she would convert were public gossip by 1863. So too, that doing so would lead to her children being taken from her (or at least made wards of Chancery) at the instigation of Herbert's sisters, their husbands, and perhaps also Gladstone.[1] Agonising more or less alone (though the unfortunate Gladstone was reported to be adding and abetting her in her spiritual journey!), Lady Herbert was finally received into the Catholic Faith on 5 January 1865. Anxieties that George, 13th Earl, 'was not of a character to withstand the influence of his mother', however, were not realised. An uneasy entente between all parties seems to have been established by the time he was of age and established at Wilton by the early 1870s. In later years, however, Lady Herbert's life was increasingly diverted by Catholic causes beyond Wiltshire. It spoke volumes that following her death in 1911 she chose to be laid to rest in the cemetery of St John's Seminary at Mill Hill in north-west London.[2]

Half a century earlier, Lady Herbert's thoughts had been turning to the question of memorials to her husband. She had been hesitant when, within days of his funeral, word reached her that 'the troops want a [...] subscription among themselves to give him a statue'. With more than a smattering of social snobbery she told Nightingale that 'I would that it could be taken up in the right way & by the right people'.[3] One of the latter was Thomas Sotheron Estcourt, Member for North Wiltshire and briefly Home Secretary in Derby's second ministry. Herbert's first memory of Estcourt, ten years his senior, was watching him ride about the countryside when he was still a boy living at Chilmark. Wiltshire politics had brought them amicably together on numerous occasions since.[4] Now, chairing a meeting in Salisbury on 24 September 1861 to discuss a memorial to his late friend, Estcourt reported that a consensus existed in favour of a statue. After some

---

1 *SWJ*, 14 Mar. 1863; Vincent, *StanleyJournals*, p. 230, 22 Mar. 1865; Herbert, *How I came Home*, pp. 10-16.
2 *ODNB*; Herbert, *How I came Home*, pp. 10-28; Quinn and Prest, *Nightingale*, p. 77, Jowett to FN, 22 Nov. 1865; *SWJ*, 8 July 1871.
3 BL Add. Mss. 43396, fols. 160-1, EH to FN, 18 Aug. 1861.
4 *SWJ*, 2 June 1860.

discussion, it was also agreed that it should be accompanied by a living memorial in the form of a convalescent hospital.[1]

Inspired by an account of the Salisbury meeting, an article appeared in *All the Year Round* calling for a national memorial. It was presumed to have been written by the magazine's editor, Charles Dickens.[2] Dickens confessed that his contribution had been limited to asking Henry Morley to 'write a few kind words in favour of the project and in recognition of the merits of the deceased'.[3] It was the exotic Count Paul Strzelecki who assumed responsibility for coordinating the initiative which followed. A Polish-born geologist and explorer who had been naturalised as a British subject in 1845, Strzelecki became known to Herbert through his relief efforts during the Irish famine and their shared interest in emigration.[4] Well over a hundred nobles and gentlemen now responded to Strzelecki's invitation to attend a meeting in Willis's Rooms on 28 November to launch the campaign for a Herbert memorial. The Duke of Cambridge took the chair. Speeches were delivered by Palmerston, General Peel, Sir John Burgoyne, Earl de Grey, Newcastle, Gladstone and Samuel Wilberforce, Bishop of Oxford. Resolutions were agreed that a statue be erected and endowments created to provide exhibitions and gold medals for the Army Medical School at Chatham. Gladstone was appointed chairman of an executive committee of sixteen to take the projects forward.[5]

Whilst the Salisbury and London meetings were clear about who they were memorialising, there was some ambiguity as to what should be commemorated. Obituaries had seized variously on Herbert's support for female emigration, his contribution to the success of the recent China war, his work coordinating the volunteers, and his championing of the Armstrong gun, a rifled breech-loading

1 *SWJ*, 28 Sept. 1861.
2 BL Add. Mss. 44212, fols. 91-2, EH to WEG, 24 Oct. 1861; *SWJ*, 26 Oct. 1861.
3 Story, *The Letters of Charles Dickens*, IX, p. 470, Dickens to Morley, 5 Oct. 1861.
4 *Dictionary of Australian Biography*.
5 *The Times*, 29 Nov. 1861.

artillery piece. Lady Herbert's poetic tribute emphasised his interest in model farms and labourers' cottages. Bishop Wilberforce esoterically singled out Herbert's establishing an institution for scrofulous children at Mudeford near Christchurch. The thorniest topic, inevitably, was the part played by Herbert during the Crimean War. One letter to Sotheron Estcourt, which remained private, expressing disgust that Salisbury would afford space for a statue to a man 'for starving the soldiers and sailors in the Crimean War', reminds us that feelings among some were still raw on the subject.[1] *The Times* dealt with the question by dismissing it as 'an old story which need not now be revived'.[2] Morley's article for Dickens confronted it head on, conceding that Herbert 'saw and was partly blamed for the breakdown of systems that had been commended to him by the Tapers and the Tadpoles'. But Herbert had more than compensated for it, Morley continued, by his later work: 'he did in his time more than any war minister who ever lived, in any age or country, to deprive war of its worst horrors, and to reduce its sacrifice of human life'.[3] The detailed case for the latter, however, had to wait until Gladstone's speech at Willis's Rooms on 28 November. His supposed killer fact was that Herbert had halved death rates in the army. But Gladstone had only been able to make his argument on the basis of information supplied to him by Nightingale. In doing so, in a remarkable act of self-effacement, she had virtually excised herself from playing any part in the enterprise. It is remarkable indeed, just how far her name is absent from these early appraisals of Herbert's accomplishments. Palmerston, Hampshire neighbour of the Nightingales and self-styled 'hereditary friend' of the Herberts, felt it incumbent upon him at the London meeting to point out that Herbert had not laboured alone. But it was Sir John Burgoyne, speaking after him, who reflected the general mood in Willis's Rooms when he said that 'it appeared to him that Lord Herbert's hobby was to promote the soldier's comfort, and that his pet was Miss Nightingale'.[4] The wider

1   Gloucestershire Record Office D1571/X199.
2   *The Times*, 3 Aug. 1861. Taper and Tadpole were malicious political hacks, fictional creations of Disraeli in *Coningsby* (1844).
3   *SWJ*, 26 Oct. 1861.
4   *SWJ*, 30 Nov. 1861.

question of how the two statues of Herbert would commemorate him for the moment went unresolved.

Various other initiatives to mark Herbert's passing were taken before either statue was ready. The most newsworthy was Queen Victoria's agreeing that the new hospital under construction on Woolwich Common should be named in Herbert's memory. 'The Herbert Hospital', reported an approving Nightingale in 1863, 'is the model for a military hospital'. She was right. When it opened in November 1865 it was the first large scale hospital in England to have been built in the pavilion style, that is to say one which allowed more daylight and fresh air by connecting wards to a central corridor.[1] Nightingale's crib notes for Gladstone, meanwhile, had been published in 1862 as a brief literary memorial under the less than snappy title of *Army Sanitary Administration And Its Reform Under the Late Lord Herbert*. In September that year, a stained glass window in Herbert's memory paid for by parishioners, was dedicated in Wilton Church. By May 1863 it had been dwarfed by T.H. Wyatt's carving of Herbert in Carrara marble.[2]

A few weeks later, on 29 June, a crowd of at least 5,000 gathered to watch the unveiling of Herbert's statue in Salisbury's Market Square. Palmerston had agreed to be guest of honour but, debilitated by gout, was unable to attend. His place was taken by Earl de Grey. In an informed address, de Grey ranged beyond Herbert's work for the cause of army sanitary reform to include his unseen work at the War Office. Appropriately enough, the band of the Wiltshire Rifle Volunteers played the national anthem as he unveiled the eight-and-a-half foot bronze of his former chief on its ten-foot pedestal of Cornish granite.[3] The statue, by Carlo Marochetti, an Italian-born French citizen who had settled in England in 1848, was much admired.[4] Lady Herbert had facilitated his task by entrusting to him her late

1   *SWJ*, 14 Sept. 1861; *CWFN*, IX, p. 269, FN to Farr, 22 Dec. 1863; Bostridge, *Nightingale*, pp. 336-7.
2   *The Times*, 18 Sept. 1862; *SWJ*, 30 May 1863.
3   WSHC 2057/F4/62, Pam to EH, 15, 30 June 1863; *SWJ*, 4 July 1863.
4   Marochetti is best known today for his equestrian bronze of Richard I outside Westminster Palace.

husband's coat, tie, boots and waistcoat. Standing with his left arm on his hip as he was apt to do when making a speech, Herbert's right hand showed him holding a copy of the plans for what became the Herbert Hospital. In truth, though it cost £2,021, 18s 10d, the statue was far from the sculptor's best work. A further £5,838 17s 1d was needed for the Herbert Convalescent Home which opened in Bournemouth in 1867.[1]

Gladstone, boasting 'an interest in the memory of Sidney Herbert', made an impromptu speech bedside Marochetti's statue when visiting Salisbury in September 1866.[2] Funds for the London memorials, the committee for which he was chairing, had been readily forthcoming. Some £5,121 16s 3d was raised, easily enough to cover the £2,969 11s 7d needed for a statue and the £1,280 set aside to provide for the first medals and exhibitions at the Army Medical School. Deciding where to locate the statue and what to put on it were more taxing questions. First thoughts inclined to an indoor location. Nightingale 'earnestly recommended' that the statue be placed in Westminster Abbey: 'He deserves a place there', she told Lady Herbert, 'for he is the initiator of a new era, that of taking the human side of the policy as regards the soldier, looking upon him as a man and not as a machine'.[3] When it was clear that the Abbey was not an option, she fell into line with Lady Herbert's preference for a marble monument in the lobby of the House of Commons. Lady Herbert found herself rebuffed, however, by Speaker Denison who informed her that majority opinion favoured a bronze memorial in Westminster Hall.[4] All suggestions then fell prey to the caveats of the Fine Arts Committee, eliciting Nightingale's priceless comment that it 'ought to be called the No Arts Committee'. It was eventually decided to place the statue in front of the War Office at Cumberland House in Pall Mall. Gladstone's committee conceded that although it was not

---

1 *SWJ*, 4 July 1863, 15 Oct. 1867; *Illustrated London News*, 1 Aug. 1863. The hospital is currently part of Dorset NHS Trust.
2 *The Times*, 8 Sept. 1866.
3 WSHC 2057/F4/65, FN to EH, nd.
4 NUL Denison Mss. Os C 330, EH to Denison, 3 June 1862.

the most prominent of locations, it was the least worst.[1] Nightingale, disheartened by the work of Herbert's successors at the War Office, did not agree: 'The sticking up a man's statue in the courtyard and destroying his work within, is an organised hypocrisy which Jesuits might envy'.[2]

John Henry Foley's nine-foot statue of Herbert was finally placed in position in June 1867. Watched by a crowd more socially exclusive than numerous, Gladstone invited the Duke of Cambridge to unveil it. Herbert, dressed in peer's robes, was cast with his head slightly forward, resting pensively on his right hand ('He was often seen unconsciously to put himself in this posture when absorbed in deep thought' affirmed the *Illustrated London News*), his left arm clutching papers.[3] Critical reaction was less than enthusiastic. 'Into the artistic merits of the monument we will not enter', ventured the *Morning Post*. 'We are not remarkable in this country for the general success of our attempts at the decoration of our towns, or the perpetuation of the memories of our great men'. In the columns of the *Pall Mall Gazette* 'An Englishman' was even more forthright:

> it conveys no impression of either confidence or power. Its attitude and mien are dejected and desponding; they denote rather a philanthropist weeping over the horrors of war – baffled administrator sinking under a task which has overpowered him – than a daring and successful servant of the public prepared to meet energetically whatever difficulties and dangers the enemies of England may have in store for her.[4]

The debate extended to the grey and red granite pedestal on which the statue stood. Three of its sides (the fourth, backing onto the War Office, was left blank) were decorated with bas-relief tablets in bronze.

1 *CWFN*, VII, p. 774, FN to H. Verney, 26 June 1862; St Deniol's 78/4/8, copy of the executive committee's report, July 1867.
2 *CWFN*, IX, pp. 642-3, FN to McNeill, 8 Feb. 1870.
3 *Illustrated London News*, 8 June 1867. Foley is best remembered now for his work on the Albert Memorial.
4 *Morning Post*, 3 June 1867; *Pall Mall Gazette*, 21 June 1867.

The front panel portrayed Nightingale visiting the Herbert Hospital; the east side depicted volunteer rifle corps; the west side, the forging of an Armstrong gun at Woolwich Foundry. Cambridge judged the panels to encapsulate perfectly Herbert's three greatest contributions to public life.[1] To this the *Pall Mall Gazette's* correspondent re-joined that the volunteers had 'little to do with real war' and that the Armstrong gun was both costly and unproven. As for the front panel:

> It represents the interior of a hospital crowded with mutilated and sick soldiers, to whose sufferings a couple of female nurses are ministering. A dentist does not unnecessarily exhibit poor wretches writhing under his key; neither does a surgeon unwisely obtrude on public view his saws and scalpels.[2]

The *Gazette's* complainant, it must be admitted, was more entertaining than typical: a large part of his objection was that 'the bas-reliefs' were 'unsuited to the *genius loci*'. But his letter does illustrate the point that Herbert was no longer being remembered primarily as a paragon of virtue who had sacrificed himself for his country. Focus was shifting more to what he had achieved. In the area of army sanitary reform far greater credit was now rightly being afforded to Nightingale. More generally, judgements were becoming more nuanced than they had been in the immediate aftermath of Herbert's death. Harriet Martineau's 1869 essay on Herbert, for example, though largely sympathetic, concluded of his work with Newcastle during the Crimean War that:

> They were morally strong; and altogether devoted; but they had not intellectual vigour or force of will sufficient to create an adequate organisation in the presence of events, or to bear down the opposition of aristocratic conceits and selfishness.

More damning still was her verdict on Herbert's final stint in office:

---

1 *The Times*, 3 June 1867.
2 *Pall Mall Gazette*, 21 June 1867.

He had not strength of will to carry through his own projects; and yet worse, he was incessantly impelled, by his ardent, generous, sanguine spirit, to pledge himself for more than he was sure of accomplishing, and to assume responsibilities belonging to others whom he could not control.[1]

Martineau's sketch of Herbert proved to be the longest biographical study for a generation. There were, however, two thinly disguised portrayals of Herbert in literature. His first appearance was as Sidney Wilton in *Endymion*, Disraeli's novel of politics and romance, published in November 1880.[2] As the politician Herbert loathed most and longest, Disraeli might reasonably have used the novel as a vehicle to exact some revenge: he had made himself conspicuous as the only political luminary who had had nothing to do with the London statue. Instead Sidney Wilton is described as being:

> in the perfection of middle life, and looked young for his years. He was tall and pensive, and naturally sentimental, though a long political career, for he had entered the House of Commons for the family borough the instant he was of age, had brought to this susceptibility a salutary hardness.[3]

By the end of the novel, Wilton has become Prime Minister. Small wonder that when he read it, George Russell (Lord John's nephew) characterised Wilton's as 'a sympathetic and admiring portrait'.[4] One can only surmise that Disraeli's generosity stemmed from his regard for Herbert's two eldest sons.

Herbert, incarnated as Percy Dacier in George Meredith's 1885 *Diana of the Crossways*, fared less well. Meredith was a close friend of Caroline Norton; the novel, through the character of Diana Warwick, an obvious catalogue of her many travails. She encounters Dacier, a rising star in the political firmament, whose 'build of limbs were those

---

1 Martineau, *Biographical Sketches*, pp. 323, 326.
2 Blake, *Disraeli*, pp. 732-9.
3 Disraeli, *Endymion*, p. 204.
4 BL Add. Mss. 49270, fols. 183-4, Russell to Stanmore, 13 Dec. 1906.

of the finely-bred English; he had the English taste for sports, games, manly diversions'. He had a taste for Diana too. Dacier implores her to elope with him, but ends the relationship when he discovers that she has sold the press his secret that Peel is about to jettison the Corn Laws.[1] Bowing to protests, not from the Herberts but Lord Dufferin (Mrs Norton's nephew), Meredith agreed to insert the disclaimer that the novel 'is intended to be read as fiction'.[2] Curiously, the 13th Earl of Pembroke, who read it on publication, made no connection between Dacier and his father, and revealed only scant knowledge of the real Diana. 'Mrs Norton', he wrote to his mother, 'seems as far as I can gather to have been a very free spoken lady at all times [...] Diana is Mrs Norton & the story is that of the unlucky revelation of the Repeal of the Corn laws to Delane – I wonder where Meredith got the story from'.[3]

Meredith's resurrecting the lurid tale of confidences betrayed was presumably one reason why Lady Augusta Gregory included a colourful version of the story in the 1894 life of her husband, Sir William. Dufferin dusted down his cudgels, fulminated that it 'ought never to have been published', and secured Lady Herbert's blessing in his determination to rebut the innuendoes.[4] Dufferin's star witness was Henry Reeve, who had written for *The Times* during the 1840s. Reeve swore that Gregory's version of events was 'absolutely false in every particular', and confirmed that the source of the leak had been Lord Aberdeen.[5] Fearful of libel suits, Lady Gregory replaced the offending passage with a paragraph in the second printing: 'various discrepancies have been pointed out to me in the story connecting Sidney Herbert with the disclosure of the secret of the Repeal of the Corn Laws. I have, therefore, thought it best to withdraw it altogether'.[6]

---

1 Meredith, *Diana of the Crossways*, especially chapters 31-4 and pp. 170, 442.
2 Dufferin was Governor-General of India at the time.
3 WSHC 2057/F4/71, Pembroke to EH, 22 Feb. 1885.
4 WSHC 2057/F4/52, Dufferin to EH, 8, 13 Nov. 1894.
5 *St James's Gazette*, 12 Dec. 1895.
6 Gregory, *Sir William Gregory*, p. 86; Stanmore, I, pp. 61-3.

Herbert's reputation in learned circles was anyway safely intact. John Andrew Hamilton (later Viscount Sumner), an eminent lawyer and judge, who penned the 1891 article on Herbert for the *Dictionary of National Biography*, drew neither on popular literature nor doubtful autobiography. His sources included Martineau's essay, Herbert's obituary from *The Times*, and more recently published works such as Morley's life of Richard Cobden and Ashley's biography of Lord Palmerston. More narrative than analytical, Hamilton was adamant that only death blocked Herbert's path to the premiership.

By now though, Lady Herbert was set upon seeing a full scale biography of her husband in print before she died. Wary that it might be considered premature, she had first mooted the project to Gladstone in 1875. On the grounds that Herbert was not a 'polemical' subject, Gladstone was encouraging. But he declined the suggestion that he might write it, being 'very doubtful whether I possess the fund of monumental energy it would require'.[1] Fourteen years and two Gladstone premierships later, she approached him again, this time for help in trying to persuade his erstwhile assistant private secretary, John Arthur Godley (later Lord Kilbracken), to take on the task.[2] When Godley, happily ensconced at the India Office declined, their attentions turned instead to Lord Stanmore, soon to return home from his posting as Governor of Ceylon. Gladstone, who had read Stanmore's history of New Zealand, enthused that his 'literary faculty cannot be denied'. Stanmore accepted the commission.[3]

Stanmore's first biographical priority, however, was a life of his father, Lord Aberdeen. It was the summer of 1894 before he completed his first draft on Herbert. He then felt 'so disgusted with its general feebleness and inadequacy that, with the exception of a few chapters, I destroyed it entirely'. Stanmore nevertheless reassured Lady Herbert that he expected to complete his labours by the end of 1895; she was presumably nonplussed when he repeated his promise in revised form in 1896. More in hope than expectation, Lady Herbert asked for

1   WSHC 2057/F4/60, WEG to EH, 2 Dec. 1875.
2   WSHC 2057/F4/60, WEG to EH, 13 Sept. 1889.
3   WSHC 2057/F4/60, WEG to EH, 13 Sept. 1889; BL Add. Mss. 44212, fols. 189-90, 193, EH to WEG, 15 Sept., 14 Oct. 1889.

an update on his progress as the century turned. Admitting that he 'should never have undertaken the task', Stanmore remained adamant that he wanted to complete it.[1]

Although Stanmore pleaded guilty to being a perfectionist, his torpor was chiefly the consequence of being unable to access letters and papers essential to his research. Such lacunae, he observed with wry humour, could only lead to a book that would be 'what is technically called "thin."' Gladstone, for example, despite his promise to place correspondence at Stanmore's disposal, had 'much procrastinated'. His death, in 1898, raised new obstacles: permission to cite from his archive now rested with John Morley, engrossed in writing the Grand Old Man's biography. It might not be 'easy to obtain'.[2] In the event, Morley was accommodating. This compensated, to some extent, for communications from Lord Pembroke in which apologies were offered for his father's propensity to illegible scrawl, and the fact that his papers at Wilton were 'in great confusion'.[3]

By far the biggest obstacle blocking Stanmore's biographical path, though, was Florence Nightingale. He bemoaned the prospect that if forced to rely only on official sources, 'dull as ditchwater', for the chapters on the Crimea and after, 'the book becomes, not a book, but a fragment'.[4] The reasons for Nightingale's reluctance to assist Stanmore in his Herbert biography – for more than a decade – were various. Partly she objected on principle: 'the publishing of all private letters not only is a treachery and a theft but a treachery and a theft which recoils upon the head of the very memory, so sacred, which they are meant to exalt'. She had even 'steadily refused' Lady Herbert's entreaties during the 1860s to let her see any letters that she had received from Herbert.[5] But Nightingale obfuscated further

---

1 WSHC 2057/F4/52, Stanmore to EH, 7 Aug. 1895, 22 July 1896, 14 Nov. 1901.
2 WSHC 2057/F4/52, Stanmore to EH, 7 Aug. 1895, 7 Nov. 1899, 23 Aug. 1902, 17 Mar. 1904.
3 WSHC 2057/F4/71, Pembroke to EH, 22 Feb. 1885; WSHC 2057/F4/52, Stanmore to EH, 22 July 1896, 12 Oct. 1900.
4 WSHC 2057/F4/52, Stanmore to EH, 12 Oct. 1900.
5 *CWFN*, I, p. 191, FN to her mother, 25 Apr. 1868.

with Stanmore. She claimed in 1890 that the letters she had received from Herbert during the Crimean War were 'not on very important business, and not such as she cared to preserve'. For the years after the war, Nightingale pleaded that Stanmore was asking for something which did not exist, that 'letters do not pass between those who see each other day after day'. This was patently untrue: she had told Dr McNeill in 1861 that 'I have hundreds of Sidney Herbert's letters'.[1] A joint approach from Stanmore and Lady Herbert in 1896 nevertheless proved equally sterile. By now, Nightingale's intransigence was increased (she took legal opinion on the issue) by the knowledge that Lady Herbert was allowing Stanmore to cite letters which she (Nightingale) had sent to Herbert. In 1900, working on the basis that there would be a quid pro quo, Lady Herbert gave the offending letters to Nightingale. But, as Stanmore recalled, there was not.[2] Towards the end of 1901, he approached Nightingale again, risking the suggestion that she might be in 'some degree mistaken' in her view that she held nothing from Herbert of any value. Privately, he believed that Nightingale was deliberately holding back evidence of 'how thoroughly they worked together', and that she was determined to have first use of the correspondence for her own biography. Complaining that Nightingale was being 'singularly ungracious', he persuaded Lady Herbert to see her in person. The meeting 'somewhat moved her'. Stanmore was able to relay the 'excellent news' at the close of 1901 that the impasse appeared to have been broken.[3]

John Murray finally received Stanmore's completed manuscript in May 1905. It was published in two volumes, in January and December 1906, priced 24 shillings for the pair. The 14th Earl had 'nothing but praise' for them.[4] Critics were less generous. Easily the most common complaint was that they were too long. The *London Evening Standard* thought them 'written in the old formal style of biography which taxes

1   BL Add. Mss. 43396, fols. 226-9, FN to EH, 24 Feb. 1890; Smith, *Nightingale*, p. 107.
2   WSHC 2057/F4/52, Stanmore to EH, 22 July 1896, 12 Oct. 1900.
3   WSHC 2057/F4/52, Stanmore to EH, 11, 21, 27 Nov., 26 Dec. 1901.
4   BL Add. Mss. 49270, fols. 165-6, 176-7, H. Murray to Stanmore, 23 May 1905, Pembroke to Stanmore, 22 Mar. 1906.

the mood of today'. George Russell, writing in the *London Daily News*, suggested that they had appeared forty years too late. He had been more generous in a private letter to Stanmore, bemused to discover 'what a very uncomfortable colleague Mr G was in those days! – almost as tiresome as poor Uncle John!!!'[1] Lord Pembroke's eye, meanwhile, had been drawn to the sections on Nightingale, concerned that they 'may give rise to some complaint'. Presumably he had come across Stanmore's writing that she showed 'jealous impatience of any rival authority, and an undue intolerance of all opposition or difference of opinion'; worse, that her great strengths 'were combined with some womanly weaknesses'. Nightingale's biographers have indeed taken exception to what they see as Stanmore's chauvinism and spite, suggesting that he was exacting retribution for her lack of cooperation. Given the frustrations which he had had to endure, one is tempted to suggest rather that Stanmore was still exercising his long-honed skills in diplomacy.[2] Either way, the substantive point is that through him Lady Herbert had lived to see the biographical memorial to El Cid which she craved.

This victory of a sort was shortlived, for Nightingale's death in August 1910 paved the way for the official biography which she had anticipated. Sir Edward Cook's *The Life of Florence Nightingale* appeared as early as November 1913. It is a superb work, much superior to Stanmore's. And Herbert features prominently in it. Cook judges that had he gone out to the Crimea in person for a month in October 1854, many of the evils of which Nightingale complained might have been prevented.[3] Thereafter, he is 'worn out prematurely by unceasing labours for the British Army'. The fact that Cook then entitles the final chapter in volume one 'The Death of Sidney Herbert', and that 1861 is thus acknowledged as a seminal moment in Nightingale's life, largely reinforces Stanmore's image of Herbert as El Cid. But

1   *London Evening Standard*, 12 Dec. 1906; *London Daily News*, 21 Dec. 1906; BL Add. Mss. 49270, fols. 183-4, G. Russell to Stanmore, 13 Dec. 1906.
2   BL Add. Mss. 49270, fols. 176-7, Pembroke to Stanmore, 22 Mar. 1906; Stanmore, I, p. 404; Bostridge, *Nightingale*, pp. 525-6.
3   Cook, *Nightingale*, I, p. 178.

not quite: Cook also endorses Nightingale's record of 'Lord Herbert's confession of failure' in having failed to complete the reorganisation of the War Office.[1] And his biography as a whole necessarily sees Herbert through Nightingale's lens. Understandably, there is very little mention of his life before 1854. No less reasonably, Cook considers Herbert's career after 1854 only insofar as he was working for (far more than with) Nightingale. As a consequence, in the absence of a fresh life of Herbert, the latter was thenceforth condemned to be remembered in the popular mind as a man whose contribution to public life was contingent upon one woman during the last seven years of his life.[2] Compared to how Herbert had been understood in 1861, this represented a shift of seismic proportions.

The popular mind would be confirmed in this revised appreciation of Herbert by a new debate about statues. Commemorating the Lady with the Lamp in bronze was inevitable; asking Herbert's son (Sidney Pembroke had placed a wreath on her grave) to head a fund-raising committee to that end only slightly less so. The Earl found the task hard-going: towards the end of 1911 only £2,800 of the required £6,000 had been contributed. But matters improved, and by 1912 some newspapers were speculating that the Nightingale statue might in some way be linked with Herbert's.[3] The idea made undeniable sense. In 1906 the War Office had moved from Cumberland House in Pall Mall to new premises in Whitehall. Herbert's statue, though it was presumed that it would 'very properly be transferred with that department to its new quarters in Whitehall', had not moved with it. Were he to remain where he was, he would now be in front of 89 Pall Mall, home to the Royal Automobile Club. For all that Herbert enjoyed travel, the juxtaposition would be a curious one.

Foley's statue, it was therefore decided, would join the new one of Nightingale by A. G. Walker. They would stand alongside each other in front of John Bell's memorial to the 2,162 Guardsmen who fell in the Crimea (in deference to aesthetics, and its illustrious newcomers,

1   Cook, *Nightingale*, I, pp. 312, 394-412.
2   Cook, *Nightingale*, I, pp. 312, 394-412.
3   WSHC 2057/F4/64, for Pembroke's circular letter of Nov. 1911; *The Times*, 4 Jan. 1912, 17 Dec. 1913.

now set back thirty feet) which had been erected in Waterloo Place in 1861.[1] As *The Times* explained when tenders for the project were being sought in 1914: 'The idea of the grouping is to bring into association the statues of Florence Nightingale and Sidney Herbert, who were so closely associated through the Crimean War, with the memorial to the brave men who died in that war, and with the great figure of Peace crowning that memorial'.[2]

Herbert duly assumed his new position in time for the formal unveiling on 24 February 1915.[3] As a grouping the statues proved popular with the public. The new location certainly afforded Herbert's statue greater public prominence than it had enjoyed at the War Office. But did it make him any better known? Just a few years earlier, the *Daily Graphic* had written that he enjoyed 'an imperishable position in the heart of the nation'; the *Nottingham Daily Mail* that his name was 'household words'. The *Daily Mail*, by contrast, insisted that Herbert had never been 'more than a secondary star in the murky sky of British politics', that nine-tenths of the population 'have never heard of him; and the remaining tenth know little more of him than his name'.[4] The *Mail* was probably nearer the mark. When Herbert's portrait was included in an auction of Sir Robert Peel's paintings in 1917, *The Times* regretted that the catalogue said nothing 'to enlighten the company of buyers, who are bound to be mostly ignorant [...] as to the careers and characters of such men'.[5] What is certain is that the new configuration of statuary confirmed the *Sheffield Telegraph's* assessment that Herbert 'is only remembered now as the man who was chiefly instrumental in sending Florence Nightingale to the Crimea'. Worse, it has been suggested that the relocation of Foley's statue helped popularise the fanciful notion of Sydney Holland, treasurer to the committee commissioning the Nightingale statue, 'that Sidney Herbert wished to marry Florence Nightingale and, therefore, in every respect it is

1 https://www.iwm.org.uk/memorials/item/memorial/11608 accessed 8 Dec. 2018.
2 *The Times*, 14 June 1914.
3 *The Times*, 24 Feb. 1915, 22 Mar. 1915.
4 WSHC 2057/F6/102, press cuttings.
5 *The Times*, 6 Dec. 1917.

appropriate and desirable that their statues should stand near each other'.[1] Well might Herbert's statue be in contemplative posture.

Alluding to the nature of the personal relations between Herbert and Nightingale, Lytton Strachey wrote that 'the tongue of scandal was silent'. He did so in his famous 1918 essay about Nightingale in *Eminent Victorians*. Given that his overall contention was that Nightingale had had feet of clay ('If Miss Nightingale had been less ruthless, Sidney Herbert would not have perished'), one might be forgiven for thinking that his assessment of Herbert would be commensurately sympathetic.[2] It was not. Rather, the 'man upon whom the good fairies seemed to have showered, as he lay in his cradle, all their most enviable goods', was weak: 'the qualities of pliancy and sympathy fell to the man, those of command and initiative to the woman'. Strachey concluded that Herbert 'was a failure, a beaten man'.[3]

It is doubtful that many recognised Percy Dacier as a fictionalised Herbert in the film version of *Diana of the Crossways*, released in 1922. The story of Herbert's leaking Peel's intentions with respect to the Corn Laws was given further life in Reginald Berkeley's 1929 play, *The Lady with a Lamp*. Successful drama it might have been, but it was poor history. Herbert is 'fair-haired, dark-eyed', with the 'eyes and brow of a poet [...] and unhappily a vitiating touch of weakness sprung from inherited disease'. Whilst he dotes on Nightingale, Elizabeth Herbert is traduced as 'kittenish' (she cannot recall what the Italian revolutionaries are fighting for), and jealous of Nightingale's 'intimacy with her husband'.[4] The play was the basis, albeit loosely, for Herbert Wilcox's iconic film of the same name (1951) starring Anna Neagle. Sidney Herbert was played in suitably debonair fashion by Michael Wilding, then at the height of his fame as a British heartthrob actor. Patently in love, the Herbert and Nightingale of the silver screen just about manage to suppress their feelings for each other. Rosalie

1   *CWFN*, VII, pp. 774-5; Bostridge, *Nightingale*, pp. 523-5.
2   Strachey, *Eminent Victorians*, p. 158.
3   Strachey, *Eminent Victorians*, pp. 136-9, 146-8, 156-9.
4   Berkeley, *The Lady with a Lamp*, pp. 9-10, 38, 98, 108.

Crutchley, meanwhile, cast as Lady Herbert, was reduced to a bit part.[1] Paradoxically, the film did Herbert both a service and disservice. It is hard to think of any other film, certainly not a commercially successful one, in which a nineteenth-century British politician features so prominently. But it is a Herbert once more defined entirely in terms of the Crimean War (the film affords him virtually sole blame for it), and the work with Nightingale which followed it.

Many of those who saw the film may already have bought Cecil Woodham-Smith's biography of Nightingale. Published in 1950, it was a huge success and would hold the field for the next half century. So far as Herbert was concerned, its author's comments were a melange of the insightful and the dubious. Herbert did not inherit vast estates in Scotland. Neither was it true that 'he was without zest for life' and 'turned for consolation to religion'. And there is more melodrama than accuracy in the verdict that Herbert 'died with a broken heart'. But Woodham-Smith was right to say that Nightingale was too hard on him and that he has 'left little impression'.[2] Essentially however, Woodham-Smith's Nightingale was a popularisation of Sir Edward Cook's.

It seems almost unconscionable, given the recent success of Wilcox's film and Woodham-Smith's book, that Salisbury City Council could contemplate moving Marochetti's statue in 1953. In 1863 the mayor had promised that 'we shall always esteem and venerate the memory of Lord Herbert, and that the Corporation will ever feel it a great privilege to take the utmost charge and care of this statue'.[3] Ninety years later, with the Coronation looming, that privilege took second place to the view that a Market Square denuded of Herbert would create more room for the impending celebrations. The decisive moment came at the council meeting of November 1952. Councillor A.E.G. Herbert read a message from his father, Lord Pembroke, Sidney Herbert's grandson, stating 'his hopes that a Herbert – dead or live – will never stand in the way of improvement of the amenities of this

---

1 Bostridge, *Nightingale*, pp. 536-9. Wilding was the second husband of Elizabeth Taylor.
2 Woodham-Smith, *Florence Nightingale*, pp. 70-1, 369, 372.
3 *SWJ*, 4 July 1863.

ancient city'. On 4 May 1953, by a decisive majority, it was decided that the statue would be transported to Victoria Park, north of the city centre, 'where it will face the southern boundary of the bowling green'. Alderman Wort's objections to what he called 'this absolute comic opera', and his protest that they 'were desecrating his memory', were in vain. It took four men (armed with scaffolding and a lorry) two days to commit the act of desecration. Herbert's pedestal, they discovered, had never been secured.[1] A modicum of imagination and a few more pounds would have taken it the three miles to its natural home at Wilton.

Herbert's fortunes, statuary or otherwise, have not much improved since. Colin Matthew's revised version of the article on Herbert for the new *Oxford Dictionary of National Biography*, whilst providing a brief narrative of Herbert's life, adopted a decidedly less effusive line than J.A. Hamilton's original: 'in the confused politics of his time', Matthew concludes, 'he had some success'. Of the plethora of Nightingale biographies to appear in the second half of the twentieth century, meanwhile, the most controversial was F.B. Smith's 1982 *Florence Nightingale. Reputation and Power*. Overly iconoclastic, it might be characterised as Strachey with footnotes. Smith viewed Herbert as being congenitally incapable of standing up to any woman. Although he suggested that Herbert's relationship with Nightingale should be painted in more nuanced colours than earlier Nightingale biographers had allowed (arguing, for example, that Herbert often took the initiative in the work they undertook), he concluded that without her, 'his efforts would have been limited and weakly pursued'.[2] It was not until 2008 and the publication of Mark Bostridge's *Florence Nightingale. The Woman And Her Legend* that a Nightingale biographer properly intimated that there was something more to Herbert:

> She failed [...] to understand fully enough that the renewed strains of Herbert's political life from the summer of 1859 [...] along with his family responsibilities at Wilton, did not allow him the freedom

---

1 *SWJ*, 8, 15 May 1953.
2 Smith, *Nightingale*, especially, pp. 37, 76, 83, 94, 100-4.

from distraction and opportunity to conserve his energy that her own lifestyle provided [...] Herbert's attention had been diverted on many fronts [...] He had overseen the development of the volunteer movement, a war against China [...] the reorganisation of the national defences, and had been embroiled in a wounding battle with the Chancellor.[1]

This, even if it only refers to Herbert's final period in office, at least provides signposts pointing in the right direction. Herbert does not need to be set free from Nightingale but he does need to be reset in a fuller context if we want to attempt a proper full re-evaluation of his life.

We might begin with a resume of his relationship with Nightingale. When they met in 1847 Herbert was a rising political star, Nightingale an unknown lady ten years his junior. Their paths crossed increasingly frequently over the next half decade. This was principally because Nightingale and Elizabeth Herbert found themselves so simpatico. It was Elizabeth Herbert who helped secure Nightingale the position of Superintendent at the Institute for the Care of Sick Gentlewomen in Upper Harley Street in 1853. Had she not done so, Herbert could hardly have provided Nightingale with the platform for fame by inviting her to go to the Crimea in 1854. Their reputations intersected in the autumn of 1854. For what remained of Herbert's life, they often worked together. Herbert's was, of necessity, the public face of that relationship. As a result, he received more than his due share of the credit at the time of his death. Thereafter, Nightingale's reputation rose, to the point where Herbert's was smothered. He came to be remembered as her helpmate; in less reverent accounts as the lackey whom she worked to death. A perplexed Lord Stanmore, reporting to Lady Herbert on the progress of his research in 1901, wrote that 'You probably hardly know how largely, in the world, his work is given to her'. Even one former Secretary for War had told him that Herbert had been no more than a 'conduit' between Nightingale and the War Office. Herbert unwittingly contributed to the legend

1 Bostridge, *Nightingale*, pp. 377-8.

himself: his last recorded words were 'Poor Florence! Who will carry on our joint work?'[1]

Insofar as both Herbert and Nightingale were looking to advance the well-being of the army, 'joint' was true. But 'joint' does not necessarily equate to 'same'. Reality in this instance is better reflected by equating 'joint' with 'complementary'. From June 1859, the competing demands on Herbert's time meant that he had to relinquish the chair of the four sub-commissions spawned by the Royal Commission on the Sanitary Condition of the Army. He remained only nominal head of the body considering sanitary affairs in India. Herbert rightly anticipated that Nightingale would be disappointed to see him going back to the War Office. But he was still endeavouring to promote the cause of the army from 1859, whether it was by attempting to reform the system of purchase and sale of commissions, reorganising the War Office, or overseeing a major military expedition to China. Nightingale was therefore patently exaggerating when she wrote to Sir John Lawrence, Viceroy of India in the 1860s, that Herbert was 'a statesman with whom I worked not daily, but hourly, for five years'.[2] It is truer to say that they were very close at the heart of a team on army sanitary matters between 1857 and 1859.

Further corrective is provided by seeing the Herbert-Nightingale partnership in the context of Herbert's relationships with other women. He was unusual in facilitating and supporting the work of several women who pursued philanthropic causes. Caroline Norton's unhappy history propelled her into campaigning for changes to custody and divorce law. The Female Emigration Fund brought Herbert into contact with Caroline Chisholm. Work on the Nightingale Fund brought him into the orbit of Anna Hall. And he had known Mary Stanley, another advocate of female nursing, as long as he had known Nightingale. F.B. Smith's claims, however, that Herbert was thus 'habituated to acquiescing in the plans of handsome, determined women', and that he 'tamely accepted his subjection', are baseless.[3] It

1 WSHC 2057/F4/52, Stanmore to EH, 21 Nov. 1901; WSHC 2057/F6/98, 'Account of Sidney Herbert', p. 45.
2 Cook, *Nightingale*, II, p. 44.
3 Smith, *Nightingale*, p. 37.

was rather that Herbert, more than most of his time, evinced a sort of gender neutrality. Certainly it is suggestive that Nightingale could write to her old friend, Mary Clarke Mohl, in December 1861, that 'Sidney Herbert and I were together exactly like two men – exactly like him and Gladstone'.[1] And the fact that resonated with contemporaries about his inviting Nightingale to go to the Crimea was that he had 'in defiance of all official tradition, appealed to the devotion and organising power of a woman'.[2] Insofar as Herbert was ever subjugated, it was to his sense of duty and God.

Herbert's ties with Nightingale were admittedly of a different order from the examples listed above. The 'other woman' who really matters is Elizabeth Herbert. Lady Herbert was not the supine figure marginalised in later popular perceptions of the alliance between Nightingale and her husband. She assisted Herbert variously as his political secretary, a co-campaigner in furtherance of the cause of female emigration, and as one of the organisers of the nursing expedition to the Crimea. A tantalising fragment addressed to her from 'M.S'. (presumably Mary Stanley), dated October 1854 hints at even more: 'Now it is clear that there is something to do. You have certainly founded the whole thing & yr. Sid launched it'.[3] Elizabeth Herbert was the figure to whom the Queen turned for information in December 1854: in convoluted language she asked Mr Herbert to enquire whether Mrs Herbert had received any fresh information about the state of the army in the Crimea. A year later, when writing to explain the rationale for trying to raise £50,000 for the Nightingale Fund, Herbert said to Palmerston that he was doing so on behalf of his wife.[4] Doubtless these latter two examples were maintaining something of a fiction; Elizabeth was more a symbolic than an actual head of affairs. But during the late 1850s, Elizabeth Herbert went well beyond the remit of an ordinary secretary, not only reading but actioning reports on her husband's behalf. She also took the lead

1 Cook, *Nightingale*, I, pp. 411-12.
2 *Fraser's Magazine*, p. 210.
3 WSHC 2057/F4/52.
4 *Norfolk News*, 6 Jan.1855; WSHC 2057/F4/61, SH to Pam, 17 Oct. 1855.

in having him elevated to the Lords. As she reflected to Palmerston in 1863, few women had 'lived' in politics as she had. For his part, Palmerston was far from being alone in his view that she 'combined in an unusual degree Beauty that fascinates, warmth of heart that endears, and powers of intellect that assist and enliven'. For a while after Herbert's death, he took to calling her his 'dearest colleague'.[1] By restoring and acknowledging Elizabeth Herbert's due prominence in her husband's world, the Herbert-Nightingale relationship comes into focus as one that often comprised not two but three partners.

This being so, we need to be clear that Nightingale was the third party. An element of jealous rivalry between the two women was perhaps inevitable following Herbert's death. An intimation of what would follow came within hours. Nightingale wrote to Elizabeth that 'No one ever loved him and served him as I did [...] After you, no one can mourn him as I do'.[2] To her sister, Nightingale did not even make the exception of Lady Herbert. And by 1865, in a letter to her cousin, Douglas Galton, marked 'most private', 'burn', she was complaining about 'How little his wife knows him'.[3] The conviction that Herbert and Nightingale fell in love and wanted to marry – a recent pseudo-fact based book has posited the idea that Herbert fathered a child by Nightingale – has proved remarkably durable. In the absence of a shred of documentary evidence, it must be dismissed as nonsense.[4] But Nightingale, by her own admission had loved Herbert: 'I knew him and loved him for the sake of God and mankind'.[5] This, she persuaded herself, was a different and higher form of love than that which existed between husband and wife. But was there, perhaps, a modicum of self-delusion here? The guilt that Nightingale felt at the thought that she had been partly responsible for Herbert's death, no less than the jealousy she felt towards Lady Herbert as her rival to be keeper of his flame, are emotions perfectly compatible with something

---

1 WSHC 2057/F4/62, Pam to EH, 13, 21, 31 Oct. 1861.
2 WSHC 2057/F4/65, FN to EH, 3 Aug. 1861.
3 *CWFN*, I, pp. 327-8, FN to Lady Verney, 7 Aug. 1861; *CWFN*, IX, p. 540, FN to Galton, 9 Nov. 1865.
4 *CWFN*, VII, pp. 774-5; Johnson, *A Divine Experience*.
5 WSHC 2057/F4/65, FN to EH, 3 Aug. 1861.

more than platonic love. In the final analysis such speculation is otiose. To Herbert she was always 'Dear Miss Nightingale', never 'My Dearest Heart'.

In trying to assuage fears that she had been the cause of his death, Benjamin Jowett assured Nightingale that 'It is not true that you killed poor S. Herbert [...] I think that you gave Lord Herbert [...] the idea which made life worth having [...] where would Lord Herbert's work or memory have been if he had died six years sooner?'[1] Leaving aside the obvious rejoinder that Nightingale's work and memory would never have prospered without Herbert, the question is a fair one. To answer it, however, we must escape Jowett's demarcation of before and after Nightingale. Properly understood, there was no bifurcation in Herbert's career. His active years as an administrator spanned not the five years of which Nightingale spoke so reverently but the twenty years from 1841.

Thanks to Peel, who realised that a High Churchman was less likely to get himself into a political scrape in a department which dealt with temporal matters, Herbert's ministerial career was one in which he was preoccupied by war, or at least the fear of it. Indeed, there is considerable congruity between his periods in office and the three war scares with France of 1846-8, 1852, and 1858-9. The coincidence is compounded by the irony that Herbert's two longer stints at the War Office involved him with preparations for wars against Russia and China in which France was Britain's ally. What this meant was that Herbert never enjoyed the luxury of peace which would have allowed him the time to devote his energies to a systematic programme of reform. Even if the international picture had been pacific, his efforts would have been impeded by the Corn Law crisis in 1845-6, and his debilitating illness during the 1850s.

Identifying achievements which were specifically Herbert's is difficult; the cynic might say that they were as evanescent as his charm. A more sympathetic writer in *Fraser's Magazine* said that 'Their relative importance and completeness are not easily discerned through the mist

---

1   Quinn and Prest, *Nightingale*, pp. 141-2, Jowett to FN, Easter 1868.

of official reserve or of technical obscurity'.[1] The point is exemplified by the plinths on Foley's statue. Although it bore his name, the Herbert Hospital and the associated reforms it brings to mind, owed more to Nightingale and more than a little to people like Farr, Sutherland and Alexander. The raising of the volunteers, Herbert himself insisted (though de Grey insisted to the contrary), owed much to de Grey. And the initiative which led to the army's adopting the Armstrong gun, Herbert told parliament, was taken by his predecessor as Secretary for War, General Peel.[2] Neither does it help Herbert's pretensions to be remembered as a reformer that each of these areas can be argued to have been only a qualified success. Spending on army hospitals and barracks was being reined in during the early 1860s; volunteer numbers soon peaked and did not provide the sort of reserve force that the regular army needed. And, most pointedly, the breech-loading rifled Armstrong gun did not prove entirely reliable when first used in anger in the China war; the army reverted to using muzzle-loading artillery pieces until 1885.[3] Herbert further undermines his case by his modesty; he lacked the modern politician's propensity to self-advertisement. Lord Aberdeen told the Queen that he was 'astounded' by Herbert's modesty, 'it is quite extraordinary how he undervalues his powers'.[4] Though it sounds too saccharine to be entirely true, Lady Herbert's recording her husband as having said, 'what <u>does</u> it signify who gets the credit of it <u>so long as the thing is done</u>?' does have some substance to it.[5]

It is by aggregating Herbert's contributions out of, as well as in government, sometimes piecemeal, and often working alongside others as encourager and enabler, that he can be argued to have been a reformer of some significance. His most salient initiatives included: advancing the cause of officer education; attempting to limit the buying and selling of commissions; trying to create a sustainable system for

1 *Fraser's Magazine*, 'Herbert', p. 203.
2 Wilton House Mss., Houghton to Strzelecki, 8 Nov. 1861; Hansard, 14 Feb. 1861, CLXI, cols. 372-3.
3 David, *Victoria's Wars*, p. 369.
4 WSHC 2057/F6/98, 'Character of Sidney Herbert', p. 9.
5 WSHC 2057/F6/98, 'Character of Sidney Herbert', pp. 10-12.

advancement in the senior ranks; embracing new military technology; improving the lot of the ordinary rank and file serviceman; looking for ways of using irregular forces to augment the army in times of crisis; and rationalising (without over-centralising) military administration. That is why, even if he exaggerated, Dickens echoed the view of many when he wrote that Herbert 'has beaten the twisted iron into shape, and many many more long years must pass away before it can be beaten out of form again'.[1] Certainly no civilian politician of his generation was better versed in the panoply of military affairs.

Taking the nineteenth century as a whole, the army reformer who stands pre-eminent today is Edward Cardwell, Secretary for War (1868-74) under Gladstone. In more advantageous circumstances than those enjoyed by Herbert, Cardwell was able to bring to fruition many of the things – he abolished the purchase of commissions, overhauled the regimental structure and reorganised the War Office – which had engrossed Herbert.[2] But Cardwell anticipated the debt. He told Herbert on the occasion of the latter's leaving the Commons that he only remembered 'one or two occasions, on which I have not found myself taking counsel with, & acting on the same side with you'. Speaking at the Jubilee dinner of the Oxford Union in 1873, a Mr Mowbray made much the same connection when he referred to Foley's statue 'still watching over the fortunes of the British Army and ever ready to act as Mentor to his hon friend and colleague Mr Cardwell'. The more sober verdict of the standard academic survey of the period is that Cardwell 'consolidated and developed the departmental reconstruction begun by Sidney Herbert after the Crimean War'.[3]

The shorter perspective of Herbert's career in government allows us to see that his overarching objective was national security. This was something largely missed by contemporaries, blinded as they were by his high profile association with Nightingale and their myopic focus

---

1   Story, *Letters of Charles Dickens*, IX, p. 483, Dickens to EH, 25 Oct. 1861.
2   Spiers, 'The Late-Victorian Army 1868-1914' in Chandler, *Oxford History of the British Army*, pp. 187-90.
3   WSHC 2057/F4/53, Cardwell to SH, 4 Jan. 1861; *The Times*, 23 Oct. 1873; Spiers, *Army and Society*, p. 187.

on his record as Secretary for War after 1859. One exception was de Grey, whose astute address when he unveiled Marochetti's statue in Salisbury, dwelt on Herbert's contribution to 'measures for the better defence of our ports and arsenals'. Another was the *Morning Post* which reflected, following the unveiling of Foley's statue, that Herbert had worked to prepare his country 'so that she should ever be ready to place her strength in the field should her safety or her honour demand it'.[1] And Lady Herbert grasped in her grief that her husband had been 'strongly impressed with the belief that the only way to prevent a French invasion was to prove that we were prepared to resist it'.[2] On the basis, to adapt a phrase, that the price of English constitutional liberties was eternal vigilance, Herbert's ultimate success in government could only ever be provisional. But it does make sense of Foley's statue: Armstrong guns were the most recent technology adopted to assist in protecting home shores; volunteers the latest attempt to find sufficient manpower for defence; and improved military hospitals the best way to render some of those defenders fit for action. It is only too obvious now that Herbert's statue should have moved with the War Office in 1906. Renamed the Ministry of Defence in 1964, what better location could there have been for a man who devoted so much of his life to defending his nation and those who defended it?

But what of Herbert the politician? Lord Houghton, musing how best to commemorate his friend, had been:

> especially anxious that there should be a memorial of him in connexion with the Houses of Parliament which are the real theatre of his eminence & his exertions [...] His administration of the war office was coincidental & short: He got the discredit of the Crimea campaign & I & the public know nothing of anything he has done for the Army since.[3]

---

1   *SWJ*, 4 July 1863; *Morning Post*, 3 June 1867.
2   WSHC 2057/F6/98, 'Account of Sidney Herbert', pp. 3-4.
3   Wilton House Mss., Houghton to Strzelecki, 8 Nov. 1861.

Only carping members of the Fine Arts Committee, it might be remembered, had prevented Herbert's memorial from finding its home inside Westminster Palace.

From uncertain beginnings, Herbert had been regarded as one of the star performers in the Commons during the 1850s. He was also a good committee man. In addition to his headline work chairing the 1858 Royal Commission on the Sanitary Condition of the Army, he chaired the 1854 Royal Commission on Promotion in the Army, and served on both the 1857 Royal Commission into the System of Purchase and Sale of Commissions in the Army, and the 1858 Royal Commission on the Promotion and Retirement in the Higher Ranks of the Army. For a while Herbert chaired the Royal Commission on the Sanitary State of the Army in India, and the Select Committee on Military Organisation, both set up in 1859. His last significant contribution to parliamentary life was a lengthy, informed testimony to the Select Committee on Colonial Military Expenditure on 30 May 1861.[1]

More politically consequential was Herbert's role in the making and unmaking of governments. He declined to help Derby in his attempt to form a ministry in 1851. In helping to bring him down in 1852, he played a part in burning the bridge which ended prospects for the reunion of Peel's Conservative party. He was close to Aberdeen throughout the manoeuvrings which led to the latter heading the coalition ministry of 1852-5. With Aberdeen's blessing, he was a central figure in the political crisis which led to Palmerston becoming Prime Minister in February 1855. He was one of the leading speakers in the debate which led to Palmerston's temporary defeat in March 1857, and he helped draft the motion which presaged Derby's fall from office in June 1859. If all this amounts to a balance sheet which is more destructive than constructive, it is only fair to add that Herbert's finest hour in the game of high politics came in helping to orchestrate the meeting in Willis's Rooms which is now generally regarded as having marked the birth of the modern Liberal party. With Palmerston's

---

1   PP 1861 (423), XIII, pp. 328-42.

Liberal government unstable at the time of Herbert's death, it was, of course, an achievement unknowable to his contemporaries.

Herbert never held one of the great offices of State, though he turned down Palmerston's offer of the Home Office in 1855. The most senior post he held, and then only for days, was Secretary for the Colonies. Had he lived, he would surely have progressed further up the ministerial ladder. The most suitable rung, by general consent, was the one identified by Speaker Denison. He told Herbert in 1861 that he possessed 'those rare qualities & powers, wh mark their possessor as Leader of the House of Commons'.[1] This might have provided a springboard for the highest place. Malmesbury's diary recorded, on Herbert's passing, that he was 'one of those who was looked upon as likely to be a future Prime Minister'.[2] A cryptic entry in Lord Stanley's journal related how 'Lord Granville lately told Lord D[erby]. that if Herbert had retained his health, he must have been Palmerston's successor, and even hinted that an arrangement to that effect had been made!'[3] Four years later, when emotions had subsided, Jowett judged that Herbert 'had grown so rapidly, in himself & in public estimation, that there seemed to be no limit to what he might have effected. He might have been one of the most popular & powerful prime ministers in this country – the man to carry us through the social & ecclesiastical questions that are springing up'.[4]

Modern scholarship currently takes a contrary view, endorsing the Duke of Argyll's conviction 'that he never would have been a leader of men'.[5] Leaving aside the fact that Argyll's view is principally striking for being untypical, a good resume of the case for Herbert's being unsuited for the premiership appears in a seminal article on the formation of the Aberdeen Coalition:

> He had some intelligence and judgement but neither the vigour nor the stamina to use them [...] Herbert's sweetness of character and

---

1 WSHC 2057/F4/54, Denison to SH, 5 Jan. 1861.
2 Malmesbury, *Memoirs*, II, p. 257, 3 Aug. 1861.
3 Vincent, *Stanley Journals*, p. 174, 14 July 1861.
4 Quinn and Prest, *Nightingale*, pp. 66-7, Jowett to FN, 7 Aug. 1865.
5 Argyll, *Autobiography*, pp. 380-1.

great personal charm concealed this political weakness, whilst his genuine piety increased it. He made his political yardstick the spirit of the Gospel, and so pure a view of the world severely limited him as a politician.[1]

One can only observe that the Herbert who exuded energy during the Crimean War, who worked into the early hours on committees and commissions, and who criss-crossed the country inspecting barracks, was a very different man from the one described above. Moreover, one searches in vain amongst Herbert's papers relating to militia business, the military estimates, fortifications, Armstrong guns and the like, for references to the Gospel. Neither did the Gospel inform Herbert's approach to international affairs. Hard-headed judgements about the balance of power left him in no doubt that Britain should support Muslim Turkey in a struggle against a Russia ostensibly defending the rights of Christians. As to the insinuation that Herbert was essentially too nice to be Prime Minister, it was the very fact of his being so personable that contemporaries believed that outcome to be likely. *Fraser's Magazine* was unequivocal that 'Everyone perceived in him a special social faculty, sure to conciliate such men as form the staple of our Cabinets'.[2]

Gladstone was the only obvious impediment blocking Herbert's way. Their careers followed a similar path: from Oxford to junior minsters under Peel, then cabinet ministers under Aberdeen and Palmerston. They became intimates from the late 1840s. It was an intimacy that reached its apogee in 1854: the Gladstones named their fourth son Herbert; the Herberts responded by naming their third son William Reginald, with the profession that 'should it please God that anything should happen to us there is no one to whom we could with such confidence entrust the oversight of our Boz as to yourself'.[3] Professional disagreements over the military estimates from 1859, what Herbert called 'unhappy differences between two very old and close friends', briefly threatened their relations, but they survived intact.

1 Stuart,' 'The Formation of the Coalition Cabinet of 1852', p. 55.
2 *Fraser's Magazine*, 'Herbert', p. 203
3 BL Add. Mss. 44212, fols. 13-14, EH to WEG, 29 May 1854.

Even so, Gladstone, no less than Nightingale, clearly felt an element of guilt amid the anguish which engulfed him when Herbert died. Lady Herbert, who believed that Gladstone was right to feel that way, could not even bring herself to refer to him by name in her memoir of Herbert's final months.[1]

In the wider scheme of things, however, nobody doubted that Gladstone was more brilliant than Herbert. But Gladstone's brilliance was mercurial; it raised doubts. Henry Goulburn, Chancellor of the Exchequer under Peel, who observed the progress of both men's careers over more than twenty years put the case well:

> He [Gladstone] weighs questions by themselves without references to consequences. He presents to his own mind all that can be argued for or against the abstract question and as soon as he fancies there is a preponderance however subtly discovered, he applies in support of that preponderating opinion his own unrivalled powers of argument & treating it as a matter of conscience will not look at the incidental evils which his course of conduct may produce; still less will he regard the effect which it may have on those who are politically associated with him. It was this that made me long ago determine that Sidney, not Gladstone, should be my leader. He is not, I admit, gifted with the power of oratory that Gladstone possesses, but to very high ability he adds a fund of correct judgement which, as a useful public servant outweighs all other considerations.[2]

Herbert, therefore, partly by virtue of the fact that he was not Gladstone, could very well have been heir to Palmerston and Russell as leader of the Liberal party. As such, blessed with even reasonable health, Sidney, 13th Earl of Pembroke, would probably have entered Downing Street.

Any further counterfactual speculation is best left to others. Herbert had need of the keys to heaven before he could be handed those to Number 10. Meeting his Maker was something about which

---

1 BL Add. Mss. 79658, fols. 105-6, SH to JRG, 1 Apr. 1860; WSHC 2057/F6/98, 'Account of Sidney Herbert', p. 5.
2 WSHC 2057/F4/52, Goulburn to EH, 29 June 1855.

Herbert was perfectly sanguine. For though C.H. Stuart was wrong to say that Herbert as a politician was hamstrung by his piety, there can be no doubt about the centrality of Christian Faith in his life. Like Gladstone he was a churchman in politics. It is telling that even though his work in government during the 1850s was focused on defence, contemporaries still defined him by his High Churchmanship. When the composition of Palmerston's 1859 cabinet was revealed, *The Record* characterised Herbert as 'a member of the Tractarian trio'. Panmure, meanwhile, 'angry' that Herbert and not he had been restored to the War Office, talked 'of sitting on the cross benches on account of the Puseyite principles of Gladstone and S. Herbert'.[1]

Herbert set out his view on the relationship between God and politics during a debate on the Jewish Disabilities Bill in 1853:

> I am so far from thinking that religion has nothing to do with politics that I believe unless religion be the animating spirit to guide us in all our measures – unless we infuse into our measures the real spirit of Christianity, our legislation will be nothing worth, and the prosperity of the country will pass away.[2]

Numerous examples could be instanced: the desire to advance education to combat ungodliness, the Christian charity which made it imperative to allow cheap corn into Ireland, or the Christian's duty to alleviate the suffering of soldiers in the Crimea. Nightingale was adamant that Herbert's Faith was his chief motivator when at the War Office and in their work together. 'I can truly say', she told Dr McNeill, 'that, during the five years that I worked with Sidney Herbert every day and nearly all day, from the moment he came into the room no other ideas came in but that of doing the work, with the best of our powers, in the service of God'.[3] God's service would also have informed Herbert's work had he stayed in office from 1855 as

---

1 *SWJ*, 25 June 1859; TNA 30/29/31/I, Granville to Canning, 10 Aug. 1859.
2 Hansard, 11 Mar. 1853, CXXV, cols. 104-8.
3 Cook, *Nightingale*, I, p. 366, FN to McNeill, 15 Nov. 1857.

Palmerston's Secretary for the Colonies. He told his listeners at the South Wiltshire by-election in February 1855 that the office imposed:

> the task of assisting in the development of the material, moral, and religious progress of those great dependencies, which are the foundations, perhaps, of what will, in the future, be mighty empires, and which will spread over the world the traditions of English life, will carry to the furthest parts of the globe those institutions of tempered freedom and that liberty of religion and that love of order combined with freedom which have been the distinguishing features of this country.[1]

It is in Wiltshire too, that we find the most tangible manifestations of Herbert's godliness during the 1850s. As chairman of the governing body of Salisbury Infirmary, he 'took special pains' to have a crucifix displayed in the operating wards; of less solace, perhaps, to ungodly patients, an engraving of 'the agony in the garden'. He continued a programme of restoring all churches on the Wilton estate, 'putting in painted glass windows of the Crucifixion in the East End of most of them'. Pews were taken out; altars put in; the names of patron saints restored. Herbert personally selected biblical texts for display in the porches.[2] Easily the biggest project, one that came close to rivalling the new parish church for Wilton in the 1840s, was the public subscription for a new church at Bemerton, not far from Wilton House. Raised as a monument to his ancestor, the Reverend George Herbert, it was predominantly a Herbert family affair. Robert Pembroke had given the land, Herbert subscribed £150, and Elizabeth Herbert laid the foundation stone in April 1859. A mix of early and middle Gothic, the salient feature of the church of St John the Evangelist was the stained glass east window by Michael O'Connor, featuring the crucifixion. Although weak and busy, Herbert insisted on

1   *SWJ*, 10 Feb. 1855.
2   BL Add. Mss. 49270, fols. 145-7.

coming down from London to be present for the consecration service in December 1860.[1]

Writing in the 1890s, from the perspective of a convert to Roman Catholicism, Lady Herbert adduced much of the above as evidence for her belief that Herbert was, to all intents and purposes, himself a Roman Catholic. In further support of her case she noted that he felt no compunction in attending Catholic Masses on their travels abroad, that all priests on his Irish estate, regardless of their denomination, received £100 a year, and that Cardinal Cullen, Roman Catholic Archbishop of Dublin, had told her that her husband 'was his most efficient helper in every good work'. The last cheque Herbert wrote, for £700, was in favour of the Catholic church of St Mary's, Star of the Sea, at Sandymount. Lady Herbert also set down, with respect to their various church-improving initiatives, that 'He used to say smiling "When Henry" (that was Cardinal Manning) comes, he will only have to add the Tabernacle and the relics in the altar stone'.[2]

The last sounds more like an example of Herbert's facetiousness. And Lady Herbert prefaced her remarks to Stanmore about Herbert's religion with the admission that they 'might be supposed to be coloured by my own convictions'.[3] In her earlier paper on Herbert's character drawn up for their children, she had noted that from the early 1850s, 'On direct religious matters he never spoke much [...] He disliked theological discussions and any extremes of Party. He believed – and he loved (both God and man) and he acted on that belief and that love'.[4] The historical record for his last decade affords us only fleeting glimpses of his religiosity – and then from the pen of others. Elizabeth noted that 'However tired he might be, he always read to himself or asked me to read to him, the Evening lesson of each day'.[5] Nightingale was struck by the touching way he invariably said 'God bless you'

1 SWJ, 16 Apr. 1859, 16 Dec. 1860; BL Add. Mss. 49270, fols. 145, 148. George Herbert was rector of St Andrew's, Bemerton 1629-1633.
2 BL Add. Mss. 49270, fol. 147-9.
3 BL Add. Mss. 49270, fol. 148.
4 BL Add. Mss. 49270, fol. 148; WSHC 2057/F6/98, 'Account of Sidney Herbert', p. 16.
5 WSHC 2057/F6/98, 'Account of Sidney Herbert', p. 38.

each time they parted.¹ It was to Nightingale, during a seemingly interminable trip to Scotland in 1858, that he confided as much as he did to anybody: 'My scepticism is shaking. I read a book coming down here in which a man who has been argued into infidelity is reconverted to Xtianity by the breaking of a cord in a piano forte'.² We may safely presume that this was another instance of Herbert whimsy.

The most telling point that Lady Herbert made in her attempt to unravel the truth of her husband's religious convictions was that he had been perfectly content to entrust their children's upbringing to her sole care. He did so in the knowledge that she might become a Roman Catholic 'as I had gone further in that direction than he had'.³ It was clearly a scenario that he could contemplate with equanimity. In life we can go no further than to say that Herbert believed in a catholic (that is to say, emphatically lowercase 'c') church. However pragmatically he adapted his religion to his politics, he would not have concealed the truth of his Roman Catholicism on his deathbed. He would mostly have approved of Nightingale's retort when assailed about her religion whilst effecting good works that: 'I am so glad my God is not the God of the High Church or of the Low – that He is not a Romanist or an Anglican – or an Unitarian […] I don't believe he is even a Russian'.⁴

Lady Herbert was probably right, therefore, in saying of her husband's lodestar that 'His Faith was, like his mother's, peculiarly child-like, simple and humble'.⁵ The words which he penned at the age of 14 in August 1825 suggested both a philosophy for life and his hopes for the hereafter:

> What are all the dreams of man,
> Of fame, and pow'r and wealth to me
> When on meditations wings
> I soar, celestial things to see
>   Leaving its body low on earth

1   BL Add. Mss. 43396, fol. 192, FN to EH, 30 Sept. 1863.
2   BL Add. Mss. 43395, fols. 39-40, SH to FN, 1 Apr. 1858.
3   BL Add. Mss. 49270, fols. 149-50.
4   BL Add. Mss. 43393, fol. 113, FN to SH, 28 Jan. 1855.
5   WSHC 2057/F6/98, 'Account of Sidney Herbert', p. 16.

Leaving its Fetters and its Chain
The soul flies up to heavn'ly joy
Ah! only to return again
    But if so short a freedom can
A momentary bliss bestow
Oh for that time when in the skies
That bliss eternal I shall know.[1]

---

1   WSHC 2057/F4/50, poem dated 7 Aug. 1825

Bibliography

Manuscript Sources

Bodleian Library, University of Oxford
    Kimberley Papers
    Manning Papers
British Library
    Aberdeen Papers
    Balfour Papers
    Canning Papers
    Gladstone Papers
    Graham Papers
    Herbert of Lea Papers
    Nightingale Papers
    Peel Papers
    Ramsay Papers
    Ripon Papers
    Stanmore Papers
Gloucestershire Record Office
    Sotheron Estcourt Papers
Hampshire Record Office
    Normanton Papers
Hartley Library, University of Southampton
    Palmerston Papers
    Shaftesbury Diary
    Wellington Papers
Hawarden, St Deniol's Library
    Glynne-Gladstone Papers
Liverpool Record Office
    Derby Papers
London Metropolitan Archives
    Nightingale Fund Papers

Manuscripts and Special Collections, University of Nottingham
  Denison Papers
  Newcastle Papers
Palace Green Library, University of Durham
  Grey Papers
Surrey History Centre
  Goulburn Papers
The National Archives
  Granville Papers
  Russell Papers
  War Office Papers
Wellcome Library
  Longmore Papers
West Sussex Record Office
  Goodwood House Papers
Wilton House
  Pembroke Papers
Wiltshire and Swindon History Centre
  Grove Papers
  Pembroke Papers

Parliamentary Papers

1847-8 (555), XXI Select Committee on Navy, Ordnance and Army Estimates.

1851 (632), XIX Report from the Select Committee on the Passengers' Act.

1852-3 (705), XXIV Minutes of Evidence taken before the Select Committee on the Devon and Dorset Railway Bill.

1854 (1802), XIX Report of Commissioners on Promotion in the Army.

1854-5 (247), IX Fourth Report from the Select Committee on the Army Before Sebastopol.

1854-5 (317), XII Report from the Select Committee on Sandhurst Royal Military College.

1854-5 (519), XXXII Strength of Militia Embodied for Service in the United Kingdom.

1857 [2267], XVIII Report of the Commissioners Appointed to Inquire into the System of Purchase and Sale of Commissions in the Army.

1857-8 [2318], XXXIV Report of the Commissioners Appointed to Inquire into the Regulations Affecting the Sanitary Condition of the Army, the Organisation of Military Hospitals, and the Treatment of the Sick and Wounded.

1857-8 [2418], XIX Report of the Commissioners Appointed to Inquire into the Question of Promotion and Retirement in the Higher Ranks of the Army.
1859 [2553], IX Report of the Commission Appointed to Inquire into the Establishment, Organisation, Government, and Direction of the Militia of the United Kingdom.
1860 (441), VII Report from the Select Committee on Military Organisation.
1860 [2682], XXIII Report of the Commissioners Appointed to Consider the Defences of the United Kingdom.
1861 [2762], V Report of the Commissioners Appointed to Inquire into the Present System of Recruiting in the Army.
1861 [2817], XXXVI Report of the Committee to Inquire into the Present Organisation and Establishment of the Yeomanry Cavalry.
1861 (423), XIII Select Committee on Colonial Military Expenditure.
1862 [3053], XXVII Report of the Commissioners Appointed to Inquire into the Condition of the Volunteer Force in Great Britain.
1863 (3184) Royal Commission on the Sanitary State of the Army in India.

Newspapers and Periodicals
Bell's Weekly Messenger
Berkshire Chronicle
Cork Examiner
Derry Journal
Devizes and Wiltshire Gazette
Dublin Evening Mail
Dublin Evening Packet
Dublin Monitor
Dublin Morning Register
Dublin Observer
Dublin Weekly Herald
Evening Standard
Exeter Flying Post
Fraser's Magazine
Freeman's Journal
Hampshire Advertiser
Hampshire Chronicle
Illustrated London News
Inverness Courier
Kilkenny Journal
Liverpool Daily Post
Lloyd's Weekly London Newspaper
London Daily News

London Gazette
Morning Advertiser
Morning Chronicle
Morning Herald
Morning Post
Northern Whig
Pall Mall Gazette
Public Ledger and Daily Advertiser
Punch
Quarterly Review
Reading Mercury
Royal Cornwall Gazette
St. James's Gazette
Salisbury and Winchester Journal
Saunders's News-letter
The Era
The Examiner
The Globe
The London Dispatch
The London Evening Standard
The Pilot
The Speaker
The Times
United Service Gazette
Westminster Review
Wiltshire Independent
Worcestershire Chronicle

Secondary Sources

Acland, A., *Caroline Norton* (1948).
Adelman, P., *Peel and the Conservative Party 1830-1850* (1989).
Aldous, R., *The Lion and the Unicorn* (2006).
Anderson, O., *A Liberal State at War. English Politics and Economics during the Crimean War* (1967).
Anon., 'Sidney Herbert, First Baron Herbert of Lea', *Fraser's Magazine*, LXV (February 1862), pp. 198-212.
Argyll, Duchess of, *George Douglas, Eighth Duke of Argyll, Autobiography and Memoirs*, 2 vols (1906).
Ashley, E., *The Life and Correspondence of Henry John Temple Viscount Palmerston*, 2 vols (1879).
Atkinson, D., *The Criminal Conversation of Mrs Norton* (2012).
Baly, M.E., *Florence Nightingale and the Nursing Legacy* (Beckenham, 1986).

Bart, Sir G.D., and Ramsay, Sir G.D., *The Panmure Papers*, 2 vols (1908).
Bateman, J., *The Great Landowners of Great Britain and Ireland* (4th edn, 1883).
Beales, D.E.D., *England and Italy 1859-1860* (1961).
Beckett, I.F.W., *Britain's Part-Time Soldiers. The Amateur Military Tradition 1558-1945* (Barnsley, 2011).
Benson, A.C., and Esher, Viscount (eds), *The Letters of Queen Victoria. A Selection from Her Majesty's Correspondence between the years 1837 and 1861*, 3 vols (1907).
Berkeley, R., *The Lady with a Lamp* (1929).
Blake, R., *Disraeli* (1966).
Blake, R., *The Conservative Party from Peel to Churchill* (1970).
Bond, B., 'Prelude to the Cardwell Reforms, 1856-68', *Royal United Services Institution Journal*, CVI (1961), pp. 229-36.
Bostridge, M., *Florence Nightingale. The Woman and Her Legend* (2008).
Bourne, K. (ed.), *The Letters of the Third Viscount Palmerston to Laurence and Elizabeth Sulivan 1804-1863*, Camden, Fourth Series, XXIII (1979).
Brighton, P., *Original Spin: Downing Street and the Press in Victorian Britain* (2016).
Brock, M.G., and Curthoys, M.C. (eds), *The History of the University of Oxford: Volume VI: Nineteenth-Century Oxford, Part 1* (Oxford, 1997).
Brooke, J. and Sorensen, M. (eds), *W.E. Gladstone III: Autobiographical Memoranda 1845-1866* (1978).
Brown, D., *Palmerston. A Biography* (2010).
Caird, J., *English Agriculture in 1850-1* (1968 reprint).
Chadwick, O., *The Victorian Church. Part 1* (1966).
Chamberlain, M.E., *Lord Aberdeen. A Political Biography* (1983).
Chandler, D.G., and Beckett, I.F.W. (eds), *The Oxford History of the British Army* (Oxford, 1994).
Conacher, J.B., *The Aberdeen Coalition 1852-1855* (Cambridge, 1968).
Conacher, J.B., *The Peelites and the Party System 1846-52* (Newton Abbot, 1972).
Conacher, J.B., *Britain and the Crimea, 1855-56. Problems of War and Peace* (New York, 1987).
Cook, Sir E.T., *The Life of Florence Nightingale*, 2 vols (1913).
Crumplin, M.K.H., *Guthrie's War* (Barnsley, 2010).
Cunningham, H., *The Volunteer Force* (1975).
Curtis, J., *Mount Merrion* (Dublin, 2012).
David, S., *Victoria's Wars. The Rise of Empire* (2006).
Disraeli, B., *Endymion* (Bradenham edition, 1927).
Dossey, B.M., *Florence Nightingale: Mystic, Visionary, Healer*, (Philadelphia, 2010).

Edsall, N.C., *Richard Cobden. Independent Radical* (1986).
Evans, E.J., *The Forging of the Modern State. Early Industrial Britain 1783-1870* (1983).
Feuchtwanger, E.J., *Gladstone* (1975).
Figes, O., *Crimea. The Last Crusade* (2010).
Finlayson, G.B.A.M., *The Seventh Earl of Shaftesbury 1801-1885* (1981).
Fitzmaurice, E., *The Life of Granville George Leveson Gower Second Earl Granville*, 2 vols (1905).
Foster, R. E., *The Politics of County Power. Wellington and the Hampshire Gentlemen 1820-1852* (Hemel Hempstead, 1990).
Foster, R.E., *Wellington and Waterloo. The Duke, the Battle and Posterity 1815-2015* (Stroud, 2014).
Foster, R.F., *Modern Ireland 1600-1972* (1988).
Gash, N., *Politics in the Age of Peel* (1953).
Gash, N., *Sir Robert Peel. The Life of Sir Robert Peel after 1830* (1972).
Gash, N., *Aristocracy and People. Britain 1815-1865* (1979).
Gash, N., *Pillars of Government and Other Essays on State and Society c. 1770-1880* (1986).
Gash, N. (ed.), *Wellington. Studies in the Military and Political Career of the First Duke of Wellington* (Manchester, 1990).
Gaunt, R.A., *Sir Robert Peel. The Life and Legacy* (2010).
Goldie, S.M. (ed.), *"I have done my duty." Florence Nightingale in the Crimean War 1854-1856* (Manchester, 1987).
Gregory, E. (ed.), *Sir William Gregory. An Autobiography* (1894).
Hamilton, C.I., *Anglo-French Naval Rivalry 1840-1870* (Oxford, 1993).
Hamilton, C.I., *The Making of the Modern Admiralty: British Naval Policy-making, 1805-1927* (Cambridge, 2011).
Hammerton, A., *Emigrant Gentlewomen: Genteel Poverty and Female Emigration, 1830-1914* (1979).
Haultain, A. (ed.), *Reminiscences by Goldwin Smith, DCL* (1910).
Hawkins, A., *Parliament, Party and the Art of Politics in Britain, 1855-1859* (1987).
Hawkins, A., *British Party Politics, 1852-1886* (1988).
Hawkins, A., *The Forgotten Prime Minister. The 14th Earl of Derby*, 2 vols (Oxford, 2007, 2008).
Hawkins, D. (ed.), *The Grove Diaries. The Rise and Fall of an English Family 1809-1925* (Wimborne, 1995).
Herbert, Lord (ed.), *Pembroke Papers (1780-1794). Letters and Diaries of Henry, Tenth Earl of Pembroke and his Circle* (1950).
Herbert, Lady E., *How I Came Home* (1894).
Hilton, B., *A Mad, Bad & Dangerous People? England 1783-1846* (Oxford, 2006).

Hoppen, K.T., *The Mid-Victorian Generation 1846-1886* (Oxford, 1998).
Howe, A. (ed.), *The Letters of Richard Cobden* , 4 vols (Oxford, 2007-2015).
Jenkins, S., *England's Thousand Best Churches* (1999).
Jenkins, T.A., *The Liberal Ascendancy, 1830-1886* (1994).
Jenkins, T.A. (ed.), *The Parliamentary Diaries of Sir John Trelawny, 1858-1865*, Camden, Fourth Series, XL (1990).
Jennings, L.J. (ed.), *The Croker Papers*, 3 vols (1884-5).
Johnson, E., *A Divine Inspiration* (Woodstock, 2017).
Jones, P.D., 'The British Army in the Age of Reform, 1830-1854' (Duke University PhD thesis, 1968).
Jones, N., *The Plimsoll Sensation* (2007).
Jupp, J. (ed.), *The Australian People* (Cambridge, 2001).
Kinglake, A.W., *The Invasion of the Crimea*, 8 vols (1863-87).
Kitson Clark, G.S.R., *Peel and the Conservative Party. A Study in Party Politics 1832-1841* (1964).
Koss, S., *The Rise and Fall of the Political Press in Britain*, 2 vols (1981, 1984).
Lever, T., *The Herberts of Wilton* (1967).
Lewis, Reverend Sir G., *Letters of the Right Hon. Sir George Cornewall Lewis, Bart.* (1870).
Lewis, M., *The Navy in Transition 1814-1864. A Social History* (1965).
Lieven, D., *Russia Against Napoleon* (2009).
Longford, E., *Wellington. Pillar of State* (1972).
McCord, N., *The Anti-Corn Law League 1838-1846* (2nd edn, 1968).
McDonald, L., et al (eds), *The Collected Works of Florence Nightingale*, 16 vols (Ontario, 2001-2012).
Magnus, P., *Gladstone. A Biography* (1954).
Malmesbury, 3rd Earl of, *Memoirs of an Ex-Minister*, 2 vols (1885).
Martineau, H., *Biographical Sketches* (New York, 1869).
Martineau, J., *The Life of Henry Pelham Fifth Duke of Newcastle 1811-1864* (1908).
Mather, F.C., *Public Order in the Age of the Chartists* (Manchester, 1959).
Matthew, H. C. G., and Foot, M.R.D. (eds), *The Gladstone Diaries*, 14 vols (Oxford, 1968-1994).
Matthew, H. C. G., *Gladstone 1809-1874* (Oxford, 1986).
Matthew, H. C. G., and Harrison, B. (eds), *Oxford Dictionary of National Biography*, 61 vols (Oxford, 2004).
Maxwell, Sir H., *The Life and Letters of George William Frederick Fourth Earl of Clarendon*, 2 vols (1913).
Meredith, G., *Diana of the Crossways* (memorial edition, 1910).
Monypenny, W.F., and Buckle, G.E., *The Life of Benjamin Disraeli, Earl of Beaconsfield*, 6 vols (1910).
Moody, R., *Mr Benett of Wiltshire* (Salisbury, 2005).

Morley, J., *The Life of William Ewart Gladstone*, 3 vols (1903).
Morley, J., *The Life of Richard Cobden*, 2 vols (1908).
Mozley, T., *Reminiscences Chiefly of Oriel College and the Oxford Movement*, 2 vols (Cambridge, Massachusetts, 1882).
Muir, R., *Wellington. Waterloo and the Fortunes of Peace 1814-1852* (2015).
Munsell, F.D., *The Unfortunate Duke. Henry Pelham, Fifth Duke of Newcastle, 1811-1864* (Columbia, 1985).
Newbould, I.D.C., *Whiggery and Reform 1830-1841. The Politics of Government* (Stanford, 1990).
Nightingale, F., *Army Sanitary Administration, and its reform under the late Lord Herbert* (1862).
Norton, Hon. Mrs C., *The Lady of Garaye* (1863).
O'Malley, I., *Florence Nightingale 1820-1856* (1931).
Parker, C. S., *Sir Robert Peel from His Private Papers*, 3 vols (1891).
Parker, C. S., *Life and Letters of Sir James Graham*, 2 vols (1907).
Parry, J., *The Rise and Fall of Liberal Government in Victorian Britain* (1993).
Partridge, M., *Military Planning for the Defence of the United Kingdom, 1814-1870* (New York, 1989).
Perkins, J.G., *The Life of Mrs Norton* (1909).
Prest, J.M., *Lord John Russell* (1972).
Pugh, R.B. (ed.), *The Victoria History of the Counties of England. A History of Wiltshire. Volume VI* (1962).
Purcell, E.S., *Life of Cardinal Manning*, 2 vols (1896).
Quinn, E.V., and Prest, J.M. (eds.), *Dear Miss Nightingale. A Selection of Benjamin Jowett's Letters 1860-1893* (Oxford, 1987).
Read, D., *Peel and the Victorians* (Oxford, 1987).
Reeve, H. (ed.), *The Greville Memoirs. A Journal of the Reigns of King George IV, King William IV and Queen Victoria*, 8 vols (1888).
Reid, T. W., *The Life, Letters, and Friendships of Richard Monckton Milnes, First Lord Houghton*, 2 vols (1891).
Richards, E., *Britannia's Children: Emigration from England, Scotland, Wales and Ireland since 1600* (2004).
Ridley, J., *The Young Disraeli 1804-1846* (1985).
Ridley, J., *Lord Palmerston* (1970).
Robinson, M., *Mary Seacole. The Charismatic Black Nurse Who Became a Heroine of the Crimean War* (2005).
Royle, T., *Crimea. The Great Crimean War 1854-1856* (New York, 2000).
Salih, S. (ed.), *Wonderful Adventure of Mrs Seacole in Many Lands* (Penguin Classic edition, 2005).
Shannon, R.T., *Gladstone. Peel's Inheritor 1809-1865* (1982).
Shannon, R.T., *Gladstone. God and Politics* (2007).
Smith, F.B., *Florence Nightingale. Reputation and Power* (1982).

Smith, J., *Wilton and its Associations* (1851).
Southgate, D., *The Passing of the Whigs 1832-1886* (1962).
Southgate, D., *The Most English Minister. The Policies and Politics of Palmerston* (1966).
Spiers, E.M., *The Army and Society 1815-1914* (1980).
Stanmore, Arthur, Lord, *Sidney Herbert, Lord Herbert of Lea. A Memoir*, 2 vols (1906).
Stewart, R., *The Politics of Protection. Lord Derby and the Protectionist Party 1841-1852* (Cambridge, 1971).
Stewart, R., *The Foundation of the Conservative Party 1830-1867* (1978).
St Lawrence, R., 'Lady Elizabeth Herbert of Lea, 1821-1911', *Sarum Chronicle* (2001), pp. 37-43.
Story, G. (ed.), *The Letters of Charles Dickens. Volume VI* (Oxford, 1988).
Strachan, H., *Wellington's Legacy. The Reform of the British Army 1830-1854* (Manchester, 1984).
Strachey, L., *Eminent Victorians. The Definitive Edition* (2002).
Struve, G., 'An Anglo-Russian Medley: Woronzows, Pembrokes, Nicolays, and others: unpublished Letters and Historical Notes', *California Slavic Studies*, V (1970), pp. 93-135.
Stuart, C.H., 'The Formation of the Coalition Cabinet of 1852', *Transactions of the Royal Historical Society*, Fifth Series, IV (1954), pp. 45-68.
Sudley, Lord (ed.), *The Lieven-Palmerston Correspondence 1828-1856* (1943).
Sweetman, J., *War and Administration. The Significance of the Crimean War for the British Army* (Edinburgh, 1984).
Sweetman, J., *Raglan. From the Peninsula to the Crimea* (Barnsley, 1993).
Thompson, F.M.L., *English Landed Society in the Nineteenth Century* (1963).
Vincent, J.R., *The Formation of the British Liberal Party 1857-1868* (1966).
Vincent, J.R. (ed.), *Disraeli, Derby and the Conservative Party. The Political Journals of Lord Stanley 1849-1869* (Hassocks, 1978).
Vincent, J.R., 'The Parliamentary Dimension of the Crimean War', *Transactions of the Royal Historical Society*, Fifth Series, XXXI (1981), pp. 37-49.
Ward, J.T., *Sir James Graham* (1967).
Williamson, B., *The Arundells of Wardour* (Salisbury, 2011).
Woodham-Smith, C., *Florence Nightingale 1820-1910* (1950).
Woolley, S.F., 'The Personnel of the Parliament of 1833', *English Historical Review*, LIII (1938), pp. 240-62.
Wrottesley, G., *Life and Correspondence of Field Marshal Sir John Burgoyne*, 2 vols (1873).
Yates, N., *The Oxford Movement and Anglican Ritualism* (1983).

Index

Abdul I, Sultan, 241-2, 246
Aberdeen, George Hamilton Gordon, 4th Earl (1784-1860), For. Sec. 1841-6, PM 1852-5, 3, 5, 13, 98, 129, 180, 198, 200-1, 204, 209, 210, 213, 251, 252, 253, 255, 257, 293, 302, 303, 304, 307, 309, 313, 317, 333, 337-8, 357, 363, 370, 372, 401, 442, 459, 460, 461; opinion of SH, 2, 229, 254, 456; Francophile, 95; Corn Law leak, 130, 441; on emigration, 172-3; forms government 215-17; as Prime Minister, 220-9; on outbreak of Crimean War, 242-8; fall of government, 282-8; advises Peelites in Jan. 1855, 289-91; death of, 417
A'Court, Lt-Gen. Charles (SH's father-in-law), 146
A'Court, Elizabeth; see (Mary) Elizabeth, Lady Herbert of Lea
A'Court, Charles Henry, later A'Court Repington (SH's brother-in-law), 208, 222
Adam Bede, 82
Admiralty, 86-93, 96-9, 103, 107, 111, 114, 181, 216, 281, 390
Ailesbury, George Brudenell-Bruce, 2nd Marquis, 19
Ailesbury, Mary, Marchionesss (SH's sister), 19, 23, 62, 81, 100, 212, 421
Airey, Gen. Sir Richard, 271, 304
Albert of Saxe Coburg, Prince Consort, 132, 172, 229, 235, 247-8, 323, 385, 392
Aldershot, 236, 350, 385, 429
Alexander II, Czar, 308, 314, 383
Alexander, Dr Thomas, 343, 345, 346, 353, 359, 362, 386, 456

Alma, Battle of the River, 257-8, 261, 283-4, 317
Amedroz, H.F., 87
Amherst, Sarah, Lady, 8
Amington Hall, Warwickshire, 147
Anti-Corn Law League, 73
Anti-League, 105
Antrobus, Sir Edmund, 2nd bt, 57, 336
Antrobus, Sir Edmund, 3rd bt, 336
Argyll, George Douglas Campbell, 8th Duke of, 10, 223, 290, 358, 371, 380, n. 3, 460
Armstrong gun, 434-5, 439, 456, 458, 461
Army, 12, 88-9, 109-20, 181-2, 212, 231-41, 249-54, 257-72, 278, 283-97, 292, 297-9, 302-3, 308-11, 315, 318-23, 339-46, 349-51, 353-4, 357-9, 361-3, 366-8, 381, 385-90, 399,403, 404, 445, 452, 456-7, 459; barracks, 110, 347, 349-50, 353-6, 359, 362, 363, 365-7, 385, 387-8, 456, 461; cost and size, 111, 115-6, 119-20, 182, 231-2, 233-4, 250-1, 261-5, 399-400; discipline, 46, 112, 181-2, 384; enlistment, 111-12, 181-2, 232-4; hospitals, 267, 270-3, 277, 279-81, 299, 339, 341, 342, 346, 349-50, 354, 359, 365, 366, 386-8, 456, 458; Medical Department, 271-2, 279-80, 341-2, 345, 350, 354, 386, 390; Medical School, 350, 354, 386-7, 434, 437; promotion in, 239-40, 360; sale and purchase of commissions, 12, 114, 235, 319-21, 384-5, 456, 457; Staff College, 238-9, 322-3; schools and education, 12, 112-13, 114, 234, 237-41, 321-3, 329, 368, 384, 456;

statistical department, 350, 353-4
Army pensioners, 111, 116, 222, 232
Arrow (ship), 333-4, 392
Arundells of Wardour, 50
Ashburton, William, 2nd Lord, 418
Astley, Sir John Dugdale, 42
Athenaeum, 229-30
Auckland, George Eden, 1st Earl, 186
Australia, 170, 171, 174, 176, 177, 399-400,

Baines, Edward, 364
Baker, Col Edward, 77-8
Balaclava, 258, 259, 260, 268, 272
Balaclava, Battle of, 258, 273, 304, 317
Balfour, Dr Thomas Graham, 343, 345, 346, 347, 351
Ballinteer, 167
Ballsbridge, 34
Bankes, William John, 23
Baring, Sir Francis Thornhill, 3rd bt, 74
Barnum, Phineas Taylor, 327
Barrow, Sir John, 87
Bath, John Alexander Thynne, 4th Marquis, 335, 418-19
Batkin, Mrs, 173
Batten, Revd Samuel Ellis, 22, 23, 29-30
Belgrave Square, 49 (SH's home), x-xi, 2, 9, 154, 167, 189, 203, 205, 215, 216, 225, 230, 275-6, 278, 291, 347, 357, 418, 421, 423
Bemerton, 11 n. 1, 352, 418, 464
Benett, John, 42-3, 47, 57, 58, 64, 104, 127, 208
Bentinck, Lord George, 137, 448-9
Berkeley, Reginald, 448
Birmingham, 38, 41, 78, 272, 356
Bishopstone, 30
Black Sea, 66, 242, 244, 245, 248, 308, 314, 315-16
Bleak House, 170
Blomfield, Revd Charles, Bp of London, 172, 189
Bostridge, Mark, 450-1
Bournemouth, 274, 437
Bowring, Sir John, 334
Bracebridge, Charles, 150-1, 267, 277, 341
Bracebridge, Selina, 150-1, 267, 275-6, 341

Brandon, David, 161
Bright, John, 104, 296, 326, 370, 377
Bright's disease, 62-3, 420
Brighton, 94
Broadstairs, 37, 256
Brodie, Sir Benjamin, 346, 387
Brougham, Henry, Lord, 38, 322
Brown, Sidney Herbert, 2
Bruce, Lord George, 80-1
Brunel, Isambard Kingdom, 270
Buckingham and Chandos, Richard, 2nd Duke of, 104
Buckingham Palace, 229, 246
Burgoyne, Sir John Fox, 239, 406, 434, 435
Burrell, W.H., 387

Cadogan, Lady Honoria, 51
Caird, James, 157
Cambridge, 23, 25, n. 1
Cambridge, H.R.H. George, Duke of, 61, 230, 323, 325, 345, 360, 383, 384, 388, 389, 392, 423, 430, 434, 438-9
Canada, 2, 176, 343, 345, 399, 408, 420
Canning, Charles John, Viscount, 31, 291, 394
Canning, Stratford, later Viscount de Redcliffe, 243
Canterbury Association, 169-70, 343
Canton, 67-8, 334, 336, 392
Captain, HMS, 431
Cardigan, James Brudenell, 7th Earl, 304
Cardwell, Edward, 309, 330, 380, 457
Carlisle, 205, 215
Carlos, Don, 67
Carlsbad, 255, 331
Carlton Club, 65, 179
Carlton Gardens, 153
Carlyle, Thomas, 107
Carnarvon, Henry Herbert, 4th Earl, 378
Cathcart, Sir George, 239
Cautley, Sir Proby, 363
Cavendish, Lord Richard, 284
Ceylon, 420, 442
Chatham, 93, 347, 386, 434
Charmouth, 273-4, 355

INDEX 481

Chartism, 72-3, 120
Chenery, Thomas, 273
Cherbourg, 398
Chichester, 163, 365
Chichester, Henry Pelham, 3rd Earl, 132
Chilhampton, 158
Chilmark, 25-6, 29-30, 433
China, 7, 68, 92, 111, 191, 333-5, 392-8, 400, 420, 434, 451, 452, 455, 456
Chisholm, Caroline, 170, 177-8, 452
Chlodwig, Prince of Hohenlohe-Schillingsfürst, 381
Chobham, 236
Church of England, 28-9, 48-50, 60, 65, 80, 84-5, 103, 107, 118, 122-4, 160-2, 191-3, 194-6, 217, 220-2, 327, 352, 418, 429-30, 464-6; see also Ireland, Nonconformists, Oxford Movement, Roman Catholicism
Church rates, 60, 65, 335, 358, 371, 405
Churchill, Sir Winston, 281
Clanwilliam, Richard Meade, 3rd Earl, 19
Clanwilliam, Elizabeth, Countess (SH's sister), 19, 212, 363, 418
Clarendon, George Villiers, 4th Earl, For. Sec. 1853-8, 185, 244, 247, 248, 250, 270, 295, 330, 408
Clark, Sir James, 343
Clontarf, meeting at, 99
Cobden, Richard, 104-5, 124-6, 218, 296, 334-5, 408-9, 442
Cockburn, Sir George, 87, 89, 93, 390
Commissariat, 110, 252, 254, 268-9, 271, 280, 299, 304, 345-6, 390, 396-7
Constantinople, 243, 244, 248, 272, 275
Cook, Sir Edward, 445-6, 449
Cooke, J.D., 184-5
Cooper, Hon. Anthony John Ashley, 77
Cork, 406
Corn Laws, 73, 76, 83, 84, 103-6, 107, 109, 120, 124-34, 137, 165, 180, 182, 183, 209, 217, 441
County Meetings, 79, 191, 194, 195, 208

Craven, Augustus, 207
Crimean War, 1, 3, 12, 234, 238, 255, 301, 302, 303, 306, 327, 336, 339, 369, 403, 435, 439, 447, 458; outbreak, 241-6; course of, 248-51, 256, 257-61, 265-73, 278-81, 311-12; peace negotiations, 308-11, 314-16
Croker, John Wilson, 16, 61-2, 128
Cromwell, Oliver, 9
Crutchley, Rosalie, 448-9
Cubitt, Thomas, x-xi, 154
Cullen, Cardinal Paul, 465
Cumming, Dr John, 327
Cunard, Samuel, 270

Dalhousie, James Broun-Ramsay, 1st Marquis, 31
Dante, 9
Danube, River 244, 308, 314
Dardanelles, 242, 244
Davis, Revd, 8
De Grey, George Frederick Samuel Robinson (1827-1909), 3rd Earl de Grey and Ripon, 410-11, 412, 417, 429, 432, 434, 436, 456, 458
Delane, John Thaddeus, 130-1, 348-9, 441
Denison, John Evelyn, 2, 331, 416, 437, 460
Derby, Edward Geoffrey Smith Stanley, 14th Earl (1799-1869), PM 1852, 1858-9, 13, 65, 97, 118, 129, 136, 180, 185, 199, 205, 207, 209-11, 215, 217, 218, 220, 292, 332, 333, 335, 360, 379, 419, 423, 433, 459; on emigration 172-3; forms government in 1852, 203; seeks SH's support in Jan. 1855, 288-9; seeks SH's support in 1858, 357, 359; defeat over 1859 Reform Bill, 369-72; fall of government, 373-4
Derby, 15th Earl; see Lord Stanley
De Vesci, Emma, Lady (SH's sister), 19
De Vesci, Thomas Vesey, 3rd Viscount (SH's brother-in-law), 19, 430
Devizes, 79, 84, 102, 105, 106, 191, 301
Devonport, 93
Diana of the Crossways, 131, 440, 448

Dickens, Charles, 143, 144, 170, 434, 435, 457
Disraeli, Benjamin, Earl of Beaconsfield (1804-1881), Ch. of Exch. 1852, 1858-9, 5-6, 8, 13, 69, 125, 180, 186, 187, 199, 200, 202, 206, 209-11, 217, 220, 223, 230, 284, 288, 310, 330, 333, 336, 360, 370, 378, 431, 440; attacks SH as Peel's valet, 126-7; on emigration, 174-5, 178; on SH's religion, 189-90; attacked by SH in Nov. 1852, 213-15; SH's dislike of, 218
Disraeli, Sarah, 295
Dissenters; see nonconformists
Dover, 347, 406, 423
Drummartin, 166
Dublin, 2, 25, 34-5, 41, 70-2, 82, 88, 101, 121, 165, 166-7, 169, 207, 222, 272, 365, 367, 465
Dufferin, Frederick, 1st Marquis, 420, 441
Duncombe, Thomas Slingsby, 120-1
Dunmore, Alexander Murray, 6th Earl, 19
Dunmore, Catherine, Countess (SH's sister), 19, 204, 358, 423
Dunmore, Charles Murray, 7th Earl (SH's nephew), 368-9
Durham Letter, 190

Easthope, John, 184
Ebrington, Hugh Fortescue, Viscount, 359
Ecclesiastical Commission, 195
Ecclesiastical Duties and Revenues Bill, 84, 195
Ecclesiastical Titles Bill, 191-2, 194, 199, 208, 217
Edinburgh, 414, 416
Edinburgh Letter, 129
Education, 48-9, 196-8, 223, 225, 463; in Wilton, 159-60, 196, 256, 273; in Ireland, 167, 168, 196; cathedral schools, 194
Eklees, John, 135
Elcho, Lady Anne, 316
Elgin, James Bruce, 8th Earl, 31
Eliot, Edward, Lord, 82
Ellenborough, Edward Law, 1st Earl, 58

Ellice, Edward, 301
Endymion, 5-6, 440
Ennis, Revd J., 164
Estcourt, Maj-Gen. James Bucknall, 266, 268, 271, 282, 306
Estcourt, Thomas Sotheron, 19, 427, 433, 435
Evans, Lt-Gen. Sir George de Lacy, 319-20, 385
Ewart, Joseph, 361
Exeter, 233, 365, 367
Exeter Flying Post, 316

Fairfield, Maj., 222
Family Colonisation Loan Society, 170, 177-8
Farnham, 322
Farr, Dr William, 346, 349, 353, 354, 362, 456
Female Emigration Fund, 165, 170-8, 186, 219, 275, 434, 452
Filder, William, 269, 304
Finn, Revd V., 164
Fisherton, 195, 221
Fitzharris; see Malmesbury
Fitzroy Somerset; see Raglan
Fitzwilliam, Richard, 7th Viscount, 23-5, 34, 419
Foley, John Henry, 438, 446, 447, 456, 457, 458
Foreign Enlistment Bill, 263-4
Forester, Lady Maria, 273, 276
Fortifications, 406-10
Fox, William John, 197-8
France, 16, 47, 82, 92, 94, 107, 116, 171, 241-5, 250, 262, 265, 270-1, 311, 314, 356, 381, 392-5, 398-401, 455
Franklin, Benjamin, 9
Free trade; see Corn Laws
Freemantle, Sir Thomas, 101
Froude, Revd Richard Hurrell, 28-9

Gage, Sir William, 87
Gallot, Alexina Sophie, 142
Galton, Sir Douglas, 454
Galton, Sir Francis, 355, 365
Gaskell, James Milnes, 294
Gaskell, Samuel, 346
Gawen, Admiral John, 429

INDEX 483

General Elections, 36, 37, 45 (1831), 36-7, 40, 45 (1832); 53-4, 58, 71 (1835); 62, 65 (1837); 76, 82 (1841); 183 (1847); 207, 209 (1852); 336-7 (1857); 373 (1859)
Gibson, Thomas Milner, 308-9, 310, 374
Gladstone, Catherine, 224,
Gladstone, Herbert, 2, 461
Gladstone, John Neilson, 301
Gladstone, William Ewart (1809-1898), Ch. of Exch. 1852-5, 1859-65, 2, 8, 12-13, 19, 46, 48, 50, 54, 55, 82, 99, 106, 118, 139, 145, 153-4, 179, 191, 192, 213, 215, 221, 230, 255, 282, 295-6, 303, 312-13, 314, 316, 326, 329-31, 333, 337, 380, 382, 405, 426-7, 429, 431, 433, 453, 457, 461-2, 463; early acquaintance with SH, 29, 31, 32, 37; on Gorham Judgement, 189; assumes lead of Peelites with SH in 1851-2, 199-201, 203-5; wooed by Derby and Russell in 1852, 209-10; joins Aberdeen coalition, 215-18; as Ch. of Exch., 223, 224-5, 231, 240; on SH as Sec at War, 267-8, 275, 281, 306-8; contemplates political future, Jan. 1855, 288-92; resigns, 293; argues with SH over foreign policy, 309-10, 312; declines office under Derby, Feb.1858, 357; declines office under Derby, May 1858, 359-60; goes to Ionian Islands, 369-70; wooed into Liberal camp during 1859, 373, 374, 376, 378-9; clashes with SH over defence spending, 1859-61, 388, 400-3, 407-9, 421; agonises over SH's dying, 423-4, 426; chairs memorial committee, 434-5, 437-8; assists Stanmore's memoir, 442-3; Goulburn's view of, 462
Glasgow, 272
Gleig, Revd George Robert, 88, 112-13, 169, 234, 238
Globe, The, 275
Gloire (ironclad), 398
Goderich, Frederick Robinson, Viscount, 319

Godley, John Arthur, 442
Godley, John Robert, 169
Gordon, Hon. Alexander, 304
Gordon, Hon. William, 87
Gorham Judgement, 189, 193
Goulburn, Henry, 23, 169, 281, 310, 462
Grafton Street, 153
Graham, Sir James Robert George, 2nd bt (1792-1861) 1st Lord of Admiralty 1830-4, Home Sec. 1841-6, 1st Lord of Admiralty 1852-5, 13, 61, 65, 87, 129, 135, 180, 185, 186, 210, 215, 243, 244-5, 286, 303, 307, 309, 312-13, 314, 332, 374, 388, 389, 392, 417, 418, 423; view of SH, 1-2; appearance, 117; works with SH on militia, 116-19; letter-opening controversy, 120-1; rapprochement with Liberals, 199, 205; joins Aberdeen coalition, 223; during Crimean War, 270, 272, 281-2; joins Palmerston government 289-90; Jan. 1855 resignation, 293, 295-6, 329-30; political stance in 1857, 333, 337-8, 350; against joining Conservatives in 1858, 357, 359-60; political stance in 1859, 370-1; advises SH to go to Lords, 379-80; advises SH over militia estimates, 401-2; on Volunteers, 413; death of, 429
Granby, Charles Manners, Marquis of, 175
Grant, Sir Francis, 10, 394 n. 2
Grant, Sir James Hope, 394, 395, 396, 397
Granville, Granville Leveson-Gower, 2nd Earl (1815-1891), For. Sec. 1851-2, Lord President 1852-8, 1859-65, 255, 281, 282, 294, 312, 332, 375, 376, 383, 405, 416, 419, 422, 460
Great Exhibition, 160
Great Industrial Exhibition, 222
Greathed, Col Edward, 363
Greene, Jeremiah, 208
Greenwich, 90-1, 93,
Gregory, Lady Augusta, 441
Gregory, Sir William, 131, 441

Greville, Charles Cavendish Fulke, 29, 45, 55, 59, 99, 130, 200, 201
Grey, Charles, 2nd Earl (1764-1845), PM 1830-4, 37, 38, 48, 53, 61, 87
Grey, Sir George, 2nd bt (1799-1882), Home Sec. 1846-52, 1855-8, 1861-5, Sec. for Cols 1855, Ch. of D. of Lancaster 1859-61, 254, 403-4
Grey, Henry 3rd Earl, formerly Viscount Howick, (1802-1894), Sec. at War 1835-9, Col Sec. 1846-52, 118, 131, 232, 266, 282, 352,
Grote, George, 46
Grove, Thomas, 56-7
Grove, Sir Thomas Fraser, 418-19
Guy, Dr, 358

Haddington, Thomas Hamilton, 9th Earl, 87, 93, 98
Hall, Anna Maria, 324, 452
Hall, Dr Sir John, 346, 359
Hall, Samuel Carter, 324-5
Hall Place School, 20-1
Hamilton, John Andrew, 3, 442, 450
Hamilton, Walter Kerr, Bp of Salisbury, 221
Hamilton-Gordon, Arthur; see Stanmore
Hardinge, Henry, Field-Marshal Viscount, 61, 99, 112, 113, 233-8, 249, 251, 264, 323
Harrow, 21, 26, 27, 29-30, 51
Harrowby, Dudley Ryder, 2nd Earl, 195
Hawes, Sir Benjamin, 391-2
Heathcote, Mr, 173
Heathcote, Sir William, 5th bt, 330-1
Herbert, Hon. A.E.G., 449
Herbert, Lady Catherine (SH's sister); see Lady Dunmore
Herbert, Lady Constance Gwladys (SH's daughter), 431-2
Herbert, Lady Diana (SH's half-sister); see Lady Normanton
Herbert, Lady Elizabeth (SH's sister); see Lady Clanwilliam
Herbert, Lady Elizabeth Maud (SH's daughter), 432
Herbert, Lady Emma (SH's sister); see Lady de Vesci
Herbert, Revd George, 10-11, 464

Herbert, Hon. George Robert (SH's son); see 13th Earl of Pembroke
Herbert, Lady Georgiana (SH's sister); see Lady Shelburne
Herbert, Lady Mary (SH's sister); see Lady Ailesbury
Herbert, Lady Mary Catherine (SH's daughter), 431
Herbert, (Mary) Elizabeth, Lady Herbert of Lea, 13, 28, 52, 154, 165-6, 281, 284, 297, 302, 347, 355, 360, 372-3, 380, n. 1, 432, 458, 464; early life, 146-8; engagement and marriage 148-9; honeymoon tour, 149-53; children, 155-6, 430-2; as patroness, 159-60; her religion, 6, 162-4, 192-4; in Ireland, 166-8; assists Female Emigration Fund, 175-6; interviews nurses in 1854, 275-8; and Wellington, 212; furious with Newcastle, 298; relations with FN, 150-1, 273-4, 276, 426, 454-5; work for Nightingale Fund, 323-4; disapproves of 12th Earl's lifestyle, 351-2; on WEG, 374, 379, 400-1, 462; on JRG, 401, n. 4; on SH, 4, 8, 9, 148-9, 190, 192-4, 328, 335-6, 456, 465; concern for his health, 379, 381, 382-3, 416-23; death of, 423-4; response to SH's passing, 426-30, 433, 435, 436-7, 441; collaborates with Stanmore on memoir of SH, 3-6, 442-5; converts to Catholicism 432-3; perceptions of, 448-9, 451, 453-4
Herbert, Hon. Michael (SH's son), 431

Herbert, Hon. Sidney, Lord Herbert of Lea (1810-1861), family background, 14-19; early years, 19-20; at school, 20-3; father's death, 23, 29; inheritance, 24-5; at Oxford, 26-32; enters Parliament, 42-5; rumoured engagement, 50-1; assumes control at Wilton, 52-3; declines office as Lord of Treasury, 54-5; as Sec. of Bd of Control, 58-60; on war in Spain, 67; 1st Opium War, 67-8; alleged interference in Salisbury election,

INDEX

77; Sec. to Admiralty, 1841-5, 86-99; and naval schools, 90-1; 1845-6 war scare, 94-6, 115-16; on naval promotions, 96-7; declines office in Ireland, 100-2; Sec. at War 1845-6, 109-20; and military education, 112-13; and commissions, 114; on army pensioners, 116; assists JRG in reviving militia, 116-20; defends JRG, 120-1; on Maynooth, 122-3; attacked by Disraeli, 126-7; during Corn Law crisis, 124-39; alleged leak to *The Times*, 130-1; attacks Malmesbury, 136; Irish Crimes Bill, 137-8; and Caroline Norton, 143-6; engagement and marriage, 146-9; extended honeymoon, 149-53; moves into Belgrave Square, 154; and high farming, 156-8; and Female Emigration Fund, 169-78; declines office under JR, July 1846, 181; favours Reform, 184; buys *Morning Chronicle*, 184-6; and Don Pacifico, 187-8; and Gorham Judgement, 189-90; and Ecclesiastical Titles, 190-2; and church reform, 194-6; and education, 196-8; on 1852 Militia Bill, 201-2, 206; declines office under Derby, Feb. 1852, 203-4; visits Robert Pembroke, 204-5; fall of Derby, 212-15; excoriates Disraeli, 213-15; formation of Aberdeen coalition, 215-16; supports Jewish Disabilities Bill, 223-4; and 1853 budget, 224-5; and 1853 India Act, 225; and Oxbridge reform, 225-6; and constitutional reform, 226-9; returns to War Office, 230-1; militia, 232; railways, 233; and army reform, 234-41; and outbreak of Crimean War, 241-6; defends government's handling of, 248-50; raises reinforcements, 250-1; admits case for administrative reorganisation, 252-3; official status downgraded, 253-4; on course of the war, 257-60; attempts to galvanise war effort, 260-82; pilots Foreign Enlistment Bill, 263-4; attempts to coordinate military departments, 284-6; fall of Aberdeen, 286-8; accepts office under Pam, 288-92; resigns as Sec. for Colonies, Feb. 1855, 292-3; and Roebuck committee of inquiry, 297-302, 306-8; defends McNeill and Tulloch, 304-6; and end to Crimean War, 308-12, 314-16; declines office under Pam, Nov. 1855, 312-14; on sale of commissions, 319-21; advocates military education, 321-3; and Nightingale Fund, 323-9; death of mother, 328; defeat of Pam, Mar. 1857, 333-5; lobbies for army sanitary commission, 341-4; work on army sanitary commission, 344-50, 351; secures sub-commissions, 352-3; work on sub-commissions, 353-4, 355, 359, 363, 365-6; Orsini affair, 356-7; declines office under Derby, Feb. 1858, 357; on Indian Mutiny, 360-1; accepts chair of Indian sanitary commission, May 1859, 362-3; Warminster speech, 364-5; article for *Westminster Review*, 366-8; on Conservative Reform Bill, Mar. 1859, 370-2; and fall of Derby, June 1859, 373-8; becomes Sec. for War, 379-80; army reform, 384-8; relative failure to reform War Office, 388-92; role in 2nd Opium War, 392-8; supports calls for programme of fortifications, 398-9, 406-10; clashes with WEG over militia estimates, 400-3; offers resignation Feb. 1860, 402; attempts to revive militia, 403-5; on paper duties, 405; and Volunteer Movement, 410-16; persuaded to quit Commons, 417-19; ennobled, 419; in House of Lords, 419; last months, 420-3; dies, 423-4; reactions to his death, 425-9; funeral, 429; will, 430; public memorials to, 433-4, 436-9, 446-7, 449-50; achievements, 455-60; the lost leader, 460-2

Political evolution of: before 1832, 7, 12-13, 36-9; during 1832 parliament, 45, 46, 47; during 1835 parliament, 60-1, 63; during 1837 parliament, 65-8, 71, 73, 82-5; during 1841 parliament, 86, 103-5, 106-8, 127, 133-5; during 1847 parliament, 179-81, 183-4, 186-7, 198-201, 203-4, 205-7; during 1852 parliament, 210-11, 216-19, 223-4, 229, 295-6, 329-333; during 1857 parliament, 336-8, 350, 357-8, 359-60, 369-70

Major speeches of: maiden speech, June 1834, 48-50; Ireland, Apr. 1839, 69; confidence motion, Jan. 1840, 73-4; sugar duties, May 1841, 74-6; Ireland, Feb. 1844, 99-100, 121-2; Corn Laws, Feb.1844, 105; 'whining' speech, Mar. 1845, 125-7; Repeal of the Corn Laws, Jan. 1846, 133-5; Don Pacifico, June 1850, 188; progressive Conservatism, Apr. 1852, 206-7; free trade, Nov. 1852, 213-14; outbreak of Crimean War, Feb. 1854, 245-6; defends conduct of war, Dec.1854, 283-4; opposes Roebuck censure, Jan. 1855, 286-8; resignation statement, Feb. 1855, 293-4; Roebuck's censure motion, July 1855, 303-4; on end to Crimean War, May 1856, 314-15; Canton, Mar. 1857, 333-5; Orsini, Feb.1858, 356; Warminster speech, Oct. 1858, 364-5; Reform Bill, Mar. 1859, 371-2; no confidence debate, June 1859, 378; fortifications, Aug. 1860, 408

Elections for South Wiltshire, 42-5 (1832); 56-8 (1835); 64-5 (1837); 76-7, 84-5 (1841); 142-3 (Feb. 1845); 165, 182-3 (1847); 175, 192, 208-10 (1852); 223, 226, 294-5 (Jan. 1853); 464 (Feb. 1855); 335-6 (1857); 372-3 (1859); 418-19 (Feb. 1861)

As a father, 20, 155-6, 430-2; as sportsman, 11, 53, 61, 81, 103, 331, 332, 383; as landlord and patron, 4, 61-2, 77-81, 102-3, 157-62, 331; religious convictions, 6, 11, 27-9, 47, 123-4, 162-4, 189-90, 192-4, 220-1, 277, 327, 373, 462-7; and church building, 1-2, 70, 84, 103, 160-2, 168-9, 195, 221-2, 464-5; in Ireland, 34-6, 69-72, 121, 164-9, 222-3, 341, 351; foreign travel, 25-6, 33, 47, 62, 66, 149-53, 204-5, 311, 331, 360, 422-3; alleged pro-Russian tendencies, 11, 247-8, 316-18; and FN: first encounter, 150-1; collaboration during Crimean War, 273-81; and Nightingale Fund, 324, 329; collaboration on army sanitary reform, ch. 11, *passim*; evaluation of relations with, 451-5; contemporary assessments of SH, 2, 4, 8-10, 99, 106-7, 138, 139, 229-30, 282-3, 294-5, 306-8, 358, 384, ill-health of, 37, 46-7, 60, 62-3, 293, 296, 302, 331, 343, 354-5, 357-8, 360, 416-17ff; view of: Disraeli, 214-15, 218; EH, 146-7; WEG, 31, 369-70; JRG, 205, 401, n. 4; Pam, 68-9, 201-3, 211, 217, 313, 332; Peel, 56, 188-9; Russell, 210, 217-18; Wellington, 211-12; posthumous reputation, 1-3, 10-11, 434-6, 439-42, 445-6, 447-9, 450-1; Stanmore's Memoir of, 3-7, 442-5

Herbert, Hon. Sidney (SH's son); see 14th Earl of Pembroke
Herbert, Hon. William Reginald (SH's son), 431
Herbert, New Zealand, 2
Herbert Convalescent Home, 437
Herbert Sound, Antarctica, 2
Herbert earls of Pembroke; see Pembroke
Heytesbury, William A'Court, Lord, 60-1, 101, 146, 212
Heywood, James, 225-6
High farming, 132-3, 156-7, 186
Hong Kong, 68, 334, 393, 394, 420
Horse Guards, 110, 113, 114, 235, 252, 260, 273, 305, 318, 323, 390
House of Lords, 38, 53, 64, 65, 69, 189, 204, 226, 405
Howick; see Grey, 3rd Earl
Hügel, Friedrich von, 431
Hume, Joseph, 46, 252

INDEX 487

Hyde Park, 414

Illustrated London News, 106, 323, 438
Income tax, 200, 224, 333, 407
India, 58-61, 116, 225, 361-3, 382, 394, 400, 452
Indian Mutiny, 321, 339, 350-1, 360-1
Inkerman, Battle of, 258-9, 261, 284, 317
Ionian Islands, 369
Ireland, 33-6, 69-72, 99-101, 106, 116, 121-3, 128-9, 137-8, 151, 164-9, 193, 222-4, 244-5, 256, 331, 341, 351, 352, 365-6, 463
Irishtown, 34, 164, 168
Italy, 9, 24, 47, 53, 61, 154, 161, 163, 379, 398, 417

Jebb, Sir Joshua, 346
Jewish disabilities, 186, 215, 223-4, 463
Joinville, Francois, Duc de, 94-5
Jones, Dr Henry Bence, 417, 422
Jones, Inigo, 15
Jowett, Revd Benjamin, 425, 455, 460

Kaiserwerth, 273
Keble, Revd John, 28
Kilmainham Hospital, 222
Kinglake, Alexander William, 144, 306

Land Transport Corps, 318
Lansdowne, Henry Petty-Fitzmaurice, 3rd Marquis, 81, 211, 247, 283, 288
Lansdowne, 4th Marquis; see Shelburne
Lawrence, Sir John, 452
Layard, Capt. Brownlow, 111-12
Lear, Revd Francis, 25, 26, 30
Leopold, Duke of Albany, 229
Lewis, Sir George Cornewall (1806-1863), Ch. of Exch. 1855-8, Home Sec. 1859-61, Sec. for War 1861-3, 370, 375, n. 5, 376, 382, 407, 419
Lichfield House Compact, 58
Lieven, Princess Dorothea, 143
Lincoln, Lord; see Newcastle
Liverpool, 31, 33, 309, 326
Liverpool, Robert Banks Jenkinson, 2nd Earl, 110
London Daily News, 384, 445
Long, Richard Penruddocke, 175, 208

Long, Walter, 80
Longfellow, Henry Wadsworth, 278
Louis Phillipe, King, 94, 153,
Lowry-Corry, Hon. Henry 87
Lucan, George Bingham, 3rd Earl, 304
Lyndhurst, John Singleton Copley, Lord, 99
Lytton, Sir Edward Bulwer, 380

Macdonald, Lawrence, 10
McNeill, Sir John, 304-6, 345-6, 444, 463
Magenta, 398
Mahon, Philip, Viscount, later 5th Earl Stanhope, 37
Maidstone, 322
Majendie, George, 25, 27, 30
Malmesbury, 419
Malmesbury, James Howard Harris, 3rd Earl (1807-1889), For. Sec. 1852, 1858-9, 8, 20, 54, 136, 144, 187, 215, 288, 330, 389; 1841 Wilton election, 78; attacked in *Morning Chronicle*, 185; accuses SH of Russian bias, 316-17; 1857 election, 335; Crimean dead, 369; reaction to SH's death, 426, 460
Malt tax, 48
Manchester, 198, 326-7, 352
Manchester School, 308-9, 310
Manning, Revd Henry Edward, later Cardinal, 6, 31, 152-3, 163, 170-1, 188, 189-90, 193, 194, 277, 431, 465
Mansel, Maj-Gen., 346
Mapleton, Dr Henry, 346
March, Charles Gordon-Lennox, Earl of, 132, 135
Maria, Grand Duchess, 246
Marochetti, Carlo, 436-7, 449, 458
Martin Chuzzlewit, 272, 324
Martin, Dr Ranald, 342, 346, 353, 362
Martineau, Harriet, 3, 18, 40, 50, 83, 296, 421, 439-40, 442
Matthew, Professor Henry Colin Gray, 450
Maule, Fox; see Panmure
Mayhew, Henry, 176
Mayne, J.T., 58
Maynooth, 122-4, 163

Mazzini, Giuseppe, 120
Melbourne, William Lamb, 2nd Viscount (1779-1848), Home Sec. 1830-4, PM 1834, 1835-41, 53, 60-1, 65, 67, 69, 74, 75, 80, 82, 92, 143, 377
Menshikov, Prince Alexander, 317
Merchant Seaman Act, 89-90
Meredith, George, 131, 440-1
Mexico, 420
Militia, 6, 110, 182, 205-6, 318, 390, 410, 411, 412, 421, 461; 1845-6 revival of, 116-20; 1852 Militia Act, 201-2, 231-4; in 1854-5, 251, 262-3; in 1859, 400-5
Mill, John Stuart, 362-3
Milnes, Richard Monckton, afterwards Lord Houghton, 326, 458
Moberly, George, 33
Model farms, 140, 157-8, 435
Moldavia, 241, 242, 248, 255, 308, 314
Morley, Henry, 434-5
Morley, John, 124, 442, 443
Morning Chronicle, 5, 8, 41, 112, 145, 159, 171, 176, 177, 184-6, 187, 243, 275, 279, 294
Morning Herald, 180
Morning Post, 438, 458
Morocco, 94
Mount Herbert, New Zealand, 2
Mount Merrion, 34, 35, 70, 166, 222, 351
Mowbray, Mr, 457
Mozley, Revd Thomas, 28, 29
Mudeford, 435
Murray, John, 284, 444

Nanking, Treaty of, 68
Napier, Admiral Sir Charles, 97, 98
Napier, Gen. Sir William, 301
Naples, 161, 193, 351
Napoleon Bonaparte, 17, 18, 21
Napoleon III, Louis Napoleon Bonaparte, 201, 202, 205, 241, 259, 265, 270, 314, 356, 364, 409
National Gallery, 9
National Portrait Gallery, 9, 331
Navigation Laws, 186
Neagle, Dame Anna, 448
Neison, Francis, 346, 347, 367

Nelson's Column, 93
Nesselrode, Karl Robert, Count, 243
Netley Hospital, 350, 355, 387
Newcastle, Henry Pelham Clinton, 5th Duke, formerly Lord Lincoln, (1811-1864), Sec. for War 1852-5, Col Sec. 1859-64, 9, 31, 46, 46, 54, 82, 93, 99, 101, 127, 144, 169, 173, 179, 180-1, 210, 223, 224, 250, 253-4, 296, 311-12, 314, 380, 408, 420, 429, 434; teases SH, 148; domestic woes, 141, 154-5; buys *Morning Chronicle*, 184-5; on Peelite position in 1851-2, 198-201; joins Aberdeen coalition, 215-17; as Sec. for War, 257-9, 260, 261, 264, 266-70, 272-3, 282-4, 286, 299, 302, 307, 439; upsets EH, 298; backs Nightingale Fund, 324-5
Newman, John Henry, Cardinal, 28, 123-4, 162-3
New Zealand, 2, 3, 169, 400, 442
Nice, 66, 398, 400, 422
Nicholas I, Czar, 20, 242, 247, 308
Nightingale, Florence (1820-1910), 1, 12, 13, 156, 172, 257, 267, 281, 297, 304-5, 339, 350, 351, 353, 355-6, 359, 366, 383, 421, 432, 436, 439; meets Herberts in Rome, 150-1; invited to take nurses to Scutari, 273, 274-6; communications with SH during Crimean War, 278-81; alleged religious affiliations of, 150, 276-8, 326-7, 466; view of Nightingale Fund, 324-5, 329; lobbies for army sanitary commission, 339-44; work on sanitary commission, 344-6, 347-9; publicises commission's report, 366-7; lobbies for Indian sanitary commission, 360-3, 382; on army reforms effected, 385-6, 387-8; SH's failure to reform War Office, 391-2; praises medical arrangements in 2nd Opium War, 396-7; on SH's ill-health, 343, 417, 420; final meeting with, 423; reaction to SH's death, 425-6, 462; supports memorial efforts, 435-6, 437-8; non-cooperation over Stanmore's memoir, 443-5; statue of FN, 425,

446-7; FN's posthumous reputation, 445-6, 448-9, 450-1; relationship with EH, 155, 273-4, 426, 454-5; relations with SH in life and death, 2, 9, 10, 150-1, 193-4, 273-4, 306, 346-7, 447-9, 451-3, 455-6, 457-8, 463, 465-6
Nightingale, Frances, 150
Nightingale, Parthenope, 276
Nightingale, William, 150
Nightingale Fund, 323-9, 452, 453
Nonconformists, 36, 48-9, 55, 57-8, 65, 83, 122, 124, 162, 195-7, 225-6
Normanton, Diana Herbert, Countess of (SH's half-sister), 17, 18, 44
Normanton, Welbore Ellis Agar, 2nd Earl, 18, 44, 78
Norton, Caroline, 11, 130-1, 143-6, 147, 148, n. 1, 152, 427, 431, 440-1, 452
Nursing, 1, 2, 150, 257, 267, 271-9, 324-5, 327-8, 342, 439, 452, 453

O'Brien, William Smith, 136, 169
O'Connell, Revd, 168
O'Connell, Daniel, 33-4, 65, 72, 99, 121
O'Connell, John, 169
O'Connor, Michael, 464
Oriel College, Oxford 26-8, 36, 169
Orsini, Felice, 356
Osborne House, IOW, 256, 383
Osborne, Revd Sidney Godolphin, 267, 317
Owen, William, 9
Oxford, 326, 327, 328
Oxford, Edward, 79
Oxford Movement, 28, 29, 31, 123-4, 162-3, 192
Oxford Union, 9, 36-7, 457
Oxford University, 10, 15, 23, 26, 28, 29, 30, 32, 36-7, 39, 43, 56, 62, 123-4, 155, 162-3, 225-6, 330, 461

Pacifico, David ('Don'), 187-8, 335
Pakington, Sir John, 301
Paley, William, 22
Pall Mall Gazette, 438, 439
Palmerston, Amelia (Emily), Viscountess, 136, 316

Palmerston, Henry John Temple, 3rd Viscount (1784-1865), For. Sec. 1830-4, 1835-41, 1846-5, Home Sec. 1852-5, PM 1855-8, 1859-65, 13, 18-19, 23, 153-4, 184, 186, 201, 209, 213-14, 223, 230, 293, 303, 305-6, 318, 328, 330, 335, 336, 337, 354, 355, 382, 385, 392, 416, 418-19, 422-3, 434-5, 436, 442, 459-60, 461, 462, 463, 464; character and SH's low view of, 10, 13, 68-9, 131, 211, 216, 294, 313-14, 332, 367, 370, 371; 1st Opium War 67-8; 2nd Opium War, 393-5; on national defence, 95, 118-9, 407-9; and Don Pacifico, 187-8; on the militia, 201-2, 262-3, 400; joins Aberdeen coalition, 215-16; and Crimean War, 242, 243, 247, 255, 262-3, 270, 282-3, 284, 294, 307, 308-9, 311, 314; becomes PM, 288-292; and SH's resignation, 295; and Orsini affair, 356-7; during 1859 political manoeuvrings, 373-6, 378-80; pleads to keep SH in government, 402-3; high regard for EH, 453-4; view of SH, 202-3, 211, 287, 312-13
Panmure, Fox Maule, 2nd Baron, later 11th Earl of Dalhousie (1801-1874), Sec. at War 1846-52, Sec. for War 1855-8, 113, 201, 318, 320-1, 323, 330, 333, 341-4, 351, 352, 353-4, 359, 366, 388, 463
Paper duties, 405
Paris, 24, 51, 53, 61, 82, 141-3, 161, 204, 210, 244, 262, 272, 325, 352, 356, 415, 420, 432
Paris, Treaty of, 315-16, 328
Parliamentary Reform, 13, 183-4, 203-4, 223, 226-7, 333, 350, 370, 374, 405; 1832 Reform Act, 36, 36-8, 41-2, 43, 45, 54, 117; 1854 Reform Bill, 226-9; 1859 Reform Bill, 370-1
Parr, Anne, 14
Parry, Sir Hubert, 432
Patriotic Fund, 258
Paulet, General Lord William, 280, 302
Pavlovich, Baron Nikolay, 247
Peel, Gen. Jonathan, 301, 304, 359, 386, 411, 434, 456

Peel, Sir Robert, 2nd bt (1788-1850), PM 1834-5, 1841-6, 13, 45, 57, 60-1, 63, 71, 79, 81, 86, 95-7, 107, 115, 117, 122, 147, 148, 180, 182, 185, 193, 195, 212, 213, 230, 235, 441, 447, 448, 455, 459, 461; 1834-5 government, 53-6, 58, 59; promotes SH to cabinet, 99-100; Corn Laws, 103-4, 109, 120, 124-5, 128-38; tips SH for premiership, 139; on emigration 172-3; death of, 188-9

Peelites, 5, 63, 64-5, 83, 97, 123, 310, 312; in 1847 parliament, 179-81, 183, 184, 186-8, 191, 198-206; at 1852 election, 209; enter coalition, 212-18; in Aberdeen's government, 220, 223; agree to serve under Pam, 289-92; resignation of, 292-3; in 1857, 329-30, 333; and 1857 election, 336-8; decline to join Derby in 1858, 356-7; and 1859 election, 373

Peking, 392, 295

Pembroke, Canada, 2

Pembroke, Herbert earls of, 14-15, 27, 41, 77, 81, 86, 117, 208
  Thomas, 8th Earl, 15, 86
  Henry, 9th Earl, 15
  Henry, 10th Earl (grandfather of SH), 15-17, 25
  George, 11th Earl (father of SH), 9, 17-20, 23, 24-5, 26-7, 29, 51, 52, 68, 77, 78, 153, 203, 431
  Robert, 12th Earl (half-brother of SH), 6, 23-4, 41-2, 45, 51-3, 61, 82, 141-3, 204, 210, 351-2, 419, 432, 464
  George, 13th Earl (son of SH), 431, 441, 443, 446
  Sidney, 14th Earl (son of SH), 431, 444-5
  Reginald, 15th Earl (grandson of SH), 449-50

Pembroke House, 23, 153

Pembroke Lodge (SH's birthplace), 19, 153, 375

Pepys, Samuel, 86

Percy, Hon. Josceline, 267

Phillimore, Robert, 426

Phillips, Sir Thomas, 343, 347

Phillpotts, Henry, Bp of Exeter, 189

Pius IX, Pope 151, 190

Place, Francis, 38

Plymouth, 233, 251, 406, 407,

Poor law, 65, 72, 73, 79-80, 83, 167

Portsmouth, 93, 233, 251, 255, 355, 406, 407

Praed, Winthrop Mackworth, 58-9

Prince, SS, 259

Protection; see Corn Laws

Punch, 9

Purveyor-General, 271, 279-80, 300, 385

Pusey, Edward Bouverie, 28, 162, 192, 276, 463

Quidhampton, 158

Radnor, William Pleydell-Bouverie, 3rd Earl, 43-4, 183

Raglan, Field-Marshal Fitzroy James Henry Somerset, 1st Baron, 103, 118, 234, 250, 255, 258, 259, 261, 262, 265-6, 268, 270, 271, 279, 281, 282, 284, 294, 295, 311

Railways, 62, 70, 154, 233

Ramsay, George, 268

Ray, Sidney Herbert, 2

Reeve, Henry, 441

Resolute (supply ship), 259

Richmond, Charles Gordon Lennox, 5th Duke, 118, 132

Richmond, George, 10

Richmond Park, 19

Riddle, Edward, 91

Riddle, John, 91

Ringsend, 34, 167, 168

Ripon, Frederick Robinson, 2nd Marquis, 432

Ripon, 89, 195, 417

Roche, Revd A., 164

Roebuck, John Arthur, 286, 288, 292-3, 294, 298-9, 301-4, 306, 308, 311, 316, 344

Roman Catholicism, 6, 11, 28-9, 33-4, 37, 50, 70-1, 83, 100, 121-4, 162-4, 168, 189-97, 207, 241, 276-8, 327, n. 1, 392, 432-3, 465-6

Roman Catholic Emancipation (1829), 34, 36, 56

Rome, 25, 31, 66, 150, 153, 163, 273, 432
Royal Commissions, 225, 258, 305; army promotion (1854), 239-40, 459; sale of commissions (1857), 320-1, 459; sanitary condition of the army (1857-8), 338, 339, 341-51, 357, 367-8, 452, 459; promotion and retirement (1857-8), 344, 358, 360, 384-5, 452, 459; militia organisation (1859), 403; defence of the UK (1860), 398-9, 406; sanitary state of army in India (1863), 362-3, 373, 381, 382, 459
Royal Herbert Hospital, 2, 436, 437, 439, 456
Royal Military Academy Sandhurst, 237-8, 322, 323
Russell, Lady Frances, 375
Russell, George, 5-6, 440, 445
Russell, Lord John, later Earl (1792-1878), Paymaster-Gen. 1831-4, Leader of House 1835-41, PM 1846-52, For. Sec. 1852-3, Leader of House 1853-4, Col Sec. 1855, For. Sec. 1859-65, 13, 53, 78, 97, 129, 131, 153, 164, 165, 172, 186-7, 196-7, 199, 200, 209-10, 217-18, 223, 230, 233, 242, 247, 253, 260, 288, 303, 332, 333, 350, 357, 382, 392, 394, 420, 462; 1845 *Edinburgh Letter*, 149; 1846 overtures to SH, 181; 1850 *Durham Letter*, 190; resigns in 1851, 199; resigns in 1852, 201-3; on Reform, 226-9, 370-2, 405; fall of Aberdeen, 283, 285-6; machinations in 1859, 373-7
Russell, William Howard, 249, 266
Russia, 18, 66, 163, 227, 242-8, 250, 25, 258, 264, 308, 312, 314-18, 369, 396, 403, 455, 461

St Thomas's Hospital, 329
Salerno, 152
Salisbury, 41, 42, 44, 50, 52, 53, 57, 58, 62, 64, 76, 79, 81, 84, 103, 104-5, 135, 146, 154, 158, 221, 266, 327, 336, 372-3, 393, 413; city council, 1, 449-50; 1841 election in, 77-8; Infirmary, 79, 103, 430, 464 ; SH statue in, 425, 433-5, 436-7, 449-50, 458
Salisbury Cathedral, 20, 30, 224, 421
Sandymount, 34, 70, 167-8, 465
Savoy, 398, 400
Schöeffer, Marie, 142, 204, 351-2, 432
Schools; see education, military education
Scotland, 156, 341, 365, 404, 417, 430, 449, 466
Scutari, 248, 257, 267, 268, 272, 275, 278, 279, 280, 281, 299, 300, 323, 325, 343, 348
Seacole, Mary, 276
Sebastopol, 246, 255, 256, 257, 258, 259, 284, 286, 297, 308, 311, 315, 369
Secret ballot, 46, 66, 70-1, 73, n. 1, 83, 226
Select committees, 46, 48, 60, 71, 182, 186; Passengers' Act (1851), 198; Devon and Dorset Railway Bill (1852-3), 233; Army before Sebastopol (1854-5), 286, 297ff, 344; Sandhurst Royal Military College (1854-5), 323; 1860 Military Organisation (1860), 11, 382, 389-92, 459; Colonial Military Expenditure (1861), 459
Seymour, Sir George, 87
Shaftesbury, Anthony Ashley Cooper, 7th Earl, 169, 171-2
Shelburne, Georgiana, Lady (SH's sister), 19, 20, 81-2, 143
Shelburne, Henry Petty-Fitzmaurice, Lord, later 4th Marquis of Lansdowne, 19, 81, 143
Sidney, Mary, 15
Sidney, Sir Philip, 15
Sillery, Maj. Charles, 280
Sinope, 245
Slavery, 74-5, 83, 150
Smith, Robert Vernon, 352
Solferino, 398
Spa, 422-3, 429
Spain, 67, 83, 208, 301
Spinelli, Octavia, 24, 351
Smith, Dr Andrew, 271-2, 279-80, 297-8, 302, 324, 346, 350, 359
Smith, F.B., 450, 452-3

Smith, James, 160
Smith, William, 150
Somerset, Edward Adolphus St Maur, 12th Duke, 320, 380 n. 3
Somerton, James Ellis Agar, Viscount, later 3rd Earl of Normanton, 78, 183, 207-8
Southampton, 276, 350
South Newton, 158, 159
Spencer, Elizabeth, Countess of Pembroke (SH's grandmother), 16
Stafford, Augustus, 343
Stanley, Edward Henry, Lord, later 15th Earl of Derby, 8, 288, 315, 326, 361-2, 382, 420, 460
Stanley, Mary, 267, n. 4, 275-6, 277, 278, 452, 453
Stanmore, Arthur, Lord, 3; 130, 442, 465; views on SH, 45, 50, 66, 127, 279; writes life of SH, 3-8, 442-4, 451
Staunton, Sir George Thomas, 68
Stonehenge, 20, 224
Storks, Gen. Henry, 343
Strachey, Lytton, 10, 448, 450
Straits Convention, 308
Straubenzee, Maj-Gen. Sir T.C., 393
Strutt, Edward, 220-1
Strzelecki, Sir Paul, 337, 429, 434
Stuart, C.H., 460-1, 463
Sugar duties, 74-6, 83
Sullivan, Cornelius, 34-5, 166, 168
Sumner, John Bird, Abp of Canterbury, 169
Sutherland Dr John, 342, 346, 347, 349, 353, 355, 362, 365, 456
Symonds, Sir William, 94

Taku forts, 393, 395
Tamworth Manifesto, 53-4, 57, 206
Taney, 35
Tennyson, Alfred, Lord, 406, 410
The Lady of Garaye, 145-6, 427
The Lady with a Lamp, 448
Thynne, Lord Henry, 335-6, 372
Tientsin, Treaty of, 392-3, 394, 397 n. 2
Times, The, 82-3, 92, 101, 129, 130, 135, 138, 174, 184, 189, 249, 252, 265, 266, 267, 273, 274, 295, 301, 326, 348, 364, 427, 435, 441, 442, 447
Tottenham Park, Savernake, 81, 149, 331, 418
Tractarianism; see Oxford Movement
Trelawny, Sir John, 371, 378, 384, 385
Tulloch, Maj-Gen. Sir Alexander Murray, 304-6, 346, 354
Turkey, 241-4, 246, 247, 314, 461
Tweeddale, George Hay, 8th Marquis, 410, 411
Tyrrell, Sir John, 131-2

United Services Institute, 358
United States of Amercia, 92

Varna, 248
Vectis (ship), 276
Ventura, Giaocchino, 165-6
Victoria, Queen, 153, 172, 229, 270, 288, 350, 392, 414, 429, 436
Vienna, 272, 308, 309, 315
Vienna Note, 242, 244
Villiers, Charles Pelham, 213
Vivian, Sir Robert Hussey, 363
Volunteer Movement, 116, 390, 404-5, 410-16, 434, 436, 439, 451, 456, 458

Wakefield, Edward Gibbon, 169
Wales, 32, 50, 211
Walewski, Alexandre Florian, Comte de, 356
Walker, Alexander Graham, 446
Wallachia, 241, 242, 248, 255, 308
Walpole, Horace, 16, 161
Walpole, Spencer, 205, 360
War Office, 98, 101, 109-13, 230-9, 255, 260, 265, 273, 276, 298, 302, 318, 323, 330, 333, 353, 354, 367, 379, 382-4, 410-11, 422, 425, 437-8, 446, 458; reform of, 251-3, 341, 382, 388-92, 413, 446, 452, 457
Ward, Revd William George, 123-4
Warminster, 80, 102, 361, 364, 368, 413
Warner, Capt. Samuel Alfred, 94
Waterloo, Battle of, 61-2, 76, 239, 241, 263, 369 n. 1
Waterloo Place, 425, 427
Watts, James, 326, 327

Wellesley, Lord Charles, 212
Wellington, Arthur Wellesley, 1st Duke of (1769-1852), PM 1828-30, 1834, For. Sec. 1834-5, 31, 33-4, 36, 37, 45, 53, 61-2, 69, 72, 88, 95, 98, 110, 113, 114, 115, 116, 118, 129, 148, 211-12, 219, 235, 236, 237, 239, 241
Westbury, 103, 209
Westminster Review, 366-7, 373, 407
Whitehall, 23, 153, 446
Wilberforce, Samuel, Bp of Oxford, 172, 434, 435
Wilcox, Herbert, 448, 449
Wilde, Oscar, 432
William IV, King, 36, 53
Williams, Dr, 422, 424
Willis's Rooms, 325, 377, 378, 379, 434-5, 459
Wilson, George, 104
Wilson, James, 209-10
Wilton, 15, 23, 41, 79-80, 149, 160, 274, 296, 317, 344, 429; Church, 1-2, 9, 160-2, 363, 430, 436; elections for, 40-2 (1832), 77-8 (1841), 183 (1847), 207-8 (1852), 336 (1857), 431
Wilton House and Estate, 9, 14-17, 19-20, 24, 26, 27, 43-4, 51-3, 57, 61-2, 80, 140, 149, 154, 156-60, 352, 360-1, 429, 430, 432; social and political gatherings at, 21, 103, 117, 149, 224, 247, 256, 266, 273-4, 332, 333, 370, 374-5, 383-4, 402, 418, 421-4

Wiltshire Agricultural Protection Society, 182
Wishford, 158, 159
Wolverhampton, 38-9
Wombwell, George, 141
Wood, Sir Charles, 3rd bt (1800-1885), Ch. of Exch. 1846-52, Pres. Bd of Control 1852-5, 1st Lord of Admiralty 1855-8, Sec. for India 1859-65, 296, 312, 332, 376
Woodham-Smith, Cecil, 449
Woolwich, 88, 390, 436, 439
Wordsworth, Christopher, 37
Woronzow, Catherine, Lady Pembroke (SH's mother), 18-22, 23, 25, 27, 29, 32, 33, 34, 36, 46, 51-2, 66, 80, 102, 109, 120, 137, 146, 149, 152, 153, 160-1, 178, 218-19, 328, 422, 466
Woronzow, Michael (SH's uncle), 18, 66, 103, 247, 318, 328
Woronzow, Simon (SH's grandfather), 18
Woronzow Road, 258, 259-60
Wort, Alderman F.H., 1, 450
Wreford, Thomas, 280
Wyatt, James, 17
Wyatt, Thomas Henry, 161, 436
Wyndham, William, 208-9, 372

Yeomanry cavalry, 80, 102, 110, 116, 140, 231-2, 331, 411, 415
Young, Sir John, 430

www.ingramcontent.com/pod-product-compliance
Lightning Source LLC
Chambersburg PA
CBHW070305230426

43664CB00015B/2643